Brief Contents

Focus on Writing

Paragraphs and Essays

Fourth Edition

Laurie G. Kirszner
University of the Sciences, Emeritus

Stephen R. Mandell
Drexel University

bedford/st.martin's
Macmillan Learning
Boston | New York

For Bedford/St. Martin's

Vice President, Editorial, Macmillan Learning Humanities: Edwin Hill
Editorial Director, English: Karen S. Henry
Senior Publisher for Composition, Business and Technical Writing,
   Developmental Writing: Leasa Burton
Executive Editor: Karita dos Santos
Senior Developmental Editor: Jill Gallagher
Senior Production Editor: Jessica Gould
Media Producer: Sarah O'Connor
Senior Production Supervisor: Jennifer Wetzel
Executive Marketing Manager: Joy Fisher Williams
Copy Editor: Wendy Annibell
Senior Photo Editor: Martha Friedman
Photo Researcher: Susan Doheny
Senior Permissions Editor: Kalina Ingham
Senior Art Director: Anna Palchik
Text Design: Jerilyn Bockorick
Cover Design: John Callahan
Cover Photo: cristinagonzalez/Getty Images
Composition: Jouve
Printing and Binding: LSC Communications

Manufactured in the United States of America.

1   0   9   8   7   6
f   e   d   c   b   a

For information, write: Bedford/St. Martin's, 75 Arlington Street, Boston, MA 02116 (617-399-4000)

ISBN 978-1-319-03529-7 (Student Edition)
ISBN 978-1-319-03619-5 (Loose-leaf Edition)

Acknowledgments

Text acknowledgments and copyrights appear at the back of the book on pages 696–697, which constitute an extension of the copyright page. Art acknowledgments and copyrights appear on the same page as the art selections they cover.

Preface

Our goal with the first edition of *Focus on Writing: Paragraphs and Essays* was to create an appealing text that motivates students to improve their writing and gives them the tools to do so. We developed the popular **TEST** tool specifically for this purpose. The letters that spell **TEST** stand for **T**opic sentence or **T**hesis statement, **E**vidence, **S**ummary statement, and **T**ransitions; this acronym helps students understand how paragraphs and essays are constructed and teaches them how to revise their own writing by checking for unity, support, and coherence.

In addition to retaining this important and successful feature, the fourth edition of *Focus on Writing* continues to reflect two of our central beliefs: that in college, writing comes first; and that students learn writing and grammar skills best in the context of their own writing. Accordingly, the text's activities not only get students writing immediately, but also encourage them to return to their own writing to apply the new skills they are learning and—with the help of **TEST**—to create a polished draft. Similarly, Grammar in Context boxes introduce fundamental concepts where they are most relevant to the student's writing.

In this fourth edition, we have used engaging images and a contemporary design to appeal to today's visual learners. The text's explanations and instructions are streamlined throughout to make them as useful as possible. In addition, to meet student needs expressed by many instructors, we have added a new Introduction, How Writing Can Help You Succeed, and a new Appendix on college success strategies. We've also expanded our step-by-step guidance for developing paragraphs, and now offer more coverage of critical reading and thinking, as well as updated exercises and readings that reflect the concerns of contemporary students.

It is our hope that this new edition of *Focus on Writing* will continue to motivate and empower students to become confident writers and capable editors of their own writing.

Organization

Focus on Writing has a flexible organization that permits instructors to teach various topics in the order that works best for them and their students. The book is divided into three sections, which are color-coded to help students and instructors more easily navigate the book:

- **Becoming a Critical Reader** introduces students to critical reading skills such as note taking and highlighting, and also teaches students how to differentiate between the various types of reading they need to do. Chapter 36, Readings for Writers, includes even more model essays to show students how to effectively read and comprehend texts.
- **Writing Paragraphs and Essays**, Chapters 2–16, is a comprehensive discussion of the writing process.
- **Revising and Editing Your Writing**, Chapters 17–35, is a thorough review of sentence skills, grammar, punctuation, and mechanics.

Features

TEST

- Topic Sentence
- Evidence
- Summary Statement
- Transitions

Although most people do not know it, the modern roller coaster got its start in Coney Island in Brooklyn, New York. First, in 1888, the Flip Flap Railway, which featured a circular loop, was built. The coaster was the first to go upside down, but it frequently injured riders' necks. Next, in 1901, the Loop-the-Loop, which was safer than the Flip Flap Railway, was built. Then, from 1884 through the 1930s, over thirty roller coasters were constructed in Coney Island. Finally, in 1927, the most famous roller coaster in history, the Cyclone, was built at a cost of over $100,000. Although it began operating over eighty years ago, it is still the standard by which all roller coasters are measured. It has steep drops, a lot of speed, and only lap belts to hold riders in their seats. Still in operation, the Cyclone is the most successful ride in Coney Island history. It is the last survivor of the wooden roller coasters that once drew crowds to Coney Island. With their many innovations, Coney Island's roller coasters paved the way for the high-tech roller coasters in amusement parks today.

Central to this text is our philosophy that students learn to write best by working with their own writing. This philosophy is supported by innovative features designed to make students' writing practice meaningful, productive, and enjoyable.

TEST helps students write and revise. This easy-to-remember tool, introduced in Chapter 2, helps students check their paragraphs and essays for unity, support, and coherence. By applying TEST to their writing, students can quickly see where their drafts need more work.

Focus on Writing activities engage and motivate students. These activities ask students to begin writing immediately by responding to a chapter-opening visual and prompt. An end-of-chapter prompt sends students back to their initial writing to apply the new skills they have learned and to work toward a final draft.

Students get the writing help they need — in a clear, step-by-step format. Eleven chapters on paragraph writing and four on essay writing cover the writing process and nine patterns of development. Each chapter includes a student-focused case study and an abundance of clear examples and engaging exercises.

Instruction and activities emphasize critical reading and thinking skills. With a full chapter on reading critically and a set of critical reading/thinking questions for each professional reading, *Focus on Writing* helps students build essential critical thinking and reading skills.

Grammar coverage is thorough yet accessible. Nineteen grammar chapters clearly and concisely convey the rules of English grammar.

New to This Edition

New support to inspire academic and college success.

- **A new Introduction—How Writing Can Help You Succeed—** helps students pinpoint exactly how writing will help them in their courses and beyond the classroom.
- **A new chapter on Strategies for College Success.** This new appendix gives students practical advice on how to succeed in college, with an emphasis on taking exams and how to manage time effectively.

New chapter organization features updated model essays integrated with instruction. Patterns of essay development have been broken up into two chapters in order to provide students and instructors model essays right in the chapter instead of at the back of the book, making clear the connections between reading and writing processes and better supporting students as they write.

New readings in Readings for Writers. Updated readings include essays by Tom Hanks, Marina Keegan, LeBron James, Jennine Capó Crucet, and Estelle Tang on a wealth of topics including the value of community college, e-readers, basketball, gun control, the Americans with Disability Act, women in technology, and sexual harassment.

Revised and enhanced exercises. New exercises help students practice the writing and grammar strategies they'll use in their own essays.

New in-depth coverage of Strategies for Doing Research. This appendix guides students through the process of writing a research paper, from choosing a topic to documenting sources. Special attention is given to finding, evaluating, integrating, and citing sources, as well as how to avoid plagiarism, which are especially challenging issues for today's students.

Narration in Action

In "The Sanctuary of School," Lynda Barry uses **narration** to structure her essay.

THE SANCTUARY OF SCHOOL

Lynda Barry

In her many illustrated works—including graphic novels, comic books, and a weekly cartoon strip, *Ernie Pook's Comeek*, which appears in a number of newspapers and magazines—Lynda Barry looks at the world through the eyes of children. Her characters remind adult readers of the complicated world of young people and of the clarity with which they see social situations. In "The Sanctuary of School," first published in the *Baltimore Sun* in 1992, Barry tells a story from her own childhood. As you read this essay, note how Barry relates her personal experience to a broader issue.

I was 7 years old the first time I snuck out of the house in the dark. It was winter and my parents had been fighting all night. They were short on money and long on relatives who kept "temporarily" moving into our house because they had nowhere else to go.

My brother and I were used to giving up our bedroom. We slept on the couch, something we actually liked because it put us that much closer to the light of our lives, our television.

At night when everyone was asleep, we lay on our pillows watching it with the sound off. We watched Steve Allen's mouth moving. We

Support for Instructors and Students

Focus on Writing is accompanied by comprehensive teaching and learning support.

Student Resources

Pairing *Focus on Writing* with *LaunchPad Solo for Readers and Writers* helps students succeed at their own pace. Available at a significant discount when packaged with *Focus on Writing*, *LaunchPad Solo for Readers and Writers* provides you with a quick and flexible solution for targeting instruction on critical reading, the writing process, grammar, mechanics, style, and punctuation. By combining formative and summative assessments with opportunities to study, practice, and review specific skills, *LaunchPad Solo for Readers and Writers* helps students gain confidence as they work through sequenced units that guide them from concept to mastery.

To order *Focus on Writing* packaged with *LaunchPad Solo for Readers and Writers* please use the package ISBN 978-1-319-08265-9.

To learn more about how to teach your course using *LaunchPad Solo for Readers and Writers*, see page xii or visit **macmillanlearning.com /readwrite**.

LearningCurve for Readers and Writers. LearningCurve, Bedford/St. Martin's adaptive quizzing program, quickly learns what students already know and helps them practice what they don't yet understand. Game-like quizzing motivates students to engage with their course, and reporting tools help teachers discern their students' needs.

With LearningCurve, students receive as much practice as they need to master a given concept and are provided with immediate feedback and links back to online instruction. A personalized study plan with suggestions for further practice completes Bedford's plan to give your students just what they need to be successful in the college classroom.

Please note: *LearningCurve for Readers and Writers* is included with *LaunchPad Solo for Readers and Writers*.

The *Bedford/St. Martin's Planner* includes everything that students need to plan and use their time effectively, with advice on preparing schedules and to-do lists plus blank schedules and calendars (monthly and weekly). The planner fits easily into a backpack or purse, so students can take it everywhere. **Free** when packaged with the print text. ISBN: 978-0-312-57447-5.

The Bedford/St. Martin's ESL Workbook, by Sapna Gandhi-Rao, Maria McCormack, and Elizabeth Trelenberg, provides ESL students with a broad range of exercises. This outstanding resource covers grammatical issues for multilingual students with varying English-language skills and cultural backgrounds. To reinforce each lesson, instructional introductions are followed by examples and exercises. ISBN: 978-0-312-54034-0.

E-Book Options

Focus on Writing is available in a variety of e-book formats. For details about our e-book partners, visit **macmillanlearning.com/ebooks**.

Instructor Resources

The *Instructor's Annotated Edition of Focus on Writing*, Fourth Edition, contains answers to all practice exercises, in addition to numerous teaching ideas, reminders, and cross-references useful to teachers at all levels of experience. ISBN: 978-1-319-03621-8.

The Bedford/St. Martin's English Community is now Bedford/St. Martin's home for professional resources, featuring Bedford *Bits*, our popular blog site offering new ideas for your course. Connect and converse with a growing team of Bedford authors and top scholars who blog on *Bits*, including Andrea Lunsford, Miriam Moore, Nancy Sommers, Susan Bernstein, and Elizabeth Wardle.

In addition, you'll find an expanding collection of additional resources that support your teaching.

- Find redesign resources ranging from webinars and lecture slides to state correlations and Lexile levels.
- Sign up for webinars.
- Download resources from our professional resource series that support your teaching.
- Start a discussion or ask a question.
- Follow your favorite members.
- Review projects in the pipeline.

Visit **community.macmillan.com** to join the conversation with your fellow teachers.

The *Instructor's Manual for Focus on Writing*, Fourth Edition, offers advice for teaching developmental writing as well as chapter-by-chapter pointers for using *Focus on Writing* in the classroom. It contains sample syllabi, additional teaching materials, and full chapters on collaborative learning. To download, see the *Focus on Writing* catalog page on our website, **macmillanlearning.com**.

Teaching Developmental Reading: Historical, Theoretical, and Practical Background Readings, **Second Edition,** is a professional development resource edited by Sonya L. Armstrong, Norman A. Stahl, and Hunter R. Boylan. It offers a wealth of readings from the historical foundations of the developmental reading field to the latest scholarship. ISBN: 978-1-4576-5895-2.

Teaching Developmental Writing: Background Readings, **Fourth Edition,** is a professional resource edited by Susan Naomi Bernstein, former co-chair of the Conference on Basic Writing. It offers essays on topics of interest to basic writing instructors, along with editorial apparatus pointing out practical applications for the classroom. ISBN: 978-0-312-60251-2.

The Bedford Bibliography for Teachers of Basic Writing, **Third Edition**, has been compiled by members of the Conference on Basic Writing under the general editorship of Gregory R. Glau and Chitralekha Duttagupta. This annotated list of books, articles, and periodicals was created specifically to help teachers of basic writing find valuable resources. ISBN: 978-0-312-58154-1.

Ordering Information

To order any of these ancillaries for *Focus on Writing*, you can contact your local Bedford/St. Martin's sales representative, send an email to **sales_support@bfwpub.com**, or visit our website at **macmillanlearning .com**.

Acknowledgments

In our work on *Focus on Writing*, we have benefited from the help of a great many people.

We are grateful to Linda Crawford of McLennan Community College, who lent her expertise and a fresh eye to existing ESL teaching tips and also wrote new tips. We are grateful to Timothy Jones of Oklahoma City Community College, who used his tech savvy to contribute advice for instructors and students on using technology both inside and outside the classroom. Additionally, we thank Elizabeth Rice, who made important contributions to the exercises and writing activities in the text.

Instructors throughout the country have contributed suggestions and encouragement at various stages of the book's development. For their collegial support, we thank Sandra Albers, Leeward Community College; Jaclyn Allen, Bismarck State College; Monique Blake, Broward College; Reed Breneman, Wake Technical Community College; Robyn Browder, Tidewater Community College; Susan Buchler, Montgomery County Community College; Joanna Christopher, John A. Logan College;

Shari Clevenger, Northeastern State University; Mary Copeland, San Bernardino Valley College; Karin Deol, Imperial Valley College; Rita Fernandez-Sterling, Miami Dade College, Kendall Campus; Jennifer Ferguson, Cazenovia College; Katherine Firkins, California State University, Northridge; David Freeman, Valencia College; Joyce Gatta, Middlesex Community College; Kendra Haggard, Northeastern State University; Karin Hauschild, Northern Kentucky University; Curt Hutchison, Leeward Community College; Patrice Johnson, Eastfield College; Therese Jones, Lewis University; Tracie Justus, Georgia Perimeter College; Ken Kouba, Prairie State College; Kevin Lamkins, Capital Community College; Katherine Lang, Community College of Allegheny County; Jonathan Lowndes, Broward College; Angelina Misaghi, California State University, Northridge; Ela Newman, University of Texas at Brownsville; Thomas Nicholas, Prairie State College; John Nordlof, Eastern University; Donna Obrzut, Henry Ford Community College; Donna Pallanti, Albertus Magnus College; Charles Porter, Wor-Wic Community College; Patricia Pullenza, Mesa Community College; Margaret Quinn, Montgomery County Community College; Minati Roychoudhuri, Capital Community College; Robin Smith, Towson University; Selena Stewart-Alexander, Eastfield College; Qiana Towns, Davenport University; Brenda Tuberville, Rogers State University; Elizabeth Wallace, Georgia Perimeter College; and Eliza Warren, Christian Brothers University.

At Bedford/St. Martin's, we thank founder and former president Charles Christensen, former president Joan Feinberg, and former editor in chief Nancy Perry, who believed in this project and gave us support and encouragement from the outset. We thank vice president for the humanities Edwin Hill, publisher Leasa Burton, and executive editor for developmental studies Karita dos Santos for overseeing this edition. We are also grateful to Elise Kaiser, managing editor; Jennifer Wetzel, senior production supervisor; and Jessica Gould, senior project editor, for guiding the book ably through production. Thanks also go to Joy Fisher Williams, executive marketing manager, and to our outstanding copy editor Wendy Annibell. And finally, we thank our talented editor, Jill Gallagher, whose patience, hard work, and dedication kept the project moving along.

It almost goes without saying that *Focus on Writing* could not exist without our students, whose words appear on almost every page of the book in sample sentences, paragraphs, and essays. We thank all of them, past and present, who allowed us to use their work.

Finally, we are grateful for the survival and growth of the writing partnership we entered into when we were graduate students. We had no idea then of the wonderful places our collaborative efforts would take us. Now, we know.

Laurie G. Kirszner
Stephen R. Mandell

Teaching with *LaunchPad Solo for Readers and Writers*

Pairing *Focus on Writing* with *LaunchPad Solo for Readers and Writers* helps students succeed at their own pace. Available at a significant discount when packaged, you can use *LaunchPad Solo for Readers and Writers* to integrate skills-based practice into your teaching with *Focus on Writing*, allowing you to more efficiently track students' progress with reading, writing, and grammar skills in an active learning arc that complements the book.

To package *LaunchPad Solo for Readers and Writers* with *Focus on Writing*, use ISBN 978-1-319-08265-9.

Assigning a project for which students will need to develop a strong thesis?

Start with the skill-specific unit in *LaunchPad Solo for Readers and Writers* to assess what students know.

Before turning to section 13d, "Stating Your Thesis," in Chapter 13, Writing an Essay, in *Focus on Writing*, have students complete the **pre-test** to get a sense of students' background knowledge of the topic. With this insight, you can meet them where they are.

After students have completed the pre-test, have them watch the **introductory video** on thesis statements.	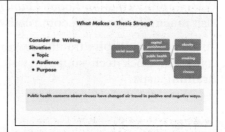

Then, from *Focus on Writing*, assign appropriate Practice exercises based on the results of the pre-test. For example, if the pre-test shows that many students are having trouble writing effective thesis statements, you might choose to assign and focus considerable class time on Practices 13-6 and 13-7.

In the writing lab or at home, students can build confidence and practice thinking like a writer using LearningCurve, game-like quizzing that adapts to students' responses and helps them practice what they don't yet understand — what it means to write for an audience, for instance, or how to evaluate a thesis in terms of its interest, specificity, or manageability.

The post-test in *LaunchPad Solo for Readers and Writers* can help you to assess how well students have mastered the topic, and to determine whether some students will require more help as they begin building theses for their projects. Students who require further practice can complete relevant LearningCurve activities.

For more information about *LaunchPad Solo for Readers and Writers*, visit **macmillanlearning.com/readwrite**.

To sign up for WebEx trainings with pedagogical specialists and access round-the-clock tech support, visit **macmillanlearning.com/catalog /training.aspx**.

Contents

Introduction: How Writing Can Help You Succeed 1

BECOMING A CRITICAL READER

Unit 1 Becoming a Critical Reader 5

1 Reading to Write 7

WRITING PARAGRAPHS AND ESSAYS

REVISING AND EDITING YOUR WRITING

Unit 4 Writing Effective Sentences 321

Unit 5 Solving Common Sentence Problems 409

23 Run-Ons 411

24 Fragments 426

25 Subject-Verb Agreement 447

32 Grammar and Usage for ESL Writers 546

Unit 7 Understanding Punctuation and Mechanics 577

33 Using Commas 579

Unit 8 Reading Essays 621

36 Readings for Writers 623

Appendix A: Strategies for College Success 668

Appendix B: Strategies for Doing Research 675

Thematic Table of Contents

Media and Society

Relationships

Race and Culture

Sports

About the Authors

During their long collaboration, Laurie Kirszner and Stephen Mandell have written a number of best-selling college texts for Bedford/St. Martin's, including *Patterns for College Writing*, *Foundations First*, *Writing First*, *Focus on Writing*, *Practical Argument*, and most recently, *Focus on Reading and Writing*. **Laurie Kirszner** is a Professor of English, Emeritus at the University of the Sciences, where she has taught composition, literature, creative writing, and scientific writing, and served as coordinator of the first-year writing program. **Stephen Mandell** is a Professor of English at Drexel University, where he founded and directed the basic writing program and has taught composition, literature, speech, and technical and business writing.

Introduction: How Writing Can Help You Succeed

Writing is not just something you do in school; writing is a life skill. If you can write clearly, you can express your ideas convincingly to others—in school, on the job, and in your community.

Writing is important. If you can write, you can communicate; if you can communicate effectively, you can succeed in school and beyond.

Most people agree that the best way to learn to write is by writing. In a sense, then, you are already something of an expert when it comes to writing; after all, you have been writing for years—not just for your classes but also in your everyday life. For example, on your Facebook page, you update your profile, post and respond to comments, and send messages; you probably text or tweet every day. In these situations, you write fluently, confidently, and concisely, without self-consciousness, because you know your audience and you know what you want to say.

Of course, this informal writing has its limitations. As you probably already know, college writing is different from informal writing; "text-speak," abbreviations, and shorthand are not acceptable in college writing assignments, and spontaneous bursts of words are acceptable only in the very roughest of first drafts or in activities like brainstorming and freewriting (see 2c). The trick is to use the experience you have with informal writing and to make it work for you in an academic context.

College writing requires you to pull your thoughts together so you can develop (and support) ideas and opinions and express them clearly for a variety of audiences. When you write informally to someone you know well, there is no need to explain, give examples, or support claims; you assume your reader will understand what you mean (and often agree with you). When your audience is a college instructor or your classmates, however, you can't always count on your readers' knowing exactly what you mean or understanding the context for your writing.

Academic writing also needs to be grammatically correct. You cannot assume that your readers will be willing to tolerate (or ignore) errors you might make in grammar, sentence structure, punctuation, or mechanics. In addition, your writing has to follow certain formal conventions and formats, so you cannot produce shapeless, slang-filled, punctuation-free documents and expect your readers to figure out what you mean.

1

Much of the writing you do every day—texts, social media posts, emails, and so on—use first person (*I*) and informal style, including contractions and slang. For example, if you are planning to see your academic adviser, you might text a friend about your appointment.

An email to your adviser, however, should not use abbreviations or shorthand, and it should not omit words or punctuation to save time or space. For example, if you have concerns about a course, you might send the following email to your instructor.

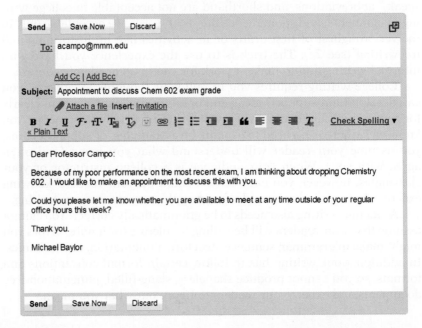

FYI

Using Email

Although you may not use email much in your personal communications, your instructors will likely use it to communicate with their students. For this reason, you should check your school email account regularly for schedule or assignment updates. When you contact your instructors by email, you should be sure to include a specific subject line to let them know what the message is about, and your message should get to the point right away.

To succeed in college, you need to learn how to write well. As you go through this book, you will learn skills and strategies that will help you write with clarity and confidence.

1 Reading to Write

In this chapter, you will learn to

- preview (1a), highlight (1b), annotate (1c), outline (1d), and summarize (1e) a reading assignment
- write a response (1f)
- use active reading skills in the classroom, in the community, and in the workplace (1g)

Reading is essential in all your college courses. To get the most out of your reading, you should approach the **texts** you read—books, articles, websites, and so on—in a practical way, always asking yourself what information they can offer you. You should also approach assigned readings critically, just as you approach your own writing when you revise.

Reading critically does not mean challenging or arguing with every idea; rather, it means considering, commenting, questioning, and assessing. Most of all, it means being an active rather than a passive reader. Being an **active reader** means participating in the reading process: approaching a reading assignment with a clear understanding of your purpose, previewing a text, highlighting and annotating it, and perhaps outlining it—all *before* you begin to respond in writing to what you have read.

To gain an understanding of your **purpose**—your reason for reading—you should start by answering some questions.

QUESTIONS ABOUT YOUR PURPOSE

- Why are you reading?
- Will you be expected to discuss what you are reading? If so, will you discuss it in class or in a conference with your instructor?
- Will you have to write about what you are reading? If so, will you be expected to write an informal response (for example, a journal entry) or a more formal one (for example, an essay)?
- Will you be tested on the material?

Once you understand your purpose, you are ready to begin the reading process.

1a Previewing

Your first step is to *preview* the material you have been assigned to read. When you **preview**, you do not read a passage word for word; instead, you **skim** it, reading it quickly to get a sense of the writer's main idea and key supporting points as well as the general emphasis. This strategy is particularly useful when you need to read many pages in a short amount of time. (Skimming can also help you determine if a particular text will be useful to you.) When you skim, you focus on just the key ideas, skipping details and examples. You look at the title, the author's name, the first paragraph (which often contains a statement of the writer's main idea or an overview of the text), and the last paragraph (which often contains a summary of the writer's points). You also look at each paragraph's first sentence. As you skim a text, you should also look for clues to content and emphasis in **visual signals**, such as headings, boxed text, images, and others listed in the following box.

Guidelines for Previewing

- Look at the title.
- Look at the author's name.
- Look at the opening paragraph, searching for the sentence that best expresses the main idea.
- Look at the closing paragraph, searching for a summary of the writer's ideas.
- Look at each paragraph's first sentence.
- Look at headings and subheadings.
- Look at *italicized* and **boldfaced** words.
- Look at numbered lists.
- Look at bulleted lists (like this one).
- Look at graphs, charts, tables, diagrams, photographs, and other images.
- Look at any information that is boxed.
- Look at any information that is in color.

When you have finished previewing, you should have a general sense of what the writer wants to communicate.

PRACTICE
1-1   "No Comprendo" ("I Don't Understand") is a newspaper opinion article by Barbara Mujica, a professor of Spanish at Georgetown University in Washington, D.C. In this article, which was published in the *New York Times*, Mujica argues against bilingual education (teaching students in their native language as well as in English).

In preparation for class discussion and for other activities that will be assigned later in this chapter, preview the article. As you skim, identify the writer's main idea and key supporting points. Then, write them on the lines that follow the article.

NO COMPRENDO

Barbara Mujica

Last spring, my niece phoned me in tears. She was graduating from high school and had to make a decision. An outstanding soccer player, she was offered athletic scholarships by several colleges. So why was she crying?   1

My niece came to the United States from South America as a child. Although she had received good grades in her schools in Miami, she spoke English with a heavy accent, and her comprehension and writing skills were deficient. She was afraid that once she left the Miami environment, she would feel uncomfortable and, worse still, have difficulty keeping up with class work.   2

Programs that keep foreign-born children in Spanish-language classrooms for years are only part of the problem. During a visit to my niece's former school, I observed that all business, not just teaching, was conducted in Spanish. In the office, secretaries spoke to the administrators and the children in Spanish. Announcements over the public-address system were made in an English so fractured that it was almost incomprehensible.   3

I asked my niece's mother why, after years in public schools, her daughter had poor English skills. "It's the whole environment," she replied. "All kinds of services are available in Spanish or Spanglish. Sports and after-school activities are conducted in Spanglish. That's what the kids hear on the radio and in the street."   4

> **WORD POWER**
>
> **Spanglish** A mixture of Spanish and English

Until recently, immigrants made learning English a priority. But even when they didn't learn English themselves, their children grew up speaking it. Thousands of first-generation Americans still strive to learn English, but others face reduced educational and career opportunities because they have not mastered this basic skill they need to get ahead.   5

According to the 1990 census, 40 percent of the Hispanics born in the United States do not graduate from high school, and the Department of Education says that a lack of proficiency in English is an important factor in the drop-out rate.   6

People and agencies that favor providing services only in foreign languages want to help people who do not speak English, but they may be doing these people a disservice by condemning them to a linguistic ghetto from which they cannot easily escape.   7

And my niece? She turned down all of her scholarship opportuni- 8
ties, deciding instead to attend a small college in Miami, where she will
never have to put her English to the test.

Writer's main idea

_____

_____

Key supporting points

1. _____

2. _____

3. _____

4. _____

1b Highlighting

After you preview the assigned material, read it carefully, *highlighting* as
you read. **Highlighting** means using underlining and symbols to identify key ideas. This active reading strategy will help you understand the
writer's ideas and make connections among them when you reread. Be
selective when you highlight. Because you will eventually be rereading
every highlighted word, phrase, and sentence, highlight only the most
important, most useful information.

Using Highlighting Symbols

- Underline key ideas—for example, topic sentences.
- Box or circle words or phrases you want to remember.
- Place a check mark (✓) or star (∗) next to an important idea.
- Place a double check mark (✓✓) or double star (∗∗) next to an
  especially significant idea.
- Draw lines or arrows to connect related ideas.
- Put a question mark (?) beside a word or an idea that you need
  to look up.
- Number the writer's key supporting points or examples.

FYI

Knowing What to Highlight

You want to highlight what's important—but how do you *know* what's important?

- *Look for visual signals.* As a general rule, you should look for the same **visual signals** you looked for when you did your previewing. Many of the ideas you will need to highlight will probably be found in material that is visually set off from the rest of the text—opening and closing paragraphs, lists, and so on.

- *Look for verbal signals.* Also look for **verbal signals**—words and phrases that often introduce key points. (Some of these verbal signals are listed in the following box.)

Together, these visual and verbal signals will give you useful clues to the writer's meaning and emphasis.

Recognizing Verbal Signals

- Phrases that signal emphasis ("The *primary* reason"; "The *most important* idea")
- Repeated words and phrases
- Words that signal addition (*also, in addition, furthermore*)
- Words that signal time sequence (*first, after, then, next, finally*)
- Words that identify causes and effects (*because, as a result, for this reason*)
- Words that introduce examples (*for example, for instance*)
- Words that signal comparison (*likewise, similarly*)
- Words that signal contrast (*unlike, although, in contrast*)
- Words that signal contradiction (*however, on the contrary*)
- Words that signal a narrowing of the writer's focus (*in fact, specifically, in other words*)
- Words that signal summaries or conclusions (*to sum up, in conclusion*)

Here is how one student highlighted a passage from a newspaper column, "Barbie at Thirty-Five" by Anna Quindlen.

> *   But consider the recent study at the University of Arizona investigating the attitudes of white and black teenage girls toward body image. The attitudes of the white girls were a nightmare. Ninety percent expressed dissatisfaction with ✓ their own bodies, and many said they saw dieting as a kind of all-purpose panacea? "I think the reason I would diet would be to gain self-confidence," said one. "I'd feel like it was a way of getting control," said another. And they were curiously united in their description of the perfect girl. She's 5 feet 7 inches, weighs just over 100 pounds, has long legs and flowing hair. The researchers concluded, "The ideal girl was a living manifestation of the Barbie doll."
>
> While white girls described an impossible ideal, black teenagers talked about appearance in terms of style, attitude, pride, and personality. White respondents talked "thin," black ones "shapely." Seventy percent of the black
> ✓   teenagers said they were satisfied with their weight, and there was little emphasis on dieting. "We're all brought up and taught to be realistic about life," said one, "and we don't look at things the way you want them to be. You look at them the way they are."

The student who highlighted the passage was preparing to write an essay about eating disorders. Because the passage included no visual signals apart from the paragraph divisions, she looked carefully for verbal signals.

The student began her highlighting by underlining and starring the writer's main idea. She then boxed the names of the two key groups the passage compares—*white girls* and *black teenagers*—and underlined two phrases that illustrate how the attitudes of the two groups differ (*dissatisfaction with their own bodies* and *satisfied with their weight*). Check marks in the margin remind the student of the importance of these two phrases, and arrows connect each phrase to the appropriate group of girls.

The student also circled three related terms that characterize white girls' attitudes—*perfect girl, Barbie doll,* and *impossible ideal*—drawing lines to connect them. Finally, she circled the unfamiliar word *panacea* and put a question mark beside it to remind herself to look up the word's meaning.

PRACTICE

1-2　Review the highlighted passage. How would your own highlighting of this passage be similar to or different from the sample student highlighting?

PRACTICE

1-3　Reread "No Comprendo" (pp. 10–11). As you reread, highlight the article by underlining and starring main ideas, boxing and circling key words, checkmarking important points, and drawing lines and arrows to connect related ideas. Be sure to circle each unfamiliar word and to put a question mark beside it.

1c　Annotating

As you highlight, you should also *annotate* what you are reading. **Annotating** a passage means reading critically and making notes—of questions, reactions, reminders, and ideas for writing or discussion—in the margins or between the lines. (If you run out of room on the page, you use sticky notes.) Keeping an informal record of ideas as they occur to you will prepare you for class discussion and for writing.

As you read, thinking about the following questions will help you make useful annotations.

Questions for Reading Critically

- What is the writer saying? What do you think the writer is suggesting or implying? What makes you think so?
- What is the writer's purpose (his or her reason for writing)?
- What kind of audience is the writer addressing?
- What is the writer's main idea?
- Is the writer responding to another writer's ideas?
- How does the writer support his or her points? Does the writer use facts? Opinions? Both?
- What kind of supporting details and examples does the writer use?
- Does the writer include enough supporting details and examples?
- Does the writer seem well informed? Reasonable? Fair?
- Do you understand the writer's vocabulary?
- Do you understand the writer's ideas?
- Do you agree with the points the writer is making?
- How are the ideas presented like (or unlike) those presented in other texts you have read?

FYI

Making Useful Annotations

As you annotate, be careful not to write too much or too little; good annotations fit in the margins or between the lines or on a small sticky note on the page. You should *not* write your annotations on a separate sheet of paper. If you do, you will be tempted to write too much, and you can easily lose track of where a particular note belongs or what point it comments on. (And if you lose the sheet of paper, you will lose all of your notes and thoughts.) Think of your annotations as a study aid that you can consult when you return to the text a few days later. If you have made useful annotations, they will help you follow the writer's ideas and remember what is most important in the text.

The following passage, which reproduces the student's highlighting from page 13, also illustrates her annotations.

But consider the recent study at the University of Arizona investigating the

✳ attitudes of white and black teenage girls toward body image. The attitudes of

the white girls were a nightmare. Ninety percent expressed dissatisfaction with ✓

their own bodies, and many said they saw dieting as a kind of all-purpose

panacea? "I think the reason I would diet would be to gain self-confidence,"   = cure-all

said one. "I'd feel like it was a way of getting control," said another. And they   Need for control,
perfection. Why?
Media? Parents?

were curiously united in their description of the perfect girl. She's 5 feet 7 inches,

weighs just over 100 pounds, has long legs and flowing hair. The researchers

concluded, "The ideal girl was a living manifestation of the Barbie doll."   Barbie doll
= plastic, unreal

While white girls described an impossible ideal, black teenagers talked

about appearance in terms of style, attitude, pride, and personality. White

respondents talked "thin," black ones "shapely." Seventy percent of the black   "Thin" vs. "shapely"

✓ teenagers said they were satisfied with their weight, and there was little   Only 30% dissatisfied—
but 90% of white girls

emphasis on dieting. "We're all brought up and taught to be realistic about

life," said one, "and we don't look at things the way you want them to be.

You look at them the way they are."

                overgeneralization?   vs. Barbie doll (= unrealistic)

In her annotations, this student wrote down the meaning of the word *panacea*, put the study's conclusions and the contrasting statistics into her own words, and recorded questions she intended to explore further.

PRACTICE

1-4 Reread "No Comprendo" (pp. 10–11). As you reread, refer to the Questions for Reading Critically (p. 14), and use them to guide you as you write down your own thoughts and questions in the margins of the article. Note where you agree or disagree with the writer, and briefly explain why. Quickly summarize any points you think are particularly important. Take time to look up any unfamiliar words you have circled and to write brief definitions. Think of these annotations as your preparation for discussing the article in class and eventually writing about it.

1d Outlining

Outlining is another technique you can use to help you understand a reading assignment. Unlike a **formal outline**, which follows strict conventions, an **informal outline** enables you to record a text's ideas in the order in which they are presented. After you have made an informal outline, you should be able to see the writer's emphasis (which ideas are more important than others) as well as how the ideas are related.

FYI

Constructing an Informal Outline

To construct an informal outline, follow these guidelines.

1. Write or type the text's main idea at the top of a sheet of paper. (This will remind you of the writer's focus and help keep your outline on track.)

2. At the left margin, write down the most important idea of the first paragraph or first section.

3. Indent the next line a few spaces, and list the examples or details that support this idea. (You can use your computer's Tab key to help you set up your outline.)

4. As ideas become more specific, indent further. (Ideas that have the same degree of importance are indented the same distance from the left margin.)

5. Repeat the process with each paragraph or section.

The student who highlighted and annotated the excerpt from Anna Quindlen's "Barbie at Thirty-Five" (pp. 13 and 15) made the following informal outline to help her understand the writer's ideas.

Main idea: White and African American teenage girls have very different attitudes about their body images.

White girls dissatisfied
    90% dissatisfied with appearance
    Dieting = cure-all
      –self-confidence
      –control
    Ideal = unrealistic
      –tall and thin
      –Barbie doll

African American girls satisfied
    70% satisfied with weight
    Dieting not important
    Ideal = realistic
      –shapely
      –not thin

PRACTICE
1-5 Working on your own or in a small group, make an informal outline of "No Comprendo" (pp. 10–11). Refer to your highlighting and annotations as you construct your outline. When you have finished, check to make certain your outline accurately represents the writer's emphasis and the relationships among her ideas.

1e Summarizing

Once you have previewed, highlighted, annotated, and outlined a text, you may want to *summarize* it to help you understand it better. A **summary** retells, *in your own words*, what a text is about. A summary condenses, so it leaves out all but the main idea and perhaps the key supporting points. A summary omits supporting examples and details, and it does *not* include your own ideas or opinions.

To summarize a text, follow these guidelines.

1. Review your outline.
2. Consulting your outline, restate the main idea *in your own words*.

3. Consulting your outline, restate the key supporting points. Add linking words and phrases between sentences where necessary.

4. Reread the original text to make sure you have not left out anything significant.

FYI

To avoid accidentally using the exact language of the original, do not look at the original while you are writing your summary. If you want to use a distinctive word or phrase from the original, put it in quotation marks.

The student who highlighted, annotated, and outlined the excerpt from "Barbie at Thirty-Five" (pp. 13, 15, and 17) wrote the following summary.

As Anna Quindlen reports in "Barbie at Thirty-Five," a University of Arizona study found that white and African American teenage girls have very different attitudes about their body images. Almost all white girls said they were dissatisfied with their appearance; African American girls in the study, however, were generally happy with their weight.

PRACTICE

1-6   Write a brief summary of "No Comprendo" (pp. 10–11). Use your outline to guide you, and keep your summary short and to the point. Your summary should be about one-quarter to one-third the length of the original article.

1f   Writing a Response

Once you have highlighted and annotated a reading selection, you are ready to write about it—perhaps in a **response paragraph** in which you record your informal reactions to the writer's ideas.

The student who highlighted, annotated, outlined, and summarized "Barbie at Thirty-Five" wrote the following response paragraph.

Why are white and African American girls' body images so different? Why do African American girls think it's okay to be "shapely" while white girls want to be thin? Maybe it's because music videos and movies and fashion magazines show so many more white models, all half-starved, with perfect hair and legs. Or maybe white girls get different messages from their parents or from the people they date. Do white and African American girls' attitudes about their bodies stay the same when they get older? And what about <u>male</u> teenagers' self-images? Do white and African American <u>guys</u> have different body images, too?

The process of writing this response was very helpful to the student. The questions she asked suggested some interesting ideas that she could explore in class discussion or in a more fully developed piece of writing.

PRACTICE

1-7   Write a response expressing your reactions to "No Comprendo" (pp. 10–11) and to the issue of bilingual education.

1g Reading in the Classroom, in the Community, and in the Workplace

In college, in your life as a citizen of your community, and in the workplace, you will read material in a variety of formats—for example, textbooks, newspapers, websites, and job-related documents.

Although the active reading process you have just reviewed can be applied to all types of material, various kinds of reading require slightly different strategies during the previewing stage. One reason for this is that different kinds of reading may have different purposes (for example, to present information or to persuade). Another reason is that the various documents you read are aimed at specific audiences, and different readers require different signals about content and emphasis. For these reasons, you need to look for specific kinds of verbal and visual signals when you preview different kinds of reading material.

Reading Textbooks

Much of the reading you do in college is in textbooks (like this one). The purpose of a textbook is to present information, and when you read a textbook, your goal is to understand that information. To do this, you need to figure out which ideas are most important as well as which points support those ideas and which examples illustrate them.

checklist

Reading Textbooks

Look for the following features as you preview:

- [ ] **Boldfaced** and *italicized* words, which can indicate terms to be defined

- [ ] Boxed checklists or summaries, which may appear at the ends of sections or chapters

- [ ] Bulleted or numbered lists, which may list key reasons or examples or summarize important material

- [ ] Diagrams, charts, tables, graphs, photographs, and other visuals that illustrate the writer's points

- [ ] Marginal quotations and definitions

- [ ] Marginal cross-references

- [ ] Web links

PRACTICE

1-8 Using the checklist for reading textbooks as a guide, preview the page from the textbook *Psychology*, Seventh Edition (2016), by Don H. Hockenbury and Sandra E. Hockenbury, on page 21. When you have finished, highlight and annotate it.

What We Hear

THE NATURE OF SOUND

Whether it's the ear-splitting screech of metal on metal or the subtle whir of a grasshopper's wings, *sound waves* are the physical stimuli that produce our sensory experience of sound. Usually, sound waves are produced by the rhythmic vibration of air molecules, but sound waves can be transmitted through other media, such as water, too. Our perception of sound is directly related to the physical properties of sound waves (see Figure 3.7).

One of the first things that we notice about a sound is how loud it is. **Loudness** is determined by the intensity, or **amplitude,** of a sound wave and is measured in units called **decibels.** Zero decibels represents the loudness of the softest sound that humans can hear, or the absolute threshold for hearing. As decibels increase, perceived loudness increases.

Pitch refers to the relative "highness" or "lowness" of a sound. Pitch is determined by the frequency of a sound wave. **Frequency** refers to the rate of vibration, or number of waves per second, and is measured in units called *hertz*. Hertz simply refers to the number of wave peaks per second. The faster the vibration, the higher the frequency, the closer together the waves are—and the higher the tone produced. If you pluck the high E and the low E strings on a guitar, you'll notice that the low E vibrates far fewer times per second than does the high E.

Most of the sounds we experience do not consist of a single frequency but are *complex,* consisting of several sound-wave frequencies. This combination of frequencies produces the distinctive quality, or **timbre,** of a sound, which enables us to distinguish easily between the same note played on a saxophone and on a piano. Every human voice has its own distinctive timbre, which is why you can immediately identify a friend's voice on the telephone from just a few words, even if you haven't talked to each other for years.

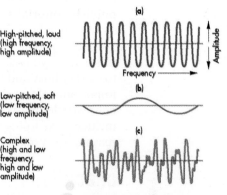

High-pitched, loud (high frequency, high amplitude)

Low-pitched, soft (low frequency, low amplitude)

Complex (high and low frequency, high and low amplitude)

FIGURE 3.7 Characteristics of Sound Waves The length of a wave, its height, and its complexity determine the loudness, pitch, and timbre that we hear. The sound produced by (a) would be high-pitched and loud. The sound produced by (b) would be soft and low. The sound in (c) is complex, like the sounds we usually experience in the natural world.

How We Hear

THE PATH OF SOUND

The ear is made up of the outer ear, the middle ear, and the inner ear. Sound waves are *collected* in the outer ear, *amplified* in the middle ear, and *transduced,* or *transformed into neural messages,* in the inner ear (see Figure 3.8 on the next page).

The **outer ear** includes the *pinna,* the *ear canal,* and the *eardrum.* The pinna is that oddly shaped flap of skin and cartilage that's attached to each side of your head. The pinna helps us pinpoint the location of a sound. But the pinna's primary role is to catch sound waves and funnel them into the ear canal. The sound wave travels down the ear canal and then bounces into the **eardrum,** a tightly stretched membrane. When the sound wave hits the eardrum, the eardrum vibrates, matching the vibrations of the sound wave in intensity and frequency.

The eardrum separates the outer ear from the **middle ear.** The eardrum's vibration is transferred to three tiny bones in the middle ear—the *hammer,* the *anvil,* and the *stirrup.* Each bone sets the next bone in motion. The joint action of these three bones almost doubles the amplification of the sound. The innermost bone, the stirrup, transmits the amplified vibration to the *oval window.* If the tiny bones of the middle ear are damaged or become brittle, as they sometimes do in old age, *conduction deafness* may result. Conduction deafness can be helped by a hearing aid, which amplifies sounds.

Like the eardrum, the oval window is a membrane, but it is many times smaller than the eardrum. The oval window separates the middle ear from the **inner ear.** As the oval window vibrates, the vibration is next relayed to an inner structure called the **cochlea,** a fluid-filled tube that's coiled in a spiral. The word *cochlea* comes from the

frequency The rate of vibration, or the number of sound waves per second.

timbre (TAM-ber) The distinctive quality of a sound, determined by the complexity of the sound wave.

outer ear The part of the ear that collects sound waves; consists of the pinna, the ear canal, and the eardrum.

eardrum A tightly stretched membrane at the end of the ear canal that vibrates when hit by sound waves.

middle ear The part of the ear that amplifies sound waves; consists of three small bones: the hammer, the anvil, and the stirrup.

inner ear The part of the ear where sound is transduced into neural impulses; consists of the cochlea and semicircular canals.

cochlea (COKE-lee-uh) The coiled, fluid-filled inner-ear structure that contains the basilar membrane and hair cells.

Reading News Articles

As a student, as a citizen, and as an employee, you read school, community, local, and national newspapers in print and online. Like textbooks, news articles communicate information. In addition, newspapers publish editorials (which aim to persuade) as well as feature articles (which may be designed to entertain as well as to inform).

Many people read news articles online rather than in print form. If this is what you usually do, keep in mind that newspaper web pages tend to be very busy and crowded, so you may need to work hard to distinguish important information from not-so-important material. For example, a news article that you read online may be surrounded by advertising and include links to irrelevant (and potentially distracting) material. For this reason, it is very important to read online material with care.

checklist

Reading News Articles

Look for the following features as you preview:

- Headlines
- **Boldfaced** headings within articles
- Labels like *editorial*, *commentary*, or *opinion*, which indicate that an article communicates the writer's own views
- Brief biographical information at the end of an opinion piece
- Phrases or sentences in **boldface** (to emphasize key points)
- The article's first sentence, which often answers the questions *who*, *what*, *why*, *where*, *when*, and *how*
- The **dateline**, which tells you the date and the city the writer is reporting from
- Photographs, charts, graphs, and other visuals
- In *print news articles*, related articles that appear on the same page, such as boxed information and **sidebars**—short related articles that provide additional background on people and places mentioned in the article
- In *online news articles*, links to related articles, reader comments, and other useful material

PRACTICE

1-9 Using the checklist for reading news articles as a guide, preview the online news article on page 23. Then, highlight and annotate it.

THE CHRONICLE OF HIGHER EDUCATION

Home   News ▾   Global   **Opinions & Ideas** ▾   Facts & Figures   Blogs ▾   Advice   Forums   Jobs ▾ | Search the Chronicle | Go

COMMENTARY   ☒ ☒ ☒ ☒ | Comments (55)

Time Is Right for Colleges to Shift From Assembly-Line Education

Tim Foley for The Chronicle

By Arthur Levine | SEPTEMBER 14, 2015

Competency-based education, which focuses on the *results* of education — what students have learned — rather than the *process* of education — number of courses taken, credits earned, seat time served — is hot. Google it and you get hundreds of thousands of choices.

The federal government is paying for it. Colleges and universities are adopting it, with 150 institutions enrolling some 200,000 students in such programs. Western Governors University, Southern New Hampshire University, and Alverno College, among other institutions, have built national reputations based on their work in this area.

In June the Council of Regional Accrediting Commissions outlined the criteria that accreditors will now use in defining and approving competency-based education programs.

Yet recently, as I talked with two education reporters about what they considered the "big" issues in higher education, they rolled their eyes when I mentioned competency-based education. One characterized the term as incomprehensible jargon, a buzzword, and the other dismissed it as the latest education fad. The MOOC of 2015.

Their skepticism is not surprising. Thirty years of a national school-reform movement have produced a seemingly endless number of silver bullets. But competency-based education is not the fad du jour. It's here to stay, and it promises to become the norm in education. Here are a few reasons why.

First, the United States is making a transition from a national, analog, industrial economy to a global, digital, information economy. Industrial economies, epitomized by the assembly line, focus on common processes. They are time-based and fixed in length. In education, this translates into a common four-year undergraduate program, preceded by 12 years of schooling, semester-long courses, credit hours, and Carnegie units. Industrial education systems are rooted in seat time, the amount of instruction students receive. The programs assume that all students can learn the same things in the same period of time.

In contrast, information economies focus on outcomes: process and time are variable. In education, this shifts the focus from teaching to learning. The emphasis is on the skills and knowledge that students must master in order to graduate rather than on the number of

Reading on the Job

In your workplace, you may be called on to read email messages, memos, letters, and reports. These documents, which may be designed to convey information or to persuade, are often addressed to a group rather than to a single person. (Note that the most important information is often presented *first*—in a subject line or in the first paragraph.)

checklist

Reading on the Job

Look for the following features as you preview:

- ☐ Numbered or bulleted lists of tasks or problems (numbers indicate the order of the items' importance)

- ☐ The first and last paragraphs and the first sentence of each body paragraph, which often contain key information

- ☐ **Boldfaced**, <u>underlined</u>, or *italicized* words

- ☐ In a report, visuals that illustrate key concepts

- ☐ In electronic communications, the person(s) addressed, the subject line, and links to the web

- ☐ In a memo or a report, headings that highlight key topics or points

PRACTICE

1-10   Using the checklist for reading on the job as a guide, preview the email message on page 25. What is the writer's purpose? What is the most important piece of information she wants to communicate? Highlight and annotate the email, and then write a two-sentence summary of it.

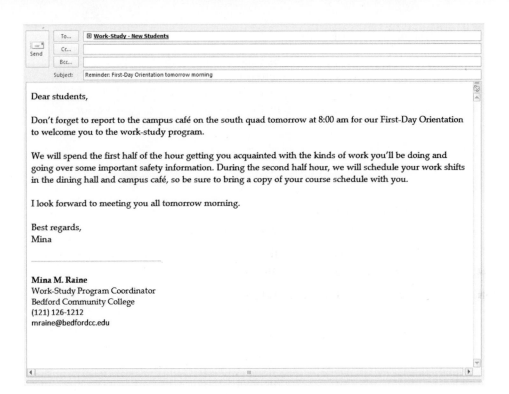

To... ⊞ **Work-Study - New Students**

Cc...

Bcc...

Subject: Reminder: First-Day Orientation tomorrow morning

Dear students,

Don't forget to report to the campus café on the south quad tomorrow at 8:00 am for our First-Day Orientation to welcome you to the work-study program.

We will spend the first half of the hour getting you acquainted with the kinds of work you'll be doing and going over some important safety information. During the second half hour, we will schedule your work shifts in the dining hall and campus café, so be sure to bring a copy of your course schedule with you.

I look forward to meeting you all tomorrow morning.

Best regards,
Mina

Mina M. Raine
Work-Study Program Coordinator
Bedford Community College
(121) 126-1212
mraine@bedfordcc.edu

review checklist

Reading to Write

☐ Preview the material. (See 1a.)

☐ Highlight the material. (See 1b.)

☐ Annotate the material. (See 1c.)

☐ Outline the material. (See 1d.)

☐ Summarize the material. (See 1e.)

☐ Write a response. (See 1f.)

☐ Use active reading strategies when reading textbooks, news articles, and workplace communications. (See 1g.)

Focus on Paragraphs

2 Writing a Paragraph

Rene Sheret (left), © Bill Aron/PhotoEdit (right)

focus on writing

Today's college students may find themselves in either a traditional classroom or a career-oriented setting. What do you think is the primary purpose of college—to give students a general education or to prepare them for specific careers? Think about this question as you read the pages that follow.

In this chapter, you will learn to

- understand paragraph structure (2a)
- focus on your assignment, purpose, and audience (2b)
- find ideas to write about (2c)
- identify your main idea and write a topic sentence (2d)
- choose supporting points (2e)
- develop supporting points (2f)
- make an outline (2g)
- draft, TEST, revise, edit, and proofread your paragraph (2h–2k)

2a Understanding Paragraph Structure

Because paragraphs are central to almost every kind of writing, learning how to write one is an important step in becoming a competent writer. (Although a paragraph can be a complete piece of writing in itself—as it is in a short classroom exercise or an exam answer—most of the time, a paragraph is part of a longer piece of writing.)

A **paragraph** is a group of sentences that is unified by a single main idea. The **topic sentence** states the main idea, and the rest of the sentences in the paragraph provide **evidence** (examples and details) to support the main idea. The sentences in a paragraph are linked by **transitions**, words and phrases (such as *also* and *for example*) that show how ideas are related. At the end of the paragraph, a **summary statement** reinforces the main idea.

Paragraph Structure

Topic sentence —

Evidence —

Summary statement

In every paragraph you write, you need to include a main idea, supporting evidence, transitions, and a summary statement. First, state the main idea of the paragraph in a topic sentence. This idea will unify your paragraph. Then, add sentences to provide support for your topic sentence. In these sentences, you present and develop the evidence that will help readers understand your main idea. Next, check to make sure you have linked these sentences with transitions. Finally, write a summary statement, a sentence that reinforces your paragraph's main idea. If you follow this general structure, you are on your way to writing an effective paragraph.

Transitions
(boxed)

The first letters of these four elements—**T**opic sentence, **E**vidence, **S**ummary statement, and **T**ransitions—spell **TEST**. Whenever you write a paragraph, you should **TEST** it to make sure it is complete.

FYI

The first sentence of a paragraph is **indented**, starting about half an inch from the left-hand margin. Every sentence begins with a capital letter and, in most cases, ends with a period. (Sometimes a sentence ends with a question mark or an exclamation point.)

PRACTICE

2-1   Bring two paragraphs to class—one from a newspaper or magazine article and one from a textbook. Compare your paragraphs with those brought in by other students. What features do all your paragraphs share? How do the paragraphs differ from one another?

The Writing Process

Writing is a **process**, a series of steps that begins in your college classes when you get an assignment:

- You start by thinking about what you want to say and finding ideas to write about. Then, you identify the main idea you want to get across.
- Once you have material to write about, you arrange the points that support your main idea in an order that makes sense to you.
- When you have decided how to arrange your ideas, you write a draft.
- When you finish your draft, you **TEST** it to make sure it includes all the elements of an effective paragraph.
- Finally, you revise, edit, and proofread.

Plan

Organize

Draft

TEST

Revise, edit, and proofread

The steps in the writing process are explained and illustrated in the pages that follow.

2b Focusing on Your Assignment, Purpose, and Audience

In college, a writing task usually begins with an assignment that gives you a topic to write about. Instead of jumping in headfirst and starting to write, take time to consider some questions about your **assignment** (*what* you are expected to write about), your **purpose** (*why* you are writing), and your **audience** (*for whom* you are writing). Answering these questions at this point will save you time in the long run.

Questions about Assignment, Purpose, and Audience

Assignment

- What is your assignment? Is it included on your course syllabus or posted on the class web page?
- Do you have a word or page limit?
- When is your assignment due?
- Will you be expected to do all of your work outside of class, or will you be doing some work in class?
- Will you be expected to work on your own or with others?
- Will you be allowed to revise before you hand in your assignment?
- Will you be allowed to revise after your assignment is graded?
- Does your instructor require a particular **format**?

Purpose

- Are you expected to express your personal reactions—for example, to tell how you feel about a piece of music or a news event?
- Are you expected to present information—for example, to answer an exam question, describe a scientific process, or summarize a story or essay you have read?
- Are you expected to argue for or against a position on a controversial issue?

Audience

- Who will read your paper—just your instructor or other students as well?
- How much will your readers know about your topic?
- Will your readers expect you to use **formal** or **informal** language?

WORD POWER

format specified arrangement of elements in a document—for example, where to type your name, the date, and the course number

---

WORD POWER

formal language language that is grammatically precise and uses words familiar to an educated audience

informal language language that is used in conversation and personal email; may include contractions and slang

PRACTICE

2-2   Each of the following writing tasks has a different audience and purpose. Think about how you would approach each task. (Use the Questions about Assignment, Purpose, and Audience listed on page 32 to help you decide on the best strategy.) Be prepared to discuss your ideas with your class or in a small group.

1. For the other students in your writing class, a description of your best or worst educational experience

2. For the instructor of an education course, a discussion of your first day of kindergarten

3. An email to your community's school board in which you try to convince members to make two or three changes that you believe would improve the schools you attended (or those your children might attend)

4. A thank-you note to a work supervisor—either past or current—telling what you appreciate about his or her guidance and how it has helped you develop and grow as an employee

5. A letter to a restaurant where you received poor service and were served terrible food, describing your experience and suggesting ways the service and food could be improved

2c   Finding Ideas to Write About

Once you know what, why, and for whom you are writing, you can begin the process of finding material to write about. This process is different for every writer.

In this chapter, you will be following the writing process of Stella Drew, a student in an introductory writing course, who was given the following assignment:

> Should community service—unpaid work in the community—be a required part of the college curriculum? Write a paragraph in which you answer this question.

Before she drafted her paragraph, Stella used a variety of strategies to find ideas to write about. The pages that follow illustrate the four strategies her instructor asked the class to try:

- Freewriting
- Brainstorming
- Clustering
- Journal writing

WORD POWER

curriculum all the courses required by a school

FYI

Keep in mind that you do not have to use all four of the strategies listed on page 33 every time you write a paragraph. Try out the various strategies, and see which ones work best for you.

Freewriting

When you **freewrite**, you write for a set period of time—perhaps five minutes—without stopping, and you keep writing even if what you are writing doesn't seem to have a point or a direction. Your goal is to relax and let ideas flow without worrying about whether or not they are related—or even make sense. (If you have trouble thinking of something to say, keep repeating the last word of your freewriting until something else comes to mind.) Sometimes you can freewrite without a topic in mind, but at other times you will focus your attention on a particular topic. This strategy is called **focused freewriting**.

When you finish freewriting, read what you have written. Then, underline any ideas you think you might be able to use. If you find an idea you want to explore further, freewrite again, using that idea as a starting point.

Stella's focused freewriting on the topic of whether or not community service should be a required part of the college curriculum appears below.

Community service. Community service. Sounds like what you do instead of going to jail. Service to the community—service in the community. Community center. College community—community college. Community service—I guess it's a good idea to do it—but when? In my spare time—spare time—that's pretty funny. So after school and work and all the reading and studying I also have to do <u>service</u>? Right. And what could I do anyway? Work with kids. Or homeless people. Old people? Sick people? Or not people—maybe animals. Or work for a political candidate. Does that count? But when would I do it? Maybe other people have time, but I don't. OK idea, could work—but not for me.

Stella's freewriting

PRACTICE

2-3 Reread Stella's freewriting on the topic of community service for college students (p. 34). If you were advising her, which of her ideas would you suggest she explore further? Underline these ideas in her freewriting, and be prepared to discuss your suggestions with the class or in a small group.

---

freewrite

Write (or type) for at least five minutes on the following topic: What is the primary purpose of college—to give students a general education or to prepare them for careers?

When you are finished, reread your freewriting, and underline any ideas you think you might be able to use in your paragraph.

Rene Sheret

FYI

To experience genuine freewriting, try darkening your computer screen while you type. This strategy will prevent you from stopping to reread and analyze what you have already written.

Brainstorming

When you **brainstorm**, you quickly record all the ideas about your topic that you can think of. Unlike freewriting, brainstorming is sometimes written in list form and sometimes scattered all over the page. You don't have to use complete sentences; single words or phrases are fine. You can underline, star, or box important points. You can also ask questions, draw arrows to connect ideas, and even draw pictures or diagrams.

Stella's brainstorming notes on community service appear below.

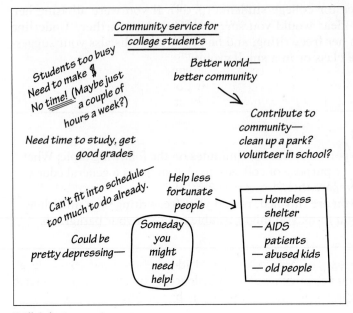

Stella's brainstorming notes

PRACTICE

2-4   Reread Stella's brainstorming notes on community service (above). How is her brainstorming similar to her freewriting on the same subject (p. 34)? How is it different? If you were advising Stella, which ideas would you suggest she write more about? Which ideas should she cross out? Be prepared to discuss your suggestions with the class or in a small group.

© Bill Aron/PhotoEdit

brainstorm

On a sheet of paper or on your computer, brainstorm about your assignment: What do you think is the primary purpose of college—to give students a general education or to prepare them for careers? (Begin by writing your topic, "The purpose of college," at the top of the page.)

When you have finished, look over what you have written. Did you come up with any new ideas as you brainstormed that you did not discover while freewriting?

FYI

Usually you brainstorm on your own, but at times you may find it helpful to do **collaborative brainstorming**, working with other students to find ideas. Sometimes your instructor may ask you and another student to brainstorm together. At other times, the class might brainstorm as a group while your instructor records the ideas you think of. However you brainstorm, your goal is the same: to come up with as much material about your topic as you can.

PRACTICE

2-5 Working as a class or in a group of three or four students, practice collaborative brainstorming, following these steps:

- First, decide as a group on a topic for brainstorming. (Your instructor may assign a topic.)

- Next, choose one person to record ideas. (If your group is large enough, you might choose two people to write down ideas, and have them compare notes at the end of the brainstorming session.)

- Then, discuss the topic informally, with each person contributing at least one idea.

- Finally, review the ideas that have been written down. As a group, try to identify interesting connections among ideas, and suggest ideas that might be explored further.

Clustering

Clustering, sometimes called *mapping*, is another strategy that can help you find ideas to write about. When you cluster, you begin by writing your topic in the center of a sheet of paper. Then, you branch out, writing related ideas on the page in groups, or clusters, around the topic. As you add new ideas, you circle them and draw lines to connect the ideas to one another and to the topic at the center. (These lines will look like a spiderweb or like spokes of a wheel or branches of a tree.) As you move from the center to the corners of the page, your ideas will get more and more specific.

Sometimes one branch of your cluster diagram will give you all the material you need. At other times, you may decide to write about the ideas from several branches, or to choose one or two ideas from each branch. If you find you need additional material after you finish your first cluster diagram, you can cluster again on a new sheet of paper, this time beginning with a topic from one of the branches.

Stella's cluster diagram on the topic of community service for college students appears below.

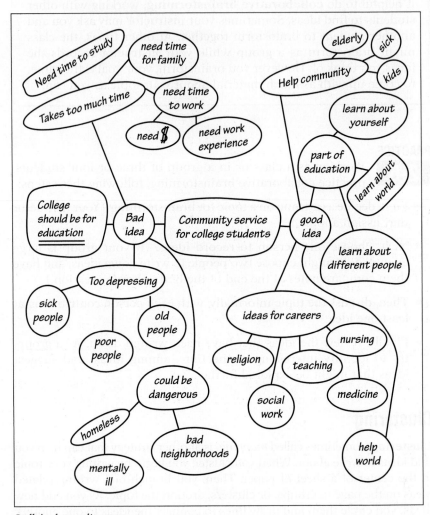

Stella's cluster diagram

PRACTICE

2-6 Look closely at Stella's cluster diagram on the topic of community service for college students. How is it similar to her brainstorming on the same subject (p. 36)? How is it different? If you were advising Stella, which branches of the cluster diagram would you suggest she develop further? Why? Would you add any branches? Be prepared to discuss your suggestions with the class or in a small group.

make a cluster diagram

Write your topic ("The purpose of college") in the center of a blank sheet of unlined paper. Circle the topic, and then branch out with specific ideas and examples, continuing to the corners of the page if you can.

Rene Sheret

When you have finished, look over what you have written. Use a highlighter to identify the branches and ideas that you could develop further. Then, add as many new details and branches as you can.

Keeping a Journal

A **journal** is a notebook or a computer file in which you keep an informal record of your thoughts and ideas. In a journal, you can reflect, question, summarize, or even complain. Your journal is also a place where you record ideas about your assignments and note possible ideas to write about. Here you can try to resolve a problem, restart a stalled project, argue with yourself about your topic, or comment on a draft. You can also try out different versions of sentences, list details or examples, or keep a record of interesting things you read, see, or hear.

Journal writing works best when you write regularly, ideally at the same time each day, so that it becomes a habit. Once you have started making regular entries in your journal, take the time every week or so to go back and reread what you have written. You may find material you want to explore in further journal entries—or even an idea for an essay.

FYI

Journals

Here are some subjects you can write about in your journal:

■ *Your schoolwork*   You can explore ideas for writing assignments, reflect on what you have learned, and ask questions about concepts you are having trouble understanding.

■ *Your job*   You can record job-related successes and frustrations, examine conflicts with coworkers, or review how you handled problems on the job. Reading over these entries can help you understand your strengths and weaknesses and become a more effective employee.

(continued)

(continued from previous page)

- *Your ideas about current events*   Expressing your opinions in your journal can be a good way to explore your reactions to social or political issues. Your journal entries may encourage you to write to your local or school newspaper or to public officials—and even to become involved in community projects or political activities.

- *Your impressions of what you see*   Many writers carry their journals with them everywhere so they can record any interesting or unusual things they observe. You can later incorporate these observations into essays or other pieces of writing.

- *Aspects of your personal life*   Although you may not want to record the intimate details of your life if your instructor will read your journal, writing about relationships with family and friends, personal problems, hopes and dreams, and so on can help you develop a better understanding of yourself and others.

Here is Stella's journal entry on the topic of community service for college students.

> I'm not really sure what I think about community service. I guess I think it sounds like a good idea, but I still don't see why we should have to do it. I can't fit anything else into my life. I guess it would be possible if it was just an hour or two a week. And maybe we could get credit and a grade for it, like a course. Or maybe it should just be for people who have the time and want to do it. But if it's not required, will anyone do it?

Stella's journal entry

© Bill Aron/PhotoEdit

write a journal entry

For your first journal entry, record your thoughts about the topic you have been working on in this chapter: the purpose of college.

2d Identifying Your Main Idea and Writing a Topic Sentence

When you think you have enough material to write about, it is time to identify your **main idea**—the idea you will develop in your paragraph.

To find a main idea for your paragraph, begin by looking over what you have already written. As you read through your freewriting, brainstorming, clustering, or journal entries, look for the central idea that your material seems to support. The sentence that states this main idea and gives your writing its focus will be your paragraph's **topic sentence**.

The topic sentence is usually the first sentence of your paragraph, and it is important because it tells both you and your readers what the focus of your paragraph will be. An effective topic sentence has three characteristics.

1. ***A topic sentence is a complete sentence.*** There is a difference between a *topic* and a *topic sentence*. The **topic** is what the paragraph is about. A **topic sentence**, however, is a complete sentence that includes a subject and a verb and expresses a complete thought. This sentence includes both a topic and the writer's idea about the topic.

TOPIC	Community service for college students
TOPIC SENTENCE	Community service should be required for all college students.

2. ***A topic sentence is more than just an announcement of what you plan to write about.*** A topic sentence makes a point about the topic the paragraph discusses.

ANNOUNCEMENT	In this paragraph, I will explain my ideas about community service.
TOPIC SENTENCE	My ideas about community service changed after I started to volunteer at a soup kitchen for homeless families.

3. ***A topic sentence presents an idea that can be discussed in a single paragraph.*** If your topic sentence is too broad, you will not be able to discuss it adequately in just one paragraph. If your topic sentence is too narrow, you will not be able to say much about it.

TOPIC SENTENCE TOO BROAD	Students all over the country participate in community service, making important contributions to their communities.

TOPIC SENTENCE TOO NARROW	Our school has a community service requirement for graduation.
EFFECTIVE TOPIC SENTENCE	Our school's community service requirement has had a number of positive results.

When Stella Drew reviewed her notes, she saw that they included two different kinds of ideas: ideas about the value of doing community service and ideas about the problems it presents. The material on the value of community service seemed more convincing, so she decided that her paragraph should support a community service requirement. She stated her main idea in a topic sentence.

> Community service is so important that college students should be required to do it.

When Stella thought about how to express her topic sentence, she knew it had to be a complete sentence, not just a topic, and that it would have to make a point, not just announce what she planned to write about. When she reread the topic sentence she had written, she felt confident that it did these things. Her topic sentence was neither too broad nor too narrow, and it made a statement she could support in a paragraph.

PRACTICE

2-7   Read the following items. Put a check mark next to each one that has all three characteristics of an effective topic sentence. Be prepared to explain why some items are effective topic sentences while others are not.

Examples

Speaking two languages, an advantage in today's workplace

_____

Our school should not abandon the foreign language requirement.

___✓___

1. The new farmers' market makes it easier for people in the neighborhood to buy fresh produce. _____

2. Eating a balanced diet with plenty of proteins and carbohydrates

_____

3. In this paragraph, I will look at the disadvantages of a large high school. _____

4. The best size for high schools: not too large, not too small. _____

5. Participation in sports is important for children because it teaches them how to compete. _____

6. The history of sports goes back to before the earliest civilizations. _____

7. Spending a quiet evening at home can have several advantages. _____

8. Television, the most popular leisure activity in the United States _____

PRACTICE

2-8 Decide whether each of the following statements could be an effective topic sentence for a paragraph. If a sentence is too broad, write *too broad* in the blank following the sentence. If the sentence is too narrow, write *too narrow* in the blank. If the sentence is an effective topic sentence, write *OK* in the blank.

Example: Unfortunately, many countries in today's world are involved in conflicts. _*too broad*_

1. Deciding what to do in life is a difficult task for many young people. _____

2. A college career counselor can help students decide what kind of work they would like to do. _____

3. The college career counseling office has three full-time employees and two part-time employees. _____

4. Safe driving reduces the number of accidents and saves lives. _____

5. Different countries, and even different states, have different rules of the road. _____

6. Texting while driving greatly increases the chance of an accident. _____

7. Some students are much happier with their college experience than other students. _____

8. Joining a study group is a good way for students who commute to get to know other students. _____

9. Flu shots are especially important for people in certain high-risk groups. _____

10. Flu shots occasionally result in soreness in the area where the shot was given. _____

Rene Sheret

identify your main idea, and write a topic sentence

Look over the work you have done so far, and try to identify the main idea your material seems to support. Do you think college should give students a general education or prepare them for careers? Write a topic sentence that expresses your main idea on the lines below.

Topic sentence: _____

_____

2e Choosing Supporting Points

After you have stated your paragraph's main idea in a topic sentence, you will need to provide specific **evidence** (examples and details) to **support** your main idea.

When you choose points to support your topic sentence, make sure they are *relevant*, *distinct*, and *specific*.

1. **Relevant** points are directly related to your main idea.

   TOPIC SENTENCE   College is important because it teaches students skills they need for their future careers.

   SUPPORTING POINTS

   ■ Students learn to write in college, and knowing how to write well is important for any job.

   ■ Students learn to think critically in college, and knowing how to think critically is necessary for almost any career.

   ■ ~~Choosing a career path is difficult.~~

   The third supporting point above is not relevant because it does not support the topic sentence. (It does not provide an example of how skills learned in college will help students in their future careers.)

2. **Distinct** points are different from other points you plan to use.

   TOPIC SENTENCE   College is important because it teaches students skills they need for their future careers.

   SUPPORTING POINTS

   ■ Students learn to write in college, and knowing how to write well is important for any job.

   ■ Students learn to think critically in college, and knowing how to think critically is necessary for almost any career.

   ■ ~~College writing courses will prepare students to write on the job.~~

   The third point above is not distinct because it says the same thing as the first point.

3. **Specific** points communicate exactly what you want to say; they are not general or vague.

   to write in college, and knowing how to write well is important
   ■ Students learn ~~things in college that will help them~~ in any job.

   The original point above is not specific because it does not tell what "things" students learn. The revision clarifies the point the writer uses to support the topic sentence.

As she continued to work on her paragraph, Stella listed several points from her notes that she thought she could write about. After she read through her list of points, she crossed out those that did not support her topic sentence or that overlapped with other points. She decided that the remaining two points on her list would give her enough material to write about in her paragraph.

TOPIC SENTENCE　Community service is so important that college students should be required to do it.

- ~~Community service helps people.~~
- ~~Some community service activities could be boring.~~
- ~~Community service can help the world.~~
- Community service helps the community.
- ~~College students are busy.~~
- ~~Community service takes a lot of time.~~
- ~~Community service might not relate to students' majors.~~
- ~~Community service can be upsetting or depressing.~~
- Community service can be part of a student's education.

PRACTICE

2-9　In each of the following two outlines, a topic sentence and a tentative list of supporting points have been provided. Read each list of points carefully, and consider whether the points support the topic sentence. Cross out any points that are not relevant, distinct, and specific.

1. *Topic Sentence:* Even though some fans may object, professional sports teams should abandon their Indian logos and nicknames.

   - Indian logos and nicknames are offensive to many people.

   - Indian logos and nicknames misrepresent Indians and perpetuate troubling stereotypes.

   - Some Indian tribes have given teams official permission to use tribal names or symbols.

   - Many high school and college teams have already abandoned their Indian names and logos.

WORD POWER

perpetuate to cause to last for a long time

- Some sports teams change their names when they move to a different city.

- Tradition is not a strong enough reason to keep racist names and logos.

- Change is difficult, but fans will get used to new names and logos.

- Many people dislike teams' Indian nicknames and logos.

- Changing a name or a logo is not a big deal.

- Team names and logos that are disrespectful of other races and cultures are unacceptable.

2. *Topic Sentence:* The government should ban unpaid student internships because they are unfair.

- Internships can be hard to find.

- Employers benefit financially from interns' free labor.

- Many unpaid interns do boring, menial work and gain few valuable job skills.

- Some students are just looking to boost their résumés and do not mind working for free.

- The government has a responsibility to protect workers from being exploited.

- Without government involvement, few employers will offer to pay their interns.

- Employers are taking advantage of their interns' unpaid work.

- A lot of unpaid interns do not benefit much from their internship experiences.

- Students from low-income families cannot afford to work without pay as wealthier students can.

- Nobody wants to work for free.

- Interns do not have enough power to negotiate with employers for paid positions.

© Bill Aron/PhotoEdit

choose supporting points

Review your freewriting, brainstorming, clustering, and journal writing to identify the points that can best support your topic sentence. Write your topic sentence on the lines below; then, list your supporting points.

Topic sentence: _____

_____

Supporting points:

- _____
- _____
- _____

Check carefully to make sure each point on your list supports your topic sentence. Cross out any points that are not relevant, distinct, and specific.

2f   Developing Supporting Points

Now that you have identified points that support your main idea, you need to **develop** them, explaining them more fully and making clear how they relate to your topic sentence. One way to develop your points is to provide specific examples. To come up with examples, ask yourself *how? why?* or *what?* for each point.

After Stella chose the two points she was going to use to support her main idea, she went back and added examples to develop each point.

SUPPORTING POINT	EXAMPLES
Community service helps the community. (How?)	— *Volunteers can help feed the homeless.* — *They can work with the elderly.* — *They can tutor in schools.*
Community service can be part of a student's education. (How?)	— *Students can learn about themselves and others.* — *Students can learn about their community and the world.* — *Students can discover what they want to do for a career.*

develop your supporting points

Review your list of supporting points, and then think of examples you can use to develop each point. (If you like, you can make a chart like the one on p. 48 to help you arrange your supporting points and examples.)

© Bill Aron/PhotoEdit

2g   Making an Outline

After you have decided which points to use to support your topic sentence and chosen examples to develop each point, your next step is to make an informal **outline**. You do this by arranging your supporting points in the order in which you plan to discuss them in your paragraph.

When Stella thought she had gathered all the examples she needed to develop the two points she planned to discuss in her paragraph, she made the following informal outline.

Outline

Topic sentence: Community service is so important that college students should be required to do it.

- Community service helps the community.
    — Volunteers can help feed the homeless.
    — Volunteers can help the elderly.
    — Volunteers can tutor students.

- Community service can be part of a student's education.
    — Students can learn about themselves.
    — Students can learn about others.
    — Students can learn about community.
    — Students can learn about the world.
    — Students can discover what they want to do for a career.

Stella's informal outline

Rene Sheret

make an outline

Look over your supporting points, and decide which ones you want to include in your paragraph. Then, make an informal outline that arranges your supporting points in the order in which you plan to write about them.

2h   Drafting Your Paragraph

Once you have written a topic sentence for your paragraph, selected the points you will discuss, and arranged them in the order in which you plan to write about them, you are ready to write a first draft.

In a **first draft**, your goal is to get your ideas down on paper. Begin your paragraph with a topic sentence that states the paragraph's main idea. Then, following your informal outline, write or type without worrying about correct wording, spelling, or punctuation. If a new idea occurs to you, include it in your draft. Don't worry about whether it fits with the other ideas. Your goal is not to produce a perfect paragraph but simply to create a working draft. Later on, when you revise, you will have a chance to rethink ideas and rework sentences.

Because you will be making changes to this first draft, you should leave wide margins, skip lines, and leave extra blank lines in places where you might need to add material.

When you have finished your first draft, don't make any changes right away. Take a break (overnight if possible), and think about something—anything—else. Then, return to your draft, and read it with a fresh eye.

Here is the first draft of Stella's paragraph on the topic of community service for college students. (Note that she included a brief working title to help her focus on her topic.)

Community Service

Community service is so important that college students should be

required to do it. When college students do community service,

they spend their time doing good for someone or for the community.

Working in a homeless shelter, doing chores for senior citizens, and

> tutoring children are all examples of community service. Community
> service activities like these are good for the community, and they can
> be more fulfilling for students than playing sports or participating in
> school activities. Community service can be an important part of a
> college education. Students can learn a lot about themselves and
> others and can discover what they want to do with their lives.
> Community service can also make the world a better place.

Stella's first draft

PRACTICE

2-10   Reread the first draft of Stella's paragraph. Working in a group
of three or four students, list the changes that you think Stella
should make. For example, what should she add? What should she cross
out? Have one member of your group record all your suggestions, and be
prepared to exchange ideas with the rest of the class.

draft your paragraph

Write a first draft of your paragraph about the purpose of a college
education. Be sure to state your main idea in the topic sentence and
support the topic sentence with specific evidence. Finally, add a
working title.

© Bill Aron/PhotoEdit

2i TESTing Your Paragraph

When you have finished your draft, the first thing you should do is "test"
what you have written to make sure it includes all the elements of an effective
paragraph. You do this by asking the following four **TEST** questions:

T ▪ **Topic sentence**—Does your paragraph have a topic sentence that
states its main idea?

E ▪ **Evidence**—Does your paragraph include specific points that support your topic sentence? Are these points developed with evidence
(examples and details)?

S ▪ **Summary statement**—Does your paragraph end with a statement that reinforces its main idea?

T ▪ **Transitions**—Does your paragraph include transitional words and phrases that show readers how your ideas are related?

If your paragraph includes these four **TEST** elements, you are off to a very good start. If it does not, you will need to add whatever is missing.

When Stella reread her draft, she **TEST**ed it to take a quick inventory of her paragraph.

- She decided that her **topic sentence** clearly stated her main idea.
- She thought she needed more **evidence** to support her topic sentence.
- She noticed that her paragraph had no **summary statement**.
- She realized she needed to add **transitions** to connect her ideas.

Rene Sheret

TEST your paragraph

TEST the first draft of your paragraph to make sure it includes all four elements of an effective paragraph: Topic sentence, Evidence, Summary statement, and Transitions. If any elements are missing, add them now.

2j Revising Your Paragraph

Once you have **TEST**ed your paragraph to make sure it is complete, you are ready to revise it.

Revision is the process of reseeing, rethinking, reevaluating, and rewriting your work. Revision involves much more than substituting one word for another or correcting a comma here and there. It means moving sentences, adding words and phrases, and even changing the direction or emphasis of your ideas.

Using a Self-Assessment Checklist

To get the most out of the revision process, you should carefully reread your draft, using the following Self-Assessment Checklist to guide your revision.

self-assessment checklist

Revising Your Paragraph

- [ ] Is your topic sentence clearly worded?

- [ ] Do you have enough evidence to support your topic sentence, or do you need to look back at your notes or try another strategy to find additional supporting material?

- [ ] Do you need to explain anything more fully or more clearly?

- [ ] Do you need to add or delete examples or details?

- [ ] Does every sentence say what you mean?

- [ ] Can you combine any sentences to make your writing smoother?

- [ ] Should you move any sentences?

- [ ] Are all your words necessary, or can you cut some?

- [ ] Should you change any words to make them more specific?

- [ ] Does your paragraph end with a summary statement that clearly reinforces its main idea?

Using Peer Review

Sometimes you revise on your own, but at other times—with your instructor's permission—you may be able to get feedback (in the form of oral or written comments) from your classmates. The process of giving and receiving constructive feedback is called **peer review**. Peer review is most productive if you know how to make helpful comments and how to use the comments you get from your peers.

WORD POWER

peer someone with equal standing; an equal

Guidelines for Peer Review

Giving Feedback

- **Be positive.** Remember that your purpose is to help other students improve their writing.

- **Be tactful.** Be sure to emphasize the good points about the writing. Mention one or two things the writer has done particularly well before you offer your suggestions for improvement.

(continued)

(continued from previous page)

- **Be specific.** Offer concrete suggestions about how the writer could do better. A general comment like "You need more support" is not as helpful as a more specific comment like "You need support for the point you make in the fourth sentence."

- **Be involved.** If you are giving feedback orally instead of in writing, make sure you interact with the writer. Ask questions, listen to responses, and explain your comments.

- **Look at the big picture.** Don't focus on issues such as spelling and punctuation, which the writer will correct at the editing and proofreading stage. At this point, the clarity of the topic sentence (or the thesis statement for an essay), the effectiveness of the support, and the organization of ideas are much more important.

- **Be thorough.** When possible, write down and explain your comments, either on a form your instructor provides or in the margins of the draft you are reviewing. (If you are reviewing another student's writing electronically, you can use the Comment function in Microsoft Word's Track Changes tool to insert your feedback.)

Using Feedback

- **Be open-minded.** Receive your peers' comments with an open mind. They might notice something important that you missed, and they might help you see something from a different angle.

- **Be selective.** It is up to you to carefully evaluate the suggestions from your peers and decide whether or not their advice will strengthen your draft. Remember, not every suggestion is worth following, but every one is worth considering.

One effective strategy to use when you are reviewing the work of your classmates is to **TEST** their writing. Just as you **TEST** your own drafts, you can use **TEST** to guide your peer review and to help you stay focused on the big picture. Here are the questions you should ask yourself as you review other students' work and make comments.

T ▪ **Topic sentence**—Does this paragraph have a topic sentence that states its main idea? If the answer is no, remind your classmate to add a topic sentence that clearly states the main idea of the paragraph.

E ▪ **Evidence**—Does this paragraph include specific points that support the topic sentence? Are these points developed with evidence (examples and details)? If the answer to these questions is no, alert the writer to this issue and suggest the kinds of examples and details that he or she might add to better support the topic sentence.

S ▪ **Summary statement**—Does this paragraph end with a statement that reinforces its main idea? If the answer is no, remind your classmate to add a summary statement that clearly reinforces the main idea of the paragraph.

T ▪ **Transitions**—Does this paragraph include transitional words and phrases that show readers how ideas are related? If the answer is no, point out specific areas where the relationship between ideas is unclear.

Classmates in Stella's peer-review group used **TEST** to make suggestions for revision, working on an electronic draft of Stella's paragraph as part of a homework assignment. Their comments on her first draft, inserted using the Comment function of Microsoft Word's Track Changes tool, follow.

Community Service

Community service is so important that college students should be required to do it. When college students do community service, they spend their time doing good for someone or for the community. Working in a homeless shelter, doing chores for senior citizens, and tutoring children are all examples of community service. Community service activities like these are good for the community, and they can be more fulfilling for students than playing sports or participating in school activities. Community service can be an important part of a college education. Students can learn a lot about themselves and others and can discover what they want to do with their lives. Community service can also make the world a better place.

> **Comment [RK1]:** Can title be more specific? What will paragraph be about?

> **Comment [AJ1]:** Good topic sentence!

> **Comment [RK2]:** Good examples

> **Comment [RK3]:** Add examples here?

> **Comment [AJ2]:** TEST element missing—you need a summary statement.

Stella's peer-reviewed draft

Guided by her **TEST** responses and the Self-Assessment Checklist, as well as by comments from her peer-review group, Stella revised her paragraph, writing her changes in by hand on her typed draft.

Why Community Service Should Be Required

Community service is so important that college students should be
required to do it. When college students do community service, they spend
helping a person or organization in their communities.   For example, they can work
their time ~~doing good for someone or for the community. Working~~ *do* in a homeless
shelter, ~~doing~~ chores for senior citizens, ~~and tutoring~~ *or tutor or mentor at-risk* children. ~~are all exam-~~
~~ples of community service.~~ Community service activities like these are good for
are also good for the students who give their time. This work
the community, and they can be more fulfilling ~~for students~~ than playing
also
sports or participating in school activities. Community service can be an important part of a college education. Students can learn a lot about themselves
, about their communities, about different kinds of people, and about their world. They
~~and others and~~ can discover what they want to do with their lives. ~~Community~~
even
~~service can also make the world a better place.~~   *For example, working in a*
school can lead a student to a career as a teacher. For all these reasons, community
service should be a required part of the college curriculum.

Stella's revised draft with handwritten revisions

As she made her revisions, Stella did not worry about being neat. She crossed out words, added material, and changed sentences and words. When she felt her revision was complete, she was ready to move on to edit and proofread her paragraph.

2k Editing and Proofreading Your Paragraph

When you **edit**, you check for correct grammar, punctuation, mechanics, and spelling. Then, you go on to **proofread** carefully for typographical errors that your spell checker may not identify, checking to make sure that you have indented the first sentence of your paragraph and that every sentence begins with a capital letter and ends with a period. Finally, you check your essay's **format** to make sure it satisfies your instructor's requirements.

Remember, editing and proofreading are vital steps in the writing process. Many readers will not take your ideas seriously if your paragraph contains grammatical or mechanical errors. You can use the following checklist to guide your editing.

self-assessment checklist

Editing and Proofreading Your Paragraph

- [ ] Are all your sentences complete and grammatically correct?
- [ ] Do all your subjects and verbs agree?
- [ ] Have you used the correct verb tenses?
- [ ] Are commas used where they are required?
- [ ] Have you used apostrophes correctly?
- [ ] Have you used other punctuation marks correctly?
- [ ] Have you used capital letters where they are required?
- [ ] Are all words spelled correctly?

For help with grammar, punctuation, mechanics, and spelling, see **Units 4–7** of this text.

Before Stella edited her paragraph, she typed in the changes she had made by hand on her first draft and printed out a revised draft. Then, she checked grammar, punctuation, mechanics, and spelling and proofread for typos. The final version of her paragraph appears below.

Why Community Service Should Be Required

TEST
- Topic Sentence
- Evidence
- Summary Statement
- Transitions

Topic sentence —
Community service is so important that college students should be required to do it. When college students do community service, they spend

Evidence —
their time helping a person or organization in their communities. For example, they can work in homeless shelters, do chores for senior citizens, or tutor or mentor at-risk children. Community service activities like these are good for the community, and they are also good for the students who give their time. This work can be more fulfilling than playing sports or participating in school activities. Community service can also be an important part of a college education. Students can learn a lot about themselves, about their communities, about different kinds of people, and about their world. They can even discover what they want to do with their lives. For example,

Summary statement —
working in a school can lead a student to a career as a teacher. For all these reasons, community service should be a required part of the college curriculum.

PRACTICE

2-11 Reread the final draft of Stella's paragraph about community service for college students (above), and compare it with her first draft (pp. 50–51). Then, working in a group of three or four students, answer the following questions about her revision. (Be prepared to discuss your responses to these questions with the class.)

1. Do you agree with Stella's decision not to revise her paragraph's topic sentence?

2. What new supporting material did Stella add to her paragraph? Can you think of any new material she *should* have added?

3. What did Stella cross out? Why do you think she deleted this material? Do you think she should cross out any additional material?

4. Why do you think Stella added "For example" and "also" to her final draft?

5. In her revision, Stella added a sentence at the end of the paragraph. Do you think this sentence is necessary? Why or why not?

Rene Sheret

revise, edit, and proofread your paragraph

Use the Self-Assessment Checklist on page 53 (and, if your instructor allows it, feedback from peer review) to help you revise your draft. Then, edit your paragraph, checking grammar, punctuation, mechanics, and spelling—and proofread carefully for typos. When you are satisfied with your paragraph, print it out.

review checklist

Writing a Paragraph

☐ Be sure you understand paragraph structure. (See 2a.)

☐ Before you start to write, consider your assignment, purpose, and audience. (See 2b.)

☐ Use freewriting, brainstorming, clustering, and journal writing to help you find ideas. (See 2c.)

☐ Identify your main idea, and write a topic sentence. (See 2d.)

☐ Choose points to support your main idea. (See 2e.)

☐ Develop your supporting points with evidence. (See 2f.)

☐ Make an informal outline by arranging your points in the order in which you plan to discuss them. (See 2g.)

☐ Write a first draft of your paragraph. (See 2h.)

☐ TEST your paragraph. (See 2i.)

☐ Revise your paragraph. (See 2j.)

☐ Edit and proofread your paragraph. (See 2k.)

3 TESTing Your Paragraphs

focus on writing

This picture shows students reading and writing on three different digital devices. Which kind of device do you use most often? What do you like about it? What, if anything, do you dislike? Write a paragraph in which you discuss the advantages and disadvantages of reading and composing on one of these devices.

As you learned in Chapter 2, you should TEST every paragraph after you finish drafting. TESTing will tell you whether or not your paragraph includes all the elements of an effective paragraph.

T opic sentence
E vidence
S ummary statement
T ransitions

If you TEST the following paragraph, you will see that it contains all four elements of an effective paragraph.

TEST

- Topic Sentence
- Evidence
- Summary Statement
- Transitions

WORD POWER

innovation something newly invented; a new way of doing something

Although most people do not know it, the modern roller coaster got its start in Coney Island in Brooklyn, New York. First, in 1888, the Flip Flap Railway, which featured a circular loop, was built. The coaster was the first to go upside down, but it frequently injured riders' necks. Next, in 1901, the Loop-the-Loop, which was safer than the Flip Flap Railway, was built. Then, from 1884 through the 1930s, over thirty roller coasters were constructed in Coney Island. Finally, in 1927, the most famous roller coaster in history, the Cyclone, was built at a cost of over $100,000. Although it began operating over eighty years ago, it is still the standard by which all roller coasters are measured. It has steep drops, a lot of speed, and only lap belts to hold riders in their seats. Still in operation, the Cyclone is the most successful ride in Coney Island history. It is the last survivor of the wooden roller coasters that once drew crowds to Coney Island. With their many innovations, Coney Island's roller coasters paved the way for the high-tech roller coasters in amusement parks today.

3a TESTing for a Topic Sentence

The first thing you do when you TEST a paragraph is look for a **topic sentence (T)**. An effective paragraph focuses on a single main idea, and it includes a topic sentence that states this main idea.

A paragraph is **unified** when all its sentences support the main idea stated in the topic sentence. When you revise, you can make your paragraphs unified by crossing out sentences that do not support your topic sentence and, if necessary, adding sentences that do.

The following paragraph is not unified because it contains sentences that do not support the paragraph's topic sentence. (These sentences have been crossed out.)

The weak economy has led many people to move away from the rural Ohio community where I was raised. Over the years, farmland has become more and more expensive. Years ago, a family could buy each of its children twenty-five acres on which they could start farming. Today, the average farmer cannot make enough money to buy this amount of land, and those who choose not to farm have few alternatives. ~~After I graduate, I intend to return to my town and get a job there. Even though many factories have moved out of the area, I think I will be able to get a job. My uncle owns a hardware store, and he told me that after I graduate, he will teach me the business. I think I can contribute something to both the business and the community.~~ Young people just cannot get good jobs anymore. Factories have moved out of the area and taken with them the jobs that many young people used to get after high school. As a result, many eighteen-year-olds have no choice but to move away to find employment.

The following revised paragraph is unified. It discusses only the idea that is stated in the topic sentence.

The weak economy has led many people to move away from the rural Ohio community where I was raised. Over the years, farmland has become more and more expensive. Years ago, a family could buy each of its children twenty-five acres on which they could start farming. Today, the average farmer cannot make enough money to buy this amount of land, and those who choose not to farm have few alternatives. Young people just cannot get good jobs anymore. Factories have moved out of the area and taken with them the jobs that many young people used to get after high school. As a result, many eighteen-year-olds have no choice but to move away to find employment.

T E S T
- Topic Sentence
- ■ Evidence
- ■ Summary Statement
- ■ Transitions

PRACTICE

3-1   The following paragraph is not unified because some sentences do not support the topic sentence. First, underline the topic sentence. Then, cross out any sentences that do not support the topic sentence.

Although many people still get down on one knee to propose, others have found more creative ways to pop the question. Using Jumbotrons, computer games, or even zero-gravity chambers, some people are making the moment truly memorable. Last year, one English graffiti artist asked his girlfriend to marry him by spray-painting his proposal on the side of a building. In 2011, a man used the Sunday crossword puzzle in the *Washington Post* to propose to his girlfriend. As she completed the puzzle, she saw that the answers to several of the clues spelled out her name and a question. Weddings are also becoming more unusual. Some couples are choosing to get married while skydiving or riding bicycles. One couple recently got married in a shark tank. Several brave people have also proposed on television. By buying ad space and recording a brief video clip, they appear on the screen during a favorite show. People are clearly using their imaginations to ask this age-old question in unexpected ways.

PRACTICE

3-2 The following paragraph has no topic sentence. Read it carefully, and then choose the most appropriate topic sentence from the list that follows the paragraph.

While continuing to make its famous interlocking plastic bricks, Lego has created a number of popular video games, such as *Lego Racer* and *Lego Star Wars*. The company also shares ownership of four Legoland amusement parks and owns dozens of retail stores in Europe and North America. In 2014, the company produced a successful feature film called *The Lego Movie*. The company also continues to make products using licensed characters from other movies, such as *Harry Potter* and *Lord of the Rings*, and has its own television series on the Cartoon Network. The Lego Group also offers special programs to accompany its products. For example, the Lego Group has developed an educational branch, Lego Education, which sponsors competitions for students and provides lesson plans and professional development for educators. With such wide-ranging programs and merchandise, the company will likely continue to thrive.

Put a check mark next to the topic sentence that best expresses the main idea of the paragraph above.

1. The Lego Group has been very successful in the video game market.

   _____

2. Because of a decline in sales, the Lego Group is now pursuing the

   education market. _____

3. Today, the Lego Group is much more than just a manufacturer of children's construction toys. _____

4. The founder of the Lego Group, a Danish man named Ole Kirk Christiansen, had a passion for making children's toys. _____

5. By diversifying its products and services, the Lego Group has spread itself too thin. _____

PRACTICE

3-3   The following paragraphs do not have topic sentences. Think of a topic sentence that expresses each paragraph's main idea, and write it on the lines above the paragraphs.

Example: _Possible answer: Rock and roll originated in African American music_

but was reinterpreted by white performers.

Early 1950s African American musicians included performers such as Johnny Ace, Big Joe Turner, and Ruth Brown. Groups like the Drifters and the Clovers were also popular. By the mid-1950s, white performers such as Bill Haley and the Comets, Jerry Lee Lewis, and Elvis Presley were imitating African American music. Their songs had a beat and lyrics that appealed to a white audience. Eventually, this combination of black and white musical styles became known as rock and roll.

1. _____

_____

First, you have to find a suitable job to apply for. Once you decide to apply, you have to compose your résumé and cover letter to send them to the potential employer. Then, when you are invited in for an interview, you need to decide what you are going to wear and prepare a list of questions to ask your potential employer. Next, review your résumé, and practice anwering questions that the interviewer might ask you. At the interview, speak slowly and clearly, make eye contact, and answer all questions directly and honestly. After the interview, send a note to the person who interviewed you, thanking him or her and reinforcing your interest in the job. Finally, if everything goes well, you will get an email or a phone call offering you the job.

2. _____

_____

There are no written records left by the Native Americans themselves. Most of the early European settlers in North America were more interested in staying alive than in writing about the Native Americans. In addition, as the westward expansion took place, the Europeans encountered the Native Americans in stages, not all at once. Also, the Native Americans spoke at least fifty-eight different languages, which made it difficult for the Europeans to speak with them. Most important, by the time scholars decided to study Native American culture, many of the tribes no longer existed. Disease and war had wiped them out.

3b TESTing for Evidence

The next thing you do when you **TEST** a paragraph is to make sure you have enough **evidence (E)** to support the main idea stated in your topic sentence.

Evidence consists of the examples and details that support your statements. To make a convincing point, you need to support it with evidence. For example, it is one thing to say that gun violence has torn your neighborhood apart, but it is much more effective to follow this general statement with examples of specific incidents of gun violence in your community. The same is true when you describe something you have observed. You could, for example, say that a certain area of campus is peaceful. This statement means little to readers, however, unless you follow it with the details—the tall trees, the grass, the silence—that explain what you mean.

A paragraph is **well developed** when it includes enough evidence to explain and support its main idea. The following paragraph does not include enough evidence to support its main idea.

Although pit bulls have a bad reputation, they actually make good pets. Part of their problem is that they can look frightening. Actually, though, pit bulls are no worse than other breeds of dogs. Even so, the bad publicity they get has given them a bad reputation. Pit bulls really do not deserve their bad reputation, though. Contrary to popular opinion, pit bulls can (and do) make friendly, affectionate, and loyal pets.

The following revised paragraph now includes enough evidence to support the main idea stated in the topic sentence.

nce added   Although pit bulls have a bad reputation, they actually make good pets. Part of their problem is that they can look frightening. Their wide, powerful jaws, short muscular legs, and large teeth are ideally suited for fighting, and they were bred for this purpose. In addition, some pit bulls—especially males—can be very aggressive toward both people and other dogs. Actually, though, pit bulls are no worse than

nce added   other breeds of dogs. As several recent newspaper articles have pointed out, the number of reported bites by pit bulls is no greater than the number of bites by other breeds. In fact, some breeds, such as cocker spaniels, bite more frequently than pit bulls. Even so, the

nce added   bad publicity they get has given them a bad reputation. The problem is that whenever a pit bull attacks someone, the incident is reported on the evening news. Contrary to popular opinion, pit bulls can (and do) make friendly, affectionate, and loyal pets.

| T | E | S | T |

- ■ Topic Sentence
- ▢ Evidence
- ■ Summary Statement
- ■ Transitions

Note: Length alone is no guarantee that a paragraph includes enough supporting evidence for your main idea. A long paragraph that consists of one generalization after another will still not include enough support for the topic sentence.

PRACTICE

3-4   Underline the specific supporting evidence in each of the following paragraphs.

1. Hearing people have some mistaken ideas about the deaf community. First, some hearing adults think that all deaf people consider themselves disabled and would trade anything not to be "handicapped." Hearing people do not realize that many deaf people do not consider themselves handicapped and are proud to be part of the deaf community, which has its own language, customs, and culture. Second, many hearing people think that all deaf people read lips, so there is no need to learn sign language to communicate with them. However, lip reading—or speech reading, as deaf people call the practice—is difficult. Not all hearing people say the same words in the same way, and facial expressions can also change the meaning of the words. If hearing people make more of an attempt to understand the deaf culture, communication between them will improve.

2. One of the largest celebrations of the passage of young girls into womanhood occurs in Latin American and Hispanic cultures. This event is called La Quinceañera, or the fifteenth year. It acknowledges that a young woman is now of marriageable age. The day usually begins with a Mass of Thanksgiving. The young woman wears a full-length white or pastel-colored dress and is attended by fourteen friends and relatives

who serve as maids of honor and escorts. Her parents and godparents surround her at the foot of the altar. When the Mass ends, other young relatives give small gifts to those who attended, while the young woman places a bouquet of flowers on the altar of the Virgin. Following the Mass is an elaborate party, with dancing, cake, and toasts. Finally, to end the evening, the young woman dances a waltz with her favorite escort. For young Hispanic women, the Quinceañera is an important milestone.

PRACTICE

3-5 Provide two or three specific pieces of evidence (examples or details) to support each of the following topic sentences.

1. When it comes to feeding a family, there are several cost-effective alternatives to fast food.

   - _____

   - _____

   - _____

2. A romantic relationship with a coworker can create serious problems.

   - _____

   - _____

   - _____

3. Choosing the right career is harder than I thought it would be.

   - _____

   - _____

   - _____

PRACTICE

3-6 The paragraph that follows does not include enough supporting evidence. Suggest some examples and details that might help the writer develop the topic sentence more fully.

Young adults who move back in with their parents after college face many challenges. Feeling dependent on one's parents after living away from home can be frustrating. Living at home can restrict a person's freedom. Also, some parents can be overbearing and treat the young graduate as if he or she is a child. Of course, the success of the living situation depends on how well the college graduate and his or her parents communicate. Despite these drawbacks, living at home for a while after college can make sense.

3c   TESTing for a Summary Statement

The third thing you do when you TEST a paragraph is to make sure it ends with a **summary statement (S)**—a sentence that reinforces your paragraph's main idea. By reminding readers what your paragraph is about, a summary statement helps to further **unify** your paragraph.

The following paragraph has no summary statement.

> Overpopulation is one of the biggest concerns for scientists. In 1900, there were 1.6 billion people on Earth, a quarter of today's population. At that time, life expectancy was also much shorter than it is now. By 2000, the world's population had grown to over 6 billion, and today, the average life expectancy worldwide is almost sixty-five years. The low death rate, combined with a high birth rate, is adding the equivalent of one new Germany to the world's population each year. According to a United Nations study, if present trends continue, by 2050 the world's population will be between 7.3 and 10.5 billion—so large that much of the world may be either malnourished or starving.

The summary statement in the following revised paragraph reinforces the paragraph's main idea and brings the paragraph to a close.

> Overpopulation is one of the biggest concerns for scientists. In 1900, there were 1.6 billion people on Earth, a quarter of today's population. At that time, life expectancy was also much shorter than it is now. By 2000, the world's population had grown to over 6 billion, and today, the average life expectancy worldwide is almost sixty-five years. The low death rate, combined with a high birth rate, is adding the equivalent of one new Germany to the world's population each year. According to a United Nations study, if present trends continue, by 2050 the world's population will be between 7.3 and 10.5 billion—so large that much of the world may be either malnourished or starving. Given these increases, it is no wonder that scientists who study population are worried.

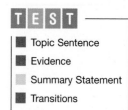

TEST

- Topic Sentence
- Evidence
- Summary Statement
- Transitions

PRACTICE

3-7   Read the following paragraph, which does not include a summary statement. Then, on the lines below the paragraph, write a summary statement that adds unity to the paragraph by reinforcing the main idea stated in the topic sentence. Be careful not to use the same wording as in the topic sentence.

> Founded more than fifty years ago, NASCAR has become one of the most successful spectator sports in the world. In December 1947, Bill France formed the National Association for Stock Car Auto Racing (NASCAR). The first NASCAR race was held at Daytona Beach's auto racecourse in 1948. From this modest start, France turned NASCAR into a highly successful business. Attendance grew 8.2 percent during 1997, and 2,102,000 fans attended the thirty-one NASCAR events in 1998. This was the first time that NASCAR attendance topped the two million mark. By 2012, more than three million people attended NASCAR events annually. Then, in 2013, NASCAR negotiated a ten-year deal with NBC and Fox for a reported $8.2 billion. As a result, these networks now televise NASCAR's most popular events.

_____

_____

_____

3d   TESTing for Transitions

The final thing you do when you TEST a paragraph is make sure the paragraph includes **transitions (T)** that connect ideas in a clear, logical order.

    Transitional words and phrases create **coherence** by indicating how ideas are connected in a paragraph—for example, in *time order*, *spatial order*, or *logical order*. By signaling the order of ideas in a paragraph, these words and phrases make it easier for readers to follow your discussion.

- You use **time** signals to show readers the order in which events occurred.

> In 1883, my great-grandfather came to this country from Russia.

- You use **spatial** signals to show readers how people, places, and things stand in relation to one another. For example, you can move from top to bottom, from near to far, from right to left, and so on.

Next to my bed is a bookcase that also serves as a room divider.

■ You use **logical** signals to show readers how ideas are connected. For example, you can move from the least important idea to the most important idea or from the least familiar idea to the most familiar idea.

Certain strategies can help you do well in college. First, you should learn to manage your time effectively.

Because transitional words and phrases create coherence, a paragraph without them can be difficult to understand. You can avoid this problem by checking to make sure you have included all the words and phrases that you need to link the ideas in your paragraph.

Frequently Used Transitional Words and Phrases

SOME WORDS AND PHRASES THAT SIGNAL TIME ORDER

after	finally	phrases that
afterward	later	include dates
at first	next	(for example,
before	now	"In June,"
during	soon	"In 1904")
earlier	then	
eventually	today	

SOME WORDS AND PHRASES THAT SIGNAL SPATIAL ORDER

above	in front	on the left
behind	inside	on the right
below	in the center	on top
beside	near	over
in back	next to	under
in between	on the bottom	

SOME WORDS AND PHRASES THAT SIGNAL LOGICAL ORDER

also	in fact
although	last
as a result	moreover
consequently	next
even though	not only . . . but also
first . . . second . . . third	one . . . another
for example	similarly
for instance	the least important
furthermore	the most important
however	therefore
in addition	

The paragraph below has no transitional words and phrases to link ideas.

> During his lifetime, Jim Thorpe faced many obstacles. Thorpe was born in 1888, the son of an Irish father and a Native American mother. He was sent to the Carlisle Indian School in Pennsylvania. "Pop" Warner, the legendary coach at Carlisle, discovered Thorpe. Thorpe left Carlisle to play baseball for two seasons in the newly formed East Carolina minor league. He returned to Carlisle, played football, and was named to the All-American team. Thorpe went to the Olympic Games in Stockholm, where he won two gold medals. Thorpe's career took a dramatic turn for the worse when a sportswriter who had seen him play baseball in North Carolina exposed him as a professional. The Amateur Athletic Union stripped him of his records and medals. Thorpe died in 1953. The International Olympic Committee returned Thorpe's Olympic medals to his family in 1982. Ironically, only in death was Thorpe able to overcome the difficulties that had frustrated him while he was alive.

The following revised paragraph is coherent because it includes transitional words and phrases that connect its ideas.

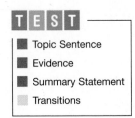

T E S T

■ Topic Sentence
■ Evidence
■ Summary Statement
  Transitions

> During his lifetime, Jim Thorpe faced many obstacles. Thorpe was born in 1888, the son of an Irish father and a Native American mother. In 1904, he was sent to the Carlisle Indian School in Pennsylvania. The next year, "Pop" Warner, the legendary coach at Carlisle, discovered Thorpe. Thorpe left Carlisle in 1909 to play baseball for two seasons in the newly formed East Carolina minor league. In 1912, he returned to Carlisle, played football, and was named to the All-American team. Thorpe then went to the Olympic Games in Stockholm, where he won two gold medals. The next year, however, Thorpe's career took a dramatic turn for the worse when a sportswriter who had seen him play baseball in North Carolina exposed him as a professional. As a result, the Amateur Athletic Union stripped him of his records and medals. Thorpe died in 1953. After years of appeals, the International Olympic Committee returned Thorpe's Olympic medals to his family in 1982. Ironically, only in death was Thorpe able to overcome the difficulties that had frustrated him while he was alive.

PRACTICE

3-8   Read the following paragraph carefully. Then, select transitional words and phrases from the accompanying alphabetized list, and write them in the appropriate blanks. When you have finished, reread your paragraph to make sure that it is coherent.

TRANSITIONS

after	for centuries
at first	however
before	in fact
by 1904	in 1897

The history of Jell-O is full of surprising setbacks. _____ Jell-O became "America's Most Famous Dessert," gelatin struggled for attention. _____, people experimented with the substance, but no one could make it appealing. By adding flavored syrup _____, Pearle B. Wait was the first to make gelatin taste good. Wait's wife, May, named the product Jell-O. _____, Wait could not market his new creation and ended up selling the company for $450 in 1899. _____, the next owner, Orator Francis Woodward, had the same problem. _____, he had supposedly tried to sell the company for even less money. _____ failing to find a buyer, Woodward started a major marketing campaign. He advertised in magazines and gave out free Jell-O cookbooks. _____, Jell-O was finally on its way to becoming the country's best-known dessert.

TEST · Revise · Edit · Proofread

Review the paragraph you drafted in response to the Focus on Writing prompt on page 59. Next, TEST your paragraph to make sure it includes a topic sentence, evidence, a summary statement, and transitions, and revise your draft accordingly. Then, edit and proofread your paragraph.

EDITING PRACTICE

TEST the following paragraph to make sure it is **unified**, **well developed**, and **coherent**. Begin by underlining the topic sentence. Then, cross out any sentences that do not support the topic sentence. If necessary, add evidence (details and examples) to support the topic sentence. Next, decide whether you need to make any changes to the paragraph's summary statement. (If the paragraph includes no summary statement, write one.) Finally, add transitional words and phrases where they are needed.

In 1979, a series of mechanical and human errors in Unit 2 of the nuclear generating plant at Three Mile Island, near Harrisburg, Pennsylvania, caused an accident that changed the nuclear power industry. A combination of stuck valves, human error, and poor decisions caused a partial meltdown of the reactor core. Large amounts of radioactive gases were released into the atmosphere. The governor of Pennsylvania evacuated pregnant women from the area. Other residents then panicked and left their homes. The nuclear regulatory agency claimed that the situation was not really dangerous and that the released gases were not a health threat. Activists and local residents disagreed with this. The reactor itself remained unusable for more than ten years. Large demonstrations followed the accident, including a rally of more than 200,000 people in New York City. Some people came just because the day was nice. By the mid-1980s, as a result of the accident at Three Mile Island, new construction of nuclear power plants in the United States had stopped.

COLLABORATIVE ACTIVITY

In a newspaper or magazine, find an illustration or photograph that includes a lot of details. Then, write a paragraph describing what you see. (Include enough details so that readers will be able to "see" it almost as clearly as you can.) Decide on a specific spatial order—from top to bottom or from left to right, for example—that makes sense to you, and follow this order as you organize the details in your paragraph. Finally, trade paragraphs with another student, and offer suggestions that could improve his or her paragraph.

review checklist

TESTing Your Paragraphs

☐ A topic sentence states a paragraph's main idea. (See 3a.)

☐ A paragraph should include enough evidence—examples and details—to support its main idea. (See 3b.)

☐ A paragraph should end with a summary statement that reinforces its main idea and helps to unify the paragraph. (See 3c.)

☐ A paragraph should include transitional words and phrases that indicate how ideas are connected. (See 3d.)

4 Exemplification Paragraphs

Student Services

FIRST FLOOR
Dean of Students
Disability Services
Student Affairs

SECOND FLOOR
Writing Center
Career Development
Advising

THIRD FLOOR
Counseling and Wellness Center
Center for International Students
Student Life

focus on writing

Most colleges have a student services center, where students can get information and advice on making the most of the programs and support the school provides. Brainstorm to develop a list of the programs and services your school offers (or should offer) to help students adjust to college. (If you prefer, you may choose a topic from the list on the following page instead.) You will return to your topic and review your brainstorming later in the chapter when you write your exemplification paragraph.

additional topics for exemplification

Effective (or ineffective) teachers
Qualities that make a great athlete
Challenges that older students face
A challenging job
Things you can't do without

In Chapters 2 and 3, you learned how to write effective paragraphs. In Chapters 4 through 12, you will learn different ways of organizing your ideas within paragraphs. Understanding these patterns of paragraph development can help you organize ideas and become a more effective, more confident writer.

4a Understanding Exemplification

What do we mean when we tell a friend that an instructor is *good* or that a football team is *bad*? What do we mean when we say that a movie is *boring* or that a particular law is *unjust*? To clarify general statements like these, we use **exemplification**—that is, we give **examples** to illustrate a general idea. In daily conversation and in school, you use specific examples to help explain your ideas.

GENERAL STATEMENT	SPECIFIC EXAMPLES
Today is going to be a hard day.	Today is going to be a hard day because I have a math test in the morning, a lab quiz in the afternoon, and work in the evening.

GENERAL STATEMENT	SPECIFIC EXAMPLES
My car is giving me problems.	My car is burning oil and won't start on cold mornings. In addition, it needs a new set of tires.

An **exemplification paragraph** uses specific examples to explain or clarify a general idea. Personal experiences, class discussions, observations, conversations, and readings can all be good sources of examples. (For information on writing exemplification essays, see 15a.)

When you **TEST** an exemplification paragraph, make sure it follows these guidelines:

T ▪ An exemplification paragraph should begin with a **topic sentence** that states the paragraph's main idea.

E ▪ An exemplification paragraph should present **evidence**—in the form of examples—that supports and clarifies the general statement made in the topic sentence. Examples should be arranged in **logical order**—for example, from least to most important or from general to specific. The number of examples you need depends on your topic sentence. A broad statement will probably require more examples than a relatively narrow one.

S ▪ An exemplification paragraph should end with a **summary statement** that reinforces the paragraph's main idea.

T ▪ An exemplification paragraph should include **transitions** that introduce the examples and connect them to one another and to the topic sentence.

Paragraph Map: Exemplification

Topic Sentence

Example #1

Example #2

Example #3

Summary Statement

Model Paragraph: Exemplification

The following paragraph uses several examples to support the idea that some countries change their names for political reasons.

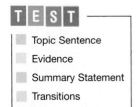

New Government, New Name

When countries change their names, it is often for political reasons. Sometimes a new government decides to change the country's name to separate itself from an earlier government. For example, Burma became Myanmar when a military government took over in 1989. Cambodia has had several name changes as well. After a coup in 1970, it was called the Khmer Republic. Then, in 1975, under communist rule, it became Kampuchea. Gaining independence from another nation is another reason for a country to change its name. For instance, in 1957, after gaining independence from Great Britain, the Gold Coast became Ghana. Another name change occurred when the French Sudan became Mali. After gaining independence from France in 1960, it decided to reject its colonial past. Finally, Zimbabwe gave up its former British name, Rhodesia, several years after winning independence. These name changes can be confusing, but they reveal the changing political climate of the countries in which they occur.

Examples presented in logical order

—Kim Seng (student)

Some Transitional Words and Phrases for Exemplification

When you write an exemplification paragraph, be sure to include appropriate transitional words and phrases. These transitions help readers follow your discussion by indicating how your examples are related and how each example supports the topic sentence.

also	furthermore	the most important
finally	in addition	example
first . . . second . . .	moreover	the next example
(and so on)	one example . . .	then
for example	another example	
for instance	specifically	

grammar in context

Exemplification

When you write an exemplification paragraph, always use a comma after the introductory transitional word or phrase that introduces an example.

> For example, Burma became Myanmar in 1989.

> For instance, the Gold Coast changed its name to Ghana in 1957.

> Finally, Zimbabwe gave up its British name after winning independence.

For information on using commas with introductory transitional words and phrases, see 33b.

Analyzing an Exemplification Paragraph

Read the exemplification paragraph below; then, follow the instructions in Practice 4-1.

Jobs of the Future

College students should take courses that prepare them for the careers that will be in demand over the next ten years. For example, the health-care field will have tremendous growth. Hundreds of thousands of medical workers—such as home-care aides, dental hygienists, and registered nurses—will be needed. Also, there will be an ongoing demand for workers who can operate and repair the specialized machines used in hospitals, labs, and other medical settings. In addition, a wide range of "green" jobs will become available as many industries work to strengthen their environmental policies. For example, construction workers, architects, and landscapers will be needed to create eco-friendly living and working spaces. Finally, education will be an attractive area for job seekers in the coming years. Many new teachers, especially those who are experienced with e-learning, will be needed to replace the teachers who retire during the next ten years. Students who know what jobs will be available can prepare themselves for the future.

—Bill Broderick (student)

PRACTICE

1. Underline the topic sentence of the paragraph above.

2. List the specific examples the writer uses to support his topic sentence. The first example has been listed for you.

health-care jobs

_____

_____

_____

3. Circle the transitional words and phrases that the writer uses to connect ideas in the paragraph.

4. Underline the paragraph's summary statement.

PRACTICE
4-2   Following are four possible topic sentences for exemplification paragraphs. Copy the topic sentences on a separate sheet of paper. Then, list three or four examples you could use to support each topic sentence. For example, if you were writing a paragraph about how difficult the first week of your new job was, you could mention waking up early, getting to know your coworkers, and learning new routines.

1. There are many things you can do to protect your online privacy.

2. Internships give students valuable opportunities to develop job skills.

3. Good advice is sometimes difficult to get.

4. Some reality television shows insult the intelligence of their viewers.

4b   Case Study: A Student Writes an Exemplification Paragraph

Here is how one student, Sarah Herman, wrote an exemplification paragraph.

When Sarah was asked to write a paragraph on a challenging job, she had little difficulty deciding what to focus on. She had just finished a summer job waiting tables in a beach community on the New Jersey shore—by far the most challenging job she had ever had. Once Sarah decided to focus her paragraph on this difficult work experience, she drafted the following topic sentence.

TOPIC SENTENCE   Waiting tables on the Jersey shore was the most challenging job I ever had.

identify your main idea, and write a topic sentence

Look back at the brainstorming you did in response to the Focus on Writing prompt on page 74, and choose several programs or services to write about. Then, draft a topic sentence that communicates the main idea your paragraph will discuss.

_____

_____

After Sarah drafted her topic sentence, she listed several examples to support it.

Restaurant too big

Boss disrespectful

No experience

Kitchen chaotic

Customers rude

Tips bad

list examples

List some examples that can support your topic sentence and help you develop your exemplification paragraph about programs or services that your school offers (or should offer) to help students adjust to college life.

_____

_____

_____

_____

_____

_____

Next, Sarah eliminated the examples on her list that she thought did not directly support her topic sentence. Then, she made an **informal outline**, arranging the remaining examples in the order in which she thought she could discuss them most effectively—in this case, from the least important to the most important example.

TOPIC SENTENCE   Waiting on tables was the most challenging job I ever had.

1. No experience
2. Customers rude
3. Tips bad
4. Boss disrespectful

make an outline

Create an informal outline for your paragraph by arranging your list of examples in a logical order—for instance, from the least important to the most important example. Make sure you include only those examples that directly support your topic sentence.

Using her informal outline as a guide, Sarah wrote the following draft of her paragraph.

> Waiting tables on the Jersey shore was the most challenging job I ever had. I had little experience as a food server. The first day of work was so bad that I almost quit. The customers were rude. All they wanted was to get their food as fast as possible so they could get back to the beach or the boardwalk. They were often impolite and demanding. The tips were bad. It was hard to be pleasant when you knew that the people you were waiting on were probably going to leave you a bad tip. Finally, the owner of the restaurant did not show us any respect. He often yelled at us, saying that if we didn't work harder, he would fire us. He never did, but his constant threats didn't do much to help our morale.

draft your paragraph

Using your informal outline as a guide, draft your exemplification paragraph.

When she finished her draft, Sarah scheduled a conference with her instructor, who suggested that her paragraph would be stronger if she made some of her examples more specific. For example, what experience did she have that made her want to quit? Exactly how were customers rude? Her instructor also reminded her that she needed to TEST her paragraph. As she TESTed her paragraph, Sarah assessed her draft.

- She checked her **topic sentence** and decided that it was effective.
- When she evaluated her **evidence**, she realized she needed to add more examples and details and delete irrelevant materials.

- She noticed that she did not have a **summary statement**, so she planned to add one at the end of her paragraph.
- She decided she needed to add more **transitions** to make it easier for readers to follow her discussion.

After TESTing her paragraph, Sarah revised her draft. The draft below, which has been edited and proofread, includes all the elements that Sarah looked for when she TESTed her paragraph.

T E S T

- Topic Sentence
- Evidence
- Summary Statement
- Transitions

My Most Challenging Job

Waiting tables on the Jersey shore was the most challenging job I ever had. First, I had never worked in a restaurant before, so I made a lot of mistakes. Once, I forgot to bring salads to a table I waited on. A person at the table complained so loudly that the owner had to calm him down. I was so frustrated and upset that I almost quit. Second, the customers at the restaurant were often rude. All they wanted was to get their food as fast as possible so they could get back to the beach or the boardwalk. They were on vacation, and they wanted to be treated well. As a result, they were frequently very demanding. No one ever said, "excuse me," "please," or "thank you," no matter what I did for them. Third, the tips were usually bad. It was hard to be pleasant when you knew that the people you were waiting on were probably going to leave you a bad tip. Finally, the owner of the restaurant never showed his workers any respect. He would yell at us, saying that if we didn't work harder, he would fire us. He never did, but his constant threats didn't do much to help our morale. Even though I survived the summer, I promised myself that I would never wait tables again.

TEST · Revise · Edit · Proofread

Look back at the draft of your exemplification paragraph. Using the TEST checklist on page 83, evaluate your paragraph to make sure it includes a topic sentence, evidence, a summary statement, and transitions, and revise your draft accordingly. Finally, edit and proofread your paragraph.

TESTing an exemplification paragraph

Topic Sentence Unifies Your Paragraph

☐ Do you have a clearly worded **topic sentence** that states your paragraph's main idea?

☐ Does your topic sentence state an idea that can be supported by examples?

Evidence Supports Your Paragraph's Topic Sentence

☐ Does all your **evidence**—the examples you present—support your paragraph's main idea?

☐ Do you need to add more examples?

Summary Statement Reinforces Your Paragraph's Unity

☐ Does your paragraph end with a **summary statement** that reinforces your main idea?

Transitions Add Coherence to Your Paragraph

☐ Do you use **transitions** to introduce each example your paragraph discusses?

☐ Do you need to add transitions to make your paragraph clearer and to help readers follow your ideas?

5 Narrative Paragraphs

"DO YOU BELIEVE IN MAGIC?" IT WAS A SONG ON THE RADIO THAT PLAYED THE SUMMER I DECIDED TO MOVE MY BEDROOM INTO THE BASEMENT.

I'LL MEETCHA TOMORROW SORTA LATE AT NIGHT

I WAS GROWING MY HAIR OUT AND IT WAS IN AN IN-BETWEEN STAGE THAT DIDN'T MAKE SENSE TO ANYBODY. I'D WANTED LONG HAIR ALL MY LIFE. I WAS WILLING TO LOOK INSANE WHILE I WAITED FOR IT.

DO YOU BELIEVE LIKE I BELIEVE

THERE WERE BIG CHANGES GOING ON IN MY HOUSE. GRANDMA MOVED OUT, AND BOTH MY PARENTS WERE "SECRETLY" SEEING OTHER PEOPLE. THEY WERE NEVER AROUND.

HALT! GET OUT OF MY WAY.

NO ONE SAID YOU COULD MOVE TO THE BASEMENT.

BUG OFF.

MAKE ME.

I WAS LEFT TO WATCH MY TWO YOUNGER BROTHERS AND KEEP HOUSE. I WAS SUPPOSED TO STAY AT HOME ALL DAY, EVERY DAY, THE SUMMER THAT SONG PLAYED ON THE RADIO.

WE'RE HUNGRY, MAN! YOU GOTTA MAKE US FOOD, MAN!

CHICKEN POT PIES, OVEN AT 350°.

WE'RE SICK OF CHICKEN POT PIE, MAN!

I'M NOT.

focus on writing

Barry, Lynda. From *One! Hundred! Demons!* (Sasquatch Books, 2002) Copyright © 2002 by Lynda Barry. All rights reserved. Used with permission.

These four panels are from Lynda Barry's book *One! Hundred! Demons!,* a graphic story about the author's childhood. Look at the panels, and then brainstorm to identify some experiences that you could discuss in a paragraph about a difficult period in your own childhood. You will return to this topic (or one of your choosing from the list on the next page) and review your brainstorming later in the chapter when you write your narrative paragraph.

In this chapter, you will learn to write a narrative paragraph.

PREVIEW

additional topics for narration

A difficult choice
An embarrassing situation
A dangerous experience
An experience that had an impact on you
An instance of injustice

5a Understanding Narration

Narration is writing that tells a story. For example, a narrative paragraph could tell how an experience you had as a child changed you, how the life of Martin Luther King Jr. is inspiring, or how the Battle of Gettysburg was the turning point in the Civil War. (For information on writing narrative essays, see 15b.)

When you TEST a **narrative paragraph**, make sure it follows these guidelines:

T ▪ A narrative paragraph should begin with a **topic sentence** that states its main idea, letting readers know why you are telling a particular story.

E ▪ A narrative paragraph should present **evidence**—events and details—in **time order**, usually in the order in which the events actually occurred. Effective narrative paragraphs include only those events that tell the story and avoid irrelevant information that could distract or confuse readers.

S ▪ A narrative paragraph should end with a **summary statement** that reinforces the paragraph's main idea.

T ▪ A narrative paragraph should include **transitions** that connect events to one another and to the topic sentence.

Paragraph Map: Narration

Topic Sentence

Event #1

Event #2

Event #3

Summary Statement

85

Model Paragraph: Narration

The student writer of the following paragraph presents a series of events to describe the creation of a viral video.

T E S T

- Topic Sentence
- Evidence
- Summary Statement
- Transitions

Fifteen Minutes of Fame

Events arranged in time order

Creating a viral video isn't easy. Before I created my first viral video, I spent hours watching some of the most famous online videos like "Charlie Bit My Finger" and "The Evolution of Dance." I even watched "The Dancing Baby," which debuted in the late 1990s and is considered one of the very first viral videos. Once I had done my research, I started drafting ideas for my own video. As soon as I finalized my concept for filming a flash mob at the local grocery store, I invited all of my friends and family to participate. We practiced four or five times and then put the plan into action. Two hours after filming, I uploaded the video to YouTube. Then I waited. Eventually, the number of views started to rise. Before I knew it, the video had over fifteen thousand views and the local newspaper was calling to see if they could interview me. Although my video only went viral locally, the hard work was worth it when I got my fifteen minutes of fame on the local news.

—Christine Clark (student)

Some Transitional Words and Phrases for Narration

As you arrange your ideas in a narrative paragraph, be sure to use clear transitional words and phrases. These signals help readers follow your narrative by indicating the order of the events you discuss.

after	first . . . second . . . third	specific dates
as	immediately	(for example, "In 2006")
as soon as	later	suddenly
before	later on	then
by the time	meanwhile	two hours (days, months,
earlier	next	years) later
eventually	now	until
finally	soon	when

grammar in context

Narration

When you write a narrative paragraph, you tell a story. As you become involved in your story, you might begin to string events together without proper punctuation. If you do, you will create a **run-on**.

INCORRECT (RUN-ON)	Two hours after filming, I uploaded the video to YouTube then I waited.
CORRECT	Two hours after filming, I uploaded the video to YouTube. Then I waited.

For information on how to identify and correct run-ons, see Chapter 23.

Analyzing a Narrative Paragraph

Read this narrative paragraph; then, follow the instructions in Practice 5-1.

Two men who risked their lives in the 1904 Harwick mine disaster were the inspiration for the Hero Fund, a charity that awards money to heroes and their families. The Harwick mine disaster began with a small explosion near the entry to the Harwick mine in Pennsylvania. Within seconds, this small explosion caused a chain reaction in which more and more coal dust was stirred up and ignited. Then, a strong blast sent materials and even a mule flying out of the mine shaft. Ten hours later, a rescue party led by Selwyn Taylor went down into the mine. The rescue party found only one survivor, but Taylor believed more men might still be alive deep within the mine. As he advanced, however, Taylor was overcome by fumes. The following day, another rescue worker, Daniel Lyle, was also overcome by fumes while searching for survivors. Neither Taylor nor Lyle found any survivors, and both men died as a result of their efforts. Three months after the mine disaster, Pittsburgh steelmaker Andrew Carnegie founded the Hero Fund to provide financial assistance to the families of those injured or killed while performing heroic acts. The Hero Fund continues to honor people like Selwyn Taylor and Daniel Lyle, ordinary people who take extraordinary risks to save others' lives.

—Kevin Smiley (student)

PRACTICE
5-1

1. Underline the topic sentence of the paragraph on page 87.

2. List the major events discussed in the paragraph. The first event has been listed for you.

A small explosion occurred near the entry to the mine.

_____

_____

_____

_____

_____

_____

3. Circle the transitional words and phrases that the writer uses to link events in time.

4. Underline the paragraph's summary statement.

PRACTICE
5-2

Following are four possible topic sentences for narrative paragraphs. List three or four events that could support each topic sentence. For example, if you were recalling a barbecue that turned into a disaster, you could tell about burning the hamburgers, spilling the soda, and forgetting to buy paper plates.

1. One experience made me realize that I was no longer as young as I thought.

2. The first time I _____, I got more than I bargained for.

3. I didn't think I had the courage to _____, but when I did, I felt proud of myself.

4. I remember my reactions to one particular event very clearly.

5b   Case Study: A Student Writes a Narrative Paragraph

Here is how one student, Todd Kinzer, wrote a narrative paragraph. When Todd's instructor asked the class to write a paragraph about an experience that had a great impact on them, Todd began by listing some experiences that he could write about.

> Accident at camp—Realized I wasn't as strong as I thought I was
>
> Breaking up with Lindsay—That was painful
>
> Shooting the winning basket in my last high school game—Sweet
>
> The last Thanksgiving at my grandparents' house—Happy and sad

As Todd looked over the experiences on his list, he realized that he could write about all of them. He decided, however, to focus on the last Thanksgiving he spent at his grandparents' house. This occasion was especially meaningful to him because his grandfather had died shortly after the holiday.

Todd began by freewriting on his topic. He typed whatever came into his mind about the dinner, without worrying about spelling, punctuation, or grammar. Here is Todd's freewriting paragraph.

> Thanksgiving. Who knew? I remember the smells when I woke up. I can see Granddad at the stove. We were all happy. He told us stories about when he was a kid. I'd heard some of them before, but so what? I loved to hear them. We ate so much I could hardly move. They say turkey has something in it that puts you to sleep. We watched football all afternoon and evening. I still can't believe Granddad is dead. I guess I have the topic for my paragraph.

freewrite

Look back at the brainstorming you did in response to the Focus on Writing prompt on page 84. Choose one experience from your notes, and then freewrite about that experience. Be sure to write nonstop, without worrying about spelling, punctuation, or grammar.

Lynda Barry © 2002. Used with permission.

After he finished freewriting, Todd arranged the main events he planned to write about in an informal outline that reflected the order in which they occurred.

Grandfather cooking

Grandfather told stories

Sat down for Thanksgiving dinner

Watched football on TV

Lynda Barry © 2002. Used with permission.

make an outline

Create an informal outline for your paragraph by arranging the events you remember from your childhood experience in the order in which they occurred. (Keep in mind that you will add details to develop these events when you draft your paragraph.)

Using his informal outline as a guide, Todd drafted the following paragraph.

> Last Thanksgiving, my grandparents were up early. My grandfather stuffed the turkey, and my grandmother started cooking the other dishes. When I got up, I could smell the turkey in the oven. The table was already set for dinner, so we ate breakfast in the kitchen. My grandfather told us about the Thanksgivings he remembered from when he was a boy. When we sat down for dinner, a fire was burning in the fireplace. My grandmother said grace. My grandfather carved the turkey, and we all passed around dishes of food. For dessert, we had pecan pie and ice cream. After dinner, we watched football on TV. When I went to bed, I felt happy. This was my grandfather's last Thanksgiving.

Lynda Barry © 2002. Used with permission.

draft your paragraph

Using your informal outline as a guide, draft your narrative paragraph.

Todd knew his draft needed a lot of work. Before he wrote the next draft, he tried to recall what other things had happened that Thanksgiving. He also tried to decide which idea was the most important and what additional supporting information could make his paragraph stronger. Todd emailed his draft to his instructor, and his instructor returned the draft along with her comments. After considering his instructor's suggestions and TESTing his paragraph, Todd decided to make the following changes.

- He decided that he needed to add a **topic sentence** that stated his paragraph's main idea.
- He decided that he needed to add some more details and examples and to delete irrelevant sentences so that all his **evidence** would support his main idea.
- He decided to write a stronger **summary statement**.
- He decided that he needed to add **transitions** to indicate the time order of the events in his paragraph.

After TESTing his paragraph, Todd revised and edited, checking grammar, punctuation, mechanics, and spelling. Then, he proofread carefully for typos. The final draft below includes all the elements Todd looked for when he TESTed his paragraph.

Thanksgiving Memories

This past Thanksgiving was happy and sad because it was the last one I would spend with both my grandparents. The holiday began early. At five o'clock in the morning, my grandfather woke up and began to stuff the turkey. About an hour later, my grandmother began cooking corn pie and pineapple casserole. At eight o'clock, when I got up, I could smell the turkey cooking. While we ate breakfast, my grandfather told us about Thanksgivings he remembered when he was a boy. Later, my grandfather made a fire in the fireplace, and we sat down for dinner. After my grandmother said grace, my grandfather carved and served the turkey. The rest of us passed around dishes of sweet potatoes, mashed potatoes, green beans, asparagus, cucumber salad, relish, cranberry sauce, apple butter, cabbage salad, stuffing, and, of course, corn pie and pineapple casserole. For dessert, my grandmother served pecan pie with scoops of ice cream. After dinner, we turned on the TV and the whole family watched football all evening. That night, I remember thinking that life couldn't get much better. Four months later, my grandfather died in his sleep. For my family and me, Thanksgiving would never be the same.

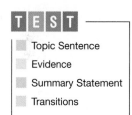

T E S T
- Topic Sentence
- Evidence
- Summary Statement
- Transitions

Lynda Barry © 2002. Used with permission.

TEST · Revise · Edit · Proofread

Look back at the draft of your narrative paragraph. Using the TEST checklist below, evaluate your paragraph to make sure it includes a topic sentence, evidence, a summary statement, and transitions, and revise your draft accordingly. Finally, edit and proofread your paragraph.

TESTing a narrative paragraph

Topic Sentence Unifies Your Paragraph

☐ Do you have a clearly worded **topic sentence** that states your paragraph's main idea?

☐ Does your topic sentence give readers an idea of why you are telling the story?

Evidence Supports Your Paragraph's Topic Sentence

☐ Do you include enough information about the events you discuss?

☐ Does all your **evidence**—events and details—support your paragraph's main idea?

☐ Do you need to include more events or details in your narrative?

Summary Statement Reinforces Your Paragraph's Unity

☐ Does your paragraph end with a **summary statement** that reinforces your main idea?

Transitions Add Coherence to Your Paragraph

☐ Do your **transitions** indicate the time order of events in your paragraph?

☐ Do you need to add transitions to make your paragraph clearer and to help readers follow your ideas?

6 Process Paragraphs

focus on writing

The picture shows a screen from the popular game *Candy Crush*, an app that so far has been installed over 500 million times. Brainstorm to develop a list of games you know well and could explain to others. (If you prefer, you may choose a topic from the list on the following page instead.) You will return to your topic and review your brainstorming later in the chapter when you write your process paragraph.

additional topics for process

How to apply for financial aid
How to shop online for bargains
A process you perform every day
How to find an apartment
How to prepare for a storm or another natural disaster

6a Understanding Process

When you describe a **process,** you tell readers how something works or how to do something. For example, you could explain how the optical scanner at the checkout counter of a food store works, how to hem a pair of pants, or how to start a blog. A **process paragraph** tells readers how to complete a process by listing steps in time order. (For information on writing process essays, see 15c.)

When you TEST a process paragraph, make sure it follows these guidelines:

T ■ A process paragraph should begin with a **topic sentence** that identifies the process you are explaining and the point you want to make about it (for example, "Parallel parking is easy once you know the secret" or "By following a few simple steps, you can design a résumé that will get noticed").

E ■ A process paragraph should discuss all the steps in the process, one at a time. These steps should be presented in strict **time order**— the order in which they occur. A process paragraph should present enough **evidence**—examples and details—to explain the steps and make the process clear to readers.

S ■ A process paragraph should end with a **summary statement** that reinforces the paragraph's main idea.

T ■ A process paragraph should include **transitions** that connect the steps in the process to one another and to the topic sentence.

Paragraph Map: Process

> **Topic Sentence**
>
> *Step #1*
>
> *Step #2*
>
> *Step #3*
>
> *Summary Statement*

There are two types of process paragraphs: *process explanations* and *instructions*.

Model Paragraph: Process Explanations

In a **process explanation**, your purpose is to help readers understand how something operates or how something happens—for example, how a hurricane forms or how fracking works. With a process explanation, you do not expect readers to perform the process.

In the following process explanation paragraph from a psychology exam, the writer explains the four stages children go through when they acquire language.

Children go through four distinct stages when they learn language. The first stage begins as soon as infants are born. By crying, they let people know when they need something or if they are in pain. The second stage begins when children are about a year old and are able to communicate with single words. For example, a child will use the word *food* to mean anything from "I'm hungry" to "feed the dog." The third stage begins at about twenty months. During this stage, children begin to use two-word sentences, such as "dada car" (for "This is dada's car"). Finally, at about thirty months, children begin to learn the rules that govern language. They learn how to form simple sentences, plurals, and the past tense of verbs. No matter what language they speak, all children follow the same process when they learn language.

—Jennifer Gulla (student)

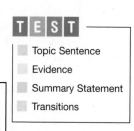

T E S T

Topic Sentence
Evidence
Summary Statement
Transitions

Steps presented
in time order

Model Paragraph: Instructions

When you write **instructions**, your purpose is to give readers the information they need to perform a task or activity—for example, to fill out an application, to operate a piece of machinery, or to help someone who is choking. Because you expect readers to follow your instructions, you address them directly, using **commands** to tell them what to do (*check the gauge . . . pull the valve*).

In the following paragraph, the writer gives a humorous set of instructions on how to get food out of a defective vending machine.

T E S T

Topic Sentence
Evidence
Summary Statement
Transitions

Step-by-step instructions presented in time order

Man vs. Machine

There is a foolproof method of outsmarting a vending machine that refuses to give up its food. First, approach the vending machine coolly. Make sure that you don't seem frightened or angry. The machine will sense these emotions and steal your money. Second, be polite. Say hello, compliment the machine on its selection of goodies, and smile. Be careful. If the machine thinks you are trying to take advantage of it, it will steal your money. Third, if the machine steals your money, remain calm. Ask nicely to get the food you paid for. Finally, it is time to get serious. Hit the side of the vending machine with your fist. If this doesn't work, lower your shoulder and throw yourself at the machine. (A good kick or two might also help.) When the machine has had enough, it will drop your snack, and you can grab it. If you follow these few simple steps, you should have no trouble walking away from vending machines with the food you paid for.

—Adam Cooper (student)

Some Transitional Words and Phrases for Process

Transitions are very important in process paragraphs. They enable readers to clearly identify each step—for example, *first, second, third,* and so on. In addition, they establish a sequence that lets readers move easily through the process you are describing.

after that,	first	subsequently
after this	immediately	the first (second,
as	later	third) step
as soon as	meanwhile	the next step
at the same time	next	the last step
at this point	now	then
during	once	when
finally	soon	while

grammar in context

Process

When you write a process paragraph, you may find yourself making **illogical shifts** in tense, person, and voice. If you shift from one tense, person, or voice to another without good reason, you may confuse readers.

CONFUSING (ILLOGICAL SHIFT)	First, the vending machine should be approached coolly. Make sure that you don't seem frightened or angry. (illogical shift from passive to active voice)
CLEAR	First, approach the vending machine coolly. Make sure that you don't seem frightened or angry. (consistent use of active voice)

For information on how to avoid illogical shifts in tense, person, and voice, see Chapter 26.

Analyzing a Process Paragraph

Read this process paragraph; then, follow the instructions in Practice 6-1.

An Order of Fries

I never realized how much work goes into making French fries until I worked at a potato processing plant in Hermiston, Oregon. The process begins with freshly dug potatoes being shoveled from trucks onto conveyor belts leading into the plant. During this stage, workers pick out any rocks that may have been dug up with the potatoes because these could damage the automated peelers. After the potatoes have gone through the peelers, they travel on a conveyor belt through the "trim line." Here, workers cut out any bad spots, being careful not to waste potatoes by trimming too much. Next, the potatoes are sliced by automated cutters and then deep-fried for about a minute. After this, they continue along a conveyor belt to the "wet line." Here, workers again look for bad spots, and they throw away any rotten pieces. At this point, the potatoes go to a second set of fryers for three minutes before being moved to subzero freezers for ten minutes. Then, it's on to the "frozen line" for a final inspection. The inspected fries are weighed by machines and then sealed into five-pound plastic packages, which are weighed again by workers who also check that the packages are properly sealed. Finally, the bags are packed into boxes and made ready for shipment to various restaurants across the western United States. This process goes on twenty-four hours a day to bring consumers the French fries they enjoy so much.

—Cheri Rodriguez (student)

PRACTICE
6-1

1. Underline the topic sentence of the paragraph on pages 97–98.

2. Is this a process explanation or instructions?

_____

How do you know? _____

3. List the steps in the process. The first step has been listed for you.

The potatoes are unloaded, and the rocks are sorted out.

_____

_____

_____

_____

_____

4. Circle the transitional words and phrases that the writer uses to move readers from one step to the next.

5. Underline the paragraph's summary statement.

PRACTICE
6-2

Following are four possible topic sentences for process paragraphs. List three or four steps that explain the process each topic sentence identifies. For example, if you were explaining the process of getting a job, you could list preparing a résumé, looking at ads in newspapers or online, writing a job application letter, and going on an interview. Make sure each step follows logically from the one that precedes it.

1. Getting the lowest prices when you shop is not a simple process.

2. Getting the most out of a student-teacher conference requires some preparation.

3. Crate-training a puppy can be a tricky process.

4. Choosing an outfit for a job interview can be challenging.

6b   Case Study: A Student Writes a Process Paragraph

Here is how one student, Manasvi Bari, wrote a process paragraph. When Manasvi was assigned to write a paragraph in which she explained a process she performed every day, she decided to write about how to get a seat on a crowded subway car. To make sure she had enough to write about, she made the following list of possible steps she could include.

Don't pay attention to heat

Get into the train

Get the first seat

Look as if you need help

Get to a pole

Don't travel during rush hour

Choose your time

Be alert

Squeeze in

After looking over her list, Manasvi crossed out steps that she didn't think were essential to the process she wanted to describe.

~~Don't pay attention to heat~~

Get into the train

Get the first seat

Look as if you need help

~~Get to a pole~~

~~Don't travel during rush hour~~

~~Choose your time~~

Be alert

Squeeze in

Bloomberg/Getty Images

list the steps in the process

Choose one game from the brainstorming you did in response to the Focus on Writing prompt on page 93, and then list the steps you need to discuss in order to explain how to play the game. (Assume that your readers know nothing about the game you are describing.)

_____

_____

_____

_____

_____

Now, cross out any steps that you don't think readers will need in order to understand how to play the game.

Once she had decided on her list of steps, Manasvi made an informal outline, arranging the steps in the order in which they should be performed.

Get into the train

Be alert

Get the first seat

Squeeze in

Look as if you need help

make an outline

Create an informal outline for your paragraph by arranging the steps for playing your game in the order in which they should be performed.

Bloomberg/Getty Images

At this point, Manasvi thought that she was ready to begin writing her paragraph. Here is her draft.

> When the train arrives, get into the car as fast as possible. Be alert. If you see an empty seat, grab it and sit down immediately. If there is no seat, ask people to move down, or squeeze into a space that seems too small. If none of this works, you'll have to use some imagination. Look helpless. Drop your books, and look as if the day can't get any worse. Sometimes a person will get up and give you a seat. If this strategy doesn't work, stand near someone who looks as if he or she is going to get up. When the person gets up, jump into the seat as fast as you can. Don't let the people who are getting on the train get the seat before you do.

draft your paragraph

Using your informal outline as a guide, draft your process paragraph.

Bloomberg/Getty Images

Manasvi showed the draft of her paragraph to a writing center tutor. Together, they TESTed her paragraph and made the following decisions.

- They decided that she needed to add a **topic sentence** that identified the process and stated the point she wanted to make about it.
- They decided that her **evidence**—the examples and details that described the steps in her process—was clear and complete.
- They decided that she needed to add a **summary statement** that reinforced the point of the process.
- They decided that she needed to add **transitions** that helped readers follow the steps in the process.

After **TEST**ing her paragraph, Manasvi revised her paragraph. The final edited and proofread draft includes all the elements that Manasvi looked for when she **TEST**ed her paragraph.

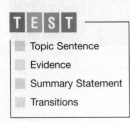

T E S T

■ Topic Sentence
■ Evidence
■ Summary Statement
■ Transitions

Surviving Rush Hour

> Anyone who takes the subway to school in the morning knows how hard it is to find a seat, but by following a few simple steps, you should be able to get a seat almost every day. First, when the train arrives, get into the car as fast as possible. Be alert. As soon as you see an empty seat, grab it and sit down immediately. Meanwhile, if there is no seat, ask people to move down, or try to squeeze into a space that seems too small. If none of this works, the next step is to use some imagination. Look helpless. Drop your books, and look as if the day can't get any worse. Sometimes a person will get up and give you a seat. Don't be shy. Take it, and remember to say thank you. Finally, if this strategy doesn't work, stand near someone who looks as if he or she is going to get up. When the person gets up, jump into the seat as fast as you can. By following these steps, you should be able to get a seat on the subway and arrive at school rested and relaxed.

Bloomberg/Getty Images

TEST · Revise · Edit · Proofread

Look back at the draft of your process paragraph. Using the **TEST** checklist on pages 102–103, evaluate your paragraph to make sure it includes a topic sentence, evidence, a summary statement, and transitions, and revise your draft accordingly. Finally, edit and proofread your paragraph.

TESTing a process paragraph

Topic Sentence Unifies Your Paragraph

☐ Do you have a clearly worded **topic sentence** that states your paragraph's main idea?

☐ Does your topic sentence identify the process you will discuss?

☐ Does your topic sentence indicate whether you will be explaining a process or giving instructions?

Evidence Supports Your Paragraph's Topic Sentence

☐ Have you included all the steps in the process?

☐ Have you included enough **evidence**—examples and details—to explain the steps and make the process clear to readers?

☐ If your paragraph is a set of instructions, have you included all the information readers need to perform the process?

Summary Statement Reinforces Your Paragraph's Unity

☐ Does your paragraph end with a **summary statement** that reinforces your main idea?

Transitions Add Coherence to Your Paragraph

☐ Do your **transitions** move readers from one step in the process to the next?

☐ Do you need to add transitions to make your paragraph clearer and to help readers follow your ideas?

7 Cause-and-Effect Paragraphs

© Karen Kasmauski/Corbis

focus on writing

Look at this picture of teen mothers with their infants. Then, freewrite to decide on a particular event that caused you to grow up in a hurry. (If you prefer, you may choose a topic from the list on the following page instead.) You will return to your topic and review your freewriting later in the chapter when you write your cause-and-effect paragraph.

additional topics for cause and effect

Why a particular video went viral
The reasons you decided to attend college
A decision that changed your life
How an event affected you
Why students drop out of high school

7a Understanding Cause and Effect

Why is the cost of college so high in the United States? How does smoking affect a person's health? What would happen if the city increased its minimum wage? How dangerous is the flu? All these questions have one thing in common: they try to determine the causes or effects of an action, event, or situation.

A **cause** is something or someone that makes something happen. An **effect** is something brought about by a particular cause.

CAUSE		EFFECT
Increased airport security	⟶	Long lines at airports
Weight gain	⟶	Health problems
Seat belt laws passed	⟶	Traffic deaths reduced

A **cause-and-effect paragraph** examines or analyzes reasons and results. It helps readers understand why something happened or is happening or shows how one thing affects another. (For information on writing cause-and-effect essays, see 15d.)

When you TEST a cause-and-effect paragraph, make sure it follows these guidelines:

T ■ A cause-and-effect paragraph should begin with a **topic sentence** that tells readers whether the paragraph is focusing on causes or on effects—for example, "There are several reasons why the cost of health care is so high" (causes) or "Going to the writing center has given me confidence as well as skill as a writer" (effects).

E ▪ A cause-and-effect paragraph should present **evidence**—examples and details—to support the topic sentence and explain each cause and effect. Causes or effects should be arranged in **logical order**—for example, from least to most important.

S ▪ A cause-and-effect paragraph should end with a **summary state-ment** that reinforces the paragraph's main idea.

T ▪ A cause-and-effect paragraph should include **transitions** that connect causes or effects to one another and to the topic sentence.

Paragraph Map: Cause and Effect

Topic Sentence

Cause (or effect) #1

Cause (or effect) #2

Cause (or effect) #3

Summary Statement

Model Paragraph: Causes

The following paragraph focuses on **causes**.

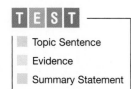

Topic Sentence
Evidence
Summary Statement
Transitions

Why Young People Don't Vote

There are several reasons why young adults don't vote in national elections. The first is that they don't think their vote is important. Nothing could be further from the truth, however. When young people vote, they help set the social agenda. By voting, they are able to weigh in on the things that they care about. By not voting, they give the impression that they don't care about issues such as abortion, gun control, and the environment. Another reason young people don't vote is that they don't realize that policies put in place now will affect them in the future. For example, will Social Security be available to them when they retire? Will student debt make it impossible for them to save or to buy a house? Only by exercising their right to vote will young people make their voices heard about these and other vital issues. Finally, many young people don't understand that it

Causes arranged in logical order

is their civic duty to vote. The right to vote—especially for women and minorites—was achieved only after a number of hard-fought battles had been won. People in many other countries are not able to vote, and for this reason, do not get to select their leaders. This situation should make it clear that for our form of government to work, everyone—including young people—must participate in the democratic process. For these reasons, young people should realize that their votes count and that they should vote in every election.

Causes arranged in logical order

—Moniquetta Hall (student)

Model Paragraph: Effects

The following paragraph focuses on **effects**.

T E S T

Topic Sentence
Evidence
Summary Statement
Transitions

The Negative Effects of Climate Change

Climate change caused by global warming would have several negative effects. One effect would be an increase in the number of intense storms. Large hurricanes and other types of storms would damage property and kill many people. Another effect would be a rise in sea level. As the earth warms, the polar ice would melt and raise the level of the earth's oceans. Coastal cities and low-lying areas would probably be flooded. Still another effect would be the spread of certain kinds of diseases. Many diseases, now found only in warm areas, would spread to areas that were once cool but then became warm. Malaria and yellow fever, for example, could become as common in the United States as they are in Africa and Southeast Asia. Finally, climate change associated with global warming would affect agriculture. Farming areas, such as the Midwest, where American farmers grow corn and wheat, would become dry. As a result, there would be food shortages, and many people could go hungry. No one knows for certain what will happen, but if global warming continues, our lives would certainly be affected.

Effects arranged in logical order

—Jackie Hue (student)

> ### Some Transitional Words and Phrases for Cause and Effect
>
> Transitions in cause-and-effect paragraphs introduce individual causes or effects. They may also show the connections between a cause and its effects or between an effect and its causes. In addition, they may indicate which cause or effect is more important than another.
>
> *(continued)*

(continued from previous page)

accordingly	moreover	the first (second, third)
another cause	since	reason
another effect	so	the most important cause
as a result	the first (second,	the most important effect
because	third, final) cause	therefore
consequently	the first (second,	
for	third, final) effect	
for this reason		

grammar in context

Cause and Effect

When you write a cause-and-effect paragraph, you should be careful not to confuse the words *affect* and *effect*. *Affect* is a verb meaning "to influence." *Effect* is a noun meaning "result."

> One ~~affect~~ ^{*effect*} would be an increase in the number of storms.
>
> (*effect* is a noun)

> No one knows for certain what will happen, but if global warming continues, our lives will certainly be ^{*affected*} ~~effected~~.
>
> (*affect* is a verb)

For more information on effect *and* affect, *see 22g.*

Analyzing a Cause-and-Effect Paragraph

Read this cause-and-effect paragraph; then, follow the instructions in Practice 7-1.

Disaster Tourism

    People taking disaster tours can have good reasons for doing so. First, disaster tourism enables people to see a disaster area in real time, without any media manipulation. For people such as educators and historians, this is important. They want to visit a disaster site so that they can understand what happened and connect the disaster to historical events. This is the case with tours of the killing fields in Cambodia and of the Auschwitz-Birkenau concentration camps in Poland. Second, some disaster tourists come to help, not just to visit. For example, after the devastating 2015 earthquake in Nepal that killed almost nine thousand people, tourists cleared rubble, prepared food for locals, and gave comfort to the injured. Finally, some disaster tourists want to help publicize the scope of the damage. They hope that by doing so, they will be able to focus attention on the area and bring in more aid. After Hurricane Katrina, for example, some New Orleans residents credited disaster tourism with helping to attract volunteers and bringing in badly needed dollars to the area. Contrary to their critics, disaster tourists can help, not hinder, efforts to rebuild devastated areas.

PRACTICE

7-1   1. Underline the topic sentence of the paragraph on pages 108–109.

2. List the causes the writer describes. The first cause has been listed for you.

Disasters are reported on by the media. Since disaster coverage can be biased,

many people want to see disaster areas for themselves.

_____

_____

_____

3. Circle the transitional words and phrases that the writer uses to identify causes.

4. Underline the paragraph's summary statement.

PRACTICE

7-2   Following are four possible topic sentences for cause-and-effect paragraphs. For each topic sentence, list the effects that could result from the cause identified in the topic sentence. For example, if you were writing a paragraph about the effects of excessive drinking on campus, you could list low grades, health problems, and vandalism.

1. Having a baby can change your life.

2. Being bilingual has many advantages.

3. College has made me a different person.

4. Impulse buying can have negative effects on a person's finances.

PRACTICE
7-3

List three causes that could support each of the following topic sentences.

1. The causes of teenage obesity are easy to identify.

2. Chronic unemployment can have many causes.

3. The high cost of college tuition is not easy to explain.

4. There are several reasons why professional athletes' salaries are so high.

7b Case Study: A Student Writes a Cause-and-Effect Paragraph

Here is how one student, Sean Jin, wrote a cause-and-effect paragraph. When Sean was asked to write a cause-and-effect essay for his composition class, he had no trouble thinking of a topic because of a debate that was going on in his hometown about building a Walmart Superstore there. He decided to write a paragraph that discussed the effects that such a store would have on the local economy.

Sean's instructor told the class the main problem to watch for in planning a cause-and-effect essay is making sure that a **causal relationship** exists—that one event actually causes another. In other words, just because one event follows another closely in time, students should not assume that the second event was caused by the first.

With this advice in mind, Sean brainstormed to develop a list of possible effects a Walmart would have on his small town. Here is Sean's list of effects.

Provide new jobs

Offer low-cost items

Pay low wages

Push out small businesses

list effects

Choose one event from the freewriting you did in response to the Focus on Writing prompt on page 104. Then, brainstorm to develop a list of the effects that the event has had on you.

© Karen Kasmauski/Corbis

_____

_____

_____

_____

_____

_____

After reviewing his list of effects, Sean drafted a topic sentence that introduced his topic and communicated the point he wanted to make about it. Here is Sean's topic sentence.

> Walmart can have good and bad effects on a small town.

write a topic sentence

Review your list of effects, and then draft a topic sentence for your cause-and-effect paragraph.

© Karen Kasmauski/Corbis

_____

_____

Next, Sean made an informal outline that arranged the effects on his list in a logical order. This outline helped him check to make sure he had included enough examples to explain each effect and to support his topic sentence. Here is Sean's outline.

Good effects

Provides new jobs

    —Store needs many employees
    —Many people out of work in rural town and need jobs

Offers low-cost items
—Families on a budget can buy things they usually can't afford
—Walmart prices lower than most other stores' prices

Bad effects

Pays low wages
—Walmart pays less than other stores

Pushes out small businesses
—Forces many small businesses to close
—Local businesses can't match low prices or wide selection

© Karen Kasmauski/Corbis

make an outline

Create an informal outline for your paragraph by arranging your list of effects in a logical order—for example, from least to most important.

After completing his outline, Sean wrote the following draft of his paragraph.

> Walmart can have good and bad effects on a small town. It provides jobs. A large store needs a lot of employees. So, many people from the area will be able to find work. Walmart's prices are low. Families that don't have much money may be able to buy things they can't afford to buy at other stores. Not all of Walmart's effects are positive. Walmart pays employees less than other stores. Walmart provides jobs, but those jobs don't pay very much. When Walmart comes into an area, many small businesses are forced to close. They just can't match Walmart's prices or stock as much merchandise as Walmart can.

© Karen Kasmauski/Corbis

draft your paragraph

Using your informal outline as a guide, draft your cause-and-effect paragraph.

When he finished his draft, Sean went to the writing center and met with a tutor. After going over his draft with the tutor and **TEST**ing his paragraph, Sean made the following decisions.

- He decided that he needed to sharpen his **topic sentence** to tie his discussion of Walmart to the small town in which he lived.
- He decided to provide more **evidence** to support his topic sentence—for example, what exactly does Walmart pay its salespeople?
- He realized that he needed to add a **summary statement** to reinforce his main idea.
- He decided to add **transitions** to identify positive and negative effects.

Now Sean was ready to revise and edit his paragraph. The final edited and proofread draft includes all the elements Sean looked for when he TESTed his paragraph.

Walmart Comes to Town

When Walmart comes to a small town like mine, it can have good and bad effects. The first and most positive effect is that it provides jobs. A large Walmart Superstore needs a lot of employees, so many people will be able to find work. In my rural town, over 15 percent of the people are out of work. Walmart could give these people a chance to improve their lives. Another positive effect that Walmart can have is to keep prices low so families on tight budgets will be able to buy things they cannot afford to buy at other stores. My own observations show that many items at a local Walmart are cheaper than those at other stores. Not all of Walmart's effects are positive, however. One negative effect Walmart can have is that it can actually lower wages in an area. My aunt, a longtime employee, says that Walmart pays beginning workers between $8 and $10 an hour. This is less than they would get in stores that pay union wages. Another negative effect Walmart can have is to drive other, smaller businesses out. When Walmart comes into an area, many small businesses are forced to close. They just cannot match Walmart's prices or selection of merchandise. It is clear that although Walmart can have a number of positive effects, it can also have some negative ones.

TEST

- Topic Sentence
- Evidence
- Summary Statement
- Transitions

TEST · Revise · Edit · Proofread

Look back at the draft of your cause-and-effect paragraph. Using the TEST checklist on page 114, evaluate your paragraph to make sure it includes a topic sentence, evidence, a summary statement, and transitions, and revise your draft accordingly. Finally, edit and proofread your paragraph.

© Karen Kasmauski/Corbis

TESTing a cause-and-effect paragraph

Topic Sentence Unifies Your Paragraph

☐ Do you have a clearly worded **topic sentence** that states your paragraph's main idea?

☐ Does your topic sentence identify the cause or effect on which your paragraph will focus?

Evidence Supports Your Paragraph's Topic Sentence

☐ Do you need to add any important causes or effects?

☐ Do you need to explain your causes or effects more fully?

☐ Does all your **evidence**—examples and details—support your paragraph's main idea?

Summary Statement Reinforces Your Paragraph's Unity

☐ Does your paragraph end with a **summary statement** that reinforces your main idea?

Transitions Add Coherence to Your Paragraph

☐ Do your **transitions** show how your ideas are related?

☐ Do your transitions clearly introduce each cause or effect?

☐ Do you need to add transitions to make your paragraph clearer and to help readers follow your ideas?

8 Comparison-and-Contrast Paragraphs

	OLD WORDS	NEW MEANINGS
GREEN	yellow + blue	good for the planet
FRIEND	a person you know	a random person
ORGANIC	living matter	made naturally in a factory

© Maria Scrivan

focus on writing

This chart shows old words that have acquired new meanings. Brainstorm to develop a list of three or four words that you think have acquired new meanings. (You can also do an Internet search with the terms "old words, new meanings.") Then, make your own chart that lists the old and new meanings of the words you have listed. (If you prefer, you may choose a topic from the list on the following page.) You will return to your topic and review your brainstorming later in the chapter when you write your comparison-and-contrast paragraph.

additional topics for comparison and contrast

Two popular sports figures
Men's and women's attitudes toward
    relationships, shopping, or conversation
Two cars you would consider buying
Two websites
Two people, places, or objects

8a Understanding Comparison and Contrast

When you buy something—for example, a hair dryer, a smartphone, a computer, or a car—you often comparison-shop, looking at various models to determine how they are alike and how they are different. In other words, you *compare and contrast*. When you **compare**, you consider how things are similar. When you **contrast**, you consider how they are different. A **comparison-and-contrast paragraph** can examine just similarities, just differences, or both similarities and differences. (For information on writing comparison-and-contrast essays, see 15e.)

When you TEST a comparison-and-contrast paragraph, make sure it follows these guidelines:

T ■ A comparison-and-contrast paragraph should begin with a **topic sentence** that tells readers whether the paragraph is going to discuss similarities, differences, or both. The topic sentence should also make clear the main point of the comparison—why you are comparing or contrasting the two subjects (for example, "The writers Toni Morrison and Maya Angelou have similar ideas about race and society" or "My parents and I have different ideas about success").

E ■ A comparison-and-contrast paragraph should include enough **evidence**—examples and details—to make the similarities and differences clear to readers. A comparison-and-contrast paragraph should discuss the same or similar points for both subjects, one by one. Points should be arranged in **logical order**—for example, from least to most important.

S ■ A comparison-and-contrast paragraph should end with a **summary statement** that reinforces the paragraph's main idea.

T ■ A comparison-and-contrast paragraph should include **transitions** that connect the two subjects being compared and link the points you make about each subject.

There are two kinds of comparison-and-contrast paragraphs: *subject-by-subject comparisons* and *point-by-point comparisons*.

Subject-by-Subject Comparisons

In a **subject-by-subject comparison**, you divide your comparison into two parts and discuss one subject at a time. In the first part of the paragraph, you discuss all your points about one subject. Then, in the second part, you discuss the same (or similar) points about the other subject. (In each part of the paragraph, you discuss the points in the same order.)

A subject-by-subject comparison is best for paragraphs in which you do not discuss too many points. In this situation, readers will have little difficulty remembering the points you discuss for the first subject when you move on to discuss the second subject.

Paragraph Map: Subject-by-Subject Comparison

Topic Sentence

Subject A
   Point #1

   Point #2

   Point #3

Subject B
   Point #1

   Point #2

   Point #3

Summary Statement

Model Paragraph: Subject-by-Subject Comparison

The writer of the following paragraph uses a subject-by-subject comparison to compare emojis and emoticons.

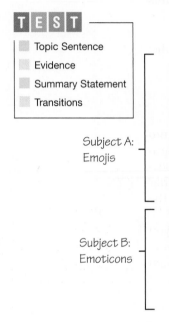

Communicating with Emojis and Emoticons

Emojis and emoticons are two different types of icons used in electronic communication. Emojis are small pictures that are used to convey not just emotions, but also events, seasons, weather, and food. In addition, emojis are limited by the operating systems that read them, meaning that Apple users and Android users do not see emojis the same way. If an operating system receives an emoji it cannot read, it will display a generic symbol or just a blank space. Finally, emojis can be used to depict entire sentences when they are strung together. However, this use can cause varying interpretations since people may see some emojis differently. In contrast, emoticons are text-only symbols that convey basic emotions or a writer's tone. Because emoticons are text-only, they can be read universally by any operating system. In addition, emoticons can convey a basic emotion to accompany a statement, but they cannot be strung together to form statements. Finally, the basic nature of emoticons reduces the risk of misinterpretation. Because they are nearly universally understood, the recipient is likely to understand the sentiment. For this reason, choosing to use either emoticons or emojis is a bigger decision than it may seem.

—Dan Lindt (student)

Point-by-Point Comparisons

When you write a **point-by-point comparison**, you discuss a point about one subject and then discuss the same point for the second subject. You use this alternating pattern throughout the paragraph.

A point-by-point comparison is a better strategy for long paragraphs in which you discuss many points. It is also a better choice if the points you are discussing are technical or complicated. Because you compare the two subjects one point at a time, readers will be able to see one point of comparison before moving on to the next point.

Paragraph Map: Point-by-Point Comparison

Topic Sentence

Point #1

    Subject A

    Subject B

> **Point #2**
>
> Subject A
>
> Subject B
>
> **Point #3**
>
> Subject A
>
> Subject B
>
> **Summary Statement**

Model Paragraph: Point-by-Point Comparison

In the following paragraph, the writer uses a point-by-point-comparison to compare two characters in a short story.

T E S T

Topic Sentence
Evidence
Summary Statement
Transitions

Two Sisters

Although they grew up together, Maggie and Dee, the two sisters in Alice Walker's short story "Everyday Use," are very different. Maggie, who was burned in a fire, is shy and has low self-esteem. When she walks, she shuffles her feet and looks down at the ground. Her sister Dee, however, is confident and outgoing. She looks people in the eye when she talks to them and is very opinionated. [Point 1: Different personalities] Maggie and Dee also have different attitudes toward life. Maggie never complains or asks for anything more than she has. She has remained at home with her mother in rural Georgia. In contrast, Dee has always wanted nicer things. She has gone away to school and hardly ever visits her mother and Maggie. [Point 2: Different attitudes toward life] The biggest difference between Maggie and Dee is their attitude toward tradition. Although Maggie values her family's rural American traditions, Dee values her African heritage. Maggie cherishes her family's handmade quilts and furniture, hoping to use them with her own family. In contrast, Dee sees the handmade objects as things to be displayed and shown off, not used every day. [Point 3: Different attitudes toward tradition] The many differences between Maggie and Dee add conflict and tension to the story.

—Margaret Caracappa (student)

Some Transitional Words and Phrases for Comparison and Contrast

Transitions make your paragraph more coherent by showing readers whether you are focusing on similarities (for example, *likewise* or *similarly*) or differences (for example, *although* or *in contrast*). Transitions also tell readers when you are changing from one point (or one subject) to another.

although	one difference . . . another difference
but	one similarity . . . another similarity
even though	on the contrary
however	on the one hand . . . on the other hand
in comparison	similarly
in contrast	though
like	unlike
likewise	whereas
nevertheless	

grammar in context

Comparison and Contrast

When you write a comparison-and-contrast paragraph, you should express the points you are comparing in **parallel** terms to highlight their similarities or differences.

NOT PARALLEL   Although Maggie values her family's traditions, the African heritage of her family is the thing that Dee values.

PARALLEL   Although Maggie <u>values</u> her family's <u>traditions</u>, Dee <u>values</u> her African <u>heritage</u>.

For more information on revising to make ideas parallel, see Chapter 21.

Analyzing a Comparison-and-Contrast Paragraph

Read this comparison-and-contrast paragraph; then, follow the instructions in Practice 8-1.

Virtual and Traditional Classrooms

Taking a course online is very different from taking a course in a traditional classroom. One difference is that students in an online course have more flexibility than students in a traditional course. They can do their schoolwork at any time, scheduling it around other commitments, such as jobs and childcare. Students in a traditional course, however, must go to class at a specific time and place. Another difference is that students in an online course can feel isolated from the teacher and other students because they never actually come into physical contact with them. Students in a traditional classroom, however, are able to connect with the teacher and their classmates because they interact with them in person. A final difference is that in an online course, students use email or a discussion board to discuss course material. A student who is a slow typist or whose Internet connection is unreliable is clearly at a disadvantage. In a traditional course, most of the discussion takes place in the classroom, so technology is not an issue. Because online and traditional courses are so different, students must think carefully about which type of course best fits their needs.

—William Hernandez (student)

PRACTICE

1. Underline the topic sentence of the paragraph above.

2. Does this paragraph deal mainly with similarities or differences?

_____ How do you know? _____

_____

3. Is this paragraph a subject-by-subject or point-by-point comparison?

_____ How do you know? _____

_____

4. List some of the contrasts the writer describes. The first contrast has been listed for you.

When it comes to their schedules, students in an online course have more flexibility

than students in a traditional course do.

_____

_____

_____

_____

_____

5. Circle the transitional words and phrases the writer uses to move from one comparison to the next.

6. Underline the paragraph's summary statement.

PRACTICE

8-2 Following are three topic sentences. For each topic sentence, list three or four similarities or differences between the two subjects. For example, if you were writing a paragraph comparing health care provided by a local clinic with health care provided by a private doctor, you could discuss the cost, the length of waiting time, the quality of care, and the frequency of follow-up visits.

1. My mother (or father) and I are very different (or alike).

2. My friends and I have different views on _____.

3. Two of my college instructors have very different teaching styles.

8b   Case Study: A Student Writes a Comparison-and-Contrast Paragraph

Here is how one student, Jermond Love, wrote a comparison-and-contrast paragraph. When Jermond was given this assignment for his composition class, he began by brainstorming to find a topic. When he reviewed his brainstorming notes, he decided that the following topics looked most promising.

Football and soccer

American and Caribbean cooking

The differences between my brother and me

Life in Saint Croix versus life in New York City

After considering each of these topics, Jermond decided to write about the differences between life in Saint Croix, the Caribbean island where he was raised, and life in New York City. He listed various points that he thought he could compare and contrast. Then, he crossed out the ones he didn't want to write about.

Size

~~Economy~~

~~Businesses~~

Lifestyle

~~Politics~~

~~Education~~

~~Music~~

~~Agriculture~~

~~Sports~~

~~Living conditions~~

~~Industry~~

~~Traditions~~

After thinking about the relative sizes of Saint Croix and New York City as well as their respective lifestyles, Jermond brainstormed again to identify some specific differences that he could discuss in his paragraph.

Population: 60,000 versus over 8 million

Laid-back versus hurried lifestyle

Christiansted and Frederiksted versus five boroughs

Friendly versus not friendly

yellow + blue
© Maria Scrivan

list differences

Look over the brainstorming you did in response to the Focus on Writing prompt on page 115, and then cross out the word pairs that you do not want to discuss in your paragraph. On the lines below, list the word pairs you do plan to discuss.

_____

_____

_____

_____

After reviewing his list of differences, Jermond drafted the following topic sentence. This sentence told readers that he was going to focus on differences, and it also identified the main point he was going to make in his comparison-and-contrast paragraph.

TOPIC SENTENCE   Life in Saint Croix is very different from life in New York City.

---

good for the planet
© Maria Scrivan

write a topic sentence

Review your list of words with new meanings, and then draft a topic sentence for your comparison-and-contrast paragraph.

_____

_____

At this point, Jermond created the following informal outline, presenting his ideas in the order in which he was going to discuss them in his paragraph.

Size
    Saint Croix
        Small size
        Small population
        Christiansted and Frederiksted

    New York City
        Large size
        Large population
        Five boroughs

Lifestyle
    Saint Croix
        Laid-back
        Friendly

    New York City
        In a hurry
        Not always friendly

Jermond thought that a point-by-point organization would be easier for his readers to follow than a subject-by-subject organization. With this organization, readers would be able to keep track of his comparison as he discussed each of his points, one at a time.

make an outline

Decide whether you will write a subject-by-subject or point-by-point comparison. Then, use the appropriate format (see the paragraph maps on pages 117 and 118–119) to help you create an outline for your comparison-and-contrast paragraph. Before you begin, decide on the order in which you will present your points—for example, from least to most important. (For a subject-by-subject comparison, begin by deciding which subject you will discuss first.)

a person you know
© Maria Scrivan

Using his informal outline as a guide, Jermond drafted his paragraph. Here is his draft.

Life in Saint Croix is very different from life in New York City. Saint Croix is much smaller than New York City. Saint Croix has a total population of about 60,000 people. The two main towns are Christiansted and Frederiksted. New York City is very large. Its residents are crowded into five boroughs. The lifestyle in Saint Croix is different from the lifestyle of New York City. In Saint Croix, almost everyone operates on "island time." Everyone is friendly. People don't see any point in getting anyone upset. In New York City, most people are always in a hurry. They don't take the time to slow down and enjoy life. As a result, people can seem unfriendly. They don't take the time to get to know anyone. I hope when I graduate I can stay in New York City but visit my home in Saint Croix whenever I can.

living matter

© Maria Scrivan

draft your paragraph

Using your informal outline as a guide, draft your comparison-and-contrast paragraph.

Jermond put his paragraph aside for a day and then reread it. Although he was generally satisfied with what he had written, he thought that his draft could be improved. To help students revise their paragraphs, his instructor divided students into peer-review groups and asked them to read and discuss each other's paragraphs. After working with a classmate on his draft and TESTing his paragraph, Jermond made the following decisions.

■ He decided that his **topic sentence** was clear and specific.

■ He saw that he needed more **evidence**—examples and details—to help his readers understand the differences between his two subjects.

■ He decided to change his **summary statement** because it didn't clearly reinforce the idea in his topic sentence.

■ Finally, he decided that he needed to add **transitional words and phrases** that would show when he was moving from one subject to another.

As Jermond revised his paragraph, he added background about Saint Croix. (The classmate who read his draft had pointed out that many people in the class would not know anything about it.) The final edited and proofread draft includes all the elements Jermond looked for when he **TEST**ed his paragraph.

Saint Croix versus New York City

Life in Saint Croix is very different from life in New York City. One difference between Saint Croix and New York is that Saint Croix is much smaller than New York. Saint Croix, the largest of the United States Virgin Islands, has a population of about 60,000. The two main towns on the island are Christiansted, with a population of about 3,000, and Frederiksted, with a population of only about 830. Unlike Saint Croix, New York City is large. It has a population of over 8 million crowded into the five boroughs of Manhattan, Brooklyn, the Bronx, Queens, and Staten Island. My neighborhood in Brooklyn is more than twice the size of Christiansted and Frederiksted combined. Another difference between Saint Croix and New York City is their lifestyles. Life in Saint Croix is slower than life in New York. In Saint Croix, almost everyone operates on "island time." Things get done, but people don't rush to do them. When workers say "later," they can mean "this afternoon," "tomorrow," or even "next week." No one seems to mind, as long as the job gets done. People don't see any point in getting anyone upset. In New York, however, most people are always in a hurry. They don't take the time to slow down and enjoy life. Everything is fast—fast food, fast cars, fast Internet access. As a result, people can seem unfriendly. Although Saint Croix and New York City are so different, life is interesting in both places.

T E S T

- Topic Sentence
- Evidence
- Summary Statement
- Transitions

TEST · Revise · Edit · Proofread

Look back at the draft of your comparison-and-contrast paragraph. Using the **TEST** checklist on page 128, evaluate your paragraph to make sure it includes a topic sentence, evidence, a summary statement, and transitions, and revise your draft accordingly. Finally, edit and proofread your paragraph.

made naturally in a factory
© Maria Scrivan

TESTing a comparison-and-contrast paragraph

Topic Sentence Unifies Your Paragraph

☐ Do you have a clearly worded **topic sentence** that states your paragraph's main idea?

☐ Does your topic sentence indicate whether you are focusing on similarities or on differences?

Evidence Supports Your Paragraph's Topic Sentence

☐ Does all your **evidence**—examples and details—support your paragraph's main idea?

☐ Do your examples and details show how your two subjects are alike or different?

☐ Do you need to discuss additional similarities or differences?

Summary Statement Reinforces Your Paragraph's Unity

☐ Does your paragraph end with a **summary statement** that reinforces your main idea?

Transitions Add Coherence to Your Paragraph

☐ Do your **transitions** indicate whether you are focusing on similarities or on differences?

☐ Do transitional words and phrases lead readers from one subject or point to the next?

☐ Do you need to add transitions to make your paragraph clearer and to help readers follow your ideas?

9 Descriptive Paragraphs

Trinette Reed/Getty Images

focus on writing

This is a picture of what many people would consider an ideal vacation spot. Brainstorm to develop a list of places that you would like to visit on vacation. (If you prefer, you may choose a topic from the list on the following page instead.) You will return to your topic and review your brainstorming later in the chapter when you write your descriptive paragraph.

additional topics for description

Your workplace
An unusual person
Your dream house
Someone you admire
A useful gadget or tool

9a   Understanding Description

In a personal email, you may describe a new boyfriend or girlfriend. In a biology lab manual, you may describe the structure of a cell. In a report for a nursing class, you may describe a patient you treated.

When you write a **description**, you use words to paint a picture for your readers. With description, you use language that creates a vivid impression of what you have seen, heard, smelled, tasted, or touched. The more details you include, the better your description will be. (For information on writing descriptive essays, see 16a.)

The following description is flat because it includes very few descriptive details.

> **FLAT**   Today, I saw a beautiful sunrise.

In contrast, the passage below is full of descriptive details that convey the writer's impression of the scene. This revised description relies on sight (*glowed red; turned slowly to pink, to aqua, and finally to blue*), touch (*the soft sandy beach; felt the cold water*), and sound (*heard the waves hit the shore*) to create a vivid picture.

> **VIVID**   Early this morning as I walked along the soft sandy beach, I saw the sun rise slowly out of the ocean. At first, the ocean glowed red. Then, it turned slowly to pink, to aqua, and finally to blue. As I stood watching the sun, I heard the waves hit the shore, and I felt the cold water swirl around my toes. For a moment, even the small grey and white birds that hurried along the shore seemed to stop and watch the dazzling sight.

When you TEST a **descriptive paragraph**, make sure it follows these guidelines:

T ■ A descriptive paragraph should begin with a **topic sentence** that conveys the main idea or general impression you want to communicate in your paragraph—for example, "The woods behind my house may seem ordinary, but to me, they are beautiful" or "The old wooden roller coaster is a work of art."

E ■ A descriptive paragraph should present **evidence**—descriptive details—that supports the topic sentence. Details should be presented in a clear **spatial order** that reflects the order in which you observed the person, place, or thing you are describing. For example, you can move from near to far or from top to bottom.

S ■ A descriptive paragraph should end with a **summary statement** that reinforces the paragraph's main idea.

T ■ A descriptive paragraph should include **transitions** that connect details to one another and to the topic sentence.

Paragraph Map: Description

Topic Sentence

Detail #1

Detail #2

Detail #3

Summary Statement

Model Paragraph: Description

The student writer of the following paragraph uses descriptive details to support the idea that the Lincoln Memorial is a monument to American democracy.

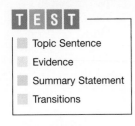

Topic Sentence
Evidence
Summary Statement
Transitions

Descriptive details
arranged in spatial
order

The Lincoln Memorial

The Lincoln Memorial was built to celebrate American democracy. In front of the monument is a long marble staircase that leads from a reflecting pool to the memorial's entrance. Thirty-six columns—which symbolize the thirty-six states reunited after the Civil War—surround the building. Inside the building are three rooms. The first room contains the nineteen-foot statue of Lincoln. Seated in a chair, Lincoln looks exhausted after the long Civil War. One of Lincoln's hands is a fist, showing his strength, and the other is open, showing his kindness. On either side of the first room are the two other rooms. Carved on the wall of the second room is the Gettysburg Address. On the wall of the third room is the Second Inaugural Address. Above the Gettysburg Address is a mural showing an angel freeing the slaves. Above the Second Inaugural Address is another mural, which depicts the people of the North and the South coming back together. As its design shows, the Lincoln Memorial was built to celebrate both the sixteenth president and the nation's struggle for democracy.

—Nicole Lentz (student)

Some Transitional Words and Phrases for Description

As you arrange your ideas in a descriptive paragraph, be sure to use appropriate transitional words and phrases to lead readers from one detail to another.

above	in	outside
at the edge	in back of	over
at the entrance	in front of	spreading out
behind	inside	the first . . . the second
below	nearby	the least important . . .
between	next to	the most important
beyond	on	the next
down	on one side . . . on the	under
farther	other side	

grammar in context

Description

When you write a descriptive paragraph, you sometimes use **modifiers**—words and phrases that describe other words in the sentence. A modifier should be placed as close as possible to the word it is supposed to modify. If you place a modifying word or phrase too far from the word it modifies, you create a **misplaced modifier** that will confuse readers.

CONFUSING (MISPLACED MODIFIER)	Seated in a chair, the long Civil War has clearly exhausted Lincoln. (Was the Civil War seated in a chair?)
CLEAR	Seated in a chair, Lincoln looks exhausted after the long Civil War.

For information on how to identify and correct misplaced modifiers, see Chapter 27.

Analyzing a Descriptive Paragraph

Read this descriptive paragraph; then, follow the instructions in Practice 9-1.

Shopping at Ikea

A trip to Ikea is a unique shopping experience. At the entrance to the store, a friendly greeter helps direct customers. Beyond the greeter is a large, white staircase—this is where the adventure begins. Next to the staircase is a bustling restaurant where visitors can take a break from shopping and sample Ikea's famous Swedish meatballs. Once you get past the restaurant, you go on a winding path through the various furniture displays of the store. Ikea visitors can explore elaborate displays for each area of the home: living room, kitchen, bathroom, and office. Typically, one decorating style will be featured to the left, and a different style will be featured to the right. On the floor below are displays of home accessories. Items such as glassware, eating utensils, pots and pans, picture frames, toys, and light fixtures are displayed on tables or in wire bins. In between this merchandise are smaller displays meant to give shoppers an idea of how they can use the accessories in their own home. Finally, the path ends at the warehouse level. There are no elaborate displays on this level; once you enter the industrial warehouse it is down to business. Here visitors use a number system to find the boxes that contain the disassembled furniture they would like to take home. Outside the warehouse level is the parking lot. Here you are sure to see cars with boxes balanced precariously on their roofs or even hanging out of windows. Ikea isn't the kind of store you stop in quickly on your way home from work; it is a full day of adventure.

PRACTICE
9-1

1. Underline the topic sentence of the paragraph above.

2. In a few words, summarize the main idea of the paragraph.

_____

3. What are some of the details the writer uses to describe the setting in Ikea? The first detail has been listed for you.

friendly greeter _____

_____

_____

_____

_____

_____

4. Circle the transitional words and phrases that the writer uses to lead readers from one detail to another.

5. Underline the paragraph's summary statement.

PRACTICE

9-2   Each of the five topic sentences below states a possible main idea for a descriptive paragraph. For each, list three details that could help convey the main idea. For example, to support the idea that sitting in front of a fireplace is relaxing, you could describe the crackling of the fire, the pine scent of the smoke, and the changing colors of the flames.

1. The most valuable possession I own is _____.

2. The most interesting place I ever visited is _____.

3. One look at my instructor told me that this was going to be a challenging semester.

4. One of my favorite stores to shop at is _____.

5. My neighborhood is full of distinctive sounds and smells.

9b   Case Study: A Student Writes a Descriptive Paragraph

Here is how one student, Jared Lopez, wrote a descriptive paragraph. When Jared was asked to write a descriptive paragraph about someone he admired, he decided to write about his uncle Manuel, who had been a father figure to him.

Because he was very familiar with his paragraph's subject, Jared did not have to brainstorm or freewrite to find material to write about. Instead, he immediately started to list the features of his uncle that he considered the most memorable.

Looks friendly

Hands

Dark eyes

Distinguished looking

Tall

Trinette Reed/Getty Images

list details

Choose a vacation spot from the brainstorming you did in response to the Focus on Writing prompt on page 129, and then list the details that best describe that place.

_____

_____

_____

After reviewing the list of features he planned to discuss, Jared arranged the features in an informal outline in the order in which he planned to discuss them.

Tall

Looks friendly

Dark eyes

Distinguished looking

Hands

Trinette Reed/Getty Images

make an outline

Create an informal outline for your paragraph by arranging the details you listed in the order in which you plan to discuss them. You might arrange them in the order in which you observe them— for example, from near to far or from top to bottom—or, as Jared did, in order of importance.

Jared decided to begin his paragraph with a general description of his uncle Manuel and then move on to concentrate on his uncle's most distinctive feature: his hands. Here is the first draft of Jared's paragraph.

My uncle's name is Manuel, but his friends call him Manny. He is over six feet tall. Uncle Manny's eyes are dark brown, almost black. They make him look very serious. When he laughs, however, he looks friendly. His nose is long and straight, and it makes Uncle Manny look very distinguished. Most interesting to me are Uncle Manny's hands. Even though he hasn't worked as a stonemason since he opened his own construction company ten years ago, his hands are still rough and scarred. They are large and strong, but they can be gentle too.

draft your paragraph

Using your informal outline as a guide, draft your descriptive paragraph.

Trinette Reed/Getty Images

After a conference with his instructor, Jared TESTed his paragraph.

- He decided that he needed to add a **topic sentence** that stated the main idea of his description.
- He decided that he needed to add more descriptive details to give readers more **evidence** of his uncle's strength and gentleness.
- He decided that he needed to add a stronger **summary statement** to unify his paragraph.
- He decided to include more **transitions** to move readers from one part of his description to the next.

After TESTing his paragraph, Jared revised and edited his draft. Then, he proofread carefully for typos. The final draft includes all the elements Jared looked for when he TESTed it.

My Uncle Manny

My uncle Manuel is a strong but gentle person who took care of my mother and me when my father died. Manuel, or "Manny" as his friends and family call him, is over six feet tall. This is unusual for a Mexican of his generation. The first thing most people notice about my uncle Manny is his eyes. They are large and dark brown, almost black. They make him look very serious. When he laughs, however, the sides of his eyes crinkle up and he looks warm and friendly. Another thing that stands out is his nose, which is long and straight. My mother says it makes Uncle Manny look strong and distinguished. The most striking thing about Uncle Manny is his hands. Even though he hasn't worked as a stonemason since he opened his own construction company ten years ago, his hands are still rough and scarred from carrying stones. No matter how much he tries, he can't get rid of the dirt under his fingernails. Uncle Manny's hands are big and rough, but they are also gentle and comforting. To me, they show what he really is: a strong and gentle man.

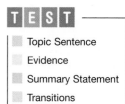

T E S T

■ Topic Sentence
■ Evidence
■ Summary Statement
■ Transitions

TEST · Revise · Edit · Proofread

Look back at the draft of your descriptive paragraph. Using the TEST checklist below, evaluate your paragraph to make sure it includes a topic sentence, evidence, a summary statement, and transitions, and revise your draft accordingly. Finally, edit and proofread your paragraph.

TESTing a descriptive paragraph

Topic Sentence Unifies Your Paragraph

☐ Do you have a clearly worded **topic sentence** that states your paragraph's main idea—the general impression you want to convey?

☐ Does your topic sentence identify the person, place, or thing you will describe in your paragraph?

Evidence Supports Your Paragraph's Topic Sentence

☐ Does all your **evidence**—descriptive details—support your paragraph's main idea?

☐ Do you have enough descriptive details, or do you need to include more?

Summary Statement Reinforces Your Paragraph's Unity

☐ Does your paragraph end with a **summary statement** that reinforces your main idea?

Transitions Add Coherence to Your Paragraph

☐ Do your **transitions** lead readers from one detail to the next?

☐ Do you need to add transitions to make your paragraph clearer and to help readers follow your ideas?

10 Classification Paragraphs

focus on writing

This picture shows fans at a basketball game. Look at the picture, and then brainstorm to identify the categories of fans you often see at a particular sporting event. (If you prefer, you may choose a topic from the list on the following page instead.) You will return to this topic and review your brainstorming later in the chapter when you write your classification paragraph.

In this chapter, you will learn to write a classification paragraph.

additional topics for classification

Types of friends
Part-time jobs
Types of drivers
Types of teachers
Kinds of YouTube videos

10a Understanding Classification

When you **classify**, you sort items (people, things, ideas) into categories or groups. You classify when you organize bills into those you have to pay now and those you can pay later, or when you sort the clothes in a dresser drawer into piles of socks, T-shirts, and underwear.

In a **classification paragraph**, you tell readers how items can be sorted into categories or groups. Each category must be **distinct**. In other words, none of the items in one category should also fit into another category. For example, you would not classify novels into mysteries, romances, and e-books, because both mystery novels and romance novels could also be e-books. (For information on writing classification essays, see 16b.)

When you **TEST** a classification paragraph, make sure it follows these guidelines:

T ■ A classification paragraph should begin with a **topic sentence** that introduces the subject of the paragraph. It may also identify the categories you will discuss (for example, "Before you go camping, you should sort the items you are thinking of packing into three categories: absolutely necessary, potentially helpful, and not really necessary").

E ■ A classification paragraph should discuss one category at a time and should include enough **evidence**—examples and details—to explain each category and show how it is distinct from the other categories. The categories should be arranged in **logical order**—for example, from least to most important or from smallest to largest.

S ■ A classification paragraph should end with a **summary statement** that reinforces the paragraph's main idea.

T ■ A classification paragraph should include **transitions** to introduce the categories you discuss and connect them to one another and to the topic sentence.

Paragraph Map: Classification

Topic Sentence

Category #1

Category #2

Category #3

Summary Statement

Model Paragraph: Classification

The writer of the following paragraph classifies bosses into three distinct groups.

Types of Bosses

TEST

- Topic Sentence
- Evidence
- Summary Statement
- Transitions

I've had three kinds of bosses in my life: the uninterested boss, the supervisor, and the micromanager. The first type is an uninterested boss. This boss doesn't care what workers do as long as they do the job. When I was a counselor at summer camp, my boss fell into this category. As long as no campers (or worse yet, parents) complained, he left you alone. He never cared if you followed the activity plan for the day or gave the kids an extra snack to keep them quiet. The second type of boss is the supervisor. This kind of boss will check you once in a while and give you helpful advice. You'll have a certain amount of freedom but not too much. When I was a salesperson at the Gap, my boss fell into this category. She helped me through the first few weeks of the job and encouraged me to do my best. At the end of the summer, I had learned a lot about retail business and had good feelings about the job. The last, and worst, type of boss is the micromanager. This kind of boss gets involved in everything. My boss at Taco Bell was this kind of person. No one could do anything right. There was always a better way to do anything you tried to do. If you rolled a burrito one way, he would tell you to do it another way. If you did it the other way, he would tell you to do it the first way. This boss never seemed to understand that people need praise every once in a while. Even though the supervisor expects a lot and makes you work, it is clear to me that this boss is better than the other types.

First type of boss

Second type of boss

Last type of boss

—Melissa Burrell (student)

> ### Some Transitional Words and Phrases for Classification
>
> Transitions tell readers when you are moving from one category to another (for example, *the first type, the second type*). They can also indicate which categories you think are more important than others (for example, *the most important, the least important*).
>
> one kind . . . another kind the first group . . . the last group
> one way . . . another way   the first type . . . the second type
> the first (second, third)   the most (or least) important group
>   category   the next part

grammar in context

Classification

When you write a classification paragraph, you may list the categories you are going to discuss. If you use a **colon** to introduce your list, make sure that a complete sentence comes before the colon.

INCORRECT Basically, bosses can be divided into: the uninterested boss, the supervisor, and the micromanager.

CORRECT Basically, I've had three kinds of bosses in my life: the uninterested boss, the supervisor, and the micromanager.

For more information on how to use a colon to introduce a list, see 35d.

Analyzing a Classification Paragraph

Read this classification paragraph; then, follow the instructions in Practice 10-1.

Unusual Smartphone Applications

Generally, there are three kinds of unusual smartphone applications: those

that are harmlessly entertaining, those that are surprisingly useful, and those

that are deadly serious. The first kind is harmlessly entertaining. The purpose of the odd apps in this category is to be amusing, silly, or fun. People enjoy using them to do unimportant things, such as "pop" bubble wrap, choose a pirate name, or look up the height of their favorite celebrity. Goofy apps include Crazy Mouth, which displays animated mouths that you can hold up in front of your face. The second kind of unusual app is also odd but surprisingly useful, helping people accomplish various tasks. For example, FileThis helps users electronically file any type of paper document, and Practice+ helps musicians during practice sessions by offering tools like a metronome, a tuner, and a pitch player. Also in this category is RockMyRun, an app that matches workout songs to a runner's pace. The third kind of unusual app is the serious kind, which can actually help save lives. Often, this kind of app is available only to select groups, not to the general public. For example, trained minesweepers use the PETAL app for the iPhone to help them determine the size and shape of landmines. Another example is TransHeat, the U.S. Army's specialized app for planning travel routes with a minimal risk of being ambushed. Although not equally important, each of these three kinds of apps has its own distinct uses.

—Emily Bentz (student)

PRACTICE

10-1

1. Underline the topic sentence of the paragraph.

2. What is the subject of the paragraph? _____

3. What three categories does the writer describe?

_____

_____

_____

4. Circle the transitional phrases the writer uses to introduce the three categories.

5. Underline the paragraph's summary statement.

PRACTICE

10-2   List items in each of the following groups; then, sort the items into three or four categories.

1. All the items on your desk

2. Buildings on your college campus

3. Websites you visit

4. The various parts of a piece of equipment you use for a course or on the job

---

10b   Case Study: A Student Writes a Classification Paragraph

Here is how one student, Corey Levin, wrote a classification paragraph. For a college composition course, Corey participated in a service-learning project at a local Ronald McDonald House, a charity that houses families of seriously ill children receiving treatment at nearby hospitals. He met several professional athletes there and was surprised to learn that many of them regularly donate time and money to charity.

When Corey was asked by his composition instructor to write a paragraph about what he had learned from his experience, he decided to write a paragraph that classified the ways in which professional athletes give back to their communities. Based on his experience, he was able to come up with the following three categories.

Starting charitable foundations

Guidance

Responding to emergencies

Andrew D. Bernstein / NBAE
via Getty Images

list categories

Look back at the brainstorming you did in response to the Focus on Writing prompt on page 139, and cross out any categories that you do not plan to discuss. List the remaining categories—the ones that you will discuss in your classification paragraph—on the lines below.

_____

_____

_____

Corey then made an informal outline, listing examples to develop each of the three categories.

Foundations

> Michael Jordan
> Troy Aikman

Guidance

> Shaquille O'Neal
> The Philadelphia 76ers

Responding to emergencies

> Ike Reese
> Vince Carter

make an outline

Create an informal outline for your paragraph by arranging the categories of sports fans in the order in which you will discuss them and listing examples to develop each of your categories.

Andrew D. Bernstein / NBAE
via Getty Images

After completing his informal outline, Corey drafted the following topic sentence for his paragraph.

Many high-profile athletes find various ways to give back to their communities.

write a topic sentence

Review your list of categories, and then draft a topic sentence for your classification paragraph.

_____

_____

Andrew D. Bernstein / NBAE
via Getty Images

Then, using his informal outline as a guide, Corey wrote the following draft of his paragraph.

> Many high-profile athletes find various ways to give back to their communities. Many athletes as well as teams do a lot to help people. I met some of them when I volunteered at the Ronald McDonald House. For example, Michael Jordan and the Chicago Bulls built a Boys and Girls Club on Chicago's West Side. Troy Aikman set up a foundation that builds playgrounds for children's hospitals. Shaquille O'Neal's Shaq's Paq provides guidance for inner-city children. The Philadelphia 76ers visit schools and have donated over five thousand books to local libraries. Ike Reese, formerly with the Atlanta Falcons, collects clothing and food for families that need help. Vince Carter of the Memphis Grizzlies founded the Embassy of Hope Foundation. It distributes food to needy families at Thanksgiving and hosts a Christmas party for disadvantaged families.

Andrew D. Bernstein / NBAE
via Getty Images

draft your paragraph

Using your informal outline as a guide, draft your classification paragraph.

Following his instructor's suggestion, Corey emailed his draft to a classmate for feedback. In her email reply to Corey, she TESTed his paragraph and made the following suggestions.

- Keep the **topic sentence** the way it is. "Various ways" shows you're writing a classification paragraph.
- Add more specific **evidence**. Give examples of each category of "giving back" to support the topic sentence. You also need to explain the athletes' contributions in more detail.
- Add a **summary statement** to sum up the paragraph's main idea.
- Add **transitions** to introduce the three specific categories you're discussing.

Corey kept these comments in mind as he revised his paragraph. The final edited and proofread draft includes all the elements Corey looked for when he **TEST**ed his paragraph.

Giving Back

Many high-profile athletes find various ways to give back to their communities. One way to give back is to start a charitable foundation to help young fans. For example, Michael Jordan and the Chicago Bulls built a Boys & Girls Club on Chicago's West Side. In addition, Troy Aikman set up a foundation that builds playgrounds for children's hospitals. Another way athletes give back to their communities is by mentoring, or giving guidance to young people. Many athletes work to encourage young people to stay in school. Shaquille O'Neal's Shaq's Paq, for example, provides guidance for inner-city children. The Philadelphia 76ers visit schools and have donated over five thousand books to local libraries. One more way athletes can contribute to their communities is to respond to emergencies. Football player Ike Reese, formerly with the Atlanta Falcons, collects clothing and food for families that need help. Basketball player Vince Carter of the Memphis Grizzlies founded the Embassy of Hope Foundation. It distributes food to needy families at Thanksgiving and hosts a Christmas party for disadvantaged families. These are just some of the ways that high-profile athletes give back to their communities.

T E S T
- Topic Sentence
- Evidence
- Summary Statement
- Transitions

TEST · **Revise · Edit · Proofread**

Look back at the draft of your classification paragraph. Using the **TEST** checklist on page 148, evaluate your paragraph to make sure it includes a topic sentence, evidence, a summary statement, and transitions, and revise your draft accordingly. Finally, edit and proofread your paragraph.

Andrew D. Bernstein / NBAE
via Getty Images

TESTing a classification paragraph

Topic Sentence Unifies Your Paragraph

☐ Do you have a clearly worded **topic sentence** that states your paragraph's main idea?

☐ Does your topic sentence identify the categories you will discuss?

Evidence Supports Your Paragraph's Topic Sentence

☐ Does all your **evidence**—examples and details—support your paragraph's main idea?

☐ Do your examples and details explain each category and indicate how each is distinct from the others?

☐ Do you need to include more examples or details?

Summary Statement Reinforces Your Paragraph's Unity

☐ Does your paragraph end with a **summary statement** that reinforces your main idea?

Transitions Add Coherence to Your Paragraph

☐ Do your **transitions** clearly indicate which categories are more important than others?

☐ Do you need to add transitions to make your paragraph clearer and to help readers follow your ideas?

11 Definition Paragraphs

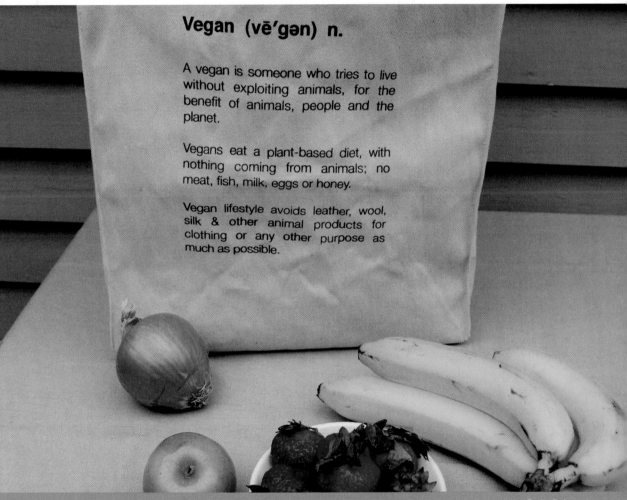

Vegan (vē′gən) n.

A vegan is someone who tries to live without exploiting animals, for the benefit of animals, people and the planet.

Vegans eat a plant-based diet, with nothing coming from animals; no meat, fish, milk, eggs or honey.

Vegan lifestyle avoids leather, wool, silk & other animal products for clothing or any other purpose as much as possible.

Emily Behrendt

focus on writing

Read the definition of the word *vegan* printed on the shopping bag pictured here, and consider how this definition could be developed further. Then, brainstorm to identify some words you have encountered in your college courses for which you could write one-paragraph definitions. (If you prefer, you may choose a topic from the list on the following page instead.) You will return to your topic and review your brainstorming later in the chapter when you write your definition paragraph.

additional topics for definition

A negative quality, such as *jealousy*

A type of person, such as an *optimist* or a *pessimist*

A controversial term, such as *right to life, affirmative action,* or *social justice*

A goal in life, such as *happiness* or *success*

11a Understanding Definition

During a conversation, you might say that a friend is stubborn, that a stream is polluted, or that a neighborhood is dangerous. In order to make yourself clear, you have to define what you mean by *stubborn, polluted,* or *dangerous*. Like conversations, academic assignments also may involve definition. In a history paper, for example, you might have to define *imperialism*; on a biology exam, you might be asked to define *mitosis*.

A **definition** tells what a word means. When you want your readers to know exactly how you are using a specific term, you define it.

When most people think of definitions, they think of the **formal definitions** they see in a dictionary. Formal definitions have a three-part structure.

- The term to be defined
- The general class to which the term belongs
- The things that make the term different from all other items in the general class to which the term belongs

TERM	CLASS	DIFFERENTIATION
Ice hockey	is a game	played on ice by two teams on skates who use curved sticks to try to hit a puck into the opponent's goal.
Spaghetti	is a pasta	made in the shape of long, thin strands.

A single-sentence formal definition is often not enough to define a specialized term (*point of view* or *premeditation,* for example), an abstract concept (*happiness* or *success*), or a complicated subject (*stem-cell research*). In these cases, you may need to expand the basic formal definition by writing a definition paragraph. In fact, a **definition paragraph** is an expanded formal definition. (For information on writing definition essays, see 16c.)

When you TEST a definition paragraph, make sure it follows these guidelines:

T ▪ A definition paragraph should begin with a formal definition in the **topic sentence**.

E ▪ A definition paragraph does not follow any one pattern of development; in fact, it may define a term by using any of the patterns discussed in this text. For example, a definition paragraph may explain a concept by *comparing* it to something else or by giving *examples*. For this reason, your discussion of each category should include **evidence**—examples and details—that is appropriate for the pattern of development that you use.

S ▪ A definition paragraph should end with a **summary statement** that reinforces the paragraph's main idea.

T ▪ A definition paragraph should include **transitions** that are appropriate for the pattern or patterns of organization you use.

Here is one possible structure for a definition paragraph. Notice that this paragraph uses a combination of **narration** and **exemplification**.

Paragraph Map: Definition

Topic Sentence

Point #1
    Narrative

Point #2
    Example

    Example

Point #3
    Example

    Example

Summary Statement

Model Paragraph: Definition

The writer of the following paragraph uses comparison and process to define the *dabbawala* system of food delivery.

The Dabbawala System

Comparison —

Fast food is a common choice for lunch in the United States. Often, this meal is high in calories and full of fat. Many workers in Mumbai, India, however, receive a daily home-cooked lunch by means of the *dabbawala system*. This distribution system consists of people (called *dabbawalas*) who collect freshly made food from the homes of office workers and deliver it to

Process —

their workplaces. First, the worker's wife or mother prepares the meal early in the morning and packs it in a container called a *tiffin*. Next, a dabbawala comes to the door to pick up the tiffin and takes it to the sorting location. Third, the tiffins are coded and loaded on to a train and delivered to offices by local dabbawalas on bicycles or motor scooters. Later, the empty tiffins

Effects —

are collected and returned to the homes. As a result of this system, over 200,000 workers a day in Mumbai have access to healthy, home-cooked meals. In addition, an important and honorable job exists for the people who pick up and deliver the tiffins. The dabbawala system is so efficient that it has been written up in the *Harvard Business Review* and studied by FedEx.

—Aran Cho (student)

Some Transitional Words and Phrases for Definition

Transitions are important for definition paragraphs. They can signal moves from one narrative event to another. Transitions can also introduce examples.

also	often
for example	one characteristic . . . another
for men (for women)	characteristic
however	one way . . . another way
in addition	sometimes
in particular	specifically
in the 1990s (or another time)	the first kind . . . the second kind
like	until recently

grammar in context

Definition

A definition paragraph often includes a formal definition of the term or concept you are going to discuss. When you write your formal definition, be careful not to use the phrases *is where* or *is when*.

consists of people (called dabbawalas) who

The *dabbawala system* ~~is when people (called *dabbawalas*)~~ collect

freshly made food from the homes of office workers and deliver it to

their workplaces.

Analyzing a Definition Paragraph

Read this definition paragraph; then, follow the instructions in Practice 11-1.

Loans That Change Lives

Microloans are small loans given to people who live in extreme poverty. The idea for such loans originated in 1974, when a Bangladeshi economist loaned $27 to a group of local women. The women used the loan to purchase bamboo to make furniture. After they sold the furniture, they repaid the loan and kept a small profit for themselves. As a result of this experience, the economist created a bank for microloans. Similar microcredit banks now exist throughout the world. For example, microcredit banks can be found in Bosnia, Peru, Ethiopia, and Russia. Microloans are different from ordinary loans because they are not awarded on the basis of credit history or financial means; instead, they are based on trust. A microcredit bank trusts a borrower to make money even if he or she has no or little income at the time of the loan. Some people see microloans as a wonderful opportunity for poor businesspeople; others criticize microloans because they can encourage governments to reduce their support for the poor. Even so, microloans have helped countless people all over the world to lift themselves out of poverty.

PRACTICE

11-1   1. Underline the topic sentence of the paragraph on page 153.

2. What is the subject of this definition? _____

3. What is the writer's one-sentence definition of the subject?

_____

4. List some of the specific information the writer uses to define his subject. The first piece of information has been listed for you.

Microloans originated in Bangladesh in 1974.

_____

_____

_____

5. Circle the transitional words and phrases the writer uses.

6. What patterns of development does the writer use in his definition? List them here.

_____

_____

_____

7. Underline the paragraph's summary statement.

PRACTICE

11-2   Following are four possible topic sentences for definition paragraphs. Each topic sentence includes an underlined word. In the space provided, list two possible patterns of development that you could use to develop a definition of the underlined word. For example, you could define the word *discrimination* by giving examples (exemplification) and by telling a story (narration).

1. During the interview, the job candidate made a sexist comment.

Possible strategy: _____

Possible strategy: _____

2. Loyalty is one of the chief characteristics of golden retrievers.

Possible strategy: _____

Possible strategy: _____

3. More than forty years after President Johnson's Great Society initiative, we have yet to eliminate <u>poverty</u> in the United States.

Possible strategy: _____

Possible strategy: _____

4. The problem with movies today is that they are just too <u>violent</u>.

Possible strategy: _____

Possible strategy: _____

11b   Case Study: A Student Writes a Definition Paragraph

Here is how one student, Lorraine Scipio, wrote a definition paragraph. On a history exam, Lorraine was asked to write a one-paragraph definition of the term *imperialism*. Lorraine had studied for the exam, so she knew what imperialism was. Because she wanted to make sure that she did not leave anything out of her definition (and because she had a time limit), she quickly listed some supporting examples and details on the inside front cover of her exam book. Then, she crossed out two items that did not seem relevant.

A policy of control

Military

~~Lenin~~

Establish empires

Cultural superiority

Raw materials and cheap labor

Africa, etc.

~~Cultural imperialism~~

Nineteenth-century term

Emily Behrendt

list examples and details

Review the brainstorming you did in response to the Focus on Writing prompt on page 149, and choose a word to define. Then, list the examples and details that can best help you develop a definition of that word.

_____

_____

_____

_____

Now, cross out the items on your list that do not seem relevant to your definition.

After reviewing her list of examples and details, Lorraine drafted the topic sentence that appears below.

The goal of imperialism is to establish an empire.

Emily Behrendt

write a topic sentence

Review your list of examples and details, and then draft a topic sentence for your definition paragraph. Include a formal definition of the term you are defining.

_____

_____

Next, Lorraine made an informal outline, quickly arranging her supporting examples and details in the order in which she planned to write about them.

Establish empires

Nineteenth-century term

Cultural superiority

Africa, etc.

Raw materials and cheap labor

A policy of control

Military

make an outline

Create an informal outline for your paragraph by arranging your examples and details in the order in which you plan to discuss them.

Emily Behrendt

Referring to the material on her list, Lorraine wrote the following draft of her definition paragraph. Notice that she uses several different patterns to develop her definition.

> The goal of imperialism is to establish an empire. The imperialist country thinks that it is superior to the country it takes over. It justifies its actions by saying that it is helping the other country. But it isn't. Countries such as Germany, Belgium, Spain, and England have been imperialist in the past. The point of imperialism is to take as much out of the occupied countries as possible. Often, imperialist countries sent troops to occupy other countries and to keep order. As a result, imperialism kept the people in occupied countries in poverty and often broke down local governments and local traditions.

draft your paragraph

Using your informal outline as a guide, draft your definition paragraph. Remember, you can use any of the patterns of development discussed in Unit 2 of this text to help you define your term. Begin by identifying the term. Then, you can describe it, give examples, tell how it works, explain its purpose, consider its history or future, or compare it with other similar terms.

Emily Behrendt

After she finished her draft, Lorraine **TEST**ed her paragraph to make sure she had answered the exam question. As a result, she decided that she needed to make the following changes.

- Because the exam question asked for a definition, she rewrote her **topic sentence** as a formal definition.
- She strengthened her **evidence**, explaining her supporting examples and details more fully. She also deleted some vague statements that did not support her topic sentence.

- She added **transitional words and phrases** to make the connections between her ideas clearer.
- She added a **summary statement** to reinforce her explanation of the negative effects of imperialism.

Lorraine made her changes directly on the draft she had written, crossing out unnecessary information and adding missing information. She also edited her paragraph for grammar, punctuation, and mechanical errors. Then, because she had some extra time, she neatly rewrote her paragraph.

Lorraine's revised, edited, and proofread paragraph appears below. (Because this is an exam answer, she does not include a title.) Notice that the final draft includes all the elements Lorraine looked for when she TESTed her paragraph.

T E S T

Topic Sentence

Evidence

Summary Statement

Transitions

Imperialism is the policy by which one country takes over the land or the government of another country. In the nineteenth century, the object of imperialism was to establish an empire. The imperialist country thought that it was superior to the country it took over. It justified its actions by saying that it was helping the other country. For instance, countries such as Germany, Belgium, Spain, and England followed their imperialist ambitions in Africa when they claimed large areas of land. The point of imperialism was to take as much out of the occupied countries as possible. For example, in South America and Mexico, Spain removed tons of gold from the areas it occupied. It made the natives slaves and forced them to work in mines. In order to protect their interests, imperialist countries sent troops to occupy the country and to keep order. As a result, imperialism kept the people in occupied countries in poverty and often broke down local governments and local traditions. Although European imperialism occasionally had benefits, at its worst it brought slavery, disease, and death.

FYI

Writing Paragraph Answers on Exams

When you write paragraph answers on exams, you do not have much time to work, so you need to be well prepared. Know your subject well, and memorize important definitions. You may have time to write an outline, a rough draft, and a final draft, but you will have to work quickly. Even so, your final draft should include all the elements of a good paragraph: a topic sentence, supporting details, transitions, and a summary statement.

TEST · **Revise** · **Edit** · **Proofread**

Look back at the draft of your definition paragraph. Using the TEST checklist below, evaluate your paragraph to make sure it includes a topic sentence, evidence, a summary statement, and transitions, and revise your draft accordingly. Finally, edit and proofread your paragraph.

Emily Behrendt

TESTing a definition paragraph

Topic Sentence Unifies Your Paragraph

☐ Do you have a clearly worded **topic sentence** that states your paragraph's main idea?

☐ Does your topic sentence identify the term you are defining?

Evidence Supports Your Paragraph's Topic Sentence

☐ Does all your **evidence**—examples and details—support your paragraph's main idea?

☐ Do you need to add more examples or details to help you define your term?

Summary Statement Reinforces Your Paragraph's Unity

☐ Does your paragraph end with a **summary statement** that reinforces your main idea?

Transitions Add Coherence to Your Paragraph

☐ Are your **transitions** appropriate for the pattern (or patterns) of development you use?

☐ Do you need to add transitions to make your paragraph clearer and to help readers follow your ideas?

12 Argument Paragraphs

David McNew / Getty Images

focus on writing

Many students, like those at the protest pictured above, are unhappy about rising student loan debt. Brainstorm to develop a list of political issues that interest you. Review your brainstorming, choose one issue, and then write a journal entry exploring your thoughts on this issue. (If you prefer, you may choose a topic from the list on the following page instead.) You will return to your journal entry later in the chapter when you write your argument paragraph.

In this chapter, you will learn to write an argument paragraph.

PREVIEW

additional topics for argument

Online courses
Campus security
Banning cell phones in class
School speech codes
College debt

12a Understanding Argument

When most people hear the word *argument*, they think of heated exchanges on television interview programs. These discussions, however, are more like shouting matches than arguments. True **argument** involves taking a well-thought-out position on a **debatable topic**—a topic about which reasonable people may disagree (for example, "Should convicted felons be allowed to vote?").

In an **argument paragraph**, you take a position on an issue, and your purpose is to persuade readers that your position has merit. You attempt to convince people of the strength of your ideas by presenting **evidence**—in this case, facts and examples. In the process, you address opposing ideas, and if they are strong, you acknowledge their strengths. If your evidence is solid and your logic is sound, you will present a convincing argument. (For information on writing argument essays, see 16d.)

FYI

Evidence

You can use two kinds of **evidence** in your argument paragraphs: *facts* and *examples*.

1. A **fact** is a piece of information (such as "Alaska officially became a state in 1959") that can be verified. If you make a statement, you should be prepared to support it with facts—using statistics, observations, or statements that are generally accepted as true.

2. An **example** is a specific illustration of a general statement. To be convincing, an example should clearly relate to the point you are making.

161

When you **TEST** an argument paragraph, make sure it follows these guidelines:

T ■ An argument paragraph should begin with a **topic sentence** that clearly states your position. Using words like *should*, *should not*, or *ought to* in your topic sentence will make your position clear to your readers.

> The federal government <u>should</u> lower taxes on gasoline.

> The city <u>ought to</u> spend 20 percent of its budget on helping businesses convert to sustainable energy sources.

E ■ An argument paragraph should present points that support the topic sentence in **logical order**. For example, if your purpose is to argue in favor of placing warning labels on unhealthy snack foods, you should give reasons—arranging them from least to most important—why this policy should be instituted. Each of these points should then be supported with **evidence**—facts and examples.

An argument paragraph should also address and **refute** (argue against) opposing arguments. By showing that an opponent's arguments are weak, inaccurate, or misguided, you strengthen your own position. If an opposing argument is particularly strong, you may want to **concede** (accept) its strengths and then point out its shortcomings.

S ■ An argument paragraph should end with a **summary statement** that reinforces the paragraph's main idea—the position you take on the issue.

T ■ An argument paragraph should include **transitions** to connect the points you are making to one another and to the topic sentence.

Paragraph Map: Argument

Topic Sentence

Point #1

Point #2

Point #3

Opposing Argument #1
(plus refutation)

Opposing Argument #2
(plus refutation)

Summary Statement

Model Paragraph: Argument

The following paragraph argues in favor of an emergency notification system for college students.

T E S T

■ Topic Sentence
■ Evidence
■ Summary Statement
■ Transitions

Why Our School Should Set Up an Emergency Notification System

Our school should set up an emergency notification system that would deliver a text message to students' cell phones in a campus crisis. The first reason why we should set up an emergency notification system is that it is needed. Currently, it takes an hour or two to inform the whole campus of something—for example, that school is closing because of bad weather or that a school event has been canceled. Another reason why we should set up an emergency notification system is that it will make our campus safer by warning students if a crime takes place on campus. For example, when a shooting took place in 2007 on the campus of Virginia Tech, the school was unable to warn students to evacuate the campus. The result was that more than thirty people were killed. An emergency notification system might have saved the lives of many of these people. One objection to an instant-messaging emergency notification system is that email notification works just as well. However, although many students check their email just once or twice a day, most students carry cell phones and read text messages whenever they get them. Another objection is that some students do not have cell phones. The same system that delivers text messages to students, however, could also deliver messages to digital message boards around campus. Because communicating with students in a crisis situation can save lives, our school should set up an emergency notification system.

— Ashley Phillips (student)

Point 1 and support

Point 2 and support

Opposing argument 1 (plus refutation)

Opposing argument 2 (plus refutation)

Some Transitional Words and Phrases for Argument

Transitions are important in argument paragraphs. For example, in the paragraph above, the transitional phrases *the first reason* and *another reason* tell readers they are moving from one point to another. In addition, the transitional phrases *one objection* and *another objection* indicate that the writer is addressing two opposing arguments.

accordingly	but	even though
admittedly	certainly	finally
after all	consequently	first . . . second . . .
although	despite	for this reason
because	even so	however

(continued)

(continued from previous page)

in addition	nevertheless	since
in conclusion	nonetheless	the first reason
in fact	of course	therefore
in summary	one . . . another	thus
meanwhile	on the one hand . . . on	to be sure
moreover	the other hand	truly

grammar in context

Argument

When you write an argument paragraph, you should use both **compound sentences** and **complex sentences**. By doing this, you not only show the relationship between ideas but also eliminate choppy sentences.

COMPOUND SENTENCE   An emergency notification system will help all of us *, and it* communicate better. ~~It~~ will ensure our school's safety.

COMPLEX SENTENCE   *Because communicating* ~~Communicating~~ with students in a crisis situation *, our* can save lives. ~~Our~~ school should set up an emergency notification system.

For more information on how to create compound sentences, see Chapter 18. For more information on how to create complex sentences, see Chapter 19.

Analyzing an Argument Paragraph

Read this argument paragraph; then, follow the instructions in Practice 12-1.

Why We Need Full-Body Scanners

Because of their advantages, airport full-body scanners are a necessary tool in the fight against terrorism. One reason why airport scanners are necessary is that the federal government needs a quick and effective way of screening passengers. Because of their ease of operation, whole-body scanners accomplish this goal. Well over a million people fly throughout the United States each day. A single airport scanner is capable of screening thousands of people a day and is much faster than other methods of screening. Another reason why airport scanners are necessary is that they provide an additional layer of security. For example, scanners are able to detect both metallic and nonmetallic items that are taped to the body. In other words, scanners will detect both weapons and bomb materials that metal detectors might miss. People who oppose scanners say that they are unsafe. However, the literature that the government distributes at airports makes it clear that airport scanners expose passengers to less radiation than they experience when they fly at high altitudes. Opponents also charge that scanners violate the Constitution's guarantee of privacy because they show a three-dimensional image of a person's naked body. To deal with this objection, the Transportation Security Administration has made sure that the TSA officer who operates a scanner never sees the images of the person being scanned. He or she sees only a screen that indicates whether the person has successfully cleared the screening. In addition, the images themselves are deleted immediately after a person has left the screening area. Given the attempts that terrorists have made to attack the United States, airport scanners are a useful and effective way of keeping people safe when they fly.

—Carl Manni (student)

PRACTICE

 12-1

1. Underline the topic sentence of the paragraph on page 164.

2. What issue is the subject of the paragraph?

_____

3. What is the writer's position?

_____

4. What specific points does the writer use to support his topic sentence?

_____

_____

5. List some evidence (facts and examples) that the writer uses to support his points. The first piece of evidence has been listed for you.

A single full-body scanner is capable of screening thousands of people a day.

_____

_____

_____

6. What other evidence could the writer have used?

_____

_____

_____

7. What opposing arguments does he mention?

_____

_____

8. How does he refute these arguments?

_____

_____

9. Circle the transitional words and phrases the writer uses to move readers through his argument.

10. Underline the paragraph's summary statement.

PRACTICE

12-2   Following are four topic sentences for argument paragraphs. List two or three points that could support each topic sentence. For example, if you were arguing in support of laws requiring motorcycle riders to wear safety helmets, you could say helmets cut down on medical costs and save lives.

1. High school graduates should perform a year of public service before going to college.

2. All student athletes should be paid a salary by their college or university.

3. College students caught cheating should be expelled.

4. The U.S. government should forgive all federal student loans.

PRACTICE

12-3   Choose one of the topic sentences from Practice 12-2. Then, list two types of evidence that could support each point you listed. For example, if you said that wearing safety helmets saves lives, you could list "accident statistics" and "statements by emergency room physicians."

_____

_____

PRACTICE

12-4   List opposing arguments for the topic sentence you selected for Practice 12-3. Then, list the weaknesses of each of these arguments.

Opposing argument #1: _____

Weaknesses: _____

Opposing argument #2: _____

Weaknesses: _____

12b Case Study: A Student Writes an Argument Paragraph

Here is how one student, Phillip Zhu, wrote an argument paragraph. Phillip, a computer science major, was asked to write an argument paragraph on an issue that interested him. Because he was taking a course in computer ethics, he decided to write about an issue that had been discussed in class: the way many employers now search social-networking sites, such as Facebook, to find information about job applicants.

Phillip had already formed an opinion about the issue, so he was ready to write the following topic sentence that expressed his position.

Employers should not use social-networking sites to find information about job applicants.

write your topic sentence

Look back at the journal entry you wrote in response to the Focus on Writing prompt on page 160. Determine your position on the issue you chose to write about, and then draft a topic sentence that clearly states the position you will take in your argument paragraph.

_____

_____

Phillip then listed the following points that he could use to support his topic sentence.

Social-networking sites should be private

People exaggerate on social-networking sites

Some posts meant to be funny

No one warns applicant

Need email address to register

Expect limited audience

Employers can misinterpret what they find

Employers going where they don't belong

Not an accurate picture

Not fair

Not meant to be seen by job recruiters

list your supporting points

Review your topic sentence, and list as many points as you can in support of your position on the issue. Then, look back at your journal entry to find evidence to support your points.

_____

_____

_____

_____

After identifying his three most important supporting points, Phillip arranged them into an informal outline.

Social-networking sites should be private
   Need email address to register
   Expect limited audience
   Employers going where they don't belong

People exaggerate on social-networking sites
   Some posts meant to be funny
   Not meant to be seen by job recruiters
   No one warns applicant

Employers can misinterpret what they find
   Not an accurate picture
   Not fair

make an outline

Create an informal outline for your paragraph by arranging the points that support your position in the order that you think will be most convincing to your readers—for example, from the least important point to the most important point. Under each point, list the evidence (facts and examples) that you will use as support.

David McNew/Getty Images

Once Phillip finished his informal outline, he tried to think of possible arguments against his position because he knew he would have to consider and refute these opposing arguments in his paragraph. He came up with two possible arguments against his position.

1. Employers should be able to find out as much as they can.

2. Applicants have only themselves to blame.

list opposing arguments

Review your informal outline, and then list one or more possible arguments against your position on the lines below.

David McNew/Getty Images

_____

_____

_____

Now, try to think of ways in which these opposing arguments are weak or inaccurate.

Phillip then wrote the following draft of his paragraph.

Employers should not use social-networking sites to find information about job applicants. For one thing, social-networking sites should be private. By visiting these sites, employers are going where they do not belong. People also exaggerate on social-networking sites. They say things that are not true, and they put things on the sites they would not want job recruiters to see. No one ever tells applicants that recruiters search these sites, so they feel safe posting all kinds of material. Employers can misinterpret what they read. Employers and recruiters need to get as much information as they can. They should not use unfair ways to get this information. Applicants have only themselves to blame for their problems. They need to be more careful about what they put up online. This is true, but most applicants don't know that employers will search social-networking sites.

David McNew/Getty Images

draft your paragraph

Guided by your informal outline and your list of opposing arguments, draft your argument paragraph. Begin your paragraph with a topic sentence that clearly states the position you are taking on the issue.

After finishing his draft, Phillip scheduled a conference with his instructor. Together, they went over his paragraph and TESTed his paragraph. They agreed that Phillip needed to make the following changes.

- They decided he needed to make his **topic sentence** more specific and more forceful.
- They decided he should add more **evidence** (facts and examples) to his discussion. For example, what social-networking sites is he talking about? Which are restricted? How do employers gain access to these sites?
- They decided he needed to delete the irrelevant discussion blaming job applicants for their problems.
- They decided he should add **transitional words and phrases** to clearly identify the points he is making in support of his argument and also to identify the two opposing arguments he discusses.
- They decided he needed to add a strong **summary statement** to reinforce his position.

As Phillip revised his paragraph, he was guided by these decisions. The final draft below includes all the elements Phillip looked for when he **TEST**ed his paragraph.

Unfair Searching

Employers should not use social-networking sites, such as Instagram and Facebook, to find information about job applicants. First, social-networking sites should be private. People who use these sites do not expect employers to access them. However, some employers routinely search social-networking sites to find information about job applicants. Doing this is not right, and it is not fair. By visiting these sites, employers are going where they do not belong. Another reason employers should not use information from social-networking sites is that people frequently exaggerate on them or say things that are not true. They may also put statements and pictures on the sites that they would not want job recruiters to see. Because no one ever tells applicants that recruiters search these sites, they feel safe posting embarrassing pictures or making exaggerated claims about drinking or sex. Finally, employers can misinterpret the material they see. As a result, they may reject a good applicant because they take seriously what is meant to be a joke. Of course, employers need to get as much information about a candidate as they can. They should not, however, use unfair tactics to get this information. In addition, prospective employers should realize that the profile they see on a social-networking site may not accurately represent the job applicant. For these reasons, employers should not use social-networking sites to do background checks.

T E S T

- Topic Sentence
- Evidence
- Summary Statement
- Transitions

TEST · **Revise · Edit · Proofread**

Look back at the draft of your argument paragraph. Using the **TEST** checklist on page 172, evaluate your paragraph to make sure it includes a topic sentence, evidence, a summary statement, and transitions, and revise your draft accordingly. Finally, edit and proofread your paragraph.

David McNew/Getty Images

TESTing an argument paragraph

Topic Sentence Unifies Your Paragraph

☐ Do you have a clearly worded **topic sentence** that states your paragraph's main idea?

☐ Does your topic sentence state your position on a debatable issue?

Evidence Supports Your Paragraph's Topic Sentence

☐ Does all your **evidence** support your paragraph's main idea?

☐ Have you included enough facts and examples to support your points, or do you need to add more?

☐ Do you summarize and refute opposing arguments?

Summary Statement Reinforces Your Paragraph's Unity

☐ Does your paragraph end with a strong **summary statement** that reinforces your main idea?

Transitions Add Coherence to Your Paragraph

☐ Do you use **transitions** to let readers know when you are moving from one point to another?

☐ Do you use transitional words and phrases to indicate when you are addressing opposing arguments?

☐ Do you need to add transitions to make your paragraph clearer and to help readers follow your ideas?

unit
3 Focus on Essays

13 Writing an Essay

focus on writing

Most people would agree that oil rig workers, like the ones pictured here, have a very challenging job. Think about the most difficult job you've ever had. This is the topic you will be writing about as you go through this chapter. (If you have never had a job, you may write about a specific task that you disliked or about a difficult job that a friend or relative has had.)

In this chapter, you will learn to

- understand essay structure (13a)
- move from assignment to topic (13b)
- find ideas to write about (13c)
- state a thesis (13d)
- choose supporting points (13e)
- make an outline (13f)
- draft, TEST, revise, and edit your essay (13g–13j)
- proofread your essay (13k)

Much of the writing you do in school will be more than just one paragraph. Often, you will be asked to write an **essay**—a group of paragraphs on a single subject. When you write an essay, you follow the same process you follow when you write a paragraph: you begin by planning and then move on to organizing your ideas, drafting, TESTing, revising, editing, and proofreading.

In this chapter, you will see how the strategies you learned for writing paragraphs can help you write essays.

13a Understanding Essay Structure

Understanding the structure of a paragraph can help you understand the structure of an essay. In a paragraph, the main idea is stated in a **topic sentence**, and the rest of the paragraph supports this main idea with **evidence** (details and examples). **Transitional words and phrases** help readers follow the discussion. The paragraph ends with a **summary statement** that reinforces the main idea.

Paragraph

The **topic sentence** states the main idea of the paragraph.

Evidence supports the main idea.

Transitional words and phrases show the connections between ideas.

A **summary statement** reinforces the main idea of the paragraph.

The structure of an essay is similar to the structure of a paragraph:

- The essay's first paragraph—the *introduction*—begins with opening remarks that create interest and closes with a **thesis statement**. This thesis statement, like a paragraph's topic sentence, presents the main idea. (For more on introductions, see 14a.)
- The *body* of the essay contains several paragraphs that support the thesis statement. Each body paragraph begins with a topic sentence that states the main idea of the paragraph. The other sentences in the paragraph support the topic sentence with **evidence** (details and examples).
- **Transitional words and phrases** lead readers from sentence to sentence and from paragraph to paragraph.
- The last paragraph—the *conclusion*—ends the essay. The conclusion includes a **summary statement** that reinforces the thesis. It ends with concluding remarks. (For more on conclusions, see 14b.)

The first letters of these four key elements—thesis statement, evidence, summary statement, and transitions—spell TEST. Just as you did with paragraphs, you can TEST your essays to see whether they include all the elements of an effective essay.

Many of the essays you will write in college will have a **thesis-and-support** structure.

Essay

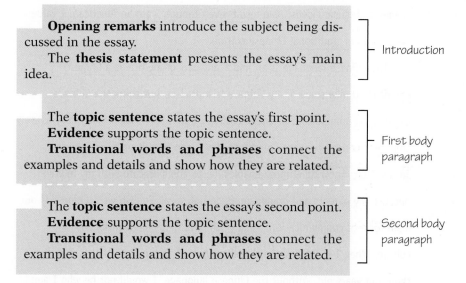

Opening remarks introduce the subject being discussed in the essay.
The **thesis statement** presents the essay's main idea.

Introduction

The **topic sentence** states the essay's first point.
Evidence supports the topic sentence.
Transitional words and phrases connect the examples and details and show how they are related.

First body paragraph

The **topic sentence** states the essay's second point.
Evidence supports the topic sentence.
Transitional words and phrases connect the examples and details and show how they are related.

Second body paragraph

The **topic sentence** states the essay's third point.
Evidence supports the topic sentence.
Transitional words and phrases connect the examples and details and show how they are related.

Third body paragraph

The **summary statement** reinforces the thesis, summarizing the essay's main idea.
Concluding remarks present the writer's final thoughts on the subject.

Conclusion

The following essay by Jennifer Chu illustrates the structure of an essay. (Note that transitional words and phrases are shaded.)

Becoming Chinese American

Introduction

Although I was born in Hong Kong, I have spent most of my life in the United States. However, my parents have always made sure that I did not forget my roots. They always tell stories of what it was like to live in Hong Kong. To make sure my brothers and sisters and I know what is happening in China, my parents subscribe to Chinese cable TV. When we were growing up, we would watch the celebration of the Chinese New Year, the news from Asia, and Chinese movies and music videos. As a result, even though I am an American, I value many parts of traditional Chinese culture.

Thesis statement

Topic sentence (states essay's first point)

First body paragraph

Evidence (supports topic sentence)

The Chinese language is an important part of my life as a Chinese American. Unlike some of my Chinese friends, I do not think the Chinese language is unimportant or embarrassing. First, I feel that it is my duty as a Chinese American to learn Chinese so that I can pass it on to my children. In addition, knowing Chinese enables me to communicate with my relatives. Because my parents and grandparents do not speak English well, Chinese is our main form of communication. Finally, Chinese helps me identify with my culture. When I speak Chinese, I feel connected to a culture that is over five thousand years old. Without the Chinese language, I would not be who I am.

Chinese food is another important part of my life as a Chinese American. One reason for this is that everything we Chinese people eat has a history and a meaning. At a birthday meal, for example, we serve long noodles and buns in the shape of peaches. This is because we believe that long noodles represent long life and that peaches are served in heaven. Another reason is that to Chinese people, food is a way of reinforcing ties between family and friends. For instance, during a traditional Chinese wedding ceremony, the bride and the groom eat nine of everything. This is because the number nine stands for the Chinese words "together forever." By taking part in this ritual, the bride and groom start their marriage by making Chinese customs a part of their life together.

Topic sentence (states essay's second point)

Second body paragraph

Evidence (supports topic sentence)

Religion is the most important part of my life as a Chinese American. At various times during the year, Chinese religious festivals bring together the people I care about the most. During Chinese New Year, my whole family goes to the temple, where we say prayers and welcome others with traditional New Year's greetings. After leaving the temple, we all go to Chinatown and eat dim sum until the lion dance starts. As the colorful lion dances its way down the street, people beat drums and throw firecrackers to drive off any evil spirits that may be around. Later that night, parents give children gifts of money in red envelopes that symbolize joy and happiness in the coming year.

Topic sentence (states essay's third point)

Third body paragraph

Evidence (supports topic sentence)

My family has taught me how important it is to hold on to my Chinese culture. When I was six, my parents sent me to a Chinese American grade school. My teachers thrilled me with stories of Fa Mulan, the Shang Dynasty, and the Moon God. I will never forget how happy I was when I realized how special it is to be Chinese. This is how I want my own children to feel. I want them to be proud of who they are and to pass their language, history, and culture on to the next generation.

Summary statement (reinforces essay's thesis)

Conclusion

PRACTICE

13-1 Following is an essay organized according to the diagram on pages 177–178. Read the essay, and then answer the questions that follow.

Enhanced Water

Flavored or "enhanced" water has grown in popularity since it was introduced in the late 1990s. Most enhanced waters are owned by soft drink companies like Coca-Cola and Pepsi. These companies have spent millions of dollars trying to convince consumers that enhanced water is better than ordinary water. In spite of their efforts, however, this is just not true.

There is no question that our bodies need fluid to stay hydrated. In fact, most experts say that people should drink about 64 ounces (eight cups) of water per day. Only athletes and people who are involved in strenuous activities, such as hiking, need to drink significantly more water. These individuals may benefit from the salt and carbohydrates found in sports drinks like Gatorade, but they are the exception. People who exercise at a normal rate, for about an hour a day, need only a few additional cups of plain water to restore lost fluids.

Despite marketing claims, it is not clear that enhanced water is more healthful than regular water. The labels on most enhanced water drinks, such as VitaminWater and SoBe Lifewater, make health claims that have not been scientifically proven. For instance, the label on VitaminWater's drink "Focus" implies that its vitamins and minerals will improve a person's focus and eyesight. Scientists generally agree, however, that this sugary beverage does not improve attention spans or eye health. Another example of a misleading claim appears on the label of SoBe's Blood Orange Mango drink, which lists B12 vitamins that are supposed to boost energy. However, the amount of vitamins found in this drink is too small to provide any health benefits and neither blood oranges nor mangoes are included in the ingredients list. Moreover, many enhanced water drinks actually contain ingredients that the body does not need—for example, caffeine, artificial flavors and colors, and sugar or artificial sweeteners.

In addition to making questionable marketing claims, manufacturers of enhanced waters present nutritional information in a confusing way. For example, just a quick glance at the label for a SoBe Lifewater drink would lead someone to believe that a serving has 40 calories, 16 grams of carbohydrates, and 10 grams of sugar. These amounts may sound reasonable, but a closer look at the label reveals that each 20-ounce bottle actually contains two and a half servings. In other words, a person who drinks the whole bottle is actually consuming 100 calories, 40 grams of carbohydrates, and 25 grams of sugar—more carbohydrates and sugar than in a glazed doughnut. Even the "zero calorie" options are concerning. They may seem healthy, but the nutrition labels reveal alarming amounts of sugar, artificial flavor, and dye.

In most cases, regular tap water is all people need to stay healthy and hydrated. The drink manufacturers ignore this fact, saying that enhanced water is lower in calories and sugar than non-diet soft drinks. They also say that, although the herbs and vitamins in their drinks may not have proven health benefits, at least they are not harmful. Finally, the drink manufacturers claim that their products get people to drink more fluids. Although all these claims are partially true, consumers do not need the ingredients in enhanced water or its extra cost.

1. Underline the essay's thesis statement.

2. Underline the topic sentence of each body paragraph.

3. What point does the first body paragraph make? What evidence supports this point?

_____

_____

_____

_____

4. What point does the second paragraph make? What evidence supports this point?

_____

_____

_____

_____

5. What point does the third body paragraph make? What evidence supports this point?

_____

_____

_____

6. What transitions does the essay include? How do they connect the essay's ideas?

_____

_____

_____

_____

7. Where in the conclusion does the writer restate the essay's thesis? Underline this statement.

13b Moving from Assignment to Topic

Many essays you write in college begin as **assignments** given to you by your instructors. Before you focus on any assignment, however, you should take time to think about your **purpose** (what you want to accomplish by writing your essay) and your **audience** (the people who will read your essay). Once you have considered these issues, you are ready to think about the specifics of your assignment.

The following assignments are typical of those given in a composition class.

- Discuss some things you would change about your school.
- What can college students do to improve the environment?
- Discuss an important decision you made during the past three years.

Because these assignments are so general, you need to narrow them before you can start to write. What specific things would you change about your school? Exactly what could college students do to improve the environment? Answering these questions will help you narrow these assignments into **topics** that you can write about.

ASSIGNMENT	TOPIC
Discuss some things you would change about your school.	Three things I would change to improve the quality of life on campus
What can college students do to improve the environment?	The campus recycling project

Jared White, a student in a first-year composition course, was given the following assignment.

ASSIGNMENT

Discuss an important decision you made during the past few years.

Jared narrowed this assignment to the following topic:

TOPIC

Deciding to go back to school

Throughout the rest of this chapter, you will be following Jared's writing process.

PRACTICE

13-2   Decide whether the following topics are narrow enough for an essay of four or five paragraphs. If a topic is suitable, write *OK* in the blank. If it is not, write in the blank a revised version of the same topic that is narrow enough for a brief essay.

Examples

Successful strategies for quitting smoking ___*OK*___

Horror movies ___*1950s Japanese monster movies*___

1. Violence in American public schools _____

_____

2. Ways to improve your study skills _____

_____

3. Using pets as therapy for nursing-home patients _____

_____

4. Teachers _____

_____

5. Safe ways to lose weight _____

_____

decide on a topic

Look back at the Focus on Writing prompt on page 175. To narrow this assignment to a topic you can write about, you need to decide which difficult job to focus on. Begin by listing several jobs you could discuss.

AP Photo/Sue Ogrocki

FYI

Visit the Study Guides and Strategies website (studygs.net /writing/prewriting.htm) to learn how to use one of the graphic organizers or to find other information about the writing process.

13c Finding Ideas to Write About

Before you start writing about a topic, you need to find ideas to write about. Sometimes ideas may come to you easily. More often, you will have to use specific strategies, such as *freewriting* or *brainstorming*, to help you come up with ideas.

Freewriting

When you **freewrite**, you write for a fixed period of time without stopping. When you do **focused freewriting**, you write with a specific topic in mind. Then, you read what you have written and choose ideas you think you can use.

The following focused freewriting was written by Jared White on the topic "Deciding to go back to school."

Deciding to go back to school. When I graduated high school, I swore I'd never go back to school. Hated it. Couldn't wait to get out. What was I thinking? How was I supposed to support myself? My dad's friend needed help. He taught me how to paint houses. I made good money, but it was boring. I couldn't picture myself doing it forever. Even though I knew I was going to have to go back to school, I kept putting off the decision. Maybe I was lazy. Maybe I was scared—probably both. I had this fear of being turned down. How could someone who had bad grades all through high school go to college? Also, I'd been out of school for six years. And even if I did get in (a miracle!), how would I pay for it? How would I live? Well, here I am—the first one in my family to go to college.

Jared's freewriting

PRACTICE

13-3   Reread Jared White's freewriting. If you were advising Jared, which ideas would you tell him to explore further? Why?

freewrite

Choose two of the difficult jobs you listed, and freewrite about each of them. Then, choose one of the jobs to write about. Circle the ideas about this job that you would like to explore further in an essay.

AP Photo/Sue Ogrocki

Brainstorming

When you **brainstorm** (either individually or with others in a group), you write down (or type) all the ideas you can think of about a particular topic. After you have recorded as much material as you can, you look over your notes and decide which ideas are useful and which ones are not.

Here are Jared's brainstorming notes about his decision to go back to school.

Deciding to Go Back to School

Money a problem

Other students a lot younger

Paying tuition—how?

No one in family went to college

Friends not in college

Couldn't see myself in college

Considered going to trade school

Computer programmer?

Grades bad in high school

Time for me to grow up

Wondered if I would get in

Found out about community college

Admission requirements not bad

Afraid—too old, failing out, looking silly

Took time to get used to routine

Found other students like me

Liked studying

Jared's brainstorming

PRACTICE

13-4   Reread Jared's brainstorming notes. Which ideas would you advise him to explore further? Why?

AP Photo/Sue Ogrocki

brainstorm

Review your freewriting. Then, brainstorm about the job for which you have found the most interesting ideas. What ideas about this job did you get from brainstorming that you did not get from freewriting?

Keeping a Journal

When you keep a **journal**, you keep an informal record of your thoughts and ideas. As you learned in Chapter 2, your journal can be a notebook (or section of a notebook) or a computer file. In your journal, you record your thoughts about your assignments, identify ideas that you want to explore further, and keep notes about things you read or see. After rereading your journal entries, you can decide to explore an idea further in another journal entry or to use material from a specific entry in an essay.

Following is an entry in Jared's journal that he eventually used in his essay about returning to school.

> When I was working as a house painter, I had a conversation that helped convince me to go to college. One day, I started talking to the guy whose house I was painting. I told him that I was painting houses until I figured out what I was going to do with the rest of my life. He asked me if I had considered going to college. I told him that I hadn't done well in high school, so I didn't think college was for me. He told me that I could probably get into the local community college. That night I looked at the community college's website to see if going to college might be a good idea.

Jared's journal entry

write journal entries

Write at least two journal entries for the topic you have been exploring for this chapter: the hardest job you ever had. Which of your entries do you want to explore further? Which could you use in your essay?

AP Photo/Sue Ogrocki

13d Stating Your Thesis

After you have gathered information about your topic, you need to decide on a thesis for your essay. You do this by reviewing the ideas from your brainstorming, freewriting, and journal entries and then asking, "What is the main point I want to make about my topic?" The answer to this question is the **thesis** of your essay. You express this point in a **thesis statement**: a single sentence that clearly expresses the main idea that you will discuss in the rest of your essay.

Keep in mind that each essay has just *one* thesis statement. The details and examples in the body of the essay all support (add to, discuss, or explain) this thesis statement.

TOPIC	THESIS STATEMENT
Three things I would change to improve the quality of life on campus	If I could change three things to improve the quality of life on campus, I would expand the food choices, decrease class size in first-year courses, and ship some of my classmates to the North Pole.
The campus recycling project	The recycling project recently begun on our campus should be promoted more actively.

Like a topic sentence in a paragraph, a thesis statement in an essay tells readers what to expect. An effective thesis statement has two important characteristics.

1. *An effective thesis statement makes a point about a topic, expressing the writer's opinion or unique view of the topic. For this reason, it must do more than state a fact or announce what you plan to write about.*

> **STATEMENT OF FACT**　Many older students are returning to school.
>
> **ANNOUNCEMENT**　In this essay, I will discuss older students going back to school.

A statement of fact is not an effective thesis statement because it gives you nothing to develop in your essay. After all, how much can you say about the *fact* that many older students are returning to school? Likewise, an announcement of what you plan to discuss gives readers no indication of the position you will take on your topic. Remember, an effective thesis statement makes a point.

2. *An effective thesis statement is clearly worded and specific.*

> **VAGUE THESIS STATEMENT**　Returning to school is difficult for older students.

The vague thesis statement above gives readers no sense of the ideas the essay will discuss. It does not say, for example, *why* returning to school is difficult for older students. Remember, an effective thesis statement is specific.

FYI

Evaluating Your Thesis Statement

Once you have a thesis statement, you need to evaluate it to determine if it is effective. Asking the following questions will help you decide:

- Is your thesis statement a complete sentence?
- Does your thesis statement clearly express the main idea you will discuss in your essay?
- Is your thesis statement specific and focused? Does it make a point that you can cover within your time and page limits?
- Does your thesis statement make a point about your topic—not just state a fact or announce what you plan to write about?
- Does your thesis statement avoid vague language?
- Does your thesis statement avoid statements like "I think" or "In my opinion"?

After freewriting, brainstorming, and reviewing his journal entries, Jared decided on a topic and wrote the following effective thesis statement for his essay.

EFFECTIVE THESIS   Although I realized it would be difficult in some ways,
STATEMENT   I decided that if I really wanted to attend college full-
time, I could.

Jared knew that his thesis statement had to be a complete sentence that
made a point about his topic and that it should be both clearly worded and
specific. When he reviewed his thesis statement, he felt sure that it satisfied these criteria and expressed an idea he could develop in his essay.

PRACTICE

13-5   In the space provided, indicate whether each of the following
items is a statement of fact (*F*), an announcement (*A*), a
vague statement (*VS*), or an effective thesis (*ET*).

Examples

My drive to school takes more than an hour. _____*F*_____

I hate my commute between home and school. _____*VS*_____

1. Students who must commute a long distance to school are at a dis-

   advantage compared to students who live close by. _____

2. In this paper, I will discuss cheating. _____

3. Schools should establish specific policies to discourage students

   from cheating. _____

4. Cheating is a problem. _____

5. Television commercials are designed to sell products. _____

6. I would like to explain why some television commercials are funny.

   _____

7. Single parents have a rough time. _____

8. Young people are starting to abuse alcohol and drugs at earlier ages

   than in the past. _____

9. Alcohol and drug abuse are both major problems in our society.

   _____

10. Families can do several things to help children avoid alcohol and

    drugs. _____

PRACTICE

13-6 Rewrite the following vague thesis statements to make them effective.

Example

My relatives are funny.

Rewrite: *My relatives think they are funny, but sometimes their humor*

can be offensive.

1. The MTV Video Music Awards are interesting.

2. Unwanted telemarketing phone calls are annoying.

3. People try to eat healthier for many reasons.

4. Slasher movies are harmful.

5. Electric cars have some advantages.

PRACTICE

13-7 Read the following groups of statements. Then, write a thesis statement that could express the main point of each group.

1. Thesis statement _____

_____

- *Gap year* is a term that refers to a year that students take off before they go to college.
- Many college students spend most of their time studying and socializing with their peers.
- Studies show that high school students who take a year off before they go to college get better grades.
- Many students take community-service jobs in order to broaden their interests and to increase their social awareness.

2. Thesis statement _____

_____

- Some people post too much personal information on social-networking sites such as Facebook.
- Child predators frequently use social-networking sites to find their victims.

- Some experts believe that people can become addicted to social-networking sites.
- Employers have fired employees because of information they have seen on their employees' social-networking sites.

3. Thesis statement _____

_____

- One way to pay for college is to get a job.
- The majority of students supplement their college tuition with loans or grants.
- According to the College Board, 43 percent of all federal aid for college was in the form of federal student loans.
- According to *U.S. News and World Report*, only 54 percent of American colleges and universities promise to provide enough scholarships to meet all students' financial needs.
- Some students enlist in the armed forces and become eligible for tuition assistance programs.

state your thesis

Review your freewriting, brainstorming, and journal entries. Then, write a thesis statement for your essay.

AP Photo/Sue Ogrocki

13e Choosing Supporting Points

Once you have decided on a thesis statement, look over your freewriting, brainstorming, and journal entries again. Identify **evidence** (details and examples) that best supports your thesis.

Jared made the following list of possible supporting points about his decision to go back to school. When he reviewed his list, he crossed out several points that he thought would not support his thesis.

Deciding to Go Back to School: Pros and Cons

Money a problem

Other students a lot younger

Paying tuition—how?

No one in family went to college

Friends not in college

Couldn't see myself in college

~~Considered going to trade school~~

~~Computer programmer?~~

Grades bad in high school

Wondered if I would get in

Found out about community college

Admission requirements not bad

Afraid—too old, failing out, looking dumb

~~Took time to get used to routine~~

Found other students like me

Liked studying

Jared's list of supporting points

PRACTICE

13-8   Review Jared's list of supporting points above. Do you see any points he crossed out that you think he should have kept? Do you see any other points he should have crossed out?

13f Making an Outline

After you have selected the points you think will best support your thesis, make an informal outline. Begin by arranging your supporting points into groups. Then, arrange them in the order in which you will discuss them (for example, from general to specific, or from least to most important). Arrange the supporting points for each group in the same way. This informal outline can guide you as you write.

When Jared looked over his list of supporting points, he saw that they fell into three groups of excuses for not going back to school: *not being able to pay tuition*, *not being a good student in high school*, and *not being able to picture himself in college*. He arranged his points under these three headings to create the following informal outline.

Excuse 1: Not being able to pay tuition

    Needed to work to live

    Didn't have much saved

    Found out about community college (low tuition)

    Found out about grants, loans

Excuse 2: Not being a good student in high school

    Got bad grades in high school: wasn't motivated and didn't work

    Looked into admission requirements at community college—doable!

    Made a commitment to improve study habits

Excuse 3: Not being able to picture myself in college

    No college graduates in family

    No friends in college

    Afraid of being too old, looking dumb

    Found other students like me

    Found out I liked studying

Jared's informal outline

PRACTICE

13-9   Look over Jared's informal outline above. Do you think his arrangement is effective? Can you suggest any other ways he might have arranged his points?

FYI

Preparing a Formal Outline

An informal outline like the one that appears above is usually all you need to plan a short essay. However, some writers—especially when they are planning a longer, more detailed essay—prefer to use formal outlines.

Formal outlines use a combination of numbered and lettered headings to show the relationships among ideas. For example, the most important (and most general) ideas are assigned a Roman numeral; the next most important ideas are assigned capital letters. Each level develops the idea above it, and each new level is indented.

Here is a formal outline of the points that Jared planned to discuss in his essay.

Thesis statement: Although I realized it would be difficult in some ways, I decided that if I really wanted to attend college full-time, I could.

I. Difficulty: Money
    A. Needed to work to live
    B. Didn't have much money saved
    C. Found out about community college (low tuition)
    D. Found out about grants/loans
II. Difficulty: Academic record
    A. Got bad grades in high school
        1. Didn't care
        2. Didn't work
    B. Found out about reasonable admissions requirements at community college
    C. Committed to improving study habits
III. Difficulty: Imagining myself as a student
    A. Had no college graduates in family
    B. Had no friends in school
    C. Felt anxious
        1. Too old
        2. Out of practice at school
    D. Found other students like me
    E. Discovered I like studying

make an outline

AP Photo/Sue Ogrocki

Review the freewriting, brainstorming, and journal entries you wrote. Then, list the points you plan to use to support your thesis statement. Cross out any points that do not support your thesis statement. Finally, group the remaining points into an informal outline that will guide you as you write.

13g Drafting Your Essay

After you have decided on a thesis for your essay and have arranged your supporting points in the order in which you will discuss them, you are ready to draft your essay.

At this stage of the writing process, you should not worry about spelling or grammar or about composing a perfect introduction or conclusion. Your main goal is to get your ideas down so you can react to them. Remember that the draft you are writing will be revised, so leave extra space between lines as you type. Follow your outline, but don't hesitate to depart from it if you think of new points.

As you draft your essay, be sure that it has a **thesis-and-support structure**—that it states a thesis and supports it with evidence. Include a **working title**, a temporary title that you will revise later so that it accurately reflects the content of your completed essay. This working title will help you focus your ideas.

Following is the first draft of Jared's essay.

Going Back to School

I was out of school for six years after I graduated from high school. The decision to return to school was one I had a lot of difficulty making. I had been around enough to know that without more education, I'd never get anywhere in life, but I always found reasons for not taking the plunge. However, after a lot of thinking, I realized that my reasons for not going to college were just excuses. Although I realized it would be difficult in some ways, I decided that if I really wanted to attend college full-time, I could.

My first excuse for not going to college was that I couldn't afford to go to school full-time. I had worked since I finished high school, but I hadn't put much money away. I kept wondering how I would pay for books and tuition. I needed to support myself and pay for rent, food, and car expenses. I was working as a house painter, and a house I was painting belonged to a college instructor. Painting wasn't hard work, but it was boring. I'd start in the morning and work without a break until lunch. We began talking. When I told him about my situation, he told me I should look at our local community college. He also told me about some loans and grants I'd probably be able to apply for. I went online

(continued)

(continued from previous page)

and looked at the college's website. I found out that tuition was one hundred dollars a credit, less than I thought it would be. If I got just one of the grants he mentioned, I might be able to make it.

Now that I had taken care of my first excuse, I had to deal with my second—that I hadn't been a good student in high school. When I was a teenager, I didn't care much about school. School bored me to death. Probably as a result, I got bad grades. Now that I was considering going back to school, though, I wondered what price I would have to pay for my laziness and immaturity. The answer to this question was not as bad as I thought it would be. According to the community college's website, all I needed to be admitted was a high school diploma and county residence. I would have to take some placement tests, but I would be judged on my ability, not my high school grades. I knew I could do better if I made a real effort to study harder and smarter. The website was easy to navigate, and I had no problem finding information.

I had a hard time picturing myself in college. No one in my family had ever gone to college. My friends were just like me; they all went to work right after high school. I had no role model or mentor who could give me advice. I thought I was just too old for college. After all, I was probably at least six years older than most of the students. How would I be able to keep up with the younger students in the class? I hadn't opened a textbook for years, and I'd never really learned how to study. Most of my fears disappeared during my first few weeks of classes. I saw a lot of students who were as old as I was, and some were even older. Studying didn't seem to be a problem either. I actually enjoyed learning. History, which had put me to sleep in high school, suddenly became interesting. So did math and English. It soon became clear to me that I was going to like being in college.

Going to college as a full-time student has changed my life, both personally and financially. I am no longer the same person I was in high school. I allowed laziness and insecurity to hold me back. Now, I have options that I didn't have before. When I graduate from community college, I plan to transfer to the state university and get a four-year degree.

Jared's first draft

PRACTICE

13-10   Reread Jared's first draft. What changes would you suggest? What might he have added? What might he have deleted? Which of his supporting details and examples do you find most effective?

---

draft your essay

Draft an essay about your most difficult job. When you finish your draft, give your essay a working title.

AP Photo/Sue Ogrocki

13h   TESTing Your Essay

Just as you **TEST** your paragraphs as you begin revising, you should also **TEST** your essays. **TEST**ing will tell you whether your essay includes the basic elements it needs to be effective.

T hesis Statement
E vidence
S ummary Statement
T ransitions

TESTing for a Thesis

The first thing you do when you **TEST** your essay is to make sure it has a clear **thesis statement (T)** that identifies the essay's main idea. By stating the main idea, your thesis statement helps to unify your essay.

When Jared **TEST**ed the draft of his essay, he decided that his thesis statement clearly stated his main idea. (His marginal note appears below.)

Jared's Introduction

I was out of school for six years after I graduated from high school. The decision to return to school was one I had a lot of difficulty making. I had been around enough to know that without more education, I'd never get anywhere in life, but I always found reasons for not taking the plunge. However, after a lot of thinking, I realized that my reasons for not going to college were just excuses. Although I realized it would be difficult in some ways, I decided that if I really wanted to attend college full-time, I could.

T E S T

☐ Topic Sentence
☐ Evidence
☐ Summary Statement
☐ Transitions

Thesis clearly states what I want to say about going to college.

TESTing for Evidence

The next thing you do when you **TEST** your essay is to check your **evidence (E)** to make sure that the body of your essay includes enough examples and details to support your thesis. Remember that without evidence, your essay is simply a series of unsupported general statements. A well-developed essay includes enough evidence to explain, illustrate, and clarify the points you are making.

When Jared **TEST**ed his draft for evidence, he decided that he should add more examples and details in his body paragraphs and delete some irrelevant ones. (His marginal notes appear below.)

Jared's Body Paragraphs

T E S T

- Topic Sentence
- Evidence
- Summary Statement
- Transitions

Are details about painting necessary?

Add more about how I thought I could cover the tuition.

Give examples of boredom.

Are details about website relevant?

My first excuse for not going to college was that I couldn't afford to go to school full-time. I had worked since I finished high school, but I hadn't put much money away. I kept wondering how I would pay for books and tuition. I needed to support myself and pay for rent, food, and car expenses. I was working as a house painter, and a house I was painting belonged to a college instructor. Painting wasn't hard work, but it was boring. I'd start in the morning and work without a break until lunch. We began talking. When I told him about my situation, he told me I should look at our local community college. He also told me about some loans and grants I'd probably be able to apply for. I went online and looked at the college's website. I found out that tuition was one hundred dollars a credit, less than I thought it would be. If I got just one of the grants he mentioned, I might be able to make it.

Now that I had taken care of my first excuse, I had to deal with my second—that I hadn't been a good student in high school. When I was a teenager, I didn't care much about school. School bored me to death. Probably as a result, I got bad grades. Now that I was considering going back to school, though, I wondered what price I would have to pay for my laziness and immaturity. The answer to this question was not as bad as I thought it would be. According to the community college's website, all I needed to be admitted was a high school diploma and county residence. I would have to take some placement tests, but I would be judged on my ability, not my high school grades. I knew I could do better if I made a real effort to study harder and smarter. The website was easy to navigate, and I had no problem finding information.

I had a hard time picturing myself in college. My friends were just like me; they all went to work right after high school. I had no role model or mentor who could give me advice. I thought I was just too old for college.

After all, I was probably at least six years older than most of the students. How would I be able to keep up with the younger students in the class? I hadn't opened a textbook for years, and I'd never really learned how to study. Most of my fears disappeared during my first few weeks of classes. I saw a lot of students who were as old as I was, and some were even older. Studying didn't seem to be a problem, either. I actually enjoyed learning. History, which had put me to sleep in high school, suddenly became interesting. So did math and English. It soon became clear to me that I was going to like being in college.

Evidence seems OK here

TESTing for a Summary Statement

The third thing you do when you **TEST** your essay is to look at your conclusion and make sure that it includes a **summary statement (S)**. Most often, your conclusion will begin with this statement, which reinforces your essay's thesis. By reinforcing your thesis, this summary statement helps to **unify** your essay.

When Jared **TEST**ed his draft for a summary statement, he thought that his summary statement adequately reinforced the main idea of his essay. (His marginal note appears below.)

T E S T
- Topic Sentence
- Evidence
- Summary Statement
- Transitions

Jared's Conclusion

Going to college as a full-time student has changed my life, both personally and financially. I am no longer the same person I was in high school. I allowed laziness and insecurity to hold me back. Now, I have options that I didn't have before. When I graduate from community college, I plan to transfer to the state university and get a four-year degree.

Conclusion is too short, but summary statement is OK.

TESTing for Transitions

The last thing you do when you **TEST** your essay is to make sure that it includes **transitions (T)**—words and phrases that connect your ideas. Make sure you have included all the transitions you need to tell readers how one sentence (or paragraph) is connected to another. Including transitions makes your essay **coherent**, with its sentences arranged in a clear, logical sequence that helps readers understand your ideas.

By linking sentences and paragraphs, transitions emphasize the relationship between ideas and help readers understand your essay's logic. By reminding readers of what has come before, transitions prepare readers for new information and help them understand how it fits into the discussion. In this sense, transitions are the glue that holds the ideas in your essay together.

Transitions are categorized according to their function. For example, they may indicate **time order** (*first, second, now, next, finally,* and so on), **spatial order** (*above, behind, near, next to, over,* and so on), or **logical order** (*also, although, therefore, in fact,* and so on). (For a full list of transitions, see 3d.)

When Jared **TEST**ed his draft for transitions, he realized that although he had included some transitional words and phrases, he needed to add more of them to connect his ideas. (His marginal notes appear below and on the following pages.)

Jared's Thesis + Body Paragraphs

Although I realized it would be difficult in some ways, I decided that if I really wanted to attend college full-time, I could.

My first excuse for not going to college was that I couldn't afford to go to school full-time. I had worked since I finished high school, but I hadn't put much money away. I kept wondering how I would pay for books and tuition. I needed to support myself and pay for rent, food, and car expenses. I was working as a house painter, and a house I was painting belonged to a college instructor. Painting wasn't hard work, but it was boring. I'd start in the morning and work without a break until lunch. We began talking. When I told him about my situation, he told me I should look at our local community college. He also told me about some loans and grants I'd probably be able to apply for. I went online and looked at the college's website. I found out that tuition was one hundred dollars a credit, less than I thought it would be. If I got just one of the grants he mentioned, I might be able to make it.

Now that I had taken care of my first excuse, I had to deal with my second—that I hadn't been a good student in high school. When I was a teenager, I didn't care much about school. School bored me to death. Probably as a result, I got bad grades. Now that I was considering going back to school, though, I wondered what price I would have to pay for my laziness and immaturity. The answer to this question was not as bad as I thought it would be. According to the community college's website, all I needed to be admitted was a high school diploma and county residence. I would have to take some placement tests, but I would be judged on my ability, not my high school grades. I knew I could do better if I made a real effort to study harder and smarter. The website was easy to navigate, and I had no problem finding information.

Need to show relationship between ideas in this paragraph.

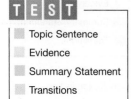

- Topic Sentence
- Evidence
- Summary Statement
- Transitions

I had a hard time picturing myself in college. No one in my family had ever gone to college. My friends were just like me; they all went to work right after high school. I had no role model or mentor who could give me advice. I thought I was just too old for college. After all, I was probably at least six years older than most of the students. How would I be able to keep up with the younger students in the class? I hadn't opened a textbook in years, and I'd never really learned how to study. Most of my fears disappeared during my first few weeks of classes. I saw a lot of students who were as old as I was, and some were even older. Studying didn't seem to be a problem, either. I actually enjoyed learning. History, which had put me to sleep in high school, suddenly became interesting. So did math and English. It soon became clear to me that I was going to like being in college.

> Add better transition between these two paragraphs.

> Add transition here.

TEST your essay

TEST your draft to make sure it includes all the elements of an effective essay. If any elements are missing, add them.

AP Photo/Sue Ogrocki

13i   Revising Your Essay

When you **revise** your essay, you do not simply correct errors; instead, you resee, rethink, reevaluate, and rewrite your work. Some of the changes you make—such as adding, deleting, or rearranging sentences or paragraphs—will be major. Others—such as adding or deleting words—will be small. Once you have TESTed your essay, there are a number of strategies that you can use to help you revise. The chart on pages 202–203 shows you the advantages of each of these revision strategies.

STRATEGIES FOR REVISING	
STRATEGY	**ADVANTAGES**
FACE-TO-FACE CONFERENCE WITH INSTRUCTOR 	■ Provides one-to-one feedback that can't be obtained in the classroom ■ Builds a student-teacher relationship ■ Enables students to collaborate with their instructors ■ Allows students to ask questions that they might not ask in a classroom setting
WRITING CENTER 	■ Offers students a less formal, less stressful environment than an instructor conference ■ Enables students to get help from trained tutors (both students and professionals) ■ Provides a perspective other than the instructor's ■ Offers specialized help to students whose first language is not English
PEER REVIEW 	■ Enables students working on the same assignment to share insights with one another ■ Gives students the experience of writing for a real audience ■ Gives students several different readers' reactions to their work ■ Enables students to benefit from the ideas of their classmates
ELECTRONIC COMMUNICATION WITH INSTRUCTOR 	■ Enables students to submit email questions before a draft is due ■ Gives students quick answers to their questions ■ Enables instructors to give feedback by annotating drafts electronically ■ Enables students to react to their instructor's responses when they have time ■ Eliminates time spent traveling to instructor's office

STRATEGY	ADVANTAGES
REVISION CHECKLIST self-assessment checklist **Revising Your Essay** ■ Does your essay have an introduction, a body, and a conclusion? ■ Does your introduction include a clearly worded thesis statement that states your essay's main idea? ■ Does each body paragraph have a topic sentence? ■ Does each topic sentence introduce a point that supports the thesis? ■ Does each body paragraph include enough examples and details to support the topic sentence? ■ Are the body paragraphs unified, well developed, and coherent? ■ Does your conclusion include a concluding statement that restates your thesis or sums up your main idea?	■ Gives students a tool that enables them to revise in an orderly way ■ Enables students to learn to revise independently ■ Enables students to focus on specific aspects of their writing

FYI

Getting the Most Out of a Conference

If you need help at any point in the writing process, you can get it from your instructor or from a tutor in your school's writing center. Following these guidelines will help you get the most out of your conference.

- Make an appointment in advance, either by phone or by email.
- Arrive on time; instructors and tutors often schedule several appointments in a row, and if you are late, you may miss your appointment entirely.
- Bring a copy of your assignment.
- Bring all drafts and prewriting notes for the assignment you are working on.
- Bring a list of specific questions you would like the instructor or tutor to answer.
- Pay attention, ask your questions, and be sure you understand the answers.
- Write the instructor's or tutor's suggestions directly on your latest draft.
- Schedule a follow-up appointment if necessary.

Remember, your instructor or tutor will answer questions and make recommendations, but he or she will *not* revise or edit your work for you. That is your job.

self-assessment checklist

Revising Your Essay

☐ Does your essay have an introduction, a body, and a conclusion?

☐ Does your introduction include a clearly worded thesis statement that states your essay's main idea?

☐ Does each body paragraph have a topic sentence?

☐ Does each topic sentence introduce a point that supports the thesis?

☐ Does each body paragraph include enough examples and details to support the topic sentence?

☐ Are the body paragraphs unified, well developed, and coherent?

☐ Does your conclusion include a concluding statement that restates your thesis or sums up your main idea?

When Jared finished **TEST**ing his essay, he decided to arrange a conference with his instructor to discuss further revisions. He made sure to follow the guidelines in the FYI box on page 203 in order to get the most out of the conference. After the conference, Jared continued revising his essay, using the Self-Assessment Checklist above to guide him.

Here is Jared's revised first draft with his handwritten revisions.

~~Going Back to School~~ _Starting Over_

The other day, my sociology instructor mentioned that half the students enrolled in college programs across the country are twenty-five or older. His remark caught my attention because I am one of those students.

I was out of school for six years after I graduated from high school. The decision to return to school was one I had a lot of difficulty making.

I had been around enough to know that without more education, I'd never get anywhere in life, but I always found reasons for not taking the plunge. However, after a lot of thinking, I realized that my reasons for not going to college were just excuses. Although I realized it would be difficult in some ways, I decided that if I really wanted to attend college full-time, I could.

My first excuse for not going to college was that I couldn't afford to go to school full-time. I had worked since I finished high school, but I hadn't put

much money away. I kept wondering how I would pay for books and tuition. I
also
needed to support myself and pay for rent, food, and car expenses. ~~The solution to my problem came unexpectedly.~~ I was

working as a house painter, and a house I was painting belonged to a college

instructor. ~~Painting wasn't hard work, but it was boring. I'd start in the morning~~
During my lunch break, we
~~and work without a break until lunch.~~ ~~We~~ began talking. When I told him about

my situation, he told me I should look at our local community college. He also
Later,
told me about some loans and grants I'd probably be able to apply for. I went

online and looked at the college's website. I found out that tuition was one

hundred dollars a credit, less than I thought it would be. If I got just one of

the grants he mentioned, I might be able to make it.

The money I'd saved, along with what I could make painting houses on the weekends, could get me through.

Now that I had taken care of my first excuse, I had to deal with my

second—that I hadn't been a good student in high school. When I was a
In fact, school
teenager, I didn't care much about school. ~~School~~ bored me ~~to death.~~ Probably

In class, I would stare out the window or watch the second hand on the clock move slowly around. I never bothered with homework. School just didn't interest me.

as a result, I got bad grades. Now that I was considering going back to school,

though, I wondered what price I would have to pay for my laziness and

immaturity. The answer to this question was not as bad as I thought it would

be. According to the community college's website, all I needed to be admitted

was a high school diploma and county residence. I would have to take some

placement tests, but I would be judged on my ability, not my high school

grades. I knew I could do better if I made a real effort to study harder and

smarter. ~~The website was easy to navigate, and I had no problem finding~~

~~information.~~
My biggest problem still bothered me:
I had a hard time picturing myself in college. No one in my family had

ever gone to college. My friends were just like me; they all went to work

right after high school. I had no role model or mentor who could give me
Besides,
advice. I thought I was just too old for college. After all, I was probably at

least six years older than most of the students. How would I be able to keep up

with the younger students in the class? I hadn't opened a textbook for years, and I'd never really learned how to study. ~~Most~~ of my fears disappeared during

However, most

my first few weeks of classes. I saw a lot of students who were as old as I was,

and some were even older. Studying didn't seem to be a problem either. I

actually enjoyed learning. ~~History,~~ which had put me to sleep in high school,

For example, history,

suddenly became interesting. So did math and English. It soon became clear

to me that I was going to like being in college.

Going to college as a full-time student has changed my life, both

personally and financially. I am no longer the same person I was in high school.

In the past,

I allowed laziness and insecurity to hold me back. Now, I have options that

I didn't have before. When I graduate from community college, I plan to

transfer to the state university and get a four-year degree. *The other day,*
one of my instructors asked me if I had ever considered becoming a teacher.
The truth is, I never had, but now I might. I'd like to be able to give kids like
me the tough, realistic advice I wish someone had given me.

PRACTICE

13-11   Working in a group of three or four students, answer the
following questions:

■ What kind of material did Jared add to his draft?
■ What did he delete?
■ Why do you think he made these changes?
■ Do you agree with the changes he made?

Be prepared to discuss your reactions to these changes with the class.

AP Photo/Sue Ogrocki

revise your essay

Using one or two of the additional revision strategies from the chart
on pages 202–203, continue revising your essay.

13j Editing Your Essay

When you **edit** your essay, you check grammar and sentence structure. Then, you look at punctuation, mechanics, and spelling. As you edit, think carefully about the questions in the following Self-Assessment Checklist. (If you have not already chosen a final title for your essay, this is a good time to do so.)

self-assessment checklist

Editing Your Essay

EDITING FOR COMMON SENTENCE PROBLEMS

☐ Have you avoided run-ons? (See Chapter 23.)

☐ Have you avoided sentence fragments? (See Chapter 24.)

☐ Do your subjects and verbs agree? (See Chapter 25.)

☐ Have you avoided illogical shifts? (See Chapter 26.)

☐ Have you avoided misplaced and dangling modifiers? (See Chapter 27.)

EDITING FOR GRAMMAR

☐ Are your verb forms and verb tenses correct? (See Chapters 28 and 29.)

☐ Have you used nouns and pronouns correctly? (See Chapter 30.)

☐ Have you used adjectives and adverbs correctly? (See Chapter 31.)

EDITING FOR PUNCTUATION, MECHANICS, AND SPELLING

☐ Have you used commas correctly? (See Chapter 33.)

☐ Have you used apostrophes correctly? Have you avoided contractions, which are usually too informal for college writing? (See Chapter 34.)

☐ Have you used capital letters where they are required? (See 35a.)

☐ Have you used quotation marks correctly where they are needed? (See 35b.)

13k Proofreading Your Essay

When you **proofread** your essay, you check for typos, proper formatting, and anything you might have missed while you were editing. Remember that your spell checker and grammar checker are helpful, but they can also introduce errors into your essay. As you proofread, be sure to double-check the spelling of any words whose spelling you are unsure of. It is also a good idea to print your essay and proofread on the hard copy because it is easy to miss typos and other small errors on a computer screen. After you have checked for typos and other lingering errors, check your essay's format.

The **format** of an essay is the way it looks on a page—for example, the size of the margins, the placement of page numbers, and the amount of space between lines. Most instructors expect you to follow a certain format when you type an essay. The model essay format illustrated below is commonly used in composition classes. Before you hand in an essay, you should make sure that it follows this model (or the format your instructor requires.)

Essay Format: Sample

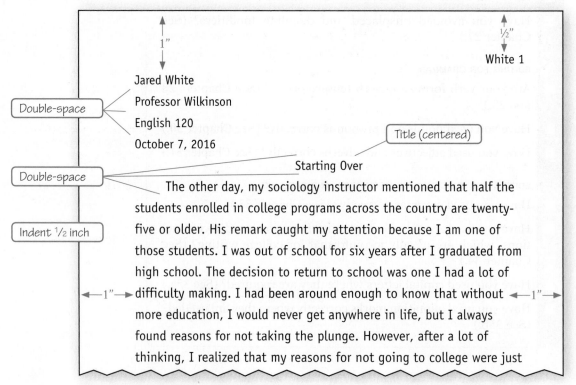

Note: The bottom margin of each page should also be one inch.

When Jared edited and proofread his essay, he deleted all the contractions, which he thought made his serious essay sound too informal. The final version of his essay appears below. (Marginal annotations have been added to highlight key features of his essay.) Note that the final draft includes all the elements Jared looked for when he **TEST**ed his essay.

Jared White

Professor Wilkinson

English 120

October 7, 2016

T E S T

☐ Topic Sentence

☐ Evidence

☐ Summary Statement

☐ Transitions

Starting Over

The other day, my sociology instructor mentioned that half the students enrolled in college programs across the country are twenty-five or older. His remark caught my attention because I am one of those students. I was out of school for six years after I graduated from high school. The decision to return to school was one I had a lot of difficulty making. I had been around enough to know that without more education, I would never get anywhere in life, but I always found reasons for not taking the plunge. However, after a lot of thinking, I realized that my reasons for not going to college were just excuses. Although I realized it would be difficult in some ways, I decided that if I really wanted to attend college full-time, I could.

Introduction

My first excuse for not going to college was that I could not afford to go to school full-time. I had worked since I finished high school, but I had not put much money away. I kept wondering how I would pay for books and tuition. I also needed to support myself and pay for rent, food, and car expenses. The solution to my problem came unexpectedly. I was working as a house painter, and a house I was painting belonged to a college instructor. During a lunch break, we began talking. When I told him about my situation, he told me I should look at our local community college. He also told me about some loans and grants I would probably be able to apply for. Later, I went online and looked at the college's website. I found out that tuition was one hundred dollars a credit, less than I thought it would be. If I got just one of the grants he mentioned, I might be able to make it. The money I had saved, along with what I could make painting houses on the weekends, could get me through.

Topic sentence (first point)

Examples and details

Body paragraphs

Topic sentence (second point)

Now that I had taken care of my first excuse, I had to deal with my second—that I had not been a good student in high school. When I was a teenager, I did not care much about school. In fact, school bored me. In class, I would stare out the window or watch the second hand on the clock move slowly around. I never bothered with homework. School just did not interest me. Probably as a result, I got bad grades. Now that I was considering going back to school, though, I wondered what price I would have to pay for my laziness and immaturity. The answer to this question was not as bad as I thought it would be. According to the community college's website, all I needed to be admitted was a high school diploma and county residence. I would have to take some placement tests, but I would be judged on my ability, not my high school grades. I knew I could do better if I made a real effort to study harder and smarter.

Examples and details

Body paragraphs

Topic sentence (third point)

My biggest problem still bothered me: I had a hard time picturing myself in college. No one in my family had ever gone to college. My friends were just like me; they all went to work right after high school. I had no role model or mentor who could give me advice. Besides, I thought I was just too old for college. After all, I was probably at least six years older than most of the students. How would I be able to keep up with the younger students in the class? I had not opened a textbook in years, and I had never really learned how to study. However, most of my fears disappeared during my first few weeks of classes. I saw a lot of students who were as old as I was, and some were even older. Studying did not seem to be a problem, either. I actually enjoyed learning. For example, history, which had put me to sleep in high school, suddenly became interesting. So did math and English. It soon became clear to me that I was going to like being in college.

Examples and details

Going to college as a full-time student has changed my life, both personally and financially. I am no longer the same person I was in high school. In the past, I allowed laziness and insecurity to hold me back. Now, I have options that I did not have before. When I graduate from community college, I plan to transfer to the state university and get a four-year degree. The other day, one of my instructors asked me if I had ever considered becoming a teacher. The truth is, I never had, but now I might. I would like to be able to give students like me the tough, realistic advice I wish someone had given me.

Conclusion

PRACTICE

13-12 Reread the final draft of Jared White's essay. Working in a group of three or four students, answer these questions.

- Do you think this draft is an improvement over his first draft (shown on pages 195–196)?
- What other changes could Jared have made?

Be prepared to discuss your group's answers with the class.

edit and proofread your essay

Edit your draft, using the Self-Assessment Checklist on page 207 to guide you. Then, proofread your essay for typos and other small errors. Finally, make sure your essay's format follows your instructor's guidelines.

AP Photo/Sue Ogrocki

EDITING PRACTICE

1. The following student essay is missing its thesis statement and topic sentences and has no summary statement. First, write an appropriate thesis statement on the lines provided. (Make sure your thesis statement clearly communicates the essay's main idea.) Then, fill in the topic sentences for the second, third, and fourth paragraphs. Finally, add a summary statement in the conclusion.

Preparing for a Job Interview

A lot of books and many websites give advice on how to do well on a job interview. Some recommend practicing your handshake, and others suggest making eye contact. This advice is useful, but not many books tell how to get mentally prepared for an interview. [Thesis statement:] _____

_____

_____

_____

   [Topic sentence for the second paragraph:] _____

_____

_____

_____

Feeling good about how you look is important, so you should probably wear a dress, or skirt, or pantsuit (or, for males, a jacket and tie or possibly a suit) to an interview. Even if you will not be dressing this formally on the job, try to make a good first impression. For this reason, you should never come to an interview dressed in jeans or shorts. Still, you should be careful not to overdress. For example, wearing a suit or a dressy dress to an interview at a fast-food restaurant might make you feel good, but it could also make you look as if you do not really want to work there.

[Topic sentence for the third paragraph:] _____

_____

_____

Going on an interview is a little like getting ready to compete in a sporting event. You have to go in with the right attitude. If you think you are not going to be successful, chances are that you will not be. So, before you go on any interview, spend some time building your confidence. Tell yourself that you can do the job and that you will do well in the interview. By the time you get to the interview, you will have convinced yourself that you are the right person for the job.

[Topic sentence for the fourth paragraph:] _____

_____

_____

Most people go to an interview knowing little or nothing about the job. They expect the interviewer to tell them what they will have to do. Most interviewers, however, are impressed by someone who has taken the time to do his or her homework. For this reason, you should always do some research before you go on an interview—even for a part-time job. Most of the time, your research can be nothing more than a quick look at the company's website, but this kind of research really pays off. Being able to talk about the job can give you a real advantage over other candidates. Sometimes the interviewer will be so impressed that he or she will offer you a job on the spot.

[Summary statement:] _____

_____

_____

Of course, following these suggestions will not guarantee that you get a job. You still have to do well at the interview itself. Even so, getting mentally prepared for the interview will give you an advantage over people who do almost nothing before they walk in the door.

2. Now, using the topic sentence below, write another body paragraph that you could add to the essay above. (This new paragraph will go right before the essay's conclusion.)

Another way to prepare yourself mentally is to anticipate and answer some typical questions interviewers ask.

_____

_____

_____

_____

COLLABORATIVE ACTIVITY

Working in a group, come up with thesis statements suitable for essays on three of the following topics.

Dealing with a cyberbully	Gun safety
Taxing junk food	Drawbacks of online dating
Voting	Patriotism
Sustainable energy	The effects of divorce
Selecting a major	Making a speech

Then, exchange your group's three thesis statements with those of another group. Choose the best one of the other group's thesis statements. A member of each group can then read the thesis statement to the class and explain why the group chose the thesis statement it did.

review checklist

Writing an Essay

☐ Be sure you understand essay structure. (See 13a.)

☐ Focus on your assignment, purpose, and audience to help you find a topic. (See 13b.)

☐ Find ideas to write about. (See 13c.)

☐ Identify your main idea, and develop an effective thesis statement. (See 13d.)

☐ List the points that best support your thesis, and arrange them in the order in which you plan to discuss them, creating an informal outline of your essay. (See 13e and 13f.)

☐ Write your first draft, making sure your essay has a thesis-and-support structure. (See 13g.)

☐ TEST your essay. (See 13h.)

☐ Revise your essay. (See 13i.)

☐ Edit and proofread your essay. (See 13j and 13k.)

☐ Make sure your essay's format is correct. (See 13k.)

14 Introductions and Conclusions

AP Photo/Jae C. Hong

focus on writing

This picture shows firefighters battling a wildfire in the Southern California mountains. Like the oil rig workers pictured on page 175, these firefighters have very difficult jobs. Think about what this picture suggests about the work they do, and then print out a copy of the essay you wrote for Chapter 13. At the end of this chapter, you will work on revising the introduction and conclusion of your essay.

In this chapter, you will learn to

- write an introduction (14a)
- choose a title (14a)
- write a conclusion (14b)

When you draft an essay, you usually spend the most time on the **body** because it is the section in which you develop your ideas. A well-constructed essay, however, is more than a series of body paragraphs. It also includes an **introduction** and a **conclusion**, both of which contribute to the essay's overall effectiveness.

14a Introductions

An **introduction** is the first thing people see when they read your essay. If your introduction is interesting, it will make readers want to read further. If it is not, readers may get bored and stop reading.

Your introduction should be a full paragraph that moves from general to specific ideas. It should begin with some general **opening remarks** that will draw readers into your essay. The **thesis statement**, a specific sentence that presents the main idea of your essay, usually comes at the end of the introduction. The following diagram illustrates the shape of an introduction.

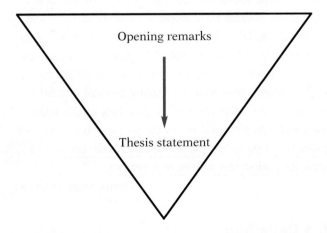

Opening remarks

Thesis statement

Here are some options you can experiment with when you write your introductions. (In each of the sample introductory paragraphs that follow, the thesis statement is underlined and labeled.)

Beginning with a Narrative

You can begin an essay with a narrative drawn from your own experience or from a current news event.

On the first day my sister and I attended school in America, our parents walked us directly to the entrance of our new classroom. Even though she barely spoke any English, Mom tried earnestly to teach us how to ask for permission to use the bathroom: "Can I go to the bathroom?" Like parrots, she had us repeat this question over and over. At the time, neither of us realized that the proper way of asking for permission is "May I go to the bathroom?" This grammar slip did not matter, though, because we forgot the question as soon as our parents left. Reluctantly, we entered the classroom, more timid than two mice trying not to awaken a sleeping cat. We didn't know yet that going to school where English was the only language spoken would prove to be very difficult.

Thesis statement

—Hilda Alvarado (student)

Beginning with a Question (or a Series of Questions)

Asking one or more questions at the beginning of your essay is an effective strategy. Because readers expect you to answer the questions, they will want to read further.

Could a text message save someone's life? If you are a Crisis Text Line volunteer, the answer is yes. Because many people are more comfortable texting than talking on the phone, Crisis Text Line is an important new service for people of all ages—especially for teenagers. Volunteers take a thirty-four-hour online training program to learn how to provide emotional support and to match people with the resources they need. The training program includes video lessons, role playing, and online observation. Once they complete the program, volunteers are able to offer guidance to the people who contact them each day. Anyone who is looking to help people should consider becoming a Crisis Text Line counselor, crisis-center partner, or supervisor.

Thesis statement

—Aleena Abbas (student)

Beginning with a Definition

A definition at the beginning of your essay can give readers important information. As the following introduction shows, a definition can help explain a complicated idea or a confusing concept.

"Getting inked" is how many people refer to the act of getting a tattoo. Although some people may see it as a form of torture, tattooing is an art form that dates back over hundreds of years. The craft has been more formally defined as the practice of permanently marking the skin through punctures or incisions, which receive various dyes or pigments. <u>Although Polynesian in origin, tattooing has a rich history in the United States.</u>   *Thesis statement*

—Kristen L. McCormack (student)

Beginning with a Quotation

An appropriate saying or some interesting dialogue can draw readers into your essay.

According to the comedian Jerry Seinfeld, "When you're single, you are the dictator of your own life. . . . When you're married, you are part of a vast decision-making body." In other words, before you can do anything when you are married, you have to talk it over with someone else. These words kept going through my mind as I thought about asking my girlfriend to marry me. The more I thought about Seinfeld's words, the more I put off asking. <u>I never thought about the huge price that I would pay for this delay.</u>   *Thesis statement*

—Dan Brody (student)

Beginning with a Surprising Statement

You can begin your essay with a surprising or unexpected statement. Because your statement takes readers by surprise, it catches their attention.

In the near future, it is likely that robots will replace us. This may sound like science fiction, but as technology continues to advance, automated machines will take over many of the jobs that humans currently perform. In fact, this has already occurred. For example, car manufacturing is almost completely done by robots. In addition, construction robots lay a brick wall in less time than a team of workers can, and drones are gradually taking the place of traditional home delivery systems. In addition, Google is developing self-driving cars that could soon replace cab drivers and truckers. As a result, people engaging in any kind of routine or repetitive work are at risk of being replaced by machines. If this trend continues—and it surely will—the country's workforce could lose millions of jobs. <u>For this reason, people should anticipate</u>   *Thesis statement*
<u>this trend and begin training for the jobs that are least likely to be automated.</u>

—Sean Murphy (student)

FYI

What to Avoid in Introductions

When writing an introduction, avoid the following:

- Beginning your essay by announcing what you plan to write about.

  PHRASES TO AVOID

  This essay is about . . .
  In my essay, I will discuss . . .

- Apologizing for your ideas.

  PHRASES TO AVOID

  Although I don't know much about this subject . . .
  I might not be an expert, but . . .

FYI

Choosing a Title

Every essay should have a **title** that suggests the subject of the essay and makes people want to read it. Here are a few tips for properly formatting your title.

- Capitalize all words except for articles (*a, an, the*), prepositions (*at, to, of, around,* and so on), and coordinating conjunctions (*and, but,* and so on), unless they are the first or last word of the title.
- Do not underline or italicize your title or enclose it in quotation marks. Do not type your title in all capital letters.
- Center the title at the top of the first page. Double-space between the title and the first line of your essay.

As you consider a title for your paper, think about the following options.

- *A title can highlight a key word or term that appears in the essay.*
  "The Barrio"
  "Migrant vs. Refugee: What's the Difference?"

- *A title can be a straightforward announcement.*
  "No, I Do Not Want to Pet Your Dog"
  "Vaccinations Are for the Good of the Nation"

- *A title can establish a personal connection with readers.*
  "I Owe It All to Community College"
  "An Open Letter to All My Male Friends"

- *A title can be a familiar saying or a quotation from your essay itself.*
  "Men Are from Mars, Women Are from Venus"
  "I Want a Wife"

PRACTICE

14-1   Look through the essays in Chapters 15 and 16, and find one introduction you think is particularly effective. Be prepared to explain the strengths of the introduction you chose.

PRACTICE

14-2   Using the different options for creating titles discussed in the FYI box above, write two titles for each of the essays described below.

1. A student writes an essay about three people who disappeared mysteriously: Amelia Earhart, aviator; Ambrose Bierce, writer; and Jimmy Hoffa, union leader. In the body paragraphs, the student describes the circumstances surrounding their disappearances.

   _____

   _____

2. A student writes an essay describing the harmful effects of steroids on student athletes. In the body paragraphs, he shows the effects on the heart, brain, and other organs.

   _____

   _____

3. A student writes an essay explaining why she joined the Navy Reserve. In the body paragraphs, she discusses her need to earn money for college tuition, her wish to learn a trade, and her desire to see the world.

   _____

   _____

14b Conclusions

Because your conclusion is the last thing readers see, they often judge your entire essay by its effectiveness. For this reason, conclusions should be planned, drafted, and revised carefully.

Like an introduction, a **conclusion** should be a full paragraph. It should begin with a **summary statement** that reinforces the essay's main idea, and it should end with some general **concluding remarks**. The following diagram illustrates the general shape of a conclusion.

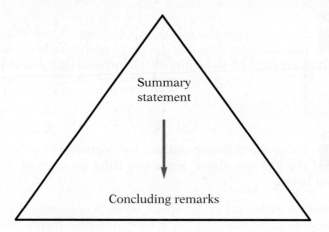

Summary
statement

Concluding remarks

Here are some options you can experiment with when you write your conclusions. (In each of the sample concluding paragraphs that follow, the summary statement is underlined and labeled.)

Concluding with a Narrative

A narrative conclusion can bring an event discussed in the essay to a logical, satisfying close.

Summary statement

I went to Philadelphia with my boys to share the thing my father and I had shared—a love for history. Unfortunately, they were more interested in horse-and-buggy rides, overpriced knickknacks, the tall buildings, and parades. As we walked into Independence Hall, though, I noticed that the boys became quiet. They felt it. They felt the thick historical air around us. I watched them look around as the guide painted a vivid picture of the times and spoke of the marches down Broad Street and the clashing of ideas as our forefathers debated and even fought for freedom. I felt my husband behind me and took my eyes off of my boys to turn to the left; I could almost see my father. I almost whispered out loud to him, "We were here."

—Shannon Lewis (student)

Concluding with a Recommendation

Once you think you have convinced readers that a problem exists, you can make recommendations in your conclusion about how the problem should be solved.

Solutions for the binge-drinking problem on college campuses are not easy, but both schools and students need to acknowledge the problem and to try to solve it. Schools that have an alcohol-free policy should aggressively enforce it, and schools that do not have such a policy should implement one. In addition, students should take responsibility for their actions and resolve to drink responsibly. No one should get hurt or die from drinking too much, but if something does not change soon, many more students will.

Summary statement

—April Moen (student)

Concluding with a Quotation

A well-chosen quotation—even a brief one—can be an effective concluding strategy. In the following paragraph, the quotation reinforces the main idea of the essay.

I'll never forget the day I caught the ball on a penalty kick, winning the game for my team. My opponent's foot made contact with the ball, and everything around me fell silent. The ball came at me, hurtling over my head toward the top right of the goal. As I dived to catch it, I closed my eyes. The ball smacked into my hands so hard I thought it must have split my gloves. When I opened my eyes, I realized that I had caught the ball and saved the game for our team. The crowd cheered wildly, and my team surrounded me as I got to my feet. As the celebration died down, my coach walked up to me and, as I handed him the game-winning ball, he said, "To the playoffs we go!"

Summary statement

—Jacob Kinley (student)

Concluding with a Prediction

This type of conclusion not only sums up the thesis but also looks to the future.

More than just another social media platform, Twitter will revolutionize the way people get information. While people once had to wait for the nightly television news, they can now find immediate, real-time information on Twitter. Since Twitter is a public platform, anyone can broadcast information, pictures, or even video. In addition, a variety of viewpoints can be presented. With millions of citizen reporters tweeting about events as they happen, Twitter is

Summary statement — making both print and televised news obsolete. <u>In the not-too-distant future, Twitter may very well be the primary news source for most people.</u>

—Mei Yamada (student)

FYI

What to Avoid in Conclusions

When writing a conclusion, avoid the following:

- Introducing new ideas. Your conclusion should sum up the ideas you discuss in your essay, not open up new lines of thought.

- Apologizing for your opinions, ideas, or conclusions. Apologies will undercut your readers' confidence in you.

  PHRASES TO AVOID

  At least that is my opinion . . .
  I could be wrong, but . . .

- Using unnecessary phrases to announce your essay is coming to a close.

  PHRASES TO AVOID

  In summary, . . .
  In conclusion, . . .

PRACTICE

14-3 Look at the essays in Chapters 15 and 16, and locate one conclusion you think is particularly effective. Be prepared to explain the strengths of the conclusion you chose.

AP Photo/Jae C. Hong

TEST · Revise · Edit · Proofread

Look back at the essay you wrote for Chapter 13. TEST what you have written one more time. Then, revise and edit your introduction and conclusion accordingly. Make sure your introduction creates interest, prepares readers for the essay to follow, and includes a clear thesis statement. Also, make sure your conclusion contains a summary statement and includes general concluding remarks. Finally, make sure your essay has an appropriate and effective title.

EDITING PRACTICE

The following student essay has an undeveloped introduction and conclusion. Decide what introductory and concluding strategies would be best for the essay. Then, rewrite both the introduction and the conclusion. Finally, suggest an interesting title for the essay.

———————

This essay is about three of the most dangerous jobs. They are piloting small planes, logging, and fishing.

Flying a small plane can be dangerous. For example, pilots who fly tiny planes that spray pesticides on farmers' fields do not have to comply with the safety rules for large airplanes. They also have to fly very low in order to spray the right fields. This leaves little room for error. Also, pilots of air-taxis and small commuter planes die in much greater numbers than airline pilots do. In some places, like parts of Alaska, there are long distances and few roads, so many small planes are needed. Their pilots are four times more likely to die than other pilots because of bad weather and poor visibility. In general, flying a small plane can be very risky.

Another dangerous job is logging. Loggers always are at risk of having parts of trees or heavy machinery fall on them. Tree trunks often have odd shapes, so they are hard to control while they are being transported. As a result, they often break loose from equipment that is supposed to move them. In addition, weather conditions, like snow or rain, can cause dangers. Icy or wet conditions increase the risk to loggers, who can fall from trees or slip when they are sawing a tree. Because loggers often work in remote places, it is very hard to get prompt medical aid. For this reason, a wound that could easily be treated in a hospital may be fatal to a logger.

Perhaps the most dangerous occupation is working in the fishing industry. Like loggers, professional fishermen work in unsafe conditions. They use heavy machinery to pull up nets and to move large amounts of fish. The combination of icy or slippery boat decks and large nets and cages makes the job unsafe. The weather is often very bad, so fishermen are at risk of falling overboard during a storm and drowning. In fact, drowning is the most common cause of death in this industry. Also, like logging, fishing is done far from medical help, so even minor injuries can be very serious.

In conclusion, piloting, logging, and fishing are three of the most dangerous occupations.

COLLABORATIVE ACTIVITY

Find a magazine or newspaper article that interests you. Cut off the introduction and conclusion, and bring the body of the article to class. Ask your group to decide on the best strategies for introducing and concluding the article. Then, collaborate on writing new opening and closing paragraphs and an interesting title.

review checklist

Introductions and Conclusions

☐ The introduction of your essay should include opening remarks and a thesis statement. (See 14a.) You can begin an essay with any of the following options.

A narrative	A quotation
A question	A surprising statement
A definition	

☐ Your title should suggest the subject of your essay and make people want to read further. (See 14a.)

☐ The conclusion of your essay should include a summary statement and some general concluding remarks. (See 14b.) You can conclude an essay with any of the following options.

A narrative	A quotation
A recommendation	A prediction

15 Patterns of Essay Development

Exemplification, Narration, Process, Cause and Effect, and Comparison and Contrast

In this chapter, you will learn to organize your essays according to the following patterns of development:

- exemplification (15a)
- narration (15b)
- process (15c)
- cause and effect (15d)
- comparison and contrast (15e)

As you learned in Chapters 4 through 12, writers have a variety of options for developing ideas within a paragraph. These options include *exemplification, narration, description, process, cause and effect, comparison and contrast, classification, definition,* and *argument*. When you write an essay, you can use these same patterns of development to help you organize your material.

In your college courses, different assignments and writing situations call for different patterns of essay development.

- If an essay exam question asked you to compare two systems of government, you would use *comparison and contrast.*

- If an English composition assignment asked you to tell about a childhood experience, you would use *narration.*

- If a research paper on environmental pollution in a particular community called for examples of dangerous waste-disposal practices, you would use *exemplification.*

As you will see in this chapter and in the chapter that follows, the skills you learned for writing paragraphs can also be applied to writing essays.

15a Exemplification Essays

Exemplification illustrates a general statement with one or more specific examples. An **exemplification essay** uses specific examples to support a thesis.

When you **TEST** an **exemplification** essay, make sure it includes all these elements:

T - **Thesis Statement**—The introduction of an exemplification essay should include a clear **thesis statement** that identifies the essay's main idea—the idea the examples will support.

E ■ **Evidence**—The body paragraphs should present **evidence**, fully developed examples that support the thesis. Each body paragraph should be introduced by a topic sentence that identifies the example or group of related examples that the paragraph will discuss.

S ■ **Summary Statement**—The conclusion of an exemplification essay should include a **summary statement** that reinforces the essay's thesis.

T ■ **Transitions**—An exemplification essay should use appropriate **transitional words and phrases** to connect examples within paragraphs and between one paragraph and another.

Moving from Assignment to Thesis

The wording of your assignment may suggest that you write an exemplification essay. For example, you may be asked to *illustrate* or to *give examples*. Once you decide that your assignment calls for exemplification, you need to develop a thesis that reflects this purpose.

ASSIGNMENT	THESIS STATEMENT
Education Should children be taught only in their native languages or in English as well? Support your answer with examples of specific students' experiences.	The success of students in a bilingual third-grade class suggests the value of teaching elementary school students in English as well as in their native languages.
Literature Does William Shakespeare's *Othello* have to end tragically? Illustrate your position with references to specific characters.	Each of the three major characters in *Othello* contributes to the play's tragic ending.
Composition Discuss the worst job you ever had, including plenty of specific examples to support your thesis.	My summer job at a fast-food restaurant was my worst job because of the endless stream of rude customers, the many boring tasks I had to perform, and my manager's insensitivity.

Organizing an Exemplification Essay

In an exemplification essay, each body paragraph can develop a single example or discuss several related examples. The topic sentence should introduce the example (or group of related examples) that the paragraph will discuss. Each example you select should clearly support your thesis.

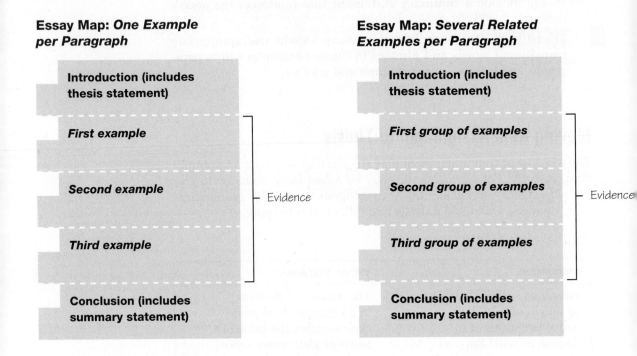

Essay Map: *One Example per Paragraph*

Introduction (includes thesis statement)

First example

Second example   ⊢ Evidence

Third example

Conclusion (includes summary statement)

Essay Map: *Several Related Examples per Paragraph*

Introduction (includes thesis statement)

First group of examples

Second group of examples   ⊢ Evidence

Third group of examples

Conclusion (includes summary statement)

Transitions in Exemplification Essays

For a list of transitions frequently used in exemplification, see page 77.

Transitional words and phrases should introduce your examples and indicate how one example is related to another.

Case Study: A Student Writes an Exemplification Essay

Kyle Sims, a student in a first-year writing course, was asked to write an essay about a popular hobby or interest. Kyle imagined that most of his classmates would write about topics like video games or sports, and while he knew a lot about sports, his knowledge came from being a spectator, not a participant. He decided to use this knowledge by writing about extreme sports.

Once he had settled on a topic, Kyle did some **freewriting**. When he read over his freewriting, he saw that he had come up with three kinds of information: ideas about the dangers of extreme sports, about the challenges they present, and about the equipment they require. He then wrote a **thesis statement** that identified the three points he wanted to make. After **brainstorming** about each of these points, he had enough material for a first draft.

As he wrote his **first draft**, Kyle devoted one paragraph to each point, using examples to develop his body paragraphs. When he finished his draft, he **TEST**ed it. He was satisfied with his thesis, which told readers what points he was going to make about extreme sports and also conveyed the idea that they were not like ordinary sports. His summary statement seemed logical and appropriate. However, realizing that his readers might not know much about extreme sports, Kyle added more examples to illustrate a range of different kinds of extreme sports. He also added more transitions to lead readers from one example to the next.

When Kyle **revised** his draft, he rewrote his topic sentences so they clearly identified the three points he wanted to make about extreme sports. After he finished his revision, he **edited** and **proofread** carefully and made sure his essay met his instructor's **format** requirements.

The following final draft includes all the elements Kyle looked for when he **TEST**ed his essay.

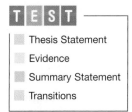

T E S T

☐ Thesis Statement
☐ Evidence
☐ Summary Statement
☐ Transitions

Model Exemplification Essay

Read Kyle's finished essay, and complete the tasks in Practice 15-1.

Going to Extremes

1   For years, sports like football, baseball, and basketball have been popular in cities, suburbs, and small rural towns. For some young people, however, these sports no longer seem exciting, especially when compared to "extreme sports," such as snowboarding and BMX racing. Extreme sports are different from more familiar sports because they are dangerous, they are physically challenging, and they require specialized equipment.

Introduction

2   First, extreme sports are dangerous. For example, snowboarders take chances with snowy hills and unpredictable bumps. They zoom down mountains at high speeds, which is typical of extreme sports. In addition, snowboarders and skateboarders risk painful falls as they do their tricks. Also, many extreme sports, like rock climbing, bungee jumping, and skydiving, are performed at very high altitudes. Moreover, the bungee jumper has to jump from a very high place, and there is always a danger of getting tangled with the bungee cord. People who participate in extreme sports accept—and even enjoy—these dangers.

Topic sentence (introduces first point)

Examples

Body paragraphs

3   In addition, extreme sports are very difficult. For instance, surfers have to learn to balance surfboards while dealing with wind and waves. Bungee

Topic sentence (introduces second point)

Examples

Body paragraphs

jumpers may have to learn how to do difficult stunts while jumping off a high bridge or a dam. Another example of the physical challenge of extreme sports can be found in BMX racing. BMX racers have to learn to steer a lightweight bike on a dirt track that has jumps and banked corners. These extreme sports require skills that most people do not naturally have. These special skills have to be learned, and participants in extreme sports enjoy this challenge.

Topic sentence
(introduces third point)

Examples

Finally, almost all extreme sports require specialized equipment. For example, surfers need surfboards that are light but strong. They can choose epoxy boards, which are stronger, or fiberglass boards, which are lighter. They can choose shortboards, which are shorter than seven feet and are easier to maneuver, or they can use longboards, which are harder and slower to turn in the water but are easier to learn on. Also, surfers have to get special wax for their boards to keep from slipping as they are paddling out into the water. For surfing in cold water, they need wetsuits that trap their own body heat. Other extreme sports require different kinds of specialized equipment, but those who participate in them are willing to buy whatever they need.

4

Conclusion

Clearly, extreme sports are very different from other sports. Maybe it is because they are so different that they have become so popular in recent years. Already, snowboarding, BMX racing, and other extreme sports are featured in the Olympics. The Summer and Winter X Games are televised on ESPN and ABC, and sports like BMX racing, snowboarding, surfing, and snowmobiling get national attention on these programs. With all this publicity, extreme sports are likely to become even more popular—despite their challenges.

5

PRACTICE
15-1

1. Restate Kyle's thesis in your own words.

2. What three points about extreme sports does Kyle make in the topic sentences of his body paragraphs?

3. What examples of extreme sports does Kyle give in paragraph 1? What examples of dangers does he give in paragraph 2? In paragraph 4, Kyle discusses surfing, giving examples of the equipment surfers need. List this equipment.

4. Is Kyle's introduction effective? How else might he have opened his essay?

5. Paraphrase Kyle's summary statement.

6. What is this essay's greatest strength? What is its greatest weakness?

grammar in context

Exemplification

When you write an exemplification essay, you may introduce your examples with transitional words and phrases like *First* or *In addition*. If you do, be sure to use a comma.

First, extreme sports are dangerous.

In addition, extreme sports are very difficult.

Finally, almost all extreme sports require specialized equipment.

For information on using commas with introductory and transitional words and phrases, see 33b.

Step-by-Step Guide: Writing an Exemplification Essay

Now, you are ready to write an exemplification essay on one of the topics listed below (or a topic of your choice).

TOPICS

Reasons to start (or not to start) college right after high school
The three best products ever invented
What kinds of people or images should appear on U.S. postage stamps? Why?
Advantages (or disadvantages) of being a young parent
Athletes who really are role models
Four items students need to survive in college
What messages do rap or hip-hop artists send to listeners?
Study strategies that work
Careers you are considering
Several recent national or world news events that gave you hope

As you write your essay, follow these steps:

- Make sure your topic calls for exemplification, and then find ideas to write about; next, identify your main idea, and write a thesis statement.

- Choose and develop examples to support your thesis; then, arrange your supporting examples in a logical order, making an outline if necessary.

- Draft your essay.

- TEST your essay, referring to the TESTing an Exemplification Essay checklist on page 234.

Plan

Organize

Draft

TEST

Revise, edit,
and proofread

Plan

Organize

Draft

TEST

Revise, edit,
and proofread

■ Revise and edit your essay, referring to the two Self-Assessment Checklists in Chapter 13.

■ Proofread your essay, and make sure it follows your instructor's format.

TESTing an exemplification essay

Thesis Statement Unifies Your Essay

☐ Does your introduction include a **thesis statement** that clearly states your essay's main idea?

Evidence Supports Your Essay's Thesis Statement

☐ Do you have enough **evidence**—fully developed examples—to support your thesis?

☐ Do all your examples support your thesis, or should some be deleted?

Summary Statement Reinforces Your Essay's Main Idea

☐ Does your conclusion include a **summary statement** that reinforces your essay's thesis?

Transitions

☐ Do you include **transitions** that move readers from one example to the next?

Exemplification in Action

In "No, I Do Not Want to Pet Your Dog," Farhad Manjoo uses **exemplification** to structure his essay.

NO, I DO NOT WANT TO PET YOUR DOG

Farhad Manjoo

Farhad Manjoo was born in South Africa in 1978 and moved with his family to the United States when he was a young boy. He graduated from Cornell University, where he served as the editor of the student newspaper. He has worked as a staff writer for *Slate* and has been a regular contributor to National Public Radio. He currently writes the "State of the Art" column for the *New York Times* and is the author of *True Enough: Learning to Live in a Post-Fact Society* (2008). In "No, I Do Not Want to Pet

Your Dog," which first appeared in *Slate,* Manjoo responds to an everyday irritation by describing an America in which dogs have "achieved
dominion" over spaces from which they were once barred. As you read,
note how he uses examples to poke fun at the way dog owners talk
about and treat their beloved pets.

The other day I walked into my gym and saw a dog. A half-dozen people   1
were crowding around him, cooing and petting. He was a big dog, a lean
and muscular Doberman with, I later learned, the sort of hair-trigger
bark you'd prize if you wanted to protect a big stash of gold bullion.

"This is Y.," the dog's owner said. No explanation was offered for   2
the pooch's presence, as if it were the most natural thing in the world to
have a dog in a place usually reserved for human beings. *Huh*, I thought.

The dog came up to me, because in my experience that's what dogs   3
do when you don't want them to come up to you. They get up real close,
touching you, licking you, theatrically begging you to respond. The dog
pushed his long face toward my hand, the canine equivalent of a high
five. And so—in the same way it's rude to leave a high-fiver hanging,
especially if the high-fiver has big teeth and a strong jaw—I was expected
to pet him. I ran my hand across his head half-heartedly. I guess I was
fairly sure he wouldn't snap and bite me, but stranger things have
happened—for instance, dogs snapping and biting people all the time.

Anyway, happily, I survived.   4

But wait a second. Come on! Why was this dog here? And why was   5
no one perturbed that this dog was here? When this beast was barking
at passersby through the window as we were all working out, why did no
one go, *Hey, just throwing this out there, should we maybe not have this
distracting, possibly dangerous animal by the free weights?*

No one was asking because no one could ask. Sometime in the last   6
decade, dogs achieved dominion over urban America. They are everywhere now, allowed in places that used to belong exclusively to humans,
and sometimes only to human adults: the office, restaurants, museums,
buses, trains, malls, supermarkets, barber shops, banks, post offices. Even
at the park and other places where dogs belong, they've been given free
rein. Dogs are frequently allowed to wander off leash, to run toward you
and around you, to run across the baseball field or basketball court, to get
up in your grill. Even worse than the dogs are the owners, who seem never
to consider whether there may be people in the gym/office/restaurant/
museum who do not care to be in close proximity to their dogs. After all,
what kind of monster would have a problem with a poor innocent wid-
dle doggie? It's a dog's world. We just live in it. And it's awful. Bad dogs!

Not everyone agrees with me on this issue. Some people—or maybe   7
even most people, since dogs, like zombies, have an insidious way of
turning opponents into allies—love that dogs abound. If you adore dogs
but aren't able to keep one, the world is now your dog park, with pooches
everywhere to pet and nuzzle and otherwise brighten your day.

WORD POWER

dominion the power
to rule

WORD POWER

proximity nearness

WORD POWER

insidious harmful
but enticing

I am not a dog person. (Could you tell?) It's not that I actively despise 8 mutts; I just don't have much time for them, in the same way I don't have time for crossword puzzles or Maroon 5. Now imagine if, everywhere you went, whatever you did, Maroon 5 was always playing and everyone pretended it was totally normal—that this permanent new situation was not in any way offensive, distracting, dirty, and potentially dangerous.

OK, bad example. 9

But here's my problem: There's now a cultural assumption that 10 everyone must love dogs. Dog owners are rarely forced to reckon with the idea that there are people who aren't enthralled by their furry friends, and that taking their dogs everywhere might not be completely pleasant for these folks.

Example: If you're in the office and someone has brought her dog 11 in for the day—because, *fun*!—the dog is sure to come around you, get between your legs, rub against your thigh, take a nap on your feet, or do some other annoying thing.

If the dog's owner notices these antics, I can promise you she won't 12 apologize for the imposition. Nor will she ask you if you mind her dog doing what he's doing. Nor will she pull on its leash, because there won't be a leash, this being an office, where dogs are as welcome as Wi-Fi and free coffee.

Instead, if the owner says anything, it will be on the order of, "Don't 13 worry, he loves people!" Oh, OK then! I guess I'll just take your word for it, and forget for the moment that 1,000 Americans a day go to emergency rooms because of dog bites. More Americans seek medical attention for dog bites than for choking or falls. You're more likely to have to go to a doctor for a bite than to call the fire department for a home fire. Like it or not, American dog owner, your pet is a hazard.

But let's leave aside the possibility that I'm scared (maybe legiti- 14 mately!) of your dog, since you've assured me your dog loves people, and there's no chance you could be wrong. What if I'm allergic? Or what if I just plain hate your dog? What if I think he's dirty, since after all he did just put his nose in another dog's butt? And what if I just want to go through my workday without being slobbered on by an animal?

I know this sounds curmudgeonly. You want to shake me and tell me 15 to snap out of it, to get over myself and just love dogs already. But that's because you like dogs and don't see anything but good in them. For you, a dog is like ice cream. What churl doesn't like ice cream? Well, I'm that churl—I'm canine intolerant.

To give you a sense of how I feel when I'm accosted by your dog, let's 16 replace that animal with my 2½-year-old son. Now, I love my son, but on any objective scale of socially acceptable behavior, he is the worst. He's loud. He's inconsiderate of people's personal space—if he's left free he won't watch where he's walking and will run into you, either on purpose or accidentally. He's jumpy and fidgety in confined spaces; in an airplane it is physically impossible to restrain him from kicking the seat in front

WORD POWER

curmudgeonly bad tempered

WORD POWER

accosted approached in an aggressive way

of him. He scratches himself often, sometimes picks his nose, sometimes offers to pick yours. He will constantly say inappropriate things. The other day at Target, he noticed a little person and commented, for pretty much everyone to hear, "That lady is short!" On top of all this, he may be packing a diaper full of urine and feces.

Weirdly, irrationally, despite all this, I feel the same way about my 17 son as you do about your dog: I love him unconditionally and just don't understand why even strangers wouldn't want him around all the time. Indeed, I think almost everything he does, even the inappropriate things, is the cutest behavior ever exhibited in human history.

And yet, still, I rein him in. I realize that, although he's impossibly 18 cute, it's possible he might aggravate some people. For this reason, whenever I go into public spaces with my toddler, I treat him as if I were handling nuclear waste or a dangerous animal. I keep him confined. I shush him. If he does anything out of turn—screams, touches people— I make a show of telling him to quit it and I apologize profusely. And, finally, there are some places that are completely off-limits to my son: nice restaurants, contemplative adult spaces like grown-up museums and coffee shops, the gym, and the office. Especially the office.

Yes, there are parents who don't act this way, awful parents who let 19 their terrible kids run free. The rest of us hate those people because they give all parents a bad name. But I'll submit there are many more such dog owners than there are overindulgent parents. Most parents I know are mortified by the thought that their children might be causing anguish for others. This is evident in the world around you: It's why your co-workers rarely bring their toddlers to work. It's why 2-year-olds don't approach you in the park and lick your leg or ask you whether you need to visit the potty. It's why, when a child is being unruly in a supermarket or restaurant, you'll usually see his parents strive to get him to knock it off.

But dog owners? They seem to suffer few qualms about their ani- 20 mals' behavior. That's why there are so many dogs running around at the park, jumping up on the bench beside you while you're trying to read a book, the owner never asking if it's OK with you. That's why, when you're at a café, the dog at the neighboring table feels free to curl up under your seat. That's why there's a dog at your office right at this moment and you're having to pretend that he's just the cutest.

Well, no more, my fellow doggie skeptics. Let's take back the peace 21 we're owed. The next time your young, happy co-worker brings in his dog for the day, tell him the office is not a canine playpen. It's time to take that dog home.

Focus on the Pattern

1. What examples does Manjoo give to support his statement that dogs "are everywhere now" (6)? What evidence does he give to support his belief that this is a problem?

2. In paragraph 10, Manjoo says, "There's now a cultural assumption that everyone must love dogs." Does he give examples to support this statement? If so, where? If not, can you think of any supporting examples?

Writing Practice

1. Do you agree with Manjoo? Write an exemplification essay that illustrates the problems dogs cause in your own life—for example, in your workplace or on the streets of your community.

2. Do you disagree with Manjoo? Write an exemplification essay that illustrates the benefits of a policy of welcoming dogs in your community, in your workplace, or on your campus.

15b Narrative Essays

Narration tells a story, usually presenting a series of events in chronological (time) order, moving from beginning to end. A **narrative essay** can tell a personal story, or it can recount a recent or historical event or a fictional story.

When you **TEST** a **narrative** essay, make sure it includes all these elements:

T ▪ **Thesis Statement**—The introduction of a narrative essay should include a **thesis statement** that communicates the main idea—the point the story is making.

E ▪ **Evidence**—The body paragraphs should tell the story, one event at a time, with each event providing **evidence**—examples and details—to support the thesis. Events are usually presented in chronological (time) order.

S ▪ **Summary Statement**—The conclusion of a narrative essay should include a **summary statement** that reinforces the essay's main idea.

T ▪ **Transitions**—Throughout a narrative essay, **transitional words and phrases** should connect events in time, showing how one event leads to the next.

Moving from Assignment to Thesis

The wording of your assignment may suggest that you write a narrative essay. For example, you may be asked to *tell, trace, summarize events,* or *recount.* Once you decide that your assignment calls for narration, you need to develop a thesis statement that reflects this purpose.

ASSIGNMENT	THESIS STATEMENT
Composition Tell about a time when you had to show courage even though you were afraid.	In extraordinary circumstances, a person can exhibit great courage and overcome fear.
American history Summarize the events that occurred during President Franklin Delano Roosevelt's first one hundred days in office.	Although many thought they were extreme, the measures enacted by Roosevelt during his first one hundred days in office were necessary to fight the economic depression.
Political science Trace the development of the Mississippi Freedom Democratic Party.	As the Mississippi Freedom Democratic Party developed in the 1960s, it found a voice that spoke for equality and justice.

Organizing a Narrative Essay

When you write a narrative essay, you can discuss one event or several in each paragraph of your essay.

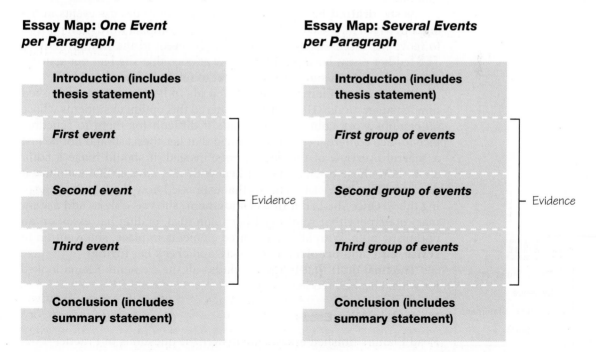

Essay Map: *One Event per Paragraph*

Introduction (includes thesis statement)

First event

Second event   — Evidence

Third event

Conclusion (includes summary statement)

Essay Map: *Several Events per Paragraph*

Introduction (includes thesis statement)

First group of events

Second group of events   — Evidence

Third group of events

Conclusion (includes summary statement)

Transitions in Narrative Essays

For a list of transitions frequently used in narration, see page 86.

Sometimes, to add interest to your narrative, you may decide not to use exact chronological order. For example, you might begin with the end of your story and then move back to the beginning to trace the events that led to this outcome. However you arrange the events, carefully worded topic sentences and clear transitional words and phrases will help readers follow your narrative.

Case Study: A Student Writes a Narrative Essay

WORD POWER

milestone an important event; a turning point

Elaina Corrato, a returning student who was older than most of her classmates, wasn't sure how to proceed when her writing instructor gave the class an assignment to write about a milestone in their lives. The first topic that came to mind was her recent thirtieth birthday, but she was reluctant to reveal her age to her classmates. However, when she learned that no one except her instructor would read her essay, she decided to write about this topic.

Elaina began by rereading entries she had made in her **writing journal** in the days before and after her birthday as well as on the day itself. Even before she began to write, she saw that her essay would be a narrative that traced her reactions to the events she experienced on that day.

As she **drafted** her essay, Elaina was careful to discuss events in the order in which they occurred and to include transitional words and phrases to move her discussion smoothly from one event to the next. When she TESTed her essay, however, Elaina saw at once that she had not stated a thesis or included a summary statement to reinforce her main idea.

At this point, Elaina emailed her draft to her instructor and asked him for suggestions. (Her instructor offered this option to students whose off-campus work commitments made it difficult for them to schedule face-to-face conferences.) He explained that her thesis should not be just a general overview of the day's events; instead, it should make a point about how those events affected her. With this advice, Elaina found it was not difficult to write a thesis that expressed how she felt about turning thirty. Once she had a **thesis statement**, she was able to add a summary statement that reinforced her main idea, ending her essay on an optimistic note. With all the required elements in place, she went on to **revise**, **edit**, and **proofread** her essay, and check her **format**.

The final draft that follows includes all the elements Elaina looked for when she TESTed her essay.

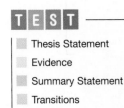

- Thesis Statement
- Evidence
- Summary Statement
- Transitions

Model Narrative Essay

Read Elaina's finished essay, and answer the questions in Practice 15-2.

Reflections

1   Turning thirty did not bother me at all. My list of "Things to Do before I Die" was far from complete, but I knew I had plenty of time to do them. In fact, turning thirty seemed like no big deal to me. If anything, it was a milestone I was happy to be approaching. Unfortunately, other people had different ideas about this milestone, and eventually their ideas made me rethink my own.

Introduction

2   As the big day approached, my family kept teasing me about it. My sister kept asking me if I felt any different. She couldn't believe I wasn't upset, but I didn't pay any attention to her. I was looking forward to a new chapter in my life. I liked my job, I was making good progress toward my college degree, and I was healthy and happy. Why should turning thirty be a problem? So, I made no special plans for my birthday, and I decided to treat it as just another day.

Topic sentence (introduces first group of events)

Events and details

3   My birthday fell on a Saturday, and I enjoyed the chance to sleep in. After I got up and had breakfast, I did my laundry and then set out for the supermarket. I rarely put on makeup or fixed my hair on Saturdays. After all, I didn't have to go to work or to school. I was only running errands in the neighborhood. Later on, though, as I waited in line at the deli counter, I caught sight of my reflection in the mirrored meat case. At first, I thought it wasn't really me. The woman staring back at me looked so old! She had bags under her eyes, and she even had a few gray hairs. I was so upset by my reflection that on my way home I stopped and bought a mud mask— guaranteed to make me look younger.

Topic sentence (introduces second group of events)

Events and details

Body paragraphs

4   As I walked up the street toward my house, I saw something attached to the front railing. When I got closer, I realized that it was a bunch of black balloons. There was also a big sign that said "Over the Hill" in big black letters. I'd been trying to think about my birthday in positive terms, but my family seemed to have other ideas. Obviously, it was time for the mud mask.

Topic sentence (introduces third group of events)

Events and details

5   After quickly unloading my groceries, I ran upstairs to apply the mask. The box promised a "rejuvenating look," and that was exactly what I wanted. I spread the sticky brown mixture on my face, and it hardened instantly. As I sat on my bed, waiting for the mask to work its magic, I heard the doorbell ring. Then, I heard familiar voices and my husband calling me to come down, saying that I had company. I couldn't answer him. I couldn't talk (or even smile) without cracking the mask. At this point, I retreated to the bathroom to make myself presentable for my friends and family. This task was not easy.

Topic sentence (introduces fourth group of events)

Events and details

Topic sentence
(introduces fifth
group of events)

Body paragraph

Events and details

When I managed to scrub off the mud mask, my face was covered with 6 little red pimples. Apparently, my sensitive skin couldn't take the harsh chemicals. At first, I didn't think the promise of "rejuvenated" skin was what I got. I had to admit, though, that my skin did look a lot younger. In fact, when I finally went downstairs to celebrate my birthday, I looked as young as a teenager—a teenager with acne.

Conclusion

Despite other people's grim warnings, I discovered that although turning 7 thirty was a milestone, it wasn't a game-changer. I learned a lot that day, and I learned even more in the days that followed. What I finally realized was that I couldn't ignore turning thirty, but having a thirtieth birthday didn't have to mean that my life was over.

PRACTICE

15-2

1. Restate Elaina's thesis statement in your own words.

2. What specific events and details support Elaina's thesis? List as many as you can.

3. Do you think paragraph 2 is necessary? How would Elaina's essay be different without it?

4. Paraphrase Elaina's summary statement. Do you think her summary statement effectively reinforces her essay's main idea?

5. What is this essay's greatest strength? What is its greatest weakness?

grammar in context

Narration

When you write a narrative essay, you tell a story. When you get caught up in your story, you might sometimes find yourself stringing a list of incidents together without proper punctuation, creating a **run-on**.

INCORRECT   As the big day approached, my family kept teasing me about it, my sister kept asking me if I felt any different.

CORRECT   As the big day approached, my family kept teasing me about it. My sister kept asking me if I felt any different.

For information on how to identify and correct run-ons, see Chapter 23.

Step-by-Step Guide: Writing a Narrative Essay

Now, you are ready to write a narrative essay on one of the topics listed below (or a topic of your choice).

TOPICS

The story of your education
Your idea of a perfect day
The plot summary of a terrible book or movie
A time when you had to make a split-second decision
Your first confrontation with authority
An important historical event
A day on which everything went wrong
A story from your family's history
Your employment history, from first to most recent job
A biography of your pet

As you write your essay, follow these steps:

- Make sure your topic calls for narration, and then find ideas to write about; next, identify your main idea, and write a thesis statement.
- Choose events and details to support your thesis, and arrange events in chronological order, making an outline if necessary.
- Draft your essay.
- **TEST** your essay, referring to the **TEST**ing a Narrative Essay checklist below.
- Revise and edit your essay, referring to the two Self-Assessment Checklists in Chapter 13.
- Proofread your essay, and make sure it follows your instructor's format.

Plan

⬇

Organize

⬇

Draft

⬇

TEST

⬇

Revise, edit, and proofread

TESTing a narrative essay

Thesis Statement Unifies Your Essay

☐ Does your introduction include a **thesis statement** that clearly states your essay's main idea?

Evidence Supports Your Essay's Thesis Statement

☐ Does all your **evidence**—events and details—support your thesis, or should some be deleted?

(continued)

☐ Do you include enough specific details to make your narrative interesting?

☐ Are the events you discuss arranged in clear chronological (time) order?

Summary Statement Reinforces Your Essay's Main Idea

☐ Does your conclusion include a **summary statement** that reinforces your essay's thesis?

Transitions

☐ Do you include enough **transitions** to make the sequence of events clear to your reader?

Narration in Action

In "The Sanctuary of School," Lynda Barry uses **narration** to structure her essay.

THE SANCTUARY OF SCHOOL

Lynda Barry
___

In her many illustrated works—including graphic novels, comic books, and a weekly cartoon strip, *Ernie Pook's Comeek*, which appears in a number of newspapers and magazines—Lynda Barry looks at the world through the eyes of children. Her characters remind adult readers of the complicated world of young people and of the clarity with which they see social situations. In "The Sanctuary of School," first published in the *Baltimore Sun* in 1992, Barry tells a story from her own childhood. As you read this essay, note how Barry relates her personal experience to a broader issue.

I was 7 years old the first time I snuck out of the house in the dark. It was winter and my parents had been fighting all night. They were short on money and long on relatives who kept "temporarily" moving into our house because they had nowhere else to go.   1

My brother and I were used to giving up our bedroom. We slept on the couch, something we actually liked because it put us that much closer to the light of our lives, our television.   2

At night when everyone was asleep, we lay on our pillows watching it with the sound off. We watched Steve Allen's mouth moving. We   3 watched Johnny Carson's mouth moving.[1] We watched movies filled with gangsters shooting machine guns into packed rooms, dying soldiers hurling a last grenade and beautiful women crying at windows. Then the sign-off finally came and we tried to sleep.

4   The morning I snuck out, I woke up filled with a panic about needing to get to school. The sun wasn't quite up yet but my anxiety was so fierce that I just got dressed, walked quietly across the kitchen and let myself out the back door.

5   It was quiet outside. Stars were still out. Nothing moved and no one was in the street. It was as if someone had turned the sound off on the world.

6   I walked the alley, breaking thin ice over the puddles with my shoes. I didn't know why I was walking to school in the dark. I didn't think about it. All I knew was a feeling of panic, like the panic that strikes kids when they realize they are lost.

7   That feeling eased the moment I turned the corner and saw the dark outline of my school at the top of the hill. My school was made up of about 15 nondescript portable classrooms set down on a fenced concrete lot in a rundown Seattle neighborhood, but it had the most beautiful view of the Cascade Mountains. You could see them from anywhere on the playfield and you could see them from the windows of my classroom—Room 2.

> **WORD POWER**
>
> **nondescript** lacking distinctive qualities; uninteresting

8   I walked over to the monkey bars and hooked my arms around the cold metal. I stood for a long time just looking across Rainier Valley. The sky was beginning to whiten and I could hear a few birds.

9   In a perfect world my absence at home would not have gone unnoticed. I would have had two parents in a panic to locate me, instead of two parents in a panic to locate an answer to the hard question of survival during a deep financial and emotional crisis.

10   But in an overcrowded and unhappy home, it's incredibly easy for any child to slip away. The high levels of frustration, depression and anger in my house made my brother and me invisible. We were children with the sound turned off. And for us, as for the steadily increasing number of neglected children in this country, the only place where we could count on being noticed was at school.

11   "Hey there, young lady. Did you forget to go home last night?" It was Mr. Gunderson, our janitor, whom we all loved. He was nice and he was funny and he was old with white hair, thick glasses and an unbelievable number of keys. I could hear them jingling as he walked across the playfield. I felt incredibly happy to see him.

12   He let me push his wheeled garbage can between the different portables as he unlocked each room. He let me turn on the lights and raise the window shades and I saw my school slowly come to life. I saw

---

1. Steve Allen and Johnny Carson were late-night television hosts.

Mrs. Holman, our school secretary, walk into the office without her orange lipstick on yet. She waved.

I saw the fifth-grade teacher Mr. Cunningham, walking under the 13 breezeway eating a hard roll. He waved.

And I saw my teacher, Mrs. Claire LeSane, walking toward us in a 14 red coat and calling my name in a very happy and surprised way, and suddenly my throat got tight and my eyes stung and I ran toward her crying. It was something that surprised us both.

It's only thinking about it now, 28 years later, that I realize I was cry- 15 ing from relief. I was with my teacher, and in a while I was going to sit at my desk, with my crayons and pencils and books and classmates all around me, and for the next six hours I was going to enjoy a thoroughly secure, warm and stable world. It was a world I absolutely relied on. Without it, I don't know where I would have gone that morning.

Mrs. LeSane asked me what was wrong and when I said "Nothing," 16 she seemingly left it at that. But she asked me if I would carry her purse for her, an honor above all honors, and she asked if I wanted to come into Room 2 early and paint.

She believed in the natural healing power of painting and drawing 17 for troubled children. In the back of her room there was always a draw- ing table and an easel with plenty of supplies, and sometimes during the day she would come up to you for what seemed like no good reason and quietly ask if you wanted to go to the back table and "make some pictures for Mrs. LeSane." We all had a chance at it—to sit apart from the class for a while to paint, draw and silently work out impossible problems on 11×17 sheets of newsprint.

Drawing came to mean everything to me. At the back table in 18 Room 2, I learned to build myself a life preserver that I could carry into my home.

We all know that a good education system saves lives, but the people 19 of this country are still told that cutting the budget for public schools is necessary, that poor salaries for teachers are all we can manage and that art, music and all creative activities must be the first to go when times are lean.

Before- and after-school programs are cut and we are told that pub- 20 lic schools are not made for baby-sitting children. If parents are neglect- ful temporarily or permanently, for whatever reason, it's certainly sad, but their unlucky children must fend for themselves. Or slip through the cracks. Or wander in a dark night alone.

We are told in a thousand ways that not only are public schools not 21 important, but that the children who attend them, the children who need them most, are not important either. We leave them to learn from the blind eye of a television, or to the mercy of "a thousand points of light"[2] that can be as far away as stars.

WORD POWER

fend to manage

2. Phrase used by former president George Herbert Walker Bush to promote volunteerism.

I was lucky. I had Mrs. LeSane. I had Mr. Gunderson. I had an abun- 22
dance of art supplies. And I had a particular brand of neglect in my
home that allowed me to slip away and get to them. But what about the
rest of the kids who weren't as lucky? What happened to them?

By the time the bell rang that morning I had finished my drawing and 23
Mrs. LeSane pinned it up on the special bulletin board she reserved for
drawings from the back table. It was the same picture I always drew—a
sun in the corner of a blue sky over a nice house with flowers all around it.

Mrs. LeSane asked us to please stand, face the flag, place our right 24
hands over our hearts and say the Pledge of Allegiance. Children across
the country do it faithfully. I wonder now when the country will face its
children and say a pledge right back.

Focus on the Pattern

1. Paragraphs 9–10 and 19–22 interrupt Barry's narrative. What purpose do these paragraphs serve? Do you think the essay would be
   more effective if paragraphs 9 and 10 came earlier? If paragraphs
   19–22 came after paragraph 24? Explain.

2. What transitional words and phrases does Barry use in her narrative
   to move readers from one event to the next? Do you think her essay
   needs more transitions? If so, where should they be added?

Writing Practice

1. Did you see elementary school as a "sanctuary" or as something
   quite different? Write a narrative essay that conveys to readers what
   school meant to you when you were a child.

2. In addition to school, television was a sanctuary for Barry and her
   brother. Did television watching (or some other activity) serve this
   function for you when you were younger? Is there some activity
   that fills this role now? In a narrative essay, write about your own
   "sanctuary."

15c Process Essays

A **process** is a series of chronological steps that produces a particular
result. **Process essays** explain the steps in a procedure, telling how
something is (or was) done. A process essay can be organized as either
a *process explanation* or a set of *instructions*.

When you TEST a **process** essay, make sure it includes all these elements:

T ■ **Thesis Statement**—A process essay should include a **thesis statement**
that expresses the essay's main idea, identifying the process you will
discuss and telling why it is important or why you are explaining it.

E ■ **Evidence**—The body paragraphs should provide **evidence**—examples and details—that explains all the steps in the process and supports the essay's thesis. Each paragraph's topic sentence should identify the step (or group of related steps) that the paragraph will explain. Steps should be presented in strict chronological (time) order.

S ■ **Summary Statement**—The conclusion of a process essay should include a **summary statement** that reinforces the essay's thesis.

T ■ **Transitions**—A process essay should include **transitional words and phrases** that link the steps in the process and show how they are related.

Moving from Assignment to Thesis

The wording of your assignment may suggest that you write a process essay. For example, you may be asked to *explain a process, give instructions, give directions,* or *give a step-by-step account.* Once you decide that your assignment calls for process, you need to develop a thesis statement that reflects this purpose.

ASSIGNMENT	THESIS STATEMENT
American government Explain the process by which a bill becomes a law.	The process by which a bill becomes a law is long and complex, involving numerous revisions and a great deal of compromise.
Pharmacy practice Summarize the procedure for conducting a clinical trial of a new drug.	To ensure that drugs are safe and effective, scientists follow strict procedural guidelines for testing and evaluating the drugs.
Technical writing　Write a set of instructions for applying for a student internship in a government agency.	If you want to apply for a government internship, you need to follow several important steps.

If your purpose is simply to help readers understand a process, not actually perform it, you will write a process explanation. **Process explanations,** like the first two examples in the chart above, often use present tense verbs ("Once a bill *is* introduced in Congress" or "A scientist first *submits* a funding application") to explain how a procedure is generally carried out. However, when a process explanation describes a specific procedure that was completed in the past, it uses past tense verbs ("The next thing I *did*").

If your purpose is to enable readers to actually perform the steps in a process, you will write instructions. **Instructions**, like the technical writing example above, always use present tense verbs in the form of commands to tell readers what to do ("First, *meet* with your adviser").

Organizing a Process Essay

Whether your essay is a process explanation or a set of instructions, you can either devote a full paragraph to each step of the process or group a series of minor steps together in a single paragraph.

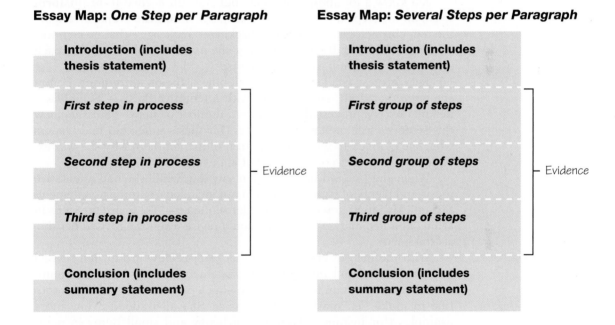

Essay Map: *One Step per Paragraph*

- Introduction (includes thesis statement)
- First step in process
- Second step in process
- Third step in process — Evidence
- Conclusion (includes summary statement)

Essay Map: *Several Steps per Paragraph*

- Introduction (includes thesis statement)
- First group of steps
- Second group of steps
- Third group of steps — Evidence
- Conclusion (includes summary statement)

As you write your process essay, discuss each step in the order in which it is performed, making sure your topic sentences clearly identify each step or group of steps. (If you are writing instructions, you may also include reminders or warnings that readers might need to know when performing the process.)

Transitions in Process Essays

Transitions are extremely important in process essays because they enable readers to follow the sequence of steps in the process and, in the case of instructions, to perform the process themselves.

For a list of transitions frequently used in a process essay, see page 96.

Case Study: A Student Writes a Process Essay

Jen Rossi, a student in a first-year writing course, was given this assignment:

> Write a set of instructions for a process that you are very familiar with but that your classmates probably do not know much about. Be sure your readers will be able not just to understand the process but also to perform the steps themselves.

When she considered what she might want to write about, Jen rejected familiar process topics like following a recipe or performing a household repair. Instead, she decided to explain how to sell items at flea markets.

Jen knew a lot about this topic, but she still needed to **brainstorm** to get all the steps down on paper. Next, she **listed the steps**, arranging them in chronological order and checking to make sure that no step was missing. When she **drafted** her essay, she made sure she identified each step with transitional words and phrases.

Jen's biggest challenge was developing a **thesis statement**. Before she wrote her draft, she came up with a tentative thesis—"Selling at a flea market is a process that requires a number of steps"—but she knew this sentence was only a placeholder. This thesis statement told readers what she planned to write about, but it didn't tell them why she was explaining this process or how she felt about it.

When she TESTed her draft, Jen saw that while she had a tentative thesis and plenty of support, she had not included a summary statement. She quickly jotted down a placeholder sentence—"These are the steps in selling at a flea market"—that she could revise when she revised her thesis statement.

With the help of classmates in her **peer-review** group, Jen revised her thesis statement and summary statement so they both communicated her essay's main idea: that following a process can establish a routine to make flea market selling easier. She also added a few more examples (for instance, examples of heavy and small items in paragraph 5 and examples of small and large items in paragraph 7) in response to suggestions from her classmates. Once she made these revisions, she went on to **edit** and **proofread** her essay and to check her **format**.

The final draft that follows includes all the elements Jen looked for when she TESTed her essay.

Model Process Essay

Read Jen's finished essay, and answer the questions in Practice 15-3.

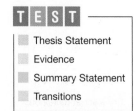

T E S T

- Thesis Statement
- Evidence
- Summary Statement
- Transitions

For Fun and Profit

1   Selling items at a flea market can be both fun and profitable. In fact, it can lead to a hobby that will be a continuing source of extra income. Your first flea market can take a lot of work, but establishing a routine will make each experience easier and more rewarding than the last one.

Introduction

2   The first step in the process is to call to reserve a spot at the flea market. If possible, try to get a spot near the entrance, where there is a lot of foot traffic. Once you have your spot, recruit a helper—for example, one of your roommates—and get to work.

Topic sentence (identifies first step)

Examples and details

3   The next step is sorting through all the items you've managed to accumulate. Your helper will come in handy here, encouraging you to sell ugly or useless things that you may want to hold on to. Make three piles—keep, sell, and trash—and, one by one, place each item in a pile. (Before you decide to sell or discard an item, check with roommates and family members to make sure you aren't accidentally throwing out one of their prized possessions.)

Topic sentence (identifies second step)

Examples and details

4   Next, price the items for sale. This can actually be the hardest step in the process. It's always difficult to accept the fact that you might have to set a low price for something that has sentimental value for you (a giant-sized stuffed animal, for example). It can be just as hard to set a high price on the ugly lamp or old record album that might turn out to be someone's treasure. In all likelihood, you will return from your first flea market with a lot of unsold items. You will also probably realize, too late, that you sold some items too cheaply. (Don't worry; you won't make these mistakes again.)

Topic sentence (identifies third step)

Body paragraphs

Examples and details

5   The next step is packing up items to be sold. You may want to borrow a friend's truck or van for the heavy, bulky items (boxes of books or dishes, for example). The small items (knickknacks, silk flowers, stray teaspoons) can be transported by car.

Topic sentence (identifies fourth step)

Examples and details

6   The final steps in your preparation take place on the day before the event. Borrow a couple of card tables. Then, go to the bank and get lots of dollar bills and quarters, and collect piles of newspaper and grocery bags. Now, your planning is complete, and you are ready for the big day.

Topic sentence (identifies fifth step)

Examples and details

7   On the day of the flea market, get up early, and (with your trusty helper's assistance) load your vehicle. When you arrive at the site where the event is to be held, have your helper unload the car. Meanwhile, set things up, placing small items (such as plates or DVDs) on the card tables and large items (such as your parents' old lawnmower) on the ground near the tables.

Topic sentence (identifies sixth step)

Examples and details

Topic sentence
(identifies
seventh step)

Body paragraph

Examples and details

Now, the actual selling begins. Before you can even set up your tables, people will start picking through your items, offering you cash for picture frames, pots and pans, and old video games. Don't panic! Try to develop a system: one of you can persuade buyers that that old meat grinder or vase is just what they've been looking for; the other person can negotiate the price with prospective buyers. Then, while one of you wraps small items in the newspapers or bags you brought, the other person can take the money and make change.

8

Conclusion

Finally, at the end of the day, the process will come to an end. Now, count your money. (Don't forget to give a share to your helper.) Then, load all the unsold items into your vehicle, and bring them back home. The process ends when you store the unsold items in the back of your closet, ready to pack them all up again and follow the same routine for the next flea market.

9

PRACTICE
15-3

1. Restate Jen's thesis statement in your own words.

2. What features identify Jen's essay as a set of instructions rather than a process explanation?

3. Review the transitional words and phrases that link the steps in the process. Are any other transitions needed? If so, where?

4. List the major steps in the process of selling at a flea market. Does Jen present these steps in strict chronological order?

5. Paraphrase Jen's summary statement. Do you think she needs to revise this sentence so it more clearly reinforces her thesis statement?

6. What is the essay's greatest strength? What is its greatest weakness?

grammar in context

Process

When you write a process essay, you may have problems keeping tense, person, and voice consistent throughout. If you shift from one tense, person, or voice to another without good reason, you will confuse your readers.

CONFUSING   Make three piles—keep, sell, and trash—and, one by one, every item should be placed in a pile. (shift from active to passive voice and from present to past tense)

CLEAR Make three piles—keep, sell, and trash—and, one by one, place every item in a pile. (consistent voice and tense)

For information on how to avoid illogical shifts in tense, person, and voice, see Chapter 26.

Step-by-Step Guide: Writing a Process Essay

Now, you are ready to write a process essay on one of the topics listed below (or a topic of your choice).

TOPICS

An unusual recipe
How to find an apartment
Applying for a job
A religious ritual or cultural ceremony
A complicated task you do at work
A do-it-yourself project that didn't get done
Your own writing process
A self-improvement program (past, present, or future)

As you write your essay, follow these steps:

Plan

- Make sure your topic calls for process, and then decide whether you want to explain a process or write instructions; next, find ideas to write about, identify your main idea, and write a thesis statement.
- Identify the most important steps in the process.
- List the steps in chronological order, making an outline if necessary.

Organize

- Draft your essay.
- TEST your essay, referring to the TESTing a Process Essay checklist below.

Draft

- Revise and edit your essay, referring to the two Self-Assessment Checklists in Chapter 13.
- Proofread your essay, and make sure it follows your instructor's format.

TEST

TESTing a process essay

Thesis Statement Unifies Your Essay

☐ Does your introduction include a **thesis statement** that expresses your essay's main idea, identifying the process you will explain and indicating why you are writing about it?

Revise, edit, and proofread

(continued)

E vidence Supports Your Essay's Thesis Statement

☐ Does all your **evidence**—examples and details—support your thesis, or should some be deleted?

☐ Do you identify and explain every step that readers will need to understand (or perform) the process? Should any steps in the process be deleted?

☐ Are the steps in the process given in strict chronological order?

☐ If you are writing instructions, have you included all necessary warnings or reminders?

S ummary Statement Reinforces Your Essay's Main Idea

☐ Does your conclusion include a **summary statement** that reinforces your essay's thesis?

T ransitions

☐ Do you include **transitions** that introduce your steps and clearly show how the steps in the process are related?

Process in Action

In "Slice of Life," Russell Baker uses **process** to structure his essay.

SLICE OF LIFE

Russell Baker

Pulitzer Prize–winning columnist and author Russell Baker was known for his keen political insight and sharp social commentary. He was also known for being funny. The source of much of Baker's humor is his dead-pan approach, in which he pretends to be completely serious. In "Slice of Life," first published in the *New York Times* in 1974, Baker uses this approach to turn what seems to be a straightforward set of instructions into a humorous discussion of a holiday ritual. As you read, think about your family's Thanksgivings.

How to carve a turkey: 1

Assemble the following tools—carving knife, stone for sharpening 2 carving knife, hot water, soap, wash cloth, two bath towels, barbells, meat cleaver. If the house lacks a meat cleaver, an ax may be substituted. If it is, add bandages, sutures, and iodine to above list.

Begin by moving the turkey from the roasting pan to a suitable carv- 3 ing area. This is done by inserting the carving knife into the posterior stuffed area of the turkey and the knife-sharpening stone into the stuffed area under the neck.

Thus skewered, the turkey may be lifted out of the hot grease with 4 relative safety. Should the turkey drop to the floor, however, remove the knife and stone, roll the turkey gingerly into the two bath towels, wrap them several times around it and lift the encased fowl to the carving place.

You are now ready to begin carving. Sharpen the knife on the stone 5 and insert it where the thigh joins the torso. If you do this correctly, which is improbable, the knife will almost immediately encounter a barrier of bone and gristle. This may very well be the joint. It could, however, be your thumb. If not, execute a vigorous sawing motion until satisfied that the knife has been defeated. Withdraw the knife and ask someone nearby, in as testy a manner as possible, why the knives at your house are not kept in better carving condition.

Exercise the biceps and forearms by lifting barbells until they are 6 strong enough for you to tackle the leg joint with bare hands. Wrapping one hand firmly around the thigh, seize the turkey's torso in the other hand and scream. Run cold water over hands to relieve pain of burns.

Now, take a bath towel in each hand and repeat the above maneuver. 7 The entire leg should snap away from the chassis with a distinct crack, and the rest of the turkey, obedient to Newton's law[1] about equal and opposite reactions, should roll in the opposite direction, which means that if you are carving at the table the turkey will probably come to rest in someone's lap.

Get the turkey out of the lap with as little fuss as possible, and con- 8 centrate on the leg. Use the meat cleaver to sever the sinewy leather which binds the thigh to the drumstick.

If using the alternate, ax method, this operation should be performed 9 on a cement walk outside the house in order to preserve the table.

Repeat the above operation on the turkey's uncarved side. You now 10 have two thighs and two drumsticks. Using the wash cloth, soap and hot water, bathe thoroughly and, if possible, go to a movie. Otherwise, look each person in the eye and say, "I don't suppose anyone wants white meat."

If compelled to carve the breast anyhow, sharpen the knife on the 11 stone again with sufficient awkwardness to tip over the gravy bowl on the person who started the stampede for white meat.

While everyone is rushing about to mop the gravy off her slacks, 12 hack at the turkey breast until it starts crumbling off the carcass in ugly chunks.

The alternative method for carving white meat is to visit around the 13 neighborhood until you find someone who has a good carving knife and borrow it, if you find one, which is unlikely.

WORD POWER

gingerly very cautiously or carefully

WORD POWER

execute to do or perform

---

1. Sir Isaac Newton, seventeenth-century physicist and mathematician known for formulating the laws of gravity and light and for inventing calculus.

This method enables you to watch the football game on neighbors' 14 television sets and also creates the possibility that somebody back at your table will grow tired of waiting and do the carving herself.

In this case, upon returning home, cast a pained stare upon the 15 mound of chopped white meat that has been hacked out by the family carving knife and refuse to do any more carving that day. No one who cares about the artistry of carving can be expected to work upon the mutilations of amateurs, and it would be a betrayal of the carver's art to do so.

Focus on the Pattern

1. How can you tell that this essay is a set of instructions and not an explanation of a process?
2. Do you think the phrase "How to carve a turkey" is an adequate introduction for this essay? What other kind of introduction might Baker have written?
3. Identify the various cautions and warnings that Baker provides for readers. Are they all necessary? Explain.

Writing Practice

1. Write a new introductory paragraph for this essay. Then, turn Baker's instructions into a straightforward process explanation, deleting any material you consider irrelevant to your purpose. Be sure to include all necessary articles (*a, an, the*) and transitions.
2. List the steps in a recipe for preparing one of your favorite dishes. Then, expand your recipe into an essay, adding transitions and cautions and reminders. Finally, add opening and closing paragraphs that describe the finished product and tell readers why the dish is worth preparing.

15d   Cause-and-Effect Essays

A **cause** makes something happen; an **effect** is a result of a particular cause or event. **Cause-and-effect essays** identify causes or predict effects; sometimes, they do both.

When you **TEST** a **cause-and-effect** essay, make sure it includes all these elements:

T ■ **Thesis Statement**—The introduction of a cause-and-effect essay should include a **thesis statement** that communicates the essay's main idea and indicates whether it will focus on causes or on effects.

E ▪ **Evidence**—The body paragraphs should include **evidence**—examples and details—to illustrate and explain the causes or effects you examine. The topic sentence of each paragraph should identify the causes or effects the paragraph will discuss.

S ▪ **Summary Statement**—The conclusion of a cause-and-effect essay should include a **summary statement** that reinforces the essay's thesis.

T ▪ **Transitions**—A cause-and-effect essay should include **transitional words and phrases** that make clear which causes lead to which effects.

Moving from Assignment to Thesis

The wording of your assignment may suggest that you write a cause-and-effect essay. For example, the assignment may ask you to *explain why, predict the outcome, list contributing factors, discuss the consequences,* or tell what *caused* something else or how something is *affected* by something else. Once you decide that your assignment calls for cause and effect, you need to develop a thesis statement that reflects this purpose.

ASSIGNMENT	THESIS STATEMENT
Women's studies What factors contributed to the rise of the women's movement in the 1970s?	The women's movement of the 1970s had its origins in the peace and civil rights movements of the 1960s.
Public health Discuss the possible long-term effects of smoking.	In addition to its well-known negative effects on smokers themselves, smoking also causes significant problems for those exposed to secondhand smoke.
Media and society How has the Internet affected the lives of those who have grown up with it?	The Internet has created a generation of people who learn differently from those in previous generations.

A cause-and-effect essay can focus on causes or on effects. When you write about causes, be sure to examine *all* relevant causes. You should emphasize the cause you consider the most important, but do not forget to consider other causes that may be significant. Similarly, when you write about effects, consider *all* significant effects of a particular cause, not just the first few that you think of.

If your focus is on finding causes, as it is in the first assignment in the chart on page 257, your introductory paragraph should identify the effect (the women's movement). If your focus is on predicting effects, as it is in the second and third assignments in the chart, you should begin by identifying the cause (smoking, the Internet).

Organizing a Cause-and-Effect Essay

In the body of your essay, you will probably devote a full paragraph to each cause (or effect). You can also group several related causes (or effects) together in each paragraph.

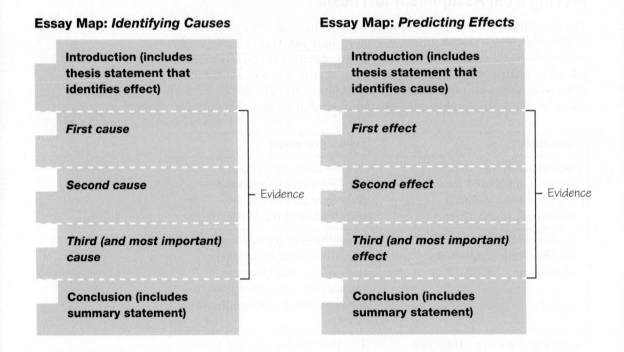

Essay Map: *Identifying Causes*

Introduction (includes thesis statement that identifies effect)

First cause

Second cause — Evidence

Third (and most important) cause

Conclusion (includes summary statement)

Essay Map: *Predicting Effects*

Introduction (includes thesis statement that identifies cause)

First effect

Second effect — Evidence

Third (and most important) effect

Conclusion (includes summary statement)

Transitions in Cause-and-Effect Essays

For a list of transitions frequently used in cause and effect, see pages 107–108.

Transitions are important in cause-and-effect essays because they establish causal connections, telling readers that A caused B and not the other way around. They also make it clear that events have a *causal* relationship (A *caused* B) and not just a *sequential* relationship (A *came before* B). Remember, when one event follows another, the second is not necessarily the result of the first. For example, an earthquake may occur the day before you fail an exam, but that doesn't mean the earthquake caused you to fail.

Case Study: A Student Writes a Cause-and-Effect Essay

In an orientation course for first-year education majors, Andrea DeMarco was asked to write a personal essay about an event that changed her life. The wording of the assignment indicated to Andrea that her essay would have a cause-and-effect structure. She remembered writing a cause-and-effect paragraph, in response to a composition assignment, about how her parents' separation had led her to grow up quickly. Now, she thought she could develop some of the ideas she had explored in that paragraph into an essay.

Before she wrote her first draft, Andrea talked to her older sister and brother to see what they remembered about the separation. As they spoke, Andrea **took notes** so she wouldn't forget any details. Armed with her siblings' and her own memories, as well as the paragraph she'd written earlier, Andrea **drafted** her essay.

In her draft, she included a **thesis statement**—"My parents' separation made everything different"—that echoed the wording of the assignment. As she wrote, she was careful to include transitional words and phrases like *because* and *as a result* to make the cause-and-effect emphasis clear and to distinguish between the cause (the separation) and its effects. Her summary statement also reinforced the cause-and-effect emphasis of her essay.

When Andrea TESTed her draft, she saw that it included all the required elements—thesis statement, evidence, summary statement, and transitions—so she continued **revising** her draft. When she finished her revisions, she **edited** and **proofread** her essay and checked her **format**.

The final draft that follows includes all the elements Andrea looked for when she TESTed her essay.

Model Cause-and-Effect Essay

Read Andrea's finished essay, and answer the questions in Practice 15-4.

How My Parents' Separation Changed My Life

1   Until I was eight, I lived the perfect all-American life with my perfect all-American family. I lived in a suburb of Albany, New York, with my parents, my sister and brother, and our dog, Daisy. We had a Ping-Pong table in the basement, a barbecue in the backyard, and two cars in the garage. My dad and mom were high school teachers, and every summer we took a family vacation. Then, it all changed. My parents' separation made everything different.

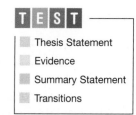

Thesis Statement

Evidence

Summary Statement

Transitions

Introduction

*Topic sentence
(identifies first effect)*

> One day, just before Halloween, when my sister was twelve and my brother was fourteen (Daisy was seven), our parents called us into the kitchen for a family conference. We didn't think anything was wrong at first; they were always calling these annoying meetings. We figured it was time for

Examples and details

> us to plan a vacation, talk about household chores, or be nagged to clean our rooms. As soon as we sat down, though, we knew this was different. We could tell Mom had been crying, and Dad's voice cracked when he told us the news. They were separating—they called it a "trial separation"—and Dad was moving out of our house.

2

*Topic sentence
(identifies
second effect)*

> After that day, everything seemed to change. Every Halloween we always had a big jack-o'-lantern on our front porch. Dad used to spend hours at the kitchen table cutting out the eyes, nose, and mouth and hollowing out the insides. That Halloween, because he didn't live with us, things were

Examples and details

> different. Mom bought a pumpkin, and I guess she was planning to carve it up. But she never did, and we never mentioned it. It sat on the kitchen counter for a couple of weeks, getting soft and wrinkled, and then it just disappeared.

3

*Topic sentence
(identifies third effect)*

> Other holidays were also different because Mom and Dad were not living together. Our first Thanksgiving without Dad was pathetic. Christmas was different, too. We spent Christmas Eve with Dad and our relatives on his side

4

Body paragraphs

Examples and details

> and Christmas Day with Mom and her family. Of course, we got twice as many presents as usual. I realize now that both our parents were trying to make up for the pain of the separation. The worst part came when I opened my big present from Mom: Barbie's Dream House. This was something I had always wanted. Even at eight, I knew how hard it must have been for Mom to afford it. The trouble was, I had gotten the same thing from Dad the night before.

*Topic sentence
(identifies
fourth effect)*

> The separation affected each of us in different ways. The worst effect of my parents' separation was not the big events but the disruption in our everyday lives. Dinner used to be a family time, a chance to talk about our day and make plans. But after Dad left, Mom seemed to stop eating.

5

Examples and details

> Sometimes she would just have coffee while we ate, and sometimes she wouldn't eat at all. She would microwave some frozen thing for us or heat up soup or cook some hot dogs. We didn't care—after all, now she let us watch TV while we ate—but we did notice.

*Topic sentence
(identifies fifth effect)*

> Other parts of our routine changed, too. Because Dad didn't live with us anymore, we had to spend every Saturday and every Wednesday night at his apartment, no matter what else we had planned. Usually, he would take us to dinner at McDonald's on Wednesdays, and then we would go back to his place and do our homework or watch TV. That wasn't too bad. Saturdays

6

Examples and details

> were a lot worse. We really wanted to be home, hanging out with our friends

in our own rooms in our own house. Instead, we had to do some planned activity with Dad, like go to a movie or a hockey game.   ⌐ Body paragraph

7   As a result of what happened in my own family, it is hard for me to believe any relationship is forever. By the end of the school year, my parents had somehow worked things out, and Dad was back home again. That June, at a family conference around the kitchen table, we made our summer vacation plans. We decided on Williamsburg, Virginia, the all-American   Conclusion
vacation destination. So, things were back to normal, but I wasn't, and I'm still not. Now, ten years later, my mother and father are all right, but I still worry they'll split up again. And I worry about my own future husband and how I will ever be sure he's the one I'll stay married to.

PRACTICE

15-4   1. Restate Andrea's thesis statement in your own words. Does this statement identify a cause or an effect?

2. List the specific effects of her parents' separation that Andrea identifies.

3. Review the transitional words and phrases Andrea uses to make cause-and-effect connections clear to her readers. Do you think she needs more of these transitions? If so, where?

4. Is Andrea's relatively long concluding paragraph effective? Why or why not? Do you think it should be shortened or divided into two paragraphs?

5. Is Andrea's straightforward title effective, or should she have used a more creative or eye-catching title? Can you suggest an alternative?

6. What is this essay's greatest strength? What is its greatest weakness?

grammar in context

Cause and Effect

When you write a cause-and-effect essay, you may have trouble remembering the difference between *affect* and *effect*.

        effect
The worst ~~affect~~ of my parents' separation was not the big
events but the disruption in our everyday lives. (*effect* is a noun)

           affected
The separation ~~effected~~ each of us in different ways.

(*affect* is a verb)

For information on affect *and* effect, *see Chapter 22.*

Step-by-Step Guide: Writing a Cause-and-Effect Essay

Now, you are ready to write a cause-and-effect essay on one of the topics listed below (or a topic of your choice).

TOPICS

A teacher's positive (or negative) effect on you

Why you voted a certain way in a recent election (or why you did not vote)

How your life would be different if you dropped out of school (or quit your job)

How a particular invention has changed your life

Why texting is so popular

A movie or book that changed the way you look at life

How a particular season (or day of the week) affects your mood

How having a child would change (or has changed) your life

How a particular event made you grow up

As you write your essay, follow these steps:

Plan

Organize

Draft

TEST

Revise, edit, and proofread

■ Make sure your topic calls for cause and effect, and then decide whether your essay will focus on causes, effects, or both; next, find ideas to write about, identify your main idea, and write a thesis statement.

■ Choose causes or effects to support your thesis, and arrange causes and effects in an effective order, making an outline if necessary.

■ Draft your essay.

■ **TEST** your essay, referring to the **TEST**ing a Cause-and-Effect Essay Checklist below.

■ Revise and edit your essay, referring to the two Self-Assessment Checklists in Chapter 13.

■ Proofread your essay, and make sure it follows your instructor's format.

TESTing a cause-and-effect essay

Thesis Statement Unifies Your Essay

☐ Does your introduction include a **thesis statement** that indicates your main idea and makes clear whether your essay will focus on causes or effects?

Evidence Supports Your Essay's Thesis Statement

☐ Does all your **evidence**—examples and details—support your thesis, or should some be deleted?

☐ Do you identify and explain all causes or effects relevant to your topic, or do you need to add any?

☐ Do you arrange causes and effects to indicate which are more important than others?

☐ Does each body paragraph identify and explain one particular cause or effect (or several closely related causes or effects)?

Summary Statement Reinforces Your Essay's Main Idea

☐ Does your conclusion include a **summary statement** that reinforces your essay's thesis?

Transitions

☐ Do you include **transitions** that introduce each of your causes or effects and make your essay's cause-and-effect connections clear?

Cause and Effect in Action

In "Facing the Concussion Risks of Youth Football," Kathleen E. Bachynski and Daniel S. Goldberg use **cause and effect** to structure their essay.

FACING THE CONCUSSION RISKS OF YOUTH FOOTBALL

Kathleen E. Bachynski and Daniel S. Goldberg

Kathleen E. Bachynski is a PhD candidate in the Department of Sociomedical Sciences at Columbia University's Mailman School of Public Health. She studies the history and ethics of public health, with a focus on injury prevention. Daniel S. Goldberg is an assistant professor of Bioethics at East Carolina University. He is trained as an attorney, an historian, and a public health ethicist, and researches a variety of issues related to health inequalities. This article originally appeared in the Public's Health section of Philly.com in 2014.

After years of denying the link between football and brain disease, this month the National Football League's own experts calculated that nearly one third of its players will go on to develop long-term cognitive problems after retirement. The league's new stance might help shift public   1

WORD POWER

cognitive related to the mental process of acquiring knowledge; thinking perceptions of football's extraordinary risks to professional players' brains. From a public health perspective, examining the sport's impact on millions of youth players is of even greater importance.

2   Children as young as seven and eight continue to play tackle football across the United States in far greater numbers than NFL stars. Accumulating evidence suggests that the repeated collisions inherent in the youth sport may cause significant harm. The players might be smaller, but the hits are still dangerous. Researchers have found that nine to twelve year olds can experience head impacts of a similar magnitude to those that occur in high school and college football. Furthermore, because children's brains are still developing and because they have weaker necks than adults, they may be more vulnerable to brain trauma.

3   Why do parents allow their children to participate in a sport that poses significant risks to developing brains? One reason is that organizers of youth football leagues portray the youth game as much safer than the professional game. The Pop Warner website, for example, states that there is "an absence of catastrophic head and neck injuries and disruptive joint injuries found at higher levels" in their league. Such assertions seem to discount the potential severity of concussions, which are common in youth football and can have major short-term and long-term consequences. Parents may not fully appreciate the risks associated with football head injuries. A recent study of over three hundred football parents found that most did not realize that a concussion is considered a mild traumatic brain injury, or that a direct blow to the head is not necessary for a concussion to occur.

4   Yet even if parents acknowledge that concussions are a significant injury, most people believe that strategies such as improved helmets, return-to-play guidelines, and "safer" tackling techniques can help significantly reduce the risks of concussion. Indeed, the NFL has helped promote this prevailing view, most notably with its "Heads Up Football" partnership with youth leagues, intended to teach proper tackling techniques to children.

5   There is no evidence that the "Heads Up Football" program reduces the risk of concussion or of long-term brain damage: As former Denver Broncos tight end Nate Jackson has observed, no matter what tackling technique children use, "you can't remove the head from play in the football field."

6   Unfortunately, improved helmet design is not a silver bullet either. Although helmets are very effective in preventing catastrophic head injuries such as skull fractures, they are not designed to prevent concussions. Even the best designed helmet cannot prevent the forces that occur when the head rotates on the neck. Kevin Walter of the American Academy of Pediatrics' Council on Sports Medicine and Fitness recently stated that currently, "no protective equipment can prevent concussion."

Although education, training, and improved equipment are all worth 7 encouraging, they do not change the fundamental risks of the sport. Football is a contact game in which repeated full-body collisions place players' brains at risk of chronic trauma. We must acknowledge that the risk of head injuries is inherent to tackle football, even at the youth level, and will remain significant even with new equipment designs or the best tackling techniques.

We need to ask different questions. At what point are the risks of head 8 injuries so high or severe that even fully informed parents should not be permitted to let their children play? And at what age can players consent to the risk of brain trauma and the elevated risks of neurological diseases later in life?

These are complex ethical issues that involve not only examining the 9 latest concussion research, but also our values and beliefs about how much risk is appropriate for children. Of course, children should be encouraged to play and lead active lives, and experiencing some amount of risk in childhood is inevitable. But how much risk is too much?

WORD POWER

inevitable unavoidable

Addressing this question will require a robust public discussion 10 involving parents, coaches, school administrators, fans, trainers, physicians, sporting goods manufacturers, and the players themselves. While children certainly benefit from participation in team sports, it remains a question whether other sports can offer those same benefits while posing less risk of brain injury than tackle football. Do the risks of America's most popular sport outweigh its benefits for young children?

WORD POWER

robust healthy; significant

Focus on the Pattern

1. This essay focuses on the risks of youth football. Are risks the same as causes? Why or why not? What do you think the effects of these risks are for the players, for parents, and for society in general?

2. Write a one-sentence thesis statement for this essay. Include at least one word or phrase (such as *because*, *for this reason*, or *as a result*) that indicates it is a cause-and-effect essay.

Writing Practice

1. Do you think parents are to blame for the negative consequences that may occur if they allow their children to participate in youth football programs? If not, whom (or what) do you think is at fault? Write a cause-and-effect essay in response to these questions.

2. Write a cause-and-effect essay in which you discuss the *positive* effects of youth football on players and on their communities. You may briefly acknowledge the possible negative results identified in Bachynski and Goldberg's essay, but be sure to focus on the benefits. If you like, you may use your own experiences to support your thesis.

15e　Comparison-and-Contrast Essays

Comparison identifies similarities, and **contrast** identifies differences. **Comparison-and-contrast essays** explain how two things are alike or how they are different; sometimes, they discuss both similarities and differences.

When you **TEST** a **comparison-and-contrast** essay, make sure it includes all these elements:

T ■ **Thesis Statement**—The introduction of a comparison-and-contrast essay should include a **thesis statement** that communicates the essay's main idea, telling readers what two items you are going to compare or contrast and whether you are going to emphasize similarities or differences.

E ■ **Evidence**—The body paragraphs should include **evidence**—examples and details—that supports the thesis statement. The topic sentence of each paragraph should identify the similarity or difference the paragraph will examine, and the examples and details should explain the similarity or difference.

S ■ **Summary Statement**—The conclusion of a comparison-and-contrast essay should include a **summary statement** that reinforces the essay's thesis.

T ■ **Transitions**—A comparison-and-contrast essay should include **transitional words and phrases** to help readers move from point to point and from subject to subject.

Moving from Assignment to Thesis

The wording of your assignment may suggest that you write a comparison-and-contrast essay. For example, you may be asked to *compare*, *contrast*, *discuss similarities*, or *identify differences*. Once you decide that your assignment calls for comparison and contrast, you need to develop a thesis statement that reflects this purpose.

ASSIGNMENT	THESIS STATEMENT
Philosophy　Identify some basic similarities in the beliefs of Henry David Thoreau and Martin Luther King Jr.	Although King was more politically active, both he and Thoreau strongly supported the idea of civil disobedience.
Nutrition　How do the diets of native Japanese and Japanese Americans differ?	As they become more and more assimilated, Japanese Americans consume more fats than native Japanese do.

Literature Contrast the two sisters in Alice Walker's short story "Everyday Use."	Unlike Maggie, Dee—her more successful, better-educated sister—has rejected her family's heritage.

Organizing a Comparison-and-Contrast Essay

When you organize a comparison-and-contrast essay, you can choose either a *point-by-point* or a *subject-by-subject* arrangement. A **point-by-point** comparison alternates between the two subjects you are comparing or contrasting, moving back and forth from one subject to the other. A **subject-by-subject** comparison treats its two subjects separately, first fully discussing one subject and then moving on to consider the other subject. In both kinds of comparison-and-contrast essays, the same points are discussed in the same order for both subjects.

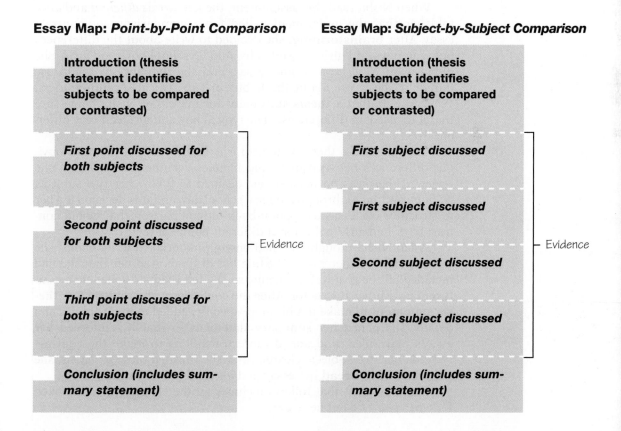

Essay Map: *Point-by-Point Comparison*

- **Introduction (thesis statement identifies subjects to be compared or contrasted)**
- **First point discussed for both subjects**
- **Second point discussed for both subjects** ⎤ Evidence
- **Third point discussed for both subjects**
- **Conclusion (includes summary statement)**

Essay Map: *Subject-by-Subject Comparison*

- **Introduction (thesis statement identifies subjects to be compared or contrasted)**
- **First subject discussed**
- **First subject discussed**
- **Second subject discussed** ⎤ Evidence
- **Second subject discussed**
- **Conclusion (includes summary statement)**

Transitions in Comparison-and-Contrast Essays

For a list of transitions frequently used in comparison and contrast, see page 120.

The transitional words and phrases you use in a comparison-and-contrast essay tell readers whether you are focusing on similarities or on differences. Transitions also help move readers through your essay from one subject to the other and from one point of comparison or contrast to the next.

Case Study: A Student Writes a Comparison-and-Contrast Essay

Nisha Jani, a student in a first-year writing course, was given the following assignment:

> Some people claim that males and females are so different that at times they seem to belong to two different species. Do you agree, or do you think males and females are more alike than different? Write an essay that supports your position.

When Nisha read this assignment, the key words *different* and *alike* told her that the assignment called for a comparison-and-contrast essay. After **brainstorming**, she decided to write about the differences between boys and girls—specifically, middle school boys and girls. She didn't want to write a serious essay, and she thought she could use humor if she wrote about the habits of two typical seventh-graders. When she drafted a **thesis statement** for her essay, Nisha made sure that it focused on differences: "The typical boy and girl lead very different lives."

Once she had a thesis statement, she **listed** some of the most obvious differences between male and female seventh-graders. When she reviewed the ideas on her list, she decided to follow her two subjects (Johnny and Jane) through a typical school day, and this decision led her to structure her essay as a point-by-point comparison that would contrast boys' and girls' behavior at different points of their day.

When Nisha thought she had enough material to write about, she **wrote a draft** of her essay. TESTing her draft showed her that she had included all the required elements, so she felt ready to schedule a **conference** with her instructor. After the conference, she **revised her thesis statement** to make it a bit more specific, added more examples and details, sharpened her summary statement so that it reinforced her essay's main idea, and added more transitions to make the contrast between her two subjects clearer. After she finished these revisions, she **edited** and **proofread** her essay and checked her **format**.

The final draft that follows includes all the elements Nisha looked for when she TESTed her essay.

Model Comparison-and-Contrast Essay

Read Nisha's finished essay, and answer the questions in Practice 15-5.

T E S T

☐ Thesis Statement
☐ Evidence
☐ Summary Statement
☐ Transitions

Another Ordinary Day

1   "Boys are from Jupiter and get stupider / Girls are from Mars and become movie stars / Boys take a bath and smell like trash / Girls take a shower and smell like a flower." As simple playground songs like this one suggest, the two sexes are very different. As adults, men and women have similar goals, values, and occupations, but as children and teenagers, boys and girls often seem to belong to two different species. In fact, from the first moment of the day to the last, the typical boy and girl live very different lives.

Introduction

2   The sun rises, and the smartphone alarm signals the beginning of another day for Johnny and Jane, two seventh-grade classmates. Johnny, an average thirteen-year-old boy, wakes up late and has to hurry. He throws on jeans or joggers, a hoodie, and a snapback hat. Then, he has a hearty high-cholesterol breakfast and runs out of the house to school, usually forgetting some vital book or homework assignment. Jane, unlike Johnny, wakes up early and takes her time. She takes a long shower and then blow-dries her hair. For Jane, getting dressed can be a very difficult process, one that often includes taking everything out of her closet and calling friends for advice. After she makes her decision, she helps herself to some food (probably low- or no-fat) and goes off to school, making sure she has with her everything she needs.

Topic sentence (identifies first difference)

Examples and details

3   School is a totally different experience for Johnny and Jane. Johnny will probably sit in the back of the classroom with a couple of other guys, throwing paper airplanes and spitballs. These will be directed at the males they do not like and the females they think are kind of cute. (However, if their male friends ever ask the boys about these girls, they will say girls are just losers and deny that they like any of them.) On the opposite side of the classroom, however, Jane is focused on a very different kind of activity. At first, it looks as if she is carefully copying the algebra notes that the teacher is putting on the board, but instead, she is writing a note to her BFF about topics that are much more important to her than the square root of one hundred twenty-one. She proceeds to fold the note into a box or other creative shape, which can often put origami to shame. As soon as the teacher turns her back, the note is passed and the process begins all over again.

Body paragraphs

Topic sentence (identifies second difference)

Examples and details

WORD POWER

origami the Japanese art of folding paper into shapes representing flowers or animals

Topic sentence (identifies third difference)

Examples and details

Body paragraphs

Topic sentence (identifies fourth difference)

Examples and details

　　Lunch, a vital part of the school day, is also very different for Johnny   4
and Jane. On the one hand, for Johnny and his friends, it is a time to
compare baseball cards, exchange sports facts, and of course tell jokes about
every bodily function imaginable. In front of them on the table, their trays
are filled with pizza, soda, fries, chips, and items from the vending machines,
and this food is their main focus. For Jane, on the other hand, lunch is not
about eating; it is a chance to exchange the latest gossip about who is
going out with whom. The girls look around to see what people are wearing,
what they should do with their hair, and so on. Jane's meal is quite a bit
smaller than Johnny's: it consists of a small low-fat yogurt and half a bagel
(if she feels like splurging, she will spread some cream cheese on the bagel).

　　After school, Johnny and Jane head in different directions. Johnny   5
rushes home to meet up with his friends. Sometimes they play video games;
at other times, they might play pick-up basketball or touch football.
Johnny and his friends play with every boy who shows up, whether they
know him or not. They may get into physical fights and arguments, but they
always plan to meet up again the next day. In contrast to the boys, Jane
and her friends are very selective. Their circle is a small one, and they do
everything together. Occasionally, they might go shopping (they will not
necessarily buy anything, but they will consider the outing productive
anyway because they will have spent time together). Most days, though,
they spend their time, alone or together, on their phones, texting, Snapchat-
ting, or posting on their favorite social media sites.

Conclusion

　　At the age of twelve or thirteen, boys and girls do not seem to have   6
very much in common. Given this situation, it is amazing that boys and girls
grow up to become men and women who interact as neighbors, friends, and
coworkers. What is even more amazing is that so many grow up to share
lives and raise families together, treating each other with love and respect.

PRACTICE
15-5

1. Restate Nisha's thesis statement in your own words.

2. Does Nisha's opening paragraph identify the subjects she
will discuss? Does it tell whether she will focus on similarities or on
differences?

3. Nisha's essay is a point-by-point comparison. What four points does
she discuss for each of her two subjects (Johnny and Jane)?

4. Review the topic sentences in Nisha's body paragraphs. What part
of the day does each topic sentence identify?

5. Review the transitional words and phrases Nisha uses to move readers from one subject (Johnny) to the other (Jane). Do you think these transitions are effective, or should they be revised to make the contrast clearer?

6. What is this essay's greatest strength? What is its greatest weakness?

grammar in context

Comparison and Contrast

When you write a comparison-and-contrast essay, be sure to present the points you are comparing or contrasting in **parallel** terms to highlight their similarities or differences.

┌──PARALLEL──┐

Johnny, an average thirteen-year-old boy, wakes up late and has

to hurry.

┌────PARALLEL────┐

Jane, unlike Johnny, wakes up early and takes her time.

For information on revising to make ideas parallel, see Chapter 21.

Step-by-Step Guide: Writing a Comparison-and-Contrast Essay

Now, you are ready to write a comparison-and-contrast essay on one of the topics listed below (or a topic of your choice).

TOPICS

Two coworkers
Two movie heroes or heroines
How you expect your life to be different from the lives of your parents
Men's and women's ideas about their body images
Two ways of studying for an exam
Risk-takers and people who play it safe
Country and city living (or, compare suburban living with either)
Two popular magazines (features, ads, target audiences, pictures) or
    websites
Leaders and followers
Designer products and counterfeit products
Optimists and pessimists

As you write your essay, follow these steps:

Plan

Organize

Draft

TEST

Revise, edit,
and proofread

- Make sure your topic calls for comparison and contrast, and then find ideas to write about; next, decide whether you want to discuss similarities, differences, or both, identify your main idea, and write a thesis statement.
- Identify specific points of comparison or contrast to support your thesis, and decide whether to structure your essay as a point-by-point or subject-by-subject comparison; then, arrange your points in a logical order, making an outline if necessary.
- Draft your essay.
- **TEST** your essay, referring to the **TEST**ing a Comparison-and-Contrast Essay checklist below.
- Revise and edit your essay, referring to the two Self-Assessment Checklists in Chapter 13.
- Proofread your essay, and make sure it follows your instructor's format.

TESTing a comparison-and-contrast essay

T hesis Statement Unifies Your Essay

☐ Does your introduction include a **thesis statement** that expresses your main idea, identifying the two subjects you will compare and indicating whether your essay will examine similarities or differences?

E vidence Supports Your Essay's Thesis Statement

☐ Do you discuss all significant points of comparison or contrast that apply to your two subjects, explaining each similarity or difference using specific examples and details?

☐ Does all your **evidence**—examples and details—support your thesis, or should some be deleted?

☐ Have you treated similar points for both of your subjects?

☐ Is your essay's organization consistent with either a point-by-point comparison or a subject-by-subject comparison?

S ummary Statement Reinforces Your Essay's Main Idea

☐ Does your conclusion include a **summary statement** that reinforces your essay's thesis, reminding readers what your two subjects are and how they are alike or different?

┌───┐
│ **T** ransitions   │
│   │
│ ☐ Do you include **transitions** that introduce each of your points │
│   of comparison or contrast and move readers from one subject │
│   or point to another?   │
└───┘

Comparison and Contrast in Action

In "Migrant vs. Refugee: What's the Difference?" Michael Martinez uses **comparsion and contrast** to structure his essay.

MIGRANT VS. REFUGEE: WHAT'S THE DIFFERENCE?

Michael Martinez

Michael Martinez has worked as a journalist in both print and online media. He was a reporter and war correspondent for the *Chicago Tribune* and is currently a newsdesk writer, editor, and media producer for CNN, where "Migrant vs. Refugee: What's the Difference?" first appeared in 2015. In this piece, Martinez attempts to distinguish the terms *migrant* and *refugee*, two words frequently used interchangeably by the media, resulting in confusion. As you read, ask yourself why the difference between these two similar words matters.

1 The difference between a migrant and a refugee marks a crucial distinction for European countries receiving new arrivals.

2 Refugees, as defined under the 1951 Refugee Convention, are entitled to basic rights under international law, including the right not to be immediately deported and sent back into harm's way.

3 "The practice of granting asylum to people fleeing persecution in foreign lands is one of the earliest hallmarks of civilization," according to the U.N. High Commissioner for Refugees. "References to it have been found in texts written 3,500 years ago, during the blossoming of the great early empires in the Middle East such as the Hittites, Babylonians, Assyrians and ancient Egyptians."

4 A refugee is someone who has been forced to flee his or her home country because of armed conflict or persecution. Syrians are a prime example.

5 The U.N.'s definition of refugee is someone who, "owing to a well-founded fear of being persecuted for reasons of race, religion, nationality, membership of a particular social group or political opinion, is outside the country of his nationality, and is unable to, or owing to such fear, is unwilling to avail himself of the protection of that country."

Migrants, however, are processed under the receiving country's im- 6
migration laws. So, ultimately, these terms have major implications for
those seeking asylum and the countries being asked to grant it.

A migrant is someone who chooses to resettle to another country in 7
search of a better life.

For example, those fleeing poverty in Nigeria, looking for work 8
in Europe, would not have refugee status and would be considered
migrants.

Not all migrants then are refugees, but refugees can fall under the 9
migrant umbrella. One of the major differences between the two des-
ignations is that while migrants may seek to escape harsh conditions
of their own, refugees could face imprisonment, deprivation of basic
rights, physical injury or worse.

"Refugees have to move if they are to save their lives or preserve 10
their freedom. They have no protection from their own state—indeed it
is often their own government that is threatening to persecute them. If
other countries do not let them in and do not help them once they are in,
then they may be condemning them to death—or to an intolerable life
in the shadows, without sustenance and without rights," the U.N. says.

So which term should you use?   11

The United Nations notes that both groups are present in Europe 12
and at its shores. It's safe to call all of them migrants because each
is migrating, but many of them—especially those fleeing Afghanistan,
Eritrea, Syria and Iraq—are also refugees.

Focus on the Pattern

1. Make an informal outline of this essay.

2. Is this essay a point-by-point or a subject-by-subject comparison?
   How can you tell? Is this structure the best choice for this topic?
   Why or why not?

3. Why is the distinction between Martinez's two subjects (*migrant* and
   refugee) important?

Writing Practice

1. Write an essay comparing two of the following terms: *undocumented
   immigrants, unauthorized immigrants, illegal aliens*.

2. Write a comparison-and-contrast essay focusing on two people you
   know who are immigrants to the United States. How are their personal stories alike and different?

review checklist

Patterns of Essay Development: Exemplification, Narration, Process, Cause and Effect, and Comparison and Contrast

- [ ] **Exemplification** essays use specific examples to support a thesis. (See 15a.)

- [ ] **Narrative** essays tell a story by presenting a series of events in chronological order. (See 15b.)

- [ ] **Process** essays explain the steps in a procedure, telling how something is (or was) done or how to do something. (See 15c.)

- [ ] **Cause-and-effect essays** identify causes or predict effects. (See 15d.)

- [ ] **Comparison-and-contrast** essays explain how two things are alike or how they are different. (See 15e.)

16 Patterns of Essay Development

Description, Classification, Definition, and Argument

In this chapter, you will learn to organize your essays according to the following patterns of development:

- description (16a)
- classification (16b)
- definition (16c)
- argument (16d)

16a Descriptive Essays

Description tells what something looks, sounds, smells, tastes, or feels like. A **descriptive essay** uses details to give readers a clear, vivid picture of a person, place, or object.

When you describe a person, place, object, or scene, you can use **objective description**, reporting only what your senses of sight, sound, smell, taste, and touch tell you ("The columns were two feet tall and made of white marble"). You can also use **subjective description**, conveying your attitude or your feelings about what you observe ("The columns were tall and powerful looking, and their marble surface seemed as smooth as ice"). Many essays combine these two kinds of description.

FYI

Figures of Speech

Descriptive writing, particularly subjective description, is frequently enriched by **figures of speech**—language that creates special or unusual effects.

- A **simile** uses *like* or *as* to compare two unlike things.

  Her smile was like sunshine.

- A **metaphor** compares two unlike things without using *like* or *as*.

  Her smile was a light that lit up the room.

- **Personification** suggests a comparison between a nonliving thing and a person by giving the nonliving thing human traits.

  The sun smiled down on the crowd.

277

When you **TEST** a **descriptive** essay, make sure it includes all these elements:

T ■ **Thesis Statement**—A descriptive essay should include a **thesis statement** that expresses the essay's main idea.

E ■ **Evidence**—The body paragraphs should include **evidence**, descriptive details that support the thesis. Details are arranged in spatial order—for example, from far to near or from top to bottom.

S ■ **Summary Statement**—The conclusion of a descriptive essay should include a **summary statement** that reinforces the essay's thesis.

T ■ **Transitions**—A descriptive essay should include **transitional words and phrases** that connect details and show how they are related.

Moving from Assignment to Thesis

The wording of your assignment may suggest that you write a descriptive essay. For example, it may ask you to *describe* or to *tell what an object looks like*. Once you decide that your assignment calls for description, you need to develop a thesis statement that reflects this purpose.

ASSIGNMENT	THESIS STATEMENT
Composition Describe a room that was important to you when you were a child.	Pink-and-white striped wallpaper, tall shelves of cuddly stuffed animals, and the smell of Oreos dominated the bedroom I shared with my sister.
Scientific writing Describe a piece of scientific equipment.	The mass spectrometer is a complex instrument, but every part is ideally suited to its function.
Art history Choose one modern painting and describe its visual elements.	The disturbing images crowded together in Pablo Picasso's *Guernica* suggest the brutality of war.

Organizing a Descriptive Essay

When you plan a descriptive essay, you focus on selecting details that help your readers see what you see, feel what you feel, and experience what you experience. Your goal is to create a single **dominant impression**, a central theme or idea to which all the details relate—for example, the liveliness of a street scene or the quiet of a summer night. This dominant impression unifies the description and gives readers an overall sense of what the person, place, object, or scene looks like (and perhaps what it sounds, smells, tastes, or feels like).

You can arrange details in a descriptive essay in many different ways. For example, you can move from least to most important details, from top to bottom (or from bottom to top or side to side), or from far to near (or near to far). Each of your essay's body paragraphs may focus on one key characteristic of the subject you are describing or on several related descriptive details.

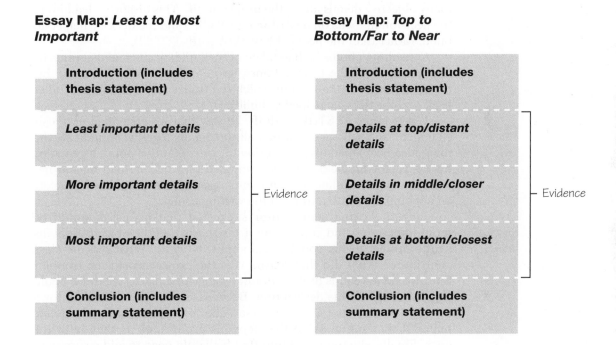

Essay Map: *Least to Most Important*

- Introduction (includes thesis statement)
- *Least important details*
- *More important details* — Evidence
- *Most important details*
- Conclusion (includes summary statement)

Essay Map: *Top to Bottom/Far to Near*

- Introduction (includes thesis statement)
- *Details at top/distant details*
- *Details in middle/closer details* — Evidence
- *Details at bottom/closest details*
- Conclusion (includes summary statement)

Transitions in Descriptive Essays

As you write, use transitional words and expressions to connect details and show how they work together to create a full picture for readers. (Many of these useful transitions indicate location or distance.)

For a list of transitions frequently used in exemplification, see page 132.

Case Study: A Student Writes a Descriptive Essay

All the students in James Greggs's first-year composition course were also enrolled in sociology, psychology, or education courses with service-learning requirements that reinforced course content. For this reason, James's composition instructor asked that the students' descriptive essays focus on a person, setting, or item related to their service-learning experiences.

Although James was enjoying his service-learning project—building a deck for elderly residents of a trailer home—he had trouble deciding which aspect of this project to write about. At first, he thought he might describe his team supervisor or one of the other students he worked with, but when he **brainstormed** to find details to include in his essay, he found he had a hard time being objective about his coworkers. However, when he reread entries in the **journal** that he was required to keep for the service-learning component of his sociology class, he found many objective details about the project itself. This discovery led him to the decision to focus on describing the trailer, and the deck he helped to build, rather than the people he worked with.

Consulting photos he had taken of the building site and diagrams he had prepared of the trailer, James wrote a **first draft**, arranging his material from far (the field in which the trailer sat) to near (the trailer itself and the deck he helped to build).

When James **TEST**ed his draft, he saw that his essay had no thesis statement—no sentence that tied all the details together to indicate the main idea he wanted his description to convey. At this point, he emailed his instructor for help, but she reminded him that he had missed her deadline for scheduling appointments and recommended that he make an appointment with a tutor in the writing center.

James's writing center tutor suggested that his essay would be more interesting and convincing if his thesis tied the objective details of the project to his conclusions about its value. What did his class contribute? What did they learn? Was the project worth the trouble? She also reviewed his draft with him, suggesting places where he could expand or clarify his description. Because his assignment called for a descriptive essay, not a process essay, she recommended that he delete material that summarized the steps his group took as they built the deck. Finally, she reminded him that he would need to add a summary statement to reinforce his thesis.

When James **revised** his draft, he incorporated his tutor's suggestions and added both a thesis statement and a summary statement. He also added transitional words and phrases to move readers through his description, added more detail, and deleted irrelevant material. Then, he **edited** and **proofread** his essay and checked his **format**.

The following final draft includes all the elements James looked for when he **TEST**ed his essay.

Model Descriptive Essay

Read James's finished essay, and answer the questions in Practice 16-1.

Building and Learning

1   Throughout the United States, houses reflect not only the lives of the people who live in them but also the diversity of the American population. Some are large and elaborate, others are modest but well maintained, and still others are in need of repair. Unfortunately, most college students know little about homes other than those in their own neighborhood. I too was fairly sheltered until I participated in a service-learning project for my sociology class. For this project, I, along with some classmates, added a deck to a trailer that was the home of three elderly sisters living on Social Security and disability. It was hard work, but my experience convinced me that all college students should be required to do some kind of service-learning project.

2   The trailer we worked on was located at the end of a small dirt road about thirty minutes from campus. Patches of green and brown grass dotted the land around the trailer, and in the far right-hand corner of the property stood three tall poplar trees. Although the bushes in front of the trailer were trimmed, the woods behind the trailer were beginning to overrun the property. (We were told that members of a local church came once a month to trim the hedges and cut back the trees.) Dominating the right front corner of the lawn, a circular concrete basin looked like a large birdbath. The basin housed a white well pipe with a rusted blue cap. About thirty feet to the left of the concrete basin stood a telephone pole and a bright red metal mailbox.

3   Like the property on which it stood, the trailer was well maintained. It was approximately thirty-five feet long and seven feet high; it rested on cinderblocks, which raised it about three feet off the ground. Under the trailer was an overturned white plastic chair. The trailer itself was covered with sheets of white vinyl siding that ran horizontally, except for the bottom panels on the right side, which ran vertically. The vinyl panels closest to the roof were slightly discolored by dirt and green moss.

4   At the left end of the trailer was a small window—about two feet wide and one foot high. Next to the window was a dark red aluminum door that was outlined in green trim. It had one window at eye level divided by metal strips into four small sections. The number "24" in white plastic letters was glued to the door below this window. To the right of the door was a lightbulb in a black ceramic socket. Next to the light was a large window that was actually two vertical rows of three windows—each the same size as the small window on the left. Further to the right were two smaller windows. Each of these small windows tilted upward and was

TEST

Thesis Statement
Evidence
Summary Statement
Transitions

Introduction

Topic sentence (introduces first group of details)

Descriptive details

Topic sentence (introduces second group of details)

Body paragraphs

Descriptive details

Topic sentence (introduces third group of details)

Descriptive details

framed with silver metal strips. On either side of each of these windows was a pair of green metal shutters.

Topic sentence (introduces fourth group of details)

Descriptive details

The deck we built replaced three wooden steps that had led up to the 5 trailer. A white metal handrail stood on the right side of these steps. It had been newly painted and was connected to the body of the trailer by a heart-shaped piece of metal. In front of the steps, two worn gray wooden boards led to the road.

Topic sentence (introduces fifth group of details)

Descriptive details

Building the deck was hard work, but the finished deck provided a much 6 better entranceway than the steps did and also gave the trailer a new look. The deck was not very large—ten feet by eight feet—but it extended from the doorway to the area underneath the windows immediately to the right of the door. We built the deck out of pressure-treated lumber so that it wouldn't rot or need painting. We also built three steps that led from the deck to the lawn, and we surrounded the deck with a wooden railing that ran down the right side of the steps. After we finished, we bought two white plastic chairs at a local thrift store and put them on the deck.

Conclusion

Now that I look back at the project, I believe that activities like this 7 should be part of every student's college education. Both the residents of the trailer and our class benefited from the service-learning project. The residents of the trailer were happy with the deck because it gave them a place to sit when the weather was nice. They also liked their trailer's new look. Those of us who worked on the project learned that a few days' work could make a real difference in other people's lives.

PRACTICE
16-1

1. Paraphrase James's thesis statement.

2. What determines the order in which James arranges the elements of his description?

3. What details does James provide to describe the property, the trailer, and the deck?

4. What kinds of signals do James's transitions give readers? Do you think he includes enough transitions? Where could he add more?

5. This essay is primarily an objective description. Does it include any subjective details? If so, where?

6. What is this essay's greatest strength? What is its greatest weakness?

grammar in context

Description

When you write a descriptive essay, you may use **modifiers**—words and phrases that describe other words in the sentence—to create a picture of your subject. If you place a modifying word or phrase too far from the word it is supposed to describe, you create a potentially confusing **misplaced modifier**.

> **CONFUSING**   Next to the window outlined in green trim was a dark red aluminum door. (Was the window outlined in green trim?)

> **CLEAR**   Next to the window was a dark red aluminum door outlined in green trim.

For information on how to identify and correct misplaced modifiers, see Chapter 27.

Step-by-Step Guide: Writing a Descriptive Essay

Now, you are ready to write a descriptive essay on one of the topics listed below (or a topic of your choice).

TOPICS

An abandoned building
A person or a fictional character who makes you laugh (or frightens you)
Your room (or your closet or desk)
A family photograph

A historical site or monument
An advertisement
An object you cherish
Someone whom everyone notices
Someone whom no one notices
The home page of a website you visit often

As you write your essay, follow these steps:

- Make sure your topic calls for description, and then find ideas to write about; next, decide what dominant impression you want to convey, and write a thesis statement that identifies your main idea.

- Choose details that help to convey your dominant impression; and arrange your details in an effective order, making an outline if necessary.

- Draft your essay.

Plan

Organize

Draft

TEST

Revise, edit,
and proofread

- **TEST** your essay, referring to the **TEST**ing a Descriptive Essay check-list below.
- Revise and edit your essay, referring to the two Self-Assessment Checklists in Chapter 13.
- Proofread your essay, and make sure it follows your instructor's format.

TESTing a descriptive essay

T hesis Statement Unifies Your Essay

- ☐ Does your introduction include a **thesis statement** that communicates your essay's main idea?
- ☐ Does your introduction identify the subject of your description?

E vidence Supports Your Essay's Thesis Statement

- ☐ Does all your **evidence**—your descriptive details—support the dominant impression communicated by your thesis, or should some details be deleted?
- ☐ Do you describe your subject in enough detail, or do you need to add details to create a more vivid picture?
- ☐ Are your supporting details arranged in an effective order within your essay and within paragraphs?

S ummary Statement Reinforces Your Essay's Main Idea

- ☐ Does your conclusion include a **summary statement** that reinforces your essay's thesis?

T ransitions

- ☐ Do you include **transitions** that introduce your details and move readers smoothly from one aspect of your subject to another?

Description in Action

In "The Barrio," Robert Ramirez uses **description** to structure his essay.

THE BARRIO

Robert Ramirez

Robert Ramirez was born and raised in Texas, where he attended Pan American College before he taught English there. He has also done work in photography, reporting, and television news announcing. "The Barrio" describes his community in vivid sensory detail. As you read, think about where you grew up. What details would you use to describe that place?

The train, its metal wheels squealing as they spin along the silvery tracks, 1 rolls slower now. Through the gaps between the cars blinks a streetlamp, and this pulsing light on a barrio streetcorner beats slower, like a weary heartbeat, until the train shudders to a halt, the light goes out, and the barrio is deep asleep.

Throughout Aztlán (the Nahuatl term meaning "land to the north"), 2 trains grumble along the edges of a sleeping people. From Lower California, through the blistering Southwest, down the Rio Grande to the muddy Gulf, the darkness and mystery of dreams engulf communities fenced off by railroads, canals, and expressways. Paradoxical communities, isolated from the rest of the town by concrete columned monuments of progress, and yet stranded in the past. They are surrounded by change. It eludes their reach, in their own backyards, and the people, unable and unwilling to see the future, or even touch the present, perpetuate the past.

Leaning from the expressway or jolting across the tracks, one enters 3 a different physical world permeated by a different attitude. The physical dimensions are impressive. It is a large section of town which extends for fifteen blocks north and south along the tracks, and then advances eastward, thinning into nothingness beyond the city limits. Within the invisible (yet sensible) walls of the barrio, are many, many people living in too few houses. The homes, however, are much more numerous than on the outside.

Members of the barrio describe the entire area as their home. It is a 4 home, but it is more than this. The barrio is a refuge from the harshness and the coldness of the Anglo world. It is a forced refuge. The leprous people are isolated from the rest of the community and contained in their section of town. The stoical pariahs of the barrio accept their fate, and from the angry seeds of rejection grow the flowers of closeness between outcasts, not the thorns of bitterness and the mad desire to flee. There is no want to escape, for the feeling of the barrio is known only to its inhabitants, and the material needs of life can also be found here.

The *tortillería* fires up its machinery three times a day, producing 5 steaming, round, flat slices of barrio bread. In the winter, the warmth of

WORD POWER

tortillería tortilla bake shop

the tortilla factory is a wool *sarape* in the chilly morning hours, but in the summer, it unbearably toasts every noontime customer.

The *panadería* sends its sweet messenger aroma down the dimly lit 6
street, announcing the arrival of fresh, hot sugary *pan dulce*.

The small corner grocery serves the meal-to-meal needs of custom- 7
ers, and the owner, a part of the neighborhood, willingly gives credit to people unable to pay cash for foodstuffs.

The barbershop is a living room with hydraulic chairs, radio, and 8
television, where old friends meet and speak of life as their salted hair falls aimlessly about them.

The pool hall is a junior level country club where *chucos*, strangers 9
in their own land, get together to shoot pool and rap, while veterans, unaware of the cracking, popping balls on the green felt, complacently play dominoes beneath rudely hung *Playboy* foldouts.

The *cantina* is the night spot of the barrio. It is the country club and 10
the den where the rites of puberty are enacted. Here the young become men. It is in the taverns that a young dude shows his *machismo* through the quantity of beer he can hold, the stories of *rucas* he has had, and his willingness and ability to defend his image against hardened and scarred old lions.

No, there is no frantic wish to flee. It would be absurd to leave the 11
familiar and nervously step into the strange and cold Anglo community when the needs of the Chicano can be met in the barrio.

The barrio is closeness. From the family living unit, familial rela- 12
tionships stretch out to immediate neighbors, down the block, around the corner, and to all parts of the barrio. The feeling of family, a rare and treasurable sentiment, pervades and accounts for the inability of the people to leave. The barrio is this attitude manifested on the countenances of the people, on the faces of their homes, and in the gaiety of their gardens.

The color-splashed homes arrest your eyes, arouse your curiosity, 13
and make you wonder what life scenes are being played out in them. The flimsy, brightly colored, wood-frame houses ignore no neon-brilliant color. Houses trimmed in orange, chartreuse, lime-green, yellow, and mixtures of these and other hues beckon the beholder to reflect on the peculiarity of each home. Passing through this land is refreshing like Brubeck, not narcoticizing like revolting rows of similar houses, which neither offend nor please.

In the evenings, the porches and front yards are occupied with men 14
calmly talking over the noise of children playing baseball in the unpaved extension of the living room, while the women cook supper or gossip with female neighbors as they water the *jardines*. The gardens mutely echo the expressive verses of the colorful houses. The denseness of multicolored plants and trees gives the house the appearance of an oasis or a tropical island hideaway, sheltered from the rest of the world.

Fences are common in the barrio, but they are fences and not the 15
walls of the Anglo community. On the western side of town, the high
wooden fences between houses are thick, impenetrable walls, built to
keep the neighbors at bay. In the barrio, the fences may be rusty, wire
contraptions or thick green shrubs. In either case you can see through
them and feel no sense of intrusion when you cross them.

Many lower-income families of the barrio manage to maintain a 16
comfortable standard of living through the communal action of family
members who contribute their wages to the head of the family. Economic
need creates interdependence and closeness. Small barefooted boys sell
papers on cool, dark Sunday mornings, deny themselves pleasantries,
and give their earnings to *mamá*. The older the child, the greater the
responsibility to help the head of the household provide for the rest of
the family.

There are those, too, who for a number of reasons have not achieved 17
a relative sense of financial security. Perhaps it results from too many
children too soon, but it is the homes of these people and their situation
that numbs rather than charms. Their houses, aged and bent, oozing
children, are fissures in the horn of plenty. Their wooden homes may
have brick-pattern asbestos tile on the outer walls, but the tile is not
convincing.

Unable to pay city taxes or incapable in influencing the city to live 18
up to its duty to serve all the citizens, the poorer barrio families remain
trapped in the nineteenth century and survive as best they can. The
backyards have well-worn paths to the outhouses, which sit near the
alley. Running water is considered a luxury in some parts of the barrio.
Decent drainage is usually unknown, and when it rains, the water stands
for days, an incubator of health hazards and an avoidable nuisance.
Streets, costly to pave, remain rough, rocky trails. Tires do not last long,
and the constant rattling and shaking grind away a car's life and spread
dust through screen windows.

The houses and their *jardines*, the jollity of the people in an ad- 19
verse world, the brightly feathered alarm clock pecking away at supper
and cautiously eyeing the children playing nearby, produce a mystifying
sensation at finding the noble savage alive in the twentieth century. It
is easy to look at the positive qualities of life in the barrio, and look at
them with a distantly envious feeling. One wishes to experience the feelings of the barrio and not the hardships. Remembering the illness, the
hunger, the feeling of time running out on you, the walls, both real and
imagined, reflecting on living in the past, one finds his envy becoming
more elusive, until it has vanished altogether.

Back now beyond the tracks, the train creaks and groans, the cars 20
jostle each other down the track, and as the light begins its pulsing, the
barrio, with all its meanings, greets a new dawn with yawns and restless
stretchings.

Focus on the Pattern

1. What specific features of the barrio does Ramirez identify in his description?
2. What dominant impression of the barrio do Ramirez's details help to convey?
3. Is this a subjective or an objective description? How can you tell?

Writing Practice

1. Write a descriptive essay (subjective or objective) about the neighborhood or community in which you grew up (or the one you live in now).
2. Write a subjective description of your childhood bedroom.

16b Classification Essays

Classification is the act of sorting items into appropriate categories. **Classification essays** divide a whole (your subject) into parts and sort various items into categories.

When you TEST a **classification** essay, make sure it includes all these elements:

T ■ **Thesis Statement**—The introduction of a classification essay should include a **thesis statement** that communicates the essay's main idea and indicates what the essay will classify.

E ■ **Evidence**—The body paragraphs should provide **evidence**—examples and details—to support the thesis statement. The topic sentence of each paragraph should identify the category it will discuss, and the examples and details should explain the category and differentiate it from other categories.

S ■ **Summary Statement**—The conclusion of a classification essay should include a **summary statement** that reinforces the essay's thesis.

T ■ **Transitions**—A classification essay should include **transitional words and phrases** to show how categories are related to one another and to the thesis.

Moving from Assignment to Thesis

The wording of your assignment may suggest that you write a classification essay. For example, you may be asked to consider *kinds*, *types*, *categories*, *components*, *segments*, or *parts of a whole*. Once you decide that your assignment calls for classification, you need to develop a thesis statement that reflects this purpose.

ASSIGNMENT	THESIS STATEMENT
Business What kinds of courses are most useful for students planning to run their own businesses?	Courses dealing with accounting, management, and entrepreneurship offer the most useful skills for future business owners.
Biology List the components of blood and explain the function of each.	Red blood cells, white blood cells, platelets, and plasma have distinct functions.
Education Classify elementary school children according to their academic needs.	The elementary school population includes special-needs students, students with reading and math skills at or near grade level, and academically gifted students.

Organizing a Classification Essay

As a rule, each paragraph of a classification essay examines a separate category—a different part of the whole. For example, a paragraph could focus on one kind of course in the college curriculum, one component of the blood, or one type of child. Within each paragraph, you discuss the individual items that you have put into a particular category—for example, accounting courses, red blood cells, or gifted students. If you consider some categories less important than others, you may decide to discuss those minor categories together in a single paragraph, devoting full paragraphs only to the most significant categories.

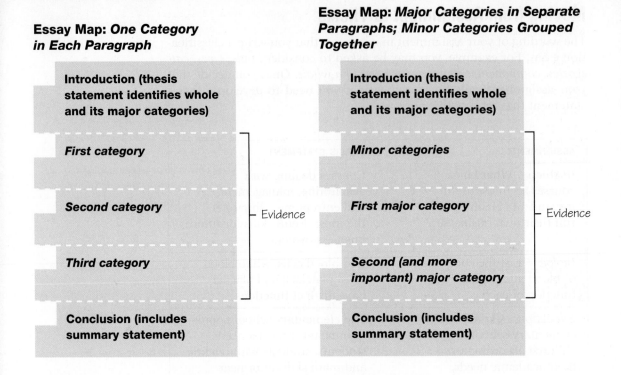

Essay Map: *One Category in Each Paragraph*

Introduction (thesis statement identifies whole and its major categories)

First category

Second category

Third category

Conclusion (includes summary statement)

— Evidence

Essay Map: *Major Categories in Separate Paragraphs; Minor Categories Grouped Together*

Introduction (thesis statement identifies whole and its major categories)

Minor categories

First major category

Second (and more important) major category

Conclusion (includes summary statement)

— Evidence

Transitions in Classification Essays

WORD POWER

For a list of transitions frequently used in classification, see page 142.

In a classification essay, topic sentences identify the category or categories discussed in each paragraph. Transitional words and phrases signal movement from one category to the next and may also tell readers which categories you consider more (or less) important.

Case Study: A Student Writes a Classification Essay

Rob O'Neal, a student in a first-year writing course, was given the following assignment.

> Write a classification essay focusing on a type of consumer product—for example, smartphones, jeans, mountain bikes, or hair gels. Discuss three or four categories of the product you select, examining the same features for each category.

At first, Rob was overwhelmed by the possibilities; after all, he was a consumer, and there were many products to choose from. Stuck in traffic on his way home from school, he started noticing the names of the different cars around him and thinking about all the different models he had learned to identify when he was younger and fascinated by everything related to cars. At this point, he realized that he could write his essay about cars, classifying them on the basis of the kinds of names they had.

When Rob got home, he **brainstormed**, listing all the car names he could think of. Then, he made a **cluster diagram** to help him sort all the names into categories. When he looked over his diagram, he saw that he could organize the car names he had listed into three categories—those that suggest exciting destinations, those that suggest toughness, and those that suggest exploration and discovery. Identifying these three categories led him to a **thesis statement** for his essay: "The names auto manufacturers choose for their cars appeal to Americans' deepest desires."

When he **drafted** his essay, Rob developed each branch of his cluster diagram into one of his body paragraphs and wrote topic sentences that clearly identified and defined each category. When he **TEST**ed his essay, he saw that it included all the required elements, but he still wasn't completely satisfied with his draft. To help him plan his revision, he made a **writing center appointment** and went over his draft with a tutor. She advised him to add more examples of each kind of car name as well as more transitional words and phrases to help readers move smoothly through his essay. When he finished making the revisions suggested by his writing center tutor (as well as some he decided on himself), he went on to **edit** and **proofread** his essay and check his **format**.

The final draft that follows includes all the elements Rob looked for when he **TEST**ed his essay.

Model Classification Essay

Read Rob's finished essay, and answer the questions in Practice 16-2.

Selling a Dream

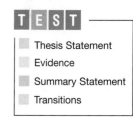

1   The earliest automobiles were often named after the men who manufactured them—Ford, Studebaker, Nash, Olds, Chrysler, Dodge, Chevrolet, and so on. Over the years, however, American car makers began competing to see what kinds of names would sell the most cars. Many car names seem to have been chosen simply for how they sound: Alero, Corvette, Neon, Probe, Caprice. Many others, however, are designed to sell specific dreams to consumers. Americans always seem to want to be, do, and become something different. They want to be tough and brave, to explore new places, to take risks. The names auto manufacturers choose for their cars appeal to Americans' deepest desires.

Introduction

2   Some American cars are named for places people dream of traveling to. Park Avenue, Malibu, Riviera, Seville, Tahoe, Yukon, Aspen, and Durango are some names that suggest escape—to New York City, California, Europe, the West. Other place names—Sebring, Daytona, and Bonneville, for example—are associated with the danger and excitement of car racing. And then there is the El Dorado, a car named for a fictional paradise: a city of gold.

Topic sentence (identifies first category)

Examples and details

Topic sentence
(identifies second
category)

Examples and details

Body paragraphs

Topic sentence
(identifies third
category)

Examples and details

Conclusion

Other car names convey rough and tough, even dangerous, images.   3
Animal names fall into this category, with models like Ram, Bronco, and
Mustang suggesting powerful, untamed beasts. The "rough and tough"
category also includes car names that suggest the wildness of the Old West:
Wrangler and Rodeo, for example. Because the American auto industry was
originally centered near Detroit, Michigan, where many cities have Indian
names, cars named for the cities where they are manufactured inherited
these names. Thus, cars called Cadillac, Pontiac, and Cherokee recall the
history of Indian nations, and these too might suggest the excitement of
the untamed West.

The most interesting car names in terms of the dream they sell, however, 4
were selected to suggest exploration and discovery. Years ago, some car names
honored real explorers, like DeSoto and LaSalle. Now, model names only sell an
abstract idea. Still, American car names like Blazer, Explorer, Navigator, Journey,
Mountaineer, Expedition, Caravan, and Voyager (as well as the names of foreign
cars driven by many Americans, such as Nissan's Pathfinder and Quest and
Honda's Passport, Pilot, and Odyssey) have the power to make drivers feel they
are blazing new trails and discovering new worlds—when in fact they may
simply be carpooling their children to a soccer game or commuting to work.

Most people take cars for granted, but manufacturers still try to make   5
consumers believe they are buying more than just transportation. Today, however,
the car is just an ordinary piece of machinery, a necessity for many people.
Sadly, the automobile is no longer seen as the amazing invention it once was.

PRACTICE

16-2

1. Restate Rob's thesis statement in your own words.

2. What three categories of car names does Rob discuss in his essay?

3. Is Rob's treatment of the three categories similar? Does he present the same kind of information for each kind of car name?

4. How do Rob's topic sentences move readers from one category to the next? How do they link the three categories?

5. Do you think Rob should have included additional examples in each category? Should he have included any additional categories?

6. What is this essay's greatest strength? What is its greatest weakness?

grammar in context

Classification

When you write a classification essay, you may want to list the categories you are going to discuss or the examples in each category. If you do, use a **colon** to introduce your list, and make sure that a complete sentence comes before the colon.

> Many car names seem to be chosen simply for how they sound: Alero, Corvette, Neon, Probe, Caprice.

For information on how to use a colon to introduce a list, see 35d.

Step-by-Step Guide: Writing a Classification Essay

Now, you are ready to write a classification essay on one of the topics below (or a topic of your own).

TOPICS

Types of teachers (or bosses)
Ways to lose (or gain) weight
Items hanging on your
    walls
Kinds of stores in your
    neighborhood
Kinds of learning styles

Traits of oldest children, middle
    children, and youngest children
Kinds of desserts
Kinds of workers you encounter
    in a typical day
College students' clothing choices
Kinds of tattoos

Plan

Organize

Draft

TEST

Revise, edit,
and proofread

As you write your essay, follow these steps:

- Make sure your topic calls for classification, and then find ideas to write about; next, identify your main idea, and write a thesis statement.

- Decide what categories you will discuss, sort examples and details into categories, and arrange your categories in an effective order, making an outline if necessary.

- Draft your essay.

- TEST your essay, referring to the TESTing a Classification Essay Checklist on page 294.

- Revise and edit your essay, referring to the two Self-Assessment Checklists in Chapter 13.

- Proofread your essay, and make sure it follows your instructor's format.

TESTing a classification essay

T hesis Statement Unifies Your Essay

- Does your introduction include a **thesis statement** that clearly identifies the subject of your classification and the categories you will discuss?

E vidence Supports Your Essay's Thesis Statement

- Does all your **evidence**—examples and details—support your thesis, or should some be deleted?
- Do you treat each major category similarly and with equal thoroughness?

S ummary Statement Reinforces Your Essay's Main Idea

- Does your conclusion include a **summary statement** that reinforces your essay's thesis?

T ransitions

- Do you include **transitions** that introduce your categories and lead readers from one category to the next?

Classification in Action

In "Mother Tongue," Amy Tan uses **classification** to structure her essay.

MOTHER TONGUE

Amy Tan

Amy Tan was born in 1952 in Oakland, California, the daughter of re-cent Chinese immigrants. In 1984, when she began to write fiction, she started to explore the contradictions she faced as a Chinese American who was also the daughter of immigrant parents. Three years later, she published *The Joy Luck Club* (1987), a best-selling novel about four immigrant Chinese women and their American-born daughters. Her later works include the novel *The Bonesetter's Daughter* (2001), two children's books, *The Opposite of Fate: A Book of Musings* (2003), and *Saving Fish from Drowning* (2005). In the following 1990 essay, Tan considers her mother's heavily Chinese-influenced English, as well as the different "Englishes" she herself uses, especially in communicating with her mother. She then discusses the potential limitations of growing up with immigrant parents who do not speak fluent English.

I am not a scholar of English or literature. I cannot give you much more than personal opinions on the English language and its variations in this country or others.

I am a writer. And by that definition, I am someone who has always loved language. I am fascinated by language in daily life. I spend a great deal of my time thinking about the power of language—the way it can evoke an emotion, a visual image, a complex idea, or a simple truth. Language is the tool of my trade. And I use them all—all the Englishes I grew up with.

Recently, I was made keenly aware of the different Englishes I do use. I was giving a talk to a large group of people, the same talk I had already given to half a dozen other groups. The nature of the talk was about my writing, my life, and my book, *The Joy Luck Club*. The talk was going along well enough, until I remembered one major difference that made the whole talk sound wrong. My mother was in the room. And it was perhaps the first time she had heard me give a lengthy speech, using the kind of English I have never used with her. I was saying things like, "The intersection of memory upon imagination" and "There is an aspect of my fiction that relates to thus-and-thus"—a speech filled with carefully wrought grammatical phrases, burdened, it suddenly seemed to me, with nominalized forms, past perfect tenses, conditional phrases, all the forms of standard English that I had learned in school and through books, the forms of English I did not use at home with my mother.

Just last week, I was walking down the street with my mother, and I again found myself conscious of the English I was using, and the English I do use with her. We were talking about the price of new and used furniture and I heard myself saying this: "Not waste money that way." My husband was with us as well, and he didn't notice any switch in my English. And then I realized why. It's because over the twenty years we've been together I've often used that same kind of English with him, and sometimes he even uses it with me. It has become our language of intimacy, a different sort of English that relates to family talk, the language I grew up with.

So you'll have some idea of what this family talk I heard sounds like, I'll quote what my mother said during a recent conversation which I video-taped and then transcribed. During this conversation my mother was talking about a political gangster in Shanghai who had the same last name as her family's, Du, and how the gangster in his early years wanted to be adopted by her family, which was rich by comparison. Later, the gangster became more powerful, far richer than my mother's family, and one day showed up at my mother's wedding to pay his respects. Here's what she said in part:

"Du Yusong having business like fruit stand. Like off the street kind. He is Du like Du Zong—but not Tsung-ming Island people. The local people call putong, the river east side, he belong to that side local people. The man want to ask Du Zong father take him in like become own family. Du Zong father wasn't looking down on him, but didn't take seriously, until

WORD POWER
wrought crafted
nominalize to convert a word into a noun

that man big like become a mafia. Now important person very hard to inviting him. Chinese way, come only to show respect, don't stay for dinner. Respect for making big celebration, he shows up. Mean gives lots of respect. Chinese custom. Chinese social life that way. If too important won't have to stay too long. He come to my wedding. I didn't see. I heard it. I gone to boy's side, they have YMCA dinner. Chinese age I was nineteen."

You should know that my mother's expressive command of English 7
belies how much she actually understands. She reads the *Forbes* report, listens to *Wall Street Week*, converses daily with her stockbroker, reads all of Shirley MacLaine's books with ease—all kinds of things I can't begin to understand. Yet some of my friends tell me they understand 50 percent of what my mother says. Some say they understand 80 to 90 percent. Some say they understand none of it, as if she were speaking pure Chinese. But to me, my mother's English is perfectly clear, perfectly natural. It's my mother's tongue. Her language, as I hear it, is vivid, direct, full of observation and imagery. This was the language that helped shape the way I saw things, expressed things, made sense of the world.

Lately, I've been giving more thought to the kind of English my 8
mother speaks. Like others, I have described it to people as "broken" or "fractured" English. But I wince when I say that. It has always bothered me that I can think of no way to describe it other than "broken," as if it were damaged and needed to be fixed, as if it lacked a certain wholeness and soundness. I've heard other terms used, "limited English," for example. But they seem just as bad, as if everything is limited, including people's perceptions of the limited English speaker.

I know this for a fact, because when I was growing up, my mother's 9
"limited" English limited *my* perception of her. I was ashamed of her English. I believed that her English reflected the quality of what she had to say. That is, because she expressed them imperfectly her thoughts were imperfect. And I had plenty of empirical evidence to support me: the fact that people in department stores, at banks, and at restaurants did not take her seriously, did not give her good service, pretended not to understand her, or even acted as if they did not hear her.

My mother has long realized the limitations of her English as well. 10
When I was fifteen, she used to have me call people on the phone to pretend I was she. In this guise, I was forced to ask for information or even complain and yell at people who had been rude to her. One time it was a call to her stockbroker in New York. She had cashed out her small portfolio and it just so happened we were going to go to New York the next week, our very first trip outside California. I had to get on the phone and say in an adolescent voice that was not very convincing, "This is Mrs. Tan."

And my mother was standing in the back whispering loudly, "Why 11
he don't send me check, already two weeks late. So mad he lie to me, losing me money."

WORD POWER

command the ability to use something
belies disguises

WORD POWER

empirical evidence knowledge gained by experience
guise the way someone or something appears

And then I said in perfect English, "Yes, I'm getting rather concerned. 12 You had agreed to send the check two weeks ago, but it hasn't arrived."

Then she began to talk more loudly. "What he want, I come to New 13 York tell him front of his boss, you cheating me?" And I was trying to calm her down, make her be quiet, while telling the stockbroker, "I can't tolerate any more excuses. If I don't receive the check immediately I am going to have to speak to your manager when I'm in New York next week." And sure enough, the following week there we were in front of this astonished stock-broker, and I was sitting there red-faced and quiet, and my mother, the real Mrs. Tan, was shouting at his boss in her impeccable broken English.

We used a similar routine just five days ago, for a situation that 14 was far less humorous. My mother had gone to the hospital for an appointment, to find out about a benign brain tumor a CAT scan had revealed a month ago. She said she had spoken very good English, her best English, no mistakes. Still, she said, the hospital did not apologize when they said they had lost the CAT scan and she had come for noth-ing. She said they did not seem to have any sympathy when she told them she was anxious to know the exact diagnosis, since her husband and son had both died of brain tumors. She said they would not give her any more information until the next time and she would have to make another appointment for that. So she said she would not leave until the doctor called her daughter. She wouldn't budge. And when the doctor finally called her daughter, me, who spoke in perfect English—lo and behold—we had assurances the CAT scan would be found, promises that a conference call on Monday would be held, and apologies for any suffering my mother had gone through for a most regrettable mistake.

> **WORD POWER**
> **benign** not dangerous

I think my mother's English almost had an effect on limiting my possi- 15 bilities in life as well. Sociologists and linguists probably will tell you that a person's developing language skills are more influenced by peers. But I do think that the language spoken in the family, especially in immigrant fami-lies which are more insular, plays a large role in shaping the language of the child. And I believe that it affected my results on achievement tests, IQ tests, and the SAT. While my English skills were never judged as poor, com-pared to math, English could not be considered my strong suit. In grade school I did moderately well, getting perhaps B's, sometimes B-pluses, in English and scoring perhaps in the sixtieth or seventieth percentile on achievement tests. But those scores were not good enough to override the opinion that my true abilities lay in math and science, because in those areas I achieved A's and scored in the ninetieth percentile or higher.

> **WORD POWER**
> **insular** uninterested in things outside of one's experiences

This was understandable. Math is precise; there is only one correct 16 answer. Whereas, for me at least, the answers on English tests were always a judgment call, a matter of opinion and personal experience. Those tests were constructed around items like fill-in-the-blank sentence completion, such as "Even though Tom was _____, Mary thought he was _____." And the correct answer always seemed to be the most bland combinations of thoughts, for example, "Even though Tom was shy,

WORD POWER

semantic relating to language

Mary thought he was charming," with the grammatical structure "even though" limiting the correct answer to some sort of semantic opposites, so you wouldn't get answers like, "Even though Tom was foolish, Mary thought he was ridiculous." Well, according to my mother, there were very few limitations as to what Tom could have been and what Mary might have thought of him. So I never did well on tests like that.

The same was true with word analogies, pairs of words in which 17 you were supposed to find some sort of logical, semantic relationship— for example, "*Sunset* is to *nightfall* as _____ is to _____." And here you would be presented with a list of four possible pairs, one of which showed the same kind of relationship: *red* is to *stoplight*, *bus* is to *arrival*, *chills* is to *fever*, *yawn* is to *boring*. Well, I could never think that way. I knew what the tests were asking, but I could not block out of my mind the images already created by the first pair, "*sunset* is to *nightfall*"—and I would see a burst of colors against a darkening sky, the moon rising, the lowering of a curtain of stars. And all the other pairs of words—red, bus, stoplight, boring—just threw up a mass of confusing images, making it impossible for me to sort out something as logical as saying: "A sunset precedes nightfall" is the same as "a chill precedes a fever." The only way I would have gotten that answer right would have been to imagine an associative situation, for example, my being disobedient and staying out past sunset, catching a chill at night, which turns into feverish pneumonia as punishment, which indeed did happen to me.

I have been thinking about all this lately, about my mother's English, 18 about achievement tests. Because lately I've been asked, as a writer, why there are not more Asian Americans represented in American literature. Why are there few Asian Americans enrolled in creative writing programs? Why do so many Chinese students go into engineering? Well, these are broad sociological questions I can't begin to answer. But I have noticed in surveys—in fact, just last week—that Asian students, as a whole, always do significantly better on math achievement tests than in English. And this makes me think that there are other Asian-American students whose English spoken in the home might also be described as "broken" or "limited." And perhaps they also have teachers who are steering them away from writing and into math and science, which is what happened to me.

Fortunately, I happen to be rebellious in nature and enjoy the chal- 19 lenge of disproving assumptions made about me. I became an English major my first year in college, after being enrolled as pre-med. I started writing nonfiction as a freelancer the week after I was told by my former boss that writing was my worst skill and I should hone my talents toward account management.

But it wasn't until 1985 that I finally began to write fiction. And at 20 first I wrote using what I thought to be wittily crafted sentences, sentences that would finally prove I had mastery over the English language.

WORD POWER

hone improve

Here's an example from the first draft of a story that later made its way into *The Joy Luck Club*, but without this line: "That was my mental quandary in its nascent state." A terrible line, which I can barely pronounce.

Fortunately, for reasons I won't get into today, I later decided I should 21 envision a reader for the stories I would write. And the reader I decided upon was my mother because these were stories about mothers. So with this reader in mind—and in fact she did read my early drafts—I began to write stories using all the Englishes I grew up with: the English I spoke to my mother, which for lack of a better term might be described as "simple"; the English she used with me, which for lack of a better term might be described as "broken"; my translation of her Chinese, which could certainly be described as "watered down"; and what I imagined to be her translation of her Chinese if she could speak in perfect English, her internal language, and for that I sought to preserve the essence, but neither an English nor a Chinese structure. I wanted to capture what language ability tests can never reveal: her intent, her passion, her imagery, the rhythms of her speech and the nature of her thoughts.

Apart from what any critic had to say about my writing, I knew I 22 had succeeded where it counted when my mother finished reading my book and gave me her verdict: "So easy to read."

Focus on the Pattern

1. What is Tan classifying in this essay? What categories does she discuss?

2. Why is classification a good choice for her subject? What other patterns of essay development might Tan have used to structure her essay?

Writing Practice

1. What different languages do you use when you speak (or write) as a student, employee, friend, or son or daughter? Write a classification essay discussing these different levels of speech or writing.

2. Think about the mothers you know best (in addition to your own). Then, write a classification essay that assigns each of these women to one of these three categories: helicopter parents, free-range parents, and those who fall somewhere in the middle. In your essay's thesis, state which kind of mother is superior to the others.

16c Definition Essays

Definition explains the meaning of a term or concept. A **definition essay** presents an *extended definition*, using various patterns of development to move beyond a simple dictionary definition.

When you **TEST** a **definition** essay, make sure it includes all these elements:

T ■ **Thesis Statement**—The introduction of a definition essay should include a **thesis statement** that communicates the essay's main idea and identifies the term you are going to define.

E ■ **Evidence**—The body paragraphs should include **evidence**—examples and details—that supports the thesis statement and defines your term. Body paragraphs may use different patterns of development.

S ■ **Summary Statement**—The conclusion of a definition essay should include a **summary statement** that reinforces the essay's thesis.

T ■ **Transitions**—A definition essay should include **transitional words and phrases** to move readers from one section of the definition to the next.

Moving from Assignment to Thesis

The wording of your assignment may suggest that you write a definition essay. For example, you may be asked to *define* or *explain* or to answer the question *What is x?* or *What does x mean?* Once you decide that your assignment calls for definition, you need to develop a thesis statement that reflects this purpose.

ASSIGNMENT	THESIS STATEMENT
Art Explain the meaning of the term *performance art.*	Unlike more conventional forms of art, *performance art* extends beyond the canvas.
Biology Define Darwin's concept of *natural selection.*	*Natural selection*, popularly known as "survival of the fittest," is a good deal more complicated than most people think.
Psychology What is *attention deficit disorder?*	*Attention deficit disorder* (ADD), once narrowly defined as a childhood problem, is now known to affect adults as well as children.

Organizing a Definition Essay

As the thesis statements above suggest, definition essays can be developed in various ways. For example, you can define something by telling how it occurred (narration), by describing its appearance (description), by giving a series of examples (exemplification), by telling how it operates (process), by telling how it is similar to or different from something else (comparison and contrast), or by discussing its parts (classification).

Some definition essays use a single pattern of development; others combine several patterns of development, perhaps using a different one in each paragraph.

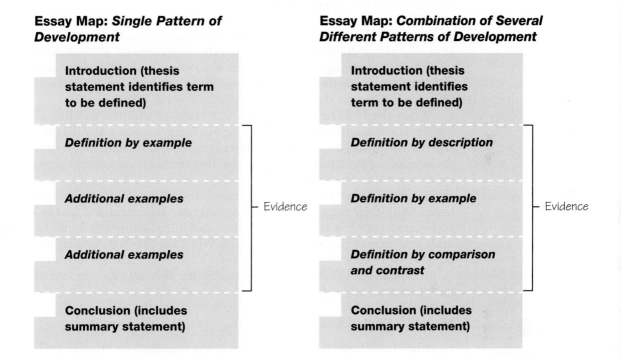

Essay Map: *Single Pattern of Development*

- Introduction (thesis statement identifies term to be defined)
- *Definition by example*
- *Additional examples*
- *Additional examples*
- Conclusion (includes summary statement)

Evidence

Essay Map: *Combination of Several Different Patterns of Development*

- Introduction (thesis statement identifies term to be defined)
- *Definition by description*
- *Definition by example*
- *Definition by comparison and contrast*
- Conclusion (includes summary statement)

Evidence

Transitions in Definition Essays

The kinds of transitions used in a definition essay depend on the specific pattern or patterns of development in the essay.

For a list of transitions frequently used in exemplification, see page 152.

Case Study: A Student Writes a Definition Essay

Kristin Whitehead, a student in a first-year writing course, was given the following assignment:

From the attached list, choose a slang term, an abbreviation or shorthand used in text messages, or a technical term used in one of your classes. Write an essay in which you define this term, developing your definition with any patterns that seem appropriate.

Because her instructor gave the class a list of topics to choose from, Kristin was able to decide on a topic quickly. She chose to define *street smart*, a term with which she was very familiar. She was particularly interested in defining this term because she thought of herself as a street-smart person and was impatient with some of her fellow first-year students, who she felt lacked this important trait.

Kristin had learned from experience how important it was to be street smart, and she **brainstormed** about her experiences to find information to guide her as she drafted her essay. In her **thesis statement**, she indicated why she was defining this term (because she saw it as a "vital survival skill"), and in her body paragraphs she defined her term by giving examples of behavior that she considered to be (and *not* to be) street smart.

When she **TEST**ed her draft, she was satisfied with the wording of her thesis statement and her supporting evidence, but she knew that she still needed to add a summary statement that did more than just repeat the wording of her thesis statement; she also needed to add clearer topic sentences. Since she knew she was going to meet with her **peer-review** group, she decided to ask her classmates for advice about these two issues. With their help, she revised her summary statement and tied her body paragraphs together by adding the same introductory phrase to the topic sentences of paragraphs 2, 3, and 4. When she finished **revising** her essay, Kristin went on to **edit** and **proofread** it and check her **format**.

The final draft that follows includes all the elements Kristin looked for when she **TEST**ed her essay.

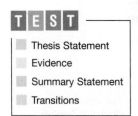

T E S T

Thesis Statement
Evidence
Summary Statement
Transitions

Model Definition Essay

Read Kristin's finished essay, and answer the questions in Practice 16-3.

Street Smart

Introduction

I grew up in a big city, so I was practically born street smart. I learned   1
the hard way how to act and what to do, and so did my friends. To us, being
street smart meant having common sense. We wanted to be cool, but we
needed to be safe, too. Now I go to college in a big city, and I realize that not
everyone here grew up the way I did. Many students are from suburbs or rural
areas, and they are either terrified of the city or totally ignorant of city life.
The few suburban or rural students who are willing to venture downtown are

Thesis statement

not street smart—but they should be. Being street smart is a vital survival
skill, one that everyone should learn.

2   For me, being street smart means knowing how to protect my possessions.   Topic sentence
Friends of mine who are not used to city life insist on wearing all their jewelry   (identifies first point)
when they go downtown. I think this is asking for trouble, and I know better.
I always tuck my chain under my shirt and leave my gold earrings home. Another
thing that surprises me is how some of my friends wave their money around.
They always seem to be standing on the street, trying to count their change   Examples and details
or stuff dollars into their wallets. Street-smart people make sure to put their
money safely away in their pockets or purses before they leave a store. A street-
smart person will also carry a backpack, a purse strapped across the chest, or no
purse at all. A person who is not street smart carries a purse loosely over one
shoulder or dangles it by its handle. Again, these people are asking for trouble.

3   Being street smart also means protecting myself. It means being aware   Topic sentence
of my surroundings at all times and looking alert. A lot of times, I have been   (identifies second point)
downtown with people who kept stopping on the street to talk about where
they should go next or walking up and down the same street over and over   — **Body paragraphs**
again. A street-smart person would never do this. It is important that I look
as if I know where I am going at all times, even if I don't. Whenever possible,   Examples and details
I decide on a destination in advance, and I make sure I know how to get there.
Even if I am not completely sure where I am headed, I make sure my body
language conveys my confidence in my ability to reach my destination.

4   Finally, being street smart means protecting my life. A street-smart person   Topic sentence
does not walk alone, especially after dark, in an unfamiliar neighborhood.   (identifies third point)
A street-smart person does not ask random strangers for directions; when lost,
he or she asks a shopkeeper for help. A street-smart person takes main streets
instead of side streets. When faced with danger or the threat of danger, a
street-smart person knows when to run, when to scream, and when to give up   Examples and details
money or possessions to avoid violence.

5   Being street smart is vitally important—sometimes even a matter of life
and death. Some people think it is a gift, but I think it is something almost
anyone can learn. Probably the best way to learn how to be street smart is to   Conclusion
hang out with people who know where they are going.

PRACTICE
16-3   1. Restate Kristin's thesis statement in your own words.

2. In your own words, define the term *street smart*. Why does
this term require more than a one-sentence definition?

3. Where does Kristin use examples to develop her definition? Where
does she use comparison and contrast?

4. What phrase does Kristin repeat in her topic sentences to tie her essay's three body paragraphs together?

5. Kristin's conclusion is quite a bit shorter than her other paragraphs. Do you think she should expand this paragraph? If so, what should she add?

6. What is this essay's greatest strength? What is its greatest weakness?

grammar in context

Definition

When you write a definition essay, you may begin with a one-sentence definition that you expand in the rest of your essay. When you write your definition sentence, do not use the phrase *is when* or *is where*.

means knowing
For me, being street smart ~~is when I know~~ how to protect my

possessions.

means protecting
Being street smart is also ~~where I protect~~ myself.

For information on how to structure a definition sentence, see the Grammar in Context box in 11a.

Step-by-Step Guide: Writing a Definition Essay

Now, you are ready to write a definition essay on one of the topics listed below (or a topic of your choice).

TOPICS

Upward mobility	Responsibility	Courage
Peer pressure	Procrastination	Happiness
Success	Security	Home
Loyalty	Ambition	Family

Plan

Organize

As you write your essay, follow these steps:

- Make sure your topic calls for definition, and then find ideas to write about; next, identify your main idea, and write a thesis statement.
- Decide what patterns of development to use to support your thesis, and arrange supporting examples and details in an effective order, making an outline if necessary.

- Draft your essay.
- **TEST** your essay, referring to the **TEST**ing a Definition Essay checklist below.
- Revise and edit your essay, referring to the two Self-Assessment Checklists in Chapter 13.
- Proofread your essay, and make sure it follows your instructor's format.

Draft

↓

TEST

↓

Revise, edit, and proofread

TESTing a definition essay

T hesis Statement Unifies Your Essay

- Does your introduction include a **thesis statement** that identifies the term your essay will define and provides a brief definition?

E vidence Supports Your Essay's Thesis Statement

- Is all your **evidence**—examples and details—clearly related to the term you are defining, or should some be deleted?
- Do you use appropriate patterns of development to support your definition, or should you explore other options?

S ummary Statement Reinforces Your Essay's Main Idea

- Does your conclusion include a **summary statement** that reinforces your essay's thesis?

T ransitions

- Do you include **transitions** that introduce your points and link your ideas?

Definition in Action

In "I Want a Wife," Judy Brady uses **definition** to structure her essay.

I WANT A WIFE

Judy Brady

Writer and activist Judy Brady helped found the Toxic Links Coalition, an organization dedicated to exposing the dangers of environmental toxins and their impact on public health. She was also active in the women's movement, and her classic essay "I Want a Wife" was published in the first issue of *Ms.* magazine (1971). As you read, think about how relevant this essay is to today's relationships.

I belong to that classification of people known as wives. I am A Wife. And, not altogether incidentally, I am a mother. 1

Not too long ago a male friend of mine appeared on the scene fresh from a recent divorce. He had one child, who is, of course, with his ex-wife. He is looking for another wife. As I thought about him while I was ironing one evening, it suddenly occurred to me that I, too, would like to have a wife. Why do I want a wife? 2

I would like to go back to school so that I can become economically independent, support myself, and, if need be, support those dependent upon me. I want a wife who will work and send me to school. And while I am going to school I want a wife to take care of my children. I want a wife to keep track of the children's doctor and dentist appointments. And to keep track of mine, too. I want a wife to make sure my children eat properly and are kept clean. I want a wife who will wash the children's clothes and keep them mended. I want a wife who is a good nurturant attendant to my children, who arranges for their schooling, makes sure that they have an adequate social life with their peers, takes them to the park, the zoo, etc. I want a wife who takes care of the children when they are sick, a wife who arranges to be around when the children need special care, because, of course, I cannot miss classes at school. My wife must arrange to lose time at work and not lose the job. It may mean a small cut in my wife's income from time to time, but I guess I can tolerate that. Needless to say, my wife will arrange and pay for the care of the children while my wife is working. 3

I want a wife who will take care of *my* physical needs. I want a wife who will keep my house clean. A wife who will pick up after my children, a wife who will pick up after me. I want a wife who will keep my clothes clean, ironed, mended, replaced when need be, and who will see to it that my personal things are kept in their proper place so that I can find what I need the minute I need it. I want a wife who cooks the meals, a wife who is a *good* cook. I want a wife who will plan the menus, do the necessary grocery shopping, prepare the meals, serve them pleasantly, and then do the cleaning up while I do my studying. I want a wife who will care for me when I am sick and sympathize with my pain and loss of time from school. I want a wife to go along when our family takes a 4

WORD POWER

nurturant providing physical and emotional care

vacation so that someone can continue to care for me and my children when I need a rest and change of scene.

I want a wife who will not bother me with rambling complaints about a wife's duties. But I want a wife who will listen to me when I feel the need to explain a rather difficult point I have come across in my course of studies. And I want a wife who will type my papers for me when I have written them.

I want a wife who will take care of the details of my social life. When my wife and I are invited out by my friends, I want a wife who will take care of the babysitting arrangements. When I meet people at school that I like and want to entertain, I want a wife who will have the house clean, will prepare a special meal, serve it to me and my friends, and not interrupt when I talk about things that interest me and my friends. I want a wife who will have arranged that the children are fed and ready for bed before my guests arrive so that the children do not bother us. I want a wife who takes care of the needs of my guests so that they feel comfortable, who makes sure that they have an ashtray, that they are passed the hors d'oeuvres, that they are offered a second helping of the food, that their wine glasses are replenished when necessary, that their coffee is served to them as they like it. And I want a wife who knows that sometimes I need a night out by myself.

I want a wife who is sensitive to my sexual needs, a wife who makes love passionately and eagerly when I feel like it, a wife who makes sure that I am satisfied. And, of course, I want a wife who will not demand sexual attention when I am not in the mood for it. I want a wife who assumes the complete responsibility for birth control, because I do not want more children. I want a wife who will remain sexually faithful to me so that I do not have to clutter up my intellectual life with jealousies. And I want a wife who understands that *my* sexual needs may entail more than strict adherence to monogamy. I must, after all, be able to relate to people as fully as possible.

If, by chance, I find another person more suitable as a wife than the wife I already have, I want the liberty to replace my present wife with another one. Naturally, I will expect a fresh new life; my wife will take the children and be solely responsible for them so that I am left free.

When I am through with school and have a job, I want my wife to quit working and remain at home so that my wife can more fully and completely take care of a wife's duties.

My God, who *wouldn't* want a wife?

WORD POWER

replenished made full or complete again

WORD POWER

adherence steady or faithful attachment

monogamy having one spouse or sexual partner at a time

Focus on the Pattern

1. Does Brady include a formal definition of *wife* anywhere in her essay? If so, where? If not, do you think she should?

2. Brady develops her definition with examples. What are some of her most important examples?

3. Besides exemplification, what other patterns of development does Brady use to develop her definition?

Writing Practice

1. Assume you are Brady's husband and feel unjustly attacked by her essay. Write her a letter in which you define *husband*, using as many examples as you can to show how overworked and underappreciated you are.

2. Write an essay in which you define your ideal teacher, parent, spouse, or boss.

16d Argument Essays

Argument takes a stand on a debatable issue—that is, an issue that has two sides (and can therefore be debated). An **argument essay** uses different kinds of *evidence*—facts, examples, and sometimes expert opinion—to persuade readers to accept a position.

When you TEST an **argument** essay, make sure it includes all these elements:

T ▪ **Thesis Statement**—The introduction of an argument essay should include a **thesis statement** that expresses the essay's main idea: the position you will take on the issue.

E ▪ **Evidence**—The body paragraphs should include **evidence**—facts, examples, and expert opinion—to support the thesis statement convincingly. The topic sentence of each body paragraph should identify one point of support for your thesis.

S ▪ **Summary Statement**—The conclusion of an argument essay should include a strong **summary statement** that reinforces the essay's thesis.

T ▪ **Transitions**—An argument essay should include logical **transitional words and phrases** that show how your points are related and move readers through your argument.

Moving from Assignment to Thesis

The wording of your assignment may suggest that you write an argument essay. For example, you may be asked to *debate, argue, consider, give your opinion, take a position,* or *take a stand.* Once you decide that your assignment calls for argument, you need to develop a thesis statement that takes a position on the topic you will write about in your essay.

ASSIGNMENT	THESIS STATEMENT
Composition Explain your position on a current social issue.	People should be able to invest some of their Social Security contributions in the stock market.
American history Do you believe that General Lee was responsible for the South's defeat at the Battle of Gettysburg? Why or why not?	Because Lee refused to listen to the advice given to him by General Longstreet, he is largely responsible for the South's defeat at the Battle of Gettysburg.
Ethics Should physician-assisted suicide be legalized?	Although many people think physician-assisted suicide should remain illegal, it should be legal in certain situations.

Organizing an Argument Essay

An argument essay can be organized *inductively* or *deductively*. An **inductive argument** moves from the specific to the general—that is, from a group of specific observations to a general conclusion based on these observations. An essay on the first topic in the chart above, for example, could be an inductive argument. It could begin by presenting facts, examples, and expert opinion about the benefits of investing in the stock market and end with the conclusion that people should be able to invest part of their Social Security contributions in the stock market.

A **deductive argument** moves from the general to the specific. A deductive argument begins with a **major premise** (a general statement that the writer believes his or her audience will accept) and then moves to a **minor premise** (a specific instance of the belief stated in the major premise). It ends with a **conclusion** that follows from the two premises. For example, an essay on the last topic in the chart above could be a deductive argument. It could begin with the major premise that all terminally ill patients who are in great pain should be given access to physician-assisted suicide. It could then go on to state and explain the minor premise that a particular patient is both terminally ill and in great pain, offering facts, examples, and the opinions of experts to support this premise. The essay could conclude that this patient should, therefore, be allowed the option of physician-assisted suicide. The deductive argument presented in the essay would have three parts.

MAJOR PREMISE   All terminally ill patients who are in great pain should be allowed to choose physician-assisted suicide.

MINOR PREMISE John Lacca is a terminally ill patient who is in great pain.

CONCLUSION Therefore, John Lacca should be allowed to choose physician-assisted suicide.

Before you present your argument, think about whether your readers are likely to be hostile toward, neutral toward, or in agreement with your position. Once you understand your audience, you can decide which points to make to support your argument. Try to achieve a balanced, moderate tone, and avoid name-calling or personal attacks.

Begin each paragraph of your argument essay with a topic sentence that clearly introduces a point in support of your thesis. Throughout your essay, include specific examples that will make your arguments persuasive. Keep in mind that arguments that rely on generalizations alone are not as convincing as those that include vivid details and specific examples.

In addition to presenting your case, your essay should also briefly summarize arguments *against* your position and **refute** them (that is, argue against them) by identifying factual errors or errors in logic. If an opposing argument is particularly strong, concede its strength—but try to point out some weaknesses as well. If you deal with opposing arguments in this way, your audience will see you as a fair and reasonable person.

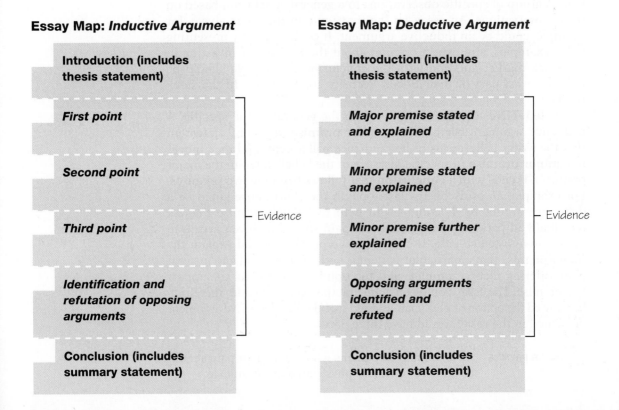

Essay Map: *Inductive Argument*

Introduction (includes thesis statement)

First point

Second point

Third point ⎱ Evidence

Identification and refutation of opposing arguments

Conclusion (includes summary statement)

Essay Map: *Deductive Argument*

Introduction (includes thesis statement)

Major premise stated and explained

Minor premise stated and explained

Minor premise further explained ⎱ Evidence

Opposing arguments identified and refuted

Conclusion (includes summary statement)

Transitions in Argument Essays

Transitions are extremely important in argument essays because they not only signal the movement from one part of the argument to another but also relate specific points to one another and to the thesis statement.

For a list of transitions frequently used in argument, see page 163.

Case Study: A Student Writes an Argument Essay

Alex Norman, a student in a first-year writing course, was assigned to write an argument essay on a controversial issue of his choice. His instructor suggested that students find a topic by reading their campus and local newspapers, going online to read national news stories and political blogs, and watching public affairs programs on television. Alex followed this advice and also talked about his assignment with friends and family members.

The issue that most interested him was one about which he had already written an argument paragraph for an earlier assignment: the question of whether the federal government should do more to subsidize the cost of college for low-income students. Now, he thought he could do some additional work to develop some of that paragraph's ideas into an argument essay.

Alex began by **brainstorming**, recording all his ideas on this complex issue, including those he had discussed in his earlier paragraph. He also included ideas he developed as he spoke to his sister, a recent college graduate, and to his boss at the bank where he worked part-time. When he read over his brainstorming notes, he saw that he had good arguments both for and against increasing government funding for low-income students. Although Alex sympathized with students who needed help paying for school, he questioned whether taxpayers should have to foot the bill. At this point, he wasn't sure what position to take in his essay, so he scheduled an appointment for a **conference** with his instructor.

Alex's instructor pointed out that he could make a good case either for or against greater government subsidies; like many controversial issues, this one had no easy answers. She encouraged him to support the position that seemed right to him and to use the information on the opposing side to present (and refute) opposing arguments. She also recommended that Alex email his first draft to her so she could review it.

After he thought about his instructor's comments, Alex decided to argue in favor of increasing government grants to help low-income students pay for college. Before he began to draft his essay, he wrote a **thesis statement** that presented his position on the issue; then, he arranged supporting points from his brainstorming notes into an **outline** that he could follow as he wrote. As he **drafted** his essay, Alex made sure to support his thesis with evidence and to explain his position as clearly and thoroughly as possible. He paid special attention to choosing transitional words and phrases that would indicate how his points were logically connected to one another.

When Alex finished his draft, he TESTed it, taking a quick inventory to make sure he had included all four necessary components of an essay. Then, he emailed the draft to his instructor. Following her suggestions, he **revised** his draft, this time focusing on his topic sentences, his presentation (and refutation) of opposing arguments, and his introductory and concluding paragraphs. When he was satisfied with his revisions, he **edited** and **proofread** his paper and checked his **format**.

The final draft that follows includes all the elements Alex looked for when he TESTed his essay.

T E S T

◻ Thesis Statement
◻ Evidence
◻ Summary Statement
◻ Transitions

Model Argument Essay

Read Alex's finished essay, and answer the questions in Practice 16-4.

Increase Grant Money for Low-Income College Students

Introduction

The price of college tuition has more than doubled over the last two   1
decades. Today, low-income students are finding it especially difficult (and sometimes impossible) to pay for school. Should the government help these students more than it does now? If so, what form should that help take? Rather than reducing aid or asking students to borrow more, the government should give larger grants to subsidize tuition for low-income students.

**Topic sentence
(introduces first point)**

If the United States is a country that is committed to equal opportunity,   2
then college should be affordable for all. To compete in today's high-tech job market, people need a college degree. However, students' access to college is too often determined by their parents' income. This unfairly excludes many people. Therefore, the government should make it a priority to support students who are being priced out of a college education. Specifically, the government should give larger grants to low-income students. Although some critics see these grants as unnecessary "handouts," such awards are the best way for the government to invest in the future and maintain our nation's core values. After all, the country's economy benefits when more of its citizens earn college degrees. Even more important, by giving low-income students the same opportunities to succeed as their more affluent peers, the United States keeps its promise to treat all its citizens fairly.

Body paragraphs

**Facts, examples,
expert opinion**

**Topic sentence
(introduces second
point)**

Some people argue that the best way to help students who are strug-   3
gling to pay for college is to offer them more loans at a lower interest rate. However, this solution is inadequate, unfair, and short-sighted. First of

all, lowering the interest rate on student loans only reduces the average monthly payments by a few dollars. Second, student loans already unfairly burden low-income students. Why should they have to take on more debt simply because their parents make less money? The government should reduce the amount these students have to borrow, not increase it. Finally, forcing graduates to start their careers with a heavy financial burden hurts the country's economy. Although loans might cost the government less in the short term, in the long term student debt makes it more difficult for Americans to be successful and competitive.

Facts, examples, or expert opinion

4   The federal government does have Pell Grant funding to help students who demonstrate need, but this program needs to be expanded. As Sara Goldrick-Rab reports, although Pell Grants once allowed students to focus their time and energy on school instead of work, the proportion of tuition the grants now cover is so low that this balance is no longer possible. In fact, Pell Grants are limited to $5,775 per student per year. At most, Pell Grants cover only a third of average college costs. Meanwhile, the education gap between rich and poor is growing. As education policy expert Andrew J. Rotherham observes, while 75 percent of wealthy students earn a four-year degree by age 24, less than 10 percent of low-income students do. To help close this gap, the government should offer more funding to those most in need of financial assistance.

Topic sentence (introduces third point)

Body paragraphs

Facts, examples, or expert opinion

5   Some would argue, however, that the government should do just the opposite. One of the most common criticisms of government subsidies is that they are to blame for the rising costs of college. Critics point out that by supplying money to colleges, government grants only make it easier for them to charge more. This may be true, but, as Andrew Rotherham points out, the government could do more to regulate college tuition. For example, the government could offer incentives to schools that keep their costs down or award more generous grants to students who attend affordable schools. Ultimately, withdrawing aid and abandoning students to the free market is irresponsible as well as counterproductive. Instead, the government should take steps to prevent colleges from taking advantage of its generosity.

Topic sentence (introduces fourth point)

Facts, examples, or expert opinion

6   With the cost of college continuing to rise, now is the time for the government to help the hardest-hit students by offering them more help to pay for their education. Rather than cutting spending on student aid, the government should increase grants to low-income students. However, it must do so in ways that discourage irresponsible increases in tuition. By acting wisely and prudently, the government can improve access to higher education for all and support the country's economic future.

Conclusion

Works Cited

Goldrick-Rab, Sara. "The Real College Barrier for Working-Poor
    Families." *Inside Higher Ed,* 10 Dec. 2013, www.insidehighered
    .com/views/2013/12/10/federal-aid-needy-students-inadequate
    -essay.

Rotherham, Andrew J. "How to Fix Pell Grants." *Time,* 24 May 2012,
    ideas.time.com/2012/05/24/how-to-fix-pell-grants/.

PRACTICE

16-4

1. In your own words, summarize the position Alex takes in his essay.

2. List the facts and examples Alex uses to support his thesis. Where does he include expert opinion?

3. Can you think of any other supporting evidence that Alex should have included but didn't?

4. Review the transitional words and phrases Alex uses. How do they move his argument along? Should he add any transitions?

5. Where does Alex address opposing arguments? Can you think of other arguments he should have addressed?

6. What is this essay's greatest strength? What is its greatest weakness?

grammar in context

Argument

When you write an argument essay, you need to show the relationships between your ideas by combining sentences to create **compound sentences** and c**omplex sentences**.

The federal government does have a program in place to help
students who demonstrate need, *, but* Pell Grant funding needs to be
expanded. (compound sentence)

Although some critics
~~Some critics~~ see these grants as unnecessary "handouts,"
^ such
~~Such~~ awards are the best way for the government to invest in the
future and to maintain our nation's core values. (complex sentence)

*For information on how to create compound sentences, see Chapter 18.
For information on how to create complex sentences, see Chapter 19.*

Step-by-Step Guide: Writing an Argument Essay

Now, you are ready to write an argument essay on one of the topics listed below (or a topic of your choice).

TOPICS

Teenagers who commit serious crimes should (or should not) be tried as adults.

All citizens without criminal records should (or should not) be permitted to carry concealed weapons.

Human beings should (or should not) be used as subjects in medical research experiments.

College financial aid should (or should not) be based solely on merit.

Government funds should (or should not) be used to support the arts.

The minimum wage should (or should not) be raised.

College athletes should (or should not) be paid to play.

Convicted felons should (or should not) lose the right to vote.

As you write your essay, follow these steps:

- Make sure your topic calls for argument, and then find ideas to write about; next, decide on the position you will support, and write a thesis statement that clearly expresses this position.

- List the key points in support of your thesis, and arrange these points in an effective order; then, list evidence (facts, examples, and expert opinion) in support of each point, list arguments against your position, and make an outline that includes key supporting and opposing points.

- Draft your essay.

- TEST your essay, referring to the TESTing an Argument Essay checklist below.

- Revise and edit your essay, referring to the two Self-Assessment Checklists in Chapter 13.

- Proofread your essay, and make sure it follows your instructor's format.

Plan

Organize

Draft

TEST

Revise, edit, and proofread

TESTing an argument essay

T hesis Statement Unifies Your Essay

☐ Does your introduction include a **thesis statement** that clearly expresses the stand you take on the issue you will discuss? Is this issue debatable—that is, does it really have two sides?

(continued)

Evidence Supports Your Essay's Thesis Statement

☐ Does all your **evidence**—facts, examples, and expert opinion— support your thesis, or should some be deleted?

☐ Do you have enough evidence to support your points?

☐ Have you considered whether readers are likely to be hostile toward, neutral toward, or in agreement with your position— and have you chosen your points accordingly?

☐ Is your evidence presented in a clear inductive or deductive order?

Summary Statement Reinforces Your Essay's Main Idea

☐ Does your conclusion include a **summary statement** that reinforces your essay's thesis?

Transitions

☐ Do you include **transitions** that introduce your points?

☐ Do you include enough transitional words and phrases to help readers follow the logic of your argument?

Argument in Action

In "Vaccinations Are for the Good of the Nation," Ben Carson uses **argument** to structure his essay.

VACCINATIONS ARE FOR THE GOOD OF THE NATION
Ben Carson

Ben Carson served as the director of pediatric neurosurgery at Johns Hopkins Hospital from 1984 until 2013, when he retired. He won the Presidential Medal of Freedom in 2008 for his contributions to the medical field, including separating conjoined twins. Originally from Detroit, Michigan, Carson is the author of many essays and books on his medical career, including 2014's *One Nation: What We Can All Do to Save America's Future*. In 2016, he made an unsuccessful bid to become the Republican Party's nominee for president of the United States. In this 2015 op-ed for the *National Review*, Carson draws on his medical experience to caution against the dangers of the anti-vaccination movement. As you read, think about whether you trust Carson's opinion more than other writers' positions, given his medical background.

There has been much debate recently over vaccination mandates, particularly in response to the measles outbreak currently taking place throughout the country.

At this juncture, there have been 102 confirmed measles cases in the U.S. during 2015, with 59 of them linked to a December 2014 visit to the Disneyland theme park in Southern California. (It is important to note that eleven of the cases associated with Disneyland were detected last year and, consequently, fall within the 2014 measles count.) This large outbreak has spread to at least a half-dozen other states, and the Centers for Disease Control and Prevention is currently requesting that all health-care professionals "consider measles when evaluating patients with febrile rash and ask about a patient's vaccine status, recent travel history and contact with individuals who have febrile rash illness."

One must understand that there is no specific antiviral therapy for measles and that 90 percent of those who are not vaccinated will contract measles if they are indeed exposed to the virus. This explains why Arizona health officials are monitoring more than 1,000 people after potential exposure to measles. These are pretty staggering numbers that should concern not only parents and children, but also the general populace.

I have been asked many times throughout the past week for my thoughts concerning the issue of vaccines. The important thing is to make sure the public understands that there is no substantial risk from vaccines and that the benefits are very significant. Although I strongly believe in individual rights and the rights of parents to raise their children as they see fit, I also recognize that public health and public safety are extremely important in our society. Certain communicable diseases have been largely eradicated by immunization policies in this country. We should not allow those diseases to return by foregoing safe immunization programs for philosophical, religious, or other reasons when we have the means to eradicate them.

Obviously, there are exceptional situations to virtually everything, and we must have a mechanism whereby those can be heard. Nevertheless, there is public policy and health policy that we must pay attention to regarding this matter. We already have policies in place at schools that require immunization records—this is a positive thing. Studies have shown over the course of time that the risk-benefit ratio for vaccination is grossly in favor of being vaccinated as opposed to not.

There is no question that immunizations have been effective in eliminating diseases such as smallpox, which was devastating and lethal. When you have diseases that have been demonstrably curtailed or eradicated by immunization, why would you even think about not doing it? Certain people have discussed the possibility of potential health risks from vaccinations. I am not aware of scientific evidence of a direct correlation. I think there probably are people who may make a

WORD POWER
mandates rules
juncture point in time

WORD POWER
febrile related to a fever

WORD POWER
communicable infectious
eradicated ended; destroyed
means ways

WORD POWER
correlation relationship

correlation where one does not exist, and that fear subsequently ignites, catches fire, and spreads. But it is important to educate the public about what evidence actually exists.

I am very much in favor of parental rights on certain types of things.   7
I am in favor of you and me having the freedom to drive a car. But do we have a right to drive without wearing our seatbelts? Do we have a right to text while we are driving? Studies have demonstrated that those are dangerous things to do, so it becomes a public-safety issue. You have to be able to distinguish our rights versus the rights of the society in which we live, because we are all in this thing together. We have to be cognizant of the other people around us, and we must always bear in mind the safety of the population. That is key, and that is one of the responsibilities of government.

I am a small-government person, and I greatly oppose government   8
intrusion into everything. Still, it is essential that we distinguish between those things that are important and those things that are just intruding upon our basic privacy. Whether to participate in childhood immunizations would be an individual choice if individuals were the only ones affected, but our children are part of our larger community. None of us lives in isolation. Your decision does not affect only you—it also affects your fellow Americans.

> **WORD POWER**
>
> **cognizant** aware

Focus on the Pattern

1. Restate Carson's thesis in your own words. Where does he state this thesis? What evidence does he use to support his position?

2. Where does Carson introduce opposing arguments? Does he refute them successfully?

3. Is this argument organized inductively or deductively? Explain.

Writing Practice

1. Write an argument essay in which you support the position that certain individuals or groups should have the right not to vaccinate their children.

2. Write an argument essay with the title "_____ Is/Are for the Good of the Nation." In your essay, support the position that a particular practice (for example, bicycle riders wearing helmets or limiting the size of soda containers) should be required despite some people's objections.

review checklist

Patterns of Essay Development: Description, Classification, Definition, and Argument

☐ **Descriptive** essays use details to give readers a clear, vivid picture of a person, place, or object. (See 16a.)

☐ **Classification** essays divide a whole into parts and sort various items into categories. (See 16b.)

☐ **Definition** essays use various patterns to develop an extended definition. (See 16c.)

☐ **Argument** essays take a stand on a debatable issue, using evidence to persuade readers to accept a position. (See 16d.)

Writing Effective Sentences

17 Writing Simple Sentences

Canine Companions for Independence, Inc.

focus on writing

This photo shows a young girl who was matched with a Skilled Companion dog through the nonprofit organization Canine Companions for Independence, which provides trained assistance dogs to people with disabilities. Imagine you had ten thousand dollars to donate to the nonprofit organization or charity of your choice. Which group would you support, and why? Write a paragraph explaining your choice.

In this chapter you will learn to

- identify a sentence's subject (17a)
- identify prepositions and prepositional phrases (17b)
- distinguish a prepositional phrase from a subject (17b)
- identify a sentence's verb (17c)

A **sentence** is a group of words that expresses a complete thought. Every sentence includes both a subject and a verb. A **simple sentence** consists of a single **independent clause**: one <u>subject</u> and one <u>verb</u>.

<u>Service animals</u> <u>help</u> people in need.

17a Identifying Subjects

Every sentence includes a subject. The **subject** of a sentence tells who or what is being talked about in the sentence. Without a subject, a sentence is not complete. In each of the following three sentences, the subject is underlined.

<u>Derek Walcott</u> won the Nobel Prize in Literature.
<u>He</u> was born in St. Lucia.
<u>St. Lucia</u> is an island in the Caribbean.

The subject of a sentence can be a noun or a pronoun. A **noun** names a person, place, or thing—*Derek Walcott, St. Lucia.* A **pronoun** takes the place of a noun—*I, you, he, she, it, we, they,* and so on.

The subject of a sentence can be *singular or plural.* A **singular subject** is one person, place, or thing (*Derek Walcott, St. Lucia, he*).

A **plural subject** is more than one person, place, or thing (*poets, people, they*).

<u>Readers</u> admire Walcott's poems.

A plural subject that joins two subjects with *and* is called a **compound subject**.

<u>St. Lucia and Trinidad</u> are Caribbean islands.

PRACTICE

17-1   In the following paragraph, underline the subject of each sentence.

Example: <u>Zombies</u> have been a part of folklore for centuries.

(1) In today's popular culture, zombies seem to be everywhere. (2) However, this trend is not a recent phenomenon. (3) For example, African slaves in seventeenth- and eighteenth-century Haiti sometimes longed for escape in death but feared becoming zombies. (4) Zombies can also be found throughout modern literature. (5) Frankenstein's monster—although not a zombie himself—inspired later interpretations of the undead. (6) In addition, zombies are popular in film. (8) *Night of the Living Dead* (1968) is a classic film featuring zombies. (9) *World War Z* (2013) continues the tradition. (10) Today, television is also being over-run by zombie tales, such as *The Walking Dead*. (11) In fact, zombies are popular in everything from comic books and video games to Halloween costumes. (12) The website of the Centers for Disease Control even features a Zombie Apocalypse Survival Guide.

PRACTICE

17-2   Underline the subject in each sentence. Then, write *S* above singular subjects and *P* above plural subjects. Remember, compound subjects are plural.

Visit *LaunchPad Solo for Readers and Writers* > **Overview: Sentences** for more practice with simple sentences.

Example: <u>Agritainment</u> introduces tourists to agriculture and entertainment at the same time.

1. Today, tourists can have fun on working farms.

2. In the past, visitors came to farms just to pick fruits and vegetables.

3. Now, some farms have mazes and petting zoos.

4. One farm has a corn maze every year.

5. Sometimes the maze is in the shape of a train.

6. Visitors can also enjoy giant hay-chute slides, pedal go-carts, and hayrides.

7. Working farms start agritainment businesses to make money.

8. However, insurance companies and lawyers worry about the dangers of agritainment.

9. Tourists have gotten animal bites, fallen from rides and machinery, and suffered from food poisoning.

10. Agritainment, like other businesses, has advantages and disadvantages.

 **LaunchPad**

Visit *LaunchPad Solo for Readers and Writers* > **Prepositions and Conjunctions** for more practice in identifying prepositional phrases.

17b Identifying Prepositional Phrases

A **prepositional phrase** consists of a **preposition** (a word such as *on, to, in,* or *with*) and its **object** (the noun or pronoun it introduces).

PREPOSITION	+	OBJECT	=	PREPOSITIONAL PHRASE
on		the stage		on the stage
to		Nia's house		to Nia's house
in		my new car		in my new car
with		them		with them

Because the object of a preposition is a noun or a pronoun, it may seem to be the subject of a sentence. However, the object of a preposition can never be the subject of a sentence. To identify a sentence's true subject, cross out each prepositional phrase. (Remember, every prepositional phrase is introduced by a preposition.)

       SUBJECT   PREP PHRASE

The cost of the repairs was astronomical.

   PREP PHRASE   PREP PHRASE   SUBJECT

At the end of the novel, after an exciting chase, the lovers flee

PREP PHRASE

to Mexico.

Frequently Used Prepositions

about	at	during	off	under
above	before	except	on	underneath
according to	behind	for	onto	until
across	below	from	out	up
after	beneath	in	outside	upon
against	beside	inside	over	with
along	between	into	through	within
among	beyond	like	throughout	without
around	by	near	to	
as	despite	of	toward	

PRACTICE

17-3   Each of the following sentences includes at least one prepositional phrase. To identify each sentence's subject, begin by crossing out each prepositional phrase. Then, underline the subject of the sentence.

Example: Bicycling ~~on busy city streets~~ can be dangerous.

(1) In many American cities, cyclists are concerned about sharing the road with cars. (2) For this reason, people are becoming more interested in "green" lanes. (3) These bike lanes are different from traditional bike lanes in one important way. (4) Green lanes are separated from the road by curbs, planters, or parked cars. (5) For years, people in Europe have been creating and using these protected bike lanes. (6) Until recently, however, few green lanes were created in the United States. (7) Now, with the help of the Bikes Belong Foundation and the Federal Highway Administration, several U.S. cities are installing green lanes. (8) For their supporters, these bike lanes are a positive step toward healthier, safer cities. (9) However, some critics worry about reduced space for traffic lanes and parking. (10) Still, despite the criticism, green lanes are increasing the number of bike riders and reducing the number of bike accidents.

17c Identifying Verbs

Visit *LaunchPad Solo for Readers and Writers* > **Overview: Parts of Speech** for more practice with verbs.

In addition to its subject, every sentence also includes a verb. This **verb** (also called a **predicate**) tells what the subject does or connects the subject to words that describe or rename it. Without a verb, a sentence is not complete.

Action Verbs

An **action verb** tells what the subject does, did, or will do.

> Eli Manning <u>plays</u> football.
> Amelia Earhart <u>flew</u> across the Atlantic.
> Renee <u>will drive</u> to Tampa on Friday.

Action verbs can also show mental and emotional actions.

> Travis always <u>worries</u> about his job.

Sometimes the subject of a sentence performs more than one action. In this case, the sentence includes two or more action verbs that form a **compound predicate**.

> He <u>hit</u> the ball, <u>threw</u> down his bat, and <u>ran</u> toward first base.

PRACTICE
17-4

In the following sentences, underline each action verb twice. Some sentences contain more than one action verb.

Example: Some new reality shows <u>introduce</u> viewers to people with disabilities.

1. The reality show *Push Girls* explores the lives of five beautiful disabled women.

2. All the women live in Los Angeles and travel in wheelchairs.

3. These women push many boundaries.

4. They drive their own cars and pursue ambitious careers.

5. Attractive and talented, they reject other people's assumptions about disability.

6. One woman works as a model and an actress.

7. Another dances for a living.

8. Like other reality shows, *Push Girls* shows us people's private lives.

9. However, this reality series also challenges stereotypes.

10. Ultimately, viewers admire these capable women and envy their fulfilling lives.

Linking Verbs

A **linking verb** does not show action. Instead, it connects the subject to a word or words that describe or rename it. The linking verb tells what the subject is (or what it was, will be, or seems to be).

A googolplex is an extremely large number.

Many linking verbs, like *is*, are forms of the verb *be*. Other linking verbs refer to the senses (*look*, *feel*, and so on).

The photocopy looks blurry.
Some students feel anxious about the future.

Frequently Used Linking Verbs		
act	feel	seem
appear	get	smell
be (am, is, are,	grow	sound
was, were)	look	taste
become	remain	turn

PRACTICE

17-5   In each of the following sentences, underline every verb twice. Remember that a verb can be an action verb or a linking verb.

Example: Airplane pilots and investment bankers <u><u>use</u></u> checklists.

(1) In *The Checklist Manifesto*, surgeon Atul Gawande argues for using checklists in operating rooms. (2) Gawande reminds readers of the complexity of modern medicine. (3) Currently, there are 6,000 drugs and 4,000 medical and surgical procedures. (4) Each year, the number of drugs and procedures increases. (5) As a result, even knowledgeable and highly trained surgeons make mistakes. (6) For some types of patients, the error rate is very high. (7) For example, doctors deliver inappropriate care to 40 percent of patients with coronary artery disease. (8) Luckily, checklists make a big difference for these and other patients. (9) In fact, checklists reduce complications by more than one-third. (10) It is hard to imagine an argument against such a simple and effective tool.

Helping Verbs

Many verbs consist of more than one word. For example, the verb in the following sentence consists of two words.

Minh <u><u>must make</u></u> a decision about his future.

In this sentence, *make* is the **main verb**, and *must* is a **helping verb**.

Frequently Used Helping Verbs

does	was	must	should
did	were	can	would
do		could	will
is	have	may	
are	has	might	
am	had		

A sentence's **complete verb** is made up of a main verb plus any helping verbs that accompany it. In the following sentences, the complete verb is underlined twice, and the helping verbs are checkmarked.

Minh should have gone earlier. ✓ ✓

Did Minh ask the right questions? ✓

Minh will work hard. ✓

Minh can really succeed. ✓

FYI

Helping Verbs with Participles

Participles, such as *going* and *gone*, cannot stand alone as main verbs in a sentence. They need a helping verb to make them complete.

INCORRECT Minh going to the library.

CORRECT Minh is going to the library.

INCORRECT Minh gone to the library.

CORRECT Minh has gone to the library.

PRACTICE

17-6 The verbs in the sentences that follow consist of a main verb and one or more helping verbs. In each sentence, underline the complete verb twice, and put a check mark above each helping verb.

Example: In 1954, the Salk polio vaccine was given to more than a million schoolchildren. ✓

(1) By the 1950s, polio had become a serious problem throughout the United States. (2) For years, it had puzzled doctors and researchers. (3) Thousands had become ill each year in the United States alone. (4) Children should have been playing happily. (5) Instead, they would get very sick. (6) Polio was sometimes called infantile paralysis. (7) In fact, it did cause paralysis in children and in adults as well. (8) Some patients could breathe only with the help of machines called iron lungs.

(9) Others would remain in wheelchairs for life. (10) By 1960, Jonas Salk's vaccine had reduced the incidence of polio in the United States by more than 90 percent.

Canine Companions for
Independence, Inc.

TEST · Revise · Edit · Proofread

Look back at your response to the Focus on Writing prompt on page 323. Circle every subject and every action verb. Then, try to replace some of them with more descriptive subjects (such as *linebacker* instead of *athlete*) and more specific action verbs (for example, *shouted* or *whispered* instead of *said*). When you have finished, TEST your paragraph. Then, revise, edit, and proofread your work.

EDITING PRACTICE

Read the following student essay. Underline the subject of each sentence once, and underline the complete verb of each sentence twice. If you have trouble locating the subject, try crossing out the prepositional phrases. The first sentence has been done for you.

A New Way to Learn

Salman Khan founded the nonprofit online Khan Academy in 2006. Khan Academy promises "a free world-class education for anyone anywhere." With the help of short videos, people can learn a subject like physics or economics at their own pace. According to some, Khan Academy is in the process of revolutionizing education.

Salman Khan was born in New Orleans in 1976. His parents had moved to Louisiana from Bangladesh. During his childhood, Khan attended public schools in New Orleans. After high school, he earned three degrees from MIT and one degree from Harvard. His degrees are in math, engineering, computer science, and business. He had never considered a career in education. However, in 2004, Khan's cousin asked him for help with algebra. He made some short YouTube videos for her. To his surprise, the lessons became extremely popular. He had a talent for teaching. In 2009, with a small donation from an investor, Salman Khan started Khan Academy.

Khan Academy has succeeded well beyond Khan's expectations. Now, the organization receives millions of dollars in donations. The Khan Academy website has more than 2,400 videos. Every video is available for free to anyone. Khan teaches many of the lessons himself. He researches his subjects. Then, without a script, he records each video in one take. These videos are not traditional lectures. The audience never sees Khan's face. Throughout each lesson,

Khan's writing appears on the screen. Related images appear as well. For viewers, each lesson feels like a one-on-one tutoring session.

The site also offers exercises for students and tools for teachers. Students can practice subjects by themselves. They can progress at their own speed. Some schools are even using Khan Academy lessons in their classrooms. With the help of Khan's videos, teachers can create a "flipped" classroom. Students learn basic concepts at night on their computers. Then, at school, students work on problems with the teacher's help. This means more time for questions. For some students, this method has been extremely effective.

Without any training in education, Salman Khan has changed people's ideas about learning. Around the world, people are using his website. They are learning new ideas. Khan is happy about this. In his view, education should be accessible for all.

COLLABORATIVE ACTIVITY

Fold a sheet of paper in half vertically. Working in a group of three or four students, spend two minutes listing as many nouns as you can in the column to the left of the fold. When your time is up, exchange papers with another group of students, and write an appropriate action verb beside each noun. (Each noun will now be the subject of a short sentence.)

Then, choose five of your sentences, and collaborate with the other students in your group to create more fully developed sentences. First, expand each subject by adding words or prepositional phrases that give more information about the subject. (For example, you could expand *boat* to *the small, leaky boat with the red sail.*) Then, expand each sentence further, adding ideas after the verb. (For example, the sentence *The boat bounced* could become *The small, leaky boat with the red sail bounced helplessly on the water.*)

review checklist

Writing Simple Sentences

☐ A sentence expresses a complete thought. The subject tells who or what is being talked about in the sentence. (See 17a.)

☐ A prepositional phrase consists of a preposition and its object (the noun or pronoun it introduces). (See 17b.)

☐ The object of a preposition cannot be the subject of a sentence. (See 17b.)

☐ An action verb tells what the subject does, did, or will do. (See 17c.)

☐ A linking verb connects the subject to a word or words that describe or rename it. (See 17c.)

☐ Many verbs are made up of more than one word. The complete verb in a sentence includes the main verb plus any helping verbs. (See 17c.)

18 Writing Compound Sentences

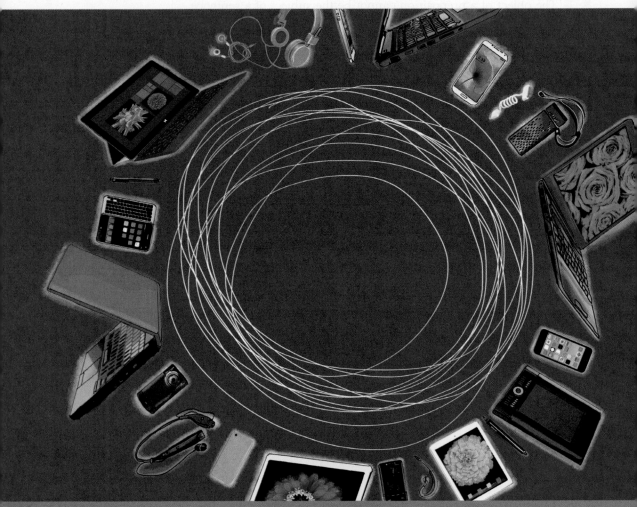

Image Source

focus on writing

Write a paragraph in which you explain the impact of a particular electronic device on your life or on the lives of your family members.

In this chapter, you will learn to

- form compound sentences with coordinating conjunctions (18a)
- form compound sentences with semicolons (18b)
- form compound sentences with transitional words and phrases (18c)

The most basic kind of sentence, a **simple sentence**, consists of a single **independent clause**: one <u>subject</u> and one <u>verb</u>.

European <u>immigrants</u> <u>arrived</u> at Ellis Island.

A **compound sentence** is made up of two or more simple sentences (independent clauses).

18a Using Coordinating Conjunctions

One way to form a compound sentence is by joining two independent clauses with a **coordinating conjunction** preceded by a comma.

Many European immigrants arrived at Ellis Island, <u>but</u> many Asian immigrants arrived at Angel Island.

WORD POWER

coordinate (verb) to link two or more things that are equal in importance, rank, or degree

Coordinating Conjunctions

and	for	or	yet
but	nor	so	

FYI

Use the letters that spell *FANBOYS* to help you remember the coordinating conjunctions.

F	for
A	and
N	nor
B	but
O	or
Y	yet
S	so

LaunchPad

Visit *LaunchPad Solo for Readers and Writers* > **Prepositions and Conjunctions** for more practice with conjunctions.

Coordinating conjunctions join two ideas of equal importance. They describe the relationship between two ideas, showing how and why the ideas are related. Different coordinating conjunctions have different meanings.

■ To indicate addition, use *and*.

He acts like a child, <u>and</u> people think he is cute.

■ To indicate contrast or contradiction, use *but* or *yet*.

He acts like a child, <u>but</u> he is an adult.

He acts like a child, <u>yet</u> he wants to be taken seriously.

■ To indicate a cause-and-effect relationship, use *so* or *for*.

He acts like a child, <u>so</u> we treat him like one.

He acts like a child, <u>for</u> he needs attention.

■ To present alternatives, use *or*.

Either he acts like a child, <u>or</u> he is ignored.

■ To eliminate alternatives, use *nor*.

He does not act like a child, <u>nor</u> does he look like one.

FYI

Commas with Coordinating Conjunctions

When you use a coordinating conjunction to join two independent clauses into a single compound sentence, always put a comma before the coordinating conjunction.

We can stand in line all night, or we can go home now.

PRACTICE

18-1 Fill in the coordinating conjunction—*and, but, for, nor, or, so,* or *yet*—that most logically links the two parts of each compound sentence. Remember to insert a comma before each coordinating conjunction.

Example: Fairy tales have been told by many people around the world, <u>*but*</u> the stories by two German brothers may be the most famous.

(1) Jakob and Wilhelm Grimm lived in the nineteenth century _____ they wrote many well-known fairy tales. (2) Most people think fondly of fairy tales _____ the Brothers Grimm wrote many unpleasant and violent stories. (3) In their best-known works, children are abused _____ endings are not always happy. (4) Either innocent children are brutally punished for no reason _____ they are neglected. (5) For example, in "Hansel and Gretel," the stepmother mistreats the children _____ their father abandons them in the woods. (6) In this story, the events are horrifying _____ the ending is still happy. (7) The children outwit the evil adults _____ they escape unharmed. (8) Apparently, they are not injured physically _____ are they harmed emotionally. (9) Nevertheless, their story can hardly be called pleasant _____ it remains a story of child abuse and neglect.

PRACTICE

18-2   Add coordinating conjunctions to combine some of the simple sentences in the following paragraph. Remember to put a comma before each coordinating conjunction you add.

Example: Years ago, few Americans lived to be one hundred. ^{, *but today,*} ~~Today,~~ there are over 70,000 centenarians.

(1) Diet, exercise, and family history may explain centenarians' long lives. (2) This is not the whole story. (3) A recent study showed surprising similarities among centenarians. (4) They did not all avoid tobacco and alcohol. (5) They did not have low-fat diets. (6) In fact, they ate relatively large amounts of fat, cholesterol, and sugar. (7) Diet could not explain their long lives. (8) They did, however, share four key traits. (9) First, all

the centenarians were optimistic about life. (10) All were positive thinkers. (11) They also had deep religious faith. (12) In addition, they had all continued to lead physically active lives. (13) They remained mobile even as elderly people. (14) Finally, all were able to adapt to loss. (15) They had all lost friends, spouses, or children. (16) They were able to get on with their lives.

PRACTICE

18-3 Write another simple sentence to follow each of the sentences below. Then, connect the sentences with a coordinating conjunction and the correct punctuation.

Example: Many patients need organ transplants,/ _, but there is a serious_ _shortage of organ donors._

1. Secondhand smoke is dangerous. _____

   _____

2. Kangaroos carry their young in pouches. _____

   _____

3. Motorcycle helmet laws have been dropped in some states. _____

   _____

4. Many juice drinks actually contain very little real fruit juice. _____

   _____

5. People tend to resist change. _____

   _____

18b Using Semicolons

Another way to create a compound sentence is by joining two simple sentences (independent clauses) with a **semicolon**. A semicolon connects clauses whose ideas are closely related.

The AIDS Memorial Quilt contains thousands of panels; each panel represents a life lost to AIDS.

Also use a semicolon to show a strong contrast between two ideas.

> With new drugs, people can live with AIDS for years; many people, however, cannot get these drugs.

FYI

Avoiding Fragments

A semicolon can only join two complete sentences (independent clauses). A semicolon cannot join a sentence and a fragment.

────────── FRAGMENT ──────────

INCORRECT   Because millions worldwide are still dying of AIDS; more research is needed.

────────── SENTENCE ──────────

CORRECT   Millions worldwide are still dying of AIDS; more research is needed.

PRACTICE

18-4   Each of the following items consists of one simple sentence. Create a compound sentence for each item by changing the period to a semicolon and then adding another simple sentence.

Example: My brother is addicted to fast food; *he eats it every day.*

1. Fast-food restaurants are an American institution. _____

_____

2. Families often eat at these restaurants. _____

_____

3. Many teenagers work there. _____

_____

4. Many fast-food restaurants offer some low-fat menu items. _____

_____

5. Some offer recyclable packaging. _____

_____

6. Some even have playgrounds. _____

_____

18c Using Transitional Words and Phrases

Another way to create a compound sentence is by combining two simple sentences (independent clauses) with a **transitional word or phrase**. When you use a transitional word or phrase to join two sentences, always place a semicolon *before* the transitional word or phrase and a comma *after* it.

> Many college students apply for grants; <u>in addition</u>, they often have to take out loans.

> He had a miserable time at the party; <u>besides</u>, he lost his wallet.

Frequently Used Transitional Words

also	instead	still
besides	later	subsequently
consequently	meanwhile	then
eventually	moreover	therefore
finally	nevertheless	thus
furthermore	now	
however	otherwise	

Frequently Used Transitional Phrases

after all	in comparison
as a result	in contrast
at the same time	in fact
for example	in other words
for instance	of course
in addition	on the contrary

Adding a transitional word or phrase makes the connection between ideas in a sentence clearer and more precise than it would be if the ideas were linked with just a semicolon. Different transitional words and phrases convey different meanings.

■ Some signal addition (*also, besides, furthermore, in addition, moreover,* and so on).

> I have a lot on my mind; <u>also</u>, I have a lot of things to do.

■ Some make causal connections (*therefore, as a result, consequently, thus,* and so on).

> I have a lot on my mind; <u>therefore</u>, it is hard to concentrate.

■ Some indicate contradiction or contrast (*nevertheless, however, in contrast, still,* and so on).

> I have a lot on my mind; <u>still</u>, I must try to relax.

■ Some present alternatives (*instead, on the contrary, otherwise,* and so on).

> I have a lot on my mind; <u>otherwise</u>, I could relax.
>
> I will try not to think; <u>instead</u>, I will relax.

■ Some indicate time sequence (*eventually, finally, at the same time, later, meanwhile, now, subsequently, then,* and so on).

> I have a lot on my mind; <u>meanwhile</u>, I still have work to do.

PRACTICE

18-5 Add semicolons and commas where required to set off transitional words and phrases that join two independent clauses.

Example: Ketchup is a popular condiment ^;^ therefore ^,^ it is available in almost every restaurant.

(1) Andrew F. Smith, a food historian, wrote a book about the tomato later he wrote a book about ketchup. (2) This book, *Pure Ketchup*, was a big project in fact Smith worked on it for five years. (3) The word *ketchup* may have come from a Chinese word however Smith is not certain of the word's origins. (4) Ketchup has existed since ancient times in other words it is a very old product. (5) Ketchup has changed a lot over the years for example special dyes were developed in the nineteenth century to make it red. (6) Smith discusses many other changes for instance preservative-

WORD POWER

condiment a prepared sauce or pickle used to add flavor to food

free ketchup was invented in 1907. (7) Ketchup is now used by people in many cultures still salsa is more popular than ketchup in the United States. (8) Today, designer ketchups are being developed meanwhile Heinz once introduced green and purple ketchup in squeeze bottles. (9) Some of today's ketchups are chunky in addition some ketchups are spicy. (10) Ketchup continues to evolve meanwhile Smith has written a book about hamburgers.

PRACTICE

18-6 Consulting the lists of transitional words and phrases on page 342, choose a word or phrase that logically connects each pair of simple sentences in the following paragraph into one compound sentence. Be sure to punctuate appropriately.

Example: Red-light cameras are used worldwide; however, some ~~Some~~ people believe these cameras should be illegal.

(1) Red-light cameras are a form of traffic enforcement. The cameras have proven to be controversial. (2) Cars trigger the camera. The camera photographs the car. (3) A law-enforcement official reviews the photos. The officer issues tickets to drivers who ran the red light. (4) The cameras enforce traffic rules. They should reduce the number of crashes. (5) Some say the cameras are not a safety feature. They primarily increase revenue. (6) Opponents are concerned about danger. Drivers may stop to avoid running a red light. (7) Some people are concerned about the pictures. They think the cameras violate their privacy. (8) The risks and rewards of red-light cameras are not necessarily clear. Several states have banned their use. (9) The red-light camera controversy will likely continue for years to come. It is every driver's responsibility to drive safely. (10) Drivers should obey traffic rules. Everyone should want safe roads.

PRACTICE

18-7   Add the suggested transitional word or phrase to each of the following simple sentences. Then, add a new independent clause after it. Be sure to punctuate correctly.

Example: Commuting students do not really experience campus life. (however)

Commuting students do not really experience campus life; however, there are some

benefits to being a commuter.

1. Campus residents may have a better college experience. (still)

_____

_____

2. Living at home gives students access to home-cooked meals. (in contrast)

_____

_____

3. Commuters have a wide choice of jobs in the community. (on the other hand)

_____

_____

4. Commuters get to see their families every day. (however)

_____

_____

5. There are also some disadvantages to being a commuter. (for example)

_____

_____

6. Unlike campus residents, many commuters have family responsibilities. (in fact)

_____

_____

7. Commuters might need a car to get to school. (consequently)

_____

_____

8. Commuting to college has pros and cons. (therefore)

_____

_____

PRACTICE
18-8   Using both the specified topics and transitional words and phrases, create three original compound sentences. Be sure to punctuate appropriately.

Example
Topic: fad diets
Transitional phrase: for example

People are always falling for fad diets; for example, some people eat only

pineapple to lose weight.

1. *Topic:* laws to protect people from bullying
   Transitional phrase: in addition

   _____

   _____

2. *Topic:* single men or women as adoptive parents
   Transitional word: however

   _____

   _____

3. *Topic:* course requirements at your school
   Transitional word: instead

   _____

   _____

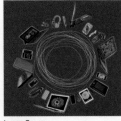
Image Source

TEST · Revise · Edit · Proofread
Look back at your response to the Focus on Writing prompt on page 336. **TEST** what you have written. Then, revise, edit, and proofread your work, checking each compound sentence to make sure you have used the coordinating conjunction or transitional word or phrase that best conveys your meaning and that you have punctuated these sentences correctly.

EDITING PRACTICE

Read the following student essay. Then, create compound sentences by linking pairs of simple sentences where appropriate, joining them with a coordinating conjunction, a semicolon, or a transitional word or phrase. Remember to put commas before coordinating conjunctions and to use semicolons and commas correctly with transitional words and phrases. The first two sentences have been combined for you.

My Grandfather's Life

My great-grandparents were born in Ukraine, *, but they* ~~They~~ raised my grandfather in western Pennsylvania. The ninth of their ten children, he had a life I cannot begin to imagine. To me, he was my big, strong, powerful grandfather. He was also a child of poverty.

My great-grandfather worked for the American Car Foundry. The family lived in a company house. They shopped at the company store. In 1934, my great-grandfather was laid off. He went to work digging sewer lines for the government. At that time, the family was on welfare. Every week, they were entitled to get food rations. My grandfather would go to pick up the food. The family desperately needed the prunes, beans, flour, margarine, and other things.

For years, my grandfather wore his brothers' hand-me-down clothes. He wore thrift-shop shoes with cardboard over the holes in the soles. He was often hungry. He would sometimes sit by the side of the railroad tracks, waiting for the engineer to throw him an orange. My grandfather would do any job to earn a quarter. Once, he weeded a mile-long row of tomato plants. For this work, he was paid twenty-five cents and a pack of NECCO wafers.

My grandfather saved his pennies. Eventually, he was able to buy a used bicycle for two dollars. He dropped out of school at fourteen and got a job. The family badly needed his income. He woke up every day at 4 a.m. He rode his bike to his job at a meatpacking plant. He worked for fifty cents a day.

In 1943, at the age of seventeen, my grandfather joined the U.S. Navy. He discovered a new world. For the first time in his life, he had enough to eat. He was always first in line at the mess hall. He went back for seconds and thirds before anyone else. After the war ended in 1945, he was discharged from the Navy. He went to work in a meat market in New York City. The only trade he knew was the meat business. Three years later, when he had saved enough to open his own store, Pete's Quality Meats, he knew his life of poverty was finally over.

COLLABORATIVE ACTIVITY

Working in a small group, pair each of the simple sentences in the left-hand column below with a sentence in the right-hand column to create ten compound sentences. Use as many different coordinating conjunctions as you can to connect the independent clauses. Be sure each coordinating conjunction you choose conveys a logical relationship between ideas, and remember to put a comma before each one. You may use some of the listed sentences more than once. *Note:* Many different combinations—some serious and factually accurate, some humorous—are possible.

Some dogs wear little sweaters.	Many are named Hamlet.
Pit bulls are raised to fight.	They live in groups.
Bonobos are pygmy chimpanzees.	One even sings Christmas carols.
	They can wear bandanas.
Many people fear Dobermans.	They can play Frisbee.
Leopards have spots.	Many live in equatorial Zaire.
Dalmatians can live in fire-houses.	Some people think they are gentle.
Horses can wear blankets.	They don't get cold in winter.
All mules are sterile.	They are half horse and half donkey.
Great Danes are huge dogs.	
Parrots can often speak.	They can be unpredictable.

review checklist

Writing Compound Sentences

☐ A compound sentence is made up of two simple sentences (independent clauses).

☐ A coordinating conjunction—*and, but, for, nor, or, so,* or *yet*—can join two independent clauses into one compound sentence. A comma always comes before the coordinating conjunction. (See 18a.)

☐ A semicolon can join two independent clauses into one compound sentence. (See 18b.)

☐ A transitional word or phrase can also join two independent clauses into one compound sentence. When it joins two independent clauses, a transitional word or phrase is always preceded by a semicolon and followed by a comma. (See 18c.)

19 Writing Complex Sentences

© Rosemary Roberts/Alamy

focus on writing

This picture shows cigarette packages from the United Kingdom, which have larger, more explicit warning labels than those sold in the United States. (Some European warning labels are even more explicit, showing pictures of diseased lungs.) Write a paragraph about whether you think cigarette companies in the United States should have similar explicit warning labels. Explain why you think such a change is (or is not) necessary.

In this chapter, you will learn to

- identify complex sentences (19a)
- use subordinating conjunctions to form complex sentences (19b)
- use relative pronouns to form complex sentences (19c)

19a Identifying Complex Sentences

As you learned in Chapter 18, an **independent clause** can stand alone as a sentence.

INDEPENDENT   The <u>exhibit</u> <u>was</u> controversial.
CLAUSE

However, a **dependent clause** cannot stand alone as a sentence.

DEPENDENT   Because the exhibit was controversial
CLAUSE

What happened because the exhibit was controversial? To answer this question, you need to add an independent clause that completes the idea begun in the dependent clause. The result is a **complex sentence**— a sentence that consists of one independent clause and one or more dependent clauses.

```
          ┌──────── DEPENDENT CLAUSE ────────┐ ┌ INDEPENDENT CLAUSE ─┐
COMPLEX    Because the exhibit was controversial, many people
SENTENCE   ──────────────┘
           came to see it.
```

PRACTICE

19-1 In the blank after each of the following items, indicate whether the group of words is an independent clause (*IC*) or a dependent clause (*DC*).

Example: When novelist Toni Morrison was born in Ohio in 1931.

  DC

1. As a young reader, Toni Morrison liked the classic Russian novelists.

   _____

2. After she graduated from Howard University with a bachelor's degree

   in English. _____

3. Morrison based her novel *The Bluest Eye* on a childhood friend's prayers to God for blue eyes. _____

4. While she raised two sons as a single mother and worked as an editor at Random House. _____

5. As her reputation as a novelist grew with the publication of *Song of Solomon* and *Tar Baby*. _____

6. Her picture appeared on the cover of *Newsweek* in 1981. _____

7. Before her novel *Beloved* won the 1988 Pulitzer Prize for Fiction. _____

8. *Beloved* was made into a film starring Oprah Winfrey. _____

9. In 1993, Morrison became the first African American woman to win the Nobel Prize in Literature. _____

10. Who published the novel *God Help the Child* in 2015 to favorable reviews. _____

19b Using Subordinating Conjunctions

WORD POWER

subordinate (adj) lower in rank or position; secondary in importance

Visit *LaunchPad Solo for Readers and Writers* > **Prepositions and Conjunctions** for more practice with conjunctions.

One way to form a complex sentence is to use a **subordinating conjunction**—a word such as *although* or *because*—to join two simple sentences (independent clauses). When the subordinating conjunction is added to the beginning of one simple sentence, the sentence becomes dependent for its meaning on the other simple sentence.

TWO SIMPLE SENTENCES	Muhammad Ali was stripped of his heavyweight title for refusing to go into the army. Many people admired his antiwar position.
COMPLEX SENTENCE	┌─── **DEPENDENT CLAUSE** ───┐ Although Muhammad Ali was stripped of his heavyweight title for refusing to go into the army, many people admired his antiwar position.

Frequently Used Subordinating Conjunctions

after	even though	since	whenever
although	if	so that	where
as	if only	than	whereas
as if	in order that	that	wherever
as though	now that	though	whether
because	once	unless	while
before	provided that	until	
even if	rather than	when	

As the chart below shows, different subordinating conjunctions express different relationships between dependent and independent clauses.

Relationship between Clauses	Subordinating Conjunction	Example
Time	after, before, since, until, when, whenever, while	When the whale surfaced, Ahab threw his harpoon.
Reason or cause	as, because	Scientists scaled back the project because the government cut funds.
Result or effect	in order that, so that	So that students' math scores will improve, many schools have begun special programs.
Condition	even if, if, unless	The rain forest may disappear unless steps are taken immediately.
Contrast	although, even though, though	Although Thomas Edison had almost no formal education, he was a successful inventor.
Location	where, wherever	Pittsburgh was built where the Allegheny and Monongahela Rivers meet.

FYI

Punctuating with Subordinating Conjunctions

In a complex sentence, use a comma after the dependent clause.

┌──── DEPENDENT CLAUSE ────────────┐ ┌── INDEPENDENT CLAUSE ──────
Although she wore the scarlet letter, Hester carried herself
┌────────┐
proudly.

Do not use a comma after the independent clause.

┌──────── INDEPENDENT CLAUSE ──┐ ┌──────── DEPENDENT CLAUSE ────────┐
Hester carried herself proudly although she wore the scarlet letter.

PRACTICE

19-2   In the blank in each of the sentences below, write an appropriate subordinating conjunction. Be sure to choose a conjunction that expresses the logical relationship between the two clauses it links.

Example: Movie cowboys are usually portrayed as white _althought_
many were African American.

(1) Few people today know about black cowboys _____ they were once common. (2) _____ the transcontinental railroad was built, cowboys were in high demand. (3) The ranchers hired cowboys to drive their cattle to the Midwest, _____ the cows were loaded on trains headed to eastern cities. (4) Many former slaves became cowboys _____ they wanted a new start. (5) Many African Americans also became cowboys _____ they had experience working with horses and cattle on Southern plantations or farms. (6) However, black cowboys faced difficulties _____ they arrived in the West. (7) African American cowboys often had to work much harder than whites _____ earn the same pay and respect. (8) _____ almost one-fourth of cowboys were black, few writers wrote about them. (9) The myth of the white-only cowboy was spread in novels, films,

and television shows _____ black cowboys never existed.
(10) Black cowboys did appear in some films of the 1970s _____
by this time Westerns were no longer popular. (11) Things started to
change in the 1970s _____ several museums honored black,
Indian, and Mexican cowboys. (12) _____ African American
cowboys have finally received some recognition, their history can now be
more fully understood.

19c Using Relative Pronouns

Another way to form a complex sentence is to use **relative pronouns**
(*who, that, which,* and so on) to join two simple sentences (independent
clauses).

TWO SIMPLE SENTENCES	Harry Potter is an adolescent wizard. He attends Hogwarts School of Witchcraft and Wizardry.
COMPLEX SENTENCE	┌──────── **DEPENDENT CLAUSE** ────────┐ Harry Potter, who attends Hogwarts School of Witchcraft and Wizardry, is an adolescent wizard.

Note: The relative pronoun always refers to a word or words in the independent clause. (In the complex sentence above, *who* refers to *Harry Potter*.)

Relative Pronouns

that	which	whoever	whomever
what	who	whom	whose

LaunchPad

Visit *LaunchPad Solo for Readers and Writers* > **Pronouns** for more practice with relative pronouns.

A relative pronoun indicates the relationships between the ideas in
the independent and dependent clauses it links.

TWO SIMPLE SENTENCES	Nadine Gordimer lived in South Africa. She won the Nobel Prize in Literature in 1991.

COMPLEX SENTENCE	Nadine Gordimer, who won the Nobel Prize in Literature in 1991, lived in South Africa.
TWO SIMPLE SENTENCES	Last week I had a job interview. It went very well.
COMPLEX SENTENCE	Last week I had a job interview that went very well.
TWO SIMPLE SENTENCES	Transistors have replaced vacuum tubes in radios and televisions. They were invented in 1948.
COMPLEX SENTENCE	Transistors, which were invented in 1948, have replaced vacuum tubes in radios and televisions.

PRACTICE

19-3   In each of the following complex sentences, underline the dependent clause once, and underline the relative pronoun twice. Then, draw an arrow from the relative pronoun to the word or words to which it refers.

Example: Research shows that vampire lengends, which you may have thought were fiction, have some truth to them.

1. Vampires, who were thought to be terrifying fiction, have been proven to be "real."

2. Recently released research debunks the myth that vampires are only found in fiction.

3. These vampires did not suck anyone's blood, which is important to note, or return from the dead.

4. Vampire rumors, which began when a person died, started because close family members often died at the same time.

5. Fear quickly turned into panic that caused the vampire folklore.

6. People assumed that the deceased, who were returning as vampires, wanted to consume the blood of their family members.

7. The real issue, which many people did not understand at the time, was germs.

8. Poor hygiene, which came from a lack of basic health knowledge, led to diseases that spread quickly.

9. Doctors, who were limited by the knowledge of the era, thought that exhuming the bodies and removing the heart of the deceased was the only way to prevent the rise of vampires.

10. Researchers, who are still discovering "real" vampire stories, now know that the origins of the vampire began with misinformation.

PRACTICE
19-4   Combine each of the following pairs of simple sentences into one complex sentence. Use the relative pronoun that follows each pair.

> **Example:**   Elias Howe invented an early type of zipper. He was too busy with his other invention—the sewing machine—to work on it. (who)
>
> _Elias Howe, who invented an early type of zipper, was too busy with his other_
>
> _invention—the sewing machine—to work on it._

1. Early zippers were just hooks and eyes. These hooks and eyes were fastened to a cloth tape. (that)

   _____

   _____

2. Gideon Sundback invented the first useful zipper. He worked endless hours to help him stop grieving for his wife. (who)

   _____

   _____

3. Their "high" price kept early zippers from becoming popular. It was about eighteen cents. (which)

   _____

   _____

4. The word *zipper* began as a brand name. It was coined by a company executive. (which)

_____

_____

5. At first, zipper manufacturers could not convince people to use zippers in clothing. They sold many zippers for boots. (who)

_____

_____

© Rosemary Roberts/Alamy

TEST · Revise · Edit · Proofread

Look back at your response to the Focus on Writing prompt on page 350. TEST what you have written. Then, revise and edit your work, making sure that you have used subordinating conjunctions and relative pronouns correctly and that your complex sentences are punctuated correctly. Finally, proofread your paragraph.

EDITING PRACTICE

Read the following student essay. Then, revise it by combining pairs of simple sentences with subordinating conjunctions or relative pronouns that indicate the relationship between them. Be sure to punctuate correctly. The first two sentences have been combined for you.

Community Art

When a   *, the*

A̶ city has a crime problem, T̶h̶e̶ police and the courts try to solve it. Some cities have come up with creative ways to help young people stay out of trouble. One example is the Philadelphia Mural Arts Program. It offers free art education for high school students.

In the 1960s, Philadelphia had a serious problem. The problem was graffiti. Graffiti artists had painted on buildings all over the city. A solution to the problem was the Philadelphia Anti-Graffiti Network. This offered graffiti artists an alternative. The artists would give up graffiti. They would not be prosecuted. The artists enjoyed painting. They could paint murals on public buildings instead. They could create beautiful landscapes, portraits of local heroes, and abstract designs. The graffiti artists had once been lawbreakers. They could now help beautify the city.

The Mural Arts Program began in 1984 as a part of the Philadelphia Anti-Graffiti Network. By 1996, the Philadelphia Anti-Graffiti Network was focusing on eliminating graffiti, and its Mural Arts Program was working to improve the community. It no longer worked with graffiti offenders. It ran after-school and summer programs for students. The Mural Arts Program got national recognition in 1997. That is when President Bill Clinton helped paint a mural. So far, the Mural Arts Program has completed more than 2,800 murals. This is more than any other public art program in the country.

Over 20,000 students have taken part in the Mural Arts Program. The students come from all parts of the city. In one part of the program, students work alongside professional artists. The students get to paint parts of the artists' murals themselves. The artwork is on public buildings. The artwork can be seen by everyone.

The Mural Arts Program continues to build a brighter future for students and their communities. It is now over a quarter of a century old. Students help bring people together to create a mural. They feel a stronger connection to their community and more confidence in themselves. They leave the program. They are equipped to make a positive difference in their communities and in their own lives.

COLLABORATIVE ACTIVITY

Working in a group of four students, make a list of three or four of your favorite television shows. Then, divide into pairs, and with your partner, write two simple sentences describing each show. Next, use subordinating conjunctions or relative pronouns to combine each pair of sentences into one complex sentence. With your group, discuss how the ideas in each complex sentence are related, and make sure you have used the subordinating conjunction or relative pronoun that best conveys this relationship.

Example: *The Walking Dead* is a horror series set in a world overrun by zombies. It appeals to many of today's viewers.

The Walking Dead, which appeals to many of today's viewers, is a horror series set in a world overrun by zombies.

review checklist

Writing Complex Sentences

▪ A complex sentence consists of one independent clause (simple sentence) combined with one or more dependent clauses. (See 19a.)

▪ Subordinating conjunctions—dependent words such as *although, after, when, while,* and *because*—can join two independent clauses into one complex sentence. (See 19b.)

▪ Relative pronouns—dependent words such as *who, which,* and *that*—can also join two independent clauses into one complex sentence. The relative pronoun shows the relationship between the ideas in the two independent clauses that it links. (See 19c.)

20 Writing Varied Sentences

focus on writing

This picture shows items about to be preserved in a time capsule at the History Center in Pittsburgh. Write a paragraph about a time capsule you might construct for your children to open when they are adults. What items would you include? How would you expect each item to communicate to your children what you and your world were like? Be sure to include explanations for your decisions.

Sentence variety is important because a paragraph of varied sentences flows more smoothly, is easier to read and understand, and is more interesting than one in which all the sentences are structured in the same way.

20a Varying Sentence Types

Most English sentences are **statements**. Others are **questions** or **exclamations**. One way to vary your sentences is to use an occasional question or exclamation where it is appropriate.

In the following paragraph, a question and an exclamation add variety.

Question

Exclamation

> Jacqueline Cochran, the first woman pilot to break the sound barrier, was one of the most important figures in aviation history. In 1996, the United States Postal Service issued a stamp honoring Cochran; the words "Pioneer Pilot" appear under her name. <u>What did she do to earn this title and this tribute?</u> Cochran broke more flight records than anyone else in her lifetime and won many awards, including the United States Distinguished Service Medal in 1945 and the United States Air Force Distinguished Flying Cross in 1969. During World War II, she helped form the WASPs, the Women's Air Force Service Pilots program, so that women could fly military planes to their bases (even though they were not allowed to go into combat). Remarkably, she accomplished all this with only three weeks of flying instruction. She only got her pilot's license in the first place because she wanted to start her own cosmetics business and flying would enable her to travel quickly around the country. Although she never planned to be a pilot, once she discovered flying she quickly became the best. <u>Not surprisingly, when the Postal Service honored Jacqueline Cochran, it was with an airmail stamp!</u>

PRACTICE

20-1 Revise the following paragraph by changing one of the statements into a question and one of the statements into an exclamation.

Example: Lewis Carroll first applied the term *portmanteau words* to certain English words. (statement)

Did Lewis Carroll first apply the term portmanteau words to certain English

words? (question)

(1) Many words in the English language are actually two words merged into one. (2) For example, combining the words *breakfast* and *lunch* creates the word *brunch*. (3) A person who works too much might be called a *workaholic*, a word we get from combining the words *work* and *alcoholic*. (4) These words have a name. (5) Word combinations like these are called *portmanteau words*. (6) In nineteenth-century English, *portmanteau* was the name for a suitcase that opens into two equal halves. (7) The two halves comprise the whole suitcase, just as the two words form a portmanteau. (8) Popular English is always developing new portmanteau words. (9) For example, a combination fork and spoon is called a *spork*, and a *turducken* is a chicken inside a duck, which is inside a turkey. (10) In fact, even the coined names of Hollywood couples, such as *Brangelina* (*Brad* plus *Angelina*), might be considered portmanteau words.

20b Varying Sentence Openings

When all the sentences in a paragraph begin the same way, your writing is likely to seem dull and repetitive. In the following paragraph, for example, every sentence begins with the subject.

> Scientists have been observing a disturbing phenomenon. The population of frogs, toads, and salamanders has been declining. This decline was first noticed in the mid-1980s. Some reports blamed chemical pollution. Some biologists began to suspect that a fungal disease was killing these amphibians. The most reasonable explanation seems to be that the amphibians' eggs are threatened by solar radiation. This radiation penetrates the thinned ozone layer, which used to shield them from the sun's rays.

WORD POWER

amphibians cold-blooded vertebrates, such as frogs, that live both in the water and on land

Beginning with Adverbs

Instead of opening every sentence in a paragraph with the subject, you can try beginning some sentences with one or more **adverbs**.

> Scientists have been observing a disturbing phenomenon. <u>Gradually but steadily</u>, the population of frogs, toads, and salamanders has been declining. This decline was first noticed in the mid-1980s. Some reports blamed chemical pollution. Some biologists began to suspect that a fungal disease was killing these amphibians. <u>However</u>, the most reasonable explanation seems to be that the amphibians' eggs are threatened by solar radiation. This radiation penetrates the thinned ozone layer, which used to shield them from the sun's rays.

PRACTICE

20-2 Underline the adverb in each of the following sentences, and then rewrite the sentence so that the adverb appears at the beginning. Be sure to punctuate correctly.

Example: An internship is <u>usually</u> a one-time work or service experience related to a student's career plans.

Usually, an internship is a one-time work or service experience related to a student's

career plans.

1. Internships are sometimes paid or counted for academic credit.

   _____

2. A prospective student intern should first talk to an academic adviser.

   _____

3. The student should next write a résumé listing job experience, education, and interests.

   _____

4. The student can then send the résumé to organizations that are looking for interns.

   _____

5. Going to job fairs and networking are often good ways to find internships.

   _____

PRACTICE

20-3 In each of the following sentences, fill in the blank with an appropriate adverb. Be sure to punctuate correctly.

Example: _Slowly,_   the sun crept over the horizon.

1. _____ the speeding car appeared from out of nowhere.

2. _____ it crashed into the guardrail.

3. _____ the car jackknifed across the highway.

4. _____ drivers behind the car slammed on their brakes.

5. _____ someone called 911.

6. _____ a wailing siren could be heard.

7. _____ the ambulance arrived.

8. _____ emergency medical technicians went to work.

9. _____ a police officer was on hand to direct traffic.

10. _____ no one was badly hurt in the accident.

Beginning with Prepositional Phrases

Another way to create sentence variety is to begin some sentences with prepositional phrases. A **prepositional phrase** (such as _along the river_ or _near the diner_) is made up of a preposition and its object.

> In recent years, scientists have observed a disturbing phenomenon. Gradually but steadily, the population of frogs, toads, and salamanders has been declining. This was first noticed in the mid-1980s. At first, some reports blamed chemical pollution. After a while, some biologists began to suspect that a fungal disease was killing them. However, the most reasonable explanation seems to be that the amphibians' eggs are threatened by solar radiation. This radiation penetrates the thinned ozone layer, which used to shield them from the sun's rays.

PRACTICE

20-4 Underline the prepositional phrase in each of the following sentences, and then rewrite the sentence so that the prepositional phrase appears at the beginning. Be sure to punctuate correctly.

Example: Very few American women did factory work before the 1940s.

Before the 1940s, very few American women did factory work.

1. Many male factory workers became soldiers during World War II.

   _____

2. The U.S. government encouraged women to take factory jobs in the war's early years.

   _____

3. Over six million women took factory jobs between 1942 and 1945.

   _____

4. A new female image emerged with this greater responsibility and independence.

   _____

   _____

5. Many women wore pants for the first time.

   _____

6. Most women lost their factory jobs after the war and returned to "women's work."

   _____

PRACTICE

20-5   In each of the following sentences, fill in the blank with an appropriate prepositional phrase. Be sure to punctuate correctly.

Example: _At the start of the New York Marathon,_ Justin felt as if he could run forever.

1. _____ he warmed up by stretching and bending.

2. _____ all the runners were crowded together.

3. _____ they crossed a bridge over the Hudson River.

4. _____ the route became more and more challenging.

5. _____ Justin grabbed some water from a helpful onlooker.

6. _____ he staggered across the finish line.

PRACTICE

20-6   Every sentence in the following paragraph begins with the subject, but several contain prepositional phrases or adverbs that could be moved to the beginning. To vary the sentence openings, move prepositional phrases to the beginnings of four sentences, and move adverbs to the beginnings of two other sentences. Be sure to place a comma after these introductory phrases.

Example: *By the early 2000s, everyone*
~~Everyone~~ had heard of Venus and Serena Williams ~~by the early 2000s.~~

(1) Venus and Serena Williams are famous for their tennis skills in the sports world. (2) Venus is older, but the sisters are just one year apart. (3) The Williams sisters were playing tennis professionally by the time they were teenagers. (4) They have played both as opponents and as doubles partners. (5) The sisters won several gold medals at the 2012 Olympics. (6) They still support each other as sisters, bravely facing intense competition. (7) Venus and Serena have also written books and produced popular fashion lines, successfully developing business careers. (8) The Williams sisters had to overcome the challenges of their childhood in a tough neighborhood in Compton, California, to achieve their dreams.

20c Combining Sentences

You can also create sentence variety by experimenting with different ways of combining sentences.

Using -*ing* Modifiers

A **modifier** identifies or describes other words in a sentence. You can use an -*ing* modifier to combine two sentences.

TWO SENTENCES   Duke Ellington composed more than a thousand songs. He worked hard to establish his reputation.

<table>
<tr><td>COMBINED WITH
-ING MODIFIER</td><td>Composing <u>more than a thousand songs</u>, Duke Ellington worked hard to establish his reputation.</td></tr>
</table>

When the two sentences above are combined, the *-ing* modifier (*composing more than a thousand songs*) describes the new sentence's subject (*Duke Ellington*).

PRACTICE

20-7   Use an *-ing* modifier to combine each of the following pairs of sentences into a single sentence. Eliminate any unnecessary words, and place a comma after each *-ing* modifier.

> **Example:** Many American colleges are setting an example for the rest of the country. They are going green.
>
> *Setting an example for the rest of the country, many American colleges are going green.*

1. Special lamps in the dorms of one Ohio college change from green to red. They warn of rising energy use.

   _____

   _____

2. A Vermont college captures methane from dairy cows. It now needs less energy from other sources.

   _____

   _____

3. Student gardeners at a North Carolina college tend a campus vegetable plot. They supply the cafeteria with organic produce.

   _____

   _____

4. A building on a California campus proves that recycled materials can be beautiful. It is built from redwood wine casks.

   _____

   _____

5. Some colleges offer courses in sustainability. They are preparing students to take the green revolution beyond campus.

   _____

   _____

Using *-ed* Modifiers

You can also use an *-ed* modifier to combine two sentences.

TWO SENTENCES Nogales is located on the border between Arizona and Mexico. It is a bilingual city.

COMBINED WITH *-ED* MODIFIER Located on the border between Arizona and Mexico, Nogales is a bilingual city.

When the two sentences above are combined, the *-ed* modifier (*located on the border between Arizona and Mexico*) describes the new sentence's subject (*Nogales*).

PRACTICE

20-8 Use an *-ed* modifier to combine each of the following pairs of sentences into a single sentence. Eliminate any unnecessary words, and use a comma to set off each *-ed* modifier. When you are finished, underline the *-ed* modifier in each sentence.

Example: Potato chips and cornflakes were invented purely by accident. They are two of America's most popular foods.

Invented purely by accident, potato chips and cornflakes are two of America's most

popular foods.

1. George Crum was employed as a chef in a fancy restaurant. He was famous for his french fries.

2. A customer was dissatisfied with the fries. He complained and asked for thinner fries.

3. The customer was served thinner fries. He was still not satisfied and complained again.

4. Crum was now very annoyed. He decided to make the fries too thin and crisp to eat with a fork.

5. The customer was thrilled with the extra-thin and crisp potatoes. He ate them all.

_____

6. Potato chips were invented to get even with a customer. They are the most popular snack food in America today.

_____

_____

7. Dr. John Kellogg was concerned about the diet of patients at his hospital. He and his brother set out to make healthy foods.

_____

_____

8. The brothers were called away on an urgent matter. They left a pot of boiled wheat on the stove.

_____

9. The wheat had hardened by the time they returned. It broke into flakes when they rolled it.

_____

10. The brothers were delighted with the results. They came up with a new flake made of corn.

_____

Using a Series of Words

Another way to vary your sentences is to combine a group of sentences into one sentence that includes a **series** of words (nouns, verbs, or adjectives). Combining sentences in this way eliminates a boring string of similar sentences and repetitive phrases and also makes your writing more concise.

GROUP OF SENTENCES College presidents want to improve athletes' academic performance. Coaches too want to improve athletes' academic performance. The players themselves also want to improve their academic performance.

COMBINED (SERIES OF NOUNS) College <u>presidents</u>, <u>coaches</u>, and the <u>players</u> themselves want to improve athletes' academic performance.

GROUP OF SENTENCES	In 1997, Arundhati Roy published her first novel, *The God of Small Things*. She won the Pulitzer Prize. She became a literary sensation.
COMBINED (SERIES OF VERBS)	In 1997, Arundhati Roy <u>published</u> her first novel, *The God of Small Things,* <u>won</u> the Pulitzer Prize, and <u>became</u> a literary sensation.
GROUP OF SENTENCES	As the tornado approached, the sky grew dark. The sky grew quiet. The sky grew threatening.
COMBINED (SERIES OF ADJECTIVES)	As the tornado approached, the sky grew <u>dark</u>, <u>quiet</u>, and <u>threatening</u>.

PRACTICE

20-9   Combine each of the following groups of sentences into one sentence that includes a series of nouns, verbs, or adjectives.

Example: Many years ago, Pacific Islanders from Samoa settled in Hawaii. Pacific Islanders from Fiji also settled in Hawaii. Pacific Islanders from Tahiti settled in Hawaii, too.

Many years ago, Pacific Islanders from Samoa, Fiji, and Tahiti settled

in Hawaii.

1. In the eighteenth century, the British explorer Captain Cook came to Hawaii. Other explorers also came to Hawaii. European travelers came to Hawaii, too.

   _____

   _____

2. Explorers and traders brought commerce to Hawaii. They brought new ideas. They brought new cultures.

   _____

   _____

3. Missionaries introduced the Christian religion. They introduced a Hawaiian-language bible. Also, they introduced a Hawaiian alphabet.

   _____

   _____

4. In the mid-nineteenth century, pineapple plantations were established in Hawaii. Sugar plantations were established there as well. Other industries were also established.

_____

_____

5. By 1900, Japanese people were working on the plantations. Chinese people were also working on the plantations. In addition, native Hawaiians were working there.

_____

_____

6. People of many different races and religions now live in Hawaii. People of many different races and religions now go to school in Hawaii. People of many different races and religions now work in Hawaii.

_____

_____

7. Schoolchildren still study the Hawaiian language. They learn about the Hawaiian kings and queens. They read about ancient traditions.

_____

_____

8. Today, Hawaii is well known for its tourism. It is well known too for its weather. It is especially well known for its natural beauty.

_____

_____

9. Tourists can swim. They can surf. They can play golf. They can ride in outrigger canoes.

_____

_____

10. Today, the state of Hawaii remains lively. It remains culturally diverse. It remains very beautiful.

_____

_____

Using Appositives

An **appositive** is a word or word group that identifies, renames, or describes an adjacent noun or pronoun. Creating an appositive is often a good way to combine two sentences about the same subject.

TWO SENTENCES	C. J. Walker was the first American woman to become a self-made millionaire. She marketed a line of hair-care products for black women.
COMBINED WITH APPOSITIVE	C. J. Walker, the first American woman to become a self-made millionaire, marketed a line of hair-care products for black women.

In the example above, the appositive appears in the middle of a sentence. However, an appositive can also come at the beginning or at the end of a sentence.

> The first American woman to become a self-made millionaire, C. J. Walker marketed a line of hair-care products for black women. (appositive at the beginning)
>
> Several books have been written about C. J. Walker, the first American woman to become a self-made millionaire. (appositive at the end)

PRACTICE

20-10   Combine each of the following pairs of sentences into one sentence by creating an appositive. Note that the appositive may appear at the beginning, in the middle, or at the end of the sentence. Be sure to use commas appropriately.

Example: *Hamilton* is a Broadway musical, It is based on a biography of Alexander Hamilton by Ron Chernow.

(1) *Hamilton* is an award-winning show about Alexander Hamilton. He was the first U.S. treasury secretary. (2) He was an immigrant from the West Indies. He was killed in a famous duel with Vice President Aaron Burr. (3) The musical numbers in *Hamilton* are notable for their hip-hop influence. They have won rave reviews. (4) The play's words and lyrics were written by Lin-Manuel Miranda. Lin-Manuel Miranda is the actor who originated the role of Alexander Hamilton on Broadway. (5) Other characters in the play include George Washington, Thomas

Jefferson, and James Madison. They are all played by African American or Hispanic actors. (6) This innovative musical has already changed the way theatergoers see American history. Some of these theatergoers are inner-city students. (7) A Rockefeller Foundation grant subsidized the cost of tickets for 20,000 New York City students. It allows them to see *Hamilton* for just ten dollars.

20d Mixing Long and Short Sentences

A paragraph of short, choppy sentences—or a paragraph of long, rambling sentences—can be monotonous. By mixing long and short sentences, perhaps combining some simple sentences to create **compound** and **complex** sentences, you can create a more interesting paragraph.

In the following paragraph, the sentences are all short, and the result is boring and hard to follow.

> The world's first drive-in movie theater opened on June 6, 1933. This drive-in was in Camden, New Jersey. Automobiles became more popular. Drive-ins did, too. By the 1950s, there were more than four thousand drive-ins in the United States. Over the years, the high cost of land led to a decline in the number of drive-ins. So did the rising popularity of television. Soon, the drive-in movie theater had almost disappeared. It was replaced by the multiplex. In 1967, there were forty-six drive-ins in New Jersey. Today, only one is still open. That one is the Delsea Drive-in in Vineland, New Jersey.

The revised paragraph that follows is more interesting and easier to read. (Note that the final short sentence is retained for emphasis.)

> The world's first drive-in movie theater opened on June 6, 1933, in Camden, New Jersey. As automobiles became more popular, drive-ins did, too, and by the 1950s, there were more than four thousand drive-ins in the United States. Over the years, the high cost of land and the rising popularity of television led to a decline in the number of drive-ins. Soon, the drive-in movie theater had almost disappeared, replaced by the multiplex. In 1967, there were forty-six drive-ins in New Jersey, but today, only one is still open. That one is the Delsea Drive-in in Vineland, New Jersey.

PRACTICE

20-11   The following paragraph contains a series of short, choppy sentences that can be combined. Revise the paragraph so that it mixes long and short sentences. Be sure to use commas and other punctuation appropriately.

> **Example:** Kente cloth has special significance for many African
> Americans/ ~~Some~~ other people do not understand this significance.
>
> *, but some* (inserted above)

(1) Kente cloth is made in western Africa. (2) It is produced primarily by the Ashanti people. (3) It has been worn for hundreds of years by African royalty. (4) They consider it a sign of power and status. (5) Many African Americans wear kente cloth. (6) They see it as a link to their heritage. (7) Each pattern on the cloth has a name. (8) Each color has a special significance. (9) For example, red and yellow suggest a long and healthy life. (10) Green and white suggest a good harvest. (11) African women may wear kente cloth as a dress or head wrap. (12) African American women, like men, usually wear strips of cloth around their shoulders. (13) Men and women of African descent wear kente cloth as a sign of racial pride. (14) It often decorates college students' gowns at graduation.

TEST · Revise · Edit · Proofread

Look back at your response to the Focus on Writing prompt on page 361. TEST what you have written. Then, using the strategies discussed in this chapter that seem appropriate, revise your writing so that your sentences are varied, interesting, and smoothly connected. Finally, edit and proofread.

Senator John Heinz History Center

EDITING PRACTICE

The following student essay lacks sentence variety. All of its sentences begin with the subject, and the essay includes a number of short, choppy sentences. Using the strategies discussed in this chapter as well as strategies for creating compound and complex sentences, revise the essay to achieve greater sentence variety. The first sentence has been edited for you.

Toys by Accident

when people

Many popular toys and games are the result of accidents. ~~People~~ try to invent one thing but discover something else instead. Sometimes they are not trying to invent anything at all. They are completely surprised to find a new product.

Play-Doh is one example of an accidental discovery. Play-Doh is a popular preschool toy. Play-Doh first appeared in Cincinnati. A company made a compound to clean wallpaper. They sold it as a cleaning product. The company then realized that this compound could be a toy. Children could mold it like clay. They could use it again and again. The new toy was an immediate hit. Play-Doh was first sold in 1956. Since then, more than two billion cans have been sold.

The Slinky was discovered by Richard James. He was an engineer. At the time, he was trying to invent a spring to keep ships' instruments steady at sea. He tested hundreds of springs of varying sizes, metals, and tensions. None of them worked. One spring fell off the desk and "walked" down a pile of books. It then went end over end onto the floor. He thought his children might enjoy playing with it. James took the spring home. They loved it. Every child in the neighborhood wanted one. The first Slinky was demonstrated at Gimbel's Department Store in Philadelphia in 1945. All four hundred Slinkys were sold within ninety minutes. The Slinky is simple and inexpensive. The Slinky is still popular with children today.

The Frisbee was also discovered by accident. According to one story, a group of Yale University students were eating pies from a local bakery. The bakery was called Frisbies. They finished eating the pies. They started throwing the empty pie tins around. A carpenter in California made a plastic version. He called it the Pluto Platter. The Wham-O company bought the patent on the product. Wham-O renamed it the Frisbee after the bakery. This is how the Frisbee came to be.

Some new toys are not developed by toy companies. Play-Doh, the Frisbee, and the Slinky are examples of very popular toys that were discovered by accident. Play-Doh started as a cleaning product. The Slinky was discovered by an engineer who was trying to invent something else. The Frisbee was invented by students having fun. The toys were discovered unexpectedly. All three toys have become classics.

COLLABORATIVE ACTIVITY

Read the following list of sentences. Working in a small group, change one sentence to a question and one to an exclamation. Then, add adverbs or prepositional phrases at the beginning of several of the sentences in the list.

Many well-known African American writers left the United States in the years following World War II.
Many went to Paris.
Richard Wright was a novelist.
He wrote *Native Son* and *Black Boy*.
He wrote *Uncle Tom's Children*.
He left the United States for Paris in 1947.
James Baldwin wrote *Another Country*, *The Fire Next Time*, and *Giovanni's Room*.
He also wrote essays.
He came to Paris in 1948.
Chester Himes was a detective story writer.

He arrived in Paris in 1953.
William Gardner Smith was a novelist and journalist.
He also left the United States for Paris.
These expatriates found Paris more hospitable than America.
They also found it less racist.

Finally, use the strategies discussed and illustrated in 20c and 20d to help you combine the sentences listed above and on the previous page into a paragraph. (You may keep the sentences in the order in which they appear.)

review checklist

Writing Varied Sentences

- [ ] Vary sentence types. (See 20a.)

- [ ] Vary sentence openings. (See 20b.)

- [ ] Combine sentences. (See 20c.)

- [ ] Mix long and short sentences. (See 20d.)

21 Using Parallelism

Andersen Ross/Getty Images

focus on writing

This picture shows patrons checking out books at a public library. Libraries, farmer's markets, and playgrounds are all important parts of building communities in U.S. cities, making them more livable. Write a paragraph discussing three positive things about your own neighborhood, school, or workplace. Support your statements with specific examples.

In this chapter, you will learn to

- recognize parallel structure (21a)
- use parallel structure (21b)

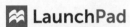 **LaunchPad**

Visit *LaunchPad Solo for Readers and Writers* > **Parallelism** for more practice with parallelism.

21a Recognizing Parallel Structure

Parallelism is the use of matching words, phrases, clauses, and sentence structure to highlight similar ideas in a sentence. When you use parallelism, you are telling readers that certain ideas are related and have the same level of importance. By repeating similar grammatical patterns to express similar ideas, you create sentences that are clearer, more concise, and easier to read.

In the following examples, the parallel sentences highlight similar ideas; the other sentences do not.

PARALLEL	NOT PARALLEL
Please leave <u>your name</u>, <u>your number</u>, and <u>your message</u>.	Please leave <u>your name</u>, <u>your number</u>, and <u>you should also leave a message</u>.
I plan to <u>graduate</u> from high school and <u>become</u> a nurse.	I plan to <u>graduate</u> from high school, and then <u>becoming</u> a nurse would be a good idea.
The grass was <u>soft</u>, <u>green</u>, and <u>sweet smelling</u>.	The grass was <u>soft</u>, <u>green</u>, and <u>the smell was sweet</u>.
<u>Making the team</u> was one thing; <u>staying on it</u> was another.	<u>Making the team</u> was one thing, but it was very difficult <u>to stay on it</u>.
We can <u>register</u> for classes in person, or <u>we can register</u> by email.	We can <u>register</u> for classes in person, or <u>registering</u> by email is another option.

PRACTICE

21-1 In the following sentences, decide whether the underlined words and phrases are parallel. If so, write *P* in the blank. If not, rewrite the sentences so that the underlined ideas are presented in parallel terms.

Examples: The missing dog had <u>brown fur</u>, <u>a red collar</u>, and <u>a long</u>

tail. ___*P*___

Signs of drug abuse in teenagers include <u>falling grades</u>, <u>mood swings</u>, and ~~they lose~~ weight/ ^{loss.} _____

1. The food in the cafeteria is <u>varied</u>, <u>tasty</u>, and <u>it is healthy</u>. _____

2. Do you want the job done <u>quickly</u>, or do you want it done <u>well</u>? _____

3. Last summer <u>I worked at the library</u>, <u>babysat for my neighbor's daughter</u>, and <u>there was a soup kitchen where I volunteered</u>. _____

4. <u>Pandas eat bamboo leaves</u>, and <u>eucalyptus leaves are eaten by koalas</u>. _____

5. Skydiving is <u>frightening</u> but <u>fun</u>. _____

6. A number of interesting people work at the co-op with me, including <u>an elderly German man</u>, <u>there is a middle-aged Chinese woman</u>, and <u>a teenaged Mexican boy</u>. _____

7. <u>The bell rang</u>, and <u>the students stood up</u>. _____

8. To conserve energy while I was away, I <u>unplugged the television</u>, <u>closed the curtains</u>, and <u>the thermostat was set at 65 degrees</u>. _____

9. He <u>wore</u> jeans, a T-shirt, and <u>had on</u> running shoes. _____

10. For several weeks after the storm, the supermarkets had <u>no eggs</u>, <u>they were out of milk</u>, and <u>they did not have any bread</u>. _____

21b Using Parallel Structure

Parallel structure is especially important in *paired items*, *items in a series*, and *items in a list or in an outline*.

Paired Items

Use parallel structure when you connect ideas with a **coordinating conjunction**—*and*, *but*, *for*, *nor*, *or*, *so*, and *yet*.

George believes in <u>doing a good job</u> and <u>minding his own business</u>.

You can <u>pay me now</u> or <u>pay me later</u>.

You should also use parallel structure for paired items joined by *both . . . and*, *not only . . . but also*, *either . . . or*, *neither . . . nor*, and *rather . . . than*.

Jan is both <u>skilled in writing</u> and <u>fluent in French</u>.

The group's new recording not only <u>has a dance beat</u> but also <u>has thought-provoking lyrics</u>.

I'd rather <u>eat one worm by itself</u> than <u>eat five worms with ice cream</u>.

Items in a Series

Use parallel structure for items in a series—words, phrases, or clauses. (Be sure to use commas to separate three or more items in a series. Never put a comma after the final item.)

Every Wednesday I have <u>English</u>, <u>math</u>, and <u>psychology</u>. (three words)

<u>Increased demand</u>, <u>high factory output</u>, and <u>a strong dollar</u> will help the economy. (three phrases)

She is a champion because she <u>stays in excellent physical condition</u>, <u>puts in long hours of practice</u>, and <u>has an intense desire to win</u>. (three clauses)

Items in a List or in an Outline

Use parallel structure for items in a numbered or bulleted list.

There are three reasons to open an Individual Retirement Account (IRA):
1. To save money
2. To reduce taxes
3. To be able to retire

Use parallel structure for the elements in an outline.

A. Types of rocks
   1. Igneous
   2. Sedimentary
   3. Metamorphic

PRACTICE
21-2 Fill in the blanks in the following sentences with parallel words, phrases, or clauses of your own that make sense in context.

Example: At the lake, we can ___*go for a swim*___, ___*paddle a canoe*___, and ___*play volleyball*___.

1. When I get too little sleep, I am _____, _____, and _____.

2. I am good at _____ but not at _____.

3. My ideal mate is _____ and _____.

4. I personally define success not only as _____ but also as _____.

5. I use my computer for both _____ and _____.

6. I like _____ and _____.

7. You need three qualities to succeed in college: _____, _____, and _____.

8. I enjoy not only _____ but also _____.

9. I would rather _____ than _____.

10. Football _____, but baseball _____.

PRACTICE
21-3 Rewrite the following sentences so that matching ideas are presented in parallel terms. Add punctuation as needed.

Example: *Game of Thrones* has been filmed in Northern Ireland and Iceland, and also some filming was done in Morocco.

Game of Thrones has been filmed in Northern Ireland, Iceland, and Morocco.

1. *Game of Thrones* is a television series on HBO that features more than 20 main characters, and 250 additional characters are also featured.

_____

_____

2. True *Game of Thrones* fans know that the story originated in a series of novels titled *A Song of Ice and Fire*, and George R. R. Martin wrote these novels, as true fans also know.

_____

_____

3. The complex plot lines follow the Stark family, and the Lannisters are also followed, as well as the Targaryens.

_____

4. In the media, *Game of Thrones* has been both praised for the performance of its actors, and many have criticized it because of its extreme violence.

_____

_____

5. *Game of Thrones* has received many honors, including Emmys and Golden Globes, and another award, a Peabody, was also won.

_____

_____

Andersen Ross/Getty Images

TEST · Revise · Edit · Proofread

Look back at your response to the Focus on Writing prompt on page 379. TEST what you have written. Then, revise, edit, and proofread your paragraph, checking carefully to make sure you used parallel structure to highlight similar ideas or items in your sentences. If you used parallel structure to present three or more items in a series, make sure you used commas to separate the items.

EDITING PRACTICE

Read the following student essay, which contains examples of faulty parallelism. Identify the sentences you think need to be corrected, and make the changes required to achieve parallelism. Be sure to supply all words necessary for clarity, grammar, and sense. Add punctuation as needed. The first error has been edited for you.

Self-Made Men and Women Helping Others

Many self-made people go from poverty to ~~achieving~~ success. Quite a few of them not only achieve such success but also they help others. Three of these people are Oprah Winfrey, Alfredo Quiñones-Hinojosa, and Geoffrey Canada. Their lives are very different, but all possess great strength, being determined, and concern for others.

Oprah is one of the most influential people in the world, and she has more money than almost anyone in the world. She came from a very poor family. First, she lived with her grandmother on a Mississippi farm, and then her mother in Milwaukee. During this time, she was abused by several relatives. When she was thirteen, she was sent to Nashville to live with her father. He used strict discipline, and she was taught by him to value education. Through her own determination and because she was ambitious, Winfrey got a job at a local broadcasting company. This started her career. However, Oprah was not satisfied with being successful. Through Oprah's Angel Network and the Oprah Winfrey Leadership Academy, she helps others and making the world a better place.

Today, Alfredo Quiñones-Hinojosa is a top brain surgeon and conducting research on new ways to treat brain cancer. At age nineteen, however, he was an illegal immigrant from Mexico, worked in the fields, and without any English. When he told his cousin he wanted to learn English and get a better job, his cousin told him he was crazy. Then, while he was a welder on a railroad crew, he fell into an empty petroleum tank and was almost dying from the fumes. However, he overcame these hardships. He enrolled in a community college, and with determination and by working hard, he began to change his life. He won a scholarship to Berkeley, went on to medical school at Harvard, and eventually winding up as director of the brain tumor program at Johns Hopkins University. In 1997, he became a citizen of the United States. At each step of the way, he has made a special effort to reach out to students from low-income backgrounds and to inspire others.

Geoffrey Canada grew up in a New York City neighborhood that was poor, dangerous, and where violence was not uncommon. His mother was a single parent who struggled to support him and his three brothers. Canada learned to survive on the streets, but he also studied a lot in school. Thanks to this hard work, he won a scholarship to Bowdoin College in Maine and went on to a master's degree from Harvard and a career in education. Deciding to leave his neighborhood in New York wasn't hard, but to decide to come back wasn't hard either. He wanted to help children in poor families to succeed in school and so they could have better lives. With this in mind, he started the Harlem Children's Zone (HCZ). HCZ includes workshops for parents, a preschool and three charter schools, and running health programs for children and families. President Obama has said he would like to see more programs like HCZ.

Oprah Winfrey, Alfredo Quiñones-Hinojosa, and Geoffrey Canada have very different careers—in entertainment, in medicine, and educating children. However, all three overcame great adversity, all three have achieved enormous success, and they have helped others. They have helped their communities, their country, and have contributed to the world.

COLLABORATIVE ACTIVITY

Working in a group, list three or four qualities that you associate with each word in the following pairs.

Brothers/sisters
Teachers/students
Parents/children
City/country
Fast food/organic food
Movies/TV shows
Work/play

Then, write a compound sentence comparing the two words in each pair. Use a coordinating conjunction to join the clauses, and make sure each sentence uses clear parallel structure, mentions both words, and includes the qualities you listed for the word pairs.

review checklist

Using Parallelism

☐ Use matching words, phrases, clauses, and sentence structure to highlight similar items or ideas. (See 21a.)

☐ Use parallel structure with paired items. (See 21b.)

☐ Use parallel structure for items in a series. (See 21b.)

☐ Use parallel structure for items in a list or in an outline. (See 21b.)

22 Using Words Effectively

Adam Crowley/Getty Images

focus on writing

This picture shows a luxury tree house. Look at the house carefully, and then write a paragraph in which you describe your dream house. Would it resemble the house in the picture, or would it be different? How? What would be inside the house? Be as specific as possible.

In this chapter, you will learn to

- use specific words (22a)
- use concise language (22b)
- avoid slang (22c)
- avoid clichés (22d)
- use similes and metaphors (22e)
- avoid sexist language (22f)
- avoid commonly confused words (22g)

PREVIEW

22a   Using Specific Words

LaunchPad

Visit *LaunchPad Solo for Readers and Writers* > **Appropriate Language** for more practice with word choice.

Specific words refer to particular people, places, things, ideas, or qualities. **General words** refer to entire classes or groups. Sentences that contain specific words are more precise and vivid than those that contain only general words.

SENTENCES WITH GENERAL WORDS	SENTENCES WITH SPECIFIC WORDS
While walking in the woods, I saw an <u>animal</u>.	While walking in the woods, I saw a <u>baby skunk</u>.
<u>Someone</u> decided to run for Congress.	<u>Rebecca</u> decided to run for Congress.
<u>Weapons</u> are responsible for many murders.	<u>Unregistered handguns</u> are responsible for many murders.
Denise bought new <u>clothes</u>.	Denise bought a new <u>blue dress</u>.
I really enjoyed my <u>meal</u>.	I really enjoyed my <u>pepperoni pizza with extra cheese</u>.
Darrell had always wanted a <u>classic car</u>.	Darrell had always wanted a <u>black 1969 Chevrolet Camaro</u>.

FYI

Using Specific Words

One way to strengthen your writing is to avoid general words like *good*, *nice*, or *great*. Take the time to think of more specific words. For example, when you say the ocean looked *pretty*, do you really mean that it *sparkled*, *glistened*, *rippled*, *foamed*, *surged*, or *billowed*?

PRACTICE

22-1 In the following passage, underline the specific words that help you imagine the scene the writer describes. The first sentence has been done for you.

Last summer, I spent three weeks backpacking through <u>the remote rural province of Yunnan in China</u>. One day, I came across four farm women playing a game of mahjong on a patch of muddy ground. Squatting on rough wooden stools around a faded green folding table, the women picked up and discarded the smooth ivory mahjong tiles as if they were playing cards. In the grassy field around them, their chestnut-colored horses grazed with heavy red and black market bags tied to their backs. A veil of shimmering white fog hung over a nearby hill, and one woman sat under a black umbrella to shelter herself from the sun. A fifth woman watched, with her wrinkled hands on her hips and a frown on her face. The only sound was the sharp click of the tiles and the soft musical talk of the women as they played.

PRACTICE

22-2 The following one-paragraph job-application letter uses many general words. Rewrite the paragraph, substituting specific words and adding details where necessary. Start by making the first sentence, which identifies the job, more specific: for example, "I would like to apply for the <u>dental technician</u> position you advertised on <u>March 15 in the *Post*</u>." Then, add information about your background and qualifications. Expand the original paragraph into a three-paragraph letter.

I would like to apply for the position you advertised in today's paper. I graduated from high school and am currently attending college. I have taken several courses that have prepared me for the duties the position requires. I also have several personal qualities that I think you would find useful in a person holding this position. In addition, I have had certain experiences that qualify me for such a job. I would appreciate the opportunity to meet with you to discuss your needs as an employer. Thank you.

22b Using Concise Language

Concise language says what it has to say in as few words as possible. Too often, writers use words and phrases that add nothing to a sentence's meaning. A good way to test a sentence for these words is to see if crossing them out changes the sentence's meaning. If the sentence's meaning does not change, you can assume that the words you crossed out are unnecessary.

> *The*
> ~~It is clear that the~~ United States was not ready to fight World War II.
> *To* ⌃
> ~~In order to~~ follow the plot, you must make an outline.
>   ⌃

Sometimes you can replace several unnecessary words with a single word.

> *Because*
> ~~Due to the fact that~~ I was tired, I missed my first class.
>   ⌃

FYI

Using Concise Language

The following wordy phrases add nothing to a sentence. You can usually delete or condense them with no loss of meaning.

WORDY	CONCISE
It is clear that	(delete)
It is a fact that	(delete)
The reason is because	Because
The reason is that	Because
It is my opinion that	I think/I believe
Due to the fact that	Because
Despite the fact that	Although
At the present time	Today/Now
At that time	Then
In most cases	Usually
In order to	To
In the final analysis	Finally
Subsequent to	After

LaunchPad

Visit *LaunchPad Solo for Readers and Writers* > **Wordiness** for more practice with concise language.

Unnecessary repetition—saying the same thing twice for no reason—can also make your writing wordy. When you revise, delete repeated words and phrases that add nothing to your sentences.

My instructor told me the book was ~~old-fashioned and~~ outdated. (An old-fashioned book *is* outdated.)

The ~~terrible~~ tragedy of the fire could have been avoided. (A tragedy is *always* terrible.)

PRACTICE

22-3 To make the following sentences more concise, eliminate any unnecessary repetition, and delete or condense wordy expressions.

> Each
> **Example:** ~~It is a fact that each individual~~ production of *Sesame*
>
> *Street* around the world is geared toward the local children ~~in that~~
>
> ~~region.~~

(1) In order to meet the needs of international children all over the world, Sesame Workshop helps produce versions of its popular show *Sesame Street* in other countries outside the United States. (2) Due to the fact that each country has different issues and concerns, the content of these shows varies. (3) In most cases, the producers focus on and concentrate on the cultural diversity in their country. (4) In order to develop the most appropriate material for their shows, producers also consult with and talk to local educators and child development experts, people who are experts in the field. (5) At the present time, versions of *Sesame Street* exist in a wide variety of places and countries. They include Mexico, Russia, South Africa, Bangladesh, and Egypt.

22c Avoiding Slang

Slang is nonstandard language that calls attention to itself. It is usually associated with a particular social group—Tumblr users or skateboarders, for example. Some slang eventually spreads beyond its original context and becomes widely used. Often, it is used for emphasis or to produce a surprising or original effect. In any case, because it is very informal, slang is not acceptable in your college writing.

> easy.
> My psychology exam was really ~~sweet.~~
> relax ^
> On the weekends, I like to ~~chill~~ and watch movies on my laptop.
> ^

If you have any question about whether a term is slang or not, look it up in a dictionary. If the term is identified as *slang* or *informal*, find a more suitable term.

FYI

Avoiding Abbreviations and Shorthand

While abbreviations and shorthand such as *BC*, *BTW*, *IMO*, and *2day* are acceptable in informal electronic communication, they are not acceptable in your college writing, in emails to your instructors, or in online class discussions.

In my opinion,
~~IMO~~ your essay needs a strong thesis statement.
^

you   *today.*
I would like to meet with ~~u~~ for a conference ~~2day~~.
                      ^   ^

PRACTICE

22-4   Edit the following sentences, replacing the slang expressions with clearer, more precise words and phrases.

yelled at me
Example: My father ~~lost it~~ when I told him I crashed the car.
                      ^

1. Whenever I get bummed, I go outside and jog.

2. Tonight I'll have to leave by 11 because I'm wiped out.

3. I'm not into movies or television.

4. Whenever we argue, my boyfriend knows how to push my buttons.

5. I really lucked out when I got this job.

22d Avoiding Clichés

Clichés are expressions—such as "easier said than done" and "last but not least"—that have been used so often that they have lost their meaning. These worn-out expressions get in the way of clear communication.

When you identify a cliché in your writing, replace it with a direct statement—or, if possible, with a fresher expression.

> **CLICHÉ**   When school was over, she felt free ~~as a bird~~.

> **CLICHÉ**   These days, you have to be ~~sick as a dog~~ before
>
> *seriously ill*
>   ^
>
> you are admitted to a hospital.

FYI

Avoiding Clichés

Here are examples of some clichés you should avoid in your writing.

a perfect storm	play God
back in the day	pushing the envelope
better late than never	reality check
connect the dots	skill set
cutting edge	bottom line
give 110 percent	think outside the box
groupthink	touched base
it goes without saying	tried and true
it is what it is	water under the bridge
keep your eye on the ball	what goes around comes around

PRACTICE

22-5 Cross out any clichés in the following sentences. Then, either substitute a fresher expression or restate the idea more directly.

free of financial worries

Example: Lottery winners often think they will be ~~on easy street~~
                                                                                         ^
for the rest of their lives.

(1) Many people think that a million-dollar lottery jackpot allows the winner to stop working like a dog and start living high on the hog. (2) All things considered, however, the reality for lottery winners is quite different. (3) For one thing, lottery winners who hit the jackpot do not always receive their winnings all at once; instead, yearly payments—for example, $50,000—can be paid out over twenty years. (4) Of that $50,000 a year, close to $20,000 goes to taxes and anything else the lucky stiff already owes the government, such as student loans. (5) Next come relatives and friends with their hands out, leaving winners between a rock and a hard place. (6) They can either cough up gifts and loans or wave

bye-bye to many of their loved ones. (7) Adding insult to injury, many lottery winners lose their jobs because employers think that, now that they are "millionaires," they no longer need to draw a salary. (8) Many lottery winners wind up way over their heads in debt within a few years. (9) In their hour of need, many might like to sell their future payments to companies that offer lump-sum payments of forty to forty-five cents on the dollar. (10) This is easier said than done, however, because most state lotteries do not allow winners to sell their winnings.

22e Using Similes and Metaphors

A **simile** is a comparison of two unlike things that uses *like* or *as*.

> His arm hung at his side <u>like</u> a broken branch.
> He was <u>as</u> content <u>as</u> a cat napping on a windowsill.

A **metaphor** is a comparison of two unlike things that does not use *like* or *as*.

> Invaders from another world, the dandelions conquered my garden.
> He was a beast of burden, hauling cement from the mixer to the building site.

The impact of similes and metaphors comes from the surprise of seeing two seemingly unlike things being compared. Used in moderation, similes and metaphors can make your writing more lively and more interesting.

PRACTICE

22-6   Use your imagination to complete each of the following items by creating three original similes.

Example: A boring class is like _____*toast without jam.*_____

_____*a four-hour movie.*_____

_____*a bedtime story.*_____

1. A good friend is like _____

_____

_____

2. A thunderstorm is like _____

_____

_____

3. A workout at the gym is like _____

_____

_____

22f Avoiding Sexist Language

Sexist language refers to men and women in insulting terms. Sexist language is not just words such as *stud* or *babe*, which people may find objectionable. It can also be words or phrases that unnecessarily call attention to gender or that suggest a job or profession is held only by a man (or only by a woman) when it actually is not.

You can avoid sexist language by using a little common sense. There is always an acceptable nonsexist alternative for a sexist term.

SEXIST	NONSEXIST
man, mankind	humanity, humankind, the human race
businessman	executive, businessperson
fireman, policeman, mailman	firefighter, police officer, letter carrier
male nurse, woman engineer	nurse, engineer
congressman	member of Congress, representative
stewardess, steward	flight attendant
man and wife	man and woman, husband and wife
manmade	synthetic
chairman	chair, chairperson
anchorwoman, anchorman	anchor
actor, actress	actor
waiter, waitress	server

FYI

Avoiding Sexist Language

Do not use *he* when your subject could be either male or female.

> **SEXIST**   Everyone should complete his assignment by next week.

You can correct this problem in three ways.

- *Use he or she or his or her.*

    Everyone should complete his or her assignment by next week.

- *Use plural forms.*

    Students should complete their assignments by next week.

- *Eliminate the pronoun.*

    Everyone should complete the assignment by next week.

PRACTICE

22-7   Edit the following sentences to eliminate sexist language.

or her (or omit "his")

Example: A doctor should be honest with his patients.

1. Many people today would like to see more policemen patrolling the streets.

2. The attorneys representing the plaintiff are Geraldo Diaz and Mrs. Barbara Wilkerson.

3. Every soldier picked up his weapons.

4. Christine Fox is the female mayor of Port London, Maine.

5. Travel to other planets will be a significant step for man.

 **LaunchPad**

Visit *LaunchPad Solo for Readers and Writers* > **Commonly Confused Words** for more practice with commonly confused words.

22g Commonly Confused Words

Accept/Except   *Accept* means "to receive something." *Except* means "with the exception of" or "to leave out or exclude."

> "I <u>accept</u> your challenge," said Alexander Hamilton to Aaron Burr.
>
> Everyone <u>except</u> Darryl visited the museum.

Affect/Effect   *Affect* is a verb meaning "to influence." *Effect* is a noun meaning "result."

> Carmen's job could <u>affect</u> her grades.
>
> Overexposure to sun can have a long-term <u>effect</u> on skin.

All ready/Already   *All ready* means "completely prepared." *Already* means "previously, before."

> Serge was <u>all ready</u> to take the history test.
>
> Gina had <u>already</u> been to Italy.

Brake/Break   *Brake* is a noun that means "a device to slow or stop a vehicle." *Break* is a verb meaning "to smash" or "to detach" and sometimes a noun meaning either "a gap" or "an interruption" or "a stroke of luck."

> Peter got into an accident because his foot slipped off the <u>brake</u>.
>
> Babe Ruth thought no one would ever <u>break</u> his home run record.
>
> The baseball game was postponed until there was a <u>break</u> in the bad weather.

Buy/By   *Buy* means "to purchase." *By* is a preposition meaning "close to," "next to," or "by means of."

> The Stamp Act forced colonists to <u>buy</u> stamps for many public documents.
>
> He drove <u>by</u> but did not stop.
>
> He stayed <u>by</u> her side all the way to the hospital.
>
> Malcolm X wanted "freedom <u>by</u> any means necessary."

Conscience/Conscious   *Conscience* is a noun that refers to the part of the mind that urges a person to choose right over wrong. *Conscious* is an adjective that means "aware" or "deliberate."

After he cheated at cards, his <u>conscience</u> started to bother him.

As she walked through the woods, she became <u>conscious</u> of the hum of insects.

Elliott made a <u>conscious</u> decision to stop smoking.

Everyday/Every day *Everyday* is a single word that means "ordinary" or "common." *Every day* is two words that mean "occurring daily."

Friends was a successful comedy show because it appealed to <u>everyday</u> people.

<u>Every day</u>, the six friends met at the Central Perk café.

Fine/Find *Fine* means "superior quality" or "a sum of money paid as a penalty." *Find* means "to locate."

He sang a <u>fine</u> solo at church last Sunday.

Demi had to pay a <u>fine</u> for speeding.

Some people still use a willow rod to <u>find</u> water.

Hear/Here *Hear* means "to perceive sound by ear." *Here* means "at or in this place."

I moved to the front so I could <u>hear</u> the speaker.

My great-grandfather came <u>here</u> in 1883.

Its/It's *Its* is the possessive form of *it*. *It's* is the contraction of *it is* or *it has*.

The airline canceled <u>its</u> flights because of the snow.

<u>It's</u> twelve o'clock, and we are late.

Ever since <u>it's</u> been in the accident, the car has rattled.

Know/No/Knew/New *Know* means "to have an understanding of" or "to have fixed in the mind." *No* means "not any," "not at all," or "not one." *Knew* is the past tense form of the verb *know*. *New* means "recent or never used."

I <u>know</u> there will be a lunar eclipse tonight.

You have <u>no</u> right to say that.

He <u>knew</u> how to install a <u>new</u> light switch.

Lie/Lay *Lie* means "to rest or recline." The past tense of *lie* is *lay*. *Lay* means "to put or place something down." The past tense of *lay* is *laid*.

Every Sunday, I lie in bed until noon.

They lay on the grass until it began to rain, and then they went home.

Tammy told Carl to lay his cards on the table.

Brooke and Cassia finally laid down their hockey sticks.

Loose/Lose *Loose* means "not fixed or rigid" or "not attached securely." *Lose* means "to mislay" or "to misplace" or "to not win."

In the 1940s, many women wore loose-fitting pants.

I always lose my car keys.

I never gamble because I hate to lose.

Passed/Past *Passed* is the past tense of the verb *pass*. It means "moved by" or "succeeded in." *Past* is a noun or an adjective meaning "earlier than the present time."

The car that passed me was doing more than eighty miles an hour.

David finally passed his driving test.

The novel was set in the past.

The statement said that the bill was past due.

Peace/Piece *Peace* means "the absence of war" or "calm." *Piece* means "a part of something."

The British prime minister tried to achieve peace with honor.

My peace of mind was destroyed when the flying saucer landed.

"Have a piece of cake," said Marie.

Principal/Principle *Principal* means "first" or "highest" or "the head of a school." *Principle* means "a law or basic assumption."

She had the principal role in the movie.

I'll never forget the day the principal called me into his office.

It was against his principles to lie.

Quiet/Quit/Quite *Quiet* means "free of noise" or "still." *Quit* means "to leave a job" or "to give up." *Quite* means "actually" or "very."

Jane looked forward to the quiet evenings at the lake.

Sammy quit his job and followed the girls into the parking lot.

"You haven't quite got the hang of it yet," she said.

After practicing all summer, Tamika got quite good at tennis.

Raise/Rise *Raise* means "to elevate" or "to increase in size, quantity, or worth." The past tense of *raise* is *raised*. *Rise* means "to stand up" or "to move from a lower position to a higher position." The past tense of *rise* is *rose*.

> Carlos <u>raises</u> his hand whenever the teacher asks for volunteers.
> They finally <u>raised</u> the money for the down payment.
> The crowd <u>rises</u> every time their team scores a touchdown.
> Kim <u>rose</u> before dawn so she could see the eclipse.

Sit/Set *Sit* means "to assume a sitting position." The past tense of *sit* is *sat*. *Set* means "to put down or place" or "to adjust something to a desired position." The past tense of *set* is *set*.

> I usually <u>sit</u> in the front row at the movies.
> They <u>sat</u> at the clinic waiting for their names to be called.
> Elizabeth <u>set</u> the mail on the kitchen table and left for work.
> Every semester I <u>set</u> goals for myself.

Suppose/Supposed *Suppose* means "to consider" or "to assume." *Supposed* is both the past tense and the past participle of *suppose*. *Supposed* also means "expected" or "required." (Note that when *supposed* has this meaning, it is always followed by *to*.)

> <u>Suppose</u> researchers were to find a cure for cancer.
> We <u>supposed</u> the movie would be over by ten o'clock.
> You were <u>supposed</u> to finish a draft of the report by today.

Their/There/They're *Their* is the possessive form of the pronoun *they*. *There* means "at or in that place." *There* is also used in the phrases *there is* and *there are*. *They're* is the contraction of *they are*.

> They wanted poor people to improve <u>their</u> living conditions.
> I put the book over <u>there</u>.
> <u>There</u> are three reasons I will not eat meat.
> <u>They're</u> the best volunteer firefighters I've ever seen.

Then/Than *Then* means "at that time" or "next in time." *Than* is used in comparisons.

> He was young and naive <u>then</u>.
> I went to the job interview and <u>then</u> stopped off for coffee.
> My dog is smarter <u>than</u> your dog.

Threw/Through *Threw* is the past tense of *throw*. *Through* means "in one side and out the opposite side" or "finished."

> Satchel Paige <u>threw</u> a baseball more than ninety-five miles an hour.
>
> It takes almost thirty minutes to go <u>through</u> the tunnel.
>
> "I'm <u>through</u>," said Clark Kent, storming out of Perry White's office.

To/Too/Two *To* means "in the direction of." *Too* means "also" or "more than enough." *Two* denotes the numeral 2.

> During spring break, I am going <u>to</u> Disney World.
>
> My roommates are coming <u>too</u>.
>
> The microwave popcorn is <u>too</u> hot to eat.
>
> "If we get rid of the Tin Man and the Cowardly Lion, the <u>two</u> of us can go to Oz," said the Scarecrow to Dorothy.

Use/Used *Use* means "to put into service" or "to consume." *Used* is both the past tense and the past participle of *use*. *Used* also means "accustomed." (Note that when *used* has this meaning, it is followed by *to*.)

> I <u>use</u> a soft cloth to clean my glasses.
>
> "Hey! Who <u>used</u> all the hot water?" he yelled from the shower.
>
> Marisol had <u>used</u> all the firewood during the storm.
>
> After two years in Alaska, they got <u>used</u> to the short winter days.

Weather/Whether *Weather* refers to temperature, humidity, precipitation, and so on. *Whether* is used to introduce alternative possibilities.

> The *Farmer's Almanac* says that the <u>weather</u> this winter will be severe.
>
> <u>Whether</u> or not this prediction will be correct is anyone's guess.

Where/Were/We're *Where* means "at or in what place." *Were* is the past tense of *are*. *We're* is the contraction of *we are*.

> <u>Where</u> are you going, and <u>where</u> have you been?
>
> Charlie Chaplin and Mary Pickford <u>were</u> popular stars of silent movies.
>
> <u>We're</u> doing our back-to-school shopping early this year.

Whose/Who's *Whose* is the possessive form of *who*. *Who's* is the contraction of either *who is* or *who has*.

> My roommate asked, "<u>Whose</u> book is this?"
>
> "<u>Who's</u> there?" squealed the second little pig as he leaned against the door.
>
> <u>Who's</u> been blocking the driveway?

Your/You're *Your* is the possessive form of *you*. *You're* is the contraction of *you are*.

> "You should have worn <u>your</u> running shoes," said the hare as he passed the tortoise.
>
> "<u>You're</u> too kind," said the tortoise sarcastically.

TEST · Revise · Edit · Proofread

Look back at your response to the Focus on Writing prompt on page 388. TEST what you have written. Then, revise and edit your paragraph, making sure that your language is specific as well as concise; that you have avoided slang, clichés, and sexist language; and that you have not made any errors in word usage. Try adding a simile or metaphor to add interest to your writing. Finally, proofread your work.

Adam Crowley/Getty Images

EDITING PRACTICE

Read the following student essay carefully, and then revise it. Make sure that your revision is concise, uses specific words, and includes no slang, sexist language, clichés, or confused words. Add an occasional simile or metaphor if you like. The first sentence has been edited for you.

Unexpected Discoveries

When we ~~here~~ *hear* the word "accident," we think of bad things. *, like dented fenders and broken glass.* But accidents can be good, too. Modern science has made advances as a result of accidents. It is a fact that a scientist sometimes works like a dog for years in his laboratory, only to make a weird discovery because of a mistake.

The most famous example of a good, beneficial accident is the discovery of penicillin. A scientist, Alexander Fleming, had seen many soldiers die of infections after they were wounded in World War I. All things considered, many more soldiers died due to the fact that infections occurred than from wounds. Fleming wanted to find a drug that could put an end to these terrible, fatal infections. One day in 1928, Fleming went on vacation, leaving a pile of dishes in the lab sink. As luck would have it, he had been growing bacteria in those dishes. When he came back, he noticed that one of the dishes looked moldy. What was strange was that near the mold, the bacteria were dead as a doornail. It was crystal clear to Fleming that the mold had killed the bacteria. He had discovered penicillin, the first antibiotic.

Everyone has heard the name "Goodyear." It was Charles Goodyear who made a discovery that changed and revolutionized the rubber industry. In the early nineteenth century, rubber products became thin and runny in hot weather and cracked in cold weather. One day in 1839, Goodyear accidentally dropped some rubber mixed with sulfur on a hot stove. It changed color and turned black. After being cooled, it could be stretched, and it would return to its original size and shape. This kind of rubber is now used in tires and in many other products.

Another thing was also discovered because of a lab accident involving rubber. In 1953, Patsy Sherman, a female chemist for the 3M company, was trying to find a new type of rubber. She created a batch of man-made liquid rubber. Some of the liquid accidentally spilled onto a lab assistant's new white canvas sneaker. Her assistant used everything but the kitchen sink to clean the shoe, but nothing worked. Over time, the rest of the shoe became dirty, but the part where the spill had hit was still clean as a whistle. Sherman new that she had found something that could actually keep fabrics clean by doing a number on dirt. The 3M Corporation named it's brand new product Scotchgard.

A scientist can be clumsy and careless, but sometimes his mistakes lead to great and important discoveries. Penicillin, better tires, and Scotchgard are examples of products that were the result of scientific accidents.

COLLABORATIVE ACTIVITY

Photocopy two or three paragraphs of description from a romance novel, a western novel, or a mystery novel, and bring your paragraphs to class. Working in a group, choose one paragraph that seems to need clearer, more specific language. As a group, revise the paragraph you chose, making it as specific as possible and eliminating any clichés or sexist language. Then, exchange your revised paragraph with the paragraph revised by another group, and check the other group's work. Make any additional changes you think the paragraph needs.

review checklist

Using Words Effectively

☐ Use specific words that convey your ideas clearly and precisely. (See 22a.)

☐ Use concise language that says what it has to say in the fewest possible words. (See 22b.)

☐ Avoid slang. (See 22c.)

☐ Avoid clichés. (See 22d.)

☐ When appropriate, use similes and metaphors to make your writing more lively and more interesting. (See 22e.)

☐ Avoid sexist language. (See 22f.)

☐ Avoid commonly confused words. (See 22g.)

Read the following student essay. Then, edit it by creating more effective sentences and correcting any misspelled words. Combine simple sentences into compound or complex sentences, use parallelism, create varied sentences, and use words that are concise, specific, and original. The first editing change has been made for you.

Eating Street Food

Street food, food cooked and served at a portable stand, is extremely popular in the United States. ~~Street~~-food customers ~~usually~~ get ~~there~~ food *(Usually, street)* *(their)* quickly*(and)*, ~~They~~ do not pay much. Some regional or ethnic foods are sold as street food. Then, they become popular There are concerns about the cleanliness and freshness of street food. These problems can be avoided. It is a fact that street food has many advantages.

Street food is the original fast food. Street food is both fast and cheap. Customers usually do not have much time to wait for it to be cooked. Vendors have to offer food that can be made beforehand or prepared quickly. The original U.S. street food is the hot dog. It can be steamed ahead of time and quickly be put into a bun. Some customers want things like relish, onions, and chili. They can be added. Street food does not cost as much as restaurant food. Vendors usually have to by a license in order to sell food at a particular location. They do not have to rent a store, pay waiters and waitresses, and supply tablecloths and dishes therefore they can charge much less then a restaurant. Street-food customers do not have to make the commitment of time and money required at a sit-down restaurant. They do not have to tip the server. Customers cannot sit at tables, however. There are no tables. They have to eat while standing or walking. Customers often do not have much time. This situation suits them. Students need fast and cheap food, especially on college campuses. Food carts make them happy as a clam.

Street food is often regional or ethnic. Vendors sell cheese steaks and soft pretzels in Philadelphia. They sell reindeer sausages in Alaska. They sell tacos and tamales in Mexican neighborhoods. In Chicago, customers can buy kielbasa sandwiches and pierogies. Often, food carts offer ethnic foods to customers who are tasting them for the first time. A person can see if he likes Indian curry, Israeli falafel, Italian panini, or a gyro from Greece. Because of the success of street vendors, many ethnic foods have gone mainstream and are now widely offered in sit-down restaurants.

There is some concern about the safety of street food. Refrigeration may be limited or nonexistent. Cleanliness sometimes can be a problem. Food from a street-corner cart may be safer than food cooked in a restaurant kitchen. In the restaurant, it may sit for a long time. Also, due to the fact that food carts may lack refrigeration, very fresh ingredients are often used. Still, customers should follow some tips for buying street food. The food should be kept covered until it is cooked. The money and food should not be touched by the same individual. Local customers are a good guide to the best street food. They know where the food is freshest. A long line usually indicates a good and safe source of street food.

In the United States, street food is especially varied. In the United States, there are many immigrants. Food is an important part of culture. The popularity of ethnic street food can be a sign that the immigrants' culture has been accepted.

unit

5 Solving Common Sentence Problems

23 Run-Ons

focus on writing

Why do you think so many American children are physically out of shape?
What do you think can be done about this problem? Write a paragraph that
answers these questions.

In this chapter, you will learn to

- recognize run-ons (23a)
- correct run-ons in five different ways (23b)

23a Recognizing Run-Ons

A **sentence** consists of at least one independent clause—one subject and one verb.

College costs are rising.

A **run-on** is an error that occurs when two sentences are joined incorrectly. There are two kinds of run-ons: *fused sentences* and *comma splices*.

■ A **fused sentence** occurs when two sentences are joined without any punctuation.

> FUSED SENTENCE [College costs are rising] [many students are concerned.]

■ A **comma splice** occurs when two sentences are joined with just a comma.

> COMMA SPLICE [College costs are rising], [many students are concerned.]

WORD POWER

fused joined together

splice (verb) to join together at the ends

PRACTICE

23-1 Some of the sentences in the following paragraph are correct, but others are run-ons. In the answer space after each sentence, write *C* if the sentence is correct, *FS* if it is a fused sentence, and *CS* if it is a comma splice.

Example: Using a screen reader is one way for blind people to access the web, two popular programs are JAWS for Windows and Window-Eyes. _____*CS*_____

(1) The Internet should be accessible to everyone, this is not always the case. _____ (2) Many blind computer users have trouble finding information on the web. _____ (3) Often, this is the result of poor web design it is the designer's job to make the site accessible. _____

(4) Most blind people use special software called screen readers, this technology translates text into speech or Braille. —————— (5) However, screen readers do not always work well the information is sometimes hard to access. —————— (6) Websites need to be understandable to all Internet users. —————— (7) The rights of blind Internet users may be protected by the Americans with Disabilities Act (ADA). —————— (8) We will have to wait for more cases to come to trial then we will know more. —————— (9) Meanwhile, we have to rely on software companies to make the necessary changes, this will take some time. —————— (10) However, there are incentives for these companies, the 1.5 million blind computer users are all potential customers. ——————

☒ LaunchPad

Visit *LaunchPad Solo for Readers and Writers* > **Run-Ons** for more practice with run-ons.

23b Correcting Run-Ons

FYI

Correcting Run-Ons

You can correct run-ons in five ways:

1. *Use a period to create two separate sentences.*

   College costs are rising. Many students are concerned.

2. *Use a coordinating conjunction (***and, but, for, nor, or, so,*** or* ***yet****) to connect ideas.*

   College costs are rising, and many students are concerned.

3. *Use a semicolon to connect ideas.*

   College costs are rising; many students are concerned.

4. *Use a semicolon followed by a transitional word or phrase to connect ideas.*

   College costs are rising; as a result, many students are concerned.

5. *Use a dependent word (***although, because, when,*** and* **so on***) to connect ideas.*

   Because college costs are rising, many students are concerned.

The pages that follow explain and illustrate the five different ways to correct run-ons.

1. ***Use a period to create two separate sentences.*** Be sure each sentence begins with a capital letter and ends with a period.

<table>
<tr><td align="right">**INCORRECT**
(FUSED SENTENCE)</td><td>Gas prices are very high some people are buying hybrid cars.</td></tr>
<tr><td align="right">**INCORRECT**
(COMMA SPLICE)</td><td>Gas prices are very high, some people are buying hybrid cars.</td></tr>
<tr><td align="right">**CORRECT**</td><td>Gas prices are very high. Some people are buying hybrid cars. (two separate sentences)</td></tr>
</table>

PRACTICE

23-2 Correct each of the following run-ons by using a period to create two separate sentences. Be sure both of your new sentences begin with a capital letter and end with a period.

Example: Stephen Colbert used to have a show called *The Colbert Report*, ~~now,~~ . Now, he is the host of *The Late Show*.

1. In 2010, David Cameron became prime minister of the United Kingdom, he replaced Gordon Brown.

2. New York–style pizza usually has a thin crust Chicago-style "deep-dish pizza" has a thick crust.

3. Last week, Soraya won a text-messaging contest the prize for texting the fastest was five hundred dollars.

4. In some parts of Canada's Northwest Territory, the only way to transport supplies is over frozen lakes, being an ice road trucker is one of the most dangerous jobs in the world.

5. In 1961, the first Six Flags opened in Arlington, Texas, the six flags represent the six former ruling governments of Texas.

2. ***Use a coordinating conjunction to connect ideas.*** If you want to indicate a particular relationship between ideas—for example, cause and effect or contrast—you can connect two independent clauses with a coordinating conjunction that makes this relationship clear. Always place a comma before the coordinating conjunction.

Coordinating Conjunctions

and	for	or	yet
but	nor	so	

> **INCORRECT**
> **(FUSED SENTENCE)**   Some schools require students to wear uniforms other schools do not.

> **INCORRECT**
> **(COMMA SPLICE)**   Some schools require students to wear uniforms, other schools do not.

> **CORRECT**   Some schools require students to wear uniforms, but other schools do not. (clauses connected with the coordinating conjunction *but*, preceded by a comma)

PRACTICE

23-3   Correct each of the following run-ons by using a coordinating conjunction (*and, but, for, nor, or, so,* or *yet*) to connect ideas. Be sure to put a comma before each coordinating conjunction.

Example: Many college students use Facebook to keep up with old
friends they also use the site to find new friends.
    , and

1. A car with soft tires gets poor gas mileage, keeping tires inflated is a good way to save money on gas.

2. It used to be difficult for football fans to see the first-down line on television, the computer-generated yellow line makes it much easier.

3. Indonesia has more volcanoes than any other country in the world the United States has the biggest volcano in the world, Hawaii's Mauna Loa.

4. Chefs can become famous for cooking at popular restaurants they can gain fame by hosting television shows.

5. Overcrowded schools often have to purchase portable classrooms or trailers this is only a temporary solution.

3. *Use a semicolon to connect ideas.* If you want to indicate a particularly close connection—or a strong contrast—between two ideas, use a semicolon.

INCORRECT (FUSED SENTENCE)	Most professional basketball players go to college most professional baseball players do not.
INCORRECT (COMMA SPLICE)	Most professional basketball players go to college, most professional baseball players do not.
CORRECT	Most professional basketball players go to college; most professional baseball players do not. (clauses connected with a semicolon)

PRACTICE
23-4

Correct each of the following run-ons by using a semicolon to connect ideas. Do not use a capital letter after the semicolon unless the word that follows it is a proper noun.

Example: From 1930 until 2006, Pluto was known as a planet ; it is

now known as a "dwarf planet."

1. Of all the states, Alaska has the highest percentage of Native American residents 16 percent of Alaskans are of Native American descent.

2. Satellites and global positioning systems (GPS) can help farmers to better understand the needs of their crops, these new tools are part of a trend called "precision agriculture."

3. Enforcing traffic laws can be difficult some cities use cameras to photograph cars that run red lights.

4. Old landfills can sometimes be made into parks, Cesar Chavez Park in Berkeley, California, is one example.

5. Freestyle motocross riders compete by doing jumps and stunts some famous FMX riders are Carey Hart, Nate Adams, and Travis Pastrana.

4. *Use a semicolon followed by a transitional word or phrase to connect ideas.* To show how two closely linked ideas are related, add a transitional word or phrase after the semicolon. The transition will indicate the specific relationship between the two clauses.

> **INCORRECT**   Finding a part-time job can be challenging
> **(FUSED SENTENCE)**   sometimes it is even hard to find an unpaid internship.

> **INCORRECT**   Finding a part-time job can be challenging,
> **(COMMA SPLICE)**   sometimes it is even hard to find an unpaid internship.

> **CORRECT**   Finding a part-time job can be challenging; in fact, sometimes it is even hard to find an unpaid internship. (clauses connected with a semicolon followed by the transitional phrase *in fact*)

Some Frequently Used Transitional Words and Phrases

after all	for this reason	now
also	however	still
as a result	in addition	then
eventually	in fact	therefore
finally	instead	thus
for example	moreover	unfortunately
for instance	nevertheless	

For more complete lists of transitional words and phrases, see 18c.

PRACTICE

23-5   Correct each of the following run-ons by using a semicolon, followed by the transitional word or phrase in parentheses, to connect ideas. Be sure to put a comma after the transitional word or phrase.

> **Example:** When babies are first born, they can only see black and
>   *; still,*
> white most infant toys are made in primary colors. (still)
>   ^

1. Restaurant goers can expect to see different condiments in different regions of the country, few tables in the Southwest are without a bottle of hot sauce. (for example)

2. Every year, millions of people participate in TV-Turnoff Week by not watching television they read, spend time with family and friends, and generally enjoy their free time. (instead)

3. Today, few workers can count on company pension plans, thirty years ago, most workers could. (however)

4. Many Americans see bottled water as a waste of money tap water is free. (after all)

5. Dog breeders who run "puppy mills" are only concerned with making money they are not particularly concerned with the dogs' well-being. (unfortunately)

FYI

Connecting Ideas with Semicolons

Run-ons often occur when you use a transitional word or phrase to join two independent clauses *without also using a semicolon.*

INCORRECT **(FUSED SENTENCE)**	It is easy to download information from the Internet however it is not always easy to evaluate the information.
INCORRECT **(COMMA SPLICE)**	It is easy to download information from the Internet, however it is not always easy to evaluate the information.

To avoid this kind of run-on, always put a semicolon before the transitional word or phrase and a comma after it.

CORRECT	It is easy to download information from the Internet; however, it is not always easy to evaluate the information.

---

5. *Use a dependent word to connect ideas.* When one idea is dependent on another, you can connect the two ideas by adding a dependent word, such as *when, who, although,* or *because.*

INCORRECT **(FUSED SENTENCE)**	American union membership was high in the mid-twentieth century it has declined in recent years.

INCORRECT (COMMA SPLICE)	American union membership was high in the mid-twentieth century, it has declined in recent years.
CORRECT	Although American union membership was high in the mid-twentieth century, it has declined in recent years. (clauses connected with the dependent word *although*)
CORRECT	American union membership, which was high in the mid-twentieth century, has declined in recent years. (clauses connected with the dependent word *which*)

Some Frequently Used Dependent Words

after	even though	until
although	if	when
as	since	which
because	that	who
before	unless	

For complete lists of dependent words, including subordinating conjunctions and relative pronouns, see 19b and 19c.

PRACTICE

23-6 Correct each run-on in the following paragraph by adding a dependent word. Consult the list above to help you choose a logical dependent word. Be sure to add correct punctuation where necessary.

Example: Harlem was a rural area $\overset{until}{\wedge}$ improved transportation linked it to lower Manhattan.

(1) Contemporary historians have written about the Harlem Renaissance, its influence is still not widely known. (2) Harlem was populated mostly by European immigrants at the turn of the last century, it saw an influx of African Americans beginning in 1910. (3) This migration from the South continued Harlem became one of the largest African

American communities in the United States. (4) Many black artists and writers settled in Harlem during the 1920s. African American art flourished. (5) This "Harlem Renaissance" was an important movement in American literary history it is not even mentioned in some textbooks. (6) Scholars recognize the great works of the Harlem Renaissance, they point to the writers Langston Hughes and Countee Cullen and the artists Henry Tanner and Sargent Johnson. (7) Zora Neale Hurston moved to Harlem from her native Florida in 1925, she began a book of African American folklore. (8) Harlem was an exciting place in the 1920s people from all over the city went there to listen to jazz and to dance. (9) The white playwright Eugene O'Neill went to Harlem to audition actors for his play *The Emperor Jones*, he made an international star of the great Paul Robeson. (10) The Great Depression occurred in the 1930s it led to the end of the Harlem Renaissance.

PRACTICE
23-7
Correct each of the following run-ons in one of these four ways: by creating two separate sentences, by using a coordinating conjunction, by using a semicolon, or by using a semicolon followed by a transitional word or phrase. Remember to put a semicolon before, and a comma after, each transitional word or phrase.

Example: Some fish-and-chip shops in Scotland sell deep-fried
                                    . Children
MARS bars ~~children~~ are the biggest consumers of these calorie-rich
                          ^
bars.

1. Fourteen percent of Americans have one or more tattoos there are over 20,000 tattoo parlors in the United States.

2. The ancient Greeks built their homes facing south this practice took advantage of light and heat from the winter sun.

3. Flamenco—a Spanish style of dancing, singing, and clapping—was traditionally informal and unplanned it has been compared to improvisational American jazz.

4. In Acadia National Park in Maine, large stones line the edges of steep trails the stones are called "Rockefeller's teeth" in honor of the trails' patron.

5. Allen Ginsberg was charged with obscenity for his book *Howl* the charges were dismissed.

PRACTICE

23-8   Correct each run-on in the following paragraph in the way that best indicates the relationship between ideas. Be sure to use appropriate punctuation.

Example: E. L. Doctorow's *Homer and Langley* tells the story of two eccentric brothers it shows that truth can be stranger than fiction.
, and

(1) The Collyer brothers were wealthy and educated they lived and died alone in a filthy apartment. (2) Langley and Homer Collyer were the sons of a doctor and an opera singer the brothers seemed to be as talented and motivated as their parents. (3) Langley played piano and studied engineering Homer had a law degree. (4) However, in their twenties and thirties, the brothers did not have jobs they lived with their parents in a Manhattan apartment. (5) Their parents died Langley and Homer inherited the apartment. (6) Gradually, they became frightened of outsiders they boarded up the windows and set traps for burglars. (7) They stopped paying their bills their heat, water, and electricity were shut off. (8) They also became compulsive hoarders, they could not throw anything away. (9) They accumulated thousands and thousands of books, numerous bundles of old newspapers, and fourteen pianos, they saved tons

of garbage. (10) They got their water from a public park they collected discarded food from grocery stores and butcher shops. (11) Eventually, Langley was caught in one of his own burglar traps, the trap sent three bundles of newspapers and a suitcase tumbling on top of him. (12) Langley died of his injuries Homer died by his side, surrounded by mountains of trash.

Donna Day/The Image Bank/Getty Images

TEST · Revise · Edit · Proofread

Look back at your response to the Focus on Writing prompt on page 411. TEST what you have written. Then, revise, edit, and proofread your work, making sure you identify and correct any run-ons.

EDITING PRACTICE: PARAGRAPH

Read the following student paragraph, and revise it to eliminate run-ons. Correct each run-on in the way that best indicates the relationship between ideas. Be sure to use appropriate punctuation. The first error has been corrected for you.

Cold Cases

    Cold cases are criminal investigations that have not been solved, *so* they are not officially closed. New evidence is found, cold cases may be reexamined. DNA tests might provide new clues, a witness may come forward with new testimony. The new evidence might lead to new suspects it might change the nature of the crime. In some cases, an accident might be reclassified a homicide, in other cases a murder might be ruled a suicide. Sometimes a person who was convicted of a crime is found to be innocent. Cold cases usually involve violent crimes, rape and murder are two examples. Investigators sometimes reopen very old cold cases, they usually focus on more recent cases with living suspects. For serious crimes, there is no limit on how much time may pass before a suspect is brought to justice, a criminal may be convicted many years after the crime was committed. When cold cases are solved, the crime is not undone, nevertheless victims' families finally feel that justice has been served.

EDITING PRACTICE: ESSAY

Read the following student essay, and revise it to eliminate run-ons. Correct each run-on in the way that best indicates the relationship between ideas, and be sure to punctuate correctly. The first error has been corrected for you.

Feng Shui

Feng shui is an ancient Chinese practice ~~it~~ . It was developed over 3,000 years

ago to balance energies and ensure both health and good fortune. A room orga-

nized according to feng shui practices is said to bring good fortune to the

occupants, a room assembled without feng shui will bring bad fortune.

Two tools are used for feng shui: the Compass and the Bagua. The Compass

is also referred to as a Luo-Pan its purpose is to discover the hidden details

about a site or a building. The Compass is composed of layers of circles sur-

rounding a magnetic needle. The Bagua is a grid in the shape of an octagon, a

symbol in each section of the grid represents an ancient oracle. The purpose of

the Bagua is to analyze the energy of the room the Bagua also reveals connec-

tions between the space and certain areas of the occupants' lives.

One of the main principles of feng shui is yin and yang this means balance.

One common example of yin and yang is black and white, another is heavy and

light. Balancing the chi, or the energy in the room, is about achieving a balance

between yin and yang. The Compass and the Bagua are the tools used to deter-

mine balance, everyone's version of balance will be different.

Many people spend several hours a day at their desks either working or

studying, for this reason, it makes sense to apply the concepts of feng shui to

workspaces. Some people may want to improve several areas of their work lives,

focusing on just one or two areas is usually best. For example, the back left corner

of the desk represents wealth, a plant could be placed there. The center left of

the desk represents family, that may be an ideal place for a family photo.

Feng shui does not guarantee immediate improvements, however, its prac-

titioners report feeling calmer and more relaxed. Perhaps practitioners have

already cleaned and organized their living spaces, or perhaps the feng shui

practice itself makes a difference, no one knows for certain. Feng shui is an

ancient art, it will undoubtedly be practiced for many years to come.

COLLABORATIVE ACTIVITY

Find an interesting paragraph in a newspaper or magazine article or on the web. Working in a small group, recopy the paragraph onto a separate sheet of paper, creating run-ons. Exchange exercises with another group. Then, work in your own group to correct each fused sentence and comma splice in an exercise prepared by another group of students. When you have finished, return the exercise to the group that created it. Finally, continuing to work with members of your group, evaluate the other group's work on your exercise, comparing it to the original newspaper, magazine, or online paragraph.

review checklist

Run-Ons

☐ A run-on is an error that occurs when two sentences are joined incorrectly. There are two kinds of run-ons: fused sentences and comma splices. (See 23a.)

☐ A fused sentence occurs when two sentences are incorrectly joined without any punctuation. (See 23a.)

☐ A comma splice occurs when two sentences are joined with just a comma. (See 23a.)

☐ Correct a run-on in one of the following ways:

1. by creating two separate sentences

☐   _____. _____.

2. by using a coordinating conjunction

☐   _____, [coordinating conjunction] _____.

3. by using a semicolon

☐   _____; _____.

4. by using a semicolon followed by a transitional word or phrase

_____; [transitional word or phrase], _____.

5. by using a dependent word

[Dependent word] _____, _____.

_____ [dependent word] _____. (See 23b.)

24 Fragments

focus on writing

The labels of Vitamin Water feature various words (such as *energy* and *power*) that attempt to convey a certain image marketers would like for you to associate with the brand. Imagine you are writing a magazine ad for your favorite beverage, footwear, or health or beauty product. Write a paragraph that describes the product as persuasively as possible. Try to include a few memorable advertising slogans.

In this chapter, you will learn to

PREVIEW

- recognize fragments (24a)
- correct missing-subject fragments (24b)
- correct phrase fragments (24c)
- correct *-ing* fragments (24d)
- correct dependent-clause fragments (24e)

24a Recognizing Fragments

A **fragment** is an incomplete sentence. Every sentence must include at least one subject and one verb, and every sentence must express a complete thought. If a group of words does not do *both* these things, it is a fragment and not a sentence—even if it begins with a capital letter and ends with a period.

The following is a complete sentence.

LaunchPad

Visit *LaunchPad Solo for Readers and Writers* > **Fragments** for more practice with fragments.

                S   **V**

SENTENCE The <u>actors</u> in the play <u><u>were</u></u> very talented. (The sentence includes both a subject and a verb and expresses a complete thought.)

Because a sentence must have both a subject and a verb and express a complete thought, the following groups of words are not complete sentences; they are fragments.

FRAGMENT (NO VERB) The actors in the play. (What point is being made about the actors?)

FRAGMENT (NO SUBJECT) Were very talented. (Who were very talented?)

FRAGMENT (NO SUBJECT OR VERB) Very talented. (Who was very talented?)

FRAGMENT (DOES NOT EXPRESS COMPLETE THOUGHT) Because the actors in the play were very talented. (What happened because they were very talented?)

FYI

Spotting Fragments

Fragments almost always appear next to complete sentences.

┌──── COMPLETE SENTENCE ────┐┌────── FRAGMENT ──────┐
Celia took two electives. Physics 320 and Spanish 101.

The fragment above does not have a subject or a verb. The complete sentence that comes before it, however, has both a subject (*Celia*) and a verb (*took*).

Often, you can correct a fragment by attaching it to an adjacent sentence that supplies the missing words. (This sentence will usually appear right before the fragment.)

Celia took two electives, Physics 320 and Spanish 101.

WORD POWER

adjacent next to

PRACTICE

24-1   Some of the following items are fragments, and others are complete sentences. On the line following each item, write *F* if it is a fragment and *S* if it is a complete sentence.

Example: Star formations in the night sky. _____*F*_____

1. To save as much as possible for college. _____

2. The judge gave her a two-year sentence. _____

3. A birthday on Christmas Day. _____

4. Because he lost ten pounds on his new diet. _____

5. Working in the garden and fixing the roof. _____

6. Sonya flew to Mexico. _____

7. Starts in August in many parts of the country. _____

8. And slept in his own bed last night. _____

9. Famous for her movie roles. _____

10. A watch that also takes photos. _____

PRACTICE

24-2 In the following paragraph, some of the numbered groups of words are missing a subject, a verb, or both. First, underline each fragment. Then, decide how each fragment could be attached to a nearby word group to create a complete new sentence. Finally, rewrite the entire paragraph, using complete sentences, on the lines provided.

Example: Gatorade was invented at the University of Florida. To help the Florida Gators fight dehydration.

Rewrite: *Gatorade was invented at the University of Florida to help the Florida Gators fight dehydration.*

(1) Doctors discovered that football players were losing electrolytes and carbohydrates. (2) Through their sweat. (3) They invented a drink. (4) That replaced these important elements. (5) Gatorade tasted terrible. (6) But did its job. (7) The Florida Gators survived a very hot season. (8) And won most of their games. (9) Now, Gatorade is used by many college and professional football teams. (10) As well as baseball, basketball, tennis, and soccer teams.

Rewrite:

_____

_____

_____

_____

_____

24b Missing-Subject Fragments

Every sentence must include both a subject and a verb. If the subject is left out, the sentence is incomplete. In the example on the following page, the first word group is a sentence. It includes both a subject (*He*) and a verb (*packed*). However, the second word group is a fragment. It includes a verb (*took*), but it does not include a subject.

┌──────── SENTENCE ────────┐ ┌──── FRAGMENT ────┐
He packed his books and papers. And also took an umbrella.

The best way to correct this kind of fragment is to attach it to the sentence that comes right before it. This sentence will usually contain the missing subject.

CORRECT He packed his books and papers and also took an umbrella.

Another way to correct this kind of fragment is to add the missing subject.

CORRECT He packed his books and papers. He also took an umbrella.

PRACTICE

24-3 Each of the following items includes a missing-subject fragment. Using one of the two methods explained above, correct each fragment.

Example: Back-to-school sales are popular with students. And with their parents.

Back-to-school sales are popular with students and with their parents. or

Back-to-school sales are popular with students. The sales are also popular

with their parents.

1. Some retailers give a lot of money to charity. And even donate part of their profits.

   _____

   _____

2. Geography bees resemble spelling bees. But instead test the contestants' knowledge of countries around the world.

   _____

   _____

3. School uniforms are often preferred by parents. And also favored by many school principals.

   _____

   _____

4. Pro-football linemen can weigh more than 300 pounds. But are still able to run fast.

_____

_____

5. Using an electric toothbrush can be good for the teeth. And promotes healthy gums.

_____

_____

24c   Phrase Fragments

Every sentence must include a subject and a verb. A **phrase** is a group of words that is missing a subject or a verb or both. When you punctuate a phrase as if it is a sentence, you create a fragment.

If you spot a phrase fragment in your writing, you can often correct it by attaching it to the sentence that comes directly before it.

Appositive Fragments

An **appositive** identifies, renames, or describes an adjacent noun or pronoun. An appositive cannot stand alone as a sentence.

To correct an appositive fragment, attach it to the sentence that comes right before it. (This sentence will contain the noun or pronoun that the appositive describes.)

┌─ FRAGMENT ─┐

INCORRECT   He decorated the room in his favorite colors. Brown and black.

CORRECT   He decorated the room in his favorite colors, brown and black.

Sometimes a word or expression like _especially, except, including, such as, for example,_ or _for instance_ introduces an appositive. Even if an appositive is introduced by one of these expressions, it is still a fragment.

┌FRAGMENT┐

INCORRECT   A balanced diet should include high-fiber foods. Such as leafy vegetables, fruits, beans, and whole-grain bread.

CORRECT   A balanced diet should include high-fiber foods, such as leafy vegetables, fruits, beans, and whole-grain bread.

Prepositional Phrase Fragments

A **prepositional phrase** consists of a preposition and its object. A prepositional phrase cannot stand alone as a sentence. To correct a prepositional phrase fragment, attach it to the sentence that comes immediately before it.

INCORRECT She promised to stand by him. ⌐———— FRAGMENT ————⌐ In sickness and in health.

CORRECT She promised to stand by him in sickness and in health.

Infinitive Fragments

An **infinitive** consists of *to* plus the base form of the verb (*to be, to go, to write*). An infinitive phrase (*to be free, to go home, to write a novel*) cannot stand alone as a sentence. You can usually correct an infinitive fragment by attaching it to the sentence that comes directly before it.

⌐———— FRAGMENT ————⌐

INCORRECT Eric considered dropping out of school. To start his own business.

CORRECT Eric considered dropping out of school to start his own business.

You can also add the words needed to complete the sentence.

CORRECT Eric considered dropping out of school. He wanted to start his own business.

PRACTICE

24-4 In the following paragraph, some of the numbered groups of words are phrase fragments. First, underline each fragment. Then, decide how each fragment could be attached to an adjacent sentence to create a complete new sentence. Finally, rewrite the entire paragraph, using complete sentences, on the lines provided.

Example: Florence Nightingale worked as a nurse. <u>During the</u> <u>Crimean War.</u>

Rewrite: *Florence Nightingale worked as a nurse during the Crimean War.*

(1) Nurses' uniforms have changed a lot. (2) Over the years. (3) Originally, nurses' uniforms looked like nuns' habits because nuns used to provide care. (4) To sick people. (5) In the late 1800s, a student of Florence Nightingale created a brown uniform. (6) With a white apron and cap. (7) This uniform was worn by student nurses at her school. (8) The Florence Nightingale School of Nursing and Midwifery. (9) Eventually, nurses began to wear white uniforms, white stockings, white shoes, and starched white caps. (10) To stress the importance of cleanliness. (11) Many older people remember these uniforms. (12) With affection. (13) Today, most nurses—both male and female—wear bright, comfortable scrubs. (14) To help patients (especially children) feel more at ease.

Rewrite:

_____

_____

_____

_____

_____

_____

_____

_____

_____

PRACTICE

24-5   Each of the following items is a phrase fragment, not a sentence. Correct each fragment by adding any words needed to turn the fragment into a complete sentence. (You may add words before or after the fragment.)

Example: During World War I. _A flu epidemic killed millions of people during_

World War I.   or   During World War I, a flu epidemic killed millions of people.

1. To be the best player on the team. _____

   _____

2. From a developing nation in Africa. _____

   _____

3. Such as tulips or roses. _____

   _____

4. Behind door number 3. _____

   _____

5. Including my parents and grandparents. _____

   _____

6. With a new car in the driveway. _____

   _____

7. To make a difficult career decision. _____

   _____

8. For a long time. _____

   _____

9. Turkey, stuffing, mashed potatoes, and cranberry sauce. _____

   _____

10. In less than a year. _____

    _____

24d *-ing* Fragments

Every sentence must include a subject and a verb. If the verb is incomplete, a word group is a fragment, not a sentence.

An *-ing* verb cannot be a complete verb. It needs a **helping verb** to complete it. An *-ing* verb, such as **looking**, cannot stand alone in a sentence without a helping verb (*is looking, was looking, were looking,* and so on). When you use an *-ing* verb without a helping verb, you create a fragment.

┌─────── FRAGMENT ───────┐

INCORRECT The twins are full of mischief. Always looking for trouble.

The best way to correct an *-ing* fragment is to attach it to the sentence that comes right before it.

CORRECT The twins are full of mischief, always looking for trouble.

Another way to correct an *-ing* fragment is to add a subject and a helping verb.

CORRECT The twins are full of mischief. They are always looking for trouble.

FYI

Being

As you write, be careful not to use the *-ing* verb *being* as if it were a complete verb.

INCORRECT I decided to take a nap. The outcome being that I slept through calculus class.

To correct this kind of fragment, substitute a form of the verb *be* that can serve as the main verb in a sentence—for example, *is*, *was*, *are*, or *were*.

CORRECT I decided to take a nap. The outcome was that I slept through calculus class.

PRACTICE

24-6 Each of the following items includes an *-ing* fragment. In each case, correct the fragment by attaching it to the sentence before it.

Example: Practical tips can help grocery shoppers. Saving them a lot of money.

Practical tips can help grocery shoppers, saving them a lot of money.

1. Always try to find a store brand. Costing less than the well-known and widely advertised brands.

_____

_____

2. Check a product's cost per pound. Comparing it to the cost per pound of similar products.

_____

_____

3. Examine sale-priced fruits and vegetables carefully. Looking for damage or spoilage.

_____

_____

4. Buy different brands of the same product. Trying each one to see which brand you like best.

_____

_____

5. Use coupons whenever possible. Keeping them handy for future shopping trips.

_____

_____

PRACTICE

24-7 Each of the following items is an *-ing* fragment. Turn each fragment into a complete sentence by adding a subject and a helping verb. Write your revised sentence on the line below each fragment.

Example: Running up and down the stairs.

Revised: *Jane and her dog are always running up and down the stairs.* ____

1. Trying to decide where to live.

   Revised: _____

   _____

2. Really feeling optimistic about the future.

   Revised: _____

   _____

3. Always complaining about the lab manual.

Revised: _____

_____

4. Deciding whether or not to get a new cell phone.

Revised: _____

_____

5. Minding their own business.

Revised: _____

_____

24e Dependent-Clause Fragments

Every sentence must include a subject and a verb. Every sentence must also express a complete thought.

A **dependent clause** is a group of words that is introduced by a dependent word, such as *although, because, that,* or *after*. A dependent clause includes a subject and a verb, but it does not express a complete thought. Therefore, it cannot stand alone as a sentence. To correct a dependent-clause fragment, you must complete the thought.

The following dependent clause is incorrectly punctuated as if it were a sentence.

FRAGMENT After Simon won the lottery.

This fragment includes both a subject (*Simon*) and a complete verb (*won*), but it does not express a complete thought. What happened after Simon won the lottery? To turn this fragment into a sentence, you need to complete the thought.

SENTENCE After Simon won the lottery, <u>he quit his night job.</u>

Some dependent clauses are introduced by dependent words called **subordinating conjunctions**.

FRAGMENT Although Marisol had always dreamed of visiting California.

This fragment includes a subject (*Marisol*) and a complete verb (*had dreamed*), but it is not a sentence; it is a dependent clause introduced by the subordinating conjunction *although*.

To correct this kind of fragment, attach it to an **independent clause** (a simple sentence) to complete the idea. (You can often find the independent clause you need right before or right after the fragment.)

> **SENTENCE** Although Marisol had always dreamed of visiting California, <u>she did not have enough money for the trip until 2011.</u>

Subordinating Conjunctions

after	even though	since	whenever
although	if	so that	where
as	if only	than	whereas
as if	in order that	that	wherever
as though	now that	though	whether
because	once	unless	while
before	provided that	until	
even if	rather than	when	

For information on how to use subordinating conjunctions, see 19b.

FYI

Correcting Dependent-Clause Fragments

The simplest way to correct a dependent-clause fragment is to cross out the dependent word that makes the idea incomplete.

~~Although~~ Marisol had always dreamed of visiting California.

However, when you delete the dependent word, readers may have trouble seeing the connection between the new sentence and the one before or after it. A better way to revise is to attach the dependent-clause fragment to an adjacent independent clause, as illustrated in the example at the top of this page.

Some dependent clauses are introduced by dependent words called **relative pronouns**.

FRAGMENT   Novelist Richard Wright, <u>who</u> came to Paris in 1947.

FRAGMENT   A quinceañera, <u>which</u> celebrates a Latina's fifteenth birthday.

FRAGMENT   A key World War II battle <u>that</u> was fought on the Pacific island of Guadalcanal.

Each of the above sentence fragments includes a subject (*Richard Wright, quinceañera, battle*) and a complete verb (*came, celebrates, was fought*). However, they are not sentences because they do not express complete thoughts. In each case, a relative pronoun creates a dependent clause.

To correct each of these fragments, add the words needed to complete the thought.

SENTENCE   Novelist Richard Wright, who came to Paris in 1947, <u>spent the rest of his life there.</u>

SENTENCE   A quinceañera, which celebrates a Latina's fifteenth birthday, <u>signifies her entrance into womanhood.</u>

SENTENCE   A key World War II battle that was fought on the Pacific island of Guadalcanal <u>took place in 1943.</u>

Relative Pronouns

that	who	whomever
what	whoever	whose
which	whom	

For information on how to use relative pronouns, see 19c.

PRACTICE

24-8   Correct each of the following dependent-clause fragments by attaching it to the sentence before or after it. If the dependent clause comes at the beginning of a sentence, place a comma after it.

Example: Before it became a state. West Virginia was part of Virginia.

Before it became a state, West Virginia was part of Virginia.

1. Because many homeless people are mentally ill. It is hard to find places for them to live. _____

   _____

2. People do not realize how dangerous raccoons can be. Even though they can be found in many parts of the United States. _____

   _____

   _____

3. I make plans to be a better student. Whenever a new semester begins.

   _____

4. Until something changes. We will just have to accept the situation.

   _____

5. Because it is a very controversial issue. My parents and I have agreed not to discuss it. _____

   _____

PRACTICE

24-9 Correct each of these dependent-clause fragments by adding the words needed to complete the idea.

Example: Many minor species of animals, which are rapidly disappearing.

Many minor species of animals, which are rapidly disappearing, need to be

protected.

1. The film that frightened me. _____

   _____

2. People who drink and drive. _____

   _____

3. Some parents who are very strict with their children. _____

   _____

4. The Vietnam War, which many Americans did not support. ————

————————————————————————————————————

5. Animals that are used in medical research. ————————

————————————————————————————————————

PRACTICE

24-10   Each of the following is a fragment. Some are missing a subject, some are phrases incorrectly punctuated as sentences, others do not have a complete verb, and still others are dependent clauses punctuated as sentences. Turn each fragment into a complete sentence, writing the revised sentence on the line below the fragment. Whenever possible, try creating two different revisions.

Example: Waiting in the dugout.

Revised: *Waiting in the dugout, the players chewed tobacco.*

Revised: *The players were waiting in the dugout.*

1. Going around in circles.

Revised: ————————————————————————

————————————————————————————————————

Revised: ————————————————————————

————————————————————————————————————

2. To win the prize for the most unusual costume.

Revised: ————————————————————————

————————————————————————————————————

Revised: ————————————————————————

————————————————————————————————————

3. Students who thought they could afford to go to college.

Revised: ————————————————————————

————————————————————————————————————

Revised: ————————————————————————

————————————————————————————————————

4. Because many instructors see cheating as a serious problem.

Revised: _____

_____

Revised: _____

_____

5. The rule that I always felt was the most unfair.

Revised: _____

_____

Revised: _____

_____

6. Finished in record time.

Revised: _____

_____

Revised: _____

_____

Erick W. Rasco/Sports Illustrated/
Getty Images

TEST · **Revise · Edit · Proofread**

Look back at your response to the Focus on Writing prompt on page 426. Reread each word group you have punctuated as a sentence, starting with the last one and working your way back; make sure that each one contains a subject and a verb. Then, underline any words ending in *-ing*; any subordinating conjunctions; and the words *which*, *that*, and *who*, making sure that the word groups they appear in are complete sentences. When you have finished, TEST the entire paragraph. Then, revise, edit, and proofread your work.

EDITING PRACTICE: PARAGRAPH

Read the following student paragraph, which includes incomplete sentences. Underline each fragment. Then, correct the fragment by attaching it to a nearby sentence that completes the thought. The first fragment has been underlined and corrected for you.

Student Debt

Debt is a serious concern, *that* ~~That~~ many students face after graduation.

Students have different options for funding their education. Such as savings, scholarships, and grants. One of the most popular options is student loans. More than 40 million people carry debt. From financing their college educations. A difficult job market has made it hard for some to repay their loans. In response to the increasing burden. President Obama introduced the Student Aid Bill of Rights. No one has the solution to this problem yet. But progress is being made. Perhaps one day in the future. Higher education will be affordable. For all students.

EDITING PRACTICE: ESSAY

Read the following student essay, which includes incomplete sentences. Underline each fragment. Then, correct the fragment by attaching it to an adjacent sentence that completes the idea. Be sure to punctuate correctly. The first fragment has been underlined and corrected for you.

Bad Behavior at the Movies

Some people have completely stopped/ ~~Going~~ *going* to the movies. They have

not stopped because they dislike the movies but because they dislike the

rude moviegoers. Who ruin their experience. One big problem is irritating

cell-phone use. There are also problems with noise. And with sharing the

theater space with strangers. All these issues can make going to the movies

seem like more trouble than it is worth.

Cell phones cause all sorts of problems. In movie theaters. People are told

to turn off their phones. But do not always do so. Loud cell-phone conversations

can be infuriating. To people who want to hear the movie. When a phone rings

during an important scene in the movie. It is especially annoying. Some

moviegoers even complain that bright text-message screens distract them. From

the movie. Of course, theaters could use jammers. To block all cell-phone signals.

Unfortunately, they would also block incoming emergency calls.

Noise in the movies also comes from other sources. Such as crying babies.

People pay money to watch a movie. Not to listen to a baby screaming. Crinkling

candy wrappers are also annoying. In addition, some moviegoers insist on talking

to each other. During the movie. In fact, they may make watching a movie an

interactive event. Talking to the actors and telling them what they should do

next. If audience members have seen the movie before, they may recite lines of

dialogue before the actors do. Spoiling the suspense for everyone else. Some-

times people even talk loudly about subjects. That have nothing to do with

the movie. In all these cases, the noise is a problem. For anyone who wants to

watch the movie and hear the actors on the screen.

Finally, going to the movies requires sharing the theater with other people.

Who are neither relatives nor friends. Unfortunately, many people behave in

movie theaters the same way they behave at home. When they are watching television. They may put their feet up on the seats in front of them. Making it impossible for others to sit there. Moviegoers become very annoyed if someone sits right in front of them. And blocks their view of the screen. Of course, these issues do not come up at home. Where friends and relatives can easily work out any problems.

Irritating movie behavior has driven many people to stop going to movie theaters. To end this rude behavior, moviegoers need to become aware of the needs of others. And make a real effort to change their behavior. Selfishness is the problem; thinking about other people is the solution.

COLLABORATIVE ACTIVITY

Working in a group of three or four students, build as many sentences as you can from the fragments listed below. Use your imagination to create as many creative sentences as you can.

Example

FRAGMENT   Knowing he has an incredible memory

SENTENCES   Zack, knowing he has an incredible memory,
wonders how he managed to forget everything
he learned about chemistry.

Knowing he has an incredible memory, Monty
the Magnificent is confident that he can amaze
his audience.

FRAGMENTS

1. Wandering in the desert
2. Never worrying about anything
3. Looking for his ideal mate
4. Always using as much ketchup as possible
5. Starting a new job

review checklist

Fragments

☐ A fragment is an incomplete sentence. Every sentence must include a subject and a verb and express a complete thought. (See 24a.)

☐ Every sentence must include a subject. (See 24b.)

☐ Phrases cannot stand alone as sentences. (See 24c.)

☐ Every sentence must include a complete verb. (See 24d.)

☐ Dependent clauses cannot stand alone as sentences. (See 24e.)

25 Subject-Verb Agreement

Courtesy Andrew Edlin Gallery and the Estate of Ralph Fasanella

focus on writing

This painting by the self-taught twentieth-century American artist
Ralph Fasanella is called *Baseball Panorama*. In a paragraph,
describe what is happening on the field and in the stands.
(Use present tense verbs.)

In this chapter, you will learn to avoid agreement problems

- with compound subjects (25b)
- with *be*, *have*, and *do* (25c)
- when words come between the subject and the verb (25d)
- with collective noun subjects (25e)
- with indefinite pronoun subjects (25f)
- when verbs come before subjects (25g)

25a Understanding Subject-Verb Agreement

A sentence's subject (a noun or a pronoun) and its verb must **agree**: singular subjects take singular verbs, and plural subjects take plural verbs.

             s   v
The <u>museum</u> <u>opens</u> at ten o'clock. (singular noun subject *museum* takes singular verb *opens*)

             s   v
Both <u>museums</u> <u>open</u> at ten o'clock. (plural noun subject *museums* takes plural verb *open*)

  s   v
<u>She</u> always <u>watches</u> the eleven o'clock news. (singular pronoun subject *she* takes singular verb *watches*)

  s   v
<u>They</u> always <u>watch</u> the eleven o'clock news. (plural pronoun subject *they* takes plural verb *watch*)

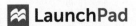 **LaunchPad**

Visit *LaunchPad Solo for Readers and Writers* > Subject-Verb Agreement for more practice with subject-verb agreement.

Subject-Verb Agreement with Regular Verbs

	SINGULAR	PLURAL
First person	I play	Molly and I/we play
Second person	you play	you play
Third person	he/she/it plays	they play
	the man plays	the men play
	Molly plays	Molly and Sam play

PRACTICE

25-1   Underline the correct form of the verb in each of the following sentences. Make sure the verb agrees with its subject.

Example: Sometimes local farmers (<u>grow</u>/grows) unusual vegetables.

(1) Locavores (choose/chooses) to eat locally grown food for a number of reasons. (2) Some locavores (eat/eats) local food simply because they (like/likes) the taste. (3) When food (travel/travels) a long distance, it (lose/loses) some of its flavor and freshness. (4) By eating locally grown food, locavores also (hope/hopes) to decrease the use of fossil fuels. (5) After all, food transportation (require/requires) a lot of energy. (6) In addition, locavores (visit/visits) farmers' markets to support local producers. (7) Local farmers (need/needs) their community's support to survive. (8) In some cases, local food supporters (buy/buys) only food produced within 50 or 100 miles. (9) In colder or drier regions, however, the climate (make/makes) such a strict policy difficult. (10) More often, a locavore diet (contain/contains) a mix of food from local and faraway places.

WORD POWER

locavore a person who eats only locally produced foods

25b Compound Subjects

The subject of a sentence is not always a single word. It can also be a **compound subject**, made up of two or more subjects joined by *and* or *or*. To avoid subject-verb agreement problems with compound subjects, follow these two rules.

1. When the parts of a compound subject are connected by *and*, the compound subject takes a plural verb.

   S   V
   <u>John and Marsha</u> <u>share</u> an office.

2. When the parts of a compound subject are connected by *or*, the verb agrees with the part of the subject that is closer to it.

>   s   v
> The mayor or the council members <u>meet</u> with community groups.
>
>   s   v
> The council members or the mayor <u>meets</u> with community groups.

PRACTICE

25-2   Underline the correct form of the verb in each of the following sentences. Make sure that the verb agrees with its compound subject.

Example: Every summer, wind and rain (<u>pound</u>/pounds) the small

shack on the beach.

1. Trophies and medals (fill/fills) my sister's bedroom.

2. Mashed potatoes and gravy (come/comes) with all our chicken dinners.

3. The instructor or his graduate students (grade/grades) the final exams.

4. A voice coach and a piano instructor (teach/teaches) each of the gifted students.

5. Pollen or cat hair (trigger/triggers) allergies in many people.

25c   *Be, Have,* and *Do*

The verbs *be, have,* and *do* are irregular in the present tense. Memorizing their present tense forms is the only sure way to avoid agreement problems.

Subject-Verb Agreement with *Be*

	SINGULAR	PLURAL
First person	I am	we are
Second person	you are	you are
Third person	he/she/it is	they are
	Tran is	Tran and Ryan are
	the boy is	the boys are

Subject-Verb Agreement with *Have*

	SINGULAR	PLURAL
First person	I have	we have
Second person	you have	you have
Third person	he/she/it has	they have
	Shana has	Shana and Robert have
	the student has	the students have

Subject-Verb Agreement with *Do*

	SINGULAR	PLURAL
First person	I do	we do
Second person	you do	you do
Third person	he/she/it does	they do
	Ken does	Ken and Mia do
	the book does	the books do

PRACTICE

25-3   Fill in the blank with the correct present tense form of the verb *be*, *have*, or *do*.

Example: Sometimes people ____*do*____ damage without really meaning to. (do)

(1) Biologists _____ serious worries about the damage that invading species of animals can cause. (have) (2) The English sparrow _____ one example. (be) (3) It _____ a role in the decline in the number of bluebirds. (have) (4) On the Galapagos Islands, cats _____ another example. (be) (5) Introduced by early explorers, they currently _____ much damage to the eggs of the giant tortoises that live on the islands. (do) (6) Scientists today _____ worried now about a new problem. (be) (7) This _____ a situation caused by wildlife agencies that put exotic fish into lakes and streams. (be) (8) They _____ this to please those who enjoy fishing. (do) (9) Although popular with people who fish, this

policy _____ major drawbacks. (have) (10) It _____ one drawback in particular: many native species of fish have been pushed close to
extinction. (have)

25d   Words between Subject and Verb

Remember that a verb must always agree with its subject. Words (for
example, a prepositional phrase) that come between the subject and the
verb do not affect subject-verb agreement.

$$\overset{s}{}\overset{v}{}$$
CORRECT   High <u>levels</u> of mercury <u>occur</u> in some fish.

CORRECT   <u>Water</u> in the fuel lines <u>causes</u> an engine to stall.

CORRECT   <u>Food</u> between the teeth <u>leads</u> to decay.

An easy way to identify the subject of the sentence is to cross out the
words that come between the subject and the verb.

High levels ~~of mercury~~ occur in some fish.

Water ~~in the fuel lines~~ causes an engine to stall.

Food ~~between the teeth~~ leads to decay.

FYI

Words between Subject and Verb

Look out for words such as *in addition to, along with, together with,
as well as, except,* and *including*. Phrases introduced by these words
do not affect subject-verb agreement.

<u>St. Thomas</u>, ~~along with St. Croix and St. John~~, <u>is</u> part of the
United States Virgin Islands.

PRACTICE
25-4   In each of the following sentences, cross out the words
that separate the subject and the verb. Then, underline the
subject of the sentence once and the verb that agrees with the subject
twice.

Example: The <u>messages</u> ~~on the phone~~ (say/<u>says</u>) that Carol is out of town.

1. Each summer, fires from lightning (cause/causes) great damage.

2. Books downloaded onto an eReader usually (cost/costs) less than print books.

3. One out of ten men (gets/get) prostate cancer.

4. The woodstove in the living room (heat/heats) the entire house.

5. Trans fat in a variety of foods (lead/leads) to increased rates of heart disease.

25e Collective Noun Subjects

Collective nouns are words (such as *family* and *audience*) that name a group of people or things but are singular. Because they are singular, they take singular verbs.

      s   v

The <u>team</u> <u>practices</u> five days a week in the gym.

Frequently Used Collective Nouns

army	club	family	jury
association	committee	gang	mob
band	company	government	team
class	corporation	group	union

PRACTICE

25-5 Fill in the blank with the correct present tense form of the verb.

Example: Our government ____*is*____ democratically elected by the people. (be)

1. The Caribbean Culture Club _____ on the first Thursday of every month. (meet)

2. The company no longer _____ health insurance for part-time employees. (provide)

3. The basketball team _____ competing in the division finals next week. (be)

4. After two days, the jury _____ been unable to reach a verdict. (have)

5. The union _____ guaranteed raises for its members. (want)

25f Indefinite Pronoun Subjects

Indefinite pronouns—*anybody, everyone*, and so on—do not refer to a particular person, place, or idea.

Most indefinite pronouns are singular and take singular verbs.

<u>No one</u> <u>likes</u> getting up early.
s   v

<u>Everyone</u> <u>likes</u> to sleep late.
s   v

<u>Somebody</u> <u>likes</u> beets.
s   v

Singular Indefinite Pronouns			
another	either	neither	somebody
anybody	everybody	nobody	someone
anyone	everyone	no one	something
anything	everything	nothing	
each	much	one	

A few indefinite pronouns (*both, many, several, few, others*) are plural and take plural verbs.

<u>Many</u> <u>were</u> left homeless by the flood.
s   v

FYI

Indefinite Pronouns as Subjects

If a prepositional phrase comes between the indefinite pronoun and the verb, cross out the prepositional phrase to help you identify the sentence's subject.

     S   V
Each ~~of the boys~~ has a bike.

    S   V
Many ~~of the boys~~ have bikes.

PRACTICE
25-6   Underline the correct verb in each sentence.

Example: As my friends and I know, anything (<u>helps</u>/help) when it comes to paying for college.

1. One of my friends (has/have) an academic scholarship.

2. Everybody (says/say) that work-study jobs are best.

3. Many of the most interesting work-study jobs (is/are) located on campus.

4. Some of the work-study jobs (tends/tend) to be better than a regular job.

5. Several of the jobs (is/are) full-time.

25g   Verbs before Subjects

A verb always agrees with its subject—even if the verb comes *before* the subject. In questions, for example, word order is reversed, with the verb coming before the subject or with the subject coming between two parts of the verb.

      V   S
Where is the bank?

  V   S   V
Are you going to the party?

If you have trouble identifying the subject of a question, answer the question with a statement. (In the statement, the subject will come before the verb.)

Where is the bank? The bank is on Walnut Street.

FYI

There Is and *There Are*

When a sentence begins with *there is* or *there are*, the word *there* is not the subject of the sentence. The subject comes after the form of the verb *be*.

There is one chief justice on the Supreme Court.

There are nine justices on the Supreme Court.

PRACTICE

25-7 Underline the subject of each sentence, and circle the correct form of the verb.

Example: Who (is/are) the baseball player who broke Hank Aaron's home-run record?

1. Where (do/does) snakes go in the winter?

2. Why (do/does) people who cannot afford them buy lottery tickets?

3. (Is/Are) there any states that do not follow Daylight Savings Time?

4. How (do/does) an immigrant become a citizen?

5. There (is/are) three branches of government in the United States.

Courtesy Andrew Edlin Gallery and the Estate of Ralph Fasanella

TEST · Revise · Edit · Proofread

Look back at your response to the Focus on Writing prompt on page 447. TEST what you have written. Then, revise and edit your work, making sure that all your verbs agree with their subjects. Pay particular attention to the agreement problems described in this chapter. Finally, proofread your paragraph.

EDITING PRACTICE: PARAGRAPH

Read the following student paragraph, which includes errors in subject-verb agreement. Decide whether each of the underlined verbs agrees with its subject. If it does not, cross out the verb, and write in the correct form. If it does, write *C* above the verb. The first sentence has been done for you.

Conflict Diamonds

Today, many people <u>know</u> about conflict diamonds, and most <u>~~wants~~</u> *want* this

violent trade to end. These illegal diamonds <u>comes</u> from countries where there

<u>are</u> civil war. Most often, the origin of these stones <u>is</u> an unstable central or

West African nation. Rebel groups in these countries <u>mines</u> the diamonds and

<u>sells</u> them to raise money for weapons. In the process, local people, who <u>does</u>

not benefit from the sale of the diamonds, often <u>gets</u> hurt or killed. How <u>does</u>

a person who wants to buy a diamond avoid buying a conflict diamond? Once a

diamond <u>reach</u> a store, neither a customer nor a gem expert <u>have</u> the ability to

determine its history just by looking at it. However, a consumer can ask for proof

that the diamond <u>is</u> "conflict-free." Each of the diamonds in a store <u>are</u> supposed

to have an official certificate to prove that it <u>is</u> legal.

EDITING PRACTICE: ESSAY

Read the following student essay, which includes errors in subject-verb agreement. Decide whether each of the underlined verbs agrees with its subject. If it does not, cross out the verb, and write in the correct form. If it does, write *C* above the verb. The first sentence has been done for you.

Party in the Parking Lot

    Fun at football games ~~are~~ ^{is} not limited to cheering for the home team. Many people arrives four or five hours early, sets up grills in the parking lot, and start cooking. Typically, fans drives to the stadium in a pickup truck, a station wagon, or an SUV. They open up the tailgate, puts out the food, and enjoys the fun with their friends. In fact, tailgating is so popular that, for some fans, it is more important than the game itself.

    What do it take to tailgate? First, most tailgaters plan their menus in advance. To avoid forgetting anything, they makes lists of what to bring. Paper plates, along with a set of plastic cups, make it unnecessary to bring home dirty dishes. Jugs of water is essential, and damp towels helps clean up hands and faces. Also, lightweight chairs or another type of seating is important.

    At the game, parking near a grassy area or at the end of a parking row are best. This location give tailgaters more space to cook and eat. If the food are ready two hours before the game start, there is plenty of time to eat and to clean up.

    Some tailgaters buys expensive equipment. The simple charcoal grill have turned into a combination grill, cooler, and foldout table with a portable awning. There is grills with their own storage space. Other grills swings out from the tailgate to provide easy access to the vehicle's storage area. Some deluxe grills even has their own beer taps, stereo systems, and sinks.

    Whatever equipment tailgaters brings to the game, the most important factors is food and companionship. There is a tradition of sharing food and swapping recipes with other tailgaters. Most tailgaters loves to meet and to compare recipes. For many, the tailgating experience is more fun than the game itself.

COLLABORATIVE ACTIVITY

Working in a group of four students, list ten nouns (five singular and five plural)—people, places, or things—along the left-hand side of a sheet of paper. Beside each noun, write the present tense form of a verb that could logically be used with the noun. Then, expand each noun-and-verb combination you listed into a complete sentence. Next, write a sentence that could logically follow each of these sentences, using a pronoun as the subject of the new sentence. Make sure the pronoun you choose refers to the noun in the previous sentence, as in this example: *Max watches three movies a week*. *He is addicted to films*. Check to be certain the subjects in your sentences agree with the verbs.

review checklist

Subject-Verb Agreement

- Singular subjects (nouns and pronouns) take singular verbs, and plural subjects take plural verbs. (See 25a.)

- Special rules govern subject-verb agreement with compound subjects. (See 25b.)

- The irregular verbs *be*, *have*, and *do* often present problems with subject-verb agreement in the present tense. (See 25c.)

- Words that come between the subject and the verb do not affect subject-verb agreement. (See 25d.)

- Collective nouns are singular and take singular verbs. (See 25e.)

- Most indefinite pronouns, such as *no one* and *everyone*, are singular and take a singular verb when they serve as the subject of a sentence. A few are plural and take plural verbs. (See 25f.)

- A sentence's subject and verb must always agree, even if the verb comes before the subject. (See 25g.)

26 Illogical Shifts

AP Photo/Paul T. Erikson, Tri-City Herald

focus on writing

This picture shows elementary school students at the annual Washington State Elementary Chess Championship. Do you believe that after-school chess clubs and similar programs can help students succeed? Write a paragraph in which you express your ideas on this subject.

In this chapter, you will learn to avoid illogical shifts in

- tense (26a)
- person (26b)
- voice (26c)

A **shift** occurs whenever a writer changes **tense**, **person**, or **voice**. As you write and revise, be sure that any shifts you make are **logical**—that is, that they occur for a reason.

26a Shifts in Tense

Tense is the form a verb takes to show when an action takes place or when a situation occurs. Some shifts in tense are necessary—for example, to indicate a change from past time to present time.

> **LOGICAL SHIFT** When they first came out, cell phones were large and bulky, but now they are small and compact.

An **illogical shift in tense** occurs when a writer shifts from one tense to another for no apparent reason.

> **ILLOGICAL SHIFT IN TENSE** The dog walked to the fireplace. Then, he circles twice and lies down in front of the fire. (shift from past tense to present tense)

> **REVISED** The dog walked to the fireplace. Then, he circled twice and lay down in front of the fire. (consistent use of past tense)

> **REVISED** The dog walks to the fireplace. Then, he circles twice and lies down in front of the fire. (consistent use of present tense)

LaunchPad

Visit *LaunchPad Solo for Readers and Writers* > **Verb Tense** for more practice with shifts in tense.

PRACTICE
26-1

Edit the sentences in the following paragraph to correct illogical shifts in tense. If a sentence is correct, write *C* in the blank.

Example: The 100th Battalion of the 442nd Infantry is the only remaining United States Army Reserve ground combat unit that fought in World War II. _____*C*_____

(1) During World War II, the 100th Battalion of the 442nd Combat Infantry Regiment was made up of young Japanese Americans who are eager to serve in the U.S. Army. _____ (2) At the start of World War II, 120,000 Japanese Americans were sent to relocation camps because the government feared that they might be disloyal to the United States. _____ (3) However, in 1943, the United States needed more soldiers, so it sends recruiters to the camps to ask for volunteers. _____ (4) The Japanese American volunteers are organized into the 442nd Combat Infantry Regiment. _____ (5) The soldiers of the 442nd Infantry fought in some of the bloodiest battles of the war, including the invasion of Italy at Anzio and a battle in Bruyeres, France, where they capture over two hundred enemy soldiers. _____ (6) When other U.S. troops are cut off by the enemy, the 442nd Infantry soldiers were sent to rescue them. _____ (7) The Japanese American soldiers suffered the highest casualty rate of any U.S. unit and receive over eighteen thousand individual decorations. _____

26b Shifts in Person

Person is the form a pronoun takes to show who is speaking, spoken about, or spoken to.

Person

	SINGULAR	PLURAL
First person	I	we
Second person	you	you
Third person	he, she, it	they

An **illogical shift in person** occurs when a writer shifts from one person to another for no apparent reason.

ILLOGICAL SHIFT IN PERSON	The hikers were told that you had to stay on the trail. (shift from third person to second person)
REVISED	The hikers were told that they had to stay on the trail. (consistent use of third person)

ILLOGICAL SHIFT IN PERSON	Anyone can learn to cook if you practice. (shift from third person to second person)
REVISED	You can learn to cook if you practice. (consistent use of second person)
REVISED	Anyone can learn to cook if he or she practices. (consistent use of third person)

PRACTICE

26-2 The sentences in the following paragraph contain illogical shifts in person. Edit each sentence so that it uses pronouns consistently. Be sure to change any verbs that do not agree with the new subjects.

Example: A person can use duct tape many more ways than
he or she
~~you~~ might realize.
^

(1) Many people do not realize how many things you can do with duct tape. (2) They think duct tape is only for ducts and that you can use it for repairs. (3) The truth is, if they are creative, you will have many more options. (4) A practical person will find that they can use duct tape to solve many everyday problems. (5) For example, practical users of duct tape can use the product to repair a hole in your shoe. (6) Other people looking for practical solutions might use duct tape to hang your Christmas lights. (7) Did you know that a more inventive person can even use duct tape to pay for your college education? (8) There is a scholarship contest for high school students who make your prom dress or tux entirely out of duct tape. (9) The people who judge

the applications expect you to feature an original design, so creativity is especially important. (10) Enthusiasts also make a variety of apparel and household goods out of duct tape, so with a little time and ingenuity your possibilities are endless!

26c Shifts in Voice

Visit *LaunchPad Solo for Readers and Writers* > **Active and Passive Voice** for more practice with shifts in voice.

Voice is the form a verb takes to indicate whether the subject is acting or is acted upon. When the subject is acting, the sentence is in the **active voice**. When the subject is acted upon, the sentence is in the **passive voice**.

ACTIVE VOICE   Nat Turner organized a slave rebellion in August 1831. (Subject *Nat Turner* is acting.)

PASSIVE VOICE   A slave rebellion was organized by Nat Turner in 1831. (Subject *rebellion* is acted upon.)

An **illogical shift in voice** occurs when a writer shifts from active to passive voice or from passive to active voice for no apparent reason.

ILLOGICAL SHIFT IN VOICE   J. D. Salinger wrote *The Catcher in the Rye*, and *Franny and Zooey* was also written by him. (active to passive)

REVISED   J. D. Salinger wrote *The Catcher in the Rye*, and he also wrote *Franny and Zooey*. (consistent use of active voice)

ILLOGICAL SHIFT IN VOICE   Radium was discovered by Marie Curie in 1910, and she won a Nobel Prize in chemistry in 1911. (passive to active)

REVISED   Marie Curie discovered radium in 1910, and she won a Nobel Prize in chemistry in 1911. (consistent use of active voice)

FYI

Correcting Illogical Shifts in Voice

You should usually use the active voice in your college writing because it is stronger and more direct than the passive voice.

To change a sentence from the passive to the active voice, determine who or what is acting, and make this noun the subject of a new active voice sentence.

> **PASSIVE VOICE**   The campus escort service is used by my friends. (*My friends* are acting.)
>
> **ACTIVE VOICE**   My friends use the campus escort service.

PRACTICE

26-3   The following sentences contain illogical shifts in voice. Revise each sentence by changing the underlined passive voice verb to the active voice.

Example:

Two teachers believed they could help struggling students in New York City schools, so "Chess in the Schools" was founded by them.

Two teachers believed they could help struggling students in New York City

schools, so they founded "Chess in the Schools."

1. Chess develops critical-thinking skills, and self-discipline and self-esteem are developed by players, too.

   _____

   _____

2. Because players face complicated chess problems, good problem-solving skills are developed by them.

   _____

   _____

3. Student chess players improve their concentration, and reading and math skills <u>can be improved</u> through this better concentration.

_____

_____

4. Chess teaches students how to lose as well as win, and that ability <u>will be needed</u> by students throughout their lives.

_____

_____

5. "Chess in the Schools" also helps keep students out of trouble because of the conflict-resolution skills <u>developed</u> by them.

_____

_____

AP Photo/Paul T. Erikson, Tri-City Herald

TEST · Revise · Edit · Proofread

Look back at your response to the Focus on Writing prompt on page 460. TEST what you have written. Then, revise and edit your work, paying particular attention to illogical shifts in tense, person, and voice. Finally, proofread your paragraph.

EDITING PRACTICE: PARAGRAPH

Read the following student paragraph, which includes illogical shifts in tense, person, and voice. Edit the passage to eliminate the unnecessary shifts, making sure subjects and verbs agree. The first error has been corrected for you.

The Origin of Baseball Cards

The first baseball cards appeared in the late 1800s. These cardboard pictures *were* ~~are~~ inserted in packs of cigarettes. Some people collected the cards, and the cigarette companies use the cards to encourage people to buy their products. By the early twentieth century, it was found by candy makers that one could use baseball cards to sell candy to children, so they developed new marketing plans. For example, each Cracker Jack box contains a baseball card. In 1933, gum manufacturers packaged bubble gum with baseball cards to make "bubble gum cards." Children could trade these cards. Sometimes children would put cards in the spokes of their bike wheels. The cards made noise when the wheels turns. Eventually, the bubble gum is dropped by the card manufacturers, and people just bought the cards. Still, collecting baseball cards was seen as a hobby for children until the 1970s, when dealers began to sell their rarest cards at high prices. Today, baseball-card collectors were mainly adults who are interested in investment, not baseball. For example, in 2007, a rare Honus Wagner baseball card sells for a record $2.8 million.

EDITING PRACTICE: ESSAY

Read the following essay, which includes illogical shifts in tense, person, and voice. Edit the passage to eliminate the illogical shifts, making sure subjects and verbs agree. The first sentence has been edited for you.

A Different Kind of Vacation

During our upcoming winter break, my sister and I ~~were~~ *are* going to Belize to help build a school. Like many people, we want to travel and see new places, but we did not want to be tourists who only see what is in a guidebook. We also want to help people who are less fortunate than we were. Volunteering gives us the opportunity to combine travel with community service and to get to know a different culture at the same time.

These days, many people are using his or her vacation time to do volunteer work. Lots of charitable organizations offer short-term projects during school or holiday breaks. For most projects, no experience was necessary. All people need is his or her interest in other people and a desire to help.

For example, last year my aunt goes to Tanzania to work in a health clinic. She loved her experience volunteering in a poor rural community where you help local doctors. She also loved the host family who shared their modest house with her. Before she left Tanzania, she and some of the other volunteers climb Mount Kilimanjaro. She said it was the best vacation she had ever had.

Although many volunteer vacations focus on improving schools or health care, a wide range of projects was available. Everyone can find work that suits their interests. For instance, people can volunteer to help preserve the environment, or you can work to protect women's rights. Countries all over the world welcome volunteers because help is needed by a lot of people.

My sister and I decided to help with the school in Belize because we believe a clean and safe place to learn is deserved by everyone. We are also eager to do some construction, get to know the local people, and enjoy the warm weather. If we have enough time, we hoped to visit some Mayan ruins as well. All in all, we are looking forward to a rewarding and unforgettable experience.

COLLABORATIVE ACTIVITY

Working in a group of three or four students, make up a test with five sentences containing illogical shifts in tense, person, and voice. Exchange tests with another group in the class. After you have taken their test, compare your answers with theirs.

review checklist

Illogical Shifts

☐ An illogical shift in tense occurs when a writer shifts from one tense to another for no apparent reason. (See 26a.)

☐ An illogical shift in person occurs when a writer shifts from one person to another for no apparent reason. (See 26b.)

☐ An illogical shift in voice occurs when a writer shifts from active to passive voice or from passive to active voice for no apparent reason. (See 26c.)

27 Misplaced and Dangling Modifiers

Shutterstock

focus on writing

Write a one-paragraph recipe explaining how to prepare your favorite food. Begin by describing the food; then, list the ingredients, and explain how to make it.

In this chapter, you will learn to recognize and correct

- misplaced modifiers (27a)
- dangling modifiers (27b)

A **modifier** is a word or word group that identifies or describes another word in a sentence. Many word groups that act as modifiers are introduced by *-ing* (present participle) or *-ed* (past participle) modifiers.

Working in his garage, Steve Jobs invented the personal computer.

Rejected by Hamlet, Ophelia goes mad and drowns herself.

 **LaunchPad**

Visit *LaunchPad Solo for Readers and Writers* > **Modifier Placement** for practice with misplaced and dangling modifiers.

Used correctly, *-ing* and *-ed* modifiers provide useful information. Used incorrectly, however, these types of modifiers can be very confusing.

The two most common problems with modification are *misplaced modifiers* and *dangling modifiers*.

27a Correcting Misplaced Modifiers

A **misplaced modifier** appears to modify the wrong word because it is placed incorrectly in the sentence. To correct this problem, move the modifier so it is as close as possible to the word it is supposed to modify (usually directly before or after it).

INCORRECT   Sarah fed the dog wearing her pajamas. (Was the

dog wearing Sarah's pajamas?)

CORRECT   Wearing her pajamas, Sarah fed the dog.

INCORRECT   Dressed in a raincoat and boots, I thought my son

was prepared for the storm. (Who was dressed in a

raincoat and boots?)

CORRECT   I thought my son, dressed in a raincoat and boots,

was prepared for the storm.

PRACTICE

27-1 Underline the modifier in each of the following sentences. Then, draw an arrow to the word it modifies.

Example: Helping people worldwide, Doctors Without Borders is a group of volunteer medical professionals.

1. Suffering from famine and other disasters, some people are unable to help themselves.

2. Feeding and healing them, Doctors Without Borders improves their lives.

3. Responding to a recent earthquake, doctors arrived within three days to help with the relief effort.

4. Setting up refugee camps in Thailand, the group quickly helped its first survivors.

5. Some doctors, chartering a ship called *The Island of Light*, once provided medical aid to people escaping Vietnam by boat.

PRACTICE

27-2 Rewrite the following sentences, which contain misplaced modifiers, so that each modifier clearly refers to the word it logically modifies.

Example: Mark ate a pizza standing in front of the refrigerator.

Standing in front of the refrigerator, Mark ate a pizza.

1. Running across my bathroom ceiling, I saw two large, hairy bugs.

_____

_____

2. Lori looked at the man sitting in the chair with red hair.

_____

_____

3. The deer was hit by a car running across the street.

_____

_____

4. Dressed in a beautiful wedding gown, the groom watched the bride walk down the aisle.

_____

_____

5. The exterminator sprayed the insect wearing a mask.

_____

_____

27b Correcting Dangling Modifiers

A **dangling modifier** "dangles" because the word it modifies does not appear in the sentence. Often, a dangling modifier comes at the beginning of a sentence and appears to modify the noun or pronoun that follows it.

Using my computer, the report was finished in two days.

In the sentence above, the modifier *Using my computer* seems to be modifying *the report.* But this makes no sense. (How can the report use a computer?) The word the modifier should logically refer to is missing.

Using my computer, I finished the report in two days.

To correct a dangling modifier, supply a word to which the modifier can logically refer.

INCORRECT Moving the microscope's mirror, the light can be

directed onto the slide. (Can the light move the

mirror?)

CORRECT Moving the microscope's mirror, you can direct

the light onto the slide.

INCORRECT   Growing up, my mom was an excellent cook.

(Was your mom growing up?)

CORRECT   Growing up, I thought my mom was an excellent cook.

INCORRECT   Paid in advance, the furniture was delivered.

(Was the furniture paid in advance?)

CORRECT   Paid in advance, the movers delivered the furniture.

PRACTICE

27-3   Each of the following sentences contains a dangling modifier. To correct each sentence, add a word to which the modifier can logically refer.

Example: Waiting inside, my bus passed by.

Waiting inside, I missed my bus.

1. Pushing on the brakes, my car would not stop for the red light.

_____

_____

2. Working overtime, his salary almost doubled.

_____

_____

3. Angered by the noise, the concert was called off.

_____

_____

4. Using the correct formula, the problem was easily solved.

_____

_____

5. Tired and hungry, the assignment was finished by midnight.

_____

_____

PRACTICE
27-4

Complete the following sentences, making sure to include a word to which each modifier can logically refer.

Example: Dancing with the man of her dreams, _she decided it was_

time to wake up.

1. Blocked by the clouds, _____

_____

2. Applying for financial aid, _____

_____

3. Settled into his recliner chair, _____

_____

4. Fearing that they might catch a cold, _____

_____

5. Hearing strange noises through the wall, _____

_____

TEST · Revise · Edit · Proofread

Look back at your response to the Focus on Writing prompt on page 470. TEST what you have written. Then, revise and edit your work, paying particular attention to -*ing* and -*ed* modifiers. Check to make sure that you do not have any misplaced or dangling modifiers. Finally, proofread your paragraph.

Shutterstock

EDITING PRACTICE: PARAGRAPH

Read the following student paragraph, which includes modification errors. Rewrite sentences where necessary to correct misplaced and dangling modifiers. In some cases, you may have to supply a word to which the modifier can logically refer. The first incorrect sentence has been corrected for you.

Beyond Mickey Mouse

For more than twenty years, Pixar computer animation studios have pro-

thousands of pictures were provided by artists

duced movies. Sketched by hand before Pixar, ~~artists provided thousands of~~

^

~~pictures~~ for traditional animated films. In 2006, Disney bought Pixar for

$7.4 billion. Now, the company that pioneered traditional animation eighty years

ago owns Pixar. Led by Steve Jobs, animation was revolutionized by Pixar. Working

with computers, special software was used by animators to create movement.

Invented by Pixar, animators were able to achieve startling lifelike effects. The

first commercially successful Pixar film was *Toy Story*. Completed in 1995, the

use of computer animation made *Toy Story* a success. Fourteen more films were

created by Pixar since the debut of *Toy Story*. The most recent film, *Inside Out,*

is about a young girl named Riley. With the help of her personified emotions,

Riley navigates life in a new town. This typical Pixar emotional development

plot resonates with audiences. Bringing in more than $9 billion in worldwide box

office sales, audiences make Pixar movies very successful.

EDITING PRACTICE: ESSAY

Read the following student essay, which includes modification errors. Rewrite sentences to correct dangling and misplaced modifiers. In some cases, you will have to supply a word to which the modifier can logically refer. The first sentence has been corrected for you.

Eating as a Sport

After eating a big meal, ~~the food often makes~~ you *often* feel stuffed. Imagine how

someone participating in competitive eating feels. To win, you have to eat more

food faster than anyone else. Training for days, many different kinds of food

are eaten in these contests. For example, contestants eat chicken wings, pizza,

ribs, hot dogs, and even matzo balls. Training for events, competitive eating is

considered a sport by participants. By winning, a good living can be made by a

competitive eater. Considered dangerous by some, competitive eaters and their

fans nevertheless continue to grow.

The way it works is that each competitor eats the same weight or portion

of food. Giving the signal, the competitors begin eating. Breaking the food

in pieces or just eating the food whole, any technique can be used. The

competitors, soaked in water, can make the food softer. They can even eat hot

dogs separately from their buns. Good competitors are usually not overweight.

In fact, some are quite thin. Keeping the stomach from expanding, competitors

are hurt by extra fat. By drinking large amounts of water, their stomachs stretch

and increase their chances of winning. This is one technique many competitors

use when they train.

The International Federation of Competitive Eating watches over the

contests to make sure they are fair and safe. Providing the dates and locations,

contests are listed on its website. Often, contests are held at state fairs. Also

listing participants, prizes, and rankings of winners, new participants are

invited. Before entering the contests, their eating specialty and personal profile

must be indicated by new participants. Competitors must also be at least eigh-

teen years old.

Many competitive eaters participate in lots of contests. For example, weigh-

ing only 100 pounds, 8.1 pounds of sausage was eaten in only 10 minutes by

Sonya Thomas. At another contest, she ate 46 crab cakes in 10 minutes. Held in the United States, some participants come from other countries. For instance, Takeru Kobayashi, who comes from Japan, once ate 18 pounds of cow brains in 15 minutes. Winners usually get cash prizes. The largest prize, $20,000, was awarded in a hot dog–eating contest at Coney Island, which was televised by ESPN. By eating 66 hot dogs and their buns in 12 minutes, the contest was won by Joey Chestnut, a professional speed eater. Almost 50,000 people attended the contest in person, and millions watched on television.

There is some concern about competitive eating. By stretching the stomach, a person's health may be affected. There is also concern about obesity and overeating. Worried about choking, events should have doctors present some people argue. Still, many people like to watch these contests, and they seem to be getting more popular each year.

COLLABORATIVE ACTIVITY

Working in a group of five or six students, make a list of five modifiers that end in *-ing* and five modifiers that end in *-ed*. Exchange your list with another group, and complete each other's sentences.

Examples

Typing as fast as he could, *John could not wait to finish his screenplay.*

Frightened by a snake, *the horse ran away.*

review checklist

Misplaced and Dangling Modifiers

☐ Correct a misplaced modifier by placing the modifier as close as possible to the word it modifies. (See 27a.)

☐ Correct a dangling modifier by supplying a word to which the modifier can logically refer. (See 27b.)

Read the following student essay, which contains run-ons, sentence fragments, errors with subject-verb agreement, illogical shifts, and dangling and misplaced modifiers. Edit the essay to correct the errors. The first error has been corrected for you.

Airplane Black Boxes

Did you know that airplane black boxes are actually orange? Many people talk about the "black box" when aviation disaster occurs, ~~Even~~ *, even* though most people do not understand how they work. Plane crashes are sometimes unexplained. Such as Malaysia Airlines Flight 370, which seemed to simply disappear. In these cases, the black box is essential because they record flight data and the voices in the cockpit. Black boxes are important technology tools. But they are not perfect.

The black box was invented by David Warren. As a result of several unexplained airplane crashes in the 1950s. Warren called his invention the "flight memory unit." Originally, critics were concerned because he thought that recording voices violated privacy. After a mysterious plane crash in Queensland, Australia, in 1960 however the value of the technology became apparent. Shortly thereafter, Australia became the first country to require black boxes in all its airplanes.

Black boxes undergo rigorous testing. Before they are installed. The devices must be able to endure 3,400-g impacts. And fire and submersion at 20,000 feet below sea level. Its capabilities are impressive, however, the devices are not without flaws. With further funding, the technology can be improved.

The biggest drawback of the current black box technology is that to unlock their data they has to be recovered. This might seem like an old-fashioned problem nevertheless, real-time reporting of a plane's information is not yet possible. In addition, the box's locator signal only lasts for thirty days. Which is not enough time in some cases.

Black boxes is an essential technology. It should be more heavily invested in. The voice and flight data it carries often explains the reason for the crash. If this information could be recovered faster, they would help rescue and recovery. It would also means that families would have more information about their loved ones. By improving black box technology, planes could be made much easier to locate after a crash. It is an investment that would benefit many people in terrible situations.

unit
6 Understanding Basic Grammar

28 Verbs: Past Tense

Ian Dickson/Getty Images

focus on writing

The obituary on the following page provides a short recap of the life of rock-and-roll icon David Bowie. Read the obituary, and then write one for yourself. (Refer to yourself by name or by *he* or *she*.) As you write, assume that you have led a long life and have achieved everything you hoped you would. Be sure to include the accomplishments for which you would most like to be remembered. Don't forget to use transitional words and phrases that clearly show how one event in your life relates to another.

- understand regular verbs in the past tense (28a)
- understand irregular verbs in the past tense (28b)
- deal with problem verbs in the past tense (28c and 28d)

Legendary musician David Bowie dies of cancer at 69

NEW YORK (AP) – David Bowie, the chameleon-like star who transformed the sound—and the look—of rock with his audacious creativity and his sexually ambiguous makeup and costumes, died of cancer Sunday.

Bowie, whose hits included "Space Oddity," "Fame," "Heroes" and "Let's Dance," died surrounded by family, representative Steve Martin said early Monday. The singer, who was 69, had fought cancer for 18 months.

Long before alter egos and wild outfits became commonplace in pop, Bowie turned the music world upside down with the release of the 1972 album, "The Rise and Fall of Ziggy Stardust and the Spiders from Mars," which introduced one of music's most famous personas. "Ziggy Stardust" was a concept album that imagined a rock star from outer space trying to make his way in the music world. The persona—the red-headed, eyeliner-wearing Stardust—would become an enduring part of Bowie's legacy, and a touchstone for the way entertainers packaged themselves for years to come.

Bowie's birthday was Friday, the same day as he released his new album, "Blackstar."

Tense is the form a verb takes to show when an action or situation takes place. The **past tense** indicates that an action occurred in the past.

28a Regular Verbs

Regular verbs form the past tense by adding either *-ed* or *-d* to the **base form** of the verb (the present tense form of the verb that is used with *I*).

We register<u>ed</u> for classes yesterday.

Walt Disney produce<u>d</u> short cartoons in 1928.

Regular verbs that end in -*y* form the past tense by changing the *y* to *i* and adding -*ed*.

tr<u>y</u>   tr<u>ied</u>

appl<u>y</u>   appl<u>ied</u>

PRACTICE

28-1 Change the regular verbs below to the past tense.

                                     visited

Example: Every year, my mother ~~visits~~ her family in Bombay.

(1) My mother always returns from India with henna designs on her hands and feet. (2) In India, henna artists create these patterns. (3) Henna originates in a plant found in the Middle East, India, Indonesia, and northern Africa. (4) Many women in these areas use henna to color their hands, nails, and parts of their feet. (5) Men dye their beards as well as the manes and hooves of their horses. (6) They also color animal skins with henna. (7) In India, my mother always celebrates the end of the Ramadan religious fast by going to a "henna party." (8) A professional henna artist attends the party to apply new henna decorations to the women. (9) After a few weeks, the henna designs wash off. (10) In the United States, my mother's henna designs attract the attention of many people.

LaunchPad

Visit *LaunchPad Solo for Readers and Writers* > **Verb Tense** for more practice with verbs.

28b   Irregular Verbs

Unlike regular verbs, whose past tense forms end in -*ed* or -*d*, **irregular verbs** have irregular forms in the past tense. In fact, their past tense forms may look very different from their present tense forms.

The following chart lists the base form and past tense form of many of the most commonly used irregular verbs. (The past tense of other irregular verbs can be found in a dictionary.)

Irregular Verbs in the Past Tense

BASE FORM	PAST	BASE FORM	PAST
awake	awoke	know	knew
be	was, were	lay (to place)	laid
beat	beat	lead	led
become	became	learn	learnt (learned)
begin	began	leave	left
bet	bet	let	let
bite	bit	lie (to recline)	lay
blow	blew	light	lit
break	broke	lose	lost
bring	brought	make	made
build	built	meet	met
buy	bought	pay	paid
catch	caught	quit	quit
choose	chose	read	read
come	came	ride	rode
cost	cost	ring	rang
cut	cut	rise	rose
dive	dove (dived)	run	ran
do	did	say	said
draw	drew	see	saw
drink	drank	sell	sold
drive	drove	send	sent
eat	ate	set	set
fall	fell	shake	shook
feed	fed	shine	shone (shined)
feel	felt	sing	sang
fight	fought	sit	sat
find	found	sleep	slept
fly	flew	speak	spoke
forgive	forgave	spend	spent
freeze	froze	spring	sprang
get	got	stand	stood
give	gave	steal	stole
go (goes)	went	stick	stuck
grow	grew	sting	stung
have	had	swear	swore
hear	heard	swim	swam
hide	hid	take	took
hold	held	teach	taught
hurt	hurt	tear	tore
keep	kept	tell	told

BASE FORM	PAST	BASE FORM	PAST
think	thought	wear	wore
throw	threw	win	won
understand	understood	write	wrote
wake	woke		

PRACTICE

28-2 Fill in the correct past tense form of each irregular verb in parentheses, using the chart on pages 486–487 to help you. If you cannot find a particular verb on the chart, look it up in a dictionary.

Example: My grandmother ___*told*___ (tell) me about the game of Mahjong.

(1) Mahjong is a game that _____ (begin) in China. (2) Traditionally, the game _____ (be) played with four players and used a special set of 144 tiles. (3) To play, participants _____ (learn) complex rules. (4) Rules varied by region, but in general players _____ (choose) tiles from the discard pile to form a winning hand. (5) Although historians do not agree on the origins of the game, some people _____ (think) that it was created by Confucius. (6) In 1949, the leaders of the People's Republic of China _____ (take) this beloved game away. (7) The government _____ (feel) that Mahjong encouraged gambling. (8) In 1985, the ban was reversed and the people _____ (get) to return to their favorite game. (9) The older generations _____ (teach) the younger generations how to play Mahjong. (10) As a result, the game _____ (find) new popularity, and is very popular today.

28c   Problem Verbs: *Be*

The irregular verb *be* causes problems because it has two different past tense forms—*was* for singular subjects and *were* for second-person singular subjects as well as for plural subjects. (All other English verbs have just one past tense form.)

> Carlo <u>was</u> interested in becoming a city planner. (singular)
>
> They <u>were</u> happy to help out at the school. (plural)

Past Tense Forms of the Verb *Be*

	Singular	Plural
First person	I <u>was</u> tired.	We <u>were</u> tired.
Second person	You <u>were</u> tired.	You <u>were</u> tired.
Third person	He <u>was</u> tired.	
	She <u>was</u> tired.	They <u>were</u> tired.
	It <u>was</u> tired.	
	The man <u>was</u> tired.	Frank and Billy <u>were</u> tired.

PRACTICE

28-3 Edit the following passage for errors in the use of the verb *be*. Cross out any underlined verbs that are incorrect, and write the correct forms above them. If a verb form is correct, label it *C*.

> **Example:** Before 1990, there ~~was~~ ^were^ no female Hispanic astronauts in the NASA program.

(1) Although there had never been a Hispanic woman astronaut, it <u>was</u> impossible for NASA to ignore Ellen Ochoa's long career in physics and engineering. (2) When Ochoa <u>was</u> young, her main interests <u>was</u> music, math, and physics. (3) After getting a degree in physics at San Diego State University, she <u>were</u> considering a career in music or business. (4) However, she <u>was</u> convinced by her mother to continue her education. (5) In 1983, Ochoa <u>was</u> studying for a doctorate in electrical engineering at Stanford University when the first female astronaut, Sally Ride, flew

on the space shuttle. (6) Ochoa <u>were</u> inspired by Sally Ride to become an astronaut. (7) More than 2,000 people <u>was</u> also inspired to apply for the astronaut program. (8) In 1990, Ochoa <u>was</u> picked to fly into space. (9) On one of her flights, she <u>was</u> a mission specialist and used a remote-controlled robotic arm to catch a satellite. (10) After four space flights, Ochoa <u>were</u> made Director of Flight Crew Operations.

28d Problem Verbs: *Can/Could* and *Will/Would*

The helping verbs *can/could* and *will/would* present problems because their past tense forms are sometimes confused with their present tense forms.

Can/Could

Can, a present tense verb, means "is able to" or "are able to."

> First-year students <u>can</u> apply for financial aid.

Could, the past tense of *can*, means "was able to" or "were able to."

> Escape artist Harry Houdini claimed that he <u>could</u> escape from any prison.

Will/Would

Will, a present tense verb, talks about the future from a point in the present.

> A solar eclipse <u>will</u> occur in ten months.

Would, the past tense of *will*, talks about the future from a point in the past.

> I told him yesterday that I <u>would</u> think about it.

Would is also used to express a possibility or wish.

> If we stuck to our budget, we <u>would</u> be better off.
> Laurie <u>would</u> like a new stuffed animal.

FYI

Will and Would

Note that *will* is used with *can* and that *would* is used with *could*.

> I will feed the cats if I can find their food.
> I would feed the cats if I could find their food.

PRACTICE

28-4 Circle the appropriate helping verb from the choices in parentheses.

Example: People who don't want to throw things away (can, could) rent a self-storage unit.

(1) In the past, warehouse storage (will, would) provide a place to store excess items. (2) However, people (will, would) have to hire moving vans and (can, could) hardly ever have access to their stored items. (3) They (will, would) have to sign an expensive long-term contract. (4) Now, however, they (can, could) take advantage of another option. (5) They (can, could) store possessions in a space as small as a closet or as large as a house. (6) With self-storage, people (can, could) easily move their belongings in and out of the storage unit. (7) When they need more space, they (will, would) be able to get it. (8) In fact, the managers of self-storage facilities (can, could) suggest how much space owners (will, would) need. (9) The only person who (can, could) get into the self-storage unit is the person who has rented it. (10) If people need a

hand truck to move their belongings, they (can, could) usually borrow one. (11) All in all, using self-storage (can, could) solve a lot of problems for people with too many possessions.

TEST · Revise · Edit · Proofread

Look back at your response to the Focus on Writing prompt on page 483. TEST what you have written. Then, revise and edit your work, making sure that you have used the correct past tense form for each of your verbs. Finally, proofread your paragraph.

Ian Dickson/Getty Images

EDITING PRACTICE

Read the following student essay, which includes errors in past tense verb forms. Decide whether each of the underlined past tense verbs is correct. If the verb is correct, write *C* above it. If it is not, cross out the verb, and write in the correct past tense form. The first sentence has been corrected for you. (If necessary, consult the list of irregular verbs on pages 486–487.)

Healing

The window seat ~~were~~ *was* our favorite place to sit. I piled pillows on the ledge and <u>spended</u> several minutes rearranging them. Then, my friend and I <u>lied</u> on our backs and propped our feet on the wall. We <u>sat</u> with our arms around our legs and <u>thinked</u> about the mysteries of life.

We stared at the people on the street below and <u>wonder</u> who they <u>was</u> and where they <u>was</u> going. We imagined that they <u>can</u> be millionaires, foreign spies, or drug smugglers. We believed that everyone except us <u>leaded</u> wonderful and exciting lives.

I <u>heard</u> a voice call my name. Reluctantly, I <u>standed</u> up, tearing myself away from my imaginary world. My dearest and oldest friend—my teddy bear—and I came back to the real world. I grabbed Teddy and <u>brung</u> him close to my chest. Together, we <u>go</u> into the cold dining room, where twelve other girls <u>sit</u> around a table eating breakfast. None of them looked happy.

In the unit for eating disorders, meals <u>was</u> always tense. Nobody <u>wants</u> to eat, but the nurses watched us until we <u>eated</u> every crumb. I <u>set</u> Teddy on the chair beside me and stared gloomily at the food on our plate. I closed my eyes and <u>taked</u> the first bite. I <u>feeled</u> the calories adding inches of ugly fat. Each swallow <u>were</u> like a nail being ripped from my finger. At last, it <u>was</u> over. I had survived breakfast.

Days passed slowly. Each passing minute <u>was</u> a victory. After a while, I learned how to eat properly. I learned about other people's problems. I also learned that people loved me. Eventually, even Teddy stopped feeling sorry for me. I <u>begun</u> to smile—and laugh. Sometimes I even considered myself happy. My doctors challenged me—and, surprisingly, I <u>rised</u> to the occasion.

COLLABORATIVE ACTIVITY

Form a group with three other students. What national or world events do you remember most clearly? Take ten minutes to list news events that you think have defined the last five years. On your own, write a few paragraphs in which you discuss the significance of the three or four events that the members of your group agree were the most important.

review checklist

Verbs: Past Tense

- The past tense is the form a verb takes to show that an action occurred in the past.

- Regular verbs form the past tense by adding either -*ed* or -*d* to the base form of the verb. (See 28a.)

- Irregular verbs have irregular forms in the past tense. (See 28b.)

- *Be* has two different past tense forms—*was* for singular subjects and *were* for second-person singular subjects as well as for plural subjects. (See 28c.)

- *Could* is the past tense of *can*. *Would* is the past tense of *will*. (See 28d.)

29 Verbs: Past Participles

Everett Collection

focus on writing

This still from the film *Mad Hot Ballroom* shows children practicing ballroom dancing. Write a paragraph about an activity—a hobby or a sport, for example—that you have been involved in for a relatively long time. Begin by identifying the activity and stating why it has been important to you. Then, describe the activity, paying particular attention to what you have gained from it over the years.

In this chapter, you will learn to

- identify regular past participles (29a)
- identify irregular past participles (29b)
- use the present perfect tense (29c)
- use the past perfect tense (29d)
- use past participles as adjectives (29e)

29a Regular Past Participles

Every verb has a past participle form. The **past participle** form of a regular verb is identical to its past tense form. Both are formed by adding either *-ed* or *-d* to the **base form** of the verb (the present tense form of the verb that is used with the pronoun *I*).

LaunchPad

Visit *LaunchPad Solo for Readers and Writers* > **Verb Tense** for more practice with past participles.

PAST TENSE

He earn<u>ed</u> a fortune.

PAST PARTICIPLE

He has earn<u>ed</u> a fortune.

PAST TENSE

He creat<u>ed</u> a work of art.

PAST PARTICIPLE

He has creat<u>ed</u> a work of art.

PRACTICE

29-1 Fill in the correct past participle form of each regular verb in parentheses.

Example: For years, volunteer vacationers have ___*visited*___ (visit) remote areas to build footpaths, cabins, and shelters.

(1) Recently, vacationers have _____ (discover) some new opportunities to get away from it all and to do good at the same time. (2) Groups such as Habitat for Humanity, for example, have _____ (offer) volunteers a chance to build homes in low-income areas. (3) Habitat's Global Village trips have _____ (raise) awareness about the lack of affordable housing in many countries. (4) Participants in Sierra Club programs have _____ (donate) thousands of work hours all over the United States. (5) Sometimes these volunteers have _____ (join) forest service workers to help restore wilderness

areas. (6) They have _____ (clean) up trash at campsites. (7) They have also _____ (remove) nonnative plants. (8) Some volunteer vacationers have _____ (travel) to countries such as Costa Rica, Russia, and Thailand to help with local projects. (9) Other vacationers have _____ (serve) as English teachers. (10) Volunteering vacations have _____ (help) to strengthen cross-cultural understanding.

29b Irregular Past Participles

Irregular verbs nearly always have irregular past participles. Irregular verbs do not form the past participle by adding -ed or -d to the base form of the verb.

The following chart lists the base form, the past tense form, and the past participle of the most commonly used irregular verbs.

Irregular Past Participles

BASE FORM	PAST TENSE	PAST PARTICIPLE
awake	awoke	awoken
be (am, are)	was (were)	been
beat	beat	beaten
become	became	become
begin	began	begun
bet	bet	bet
bite	bit	bitten
blow	blew	blown
break	broke	broken
bring	brought	brought
build	built	built
buy	bought	bought
catch	caught	caught
choose	chose	chosen
come	came	come
cost	cost	cost
cut	cut	cut
dive	dove, dived	dived
do	did	done

BASE FORM	PAST TENSE	PAST PARTICIPLE
draw	drew	drawn
drink	drank	drunk
drive	drove	driven
eat	ate	eaten
fall	fell	fallen
feed	fed	fed
feel	felt	felt
fight	fought	fought
find	found	found
fly	flew	flown
forgive	forgave	forgiven
freeze	froze	frozen
get	got	got, gotten
give	gave	given
go	went	gone
grow	grew	grown
have	had	had
hear	heard	heard
hide	hid	hidden
hold	held	held
hurt	hurt	hurt
keep	kept	kept
know	knew	known
lay (to place)	laid	laid
lead	led	led
leave	left	left
let	let	let
lie (to recline)	lay	lain
light	lit	lit
lose	lost	lost
make	made	made
meet	met	met
pay	paid	paid
quit	quit	quit
read	read	read
ride	rode	ridden
ring	rang	rung
rise	rose	risen
run	ran	run
say	said	said
see	saw	seen
sell	sold	sold

(continued)

(continued from previous page)

BASE FORM	PAST TENSE	PAST PARTICIPLE
send	sent	sent
set	set	set
shake	shook	shaken
shine	shone, shined	shone, shined
sing	sang	sung
sit	sat	sat
sleep	slept	slept
speak	spoke	spoken
spend	spent	spent
spring	sprang	sprung
stand	stood	stood
steal	stole	stolen
stick	stuck	stuck
sting	stung	stung
swear	swore	sworn
swim	swam	swum
take	took	taken
teach	taught	taught
tear	tore	torn
tell	told	told
think	thought	thought
throw	threw	thrown
understand	understood	understood
wake	woke, waked	woken, waked
wear	wore	worn
win	won	won
write	wrote	written

PRACTICE

29-2 Edit the following paragraph for errors in irregular past participles. Cross out any underlined past participles that are incorrect, and write in the correct form above them. If the verb form is correct, label it *C*.

Example: Banned book lists have ~~keeped~~ *kept* many people from reading

great novels.

(1) Banning books has became a controversial topic. (2) Many people

have spoke out about banning books, particularly in relation to freedom of speech. (3) It's very likely that some of your most beloved books have be put on banned book lists. (4) For example, *Alice in Wonderland* had made the list in Hunan, China, in 1931. (5) In Australia, the *Twilight* books have rised to the top of the banned list in several schools. (6) Many books have made the banned list in the United States as well. (7) In 2006, a Kansas school district had taked *Charlotte's Web* off of bookshelves. (8) Recently, the annual Banned Books Week celebration has grew in popularity. (9) Banned Books Week has builded awareness about censorship issues. (10) Organizers hope that if more people have readed banned books, then more people will protest the censorship of those books.

29c The Present Perfect Tense

The past participle can be combined with the present tense forms of *have* to form the **present perfect tense**.

The Present Perfect Tense

(*have* or *has* + past participle)

SINGULAR	PLURAL
I have gained.	We have gained.
You have gained.	You have gained.
He has gained.	They have gained.
She has gained.	
It has gained.	

■ Use the present perfect tense to indicate an action that began in the past and continues into the present.

PRESENT PERFECT   The nurse has worked at the clinic for two years. (The working began in the past and continues into the present.)

■ Use the present perfect tense to indicate that an action has just occurred.

PRESENT PERFECT   I have just eaten. (The eating has just occurred.)

PRACTICE

29-3   Fill in the appropriate tense (past tense or present perfect) of the verb in parentheses.

Example: Now, cell phones fit easily into a pocket, but the first mobile-phone users ___*carried*___ (carry) devices that were more than a foot long.

(1) In recent years, the size of many everyday items _____ (change) considerably. (2) Cell phones and computers _____ (undergo) the biggest changes. (3) There was a time, not long ago, when a single computer _____ (fill) an entire room and a cell phone weighed as much as two pounds. (4) Since then, we _____ (invent) smaller and smaller devices. (5) Now, we _____ (become) accustomed to tiny devices that act as both phone and computer yet weigh only a few ounces. (6) However, while these items have shrunk, other things _____ (get) bigger. (7) For example, flat-screen TVs now come in sizes up to 100 inches. (8) Moreover, as Americans _____ (grow) heavier, hospital equipment has had to get sturdier. (9) Ten years ago, manufacturers _____ (build) operating tables that supported a maximum of 700 pounds. (10) Now, medical supply companies _____ (develop) a standard table that supports up to 1,200 pounds. (11) To accommodate the growing number of overweight people, movie theater seats

and caskets _____ (increase) in size as well. (12) While movie-goers in the 1980s _____ (sit) in 20-inch seats, today's viewers sit in 26-inch seats. (13) Similarly, standard-size caskets have expanded in width from 24 to 28 inches, and some companies _____ (start) making plus-size caskets as large as 52 inches across. (14) Clearly, consumers prefer some items to be smaller even as they themselves _____ (get) bigger.

29d The Past Perfect Tense

The past participle can also be used to form the **past perfect tense**, which consists of the past tense of *have* plus the past participle.

The Past Perfect Tense

(*had* + past participle)

SINGULAR	PLURAL
I had returned.	We had returned.
You had returned.	You had returned.
He had returned.	They had returned.
She had returned.	
It had returned.	

Use the past perfect tense to show that an action occurred before another past action.

PAST PERFECT TENSE   PAST TENSE

Chief Sitting Bull had fought many battles before he defeated General Custer. (The fighting was done before Sitting Bull defeated Custer.)

PRACTICE

29-4 Underline the appropriate verb tense (present perfect or past perfect) from the choices in parentheses.

Example: Although he (has missed/<u>had missed</u>) his second free throw, the crowd cheered for him anyway.

1. Meera returned to Bangladesh with the money she (has raised/had raised).

2. Her contributors believe that she (has shown/had shown) the ability to spend money wisely.

3. The planner told the commission that she (has found/had found) a solution to the city's traffic problem.

4. It seems clear that traffic cameras (have proven/had proven) successful in towns with similar congestion problems.

5. Emily says she (has saved/had saved) a lot of money by driving a motor scooter instead of a car.

6. She sold the car she (has bought/had bought) three years before.

7. Because they are huge fans, Esteban and Tina (have camped/had camped) out in front of the theater to buy tickets.

8. The people who (have waited/had waited) all night were the first to get tickets.

9. Sam and Ryan volunteer at Habitat for Humanity, where they (have learned/had learned) many useful skills.

10. After they (have completed/had completed) five hundred hours of work, they were eligible to get their own house.

29e Past Participles as Adjectives

In addition to functioning as verbs, past participles can function as adjectives modifying nouns that follow them.

I cleaned up the broken glass.

The exhausted runner finally crossed the finish line.

Past participles are also used as adjectives after **linking verbs**, such as *seemed* or *looked*.

Jason seemed surprised.

He looked shocked.

PRACTICE

29-5   Edit the following passage for errors in past participle forms used as adjectives. Cross out any underlined participles that are incorrect, and write the correct form above them. If the participle form is correct, label it *C*.

　　　　　　inspired
Example: I am ~~inspire~~ by the lost boys of Sudan.
　　　　　　　　　　　 ^

(1) Many people are interesting in the story of the lost boys of Sudan. (2) The young boys were force to leave their homes when civil war broke out. (3) The frightening boys traveled to Ethiopia on foot. (4) Many boys died because they were dehydrate. (5) The story of the lost boys of Sudan fascinate people around the world, inspiring them to help. (6) In 2000, approximately three thousand surprised boys learned that they would be relocated to the United States. (7) Since many of them felt overwhelm by life in the United States, volunteers were recruited to help them adjust. (8) Concern groups formed fundraising efforts to help support the lost boys. (9) Although many of the boys (now men) are still locate in the United States, others have returned to Sudan to help rebuild their country.

Everett Collection

TEST · Revise · Edit · Proofread

Look back at your response to the Focus on Writing prompt on page 494. **TEST** what you have written. Then, revise and edit your work, paying particular attention to present perfect and past perfect verb forms and to past participles used as adjectives. Finally, proofread your paragraph.

EDITING PRACTICE

Read the following student essay, which includes errors in the use of past participles and perfect tenses. Decide whether each of the underlined verbs or participles is correct. If it is correct, write *C* above it. If it is not, write in the correct verb form. The first error has been corrected for you.

The Flash Mob Phenomenon

The first flash mob ~~had take~~ *took* place in 2003 when two hundred people assembled in a New York City Macy's store. Since then, these strange spontaneous gatherings had popped up in cities around the world and have involve all kinds of unusual behaviors. Occasionally, a group has organized a flash mob for criminal purposes, but in most cases, flash mobs had been harmless acts of group expression.

Organizer Bill Wasik had actually intend the first flash mob to be a social commentary. Wasik has wanted to make fun of "hipster" New Yorkers who showed up at events simply because other people did. However, almost no one had saw the first flash mob that way. In fact, people mostly have thought it was cool. As a result, admirers started organizing their own flash mobs.

So far, few of the subsequent flash mobs had have a political or social purpose. Typically, people had participate simply because these gatherings are fun. For example, over the years, people have gathered in cities around the world to dance to Michael Jackson's "Thriller." People had also enjoyed getting together in public spaces for massive pillow fights. In addition, several groups have coordinated group "freeze frames," in which participants all "freeze" at the same moment. Organized quietly by text messages or social media, most flash mobs have not publicize their plans in traditional media. Consequently, passers-by have enjoyed the feeling that the group had gathered spontaneously.

Although the majority of flash mob organizers have create these brief performances to entertain, people have occasionally use flash mobs to commit crimes. Over the last few years, several groups <u>have robbed</u> stores by entering in large numbers, stealing merchandise, and then separating quickly. Worse, several groups <u>have came</u> together to commit violent acts or destroy property. Most of today's flash mobs, however, are peaceful.

Over the last decade, flash mobs <u>have became</u> more popular than anyone could have imagined. Although they have not had the impact that creator Bill Wasik <u>had hoped</u> for, they <u>given</u> a lot of people a lot of enjoyment. Flash mobs allow people to be creative, to work together, and to have fun. Although a few flash mobs <u>have done</u> harm, most <u>have offer</u> people a way to be a part of something memorable.

COLLABORATIVE ACTIVITY

Assume that you are a restaurant employee who has been nominated for the Employee-of-the-Year Award. To win this award (along with a thousand-dollar prize), you have to explain in writing what you have done during the past year to deserve this honor. Write a letter to your supervisor and the awards committee. When you have finished, trade papers with another student and edit his or her letter. Read all the letters to the class, and have the class decide which is the most convincing.

review checklist

Verbs: Past Participles

- The past participle of regular verbs is formed by adding -*ed* or -*d* to the base form. (See 29a.)

- Irregular verbs usually have irregular past participles. (See 29b.)

- The past participle is combined with the present tense forms of *have* to form the present perfect tense. (See 29c.)

- The past participle is used to form the past perfect tense, which consists of the past tense of *have* plus the past participle. (See 29d.)

- The past participle can function as an adjective. (See 29e.)

30 Nouns and Pronouns

AP Photo/NASA/Neil A. Armstrong

focus on writing

Write a paragraph about a significant local, national, or international
event you remember. Begin by explaining what happened. Then,
tell why the event was important to you.

In this chapter, you will learn to

- identify nouns (30a) and pronouns (30c)
- form plural nouns (30b)
- understand (30d) and solve special problems with (30e) pronoun-antecedent agreement
- avoid vague and unnecessary pronouns (30f)
- understand (30g) and solve special problems with (30h) pronoun case
- identify reflexive and intensive pronouns (30i)

30a Identifying Nouns

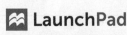

Visit *LaunchPad Solo for Readers and Writers* > **Nouns** for more practice with nouns.

A **noun** is a word that names a person (*singer, Jay-Z*), an animal (*dolphin, Flipper*), a place (*downtown, Houston*), an object (*game, Scrabble*), or an idea (*happiness, Darwinism*).

A **singular noun** names one thing. A **plural noun** names more than one thing.

FYI

When to Capitalize Nouns

Most nouns, called **common nouns**, begin with lowercase letters.

character   holiday

Some nouns, called **proper nouns**, name particular people, animals, places, objects, or events. A proper noun always begins with a capital letter.

Homer Simpson   Labor Day

30b Forming Plural Nouns

Most nouns that end in consonants add -*s* to form plurals. Other nouns add -*es* to form plurals. For example, most nouns that end in -*o* add -*es* to form plurals. Other nouns, whose singular forms end in -*s*, -*ss*, -*sh*, -*ch*, -*x*, or -*z*, also add -*es* to form plurals. (Some nouns that end in -*s* or -*z* double the *s* or *z* before adding -*es*.)

SINGULAR	PLURAL
street	streets
tomato	tomatoes
gas	gases
class	classes
bush	bushes
church	churches
fox	foxes
quiz	quizzes

Irregular Noun Plurals

Some nouns form plurals in unusual ways.

■ Nouns whose plural forms are the same as their singular forms

SINGULAR	PLURAL
a deer	a few deer
this species	these species
a television series	two television series

■ Nouns ending in *-f* or *-fe*

SINGULAR	PLURAL
each half	both halves
my life	our lives
a lone thief	a gang of thieves
one loaf	two loaves
the third shelf	several shelves

Exceptions: *roof* (plural *roofs*), *proof* (plural *proofs*), *belief* (plural *beliefs*)

■ Nouns ending in *-y*

SINGULAR	PLURAL
another baby	more babies
every worry	many worries

Note that when a vowel (*a, e, i, o, u*) comes before the *y*, the noun has a regular plural form: *monkey* (plural *monkeys*), *day* (plural *days*).

(continued)

(continued from previous page)

- Hyphenated compound nouns

SINGULAR	PLURAL
Lucia's sister-in-law	Lucia's two favorite sisters-in-law
a mother-to-be	twin mothers-to-be
the first runner-up	all the runners-up

Note that the plural ending is attached to the compound's first word: *sister, mother, runner*.

- Miscellaneous irregular plurals

SINGULAR	PLURAL
that child	all children
a good man	a few good men
the woman	lots of women
my left foot	both feet
a wisdom tooth	my two front teeth
this bacterium	some bacteria

30c　Identifying Pronouns

A **pronoun** is a word that refers to and takes the place of a noun or another pronoun. In the following sentence, the pronouns *she* and *her* take the place of the noun *Michelle*.

> Michelle was really excited because <u>she</u> had finally found a job that made <u>her</u> happy. (*She* refers to *Michelle*; *her* refers to *she*.)

Pronouns, like nouns, can be singular or plural.

LaunchPad

Visit *LaunchPad Solo for Readers and Writers* > **Pronouns** for more practice with pronouns.

- Singular pronouns (*I, he, she, it, him, her,* and so on) always take the place of singular nouns or pronouns.

> Geoff left his jacket at work, so <u>he</u> went back to get <u>it</u> before <u>it</u> could be stolen. (*He* refers to *Geoff*; *it* refers to *jacket*.)

- Plural pronouns (*we, they, our, their,* and so on) always take the place of plural nouns or pronouns.

> Jessie and Dan got up early, but <u>they</u> still missed <u>their</u> train. (*They* refers to *Jessie and Dan*; *their* refers to *they*.)

■ The pronoun *you* can be either singular or plural.

> When the volunteers met the mayor, they said, "We really admire you." The mayor replied, "I admire you, too." (In the first sentence, *you* refers to *the mayor*; in the second sentence, *you* refers to *the volunteers*.)

FYI

Demonstrative Pronouns

Demonstrative pronouns—*this*, *that*, *these*, and *those*—point to one or more items.

■ *This* and *that* point to one item: This is a work of fiction, and that is a nonfiction book.

■ *These* and *those* point to more than one item: These are fruits, but those are vegetables.

PRACTICE

30-1   In the following sentences, fill in each blank with an appropriate pronoun.

Example: Ever since _____*I*_____ had my first scuba-diving experience, _____*I*_____ have wanted to search for sunken treasure.

(1) Three friends and _____ decided to explore an area off the Florida coast where a shipwreck had occurred almost three hundred years ago. (2) The first step was to buy a boat; _____ all agreed on a used rubber boat with a fifteen-horsepower engine. (3) _____ had hardly been used and was in very good condition. (4) _____ also needed some equipment, including an anchor and metal detectors. (5) If there was treasure on the bottom of the ocean, _____ would find it. (6) _____ stayed in the boat while my friends made the first dive. (7) At first, _____ found only fish

and sea worms, but _____ didn't give up. (8) Finally, one of the metal detectors started beeping because _____ had located a cannon and two cannonballs. (9) Then, it started beeping again; this time, _____ had found some pieces of pottery and an old pistol. (10) Although our group didn't find any coins, _____ all enjoyed our search for sunken treasure.

30d Understanding Pronoun-Antecedent Agreement

The word that a pronoun refers to is called the pronoun's **antecedent**. In the following sentence, the noun *leaf* is the antecedent of the pronoun *it*.

The leaf turned yellow, but it did not fall.

A pronoun must always agree with its antecedent. If an antecedent is singular, as it is in the sentence above, the pronoun must be singular. If the antecedent is plural, as it is in the sentence below, the pronoun must also be plural.

The leaves turned yellow, but they did not fall.

If an antecedent is feminine, the pronoun that refers to it must also be feminine.

Melissa passed her driver's exam with flying colors.

If an antecedent is masculine, the pronoun that refers to it must also be masculine.

Matt wondered what courses he should take.

If an antecedent is **neuter** (neither masculine nor feminine), the pronoun that refers to it must also be neuter.

The car broke down, but they refused to fix it again.

PRACTICE

30-2   In the following sentences, circle the antecedent of each underlined pronoun. Then, draw an arrow from the pronoun to the antecedent it refers to.

Example: (Navajo Indians) were recruited by the U.S. military because <u>they</u> spoke a language that very few could understand.

(1) During World War II, approximately 400 Navajos participated in a top-secret military program in which <u>they</u> served as "code talkers." (2) The U.S. Marine Corps recruited Navajos to assist <u>them</u> with guarding military secrets. (3) Philip Johnston, a World War I veteran, developed the idea of the "code talkers" because <u>he</u> grew up on a Navajo reservation. (4) The Navajos used only oral communication, and <u>their</u> language's syntax and vocabulary were not recorded in writing. (5) In addition, the language is so specific and complex that often Navajo tribes could not even understand <u>their</u> neighboring tribes. (6) These features of the language made <u>it</u> ideal for a secret military project. (7) One major obstacle was that the Navajos did not have language for military words, so <u>they</u> had to improvise. (8) All in all, the Navajos proved <u>they</u> were important contributors to the war effort. (9) Because the code talker program was top secret, <u>it</u> was not made public until 2000. (10) Today, the Navajos are honored for <u>their</u> important contributions to the war effort.

PRACTICE

30-3   Fill in each blank in the following passage with an appropriate pronoun.

Example: Americans celebrate July 4 because _____*it*_____ is Independence Day.

(1) For some Germans, November 9 is a day to celebrate positive change; for others, _____ recalls the human potential for violence

and destruction. (2) November 9, designated "World Freedom Day," is important because _____ is the day the Berlin Wall fell. (3) On that day in 1989, residents of East and West Germany were allowed to cross the barrier that had separated _____ since the end of World War II. (4) However, Germans have mixed feelings about this date because November 9 also reminds _____ of a dark moment in their history. (5) On the night of November 9, 1938, Nazis took sledgehammers and axes to as many Jewish businesses, synagogues, and homes as _____ could find. (6) In German, this violent event is called *Kristallnacht*; in English, _____ is known as the "Night of Broken Glass." (7) Because November 9 has been so important in German history, journalists some-times refer to _____ as Germany's "day of fate." (8) Coincidentally, Albert Einstein, a German Jew, received the Nobel Prize on November 9, 1921; the theories _____ described have changed how scien-tists think. (9) Thus, November 9 in Germany is a day of opposites; like so many dates in human history, _____ marks both triumph and tragedy.

30e Special Problems with Agreement

Certain kinds of antecedents can be challenging for writers because they cannot easily be identified as singular or plural.

Compound Antecedents

A **compound antecedent** consists of two or more words connected by *and* or *or*.

■ Compound antecedents connected by *and* are plural, and they are used with plural pronouns.

> During World War II, Belgium and France tried to protect their borders.

■ Compound antecedents connected by *or* may take a singular or a plural pronoun. The pronoun always agrees with the word that is closer to it.

> Is it possible that European nations or Russia may send its [not *their*] troops?

> Is it possible that Russia or European nations may send their [not *its*] troops?

PRACTICE

30-4 In each of the following sentences, underline the compound antecedent, and circle the connecting word (*and* or *or*). Then, circle the appropriate pronoun in parentheses.

Example: Marge (and) Homer Simpson love (his or her/their) children very much in spite of the problems they cause.

1. Either *The Sopranos* or *Breaking Bad* had the highest ratings for any cable television show in (its/their) final episode.

2. In *The Office*, Jim and Pam played pranks on (his/their) coworker Dwight Shrute.

3. Both NBC and ABC offer (its/their) television shows online.

4. Both cable stations and the networks hire the most attractive anchors to host (its/their) prime-time shows.

5. Recent movies and documentaries about penguins have delighted (its/their) audiences.

6. In baseball, pitchers and catchers communicate (his or her/their) plays with hand signals.

7. Either Angry Birds or Candy Crush gives (its/their) players many hours of gaming fun.

8. In summer, many parents and children enjoy spending (his or her/their) time at water parks.

9. Hurricanes or tornadoes can be frightening to (its/their) victims.

Indefinite Pronoun Antecedents

Most pronouns refer to a specific person or thing. However, **indefinite pronouns** do not refer to any particular person or thing.

Most indefinite pronouns are singular.

Singular Indefinite Pronouns

another	everybody	no one
anybody	everyone	nothing
anyone	everything	one
anything	much	somebody
each	neither	someone
either	nobody	something

When an indefinite pronoun antecedent is singular, use a singular pronoun to refer to it.

Everything was in its place. (*Everything* is singular, so it is used with the singular pronoun *its*.)

FYI

Indefinite Pronouns with *Of*

The singular indefinite pronouns *each, either, neither,* and *one* are often used in phrases with *of—each of, either of, neither of,* or *one of*—followed by a plural noun. Even in such phrases, these indefinite pronoun antecedents are always singular and take singular pronouns.

Each of the routes has its [not *their*] own special challenges.

A few indefinite pronouns are plural.

Plural Indefinite Pronouns

both	others
few	several
many	

When an indefinite pronoun antecedent is plural, use a plural pronoun to refer to it.

> They all wanted to graduate early, but few received their diplomas in January. (*Few* is plural, so it is used with the plural pronoun *their*.)

FYI

Using *His* or *Her* with Indefinite Pronouns

Even though the indefinite pronouns *anybody*, *anyone*, *everybody*, *everyone*, *somebody*, *someone*, and so on are singular, many people use plural pronouns to refer to them.

> Everyone must hand in their completed work by 2 p.m.

This usage is widely accepted in spoken English. Nevertheless, indefinite pronouns like *everyone* are singular, and written English requires a singular pronoun.

However, using the singular pronoun *his* to refer to *everyone* suggests that *everyone* refers to a male. Using *his or her* is more accurate because the indefinite pronoun can refer to either a male or a female.

> Everyone must hand in his or her completed work by 2 p.m.

When used over and over again, *he or she*, *him or her*, and *his or her* can create wordy or awkward sentences. Whenever possible, use plural forms.

> All students must hand in their completed work by 2 p.m.

PRACTICE

30-5 In each of the following sentences, first circle the indefinite pronoun. Then, circle the pronoun in parentheses that refers to the indefinite pronoun antecedent.

Example: (Each) of the lacrosse players will have (his or her/their) own locker at training camp.

1. Everyone likes to choose (his or her/their) own class schedule.

2. Somebody left (his or her/their) laptop on the bus.

3. Most of the *Project Runway* contestants did (his or her/their) best for the judges.

4. Someone in the audience forgot to turn off (his or her/their) cell phone before the performance.

5. Neither of the dogs wanted to have (its/their) coat brushed.

6. Coach Reilly personally gave each of the players (his or her/their) trophy.

7. Both of the soldiers donated (his or her/their) cars to Purple Heart, an organization that helps veterans.

8. No one should ever give (his or her/their) Social Security number to a telephone solicitor.

9. Anyone who works hard in college can usually receive (his or her/their) degree.

10. Everyone loves receiving presents on (his or her/their) birthday.

PRACTICE

30-6 Edit the following sentences for errors in pronoun-antecedent agreement. When you edit, you have two options: either substitute *its* or *his or her* for *their* to refer to the singular antecedent, or replace the singular antecedent with a plural word.

Examples: Everyone is responsible for ~~their~~ own passport.
his or her

All
~~Each~~ of the children took their books out of their backpacks.

1. Either of the hybrid cars comes with their own tax rebate.

2. Anyone who loses their locker key must pay $5.00 for a new one.

3. Everyone loves seeing their home team win.

4. Somebody left their scarf and gloves on the subway.

5. Almost everyone waits until the last minute to file their tax returns.

6. Each student returned their library books on time.

7. Everything we need to build the model airplane comes in their kit.

8. Anyone who wants to succeed must develop their public-speaking skills.

9. One of the hockey teams just won their first Olympic medal.

10. No one leaving the show early will get their money back.

Collective Noun Antecedents

Collective nouns are words (such as *band* and *team*) that name a group of people or things but are singular. Because they are singular, collective noun antecedents are used with singular pronouns.

The band played on, but it never played our song.

Frequently Used Collective Nouns			
army	club	gang	mob
association	committee	government	posse
band	company	group	team
class	family	jury	union

PRACTICE

30-7 Circle the collective noun antecedent in each of the following sentences. Then, circle the correct pronoun in parentheses.

Example: The jury returned with (its/their) verdict.

1. The company offers comprehensive benefits to (its/their) employees.

2. All five study groups must hand in (its/their) projects by Tuesday.

3. Any government should be concerned about the welfare of (its/their) citizens.

4. The Asian Students Union is sponsoring an event to celebrate (its/their) twentieth anniversary.

5. Every family has (its/their) share of problems.

6. To join the electricians' union, applicants had to pass (its/their) test.

7. Even the best teams have (its/their) bad days.

8. The orchestra has just signed a contract to make (its/their) first recording.

9. The math class did very well with (its/their) new instructor.

10. The club voted to amend (its/their) charter.

PRACTICE
30-8 Edit the following passage for correct pronoun-antecedent agreement. First, circle the antecedent of each underlined pronoun. Then, cross out any pronoun that does not agree with its antecedent, and write the correct form above it. If the pronoun is correct, write *C* above it.

Example: Many Americans believe that the (country) is ready for its
    C

first female president.

(1) The history of woman suffrage in the United States shows that women were determined to achieve <u>her</u> equal rights. (2) Before 1920, most American women were not allowed to vote for the candidates <u>they</u> preferred. (3) Men ran the government, and a woman could not express <u>their</u> views at the ballot box. (4) However, in the mid-1800s, women began to demand <u>her</u> right to vote—or "woman suffrage." (5) Supporters of woman suffrage believed everyone, regardless of <u>their</u> gender, should be able to vote. (6) At the first woman suffrage convention, Elizabeth Cady Stanton and Lucretia Mott gave speeches explaining <u>his or her</u> views. (7) Susan B. Anthony started the National Woman Suffrage Association, which opposed the Fifteenth Amendment to the Constitution because <u>it</u> gave the vote to black men but not to women. (8) The first state to permit women to vote was Wyoming, and soon other states became more friendly to <u>her</u> cause. (9) Many women participated in marches where <u>he or she</u> carried banners and posters for <u>their</u> cause. (10) During World War I, the U.S. government found that the cooperation of women was essential to <u>their</u> military success. (11) Finally, in 1919, the House of Representatives and the states gave <u>its</u> approval to the Nineteenth Amendment, which gave American women the right to vote.

30f   Vague and Unnecessary Pronouns

Vague and unnecessary pronouns clutter up your writing and make it hard to understand. Eliminating them will make your writing clearer and easier for readers to follow.

Vague Pronouns

A pronoun should always refer to a specific antecedent. When a pronoun— such as *they* or *it*—has no antecedent, readers will be confused.

> **VAGUE PRONOUN**   On the news, <u>they</u> said baseball players would strike. (Who said baseball players would strike?)

> **VAGUE PRONOUN**   <u>It</u> says in today's paper that our schools are over-crowded. (Who says schools are overcrowded?)

If a pronoun does not refer to a specific word in the sentence, replace the pronoun with a noun.

> **REVISED**   On the news, the <u>sportscaster</u> said baseball players would strike.

> **REVISED**   An <u>editorial</u> in today's paper says that our schools are overcrowded.

Unnecessary Pronouns

When a pronoun comes directly after its antecedent, it is unnecessary.

> **UNNECESSARY PRONOUN**   The librarian, <u>he</u> told me I should check the database.

In the sentence above, the pronoun *he* serves no purpose. Readers do not need to be directed back to the pronoun's antecedent (the noun *librarian*) because it appears right before the pronoun. The pronoun should therefore be deleted.

> **REVISED**   The librarian told me I should check the database.

PRACTICE

30-9   The following sentences contain vague or unnecessary pronouns. Revise each sentence on the line below it.

Example: On their website, they advertised a special offer.

On its website, the Gap advertised a special offer.

1. In Jamaica, they love their spectacular green mountains.

_____

2. My hamster, he loves his exercise wheel.

_____

3. On *Jeopardy!* they have to give the answers in the form of questions.

_____

4. On televisions all over the world, they watched the moon landing.

_____

5. In Sociology 320, they do not use a textbook.

_____

30g   Understanding Pronoun Case

A **personal pronoun** refers to a particular person or thing. Personal pronouns change form according to their function in a sentence. Personal pronouns can be *subjective*, *objective*, or *possessive*.

Personal Pronouns		
SUBJECTIVE	**OBJECTIVE**	**POSSESSIVE**
I	me	my, mine
he	him	his
she	her	her, hers
it	it	its
we	us	our, ours
you	you	your, yours
they	them	their, theirs
who	whom	whose
whoever	whomever	

Subjective Case

When a pronoun is a subject, it is in the **subjective case**.

> Finally, she realized that dreams could come true.

Objective Case

When a pronoun is an object, it is in the **objective case**.

> If Joanna hurries, she can stop him. (The pronoun *him* is the object of the verb *can stop*.)
>
> Professor Miller sent us information about his research. (The pronoun *us* is the object of the verb *sent*.)
>
> Marc threw the ball to them. (The pronoun *them* is the object of the preposition *to*.)

Possessive Case

When a pronoun shows ownership, it is in the **possessive case**.

> Hieu took his lunch to the meeting. (The pronoun *his* indicates that the lunch belongs to Hieu.)
>
> Debbie and Kim decided to take their lunches, too. (The pronoun *their* indicates that the lunches belong to Debbie and Kim.)

PRACTICE

30-10 In the following passage, fill in the blank after each pronoun to indicate whether the pronoun is subjective (*S*), objective (*O*), or possessive (*P*).

Example: Famous criminals Bonnie and Clyde committed their

_____*P*_____ crimes in broad daylight.

(1) Bonnie Parker and Clyde Barrow are remembered today because they _____ were the first celebrity criminals. (2) With their _____ gang, Bonnie and Clyde robbed a dozen banks as well as many stores and gas stations. (3) In small towns, they _____ terrorized the police. (4) Capturing them _____ seemed impossible. (5) To many Americans, however, their _____ crimes seemed exciting. (6) Because Bonnie was

a woman, she _____ was especially fascinating to them _____.

(7) During their _____ crimes, Bonnie and Clyde would often carry a camera, take photographs of themselves, and then send them _____ to the newspapers, which were happy to publish them _____.

(8) By the time they _____ were killed in an ambush by Texas and Louisiana law officers, Bonnie and Clyde were famous all over the United States.

30h Special Problems with Pronoun Case

When you are trying to determine which pronoun case to use in a sentence, three kinds of pronouns can present challenges: pronouns in compounds, pronouns in comparisons, and the pronouns *who* and *whom* (or *whoever* and *whomever*).

Pronouns in Compounds

Sometimes a pronoun is linked to a noun or to another pronoun with *and* or *or* to form a **compound**.

> The teacher and I met for an hour.
> He or she can pick up Jenny at school.

To determine whether to use the subjective or objective case for a pronoun in the second part of a compound, follow the same rules that apply for a pronoun that is not part of a compound.

- If the compound is a subject, use the subjective case.

    > Toby and I [not *me*] like jazz.

    > He and I [not *me*] went to the movies.

- If the compound is an object, use the objective case.

    > The school sent my father and me [not *I*] the financial-aid forms.

    > This argument is between Kate and me [not *I*].

FYI

Choosing Pronouns in Compounds

To determine which pronoun case to use in a compound that joins a noun and a pronoun, rewrite the sentence with just the pronoun.

> Toby and [*I* or *me*?] like jazz.
> **I** like jazz. (not *Me like jazz*)
> Toby and **I** like jazz.

PRACTICE

30-11   In the following sentences, the underlined pronouns are parts of compounds. Check them for correct subjective or objective case. If the pronoun is incorrect, cross it out, and write the correct form above it. If the pronoun is correct, write *C* above it.

C
Example: My classmates and I were surprised by the results of a study on listening.

(1) According to a recent study, the average listener remembers only 50 percent of what <u>him</u> or <u>her</u> hears. (2) Two days later, <u>he</u> or <u>she</u> can correctly recall only 25 percent of the total message. (3) My friend Alyssa and <u>me</u> decided to ask our school to sponsor a presentation about listening in the classroom. (4) One point the speaker made was especially helpful to Alyssa and <u>I</u>. (5) We now know that <u>us</u> and the other students in our class each have four times more mental "room" than we need for listening. (6) The presenter taught the other workshop participants and <u>we</u> how to use this extra space. (7) Now, whenever one of our professors pauses to write on the board or take a sip of water, Alyssa and <u>I</u> remember to silently summarize the last point <u>he</u> or <u>she</u> made. (8) Throughout the lecture, we pay attention to the big ideas and overall structure that the professor wants the other students and <u>us</u> to take away. (9) Also, to keep ourselves actively thinking about the topic, we try to predict where the professor will lead our peers and <u>us</u> next. (10) Above all, we do not waste

our mental energy on distractions that other students and <u>us</u> ourselves create, such as dropped books or our own worries. (11) Comedian Lily Tomlin's advice to "listen with an intensity most people save for talking" now makes a lot of sense to Alyssa and <u>me</u>.

Pronouns in Comparisons

Sometimes a pronoun appears after the word *than* or *as* in the second part of a **comparison**.

> John is luckier <u>than I</u>.
> The inheritance changed Raymond as much <u>as her</u>.

- ■ If the pronoun is a subject, use the subjective case.

    > John is luckier <u>than I</u> [am].

- ■ If the pronoun is an object, use the objective case.

    > The inheritance changed Raymond as much <u>as</u> [it changed] <u>her</u>.

FYI

Choosing Pronouns in Comparisons

Sometimes the pronoun you use can change your sentence's meaning. For example, if you say, "I like Cheerios more than *he*," you mean that you like Cheerios more than the other person likes them.

> I like Cheerios more than he [does].

If, however, you say, "I like Cheerios more than *him*," you mean that you like Cheerios more than you like the other person.

> I like Cheerios more than [I like] him .

PRACTICE

30-12 Each of the following sentences includes a comparison with a pronoun following the word *than* or *as*. Write in each blank the correct form (subjective or objective) of the pronoun in parentheses. In brackets, add the word or words needed to complete the comparison.

Example: Many people are better poker players than ___*I [am]*___

(I/me).

1. The survey showed that most people like the candidate's wife as much as _____ (he/him).

2. No one enjoys shopping more than _____ (she/her).

3. My brother and Aunt Cecile were very close, so her death affected him more than _____ (I/me).

4. No two people could have a closer relationship than _____ (they/them).

5. My neighbor drives better than _____ (I/me).

6. He may be as old as _____ (I/me), but he does not have as much work experience.

7. That jacket fits you better than _____ (I/me).

8. The other company had a lower bid than _____ (we/us), but we were awarded the contract.

Who and *Whom*, *Whoever* and *Whomever*

To determine whether to use *who* or *whom* (or *whoever* or *whomever*), you need to know how the pronoun functions within the clause in which it appears.

▪ When the pronoun is the subject of the clause, use *who* or *whoever*.

> I wonder <u>who</u> wrote that song. (*Who* is the subject of the clause *who wrote that song.*)

> I will vote for <u>whoever</u> supports the youth center. (*Whoever* is the subject of the clause *whoever supports the youth center.*)

▪ When the pronoun is the object, use *whom* or *whomever*.

> <u>Whom</u> do the police suspect? (*Whom* is the direct object of the verb *suspect.*)

> I wonder <u>whom</u> the song is about. (*Whom* is the object of the preposition *about* in the clause *whom the song is about.*)

> Vote for <u>whomever</u> you prefer. (*Whomever* is the object of the verb *prefer* in the clause *whomever you prefer.*)

FYI

Who and Whom

To determine whether to use *who* or *whom*, try substituting another pronoun for *who* or *whom* in the clause. If you can substitute *he* or *she*, use *who*; if you can substitute *him* or *her*, use *whom*.

> [Who/Whom] wrote a love song? <u>He</u> wrote a love song.
>
> [Who/Whom] was the song about? The song was about <u>her</u>.

The same test will work for *whoever* and *whomever*.

PRACTICE

30-13 Circle the correct form—*who* or *whom* (or *whoever* or *whomever*)—in parentheses in each sentence.

Example: With (who/whom) did Rob collaborate?

1. The defense team learned (who/whom) was going to testify for the prosecution.

2. (Who/Whom) does she think she can find to be a witness?

3. The runner (who/whom) crosses the finish line first will be the winner.

4. They will argue their case to (whoever/whomever) will listen.

5. It will take time to decide (who/whom) is the record holder.

6. Take these forms to the clerk (who/whom) is at the front desk.

7. We will have to penalize (whoever/whomever) misses the first training session.

8. (Who/Whom) did Kobe take to the prom?

9. We saw the man (who/whom) fired the shots.

10. To (who/whom) am I speaking?

30i Identifying Reflexive and Intensive Pronouns

Two special kinds of pronouns, *reflexive pronouns* and *intensive pronouns*, end in *-self* (singular) or *-selves* (plural). Although the functions of the two kinds of pronouns are different, their forms are identical.

Reflexive and Intensive Pronouns

Singular Forms

ANTECEDENT	REFLEXIVE OR INTENSIVE PRONOUN
I	myself
you	yourself
he	himself
she	herself
it	itself

Plural Forms

ANTECEDENT	REFLEXIVE OR INTENSIVE PRONOUN
we	ourselves
you	yourselves
they	themselves

Reflexive Pronouns

Reflexive pronouns indicate that people or things did something to themselves or for themselves.

Rosanna lost herself in the novel.

You need to watch yourself when you mix those solutions.

Mehul and Paul made themselves cold drinks.

Intensive Pronouns

Intensive pronouns always appear directly after their antecedents, and they are used for emphasis.

I myself have had some experience in sales and marketing.

The victim himself collected the reward.

They themselves were uncertain of the significance of their findings.

PRACTICE
30-14

Fill in the correct reflexive or intensive pronoun in each of the following sentences.

Example: The opening act was exciting, but the main attraction ___*itself*___ was boring.

1. Aunt Mary told her visitors to make _____ at home.

2. Migrating birds can direct _____ through clouds, storms, and moonless nights.

3. The First Lady _____ gave a speech at the school.

4. We all finished the marathon without injuring _____ .

5. Even though the government offered help to flood victims, the residents _____ did most of the rebuilding.

6. Sometimes he finds _____ daydreaming in class.

7. The guide warned us to watch _____ on the slippery path.

8. The senators were not happy about committing _____ to vote for lower taxes.

9. She gave _____ a manicure.

10. Although everyone else in my family can sing or play a musical instrument, I _____ am tone-deaf.

AP Photo/NASA/Neil A. Armstrong

TEST · Revise · Edit · Proofread

Look back at your response to the Focus on Writing prompt on page 507. TEST what you have written. Then, revise and edit your work, paying special attention to your use of nouns and pronouns. Finally, proofread your paragraph.

EDITING PRACTICE

Read the following student essay, which includes noun and pronoun errors. Check for errors in plural noun forms, pronoun case, and pronoun-antecedent agreement. Then, make any editing changes you think are necessary. The first paragraph has been edited for you.

Swimming to Safety

Swimming is a favorite summertime activity for many children and adults, but it is not enjoyable for everyone. For those who cannot swim, being in or near the water can be a terrifying experience. The Swimming Saves Lives Foundation is one organization that is trying to make a difference for ~~a person~~ _people_ who never learned how to swim.

It is important for children to start swimming lessons at a young age. Children should learn how to keep himself or herself safe near the water. The Swimming Saves Lives Foundation believes that water-safety lessons are important for all children, but particularly for minorities. Reports suggest that approximately 70 percent of African American children and 60 percent of Latino children are not strong swimmeres. For all children, drowning is a common cause of death. Whom wants to take that risk? Even if a child does not want to swim recreationally, him or her should understand basic water safety.

Some adult seem to think that it is too late to learn how to swim. The Swimming Saves Lives Foundation offers their services to anyone who wants to learn to swim. Local program are available in many states. Anyone who wants to participate can sign themselves up online.

For many adults, learning to swim leads him to a new favorite sport. For these people, the Swimming Saves Lives Foundation offers a Masters Swimming program. In the Masters Swimming program, adults can continue to refine his or her swimming skills.

531

Approximately 37 percent of adults cannot swim the length of the pool, and it is time for that number to drop. Thanks to the Swimming Saves Lives Foundation, whomever wants to swim has a greater opportunity to learn. Even if adults do not choose to swim recreationally, he or she can still learn practical water safety and teach it to their children.

COLLABORATIVE ACTIVITY

Working in a group, fill in the following chart, writing one noun on each line. If the noun is a proper noun, be sure to capitalize it.

CARS	TREES	FOODS	FAMOUS COUPLES	CITIES
_____	_____	_____	_____	_____
_____	_____	_____	_____	_____
_____	_____	_____	_____	_____
_____	_____	_____	_____	_____
_____	_____	_____	_____	_____
_____	_____	_____	_____	_____
_____	_____	_____	_____	_____

Now, using as many of the nouns listed above as you can, write a one-paragraph news article that describes an imaginary event. Exchange your work with another group, and check the other group's article to be sure the correct pronoun refers to each noun. Return the articles to their original groups for editing.

review checklist

Nouns and Pronouns

- [ ] A noun is a word that names something. A singular noun names one thing; a plural noun names more than one thing. (See 30a.)

- [ ] Most nouns add *-s* or *-es* to form plurals. Some nouns have irregular plural forms. (See 30b.)

- [ ] A pronoun is a word that refers to and takes the place of a noun or another pronoun. (See 30c.)

- [ ] The word a pronoun refers to is called the pronoun's antecedent. A pronoun and its antecedent must always agree. (See 30d.)

- [ ] Compound antecedents connected by *and* are plural and are used with plural pronouns. Compound antecedents connected by *or* may take singular or plural pronouns. (See 30e.)

- [ ] Most indefinite pronoun antecedents are singular and are used with singular pronouns; some are plural and are used with plural pronouns. (See 30e.)

- [ ] Collective noun antecedents are singular and are used with singular pronouns. (See 30e.)

- [ ] A pronoun should always refer to a specific antecedent. (See 30f.)

- [ ] Personal pronouns can be in the subjective, objective, or possessive case. (See 30g.)

- [ ] Pronouns present special problems when they are used in compounds and comparisons. The pronouns *who* and *whom* and *whoever* and *whomever* can also cause problems. (See 30h.)

- [ ] Reflexive and intensive pronouns must agree with their antecedents. (See 30i.)

31 Adjectives and Adverbs

Amy Etra/PhotoEdit

focus on writing

This picture shows children being homeschooled by their mother. Write a paragraph about the advantages and disadvantages of being educated at home by parents instead of at school by professional teachers.

In this chapter, you will learn to

- understand the difference between adjectives and adverbs (31a)
- form comparatives and superlatives of adjectives and adverbs (31b)

31a Identifying Adjectives and Adverbs

Adjectives and adverbs are words that modify (identify or describe) other words. They help make sentences more specific and more interesting.

An **adjective** answers the question *What kind? Which one?* or *How many?* Adjectives modify nouns or pronouns.

> The Turkish city of Istanbul spans two continents. (*Turkish* modifies the noun *city*, and *two* modifies the noun *continents*.)
>
> It is fascinating because of its location and history. (*Fascinating* modifies the pronoun *it*.)

FYI

Demonstrative Adjectives

Demonstrative adjectives—*this*, *that*, *these*, and *those*—do not describe other words. They simply identify particular nouns.

This and *that* identify singular nouns and pronouns.

> This website is much more up-to-date than that one.

These and *those* identify plural nouns.

> These words and phrases are French, but those expressions are Creole.

 **LaunchPad**

Visit *LaunchPad Solo for Readers and Writers* > **Adjectives and Adverbs** for more practice with adjectives and adverbs.

An **adverb** answers the question *How? Why? When? Where?* or *To what extent?* Adverbs modify verbs, adjectives, or other adverbs.

> Traffic moved steadily. (*Steadily* modifies the verb *moved*.)
>
> Still, we were quite impatient. (*Quite* modifies the adjective *impatient*.)
>
> Very slowly, we moved into the center lane. (*Very* modifies the adverb *slowly*.)

535

FYI

Distinguishing Adjectives from Adverbs

Many adverbs are formed when *-ly* is added to an adjective form.

ADJECTIVE	ADVERB
slow	slowly
nice	nicely
quick	quickly
real	really

ADJECTIVE Let me give you one quick reminder. (*Quick* modifies the noun *reminder*.)

ADVERB He quickly changed the subject. (*Quickly* modifies the verb *changed*.)

PRACTICE

31-1 In the following sentences, circle the correct form (adjective or adverb) from the choices in parentheses.

Example: Beatles enthusiasts all over the world have formed tribute bands devoted to the (famous/famously) group's music.

(1) To show appreciation for their favorite musicians, tribute bands go to (great/greatly) lengths. (2) Fans who have a (real/really) strong affection for a particular band may decide to play its music and copy its style. (3) Sometimes they form their own groups and have successful careers (simple/simply) performing that band's music. (4) These groups are (usual/usually) called "tribute bands." (5) Most tribute bands are (passionate/passionately) dedicated to reproducing the original group's work. (6) They not only play the group's songs but (careful/carefully) imitate the group's look. (7) They study the band members' facial expressions and body movements and create (exact/exactly) copies of the band's costumes and instruments. (8) Some more (inventive/inventively) tribute bands take the original band's songs and interpret them (different/differently).

(9) For example, by performing Beatles songs in the style of Metallica, the tribute band Beatallica has created a (unique/uniquely) sound. (10) Some people believe such tributes are the (ultimate/ultimately) compliment to the original band; others feel (sure/surely) that tribute groups are just copycats who (serious/seriously) lack imagination.

FYI

Good and *Well*

Be careful not to confuse *good* and *well*. Unlike regular adjectives, whose adverb forms add *-ly*, the adjective *good* is irregular. Its adverb form is *well*.

> **ADJECTIVE** Fred Astaire was a good dancer. (*Good* modifies the noun *dancer*.)

> **ADVERB** He danced especially well with Ginger Rogers. (*Well* modifies the verb *danced*.)

Always use *well* when you are describing a person's health.

> He really didn't feel well [not *good*] after eating the entire pizza.

PRACTICE

31-2

Circle the correct form (*good* or *well*) in the sentences below.

Example: It can be hard for some people to find a (good/well) job that they really like.

(1) Some people may not do (good/well) sitting in an office. (2) Instead, they may prefer to find jobs that take advantage of their (good/well) physical condition. (3) Such people might consider becoming smoke jumpers—firefighters who are (good/well) at parachuting from small planes into remote areas to battle forest fires. (4) Smoke jumpers must be able to work (good/well) even without much sleep. (5) They must also handle danger (good/well). (6) They look forward to the

(good/well) feeling of saving a forest or someone's home. (7) As they battle fires, surrounded by smoke and fumes, smoke jumpers may not feel very (good/well). (8) Sometimes things go wrong; for example, when their parachutes fail to work (good/well), jumpers may be injured or even killed. (9) Smoke jumpers do not get paid particularly (good/well). (10) However, they are proud of their strength and endurance and feel (good/well) about their work.

31b Understanding Comparatives and Superlatives

The **comparative** form of an adjective or adverb compares two people or things. Adjectives and adverbs form the comparative with *-er* or *more*. The **superlative** form of an adjective or adverb compares more than two things. Adjectives and adverbs form the superlative with *-est* or *most*.

ADJECTIVES	This film is <u>dull</u> and <u>predictable</u>.
COMPARATIVE	The film I saw last week was even <u>duller</u> and <u>more predictable</u> than this one.
SUPERLATIVE	The film I saw last night was the <u>dullest</u> and <u>most predictable</u> one I've ever seen.
ADVERBS	For a beginner, Jane did needlepoint <u>skillfully</u>.
COMPARATIVE	After she had watched the demonstration, Jane did needlepoint <u>more skillfully</u> than Rosie.
SUPERLATIVE	Of the twelve beginners, Jane did needlepoint the <u>most skillfully</u>.

Forming Comparatives and Superlatives

Adjectives

■ One-syllable adjectives generally form the comparative with *-er* and the superlative with *-est*.

great greater greatest

■ Adjectives with two or more syllables form the comparative with *more* and the superlative with *most*.

> wonderful   more wonderful   most wonderful

> Exception: Two-syllable adjectives ending in *-y* add *-er* or *-est* after changing the *y* to an *i*.

> funny   funnier   funniest

Adverbs

■ All adverbs ending in *-ly* form the comparative with *more* and the superlative with *most*.

> efficiently   more efficiently   most efficiently

■ Some other adverbs form the comparative with *-er* and the superlative with *-est*.

> soon   sooner   soonest

Solving Special Problems with Comparatives and Superlatives

The following rules will help you avoid errors with comparatives and superlatives.

■ Never use both *-er* and *more* to form the comparative or both *-est* and *most* to form the superlative.

> Nothing could have been <u>more awful</u>. (not *more awfuller*)

> Space Mountain is the <u>most frightening</u> (not *most frighteningest*) ride at Disney World.

■ Never use the superlative when you are comparing only two things.

> This is the <u>more serious</u> (not *most serious*) of the two problems.

■ Never use the comparative when you are comparing more than two things.

> This is the <u>worst</u> (not *worse*) day of my life.

PRACTICE

31-3　Fill in the correct comparative form of the word supplied in parentheses.

Example:　Children tend to be _____noisier_____ (noisy) than adults.

1. Traffic always moves _____ (slow) during rush hour than late at night.

2. The weather report says temperatures will be _____ (cold) tomorrow.

3. Some elderly people are _____ (healthy) than younger people.

4. It has been proven that pigs are _____ (intelligent) than dogs.

5. When someone asks you to repeat yourself, you usually answer _____ (loud).

6. The _____ (tall) of the two buildings was damaged by the earthquake.

7. They want to teach their son to be _____ (respectful) of women than many young men are.

8. Las Vegas is _____ (famous) for its casinos than for its natural resources.

9. The WaterDrop is _____ (wild) than any other ride in the amusement park.

10. You must move _____ (quick) if you expect to catch the ball.

PRACTICE

31-4　Fill in the correct superlative form of the word supplied in parentheses.

Example:　*Match.com* and *eHarmony* are two of the _____most popular_____ (popular) online dating sites.

(1) Niche dating sites are becoming some of the _____ (popular) places to find a date online. (2) Though more general-interest sites, such as *Match.com* and *eHarmony*, are still widely used, the _____ (specialized) sites are creating new ways for people to connect. (3) For example, *FarmersOnly.com* is a dating site for people who are the _____ (enthusiastic) about the farming lifestyle. (4) If you love *Star Trek*, then *Trek Passions* is the dating site that is the _____ (likely) to help you find a like-minded Trekkie. (5) Fans of Apple products will find *Cupidtino* the _____ (simple) way to find other fans. (6) Even salad fanatics can find love using *SaladMatch*, an app that connects people with their _____ (compatible) mate based on their favorite salad toppings. (7) Many users of dating sites have proclaimed niche sites to be the _____ (effective) way to find love online. (8) Identifying common ground is the _____ (easy) way to start a conversation, and these communities emphasize users' common interests. (9) With new sites appearing all the time, even the _____ (unusual) interests are represented. (10) With so many options, choosing one site might be the _____ (intimidating) part of the process.

FYI

Good/Well and Bad/Badly

Most adjectives and adverbs form the comparative with *-er* or *more* and the superlative with *-est* or *most*. The adjectives *good* and *bad* and their adverb forms *well* and *badly* are exceptions.

ADJECTIVE	COMPARATIVE FORM	SUPERLATIVE FORM
good	better	best
bad	worse	worst

ADVERB	COMPARATIVE FORM	SUPERLATIVE FORM
well	better	best
badly	worse	worst

PRACTICE

31-5   Fill in the correct comparative or superlative form of *good*, *well*, *bad*, or *badly*.

Example: My sister is a ___*better*___ (good) runner than I am.

1. Neela was certain she was the _____ (good) chef in the competition.

2. Because he studied more, Helio earned _____ (good) grades than his sister.

3. An optimist, Mara always thinks she will do _____ (well) next time.

4. Many people drive the _____ (badly) when they are in a hurry.

5. Of all the mortgage companies Ramon researched, Plains Bank had the _____ (good) interest rate.

6. I feel bad when I get rejected, but I feel _____ (bad) when I do not try.

7. For nontraditional students, access to education is _____ (good) than it used to be.

8. Jamie sings badly, but Simon sings _____ (badly).

9. I learn the _____ (well) when I am not distracted.

10. After looking at every painting in the gallery, they decided that the landscapes were definitely the _____ (bad) paintings there.

Amy Etra/PhotoEdit

TEST · Revise · Edit · Proofread

Look back at your response to the Focus on Writing prompt on page 534. TEST what you have written. Then, revise and edit your work, paying special attention to your use of adjectives and adverbs. Finally, proofread your paragraph.

EDITING PRACTICE

Read the following student essay, which includes errors in the use of adjectives and adverbs. Make any changes necessary to correct adjectives incorrectly used for adverbs and adverbs incorrectly used for adjectives. Also, correct any errors in the use of comparatives and superlatives and in the use of demonstrative adjectives. Finally, try to add some adjectives and adverbs that you feel would make the writer's ideas clearer or more specific. The first sentence has been edited for you.

Starting Over

A wedding can be the ~~joyfullest~~ *most joyful* occasion in two people's lives, the beginning of a couple's most happiest years. For some unlucky women, however, a wedding can be the worse thing that ever happens; it is the beginning not of their happiness but of their battered lives. As I went through the joyful day of my wedding, I wanted bad to find happiness for the rest of my life, but what I hoped and wished for did not come true.

I was married in the savannah belt of the Sudan in the eastern part of Africa, where I grew up. I was barely twenty-two years old. The first two years of my marriage progressed peaceful, but problems started as soon as our first child was born.

Many American women say, "If my husband hit me just once, that would be it. I'd leave." But those attitude does not work in cultures where tradition has overshadowed women's rights and divorce is not accepted. All women can do is accept their sadly fate. Battered women give many reasons for staying in their marriages, but fear is the commonest. Fear immobilizes these women, ruling their decisions, their actions, and their very lives. This is how it was for me.

Of course, I was real afraid whenever my husband hit me. I would run to my mother's house and cry, but she would always talk me into going back and being more patiently with my husband. Our tradition discourages divorce, and wife-beating is taken for granted. The situation is really quite ironic: the religion I practice sets harsh punishments for abusive husbands, but tradition has so overpowered religion that the laws do not really work very good.

One night, I asked myself whether life had treated me fair. True, I had a high school diploma and two of the beautifullest children in the world, but all this was not enough. I realized that to stand up to the husband who treated me so bad, I would have to achieve a more better education than he had. That night, I decided to get a college education in the United States. My husband opposed my decision, but with the support of my father and mother, I was able to begin to change my life. My years as a student and single parent in the United States have been real difficult for me, but I know I made the right choice.

COLLABORATIVE ACTIVITY

Working in a small group, write a plot summary for an imaginary film. Begin with one of the following three sentences.

- Dirk and Clive were sworn enemies, but that night on Boulder Ridge they vowed to work together just this once, for the good of their country.
- Genevieve entered the room in a cloud of perfume, and when she spoke, her voice was like velvet.
- The desert sun beat down on her head, but Susanna was determined to protect what was hers, no matter what the cost.

Now, exchange summaries with another group, and add as many adjectives and adverbs as you can to the other group's summary. Finally, reread your own group's plot summary, and edit it carefully, paying special attention to the way adjectives and adverbs are used.

review checklist

Adjectives and Adverbs

- [ ] Adjectives modify nouns or pronouns. (See 31a.)

- [ ] Adverbs modify verbs, adjectives, or other adverbs. (See 31a.)

- [ ] To compare two people or things, use the comparative form of an adjective or adverb. To compare more than two people or things, use the superlative form of an adjective or adverb. (See 31b.)

- [ ] The adjectives *good* and *bad* and their adverb forms *well* and *badly* have irregular comparative and superlative forms. (See 31b.)

32 Grammar and Usage for ESL Writers

ZUMA Press, Inc./Alamy

focus on writing

This image depicts a naturalization ceremony that took place on the Fourth of July in Phoenix, Arizona. (It is during such ceremonies that noncitizens become citizens of the United States.) People from different countries and cultures bring to the United States a variety of unique holidays and celebrations. Using the present tense, write a paragraph explaining how you and your family celebrate a holiday that is important to you.

In this chapter, you will learn to

- understand how subjects are used in sentences (32a)
- understand and use determiners with count and noncount nouns (32b and 32c)
- understand articles (32d)
- form negative statements and questions (32e)
- indicate verb tense (32f)
- recognize stative verbs (32g)
- understand gerunds (32h)
- choose correct prepositions (32i)
- use prepositions in phrasal verbs (32j)

Learning English as a second language involves more than just learning grammar. In fact, if you have been studying English as a second language, you may know more about English grammar than many native speakers do. However, you will still need to learn the conventions and rules that most native speakers already know.

32a Subjects in Sentences

English requires that every sentence state its subject. Every independent clause and every dependent clause must also have a subject.

INCORRECT Elvis Presley was only forty-two years old when died. (When who died?)

CORRECT Elvis Presley was only forty-two years old when he died.

When the real subject follows the verb and the normal subject position before the verb is empty, it must be filled by a "dummy" subject, such as *it* or *there*.

INCORRECT Is hot in this room.

CORRECT It is hot in this room.

INCORRECT Are many rivers in my country.

CORRECT There are many rivers in my country.

Standard English also does not permit a two-part subject in which the second part of the subject is a pronoun referring to the same person or thing as the first part.

INCORRECT   The Caspian Sea it is the largest lake in the world.

CORRECT   The Caspian Sea is the largest lake in the world.

Visit *LaunchPad Solo for Readers and Writers* > **Resources for Multilingual Writers** for more practice with grammar for ESL writers.

PRACTICE

32-1   Each of the following sentences is missing the subject of a dependent or an independent clause. On the lines provided, rewrite each sentence, adding an appropriate subject. Then, underline the subject you have added.

Example: Because college students often have very little money, are always looking for inexpensive meals.

Because college students often have very little money, they are always looking

for inexpensive meals.

1. Ramen noodles are a popular choice for students because are cheap, tasty, and easy to prepare.

_____

_____

2. In minutes, a student can enjoy hot noodles flavored with chicken, shrimp, or beef, and sell vegetarian versions, too.

_____

_____

3. Although high in carbohydrates (a good source of energy), also contain saturated and trans fats and few vitamins or minerals.

_____

_____

4. Cookbooks provide special recipes for preparing ramen noodles; include "Ramen Shrimp Soup" and "Ramen Beef and Broccoli."

_____

_____

5. Ramen noodles are not just popular with American college students; are also popular in many other countries around the world.

_____

_____

6. The noodles have even found their way to the International Space Station, where enjoy them in space.

_____

_____

7. The noodles originated in China many years ago, where were deep fried so that they could be stored for a long time without spoiling.

_____

_____

8. For today's college students, however, spoilage is not a problem because are usually eaten long before their expiration date.

_____

_____

PRACTICE

32-2   The following sentences contain unnecessary two-part subjects. Cross out the unnecessary pronoun. Then, rewrite each sentence correctly on the lines provided.

Example: Travelers to China ~~they~~ often visit the Great Wall.

Travelers to China often visit the Great Wall.

1. The first parts of the Great Wall they were built around 200 BCE.

_____

_____

2. The Great Wall it was built to keep out invading armies.

_____

_____

3. The sides of the Great Wall they are made of stone, brick, and earth.

_____

_____

4. The top of the Great Wall it is paved with bricks, forming a roadway for horses.

_____

_____

5. The Great Wall it is so huge that it can be seen by astronauts in space.

_____

_____

32b   Count and Noncount Nouns

A **count noun** names one particular thing or a group of particular things that can be counted: _a teacher, a panther, a bed, an ocean, a cloud, an ice cube; two teachers, many panthers, three beds, two oceans, several clouds, some ice cubes._ A **noncount noun** names things that cannot be counted: _gold, cream, sand, blood, smoke, water._

Count nouns usually have a singular form and a plural form: _cube, cubes._ Noncount nouns usually have only a singular form: _water._ Note how the nouns _cube_ and _water_ differ in the way they are used in sentences.

CORRECT	The glass is full of ice cubes.
CORRECT	The glass is full of water.
INCORRECT	The glass is full of waters.
CORRECT	The glass contains five ice cubes.
CORRECT	The glass contains some water.
INCORRECT	The glass contains five waters.

Often, the same idea can be expressed with either a count noun or a noncount noun.

COUNT	NONCOUNT
people (plural of *person*)	humanity [*not* humanities]
tables, chairs, beds	furniture [*not* furnitures]
letters	mail [*not* mails]
supplies	equipment [*not* equipments]
facts	information [*not* informations]
guns	ammunition [*not* ammunitions]

Some words can be either count or noncount, depending on the meaning intended.

COUNT   He had many interesting <u>experiences</u> at his first job.

NONCOUNT   It is often difficult to get a job if you do not have <u>experience</u>.

FYI

Guidelines for Using Count and Noncount Nouns

- Use a count noun to refer to a living animal, but use a noncount noun to refer to the food that comes from that animal.

    COUNT   There are three live lobsters in the tank.

    NONCOUNT   This restaurant specializes in lobster.

- If you use a noncount noun for a substance or class of things that can come in different varieties, you can often make that noun plural if you want to talk about those varieties.

    NONCOUNT   Cheese is a rich source of calcium.

    COUNT   Many different cheeses come from Italy.

- If you want to shift attention from a concept in general to specific examples of it, you can often use a noncount noun as a count noun.

    NONCOUNT   You have a great deal of talent.

    COUNT   My talents do not include singing.

PRACTICE

32-3 In each of the following sentences, decide if the underlined word is being used as a count or a noncount noun. If it is being used as a noncount noun, circle the *N* following the sentence. If it is being used as a count noun, circle the *C*.

Examples: As a Peace Corps <u>volunteer</u> in Ecuador, Dave Schweidenback realized how important bicycles could be.   N Ⓒ

Using his <u>imagination</u>, Dave figured out an effective way to recycle America's unwanted bicycles. Ⓝ C

1. Pedals for Progress is an American nonprofit <u>organization</u>.   N   C

2. The <u>group</u> collects and repairs old bicycles and sends them to countries where they are needed.   N   C

3. Pedals for Progress aims to reduce the amount of bicycle <u>waste</u> that ends up in American landfills.   N   C

4. People in the United States throw away millions of bikes and bike parts every <u>year</u>.   N   C

5. At the same time, lack of <u>transportation</u> is a serious problem for many people in developing countries.   N   C

6. Without an efficient and affordable way to get to work, a person cannot hold a <u>job</u>.   N   C

7. A working bicycle provides an easy and environmentally friendly <u>way</u> to get around.   N   C

8. Bicycles from Pedals for Progress only cost the user a small amount of <u>money</u>.   N   C

9. To help maintain these recycled bikes, the organization also helps to establish local repair <u>shops</u>.   N   C

10. By making it easier for people to work, Pedals for Progress hopes to reduce <u>poverty</u>.   N   C

32c Determiners with Count and Noncount Nouns

Determiners are adjectives that *identify* rather than describe the nouns they modify. Determiners may also *quantify* nouns (that is, indicate an amount or a number).

Determiners include the following words.

- Articles: *a, an, the*
- Demonstrative pronouns: *this, these, that, those*
- Possessive pronouns: *my, our, your, his, her, its, their*
- Possessive nouns: *Sheila's, my friend's,* and so on
- *Whose, which, what*
- *All, both, each, every, some, any, either, no, neither, many, most, much, a few, a little, few, little, several, enough*
- All numerals: *one, two,* and so on

When a determiner is accompanied by one or more other adjectives, the determiner always comes first. For example, in the phrase *my expensive new digital watch, my* is a determiner; you cannot put *expensive, new, digital,* or any other adjective before *my*.

A singular count noun must always be accompanied by a determiner—for example, *my watch* or *the new digital watch*, not just *watch* or *new digital watch*. However, noncount nouns and plural count nouns sometimes have determiners but sometimes do not. *This honey is sweet* and *Honey is sweet* are both acceptable, as are *These berries are juicy* and *Berries are juicy*. (In each case, the meaning is different.) You cannot say, *Berry is juicy*, however; say instead, *This berry is juicy, Every berry is juicy*, or *A berry is juicy*.

FYI

Determiners

Some determiners can be used only with certain types of nouns.

- *This* and *that* can be used only with singular nouns (count or noncount): *this berry, that honey.*
- *These, those, a few, few, many, both,* and *several* can be used only with plural count nouns: *these berries, those apples, a few ideas, few people, many students, both sides, several directions.*

(continued)

(continued from previous page)

- *Much, little,* and *a little* can be used only with noncount nouns: *much affection, little time, a little honey.*
- *Some, enough, all,* and *most* can be used only with noncount or plural count nouns: *some honey, some berries; enough trouble, enough problems; all traffic, all roads; most money, most coins.*
- *A, an, every, each, either,* and *neither* can be used only with singular count nouns: *a berry, an elephant, every possibility, each citizen, either option, neither candidate.*

PRACTICE

32-4 In each of the following sentences, circle the more appropriate choice from each pair of words or phrases in parentheses.

Examples: Volcanoes are among the most destructive of ((all)/every) natural forces on earth.

People have always been fascinated and terrified by ((this)/these) force of nature.

1. Not (all/every) volcano is considered a danger.

2. In (major some/some major) volcanic eruptions, huge clouds rise over the mountain.

3. In 2010, ash from a volcano in Iceland caused (many/much) disruption for airline passengers throughout Europe.

4. (A few violent/Violent a few) eruptions are so dramatic that they blow the mountain apart.

5. (Most/Much) volcanic eruptions cannot be predicted.

6. Since the 1400s, (many/much) people—almost 200,000—have lost their lives in volcanic eruptions.

7. When a volcano erupts, (little/a little) can be done to prevent property damage.

8. By the time people realize an eruption is about to take place, there is rarely (many/enough) time to escape.

9. Volcanoes can be dangerous, but they also produce (a little/some) benefits.

10. For example, (a few/a little) countries use energy from underground steam in volcanic areas to produce electric power.

32d Articles

The **definite article** *the* and the **indefinite articles** *a* and *an* are determiners that tell readers whether the noun that follows is one they can identify (*the book*) or one they cannot yet identify (*a book*).

The Definite Article

When the definite article *the* is used with a noun, the writer is saying to readers, "You can identify which particular thing or things I have in mind. The information you need to make that identification is available to you. Either you have it already, or I am about to give it to you."

Readers can find the necessary information in the following ways.

- By looking at other information in the sentence

     Meet me at <u>the</u> corner of Main Street and Lafayette Road.

  In this example, *the* is used with the noun *corner* because other words in the sentence tell readers which particular corner the writer has in mind: the one located at Main and Lafayette.

- By looking at information in other sentences

     Aisha ordered a slice of pie and a cup of coffee. <u>The</u> pie was delicious. She asked for a second slice.

  Here, *the* is used before the word *pie* in the second sentence to indicate that it is the same pie identified in the first sentence. Notice, however, that the noun *slice* in the third sentence is preceded by an indefinite article (*a*) because it is not the same slice referred to in the first sentence.

■ By drawing on general knowledge

> The earth revolves around the sun.

Here, *the* is used with the nouns *earth* and *sun* because readers are expected to know which particular things the writer is referring to.

FYI

The Definite Article

Always use *the* (rather than *a* or *an*) in the following situations:

■ Before the word *same*: *the same day*
■ Before the superlative form of an adjective: *the youngest son*
■ Before a number indicating order or sequence: *the third time*

Indefinite Articles

When an indefinite article is used with a noun, the writer is saying to readers, "I don't expect you to have enough information right now to identify a particular thing that I have in mind. I do, however, expect you to recognize that I'm referring to only one item."

Consider the following sentences.

> We need a table for our computer.
>
> I have a folding table; maybe you can use that.

WORD POWER

hypothetical
assumed or supposed; not supported by evidence

In the first sentence, the writer is referring to a hypothetical table, not an actual one. Because the table is indefinite to the writer, it is clearly indefinite to the reader, so *a* is used, not *the*. The second sentence refers to an actual table, but because the writer does not expect the reader to be able to identify the table specifically, it is also used with *a* rather than *the*.

FYI

Indefinite Articles

Unlike the definite article (*the*), the indefinite articles *a* and *an* occur only with singular count nouns. *A* is used when the next sound is a consonant, and *an* is used when the next sound is a vowel. In choosing *a* or *an*, pay attention to sound rather than to spelling: *a house, a year, a union,* but *an hour, an uncle.*

No Article

Only noncount and plural count nouns can stand without articles: *butter*, *chocolate*, *cookies*, *strawberries* (but *a cookie* or *the strawberry*).
Nouns without articles can be used to make generalizations.

Infants need affection as well as food.

Here, the absence of articles before the nouns *infants*, *affection*, and *food* indicates that the statement is not about particular infants, affection, or food but about infants, affection, and food in general. Remember not to use *the* in such sentences; in English, a sentence like *The infants need affection as well as food* can only refer to particular, identifiable infants, not to infants in general.

Articles with Proper Nouns

Proper nouns can be divided into two classes: names that take *the* and names that take no article.

- Names of people usually take no article unless they are used in the plural to refer to members of a family, in which case they take *the*: *Napoleon*, *Mahatma Gandhi* (but *the Parkers*).
- Names of places that are plural in form usually take *the*: *the Andes, the United States*.
- The names of most places on land (cities, states, provinces, and countries) take no article: *Salt Lake City, Mississippi, Alberta, Japan*. The names of most bodies of water (rivers, seas, and oceans, although not lakes or bays) take *the*: *the Mississippi, the Mediterranean, the Pacific* (but *Lake Erie, San Francisco Bay*).
- Names of streets take no article: *Main Street*. Names of unnumbered highways take *the*: *the Belt Parkway*.

PRACTICE

32-5   In the following passage, decide whether each blank needs a definite article (*the*), an indefinite article (*a* or *an*), or no article. If a definite or an indefinite article is needed, write it in the space provided. If no article is needed, leave the space blank.

Example: Football ____*is*____ a popular sport, but its players take

some serious health risks.

Football has been (1) _____ popular American pastime for many years. Recently, more and more experts have become concerned about (2) _____ sport. Even though football players wear protective gear, (3) _____ helmets do not always protect them from severe concussions. Experts now believe that concussions are (4) _____ reason some players experience memory loss and depression. Though much of (5) _____ media coverage on this issue has been about professional football, the concern extends to college, high school, and youth football. Today, some parents are encouraging their children to choose other sports because of (6) _____ risks of football. As a result of (7) _____ increasing concern, new technology is being developed to address the problem of concussions on the field. For example, some professional players are given (8) _____ helmet with a device that records the speed of the impact when two players crash together. This technology may help doctors to better understand (9) _____ risks (10) _____ player takes and how to prevent serious injury. (11) Football is _____ essential part of American culture, so it is important that steps are taken to keep players safe.

32e Negative Statements and Questions

Negative Statements

To form a negative statement, add the word *not* directly after the first helping verb of the complete verb.

Global warming has been getting worse.
Global warming has <u>not</u> been getting worse.

When there is no helping verb, a form of the verb *do* must be inserted before *not*.

> Automobile traffic contributes to pollution.
>
> Automobile traffic <u>does not</u> contribute to pollution.

However, if the main verb is *am, is, are, was,* or *were,* do not insert a form of *do* before *not*: *Harry was late. Harry was <u>not</u> late.*

Remember that when *do* is used as a helping verb, the form of *do* used must match the tense and number of the original main verb. Note that in the negative statement above, the main verb loses its tense and appears in the base form (*contribute,* not *contributes*).

Questions

To form a question, move the helping verb that follows the subject to the position directly before the subject.

> The governor <u>is</u> trying to compromise.
> <u>Is</u> the governor trying to compromise?

> The governor <u>is</u> working on the budget.
> <u>Is</u> the governor working on the budget?

The same rule applies even when the verb is in the past or future tense.

> The governor <u>was</u> trying to lower state taxes.
> <u>Was</u> the governor trying to lower state taxes?

> The governor <u>will</u> try to get reelected.
> <u>Will</u> the governor try to get reelected?

As with negatives, when the verb does not include a helping verb, you must supply a form of *do*. To form a question, put the correct form of *do* directly before the subject.

> The governor <u>works</u> hard.
> <u>Does</u> the governor <u>work</u> hard?

> The governor <u>improved</u> life in his state.
> <u>Did</u> the governor <u>improve</u> life in his state?

However, if the main verb is *am, is, are, was,* or *were,* do not insert a form of *do* before the verb. Instead, move the main verb before the subject: *Harry was late. <u>Was</u> Harry late?*

Note: The helping verb never comes before the subject if the subject is a question word, such as *who* or *which*.

Who is talking to the governor?

Which bills have been vetoed by the governor?

PRACTICE

32-6 Rewrite each of the following sentences in two ways: first, turn the sentence into a question; then, rewrite the original sentence as a negative statement.

Example: Her newest book is selling as well as her first one.

Question: Is her newest book selling as well as her first one?

Negative statement: Her newest book is not selling as well as her first one.

1. Converting metric measurements to the system used in the United States is difficult.

Question: _____

_____

Negative statement: _____

_____

2. The early frost damaged some crops.

Question: _____

_____

Negative statement: _____

_____

3. That family was very influential in the early 1900s.

Question: _____

_____

Negative statement: _____

_____

4. Most stores in malls are open on Sundays.

   Question: _____

   _____

   Negative statement: _____

   _____

5. Choosing the right gift is a difficult task.

   Question: _____

   _____

   Negative statement: _____

   _____

6. Most great artists are successful during their lifetimes.

   Question: _____

   _____

   Negative statement: _____

   _____

7. The lawyer can verify the witness's story.

   Question: _____

   _____

   Negative statement: _____

   _____

8. American cities are as dangerous as they were thirty years ago.

   Question: _____

   _____

   Negative statement: _____

   _____

9. The British royal family is loved by most of the British people.

Question: _____

_____

Negative statement: _____

_____

10. Segregation in the American South ended with the Civil War.

Question: _____

_____

Negative statement: _____

_____

32f Verb Tense

In English, a verb's form must indicate when an action took place (for instance, in the past or in the present). Always use the appropriate tense of the verb even if the time is obvious or if the sentence includes other indications of time (such as *two years ago* or *at present*).

INCORRECT Albert Einstein emigrate from Germany in 1933.

CORRECT Albert Einstein emigrated from Germany in 1933.

32g Stative Verbs

Stative verbs usually tell that someone or something is in a state that will not change, at least for a while.

Hiro knows American history very well.

Most English verbs show action, and these action verbs can be used in the progressive tenses. The **present progressive** tense consists of the present tense of *be* plus the present participle (*I am going*). The **past**

progressive tense consists of the past tense of *be* plus the present participle (*I was going*). Unlike most verbs, however, stative verbs are rarely used in the progressive tenses.

> **INCORRECT**   Hiro is knowing American history very well.

> **CORRECT**   Hiro knows American history very well.

FYI

Stative Verbs

Verbs that are stative—such as *know, understand, think, believe, want, like, love,* and *hate*—often refer to mental states. Other stative verbs include *be, have, need, own, belong, weigh, cost,* and *mean*. Certain verbs of sense perception, like *see* and *hear*, are also stative even though they can refer to momentary events as well as to unchanging states.

Many verbs have more than one meaning, and some of these verbs are active with one meaning but stative with another. An example is the verb *weigh*.

> **ACTIVE**   The butcher weighs the meat.

> **STATIVE**   The meat weighs three pounds.

In the first sentence above, the verb *weigh* means "to put on a scale"; it is active, not stative. In the second sentence, however, the same verb means "to have weight," so it is stative, not active. It would be unacceptable to say "The meat is weighing three pounds," but "The butcher is weighing the meat" would be correct.

PRACTICE

32-7   In each of the following sentences, circle the verb or verbs. Then, correct any problems with stative verbs by crossing out the incorrect verb tense and writing the correct verb tense above the line. If the verb is correct, write *C* above it.

Example: Police officers ~~are knowing~~ *know* that fingerprint identification *C* is one of the best ways to catch criminals.

1. As early as 1750 BC, ancient Babylonians were signing their identities with fingerprints on clay tablets.

2. By 220 BCE, the Chinese were becoming aware that ink fingerprints could identify people.

3. However, it was not until the late 1800s that anyone was believing that criminal identification was possible with fingerprints.

4. Today, we know that each person is having unique patterns on the tips of his or her fingers.

5. When police study a crime scene, they want to see whether the criminals have left any fingerprint evidence.

6. There is always a layer of oil on the skin, and police are liking to use it to get fingerprints.

7. Crime scene experts are often seeing cases where the criminals are touching their hair and pick up enough oil to leave a good fingerprint.

8. The police are needing to judge whether the fingerprint evidence has been damaged by sunlight, rain, or heat.

9. In the courtroom, juries often weigh fingerprint evidence before they are deciding on their verdict.

10. The FBI is collecting millions of fingerprints, which police departments can compare with the fingerprints they find at crime scenes.

32h Gerunds

A **gerund** is a verb form ending in *-ing* that acts as a noun.

<u>Reading</u> the newspaper is one of my favorite things to do on Sundays.

Just like a noun, a gerund can be used as a subject, a direct object, a subject complement, or the object of a preposition.

- A gerund can be a subject.

    Playing tennis is one of my hobbies.

■ A gerund can be a direct object.

My brother influenced my racing.

■ A gerund can be a subject complement.

The most important thing is winning.

■ A gerund can be the object of a preposition.

The teacher rewarded him for passing.

PRACTICE

32-8 To complete the sentences below, fill in the blanks with the gerund form of the verb provided in parentheses.

Example: _____*Typing*_____ (type) is a skill that used to be taught in high school.

1. _____ (eat) five or six smaller meals throughout the day is healthier than eating two or three big meals.

2. The household task I dread the most is _____ (clean).

3. Her parents praised her for _____ (remember) their anniversary.

4. I did not like his _____ (sing).

5. The best way to prepare for the concert is by _____ (practice).

32i Choosing Prepositions

A **preposition** introduces a noun or pronoun and links it to other words in the sentence. The word the preposition introduces is called the **object** of the preposition.

A preposition and its object combine to form a **prepositional phrase**: *on the table, near the table, under the table.*

I thought I had left the book <u>on</u> the table or somewhere <u>near</u> the table, but I found it <u>under</u> the table.

The prepositions *at*, *in*, and *on* sometimes cause problems for non-native speakers of English. For example, to identify the location of a place or an event, you can use *at*, *in*, or *on*.

- The preposition *at* specifies an exact point in space or time.

  The museum is <u>at</u> 1000 Fifth Avenue. Let's meet there <u>at</u> 10:00 tomorrow morning.

- Expanses of space or time are treated as containers and therefore require *in*.

  Women used to wear long skirts <u>in</u> the early 1900s.

- *On* must be used in two cases: with names of streets (but not with exact addresses) and with days of the week or month.

  We will move into our new office <u>on</u> 18th Street either <u>on</u> Monday or <u>on</u> March 12.

FYI

Using Prepositions in Familiar Expressions

Many familiar expressions end in prepositions. The following pairs of expressions have similar meanings.

acquainted with, familiar with	interested in, fascinated by
addicted to, hooked on	interfere with, disrupt
angry with (a person), upset with	meet with, get together with
	object to, oppose
bored with, tired of	pleased with, happy with
capable of, able to	protect against, guard against
consist of, have, contain, include	reply to, answer
deal with, address (a problem)	responsible for, accountable for
depend on, rely on	similar to, almost the same as
differ from (something else), be different from	succeed in, attain success in
differ with (someone else), disagree	take advantage of, use an opportunity to
emigrate from, move from (another country)	wait for (something to happen), expect
grateful for (a favor), thankful for	wait on (in a restaurant), serve
immigrate to, move to (another country)	

PRACTICE

32-9   In the following passage, fill in each blank with the correct preposition.

Example: Like other struggling artists, writers often make a living

working ___*in*___ restaurants and waiting ___*on*___ customers.

(1) Most writers, even those who succeed _____ the literary world, need day jobs to help pay _____ food and rent. (2) Many _____ them work _____ related fields—for example, _____ bookstores, _____ publishing houses, or _____ newspapers. (3) Some take advantage _____ their talents and devote themselves _____ teaching others _____ language and literature. (4) For example, _____ the 1990s, *Harry Potter* author J. K. Rowling worked as a teacher _____ Portugal and _____ Britain. (5) _____ the 1960s and '70s, students _____ Howard University _____ Washington, D.C., could enroll _____ classes taught _____ Nobel Prize winner Toni Morrison. (6) Other writers work _____ fields unrelated _____ writing. (7) For instance, poet William Carlos Williams was a medical doctor who wrote poetry only _____ the evenings. (8) Science fiction writer Isaac Asimov worked _____ Boston University _____ the department _____ biochemistry. (9) Occasionally, an aspiring writer has friends and family who approve _____ his or her goals, and he or she can depend _____ them _____ financial help. (10) However, many family members, wanting to protect young writers _____ poverty, try to encourage them to focus _____ other goals.

32j Prepositions in Phrasal Verbs

A **phrasal verb** consists of two words, a verb and a preposition, that are joined to form an idiomatic expression. Many phrasal verbs are **separable**. This means that a direct object can come between the verb and the preposition. However, some phrasal verbs are **inseparable**; that is, the preposition must always come immediately after the verb.

Separable Phrasal Verbs

In many cases, phrasal verbs may be split, with the direct object coming between the two parts of the verb. When the direct object is a noun, the second word of the phrasal verb can come either before or after the object.

In the sentences below, *fill out* is a phrasal verb. Because the object of the verb *fill out* is a noun (*form*), the second word of the verb can come either before or after the verb's object.

> **CORRECT** Please fill out the form.

> **CORRECT** Please fill the form out.

When the object is a pronoun, however, these phrasal verbs must be split, and the pronoun must come between the two parts of the verb.

> **INCORRECT** Please fill out it.

> **CORRECT** Please fill it out.

Some Common Separable Phrasal Verbs

ask out	give away	put back	throw away
bring up	hang up	put on	try out
call up	leave out	set aside	turn down
carry out	let out	shut off	turn off
drop off	make up	take down	wake up
fill out	put away	think over	

Remember, when the object of the verb is a pronoun, these phrasal verbs must be split, and the pronoun must come between the two parts (for example, *take it down*, *put it on*, *let it out*, and *make it up*).

Inseparable Phrasal Verbs

Some phrasal verbs, however, cannot be separated; that is, the preposition cannot be separated from the verb. This means that a direct object cannot come between the verb and the preposition.

INCORRECT Please go the manual over carefully.

CORRECT Please go over the manual carefully.

Notice that in the correct sentence above, the direct object (*manual*) comes right after the preposition (*over*).

Some Common Inseparable Phrasal Verbs		
come across	run across	show up
get along	run into	stand by
go over	see to	

PRACTICE

32-10 In each of the following sentences, look closely at the phrasal verb, and decide whether the preposition is placed correctly in the sentence. If it is, write *C* in the blank after the sentence. If the preposition needs to be moved, edit the sentence.

Example: People who live in American suburbs are often surprised to come across wild animals in their neighborhoods. _____*C*_____

1. In one case, a New Jersey woman was startled when a hungry bear woke up her from a nap one afternoon. _____

2. She called the police, hung up the phone, and ran for her life. _____

3. Actually, although it is a good idea to stay from bears away, most wild bears are timid. _____

4. When there is a drought, people are more likely to run into bears and other wild animals. _____

5. The amount of blueberries and other wild fruit that bears eat usually drops in dry weather off. _____

6. Bears need to put on weight before the winter, so they may have to find food in suburban garbage cans. _____

7. It is a good idea for families to go their plans over to safeguard their property against bears. _____

8. People should not leave pet food out overnight, or else their dog may find that a hungry bear has eaten its dinner. _____

9. If people have a bird feeder in the yard, they should put away it during the autumn. _____

10. As the human population grows, more and more houses are built in formerly wild areas, so bears and people have to learn to get along with each other. _____

ZUMA Press, Inc./Alamy

TEST · Revise · Edit · Proofread

Look back at your response to the Focus on Writing prompt on page 546. **TEST** what you have written. Then, revise and edit your work, paying special attention to the grammar and usage issues discussed in this chapter. Finally, proofread your paragraph.

EDITING PRACTICE

Read the following student essay, which includes errors in the use of subjects, nouns, articles and determiners, and stative verbs, as well as errors with phrasal verbs. Check each underlined word or phrase. If it is not used correctly, write in any necessary changes. If the underlined word or phrase is correct, write *C* above it. The title of the essay has been edited for you.

How to Succeed on ⁱⁿ Multinational Business

Success in multinational business often <u>depends in</u> the ability to understand other countries' cultures. Understanding how cultures <u>differ to</u> our own, however, is only one key to <u>these</u> success. Also, <u>is</u> crucial that businesses learn to adapt to different cultures. <u>The ethnocentrism</u> is the belief that one's own culture has <u>a</u> best way of doing things. In international business, <u>is</u> necessary to set aside this belief. A company cannot <u>be using</u> the same methods or sell the same products overseas as it does at home. Though making these changes requires a lot of work, companies that choose to adjust to new markets are usually <u>happy with</u> their decision.

<u>It is</u> many aspects of a country that must be understood before successful international business can be <u>carried out</u>. To protect itself <u>from</u> legal errors, a company needs to understand the country's legal system, which may be very different from its home country's legal system. <u>May be</u> necessary to get licenses to export products <u>onto</u> other countries. The role of <u>women</u> is also likely to be different; without knowing this, businesspeople might unintentionally offend people. Also, <u>much</u> personal interactions in other countries may give the wrong impression to someone who is inexperienced. For example, in Latin American countries, people <u>are often standing</u> close together and touch each other when they are talking. Americans may feel uncomfortable in such a situation <u>unless understand</u> it.

To <u>succeed in</u> international business, companies <u>are also needing</u> to understand what people buy and why. To avoid problems, a company that wants to sell its product internationally it should do a few market research. For example, when McDonald's opened restaurants on India, realized that beef burgers would not work in a country where many people believe that cows are sacred. Instead, burgers were made from ground chickens. For India's many vegetarians, McDonald's created several different vegetable patties. McDonald's understood that both the religious and the cultural characteristic of India had to be considered if its new restaurants were going to succeed.

Looking to attract new customers in today's international market, companies they are noticing a growing demand for *halal* goods and services. The word *halal* indicates an object or action that is permissible by Islamic law. Businesses are realizing that world's Muslims depend in companies to provide acceptable *halal* foods, banks, hotels, magazines, and other services. Nestlé, KFC, Subway, LG, and Nokia are just a few of the well-known companies that have been successfully remaking their products to appeal in Muslim consumers. Because these high-quality items also appeal to non-Muslims, many of this companies are discovering that meeting cultural needs and desires are simply good business.

Over time, the marketplace is becoming more global. In those setting, individuals from numerous cultures come together. To take advantage from opportunities and perform effectively, an international company must hire people with the right experiences. To deal with other cultures, multinational companies inside today's global market must have good informations and show other cultures the highest respects.

COLLABORATIVE ACTIVITY

Working in a small group, make a list of ten prepositional phrases that include the prepositions *above, around, at, between, from, in, on, over, under,* and *with.* Use appropriate nouns as objects of these prepositions, and use as many modifying words as you wish. (Try, for example, to write something like *above their hideous wedding portrait,* not just *above the picture.*) Now, work together to compose a list of ten sentences, each including one of your ten prepositional phrases.

review checklist

Grammar and Usage for ESL Writers

☐ English sentences must state their subjects. (See 32a.)

☐ English nouns may be count nouns or noncount nouns. A count noun names one particular thing or a group of particular things (*a teacher, oceans*). A noncount noun names something that cannot be counted (*gold, sand*). (See 32b.)

☐ Determiners are adjectives that identify rather than describe the nouns they modify. Determiners may also indicate amount or number. (See 32c.)

☐ The definite article *the* and the indefinite articles *a* and *an* are determiners that indicate whether the noun that follows is one readers can identify (*the book*) or one they cannot yet identify (*a book*). (See 32d.)

☐ To form a negative statement, add the word *not* directly after the first helping verb of the complete verb. To form a question, move the helping verb that follows the subject to the position directly before the subject. (See 32e.)

☐ A verb's form must indicate when an action took place. (See 32f.)

☐ Stative verbs indicate that someone or something is in a state that will not change, at least for a while. Stative verbs are rarely used in the progressive tenses. (See 32g.)

☐ A gerund is a verb form ending in *-ing* that is always used as a noun. (See 32h.)

☐ The prepositions *at*, *in*, and *on* sometimes cause problems for nonnative speakers of English. (See 32i.)

☐ A phrasal verb consists of two words, a verb and a preposition, that are joined to form an idiomatic expression. (See 32j.)

Read the following student essay, which includes errors in the use of verbs, nouns, pronouns, adjectives, and adverbs, as well as ESL errors. Make any changes necessary to correct the basic grammar of the sentences. The first sentence has been edited for you.

The Mystery of the Bermuda Triangle

The Bermuda Triangle is an area in the Atlantic Ocean also ~~know~~ *known* as the Devil's Triangle. Its size, between 500,000 and 1.5 million square miles, depends on who you are believing. Strange events happen there.

During the past century, more than fifty ships and twenty airplanes have disappeared to these area. According to some people, a mysterious force causes ships and planes to vanish in the Bermuda Triangle. Everyone who hears about the mystery has to decide what to believe. However, according to the U.S. Coast Guard, the explanations are not mysterious.

The stories about odd these occurrences they may have started as early as 1492. When Columbus sailed through the area, him and his crew seen unusual lights in the sky. In addition, his compass reacted strangely. Now is believed that the lights came from a meteor that crashed into the ocean. The peculiar compass readings were probably cause from the fact that in this area, magnetic compasses point toward true north rather than magnetic north. These variation can cause navigators to sail off course.

The modern Bermuda Triangle legend started in 1945, when Flight 19, compose of five U.S. Navy Avenger torpedo bombers, disappeared while on a routine training mission. Rescue plane that has been sent to search for them also disappeared. Six aircraft and twenty-seven man vanished. Not only were their lifes lost, but no bodies were ever found. Were a mysterious force responsible? Although the events themselves seem strange, there are several good explanation. First, all the crew members except his leader were trainees.

It is quite possibly that they flied through a magnetic storm or that the leader's compass was not working. If so, they would have become confused of their location. Radio transmissions were unreliable because of a bad weather and a broken receiver in one of the planes. The crew leader was not functioning very good. The leader told his pilots to head east; he thinked that they were over the Gulf of Mexico. However, they were flying up the Atlantic coastline, so his instructions sent him further out to sea. If the planes crashed into the ocean at night, it is not likely there would have been any survivors. No wreckage was ever recover.

After Flight 19 disappeared, storys start to appear about the events that have occurred. The odd compass readings, the problems with radio transmissions, and the missing wreckage lead to strange tales. Some people believed that the missing ships and planes were taken by UFOs (unidentified flying objects) to a different dimension. Others thought that those whom disappeared were kidnapped from aliens from other planets. However, there are most logical explanations. The fact that magnetic compasses point toward true north in this area is now well known. It is also well known that the weather patterns in the southern Atlantic and Caribbean is unpredictable. In addition, human error may have been involved. For these reason, the tales of the Bermuda Triangle are clearly science fiction, not fact.

unit
7 Understanding Punctuation and Mechanics

REVISING AND EDITING YOUR WRITING
REVISING AND EDITING YOUR WRITING

33 Using Commas

Mario Tama/Getty Images (above), Joshua Lutz/Redux (below)

focus on writing

One of these pictures shows public housing in disrepair; one shows new affordable housing units. Write a paragraph that explains your idea of ideal affordable housing. Where should complexes for low-income families be located? What kinds of buildings should they consist of? What facilities and services should be offered to residents?

In this chapter, you will learn to

- use commas in a series (33a)
- use commas to set off introductory phrases and transitional words and phrases (33b)
- use commas with appositives (33c)
- use commas to set off nonrestrictive clauses (33d)
- use commas in dates and addresses (33e)
- avoid unnecessary commas (33f)

A **comma** is a punctuation mark that separates words or groups of words within sentences. In this way, commas keep ideas distinct from one another.

33a Commas in a Series

Use commas to separate all elements in a **series** of three or more words, phrases, or clauses.

> Leyla, Zack, and Kathleen campaigned for Representative Lewis.
>
> Leyla, Zack, or Kathleen will be elected president of Students for Lewis.
>
> Leyla made phone calls, licked envelopes, and ran errands for the campaign.
>
> Leyla is president, Zack is vice president, and Kathleen is treasurer.

FYI

Using Commas in a Series

Newspapers and magazines usually omit the comma before the coordinating conjunction in a series. However, in college writing, you should always use a comma before the coordinating conjunction.

> Leyla, Zack, and Kathleen worked on the campaign.

Exception: Do not use *any* commas if all the items in a series are separated by coordinating conjunctions.

> Leyla or Zack or Kathleen will be elected president of Students for Lewis.

LaunchPad

Visit *LaunchPad Solo for Readers and Writers* > **Commas** for more practice with commas.

PRACTICE

33-1   Edit the following sentences for the use of commas in a series. If the sentence is correct, write *C* in the blank.

Examples

Costa Rica produces bananas, cocoa, and sugarcane. _____*C*_____

The pool rules state that there is no running/ or jumping/ or diving.

_____

1. The musician plays guitar bass and drums. _____

2. The organization's goals are feeding the hungry, housing the homeless and helping the unemployed find work. _____

3. *The Price Is Right, Let's Make a Deal,* and *Jeopardy!* are three of the longest-running game shows in television history. _____

4. In native Hawaiian culture, yellow was worn by the royalty red was worn by priests and a mixture of the two colors was worn by others of high rank. _____

5. The diary Anne Frank kept while her family hid from the Nazis is insightful, touching and sometimes humorous. _____

6. A standard bookcase is sixty inches tall forty-eight inches wide and twelve inches deep. _____

7. Most coffins manufactured in the United States are lined with bronze, or copper, or lead. _____

8. Young handsome and sensitive, Leonardo DiCaprio was the 1990s answer to the 1950s actor James Dean. _____

9. California's capital is Sacramento, its largest city is Los Angeles and its oldest settlement is San Diego. _____

10. Watching television, playing video games, and riding a bicycle are some of the average ten-year-old boy's favorite pastimes. _____

33b Commas with Introductory Phrases and Transitional Words and Phrases

Introductory Phrases

Use a comma to set off an **introductory phrase** from the rest of the sentence.

> In the event of a fire, proceed to the nearest exit.
> Walking home, Nelida decided to change her major.
> To keep fit, people should try to exercise regularly.

PRACTICE

33-2 Edit the following sentences for the use of commas with introductory phrases. If the sentence is correct, write *C* in the blank.

Examples

For some medical conditions, effective treatments are hard to find.

_____

After taking placebos, some depressed patients experience relief from their symptoms. ____*C*____

(1) Sometimes known as sugar pills placebos contain no actual medicine. _____ (2) Despite this fact, placebos sometimes have positive effects on patients who take them. _____ (3) For years researchers have used placebos in experiments. _____ (4) To evaluate the effectiveness of a medication scientists test the drug on volunteers. _____ (5) To ensure that the experiment's results are reliable, researchers always have a control group. _____ (6) Instead of taking the drug the control group takes a placebo. _____ (7) Thinking they are taking an actual medicine patients in the control group may

experience the "placebo effect." _____ (8) After receiving treatment with a placebo, they feel better. _____ (9) In some cases patients feel better even when they know they have taken a placebo. _____ (10) Puzzling to researchers, this "honest placebo effect" is the subject of several new scientific studies. _____

Transitional Words and Phrases

Also use commas to set off **transitional words or phrases**, whether they appear at the beginning, in the middle, or at the end of a sentence.

In fact, Thoreau spent only one night in jail.
He was, of course, bailed out by a friend.
He did spend more than two years at Walden Pond, however.

FYI

Using Commas in Direct Address

Always use commas to set off the name of someone whom you are addressing (speaking to) directly, whether the name appears at the beginning, in the middle, or at the end of a sentence.

Molly, come here and look at this.
Come here, Molly, and look at this.
Come here and look at this, Molly.

PRACTICE

33-3   Edit the following sentences for the use of commas with transitional words and phrases. If the sentence is correct, write C in the blank.

Example: In general, many people agree that mandatory minimum sentence laws should be reformed.

(1) Recently mandatory minimum sentences have been called into question. _____ (2) Nonviolent drug offenders for example are often incarcerated when addiction treatment would be a better course of action. _____ (3) In fact an increasing percentage of the total prison population is composed of these nonviolent offenders. _____ (4) As a result taxpayers are increasingly burdened by the rising costs associated with keeping people behind bars. _____ (5) Of course, there should be consequences for breaking the law. _____ (6) For this reason supporters of mandatory minimum sentences say that they are necessary to deter people from committing crimes. _____ (7) Lawmakers in both parties have been working on reform however. _____ (8) In 2014 the Obama administration endorsed a proposal to reduce mandatory minimum sentences for nonviolent drug offenders. _____ (9) Ultimately, the laws are likely to be changed. _____

33c Commas with Appositives

Use commas to set off an **appositive**—a word or word group that identifies, renames, or describes a noun or a pronoun.

> I have visited only one country, Canada, outside the United States. (*Canada* is an appositive that identifies the noun *country*.)
>
> Carlos Santana, leader of the group Santana, played at Woodstock in 1969. (*Leader of the group Santana* is an appositive that identifies *Carlos Santana*.)
>
> A really gifted artist, he is also a wonderful father. (*A really gifted artist* is an appositive that describes the pronoun *he*.)

FYI

Using Commas with Appositives

Most appositives are set off by commas, whether they fall at the beginning, in the middle, or at the end of a sentence.

A dreamer, he spent his life thinking about what he could not have.

He always wanted to build a house, a big white one, overlooking the ocean.

He finally built his dream house, a log cabin.

PRACTICE

33-4   Underline the appositive in each of the following sentences. Then, check each sentence for the correct use of commas to set off appositives, and add any missing commas. If the sentence is correct, write *C* in the blank.

Example: Wendy Kopp, a college student developed the Teach For America program to help minority students get a better education.

_____

1. Guglielmo Marconi a young Italian inventor, sent the first wireless message across the Atlantic Ocean in 1901. _____

2. A member of the boy band 'N Sync Justin Timberlake went on to establish a successful career as a solo musician and an actor. _____

3. HTML hypertext markup language, is the set of codes used to create web documents. _____

4. William Filene, founder of Filene's Department Store, invented the "bargain basement." _____

5. Known as NPR National Public Radio presents a wide variety of programs. _____

6. On the southwest coast of Nigeria lies Lagos a major port. _____

7. Prospective home of the 2022 Olympics, Beijing continues to have serious problems with its air quality. _____

8. Lightning a strong electrical charge can be both beautiful and dangerous. _____

9. A plant that grows on mountains and in deserts, the fern is surprisingly adaptable. _____

10. Golf a game developed in Scotland, is very popular in the United States. _____

33d   Commas with Nonrestrictive Clauses

WORD POWER

restrict to keep within limits

restrictive limiting

Clauses are often used to add information within a sentence. In some cases, you need to add commas to set off these clauses; in other cases, commas are not required.

Use commas to set off **nonrestrictive clauses**, clauses that are not essential to a sentence's meaning. Do not use commas to set off **restrictive clauses**.

■ A **nonrestrictive clause** does *not* contain essential information. Nonrestrictive clauses are set off from the rest of the sentence by commas.

> Telephone calling-card fraud, which has already cost consumers and phone companies several billion dollars, is increasing.

Here, the clause between the commas (underlined) provides extra information to help readers understand the sentence, but the sentence would still communicate the same idea without this information.

> Telephone calling-card fraud is increasing.

■ A **restrictive clause** contains information that is essential to a sentence's meaning. Restrictive clauses are *not* set off from the rest of the sentence by commas.

> Many rock stars who recorded hits in the 1950s made little money from their songs.

In the sentence above, the clause *who recorded hits in the 1950s* supplies specific information that is essential to the idea the sentence is communicating: it tells readers which group of rock stars made little money. Without the clause, the sentence does not communicate the same idea because it does not tell which rock stars made little money.

Many rock stars made little money from their songs.

Compare the meanings of the following pairs of sentences with non-restrictive and restrictive clauses.

NONRESTRICTIVE Young adults, <u>who text while driving</u>, put themselves and others in danger. (This sentence says that all young adults text while driving and all pose a danger.)

RESTRICTIVE Young adults <u>who text while driving</u> put themselves and others in danger. (This sentence says that only those young adults who text and drive pose a danger.)

NONRESTRICTIVE Student loans, <u>which are based on need</u>, may not be fair to middle-class students. (This sentence says that all student loans are based on need and all may be unfair to middle-class students.)

RESTRICTIVE Student loans <u>that are based on need</u> may not be fair to middle-class students. (This sentence says that only those student loans that are based on need may be unfair to middle-class students.)

FYI

Which, That, and Who

- *Which* always introduces a nonrestrictive clause.

    The job, <u>which had excellent benefits,</u> did not pay well. (clause set off by commas)

- *That* always introduces a restrictive clause.

    He accepted the job <u>that had the best benefits</u>. (no commas)

- *Who* can introduce either a restrictive or a nonrestrictive clause.

    RESTRICTIVE Many parents <u>who work</u> feel a lot of stress. (no commas)

    NONRESTRICTIVE Both of my parents, <u>who have always wanted the best for their children,</u> have worked two jobs for years. (clause set off by commas)

PRACTICE

33-5 Edit the following sentences so that commas set off all nonrestrictive clauses. (Remember, commas are *not* used to set off restrictive clauses.) If a sentence is correct, write *C* in the blank.

> **Example:** A museum exhibition that celebrates the Alaska highway tells the story of its construction. _____*C*_____

(1) During the 1940s, a group of African American soldiers who defied the forces of nature and human prejudice were shipped to Alaska. _____ (2) They built the Alaska highway which stretches twelve hundred miles across Alaska. _____ (3) The troops who worked on the highway have received little attention in most historical accounts. _____ (4) The highway which cut through some of the roughest terrain in the world was begun in 1942. _____ (5) The Japanese had just landed in the Aleutian Islands which lie west of the tip of the Alaska Peninsula. _____ (6) Military officials, who oversaw the project, doubted the ability of the African American troops. _____ (7) As a result, they made them work under conditions, that made construction difficult. _____ (8) The troops who worked on the road proved their commanders wrong by finishing the highway months ahead of schedule. _____ (9) In one case, white engineers, who surveyed a river, said it would take two weeks to bridge. _____ (10) To the engineers' surprise, the soldiers who worked on the project beat the estimate. _____ (11) A military report that was issued in 1945 praised them. _____ (12) It said the goals that the African American soldiers achieved would be remembered through the ages. _____

33e   Commas in Dates and Addresses

Dates

Use commas in dates to separate the day of the week from the month and the day of the month from the year.

> The first Cinco de Mayo we celebrated in the United States was Tuesday, May 5, 1998.

When a date that includes commas does not fall at the end of a sentence, place a comma after the year.

> Tuesday, May 5, 1998, was the first Cinco de Mayo we celebrated in the United States.

Addresses

Use commas in addresses to separate the street address from the city and the city from the state or country.

> The office of the famous fictional detective Sherlock Holmes was located at 221b Baker Street, London, England.

When an address that includes commas falls in the middle of a sentence, place a comma after the state or country.

> The office at 221b Baker Street, London, England, belonged to the famous fictional detective Sherlock Holmes.

PRACTICE

33-6   Edit the following sentences for the correct use of commas in dates and addresses. Add any missing commas, and cross out any unnecessary commas. If the sentence is correct, write *C* in the blank.

Examples

Usher's album *Looking 4 Myself* was released on June 8, 2012.

_____

The entertainer grew up in Chattanooga, Tennessee. _____

1. On Sunday September 27, 2015, and Monday, September 28 2015, people around the world witnessed the rare astronomical phenomenon known as the super blood moon eclipse. _____

2. For traditional Venezuelan food, locals go to Café Casa Veroes on Avenida Norte in Caracas Venezuela. _____

3. Stefani Joanne Angelina Germanotta, more commonly known as Lady Gaga, was born on March 28 1986 in New York New York. _____

4. Jake Arrieta of the Chicago Cubs pitched a no-hitter on August 30, 2015. _____

5. Donations can be sent to the American Red Cross at P. O. Box 4002018 in Des Moines, Iowa. _____

6. To visit the New York Transit Museum, visitors must travel to 130 Livingston Street in Brooklyn New York. _____

7. The Anne Frank House in Amsterdam the Netherlands became a museum on May 3 1960. _____

8. First released on November 1 1997, *Titanic* remains one of the highest-grossing movies of all time. _____

9. Fans from around the world travel to visit Ernest Hemingway's houses in Key West Florida and San Francisco de Paula, Cuba. _____

10. Oprah addressed the graduating class at Harvard on Sunday May 30, 2013 in Cambridge Massachusetts. _____

33f Unnecessary Commas

In addition to knowing where commas are required, it is also important to know when *not* to use commas.

- Do not use a comma before the first item in a series.

INCORRECT	The 1933 film *Duck Soup* starred, Groucho, Chico, and Harpo Marx.
CORRECT	The 1933 film *Duck Soup* starred Groucho, Chico, and Harpo Marx.

■ Do not use a comma after the last item in a series.

INCORRECT	Groucho, Chico, and Harpo Marx, starred in the 1933 film *Duck Soup*.
CORRECT	Groucho, Chico, and Harpo Marx starred in the 1933 film *Duck Soup*.

■ Do not use a comma between a subject and a verb.

INCORRECT	Students and their teachers, should try to respect one another.
CORRECT	Students and their teachers should try to respect one another.

■ Do not use a comma before the coordinating conjunction that separates the two parts of a compound predicate.

INCORRECT	The transit workers voted to strike, and walked off the job.
CORRECT	The transit workers voted to strike and walked off the job.

■ Do not use a comma before the coordinating conjunction that separates the two parts of a compound subject.

INCORRECT	The transit workers, and the sanitation workers voted to strike.
CORRECT	The transit workers and the sanitation workers voted to strike.

■ Do not use a comma to set off a restrictive clause.

INCORRECT	People, who live in glass houses, should not throw stones.
CORRECT	People who live in glass houses should not throw stones.

■ Finally, do not use a comma before a dependent clause that follows an independent clause.

INCORRECT   He was exhausted, because he had driven all night.

CORRECT   He was exhausted because he had driven all night.

PRACTICE
33-7   Some of the following sentences contain unnecessary commas. Edit to eliminate unnecessary commas. If the sentence is correct, write *C* in the blank following it.

Example: Both the Dominican Republic, and the republic of Haiti

occupy the West Indian island of Hispaniola. _____

1. The capital of the Dominican Republic, is Santo Domingo. _____

2. The country's tropical climate, generous rainfall, and fertile soil, make the Dominican Republic suitable for many kinds of crops. _____

3. Some of the most important crops are, sugarcane, coffee, cocoa, and rice. _____

4. Mining is also important to the country's economy, because the land is rich in many ores. _____

5. Spanish is the official language of the Dominican Republic, and Roman Catholicism is the state religion. _____

6. In recent years, resort areas have opened, and brought many tourists to the country. _____

7. Tourists who visit the Dominican Republic, remark on its tropical beauty. _____

8. Military attacks, and political unrest have marked much of the Dominican Republic's history. _____

9. Because the republic's economy has not always been strong, many Dominicans have immigrated to the United States. _____

10. However, many Dominican immigrants maintain close ties to their home country, and return often to visit. _____

TEST · **Revise · Edit · Proofread**

Look back at your response to the Focus on Writing prompt on page 579. TEST what you have written. Then, make the following additions.

Joshua Lutz/Redux

1. Add a sentence that includes a series of three or more words or word groups.
2. Add introductory phrases to two of your sentences.
3. Add an appositive to one of your sentences.
4. Add a transitional word or phrase to one of your sentences (at the beginning, in the middle, or at the end).
5. Add a nonrestrictive clause to one of your sentences.

When you have made all the additions, revise, edit, and proofread your work, carefully checking your use of commas.

EDITING PRACTICE

Read the following student essay, which includes errors in comma use. Add commas where necessary between items in a series and with introductory phrases, transitional words and phrases, appositives, and nonrestrictive clauses. Cross out any unnecessary commas. The first sentence has been edited for you.

Two Nations in Conflict

The United States and Cuba, two countries with a tumultuous relationship, are regularly mentioned in the news. The countries have been at odds for centuries, but relations are finally improving. Recently diplomatic relations were restored, and this was a cause for celebration for people in the United States in Cuba and around the world.

In 1898 Spain was defeated in the Spanish-American War. As a result Cuba became a U.S. territory. Relations between the United States and Cuba which were already difficult became even more strained. Cuba was granted independence but the Platt Agreement imposed certain conditions on Cuba. From 1906 to 1922, the United States intervened with military power, in Cuban affairs. Then in 1934 the United States assisted with a military coup to bring General Fulgencio Batista into power. When he was overthrown by Fidel Castro in 1959 President Eisenhower ordered a ban on all exports to Cuba. The Bay of Pigs Invasion and the Cuban Missile Crisis followed shortly thereafter leading to further deteriorating relations.

Meanwhile many Cubans hoped to come to America. The Cuban Adjustment Act which was passed in 1966 allowed Cuban escapees to seek U.S. citizenship. In 1999, Elián González a five-year-old boy became a symbol of the tension between Cubans living in Cuba and Cubans who had fled to America. González was found floating on a raft near Miami, after his mother and the other escapees he fled with were killed. González was returned to his father in Cuba, despite the protests of his extended family in America.

For years relations between the United States and Cuba continued to be strained. Finally, in 2014 U.S. President Barack Obama and Cuban President Raúl Castro, made history when they announced an agreement to improve relations.

There is still a long road ahead. However restored diplomacy has meant that travel restrictions have been eased. Americans will also be allowed to import goods from Cuba and improved telecommunications systems will make the Internet more accessible to Cubans. Both the United States and Cuba stand to benefit from restored diplomacy. It will be exciting to watch history continue to unfold.

COLLABORATIVE ACTIVITY

Bring a homemaking, sports, or fashion magazine to class. Working in a small group, look at the people pictured in the ads. In what roles are men most often depicted? In what roles are women presented? Identify the three or four most common roles for each sex, and give each kind of character a descriptive name—*athlete* or *mother*, for example.

Working on your own, choose one type of character, and write a paragraph in which you describe his or her typical appearance and habits. Then, circle every comma in your paragraph, and work with your group to explain why each comma is used. If no one in your group can explain why a particular comma is used, cross it out.

review checklist

Using Commas

☐ Use commas to separate all elements in a series of three or more words or word groups. (See 33a.)

☐ Use commas to set off introductory phrases and transitional words and phrases from the rest of a sentence. (See 33b.)

☐ Use commas to set off appositives from the rest of a sentence. (See 33c.)

☐ Use commas to set off nonrestrictive clauses. (See 33d.)

☐ Use commas to separate parts of dates and addresses. (See 33e.)

☐ Avoid unnecessary commas. (See 33f.)

34 Using Apostrophes

Jinny Goodman/Alamy

focus on writing

Certain jobs have traditionally been considered "men's work," and others have been viewed as "women's work." Although the workplace has changed considerably in recent years, some things have remained the same. Write a paragraph about the tasks that are considered "men's work" and "women's work" at your job or in your current household. Be sure to give examples of the responsibilities you discuss. (*Note:* Contractions, such as *isn't* or *don't*, are acceptable in this informal response.)

In this chapter, you will learn to

- use apostrophes to form contractions (34a)
- use apostrophes to form possessives (34b)
- revise incorrect use of apostrophes (34c)

An **apostrophe** is a punctuation mark that is used in two situations: to form a contraction and to form the possessive of a noun or an indefinite pronoun.

34a Apostrophes in Contractions

A **contraction** is a word that uses an apostrophe to combine two words. The apostrophe takes the place of omitted letters.

> I <u>didn't</u> (*did not*) realize how late it was.
>
> <u>It's</u> (*it is*) not right for cheaters to go unpunished.

Frequently Used Contractions

I + am = I'm	are + not = aren't
we + are = we're	can + not = can't
you + are = you're	do + not = don't
it + is = it's	will + not = won't
I + have = I've	should + not = shouldn't
I + will = I'll	let + us = let's
there + is = there's	that + is = that's
is + not = isn't	who + is = who's

PRACTICE

34-1 In the following sentences, add apostrophes to contractions if needed. If the sentence is correct, write *C* in the blank.

Example: ~~Whats~~ *What's* the deadliest creature on earth? _____

(1) Bacteria and viruses, which we cant see without a microscope, kill

many people every year. _____ (2) When we speak about the deadli-

est creatures, however, usually were talking about creatures that cause

Visit *LaunchPad Solo for Readers and Writers* > **Apostrophes** for more practice with apostrophes.

illness or death from their poison, which is called venom. _____ (3) After your bitten, stung, or stuck, how long does it take to die? _____ (4) The fastest killer is a creature called the sea wasp, but it isn't a wasp at all. _____ (5) The sea wasp is actually a fifteen-foot-long jellyfish, and although its not aggressive, it can be deadly. _____ (6) People who've gone swimming off the coast of Australia have encountered this creature. _____ (7) While jellyfish found off the Atlantic coast of the United States can sting, they arent as dangerous as the sea wasp, whose venom is deadly enough to kill sixty adults. _____ (8) A person whos been stung by a sea wasp has anywhere from thirty seconds to four minutes to get help or die. _____ (9) Oddly, it's been found that something as thin as panty-hose worn over the skin will prevent these stings. _____ (10) Also, theres an antidote to the poison that can save victims. _____

34b Apostrophes in Possessives

Possessive forms of nouns and pronouns show ownership. Nouns and indefinite pronouns do not have special possessive forms. Instead, they use apostrophes to indicate ownership.

Singular Nouns and Indefinite Pronouns

To form the possessive of **singular nouns** (including names) and **indefinite pronouns**, add an apostrophe plus an *s*.

Cesar Chavez's goal (*the goal of Cesar Chavez*) was justice for American farmworkers.
The strike's outcome (*the outcome of the strike*) was uncertain.
Whether it would succeed was anyone's guess (*the guess of anyone*).

FYI

Singular Nouns Ending in -s

Even if a singular noun already ends in -s, add an apostrophe plus an s to form the possessive.

The class's next assignment was a research paper.

Dr. Ramos's patients are participating in a clinical trial.

Plural Nouns

Most plural nouns end in -s. To form the possessive of **plural nouns ending in -s** (including names), add just an apostrophe (not an apostrophe plus an s).

The two drugs' side effects (*the side effects of the two drugs*) were quite different.

The Johnsons' front door (*the front door of the Johnsons*) is red.

Some irregular noun plurals do not end in -s. If a plural noun does not end in -s, add an apostrophe plus an s to form the possessive.

The men's room is right next to the women's room.

PRACTICE

34-2   Rewrite the following phrases, changing the noun or indefinite pronoun that follows *of* to the possessive form. Be sure to distinguish between singular and plural nouns.

Examples

the mayor of the city   *the city's mayor*

the uniforms of the players   *the players' uniforms*

1. the video of the singer _____

2. the scores of the students _____

3. the favorite band of everybody _____

4. the office of the boss _____

5. the union of the players _____

6. the specialty of the restaurant ⎯⎯⎯⎯⎯⎯⎯⎯⎯⎯⎯

7. the bedroom of the children ⎯⎯⎯⎯⎯⎯⎯⎯⎯⎯⎯

8. the high cost of the tickets ⎯⎯⎯⎯⎯⎯⎯⎯⎯⎯⎯

9. the dreams of everyone ⎯⎯⎯⎯⎯⎯⎯⎯⎯⎯⎯

10. the owner of the dogs ⎯⎯⎯⎯⎯⎯⎯⎯⎯⎯⎯

34c Incorrect Use of Apostrophes

Be careful not to confuse a plural noun (*boys*) with the singular possessive form of the noun (*boy's*). Never use an apostrophe with a plural
noun unless the noun is possessive.

> Termites can be dangerous <u>pests</u> [not *pest's*].
>
> The <u>Velezes</u> [not *Velez's*] live on Maple Drive, right next door to the
> <u>Browns</u> [not *Brown's*].

Also remember not to use apostrophes with possessive pronouns
that end in -*s*: *theirs* (not *their's*), *hers* (not *her's*), *its* (not *it's*), *ours* (not
our's), and *yours* (not *your's*).

Be especially careful not to confuse possessive pronouns with sound-
alike contractions. Possessive pronouns never include apostrophes.

POSSESSIVE PRONOUN	CONTRACTION
The dog bit its master.	It's (*it is*) time for breakfast.
The choice is theirs.	There's (*there is*) no place like home.
Whose house is this?	Who's (*who is*) on first base?
Is this your house?	You're (*you are*) late again.

PRACTICE

34-3 Check the underlined words in the following sentences for
correct use of apostrophes. If a correction needs to be made,
cross out the word and write the correct version above it. If the noun
or pronoun is correct, write *C* above it.

> *C*
> **Example:** The <u>president's</u> views were presented after several other
> *speakers*   *theirs.*
> ~~speaker's~~ first presented ~~their's.~~

1. Parent's should realize that when it comes to disciplining children, the responsibility is there's.

2. It's also important that parents offer praise for a child's good behavior.

3. In it's first few week's of life, a dog is already developing a personality.

4. His and her's towels used to be popular with couple's, but it's not so common to see them today.

5. All the Ryan's spent four year's in college and then got good jobs.

6. Kanye told Kim, "You're the one who's love I've been waiting for."

7. If you expect to miss any class's, you will have to make arrangements with someone who's willing to tell you you're assignment.

8. No other school's cheerleading squad tried as many stunts as our's did.

9. Surprise test's are common in my economics teacher's class.

10. Jazz's influence on many mainstream musician's is one of the book's main subject's.

TEST · Revise · Edit · Proofread

Look back at your response to the Focus on Writing prompt on page 596. TEST what you have written. Then, revise and edit your work, checking to make sure you have used apostrophes correctly in possessive forms and contractions. (Remember, because this is an informal exercise, contractions are acceptable.) Finally, proofread your paragraph.

Jinny Goodman/Alamy

EDITING PRACTICE

Read the following student essay, which includes errors in the use of apostrophes. Edit it to eliminate errors by crossing out incorrect words and writing corrections above them. (Note that this is an informal response paper, so contractions are acceptable.) The first sentence has been edited for you.

The Women of Messina

In William ~~Shakespeares'~~ *Shakespeare's* play *Much Ado about Nothing*, the women of Messina, whether they are seen as love objects or as ~~shrew's,~~ *shrews,* have very few options. A womans role is to please a man. She can try to resist, but she will probably wind up giving in.

WORD POWER

shrew a scolding woman

The plays two women, Hero and Beatrice, are very different. Hero is the obedient one. Heroes cousin, Beatrice, tries to challenge the rules of the mans world in which she lives. However, in a place like Messina, even women like Beatrice find it hard to get the respect that should be their's.

Right from the start, we are drawn to Beatrice. Shes funny, she has a clever comment for most situation's, and she always speaks her mind about other peoples behavior. Unlike Hero, she tries to stand up to the men in her life, as we see in her and Benedicks conversations. But even though Beatrice's intelligence is obvious, she often mocks herself. Its clear that she doesn't have much self-esteem. In fact, Beatrice is'nt the strong woman she seems to be.

Ultimately, Beatrice does get her man, and she will be happy—but at what cost? Benedicks' last word's to her are "Peace! I will stop your mouth." Then, he kisses her. The kiss is a symbolic end to their bickering. It is also the mark of Beatrices defeat. She has lost. Benedick has silenced her. Now, she will be Benedick's wife and do what he wants her to do. Granted, she will have more say in her marriage than Hero will have in her's, but she is still defeated.

603 Chapter 34 Chapter Review

Shakespeares audience might have seen the plays ending as a happy one. For contemporary audience's, however, the ending is disappointing. Even Beatrice, the most rebellious of Messinas women, finds it impossible to achieve anything of importance in this male-dominated society.

COLLABORATIVE ACTIVITY

Bring to class a book, magazine, or newspaper whose style is informal— for example, a romance novel, *People*, your school newspaper, or even a comic book. Working in a group, circle every contraction you can find on one page of each publication, and substitute for each contraction the words it combines. Are your substitutions an improvement? (You may want to read a few paragraphs aloud before you reach a conclusion.)

review checklist

Using Apostrophes

- Use apostrophes to form contractions. (See 34a.)

- Use an apostrophe plus an *s* to form the possessive of singular nouns and indefinite pronouns, even when a noun ends in -*s*. (See 34b.)

- Use an apostrophe alone to form the possessive of plural nouns ending in -*s*, including names. If a plural noun does not end in -*s*, add an apostrophe plus an *s*. (See 34b.)

- Do not use apostrophes with plural nouns unless they are possessive. Do not use apostrophes with possessive pronouns. (See 34c.)

35 Understanding Mechanics

Universal Pictures/PhotoFest

focus on writing

This picture shows the movie poster for *E.T.*, a 1982 film directed by Steven Spielberg that has become one of the most iconic films of the last fifty years. Think of a movie that is significant to you and write a paragraph describing a memorable scene (such as when Elliott and E.T. touch fingers). Begin by giving the film's title and listing the names of the major stars and the characters they play. Then, tell what happens in the scene, quoting a few words of dialogue if possible.

In this chapter, you will learn to

- capitalize proper nouns (35a)
- punctuate direct quotations (35b)
- set off titles (35c)
- use minor punctuation marks correctly (35d)

35a Capitalizing Proper Nouns

A **proper noun** names a particular person, animal, place, object, or idea. Proper nouns are always capitalized. The list that follows explains and illustrates specific rules for capitalizing proper nouns.

- Always capitalize names of **races, ethnic groups, tribes, nationalities, languages, and religions**.

  > The census data revealed a diverse community of Caucasians, African Americans, and Asian Americans, with a few Latino and Navajo residents. Native languages included English, Korean, and Spanish. Most people identified themselves as Catholic, Protestant, or Muslim.

- Capitalize names of **specific people and the titles that accompany them**. In general, do not capitalize titles used without a name.

  > In 1994, President Nelson Mandela was elected to lead South Africa.

  > The newly elected fraternity president addressed the crowd.

- Capitalize names of **specific family members and their titles**. Do not capitalize words that identify family relationships, including those introduced by possessive pronouns.

  > The twins, Aunt Edna and Aunt Evelyn, are Dad's sisters.

  > My aunts, my father's sisters, are twins.

- Capitalize names of **specific countries, cities, towns, bodies of water, streets, and so on**. Do not capitalize words that do not name specific places.

  > The Seine runs through Paris, France.

  > The river runs through the city.

LaunchPad

Visit *LaunchPad Solo for Readers and Writers* > **Capitalization** for more practice with capitalization.

■ Capitalize names of **specific geographical regions**. Do not capitalize such words when they specify direction.

> William Faulkner's novels are set in the South.
>
> Turn right at the golf course, and go south for about a mile.

■ Capitalize names of **specific groups, clubs, teams, and associations**. Do not capitalize general references to such groups.

> The Teamsters Union represents workers who were at the stadium for the Republican Party convention, the Rolling Stones concert, and the Phillies-Astros game.
>
> The union represents workers who were at the stadium for the political party's convention, the rock group's concert, and the baseball teams' game.

■ Capitalize **brand names**. Do not capitalize general references to kinds of products.

> While Jeff waited for his turn at the Xerox machine, he drank a can of Coke.
>
> While Jeff waited for his turn at the copier, he drank a can of soda.

■ Capitalize **titles of specific academic courses**. Do not capitalize names of general academic subject areas, except for proper nouns— for example, a language or a country.

> Are Introduction to American Government and Biology 200 closed yet?
>
> Are the introductory American government course and the biology course closed yet?

■ Capitalize **days of the week, months of the year, and holidays**. Do not capitalize the names of seasons.

> The Jewish holiday of Passover usually falls in April.
>
> The Jewish holiday of Passover falls in the spring.

Note: Also capitalize names of specific buildings and monuments; names of specific historical periods, events, and documents; and names of businesses, government agencies, schools, and other institutions.

PRACTICE

35-1   Edit the following sentences, capitalizing letters or changing capitals to lowercase where necessary.

Example: The third-largest ₵ity in the ᵁnited ˢtates is ₵hicago, ᴵllinois.

(1) Located in the midwest on lake Michigan, chicago is an important port city, a rail and highway hub, and the site of o'hare international airport, one of the Nation's busiest. (2) The financial center of the city is Lasalle street, and the lakefront is home to Grant park, where there are many Museums and monuments. (3) To the North of the city, soldier field is home to the chicago bears, the city's football team, and wrigley field is home to the chicago cubs, a national league Baseball Team. (4) In the mid-1600s, the site of what is now Chicago was visited by father jacques marquette, a catholic missionary to the ottawa and huron tribes, who were native to the area. (5) By the 1700s, the city was a trading post run by john kinzie. (6) The city grew rapidly in the 1800s, and immigrants included germans, irish, italians, poles, greeks, and chinese, along with african americans who migrated from the south. (7) In 1871, much of the city was destroyed in one of the worst fires in united states history; according to legend, the fire started when mrs. O'Leary's Cow kicked over a burning lantern. (8) Today, Chicago's skyline has many Skyscrapers, built by businesses like the john hancock company, sears, and amoco. (9) I know Chicago well because my Mother grew up there and my aunt jean and uncle amos still live there. (10) I also got information from the Chicago Chamber of Commerce when I wrote a paper for introductory research writing, a course I took at Graystone high school.

35b Punctuating Direct Quotations

A **direct quotation** shows the *exact* words of a speaker or writer. Direct quotations are always placed in quotation marks.

A direct quotation is usually accompanied by an **identifying tag**, a phrase (such as "she said") that names the person being quoted. In the following sentences, the identifying tag is underlined.

<u>Lauren said</u>, "My brother and Tina have gotten engaged."
A <u>famous advertising executive wrote</u>, "Don't sell the steak; sell the sizzle."

When a quotation is a complete sentence, it begins with a capital letter and ends with a period (or a question mark or exclamation point). When a quotation falls at the end of a sentence (as in the two examples above) the period is placed *before* the quotation marks.

If the quotation is a question or an exclamation, the question mark or exclamation point is also placed *before* the closing quotation mark.

The instructor asked, "Has anyone read Toni Morrison's *Sula*?"
Officer Warren shouted, "Hold it right there!"

If the quotation itself is not a question or an exclamation, the question mark or exclamation point is placed *after* the closing quotation mark.

Did Joe really say, "I quit"?
I can't believe he really said, "I quit"!

FYI

Indirect Quotations

A direct quotation shows someone's *exact* words, but an **indirect quotation** simply summarizes what was said or written.
Do not use quotation marks with indirect quotations.

DIRECT QUOTATION	Martin Luther King Jr. said, "I have a dream."
INDIRECT QUOTATION	Martin Luther King Jr. said that he had a dream.

The rules for punctuating direct quotations with identifying tags are summarized below.

Identifying Tag at the Beginning

When the identifying tag comes *before* the quotation, it is followed by a comma.

> Alexandre Dumas wrote, "Nothing succeeds like success."

Identifying Tag at the End

When the identifying tag comes at the *end* of a quoted sentence, it is followed by a period. A comma (or, sometimes, a question mark or an exclamation point) inside the closing quotation mark separates the quotation from the identifying tag.

> "Life is like a box of chocolates," stated Forrest Gump.
> "Is that so?" his friends wondered.
> "That's amazing!" he cried.

Identifying Tag in the Middle

When the identifying tag comes in the *middle* of the quoted sentence, it is followed by a comma. The first part of the quotation is also followed by a comma, placed inside the closing quotation mark. Because the part of the quotation that follows the identifying tag is not a new sentence, it does not begin with a capital letter.

> "This is my life," Bette insisted, "and I'll live it as I please."

Identifying Tag between Two Sentences

When the identifying tag comes *between two* quoted sentences, it is preceded by a comma and followed by a period. (The second quoted sentence begins with a capital letter.)

> "Producer Berry Gordy is an important figure in the history of music," Tony explained. "He was the creative force behind Motown records."

PRACTICE

35-2   The following sentences contain direct quotations. First, underline the identifying tag. Then, punctuate the quotation correctly, adding capital letters as necessary.

> **Example:**   Why Darryl asked are teachers so strict about deadlines?

1. We who are about to die salute you said the gladiators to the emperor.

2. The bigger they are said boxer John L. Sullivan the harder they fall.

3. If you believe celebrity gossip my friend always says then you'll believe anything.

4. When asked for the jury's verdict, the foreperson replied we find the defendant not guilty.

5. I had felt for a long time that if I was ever told to get up so a white person could sit Rosa Parks recalled I would refuse to do so.

35c Setting Off Titles

Some titles are typed in *italics*. Others are enclosed in quotation marks. The following box shows how to set off different kinds of titles.

Italics or Quotation Marks?

ITALICIZED TITLES	TITLES IN QUOTATION MARKS
Books: *How the García Girls Lost Their Accents*	Book chapters: "Understanding Mechanics"
Newspapers: *Miami Herald*	Short stories: "The Tell-Tale Heart"
Magazines: *People*	Essays and articles: "Mother Tongue"
Long poems: *John Brown's Body*	Short poems: "Richard Cory"
Plays: *Death of a Salesman*	Songs and speeches: "America the Beautiful"; "The Gettysburg Address"
Films: *The Hunger Games*	
Television or radio series: *Battlestar Galactica*	Individual episodes of television or radio series: "The Montgomery Bus Boycott" (an episode of the PBS series *Eyes on the Prize*)
Paintings and Sculpture: *American Gothic*	
Video games: *Tetris*	

FYI

Capital Letters in Titles

Capitalize the first letters of all important words in a title. Do not capitalize an **article** (*a, an, the*), a **preposition** (*to, of, around,* and so on), the *to* in an infinitive, or a **coordinating conjunction** (*and, but,* and so on)—unless it is the first or last word of the title or subtitle (*On the Road*; "To an Athlete Dying Young"; *No Way Out*; *And Quiet Flows the Don*).

PRACTICE

35-3   Edit the following sentences, capitalizing letters as necessary in titles.

Example: New *y*ork *t*imes best-seller *t*hree *c*ups of *t*ea is about Greg

Mortenson's work building schools in Pakistan and Afghanistan.

1. When fans of reality television voted for their favorite shows, *the bachelor, the biggest loser,* and *the amazing race* were in the top ten.

2. In 2009, David Blaine delivered his famous TED Talk "how i held my breath for 17 minutes."

3. After nearly losing her life for supporting education for young girls, Malala Yousafzai published a memoir titled *i am malala: the girl who stood up for education and was shot by the taliban.*

4. Actor Johnny Depp plays the pirate Captain Jack Sparrow in the films *the curse of the black pearl, dead man's chest, at world's end,* and *on stranger tides.*

5. Singer-songwriter Bruno Mars has written songs that were performed by other artists, such as "billionaire," as well as songs he has performed himself, such as "just the way you are."

PRACTICE

35-4 In the following sentences, underline titles (to indicate italics) or place them in quotation marks. (Remember that titles of books and other long works are italicized, and titles of stories, essays, and other shorter works are enclosed in quotation marks.)

Example: An article in <u>The Atlantic</u> called "Can Campus Networks Ever Be Secure?" talks about cyber security on campus.

1. Oprah Winfrey publishes a magazine called O.

2. At the beginning of most major American sporting events, the crowd stands for The Star Spangled Banner.

3. The Farmer's Almanac is a publication that makes predictions about the weather for the upcoming year.

4. Elton John's song Empty Garden is about the death of John Lennon.

5. Edgar Allan Poe wrote several mysterious short stories, two of which are called The Tell-Tale Heart and The Black Cat.

6. The popular Broadway show The Book of Mormon was written by the creators of South Park.

7. Mindy Kaling, who starred in the hit TV show The Office, wrote two best-selling books: Is Everyone Hanging Out Without Me? and Why Not Me?

8. In the college textbook Sociology: A Brief Introduction, the first chapter is titled The Essence of Sociology.

35d Using Minor Punctuation Marks

The Semicolon

Use a **semicolon** to join independent clauses in a compound sentence.

> Twenty years ago, smartphones did not exist; today, many people cannot imagine life without them.

The Colon

- Use a **colon** to introduce a quotation.

  Our family motto is a simple one: "Accept no substitutes."

- Use a colon to introduce an explanation, a clarification, or an example.

  Only one thing kept him from climbing Mt. Everest: fear of heights.

- Use a colon to introduce a list.

  I left my job for four reasons: boring work, poor working conditions, low pay, and a terrible supervisor.

The Dash

Use **dashes** to set off important information.

  She parked her car—a red Firebird—in a tow-away zone.

Parentheses

Use **parentheses** to enclose material that is relatively unimportant.

  The weather in Portland (a city in Oregon) was overcast.

Visit *LaunchPad Solo for Readers and Writers* > **Semicolons and Colons** for more practice with punctuation.

PRACTICE

35-5   Add semicolons, colons, dashes, and parentheses to the following sentences where necessary.

Example: Megachurches (those with more than two thousand ^) worshippers at a typical service ^ have grown in popularity since the 1950s.

1. Megachurches though they are Protestant are not always affiliated with the main Protestant denominations.

2. Services in megachurches are creative preaching is sometimes accompanied by contemporary music and video presentations.

3. Although many of these churches are evangelical actively recruiting new members, people often join because of friends and neighbors.

4. Megachurches tend to keep their members because they encourage a variety of activities for example, hospitality committees and study groups.

5. Worshippers say that their services are upbeat they are full of joy and spirituality.

6. Megachurches in nearly all cases use technology to organize and communicate with their members.

7. The largest of these churches with ten thousand members would be unable to function without telecommunications.

8. Some even offer services in a format familiar to their younger members the podcast.

9. Critics of megachurches and there are some believe they take up too much tax-exempt land.

10. Other critics fear that smaller churches already struggling to keep members will lose worshippers to these huge congregations and eventually have to close.

Universal Pictures/PhotoFest

TEST · Revise · Edit · Proofread

Look back at your response to the Focus on Writing prompt on page 604. TEST what you have written.

If you have quoted any dialogue from the film you wrote about, try varying the placement of the identifying tags you have used. If you did not include any lines of dialogue, try adding one or two. Then, add an example or list to your writing, introducing this new material with a colon. Make sure that a complete sentence comes before the colon.

Finally, revise, edit, and proofread your work, paying special attention to the issues covered in this chapter.

EDITING PRACTICE

Read the following student essay, which includes errors in capitalization and punctuation and in the use of direct quotations and titles. Correct any errors you find. The first sentence has been edited for you.

A Threat to Health

Pandemics are like Ẹpidemics, only more widespread, perhaps even spreading throughout the Ẉorld. In a pandemic, a serious Disease spreads very easily. In the past, there have been many pandemics. In the future, in spite of advances in Medicine, there will still be pandemics. In fact, scientists agree that not every pandemic can be prevented, so pandemics will continue to be a threat.

Probably the best-known pandemic is the bubonic plague. It killed about one-third of the Population of europe during the middle ages. Some areas suffered more than others. According to Philip ziegler's book the black Death, at least half the people in florence, Italy, died in one year. Many years later, in 1918, a flu pandemic killed more than fifty million people worldwide, including hundreds of thousands in the United states.

Unfortunately, pandemics have not disappeared. AIDS, for example, is a current pandemic. Philadelphia the 1993 movie starring denzel washington and tom hanks is still one of the most moving depictions of the heartbreak of AIDS. The rate of AIDS infection is over 30% in parts of africa, the disease continues to spread on other Continents as well. So far, efforts to find an AIDS vaccine have failed. Dr. anthony s. Fauci discussed this problem, as well as recent AIDS research, on NPR's series All things considered in a program called Search for an HIV vaccine expands.

Although some pandemic diseases, such as Smallpox, have been wiped out by Vaccination, new pandemics remain a threat. Many viruses and Bacteria change in response to treatment, so they may become resistant to Vaccination and Antibiotics. Also, with modern transportation, a disease can move quickly from Country to Country. For example, the disease known as severe acute respiratory syndrome (SARS) began in china but was spread to other countries by travelers. Hundreds died as a result of the SARS pandemic between November 2002 and july 2003.

Birds also remain a threat because they can transmit disease. It is obviously impossible to prevent birds from flying from one country to another. Markos kyprianou, health commissioner of the European union, has said that I am concerned that birds in Turkey had been found with the bird flu Virus. He said, There is a direct relationship with viruses found in Russia, Mongolia and china. If this Virus changes so that it can move easily from birds to Humans, bird flu could become the next pandemic.

Public Health Officials are always on the lookout for diseases with three characteristics they are new, they are dangerous, and they are very contagious. Doctors try to prevent these diseases from becoming Pandemics. However, they continue to warn that some Pandemics cannot be prevented.

COLLABORATIVE ACTIVITY

Working in pairs, write a conversation between two characters, real or fictional, who have very different positions on a particular issue. Place all direct quotations within quotation marks, and include identifying tags that clearly indicate which character is speaking. (Begin a new paragraph each time a new person speaks.)

Exchange your conversation with another pair, and check their work to see that directly quoted speech is set within quotation marks and that capital letters and other punctuation are used correctly.

review checklist

Understanding Mechanics

☐ Capitalize proper nouns. (See 35a.)

☐ Always place direct quotations within quotation marks. (See 35b.)

☐ In titles, capitalize all important words. Use italics or quotation marks to set off titles. (See 35c.)

☐ Use semicolons to join independent clauses in a compound sentence. (See 35d.)

☐ Use colons, dashes, and parentheses to set off material from the rest of a sentence. (See 35d.)

Read the following student essay, which contains errors in the use of punctuation and mechanics. Identify the sentences that need to be corrected, and edit the faulty sentences. (Underline to indicate italics where necessary.) The first sentence has been edited for you.

Telenovelas

What is the most-watched kind of television program in Spanish-speaking countries, It's the telenovela, a Spanish-language soap opera. Televised on Weeknights in the prime evening hour's; telenovelas started in the early 1950s and are still popular today. In fact more telenovelas are shown in central America and South america than any other type of TV drama. In a recent study more than half the population of Latin American countries said "that they watch these shows." Telenovelas are different from american soap operas in the way they are planned and scheduled. Also they dont have the same kinds of plots. Telenovela's popularity can be seen in their websites, and by their growth in countries whose residents dont speak spanish.

Telenovelas are quite different from. American Soap Operas. In the United States, there have been some evening soap-opera dramas (dallas and dynasty are good examples but they have usually been televised only once a week, however telenovelas usually appear Monday through Friday. In the United States soap operas generally continue until viewers stop watching, and ratings fall. The writers of an american soap opera, do not know how the plot will develop; or when it will end. In contrast telenovela's are usually completely mapped out at the beginning. In general a telenovela continues for about eight months and then the short-lived drama is over. A new telenovela takes it's place.

The plots may seem strange to american viewers. In a typical telenovela the beautiful Heroine is a girl—who has no money but has a good heart. The hero—a rich, handsome man, rejects his rich but evil girlfriend in favor of the heroine. Eventually the heroine may turn out to be the secret child of a wealthy family. The unhappy villain's may wind up in the cemetery and the heroine and her hero will live "happily ever after." Other telenovelas occur in the past, or may deal with modern social problems such as drug abuse, or prejudice. Some telenovelas are really serial comedies and are more, like American sitcoms.

Telenovelas are becoming more and more popular. There are even websites dedicated to: popular telenovelas and their actors. For example viewers can go to the website called topnovelas to access: plot summaries lists of the most popular shows and downloads of episodes'. Although telenovelas started in Spanish-speaking countries they have spread to other countries. The first telenovela to be translated into another language was The Rich Cry too (Los Ricos También Lloran) which was first produced in Mexico in 1979 and was brought to, China, the Soviet Union and the United States. Other places where telenovelas are popular include the following countries; france israel japan, malaysia Singapore and indonesia.

The popularity of the telenovela in the United states is only partly a reflection of its' millions of spanish-speaking viewers. Although it is true that Networks want to attract hispanic viewers it is also true that the format, and subject matter interest English-Speaking viewers. Its quite possible that one day, telenovelas in English will appear every night?

unit
8 Reading Essays

36 Readings for Writers

The following twelve essays by professional writers offer interesting material to read, react to, think critically about, discuss, and write about. In addition, these essays illustrate some of the ways you can organize ideas in your own writing.

The essays in this chapter use many of the patterns of essay development you learned about in Chapters 15 and 16 of this book. Of course, these patterns are not your only options for arranging ideas in essays; in fact, many essays combine several patterns of development. Still, understanding how patterns work will help you to choose the most effective organization strategy when you are writing for a particular purpose and audience.

Each of the essays that follow is preceded by a short **headnote**, an introduction that tells you something about the writer and suggests what to look for as you read. Following each essay are three sets of questions.

- **Focus on Meaning** questions help you to assess your understanding of the basic ideas the essay communicates.

- **Focus on Strategy and Critical Thinking** questions ask you to consider the writer's purpose and intended audience, the essay's opening and closing strategies, and the thesis statement. These questions often ask you to make judgments about the writer's rhetorical choices.

- **Focus on Language and Style** questions ask you to think about the writer's stylistic decisions and word choice as well as the **connotations** (meanings associated with words) and **denotations** (dictionary definitions).

Two or three **Writing Practice** prompts also follow each essay.

As you read each of these essays, you should **preview**, **highlight**, and **annotate** it to help you understand what you are reading. (Previewing, highlighting, and annotating are explained and illustrated in Chapter 1.) Then, you should reread each essay more carefully in preparation for class discussion and writing.

Essays

THE CASE AGAINST E-READERS: WHY READING PAPER BOOKS IS BETTER FOR YOUR MIND

Naomi S. Baron

A renowned scholar in linguistics, Naomi Baron has taught at American University in Washington, D.C., since 1987. A recipient of Guggenheim and Fulbright fellowships, she has also taught at Brown University, the Rhode Island School of Design, and Emory University. Her most recent book, *Words Onscreen: The Fate of Reading in a Digital World* (2015), addresses the issue of language in the age of technology and social media, a popular theme in her work. In the following essay, published in the *Washington Post* in 2015, Baron compares and contrasts the practice of reading on a screen and reading in a printed book. As you read, think about the differences and similarities in your own experiences with these ways of reading.

You got an e-reader over the holidays. What should you load it up with? 1

Beach reads? Sure. *Ulysses*?[1] Probably not. 2

We know a lot about the pros and cons of reading a hard-copy 3
book vs. reading electronically. The problem is, many of us refuse to listen.

Don't get me wrong: Digital reading has some real advantages. Ask 4
people what they like most about reading on digital screens (a question I've put to several hundred university students in the United States, Germany, Japan, and Slovakia), and you hear over and over again about convenience: "easy to carry" and "compact." We also know electronic texts (especially when they are open-access or donated) are vital for democratizing learning opportunities. Just look at projects like the Digital Public Library of America or Worldreader.

More points for digital reading: e-books tend to be cheaper than 5
print versions (though outside America, tax structures sometimes complicate the comparison). There's also the environmental argument. Think of the trees!

> **WORD POWER**
> **open-access** online information that is free of all restrictions

> **WORD POWER**
> **democratizing** making more equal for all

---

1. Novel written by Irish writer James Joyce, published in 1922.

WORD POWER

soundness validity; truth

WORD POWER

aesthetic concerned with beauty

WORD POWER

hasten to be quick to do something

Yet the soundness of this case is arguable. The earth metals we're using up to build e-readers and tablets are not just rare but highly toxic. And think about all that energy needed to run servers and cooling fans. And remember, trees are a renewable resource.

Then, there's the appeal of a hard copy. What fascinates me is how many people—from teenagers to millennials to those of a certain age—prefer print when reading both for pleasure and for school or work. Drawing examples from my own research, some of the reasons are aesthetic ("charm of actually turning pages" and "scent of a new book"). Others involve a sense of accomplishment ("able to see how much I read"), ease of annotation ("I can write on the pages"), and navigation ("easy to locate where I was"). In contrast, I hear abundant complaints about eye strain and headaches when using screens.

Much of what students liked about reading print involved their minds. They said "it's easier to focus," "my spatial memory works best," and "feel like the content sticks in my head more easily." Some also acknowledged they took more time with printed text and read more carefully—not really a surprise, since digital screens encourage scrolling and hasten us along to grab the next website or tweet.

But the real nail in the coffin for one-size-fits-all electronic reading is concentration. Over 92 percent of those I surveyed said they concentrate best when reading a hard copy. The explanation is hardly rocket science. When a digital device has an Internet connection, it's hard to resist the temptation to jump ship: I'll just respond to that text I heard come in, check the headlines, order those boots that are on sale.

Readers are human. If you dangle distractions in front of us (or if we know they are just a click or swipe away), it's hard not to take the bait.

Which brings us back to the question of what sorts of reading it makes sense to do onscreen and which to reserve for paper. If digital interruptions don't threaten your enjoyment or understanding of a text (but here, you have to be honest), then medium may not matter. Casual reading like Baldacci?[2] If you break to check sports scores, little harm done. Just don't expect to understand much of Joyce this way.

Focus on Meaning

1. According to Baron, what are the advantages of reading electronically versus reading a hard copy?

2. What different kinds of readings does Baron think are better suited to digital reading? Why? What kinds of readings does she think should be read in a hard-copy book? Why?

___

2. David Baldacci, a best-selling American thriller writer.

Focus on Strategy and Critical Thinking

1. What audience does Baron seem to be addressing? Does she expect them to have a preference for one kind of reading over the other?

2. Baron's title expresses her preference for "paper books" over e-readers. Do you think she makes a convincing case for hard-copy books? Why or why not?

3. This essay is organized as a comparison and contrast. Is this the best choice? Why or why not? What other pattern of development could Baron have used to structure her essay?

Focus on Language and Style

1. In paragraph 9, Baron uses three clichés: "nail in the coffin," "hardly rocket science," and "jump ship." What does each of these expressions mean? Does Baron's use of these clichés undercut her credibility, or does it add to her essay's effectiveness? Explain.

2. What is a "beach read" (2)? Why do you think Baron uses this expression instead of a more formal term?

Writing Practice

1. Write an essay in which you compare two texts you have read—one more suitable for digital reading and one more suitable for reading as hard copy. Why is each book better suited to one method of reading than to another?

2. Write an essay that compares the way you would read an online news article or textbook passage versus the way you would read the same text in a paper book.

TAKING MY PARENTS TO COLLEGE

Jennine Capó Crucet

Jennine Cap Crucet, the daughter of Cuban immigrants, was the first in her family to be born in the United States. Her writing deals with navigating the differences between Spanish, her native language, and English, as well as with the differences between Cuban and American culture. Her first novel, *Make Your Home among Strangers* (2015), is about a young Cuban American struggling to find her identity when she leaves her home in Miami for an elite university, an issue Crucet also writes about in the following 2015 *New York Times* essay. Crucet graduated with honors from Cornell University in 2003, the first in her family to obtain a college degree. As you read, notice the details Crucet uses to tell her story.

It was a simple question, but we couldn't find the answer in any of the 1
paperwork the college had sent. How long was my family supposed to
stay for orientation? This was 1999, so Google wasn't really a verb yet,
and we were a low-income family (according to my new school) without
regular Internet access.

I was a first-generation college student as well as the first in our 2
family to be born in America—my parents were born in Cuba—and we
didn't yet know that families were supposed to leave pretty much right
after they unloaded your stuff from the car.

We all made the trip from Miami, my hometown, to what would be 3
my new home at Cornell University. Shortly after arriving on campus,
the five of us—my parents, my younger sister, my abuela and me—found
ourselves listening to a dean end his welcome speech with the words:
"Now, parents, please: Go!"

Almost everyone in the audience laughed, but not me, and not 4
my parents. They turned to me and said, "What does he mean, *Go*?"
I was just as confused as they were: We thought we *all* needed to be
there for freshman orientation—the whole family, for the entirety of
it. My dad had booked their hotel through the day after my classes
officially began. They'd used all their vacation days from work and
had been saving for months to get me to school and go through our
orientation.

Every afternoon during that week, we had to go back to the only 5
department store we could find, the now-defunct Ames, for some stupid
thing we hadn't known was a necessity, something not in our budget:
shower shoes, extra-long twin sheets, mesh laundry bags. Before the
other families left, we carefully watched them—they knew what they
were doing—and we made new shopping lists with our limited vocabulary: *Those things that lift up the bed*, we wrote. *That plastic thing to carry
stuff to the bathroom.*

My family followed me around as I visited department offices dur- 6
ing course registration. *Only four classes?* they asked, assuming I was
mistakenly taking my first semester too easy. They walked with me to
buildings I was supposed to be finding on my own. They waited outside
those buildings so that we could all leave from there and go to lunch
together.

The five of us wandered each day through the dining hall's doors. 7
"You guys are still here!" the over-friendly person swiping ID cards said
after day three. "They sure are!" I chirped back, learning via the cues of
my hallmates that I was supposed to want my family gone. But it was
an act: We sat together at meals—amid all the other students, already
making friends—my mom placing a napkin and fork at each place, setting the table as we did at home.

I don't even remember the moment they drove away. I'm told it's one 8
of those instances you never forget, that second when you realize you're

WORD POWER

abuela Spanish word
for "grandmother"

WORD POWER

defunct no longer
functional

WORD POWER

cues signals

finally on your own. But for me, it's not there—perhaps because, when you're the first in your family to go to college, you never truly feel like they've let you go.

They did eventually leave—of course they did—and a week 9 into classes, I received the topics for what would be my first college paper, in an English course on the modern novel. I might as well have been my non-English-speaking grandmother trying to read and understand them: The language felt that foreign. I called my mom at work and in tears told her that I had to come home, that I'd made a terrible mistake.

She sighed into the phone and said: "Just read me the first question. 10 We'll go through it a little at a time and figure it out."

I read her the topic slowly, pausing after each sentence, waiting for 11 her to say something. The first topic was two paragraphs long. I remember it had the word *intersectionalities* in it. And the word *gendered*. And maybe the phrase *theoretical framework*. I waited for her response and for the ways it would encourage me, for her to tell me I could do this, that I would eventually be the first in my family to graduate from college.

"You're right," she said after a moment. "You're screwed." 12

Other parents—parents who have gone to college themselves— 13 might have known at that point to encourage their kid to go to office hours, or to the writing center, or to ask for help. But my mom thought I was as alone as I feared.

"I have no idea what any of that means," she said. "I don't even know 14 how it's a *question*."

While my college had done an excellent job recruiting me, I had no 15 road map for what I was supposed to do once I made it to campus. I'd already embarrassed myself by doing things like asking my R.A. what time the dorm closed for the night. As far as I knew, there'd been no mandatory meeting geared toward first-generation students like me: Aside from a check-in with my financial aid officer when she explained what work-study was (I didn't know and worried it meant I had to join the army or something) and where she had me sign for my loans, I was mostly keeping to myself to hide the fact that I was a very special kind of lost. I folded the sheet with the paper topics in half and put it in my desk drawer.

"I don't know what you're gonna do," my mom almost laughed. 16 "Maybe—have you looked in the dictionary?"

I started crying harder, my hand over the receiver. 17

"You still there?" she eventually asked, clearly hiding her own tears. 18 I murmured *Mmmhmm*.

"Look, just stick it out up there until Christmas," she said. "We have 19 no more vacation days this year. We can't take off any more time to go get you."

"O.K.," I swallowed. I started breathing in through my nose and out 20 through my mouth, calming myself. "I can do that," I said.

My mom laughed for real this time and said, "Mamita, you don't 21 really have a choice."

She didn't say this in a mean way. She was just telling me the truth. 22 "This whole thing was your idea, remember?" she said. Then she told me she had to go, that she needed to get back to work.

So I got back to work, too, and *Get back to work* became a sort of 23 mantra for me. I tackled the paper with the same focus that had landed me, to everyone's surprise—even my own—at Cornell in the first place. I did O.K. on it, earning a "B-/C" (I never found out how a grade could have a slash in it, but now that I'm an English professor I understand what he was trying to say). The professor had covered the typed pages with comments and questions, and it was in his endnote that he listed the various campus resources available to me.

My mom didn't ask outright what grade I earned—she eventually 24 stopped asking about assignments altogether—and I learned from my peers that grades were something that I didn't have to share with my parents the way I had in high school.

My grades were the first of many elements of my new life for which 25 they had no context and which they wouldn't understand. With each semester, what I was doing became, for them, as indecipherable as that paper topic; they didn't even know what questions to ask. And that, for me, is the quintessential quality of the first-generation college student's experience. It's not even knowing what you don't know.

WORD POWER

indecipherable
impossible to
understand

WORD POWER

quintessential
the most typical
example

Focus on Meaning

1. How are Crucet and her parents different from her fellow students and their parents? What things do other students know that Crucet and her family do not know?

2. What specific mistakes do Crucet and her family make?

Focus on Strategy and Critical Thinking

1. Reread the passages of dialogue (paragraphs 16–22 and elsewhere) in this essay. Why do you think Crucet includes this dialogue? What does it contribute to the essay?

2. Why does Crucet include information about herself and her family in paragraph 2? Is this information necessary? Explain.

3. Do you think Crucet should have provided more information about her parents' economic status? About their jobs? About her neighborhood? Why or why not?

Focus on Language and Style

1. In paragraph 11, Crucet mentions some words and expressions that she does not understand. Define each of these terms. Do you think her not knowing what they mean can be explained by the fact that she is a first-generation college student, or is there some other reason?

2. What is a *mantra* (23)? What does the word mean in the context of the paragraph in which it appears?

Writing Practice

1. In her conclusion, Crucet identifies the "quintessential quality of the first-generation college student's experience." According to her, "It's not even knowing what you don't know." Write an essay in which you discuss the things you didn't know when you began college and how you learned to navigate academic life.

2. Write an essay focusing on how you decided which college to attend. Did you consult your parents, teachers, or friends? What factors— for example, geography, finances, academic programs, or social life—influenced your decision?

MEN ARE FROM MARS, WOMEN ARE FROM VENUS

John Gray

Marriage counselor, seminar leader, and author John Gray has written a number of books that examine relationships between men and women. His best-known book, *Men Are from Mars, Women Are from Venus* (1992), suggests that men and women are at times so different that they might as well come from different planets. In the following excerpt from this book, Gray contrasts the different communication styles that he believes are characteristic of men and women. As you read, consider whether Gray's comparison oversimplifies the gender differences he discusses.

The most frequently expressed complaint women have about men is that men don't listen. Either a man completely ignores [a woman] when she speaks to him, or he listens for a few beats, assesses what is bothering her, and then proudly puts on his Mr. Fix-It cap and offers her a solution to make her feel better. He is confused when she doesn't appreciate this gesture of love. No matter how many times she tells him that he's not listening, he doesn't get it and keeps doing the same thing. She wants empathy, but he thinks she wants solutions.

1

WORD POWER

empathy
identification with another person's situation and feelings

The most frequently expressed complaint men have about women 2
is that women are always trying to change them. When a woman loves
a man she feels responsible to assist him in growing and tries to help
him improve the way he does things. She forms a home-improvement
committee, and he becomes her primary focus. No matter how much he
resists her help, she persists—waiting for any opportunity to help him or
tell him what to do. She thinks she's nurturing him, while he feels he's
being controlled. Instead, he wants her acceptance.

WORD POWER

nurturing supporting
and encouraging

These two problems can finally be solved by first understanding why 3
men offer solutions and why women seek to improve. Let's pretend to
go back in time, where by observing life on Mars and Venus—before the
planets discovered one another or came to Earth—we can gain some
insights into men and women.

Martians value power, competency, efficiency, and achievement. 4
They are always doing things to prove themselves and develop their
power and skills. Their sense of self is defined through their ability to
achieve results. They experience fulfillment primarily through success
and accomplishment.

Everything on Mars is a reflection of these values. Even their dress 5
is designed to reflect their skills and competence. Police officers, soldiers, businessmen, scientists, cab drivers, technicians, and chefs all
wear uniforms or at least hats to reflect their competence and power.

They don't read magazines like *Psychology Today*, *Self*, or *People*. 6
They are more concerned with outdoor activities, like hunting, fishing,
and racing cars. They are interested in the news, weather, and sports
and couldn't care less about romance novels and self-help books.

They are more interested in "objects" and "things" rather than peo- 7
ple and feelings. Even today on Earth, while women fantasize about
romance, men fantasize about powerful cars, faster computers, gadgets,
gizmos, and new more powerful technology. Men are preoccupied with
the "things" that can help them express power by creating results and
achieving their goals.

Achieving goals is very important to a Martian because it is a way for 8
him to prove his competence and thus feel good about himself. And for
him to feel good about himself he must achieve these goals by himself.
Someone else can't achieve them for him. Martians pride themselves
in doing things all by themselves. Autonomy is a symbol of efficiency,
power, and competence.

WORD POWER

autonomy
independence or
freedom

unsolicited not
asked for

Understanding this Martian characteristic can help women 9
understand why men resist so much being corrected or being told
what to do. To offer a man unsolicited advice is to presume that he
doesn't know what to do or that he can't do it on his own. Men are
very touchy about this, because the issue of competence is so very
important to them.

Because he is handling his problems on his own, a Martian rarely 10
talks about his problems unless he needs expert advice. He reasons: "Why

involve someone else when I can do it by myself?" He keeps his problems to himself unless he requires help from another to find a solution. Asking for help when you can do it yourself is perceived as a sign of weakness.

However, if he truly does need help, then it is a sign of wisdom to get 11 it. In this case, he will find someone he respects and then talk about his problem. Talking about a problem on Mars is an invitation for advice. Another Martian feels honored by the opportunity. Automatically he puts on his Mr. Fix-It hat, listens for a while, and then offers some jewels of advice.

This Martian custom is one of the reasons men instinctively offer 12 solutions when women talk about problems. When a woman innocently shares upset feelings or explores out loud the problems of her day, a man mistakenly assumes she is looking for some expert advice. He puts on his Mr. Fix-It hat and begins giving advice; this is his way of showing love and of trying to help.

He wants to help her feel better by solving her problems. He wants 13 to be useful to her. He feels he can be valued and thus worthy of her love when his abilities are used to solve her problems.

Once he has offered a solution, however, and she continues to be 14 upset it becomes increasingly difficult for him to listen because his solution is being rejected and he feels increasingly useless.

He has no idea that by just listening with empathy and interest he 15 can be supportive. He does not know that on Venus talking about problems is not an invitation to offer a solution.

Venusians have different values. They value love, communication, 16 beauty, and relationships. They spend a lot of time supporting, helping, and nurturing one another. Their sense of self is defined through their feelings and the quality of their relationships. They experience fulfillment through sharing and relating.

Everything on Venus reflects these values. Rather than building 17 highways and tall buildings, the Venusians are more concerned with living together in harmony, community, and loving cooperation. Relationships are more important than work and technology. In most ways their world is the opposite of Mars.

They do not wear uniforms like the Martians (to reveal their compe- 18 tence). On the contrary, they enjoy wearing a different outfit every day, according to how they are feeling. Personal expression, especially of their feelings, is very important. They may even change outfits several times a day as their mood changes.

Communication is of primary importance. To share their personal 19 feelings is much more important than achieving goals and success. Talking and relating to one another is a source of tremendous fulfillment.

This is hard for a man to comprehend. He can come close to under- 20 standing a woman's experience of sharing and relating by comparing it to the satisfaction he feels when he wins a race, achieves a goal, or solves a problem.

Instead of being goal oriented, women are relationship oriented; 21 they are more concerned with expressing their goodness, love, and caring. Two Martians go to lunch to discuss a project or business goal; they have a problem to solve. In addition, Martians view going to a restaurant as an efficient way to approach food: no shopping, no cooking, and no washing dishes. For Venusians, going to lunch is an opportunity to nurture a relationship, for both giving support to and receiving support from a friend. Women's restaurant talk can be very open and intimate, almost like the dialogue that occurs between therapist and patient.

On Venus, everyone studies psychology and has at least a master's 22 degree in counseling. They are very involved in personal growth, spirituality, and everything that can nurture life, healing, and growth. Venus is covered with parks, organic gardens, shopping centers, and restaurants.

Venusians are very intuitive. They have developed this ability through 23 centuries of anticipating the needs of others. They pride themselves in being considerate of the needs and feelings of others. A sign of great love is to offer help and assistance to another Venusian without being asked.

Because proving one's competence is not as important to a Venusian, 24 offering help is not offensive, and needing help is not a sign of weakness. A man, however, may feel offended because when a woman offers advice he doesn't feel she trusts his ability to do it himself.

A woman has no conception of this male sensitivity because for her 25 it is another feather in her hat if someone offers to help her. It makes her feel loved and cherished. But offering help to a man can make him feel incompetent, weak, and even unloved.

On Venus it is a sign of caring to give advice and suggestions. 26 Venusians firmly believe that when something is working it can always work better. Their nature is to want to improve things. When they care about someone, they freely point out what can be improved and suggest how to do it. Offering advice and constructive criticism is an act of love.

Mars is very different. Martians are more solution oriented. If some- 27 thing is working, their motto is don't change it. Their instinct is to leave it alone if it is working. "Don't fix it unless it is broken" is a common expression.

When a woman tries to improve a man, he feels she is trying to fix 28 him. He receives the message that he is broken. She doesn't realize her caring attempts to help him may humiliate him. She mistakenly thinks she is just helping him to grow.

Focus on Meaning

1. What specific character traits and habits does Gray associate with men?

2. What character traits and habits does he associate with women?

3. Does Gray see one set of characteristics as superior to the other, or does he consider them to be comparable?

Focus on Strategy and Critical Thinking

1. What serious point is Gray making by characterizing men as Martians and women as Venusians?

2. If you were going to add a more fully developed conclusion to sum up Gray's point about the differences between men and women, what kind of closing strategy would you use? Do you think the essay needs such a conclusion?

3. Do you think Gray is stereotyping men and women? Explain.

4. Regardless of how you answered the previous question, do you agree with Gray that men and women seem at times to be from two different planets? Why or why not?

Focus on Language and Style

1. Do you think Gray's choice of the labels *Martians* and *Venusians* is appropriate? Explain.

2. What other labels could Gray have used to contrast men and women?

Writing Practice

1. Are young boys and girls also from two different planets? Take a position on this issue, and support it in an essay. In your thesis statement, try to account for the differences you identify between boys and girls.

2. Identify one general area in which you believe men's and women's attitudes, behavior, or expectations are very different—for example, dating, careers, eating habits, sports, housekeeping, or driving. Write an essay (serious or humorous) that explores the differences you identify.

I OWE IT ALL TO COMMUNITY COLLEGE

Tom Hanks

Tom Hanks is an award-winning actor, producer, and director whose many popular films include *Apollo 13*, *Forrest Gump*, *Saving Private Ryan*, and the *Toy Story* franchise. In addition to two Academy Awards, Hanks has won four Golden Globes, two Screen Actors Guild Awards, a BAFTA Britannia Award for Excellence in Film, and seven Emmy Awards for producing and directing. Outside of the film industry, Hanks is an advocate for environmental causes and is involved in space advocacy groups. In addition, he has published a short story in the *New Yorker*, collects (and uses) manual typewriters, has created an iOS app that mimics the sound of typewriters, and has had an asteroid named after him (*12918 Tomhanks*). The following essay, originally published as an opinion piece in the *New York Times* in 2015, explains how Hanks's two years at community college prepared him for his career. As you read, consider the effectiveness of Hanks's use of his own personal story to support a more general recommendation.

In 1974, I graduated from Skyline High School in Oakland, Calif., an underachieving student with lousy SAT scores. Allowed to send my results to three colleges, I chose M.I.T. and Villanova, knowing such fine schools would never accept a student like me but hoping they'd toss some car stickers my way for taking a shot. I couldn't afford tuition for college anyway. I sent my final set of stats to Chabot, a community college in nearby Hayward, Calif., which, because it accepted everyone and was free, would be my alma mater.

For thousands of commuting students, Chabot was our Columbia, Annapolis, even our Sorbonne,[1] offering courses in physics, stenography, auto mechanics, certified public accounting, foreign languages, journalism—name the art or science, the subject or trade, and it was probably in the catalog. The college had a nursing program that churned out graduates, sports teams that funneled athletes to big-time programs, and parking for a few thousand cars—all free but for the effort and the cost of used textbooks.

Classmates included veterans back from Vietnam, women of every marital and maternal status returning to school, middle-aged men wanting to improve their employment prospects and paychecks. We could get our general education requirements out of the way at Chabot—credits we could transfer to a university—which made those two years an invaluable head start. I was able to go on to the State University in Sacramento (at $95 a semester, just barely affordable) and study no other subject but my major, theater arts. (After a year there I moved on, enrolling in a little thing called the School of Hard Knocks, a.k.a. Life.)

By some fluke of the punch-card computer era, I made Chabot's dean's list taking classes I loved (oral interpretation), classes I loathed (health, a requirement), classes I aced (film as art—like Jean Renoir's "Golden Coach" and Luis Buñuel's "Simon of the Desert"), and classes I dropped after the first hour (astronomy, because it was all math). I nearly failed zoology, killing my fruit flies by neglect, but got lucky in an English course, The College Reading Experience. The books of Carlos Castaneda were incomprehensible to me (and still are), but my assigned presentation on the analytic process called structural dynamics was hailed as clear and concise, though I did nothing more than embellish the definition I had looked up in the dictionary.

1. Columbia is an Ivy League university in New York City; Annapolis is the site of the U.S. Naval Academy in Maryland; and the Sorbonne, in Paris, France, was one of the first universities in the world.

WORD POWER

alma mater a school a person once attended

WORD POWER

embellish to make more interesting by adding details, mostly untrue

A public speaking class was unforgettable for a couple of reasons. 5
First, the assignments forced us to get over our self-consciousness. Second, another student was a stewardess, as flight attendants called themselves in the '70s. She was studying communications and was gorgeous. She lived not far from me, and when my VW threw a rod and was in the shop for a week, she offered me a lift to class. I rode shotgun that Monday-Wednesday-Friday totally tongue-tied. Communicating with her one on one was the antithesis of public speaking.

> **WORD POWER**
> **antithesis** opposite

Classes I took at Chabot have rippled through my professional pond. 6
I produced the HBO mini-series *John Adams* with an outline format I learned from a pipe-smoking historian, James Coovelis, whose lectures were riveting. Mary Lou Fitzgerald's Studies in Shakespeare taught me how the five-act structures of *Richard III, The Tempest,* and *Othello* focused their themes.

In Herb Kennedy's Drama in Performance, I read plays like *The* 7 *Hot L Baltimore* and *Desire Under the Elms*, then saw their productions. I got to see the plays he taught, through student rush tickets[2] at the American Conservatory Theater in San Francisco and the Berkeley Repertory Theater. Those plays filled my head with expanded dreams. I got an A.

Of course, I goofed off between classes eating French fries and look- 8
ing at girls; such are the pleasures, too, of schools that cost thousands of bucks a semester. Some hours I idled away in the huge library that anchored Chabot's oval quad. It's where I first read the *New York Times*, frustrated by its lack of comics.

> **WORD POWER**
> **idled** to do nothing

If Chabot's library still has its collection of vinyl records, you will 9
find my name repeatedly on the takeout slip of Jason Robards's performance of the monologues of Eugene O'Neill.[3] On Side B he was Hickey, from *The Iceman Cometh*, a recording I listened to twenty times at least. When I worked with Mr. Robards on the 1993 film *Philadelphia*, he confessed to recording those monologues at ten in the morning after lots and lots of coffee.

President Obama hopes to make two years of free community col- 10
lege accessible for up to nine million Americans. I'm guessing the new Congress will squawk at the $60 billion price tag, but I hope the idea sticks, because more veterans, from Iraq and Afghanistan this time, as well as another generation of mothers, single parents and workers who have been out of the job market, need lower obstacles between now and the next chapter of their lives. High school graduates without the finances for a higher education can postpone taking on big loans and maybe luck into the class that will redefine their life's work. Many lives will be changed.

2. Discounted tickets sold on the same day as the performance.
3. Eugene O'Neill (1888–1957): famous American playwright.

Chabot College is still in Hayward, though Mr. Coovelis, Ms. Fitzgerald, 11 and Mr. Kennedy are no longer there. I drove past the campus a few years ago with one of my kids and summed up my two years there this way: "That place made me what I am today."

Focus on Meaning

1. Why did Hanks end up enrolling at Chabot Community College?

2. In paragraph 11, Hanks says that Chabot "made me what I am today." In what sense did Chabot do this?

Focus on Strategy and Critical Thinking

1. In paragraph 10, Hanks discusses a proposal made by President Obama. Does this paragraph explain Hanks's purpose for writing this essay, or did he have another motive? Explain.

2. Do you think Hanks should have discussed the background and academic experiences of his fellow students? Why or why not?

3. Do you agree with Hanks that community colleges are a vital part of our higher education system? What benefits do they provide that four-year schools do not?

Focus on Language and Style

1. What exactly is the "School of Hard Knocks" (3)? What is the origin of this expression? In what sense is it an appropriate choice here?

2. In his introduction, Hanks mentions his "lousy SAT scores." What other negative attributes does he describe to characterize his younger self? Why does he do this?

Writing Practice

1. Watch the 2011 film *Larry Crowne*, which Hanks says was inspired by the time he spent at Chabot Community College. Take notes as you watch. Then, write an essay identifying specific things that link the film to this essay. In your essay, evaluate the film's success in conveying Hanks's personal experiences to his audience.

2. Although Jennine Capó Crucet (p. 627) attended an Ivy League university and Hanks enrolled at a community college, in many respects their experiences were similar. Write an essay in which you explore the similar challenges these two students faced, and propose some steps schools could take to make the adjustment easier for such students.

I'M COMING HOME

LeBron James

LeBron James was the first overall NBA draft pick in 2003, drafted straight from high school by the Cleveland Cavaliers. During his career as a professional basketball player, he has won countless titles and awards—including two NBA championships, two Olympic Gold Medals, four NBA Most Valuable Player Awards, and the 2004 NBA Rookie of the Year Award—and has played on the NBA All-Star team eleven times. In addition to his work on the court, in 2004 James founded the LeBron James Family Foundation, which focuses on helping students in his hometown of Akron, Ohio, from third grade through high school graduation. Despite his popularity, James's decision to leave the Cavaliers for the Miami Heat made him one of the nation's most disliked athletes (although his popularity soared again in 2016, when he lead the Cavs to a come-from-behind victory in the NBA finals, winning the MVP award). In "I'm Coming Home," which originally appeared in *Sports Illustrated* in 2014, James explains his decision to leave the Miami Heat and return to the Cavaliers. As you read, think about how James uses his ties to home to justify his choice.

1   Before anyone ever cared where I would play basketball, I was a kid from Northeast Ohio. It's where I walked. It's where I ran. It's where I cried. It's where I bled. It holds a special place in my heart. People there have seen me grow up. I sometimes feel like I'm their son. Their passion can be overwhelming. But it drives me. I want to give them hope when I can. I want to inspire them when I can. My relationship with Northeast Ohio is bigger than basketball. I didn't realize that four years ago. I do now.

2   Remember when I was sitting up there at the Boys & Girls Club in 2010?[1] I was thinking, *This is really tough*. I could feel it. I was leaving something I had spent a long time creating. If I had to do it all over again, I'd obviously do things differently, but I'd still have left. Miami, for me, has been almost like college for other kids. These past four years helped raise me into who I am. I became a better player and a better man. I learned from a franchise that had been where I wanted to go. I will always think of Miami as my second home. Without the experiences I had there, I wouldn't be able to do what I'm doing today.

3   I went to Miami because of D-Wade and CB.[2] We made sacrifices to keep UD.[3] I loved becoming a big bro to Rio.[4] I believed we could do something magical if we came together. And that's exactly what we did!

> **WORD POWER**
>
> **franchise** a team

1. When James made his announcement that he was leaving the Cleveland Cavaliers to play for the Miami Heat.
2. Miami Heat players Dwyane Wade and Chris Bosh.
3. Miami Heat player Udonis Haslem.
4. Miami Heat player Mario Chalmers.

The hardest thing to leave is what I built with those guys. I've talked to some of them and will talk to others. Nothing will ever change what we accomplished. We are brothers for life. I also want to thank Micky Arison and Pat Riley[5] for giving me an amazing four years.

I'm doing this essay because I want an opportunity to explain my- 4 self uninterrupted. I don't want anyone thinking: *He and Erik Spoelstra didn't get along. . . . He and Riles didn't get along. . . . The Heat couldn't put the right team together.* That's absolutely not true.

I'm not having a press conference or a party. After this, it's time to 5 get to work.

When I left Cleveland, I was on a mission. I was seeking champion- 6 ships, and we won two. But Miami already knew that feeling. Our city hasn't had that feeling in a long, long, long time. My goal is still to win as many titles as possible, no question. But what's most important for me is bringing one trophy back to Northeast Ohio.

I always believed that I'd return to Cleveland and finish my career 7 there. I just didn't know when. After the season, free agency wasn't even a thought. But I have two boys and my wife, Savannah, is pregnant with a girl. I started thinking about what it would be like to raise my family in my hometown. I looked at other teams, but I wasn't going to leave Miami for anywhere except Cleveland. The more time passed, the more it felt right. This is what makes me happy.

To make the move I needed the support of my wife and my mom, who 8 can be very tough. The letter from Dan Gilbert,[6] the booing of the Cleveland fans, the jerseys being burned—seeing all that was hard for them. My emotions were more mixed. It was easy to say, "OK, I don't want to deal with these people ever again." But then you think about the other side. What if I were a kid who looked up to an athlete, and that athlete made me want to do better in my own life, and then he left? How would I react? I've met with Dan, face-to-face, man-to-man. We've talked it out. Everybody makes mistakes. I've made mistakes as well. Who am I to hold a grudge?

I'm not promising a championship. I know how hard that is to 9 deliver. We're not ready right now. No way. Of course, I want to win next year, but I'm realistic. It will be a long process, much longer than it was in 2010. My patience will get tested. I know that. I'm going into a situation with a young team and a new coach. I will be the old head. But I get a thrill out of bringing a group together and helping them reach a place they didn't know they could go. I see myself as a mentor now and I'm excited to lead some of these talented young guys. I think I can help Kyrie Irving become one of the best point guards in our league. I think I can help elevate Tristan Thompson and Dion Waiters. And I can't wait to reunite with Anderson Varejao, one of my favorite teammates.

5. Arison is the Miami Heat owner, and Riley is the Miami Heat president.
6. Owner of the Cleveland Cavaliers, Gilbert wrote an open letter calling James "disloyal" and "narcissistic" after he left the team in 2010.

But this is not about the roster or the organization. I feel my calling 10 here goes above basketball. I have a responsibility to lead, in more ways than one, and I take that very seriously. My presence can make a difference in Miami, but I think it can mean more where I'm from. I want kids in Northeast Ohio, like the hundreds of Akron third-graders I sponsor through my foundation,[7] to realize that there's no better place to grow up. Maybe some of them will come home after college and start a family or open a business. That would make me smile. Our community, which has struggled so much, needs all the talent it can get.

In Northeast Ohio, nothing is given. Everything is earned. You work 11 for what you have.

I'm ready to accept the challenge. I'm coming home. 12

Focus on Meaning

1. According to James, why did he decide to return to Cleveland? List all the reasons—both personal and professional—that he discusses. Which do you see as his primary motive? Why?

2. In paragraph 2, James says, "Miami, for me, has been almost like college for other kids." What does he mean? Do you think this analogy makes sense? Explain.

3. What did James gain by moving back to Cleveland? What did he lose?

Focus on Strategy and Critical Thinking

1. In paragraph 4, James explains what motivated him to write this essay. Paraphrase his explanation. What other reasons for writing might he have had?

2. Evaluate the two very brief paragraphs that close this essay. Do you think the essay needs a more fully developed conclusion? Why or why not?

3. In paragraph 9, James makes clear to fans what they should expect as a result of his return. Why does he do this? In what sense is he anticipating his readers' responses to his essay?

Focus on Language and Style

1. Reread James's introductory paragraph, paying particular attention to its series of relative short sentences, many of which begin with the subject. Do you think some of these short sentences (or others throughout the essay) should be combined with adjacent sentences, or do you think they are effective as they are? Explain.

---

7. The LeBron James Family Foundation, an organization dedicated to supporting children and young adults in Ohio.

2. Evaluate the title of James's essay. What different connotations does the word *home* have here?

3. In paragraph 10, James says, "I feel my calling here goes above basketball. . . ." What does he mean by *calling*? Is this word a good choice?

Writing Practice

1. In paragraph 8, James speculates, "What if I were a kid who looked up to an athlete, and that athlete made me want to do better in my own life, and then he left?" Answer his question. Then, write an essay that traces several athletes' personal and professional careers. In your thesis statement, support or challenge the idea that athletes can (or should) be seen as role models.

2. Write an essay that explains a difficult decision you made. In your introduction, tell why you made this decision and what the alternatives were; in the body of your essay, explain how you reached the decision; and in your conclusion, summarize how you feel now about the decision you made.

STABILITY IN MOTION

Marina Keegan

Marina Keegan was a Boston-born writer whose work was featured in the *New Yorker* and the *New York Times*, as well as on NPR. Keegan died in a car accident five days after graduating *magna cum laude* from Yale University in 2012. Her final essay for the *Yale Daily News*, "The Opposite of Loneliness," went viral following her premature death. During her short writing career she produced many poems, essays, articles, and stories, some of which are collected in her posthumous book *The Opposite of Loneliness* (2014). At the time of her graduation, Keegan had been hired at the *New Yorker*, and her play *The Independents* was set to be produced by the New York International Fringe Festival (it was later chosen to appear in an encore series). In "Stability in Motion," first published in *The Opposite of Loneliness*, Keegan explains how a hand-me-down car came to represent a specific stage of her life. As you read, think of an object that holds the same kind of significance for you, and consider how you would describe it.

My 1990 Camry's DNA was designed inside the metallic walls of the   1
Toyota Multinational Corporation's headquarters in Tokyo, Japan;
transported via blueprint to the North American Manufacturing nerve
center in Hebron, Kentucky; grown organ by organ in four major

assembly plants in Alabama, New Jersey, Texas, and New York; trucked to 149 Arsenal Street in Watertown, Massachusetts; and steered home by my grandmother on September 4, 1990. It featured a 200 hp, 3.0 L V6 engine, a four-speed automatic, and an adaptive Variable Suspension System. She deemed the car too "high tech." In 1990 this meant a cassette player, a cup holder, and a manually operated moon roof.

During its youth, the car traveled little. In fifteen years my grandmother accumulated a meager twenty-five thousand miles, mostly to and from the market, my family's house, and the Greek jewelry store downtown. The black exterior remained glossy and spotless, the beige interior crisp and pristine. Tissues were disposed of, seats vacuumed, and food prohibited. My grandmother's old-fashioned cleanliness was an endearing virtue—one that I evidently did not inherit.

I acquired the old Camry through an awkward transaction. Ten days before my sixteenth birthday, my grandfather died. He was eighty-six and it had been long expected, yet I still felt a guilty unease when I heard the now surplus car would soon belong to me. For my grandmother, it was a symbolic good-bye. She needed to see only *one* car in her garage—needed to comprehend her loss more tangibly. Grandpa's car was the "nicer" of the two, so that one she would keep. Three weeks after the funeral, my grandmother and I went to the bank, I signed a check for exactly one dollar, and the car was legally mine. That was that. When I drove her home that evening, I manually opened the moon roof and put on a tape of Frank Sinatra. My grandma smiled for the first time in weeks.

Throughout the next three years, the car evolved. When I first parked the Toyota in my driveway, it was spotless, full of gas, and equipped with my grandmother's version of survival necessities. The glove compartment had a magnifying glass, three pens, and the registration in a little Ziploc bag. The trunk had two matching black umbrellas, a first aid kit, and a miniature sewing box for emergency repairs. Like my grandmother's wrists, everything smelled of Opium perfume.

For a while, I maintained this immaculate condition. Yet one Wrigley's wrapper led to two and soon enough my car underwent a radical transformation—the vehicular equivalent of a midlife crisis. Born and raised in proper formality, the car saw me as *that* friend from school, the bad example who washes away naïveté and corrupts the clean and innocent. We were the same age, after all—both eighteen. The Toyota was born again, crammed with clutter, and exposed to decibel levels it had never fathomed. I filled it with giggling friends and emotional phone calls, borrowed skirts and bottled drinks.

The messiness crept up on me. Parts of my life began falling off, forming an eclectic debris that dribbled gradually into every corner. Empty sushi containers, Diet Coke cans, half-full packs of gum, sweaters, sweatshirts, socks, my running shoes. My clutter was nondiscriminatory. I had every variety of newspaper, scratched-up English paper,

WORD POWER

meager small amount

WORD POWER

tangibly physically

WORD POWER

immaculate pure, untouched

WORD POWER

eclectic coming from many sources

biology review sheet, and Spanish flash card discarded on the seats after I'd sufficiently studied on my way to school. The left door pocket was filled with tiny tinfoil balls, crumpled after consuming my morning English muffin. By Friday, I had the entire house's supply of portable coffee mugs. By Sunday, someone always complained about their absence and I would rush out, grab them all, and surreptitiously place them in the dishwasher.

My car was not gross; it was occupied, cluttered, cramped. It 7 became an extension of my bedroom, and thus an extension of myself. I had two bumper stickers on the back: REPUBLICANS FOR VOLDEMORT and the symbol for the Equal Rights Campaign. On the back side windows were OBAMA '08 signs that my parents made me take down because they "dangerously blocked my sight lines." The trunk housed my guitar but was also the library, filled with textbooks and novels, the giant tattered copy of *The Complete Works of William Shakespeare* and all one hundred chapters of *Harry Potter* on tape. A few stray cassettes littered the corners, their little brown insides ripped out, tangled and mutilated. They were the casualties of the trunk trenches, sprawled out forgotten next to the headband I never gave back to Meghan.

On average, I spent two hours a day driving. It was nearly an hour 8 each way to school, and the old-fashioned Toyota—regarded with light-hearted amusement by my classmates—came to be a place of comfort and solitude amid the chaos of my daily routine. My mind was free to wander, my muscles to relax. No one was watching or keeping score. Sometimes I let the deep baritone of NPR's Tom Ashbrook lecture me on oil shortages. Other times I played repetitive mix tapes with titles like *Pancake Breakfast, Tie-Dye and Granola*, and *Songs for the Highway When It's Snowing*.

Ravaging my car, I often found more than just physical relics. For 9 two months I could hardly open the side door without reliving the first time he kissed me. His dimpled smile was barely visible in the darkness, but it nevertheless made me stumble backward when I found my way blushingly back into the car. On the backseat there was the June 3 issue of the *New York Times* that I couldn't bear to throw out. When we drove home together from the camping trip, he read it cover to cover while I played Simon and Garfunkel—hoping he'd realize all the songs were about us. We didn't talk much during that ride. We didn't need to. He slid his hand into mine for the first time when we got off the highway; it was only after I made my exit that I realized I should have missed it. Above this newspaper are the fingernail marks I dug into the leather of my steering wheel on the night we decided to *just be friends*. My car listened to me cry for all twenty-two-and-a-half miles home.

The physical manifestations of my memories soon crowded the car. 10 My right back speaker was broken from the time my older brother and I pulled an all-nighter singing shamelessly during our rainy drive home from the wedding. I remember the sheer energy of the storm, the lights, the music—moving through us, transcending the car's steel shell, and tracing the city. There was the folder left behind from the day I drove my dad to an interview the month after he lost his job. It was coincidental that *his* car was in the shop, but I knew he felt more pathetic that it was he, not his daughter, in the passenger seat. I kept my eyes on the road, feeling the confused sadness of a child who catches a parent crying.

I talked a lot in my car. Thousands of words and songs and swears 11 are absorbed in its fabric, just like the orange juice I spilled on my way to the dentist. It knows what happened when Allie went to Puerto Rico, understands the difference between the way I look at Nick and the way I look at Adam, and remembers the first time I experimented with talking to myself. I've practiced for auditions, college interviews, Spanish oral presentations, and debates. There's something novel about swearing alone in the car. Yet with the pressures of APs and SATs and the other acronyms that haunt high school, the act became more frequent and less refreshing.

My car has seen three drive-in movies. During *The Dark Knight*, its 12 battery died and, giggling ferociously, we had to ask the overweight family in the next row to jump it. The smell of popcorn permeated every crevice of the sedan, and all rides for the next week were like a trip to the movies. There was a variety of smells in the Camry. At first it smelled like my grandmother—perfume, mint, and mothballs. I went through a chai-tea phase during which my car smelled incessantly of Indian herbs. Some mornings it would smell slightly of tobacco and I would know immediately that my older brother had kidnapped it the night before. For exactly three days it reeked of marijuana. Dan had removed the shabbily rolled joint from behind his ear and our fingers had trembled as the five of us apprehensively inhaled. Nothing happened. Only the seats seemed to absorb the plant and get high. Mostly, however, it smelled like nothing to me. Yet when I drove my friends, they always said it had a distinct aroma. I believe this functioned in the same way as not being able to taste your own saliva or smell your own odor—the car and I were pleasantly immune to each other.

In the Buckingham Browne & Nichols High School yearbook I 13 was voted worst driver, but on most days I will refute this superlative. My car's love for parking tickets made me an easy target, but I rarely received other violations. My mistakes mostly harmed me, not others— locking my keys in the car or parking on the wrong side of the road. Once, last winter, I needed to refill my windshield wiper fluid and in a rushed frenzy poured an entire bottle of similarly blue antifreeze inside. Antifreeze, as it turns out, burns out engines if used in excess. I spent the next two hours driving circles around my block in a snowstorm, urgently expelling the antifreeze squirt by thick blue squirt. I played no music during this vigil. I couldn't find a playlist called *Poisoning Your Car*.

It may have been awkward-looking and muddled, but I was attached 14 to my car. It was a portable home that heated my seat in winter and

WORD POWER
incessantly
constantly

carried me home at night. I had no diary and rarely took pictures. That old Toyota Camry was an odd documentation of my adolescence. When I was seventeen, the car was seventeen. My younger brother entered high school last September and I passed my ownership on to him. In the weeks before I left for college, my parents made me clean it out for his sake. I spread six trash bags over the driveway, filling them with my car's contents as the August sun heated their black plastic. The task was strange, like deconstructing a scrapbook, unpeeling all the pictures and whiting out the captions.

Just like for my grandmother, it was a symbolic good-bye. Standing 15 outside my newly vacuumed car, I wondered, if I tried hard enough, whether I could smell the Opium perfume again, or if I searched long enough, whether I'd find the matching umbrellas and the tiny sewing kit. My brother laughed at my nostalgia, reminding me that I could still drive the car when I came home. He didn't understand that it wasn't just the driving I'd miss. That it was the tinfoil balls, the *New York Times*, and the broken speaker; the fingernail marks, the stray cassettes, and the smell of chai. Alone that night and parked in my driveway, I listened to Frank Sinatra with the moon roof slid back.

Focus on Meaning

1. What does this essay's title mean to you? How does it sum up the main idea Keegan wanted to get across to readers?

2. How did Keegan's car change when it was transferred to her from her grandmother? How do you think the car might have changed after Keegan passed it on to her brother?

3. In one sentence, sum up what the car meant to Keegan.

Focus on Strategy and Critical Thinking

1. What dominant impression of her car does Keegan convey here? Does this essay have a thesis statement? If so, where is it? If not, does it need one? Explain.

2. In paragraph 7, Keegan describes her car as "an extension of my-self." Where else does she identify parallels between her own life and the life of her car? What does her description of the car reveal about Keegan herself?

3. Does this essay rely primarily on subjective or objective description? Explain.

4. Keegan sometimes talks about her car in human terms—for example, when she says, "We were the same age, after all—both eighteen" (5). Where else does she talk about her car as if it is human? What does she achieve by doing this?

Focus on Language and Style

1. Choose three paragraphs, and circle all the descriptive adjectives and adverbs. Are these descriptive words largely positive or negative? Explain.

2. In paragraph 4, Keegan catalogs the contents of her car's glove compartment and trunk. Where else does she present catalogs of details? What do these catalogs add to her description?

Writing Practice

1. Write a description of your own (or your family's) car, van, or truck, including information about your own experiences during the years in which the vehicle was part of your life.

2. Write an essay that focuses on a childhood possession for which you now feel a sense of nostalgia. What did this possession mean to you in the past, and what does it mean to you now? How (and why) did your feelings for it change as you grew older? What do these changes reveal about the person you were—and about the person you are now?

HOW TO HAVE A DOG'S LIFE

Caroline Knapp

After graduating from Brown University, Caroline Knapp (1959–2012) spent seven years writing and editing for the *Boston Phoenix*. Knapp invented an alter ego named Alice K for her popular column, "Out There"; some of these columns were collected and published as her first book in 1994. Her best-selling memoir, *Drinking: A Love Story* (1996), bluntly discusses her two-decade struggle with alcoholism. *Pack of Two* (1998), Knapp's next book, which examines the relationships between humans and dogs, was also a best-seller. Two of her books have been published posthumously: *Appetites: Why Women Want* (2003) and *The Merry Recluse: A Life in Essays* (2004). In "How to Have a Dog's Life," which originally appeared in the *Boston Phoenix* in 1995, Knapp humorously details the many ways in which having a dog changes a person's life. As you read, note how Knapp alternates between the advantages and disadvantages of dog ownership.

Have you ever considered, or are you currently considering, acquiring   1
a canine companion? If so, understand in advance that your life will change dramatically. When asking you to contemplate life with a dog, most experts ask you to consider a fairly standard set of questions about leisure time and household space: how many hours a day might the dog

be left alone; do you have a yard where the dog can play; are you willing to train the dog; and so on. The experts also outline a fairly predictable set of general expectations: you'll need certain equipment for the dog (dish, leash), and you'll need to walk the dog, and here and there you'll have to take it to the vet. These are all important questions and factors, but acquiring a dog is actually a far more complex matter. This is what you are likely to go through.

1. *You idealize.* This happens before you get the dog. You have a charming set of images about man's best friend. Dogs are wonderful, obedient, intuitive creatures, correct? You will acquire one for yourself, and occasionally you will walk it and feed it, but for the most part you will go about your business as before while the dog sits quietly by your side and gazes lovingly into your eyes.

2. *You have a quick reality-check.* You acquire the dog. In the car on the way home from the animal shelter, the dog sits quietly by your side and gazes lovingly into your eyes. You beam with pride at your fine judgment and wise decision. Ten minutes later, you open the door to your boyfriend's apartment, shout "Look what I got!" and watch as the new pup trots up to the boyfriend and defecates on the rug. In shame, you hustle the pup over to your own home, where she promptly urinates all over the kitchen floor. Reality sinks in: this is all going to be a little more complicated than you thought.

3. *You lose your life.* Once upon a time, you were a busy, active, articulate young professional who spent the bulk of her time engaged in serious activities: working, reading, discussing important matters with friends and co-workers. Suddenly, within the course of three days, you become a frenzied, confused person who spends the bulk of her time standing in a stooped position with her arms dangling by her sides ready to swoop the urinating, defacating puppy up off the floor and outside. Your vocabulary has degenerated with amazing speed and now appears to consist of only two or three key words and phrases. "Yes!" "No!" "Drop it!" "No . . . no . . . no! outside! outside!" Stoop-and-swoop, stoop-and-swoop: this is what your life has become.

4. *You fall in love.* So, who minds a little stooping and scooping? By day two or three, you are so enchanted with the new pup you can hardly stand it. Everything she does is cute: her paws and ears and sharp little teeth are cute, the way she curls in a circle on the farthest corner of the sofa is cute, even the way she squats to pee is cute. You worry you might literally cuddle her to death and you periodically forget your boyfriend's name ("Who?"). At first, the pup slept in a crate. Then on the floor by your bed. Now she's on, and in, the bed. Your side. You are so smitten that you find yourself doing things like standing in the kitchen boiling her a chicken for dinner. Free-range chicken, from Bread & Circus. (Notably, you have a fight with your boyfriend about this: you haven't cooked him dinner in three years.) You suddenly appreciate why people join bereavement groups when their dogs die: you're already

WORD POWER

articulate well-spoken

WORD POWER

bereavement grief

worrying about how you'll handle your dog's demise and she isn't even four months old yet.

5. *You freak out.* This phase immediately follows. You wake up at 6 3 a.m. on the second or third day with your dog and you think, Oh my God, what have I gotten myself into?! This helpless, alien creature is totally dependent upon you and you feel completely inadequate to the task of caring for it. You worry about your inability to anticipate its needs. You worry about your basic character, your capacity for giving and nurturance. You worry about failing the dog in some fundamental way, scarring it for life. You feel completely sandbagged by these feelings—no one told you a tiny pup could generate such a flood of emotion and self-doubt and intensity—and you worry that you're in way over your head.

As the pup develops, other anxieties follow. You begin to act like the 7 mother of a toddler. You take the dog to the park and find yourself worrying about her social skills: will she get along with the other dogs? Does she have the right toys? You become way overidentified with the dog: if she refuses to obey a simple command (sit; heel; stop trying to follow the pizza-delivery guy out to his car), you take it as a sign of personal failure. If she rests her head sweetly on your boyfriend's knee instead of yours, you feel betrayed and paranoid: you haven't bonded with her sufficiently; you're not good enough for her; she hates you. You realize you've got way more emotions than you anticipated tied up in this tiny creature and you find yourself actually discussing your relationship with the dog in therapy. You ponder the irony: at $125 per hour, this is vastly more expensive than the dog was.

6. *You become obnoxious.* As the dog's social skills improve, yours 8 deteriorate. You realize you are having conversations about such topics as canine stool color and consistency with total strangers at the park, often at great length. You stand on street corners and enthuse loudly, wildly, as your dog pees in public. You begin to bore your friends with lengthy descriptions of the latest incredibly cute thing the pup did, and finally, you exact a promise from your family: if they ever—ever find that you've added the dog's name to your answering machine message, they will take you out and shoot you.

7. *Your social world changes.* You develop a new set of acquaintances, 9 many of whom meet each morning at the same park to walk their dogs: the dogs romp and play; the humans stand in a clump and oooh and aaaah like mothers at a sandbox. The dogs in this particular group have names like Max, Marty, Murray, Rita, Sadie, Frannie, and Lucille. You all stand around discussing the animals, sounding as though you're talking about a group of old Jewish people in the Catskills.

8. *You develop canine empathy.* Five or six weeks pass and you begin 10 to settle in. The pup is house-trained (mostly), the two of you have established a set of routines, and you are through the most acute phases of adjustment. You notice at this point that you have begun to think

like a dog, probably because you have read nothing but tomes on dog psychology for the last month. You now consider the pup a member of your pack and you are confident about your role as the leader, or alpha wolf. You understand that your pup thinks of you as the head of the pack, and you empathize with her interpretation of the world around her. Thus, when you return from your morning foray to the bakery to purchase breakfast, you blaze into the house with a flourish and announce proudly to the dog that you've been out hunting and killing scones. The dog looks excited by this, so later, when the guy from Bertucci's comes to deliver a large pepperoni pie, you emerge from the front hall with the box and inform the dog that your alpha wolf skills are so sophisticated and acute that a pizza has actually come and died at your front door. The dog wags her tail; your heart swells with pride.

Later that night, you're actually engaged in something non-canine 11 related (reading, watching TV), when you look up and notice: sitting across the room, the dog is gazing lovingly into your eyes. You gaze lovingly back. Then you stop for an instant and relish the moment: this is it; this is the combined result of all that love, all that anxiety, all that work. This is joy, the purest sort.

Focus on Meaning

1. Look carefully at each step in this process, and consider what it actually means. Then, rewrite each step so that its meaning is clearer and more specific.

2. According to Knapp, how does a person's life change when he or she acquires a dog?

3. What misconceptions about dog ownership does Knapp think most people have? How are these mistaken assumptions different from the reality of dog ownership?

Focus on Strategy and Critical Thinking

1. Knapp begins her essay by summarizing the advice "experts" usually give to potential pet owners. Why does she introduce her essay in this way?

2. What kind of audience is Knapp writing for? Experienced dog owners? Potential first-time dog owners? Both? Explain.

3. Do you think the essay's last paragraph is necessary? Should it be a separate step in the process? If so, what would you call this step?

4. Knapp includes both positive and negative details about dog ownership. All in all, is this essay's view of owning a dog positive or negative?

Focus on Language and Style

1. The steps in this process are introduced by numbered headings. Are these headings necessary, or are they distracting? Would it have been better to delete the headings and incorporate their content into the paragraphs that explain each step—for example, in paragraph 2, adding, "Before you get the dog, you idealize pet ownership." Why or why not?

2. Knapp speaks directly to her readers in this essay, addressing them as "you." What are the advantages and disadvantages of this strategy?

3. What does the expression "a dog's life" mean? Does it have positive or negative connotations? What does it mean in the context of this essay's title?

Writing Practice

1. Write an essay advising potential dog owners of the drawbacks of owning a dog. Your goal here is to discourage your readers from dog ownership.

2. Writing from a dog's point of view, explain how you would evaluate and select a potential owner.

A NEW WAY TO TACKLE GUN DEATHS

Nicholas Kristof

Nicholas Kristof, a columnist at the *New York Times* since 2001, writes about human rights, health, and global issues. His reporting has earned him two Pulitzer Prizes and numerous other awards, such as the Anne Frank Award (2008), the Fred Cuny Award for Prevention of Deadly Conflict (2007), and the Advancing Global Health Award (2013). Writing with his wife, journalist Sheryl WuDunn, Kristof has coauthored several books, including the best-selling *Half the Sky* (2008), which explores the oppression of women around the globe. Hoping to inspire more interest in global issues, Kristof runs an annual contest whose winners he takes on a trip to report on topics such as poverty, human rights, and disease. His 2007 trip to Congo was made into an HBO documentary, *Reporter*. The following essay, originally published in 2015 in the *New York Times*, discusses how to reduce gun deaths by making guns themselves safer instead of banning them. As you read, consider the pros and cons of Kristof's argument.

We've mourned too often, seen too many schools and colleges devastated   1
by shootings, watched too many students get an education in grief. It's time for a new approach to gun violence.

WORD POWER

brazen bold; shameless

We're angry, but we also need to be smart. And frankly, liberal efforts, 2 such as the assault weapons ban, were poorly designed and saved few lives, while brazen talk about banning guns just sparked a backlash that empowered the National Rifle Association.

What we need is an evidence-based public health approach—the 3 same model we use to reduce deaths from other potentially dangerous things around us, from swimming pools to cigarettes. We're not going to eliminate guns in America, so we need to figure out how to coexist with them.

WORD POWER

deluge flood

First, we need to comprehend the scale of the problem: It's not 4 just occasional mass shootings like the one at an Oregon college on Thursday,[1] but a continuous deluge of gun deaths, an average of 92 every day in America. Since 1970, more Americans have died from guns than died in all U.S. wars going back to the American Revolution.

WORD POWER

lobbyist person who tries to influence government officials on the behalf of a particular interest or group

When I reported a similar figure in the past, gun lobbyists insisted 5 that it couldn't possibly be true. But the numbers are unarguable: fewer than 1.4 million war deaths since 1775, more than half in the Civil War, versus about 1.45 million gun deaths since 1970 (including suicides, murders and accidents).

If that doesn't make you flinch, consider this: In America, more pre- 6 schoolers are shot dead each year (82 in 2013) than police officers are in the line of duty (27 in 2013), according to figures from the Centers for Disease Control and Prevention and the FBI.

WORD POWER

scoff to dismiss in a mocking way

More than 60 percent of gun deaths are suicides, and most of the 7 rest are homicides. Gun enthusiasts scoff at including suicides, saying that without guns people would kill themselves by other means. In many cases, though, that's not true.

WORD POWER

asphyxiate to choke

In Great Britain, people used to kill themselves by putting their heads 8 in the oven and asphyxiating themselves with coal gas. This accounted for almost half of British suicides in the late 1950s, but Britain then began switching from coal gas to natural gas, which is much less lethal. Sticking one's head in the oven was no longer a reliable way to kill oneself—and there was surprisingly little substitution of other methods. Suicide rates dropped, and they stayed at a lower level.

The British didn't ban ovens, but they made them safer. We need to 9 do the same with guns.

When I tweeted about the need to address gun violence after the 10 college shooting in Roseburg, Ore., a man named Bob pushed back. "Check out car accident deaths," he tweeted sarcastically. "Guess we should ban cars."

WORD POWER

exemplify serve as a good example of something

Actually, cars exemplify the public health approach we need to apply 11 to guns. We don't ban cars, but we do require driver's licenses, seatbelts,

---

1. Mass shooting that occurred at Umpqua Community College in Roseburg, Oregon, on October 1, 2015. Nine people died, and nine others were injured in the attack.

airbags, padded dashboards, safety glass, and collapsible steering columns. And we've reduced the auto fatality rate by 95 percent.

One problem is that the gun lobby has largely blocked research on 12 making guns safer. Between 1973 and 2012, the National Institutes of Health awarded 89 grants for the study of rabies and 212 for cholera[2]— and only three for firearms injuries.

Daniel Webster, a public health expert at Johns Hopkins University, 13 notes that in 1999, the government listed the gun stores that had sold the most weapons later linked to crimes. The gun store at the top of the list was so embarrassed that it voluntarily took measures to reduce its use by criminals—and the rate at which new guns from the store were diverted to crime dropped 77 percent.

But in 2003, Congress barred the government from publishing such 14 information.

Why is Congress enabling pipelines of guns to criminals? 15

Public health experts cite many ways we could live more safely with 16 guns, and many of them have broad popular support.

A poll this year found that majorities even of gun-owners favor uni- 17 versal background checks; tighter regulation of gun dealers; safe storage requirements in homes; and a ten-year prohibition on possessing guns for anyone convicted of domestic violence, assault or similar offenses. 18

We should also be investing in "smart gun" technology, such as weapons that fire only with a PIN or fingerprint. We should adopt microstamping that allows a bullet casing to be traced back to a particular gun. We can require liability insurance for guns, as we do for cars.

It's not clear that these steps would have prevented the Oregon 19 shooting. But Professor Webster argues that smarter gun policies could reduce murder rates by up to 50 percent—and that's thousands of lives a year. Right now, the passivity of politicians is simply enabling shooters.

The gun lobby argues that the problem isn't firearms; it's crazy 20 people. Yes, America's mental health system is a disgrace. But to me, it seems that we're all crazy if we as a country can't take modest steps to reduce the carnage that leaves America resembling a battlefield.

> **WORD POWER**
> **passivity** allowing others to do things without pushing back

Focus on Meaning

1. What does Kristof mean when he says that we need "an evidenced-based public health approach" (paragraph 3) to reduce deaths from guns?

2. What steps does Kristof say the country should take to reduce gun violence? In what sense are his suggestions "evidence based"?

Focus on Strategy and Critical Thinking

1. Why does Kristof wait until nearly the end of the essay to introduce his suggestions for reducing gun violence?

2. Bacterial disease usually spread through contaminated water.

2. In paragraphs 8 and 9, Kristof compares ovens in Great Britain to guns. In paragraph 11, he compares guns to cars. What point is he trying to make with these comparisons? Is he successful?

3. Studies show that the majority of criminals use illegal guns to commit crimes. How does this fact affect Kristof's argument?

4. Where does Kristof address opposing arguments? Does he counter these arguments effectively?

Focus on Language and Style

1. In paragraph 20, Kristof uses the word *crazy* twice. Is the meaning of this word the same in both cases? Explain.

2. The essay's first sentence consists of three parallel clauses. What is the effect of these three clauses in one sentence? Why does Kristof begin his essay this way?

Writing Practice

1. What do you think should be done to reduce gun violence? Write an essay in which you agree or disagree with Kristof. Be specific, and make sure you address Kristof's suggestions in your essay.

2. Write an essay in which you argue that video games, movies, and television either encourage or discourage gun violence. Make sure your essay has a clear thesis and that you support your points by referring to specific video games, movies, or TV shows with which you are familiar.

AN ACT THAT ENABLED ACCEPTANCE

Ben Mattlin

After graduating from Harvard University with honors in 1984, Ben Mattlin began a career in editing that has taken him to many financial publications, most recently *Financial Advisor* and *Institutional Investor*. Born with spinal muscular atrophy, Mattlin has written essays on the subject of disability for such publications as *Self*, *USA Today*, and the *Los Angeles Times*. His memoir, *Miracle Boy Grows Up: How the Disability Rights Revolution Saved My Life* (2012), discusses the parallels between Mattlin's life and the fight for equality for the disabled, a subject he also covers in this 2015 essay for the *New York Times*. As you read, consider the impact the disability rights movement had on Mattlin's life.

Visit me and you'll see, prominently displayed in my living room, my   1
wedding portrait. My wife looks radiant in a lacy white cloud, standing

beside tuxedo'd me in my motorized wheelchair. I'm not propped on a sofa or lounger; my wheelchair is deliberately not cropped out of the photo. It's literally part of the picture, as it's always been for us.

We were married almost exactly one year before passage of the Americans with Disabilities Act, the 25th anniversary of which will be celebrated July 26. I'm a lifelong wheelchair user because of a genetic condition called spinal muscular atrophy; my wife is what's now called "neurotypical," a fancy term for nondisabled. But on our wedding day, my disability—and my concomitant lack of basic civil-rights protections—was far from our minds.

Of course, the A.D.A. had nothing to do with marriage equality. What it did do, the government noted, was mandate equal access in employment, public accommodations and government programs for anyone who "has a physical or mental impairment that substantially limits one or more major life activities" or "a history or record of such an impairment" or "is perceived by others as having such an impairment." This meant public spaces like stores, theaters and restaurants had to install ramps or electric lifts; many doorways had to be widened; elevators revamped with Braille buttons; and public restrooms altered. Employers, too, had to make "reasonable accommodations" for disabled workers, such as allowing flex time or providing telephone headsets or appropriate computer software.

Before the A.D.A., only public schools and other institutions that received federal funding faced similar requirements. A few states—notably, California—had already established some accessibility standards, but nothing as broad-based as the A.D.A.

Back then, I was only marginally aware that I could be—or even had been—discriminated against. I tended to minimize my disability and its impact on others. My wife and I were probably more concerned about the fact that I was a New York urbanite and she a suburban Californian. We met on summer break from college, talking endlessly during long warm-evening strolls, trying to keep pace with each other though we moved by different means. Our many differences, I think now, were part of the attraction. To me, her West Coast free-spiritedness was exotic; to her, my determination must have seemed like a force of nature. Also, she told me later, seeing the no-nonsense way my family assisted me at home helped demystify my limitations and needs. The novelty of our relationship felt like an asset, not a liability.

Certainly, the longevity of our union also owes a great debt to honest communication and creative problem solving. The wedding photo is a good example. We put it up only after we grew tired of delivery-men and repairmen and housecleaners asking if she was my sister, or my nurse. Some have even called her a saint for staying with me. It makes us want to scream: "No! The disability didn't come as a tragic surprise. It was there from day one, a strand in the very fabric of our lives together."

WORD POWER
concomitant associated

WORD POWER
mandate to require

WORD POWER
urbanite someone who lives in a city

The picture also comes in handy if my wife isn't home and some   7
clueless visitor addresses my attendant instead of me, discounting my
presence. I'll try to draw attention to the photo, as a way of saying, "Hey,
I live here, and I have a life beyond these wheels."

When I was in grade school, my parents fought to get me "main-   8
streamed" into regular classrooms rather than segregated in special
education. (Full inclusion, as it's now known, didn't become law until
I was in eighth grade.) When I started college, at Harvard, it was the
first year accessibility was required at universities and similar institutions, per the Rehabilitation Act of 1973 (which took years to be fully
implemented). One dean, I painfully recall, quashed my request for
roommates instead of the isolation of a separate dorm room. He said
he feared how my disability might affect *them*. Forget about how this
sequestration affected *me*.

More shocking still is how easily I accepted his judgment. Accom-   9
modating the disabled did seem like an impossible imposition then.
Indeed, when the A.D.A. passed, one of the biggest fears was what it
would cost businesses, even though the law plainly states that accommodations can't cause "undue hardship" for other patrons or employees
or the employer's bottom line. (The Department of Labor found that
modifications for workers with disabilities averaged only $500 each.)
Moreover, businesses that make accessibility modifications can receive
tax benefits—a deduction of up to $15,000 a year for removing barriers,
as well as a tax credit of up to $5,000 annually for small businesses.

People with disabilities also represent a huge potential market. The   10
United States Census counts nearly one in five Americans as disabled,
and we spend $17.3 billion a year on travel alone, according to the Open
Doors Organization, a Chicago-based nonprofit.

Looking back, perhaps the most unexpected achievement of the   11
A.D.A. isn't the wheelchair lifts on buses or the sign-language interpret-
ers at political conventions. It's that it gave people like me a sense of
entitlement, of belonging, of pride.

The A.D.A. is about more than ramps and Braille; it's about dis-   12
pelling stereotypes, ensuring parity and fairness, creating opportunities
and opening up our society to the full spectrum of types and needs. It's
about accepting, even welcoming, a huge and often marginalized seg-
ment of the population.

Our two teenage daughters, both able-bodied, have grown up in a   13
different world. Recently, one came home from her high school's Diversity Day incensed by a presentation about disabilities. "It was all about
being kind to people who face difficulties, which is fine," she said, "but
there was nothing about respect or empowerment or equality!"

Maybe I'll bring my wedding portrait to the next Diversity Day.   14
Whether we knew it or not at the time, our brand of mixed marriage
sends a powerful message.

WORD POWER
quashed put an end to

WORD POWER
sequestration
isolation

WORD POWER
imposition burden

WORD POWER
parity equality

WORD POWER
incensed enraged

Focus on Meaning

1. What were the specific provisions of the Americans with Disabilities Act (ADA)?

2. According to Mattlin, what is the most important result of the ADA? How did the ADA "enable acceptance" for people like him?

3. What instances of prejudice did Mattlin encounter? How did he respond in these situations? Do you think he might respond differently now? Why or why not?

4. Generally speaking, what impact did Mattlin's disability have on his life?

Focus on Strategy and Critical Thinking

1. Despite the challenges he faced, Mattlin's tone in this essay is matter-of-fact and, at times, even optimistic. Why do you think he uses this kind of tone rather than using an angry or sarcastic tone?

2. Why does Mattlin begin and end his essay by discussing his wedding portrait (also discussed in paragraphs 6 and 7)?

3. In paragraph 10, Mattlin notes that "people with disabilities . . . represent a huge potential market" for businesses. Why does he include this information?

4. Contrast the content of paragraph 3 with the content of paragraph 12. What is the difference between the kinds of information these two paragraphs present?

Focus on Language and Style

1. In characterizing people like himself, Mattlin uses the terms "wheelchair user" and "disabled" where some might use the older terms *wheelchair bound* and *handicapped*. What is the difference?

2. What does the word "mainstreamed" (8) mean? In what sense is this an appropriate term for what it denotes?

Writing Practice

1. Suppose you are organizing a Diversity Day at a middle school or a workplace. What kind of speakers, exhibits, presentations, and materials would you include? Write an essay identifying your goals and explaining how you would achieve them.

2. If you suddenly became disabled, how would your life change? Write an essay in which you explain how a specific disability might affect your personal and professional life.

GROUP MOBILIZATION AS A DESPERATE CRY FOR HELP

Christopher Monks

Christopher Monks is the editor of the popular humor website *McSweeney's Internet Tendency*, where the following essay first appeared in 2003. Founded by writer Dave Eggers in 1998, *McSweeney's* is known for its irreverent and quirky writing and has grown into a separate publishing company. Monks began contributing to the *Internet Tendency* in 2003 and took over as editor in 2007. As you read, think about how Monks uses humor to present the steps in a process.

1 HELLO! You are invited to take part in a flash mob, the project that creates an inexplicable mob of people for ten minutes or less, in the front yard of my ex-girlfriend Deborah's house, tomorrow at 6:13 p.m. Please tell anybody else who you think might be interested in joining us.

2 INSTRUCTIONS: 1. We'll meet outside the Crazy Pizza around the corner from Deborah's place. Be there by 6 p.m. Please be respectful of Crazy Pizza's employees and patrons, and refrain from ordering pizza or Crazy Cinnaballs.

3 2. At exactly 6:05 p.m. I will pass out slips of paper with general instructions and poster boards. One-third of the poster-boards will read "I will never stop lovin' you, Deborah"; one-third will read "Why do you insist on ruining my life?"; and one-third will read "Please don't throw out my comic book collection."

4 3. Once the instructions and poster boards have been passed out, I will organize the group. All of the guys who are better looking than me will be sent to the back and will be required to wear sad clown masks. If I find that a better-looking-than-me guy in a sad clown mask is still better-looking than me I will ask him to leave. This may seem a little paranoid, but you don't know Deborah like I know Deborah. All of the just-as-good-looking-as-me guys will be placed in the middle of the line, and the guys who I think are uglier than me will get to be in the front. Women can choose to be wherever they want.

5 4. At 6:10 p.m. we will walk over in a silent and orderly fashion to Deborah's place. Really hot-looking women are encouraged to walk with me, hold my hand, and act like I'm their new boyfriend.

6 5. We will arrive at Deborah's at 6:13 p.m. sharp. Please arrange yourself in Deborah's front yard in the same order you were in while walking over. Depending on the size of the mob, some of the better-looking-than-me guys in sad clown masks may have to stand on the sidewalk. Please don't complain about it if this is necessary. Be tough.

7 6. Once we are organized in our appropriate places, everyone should take a moment to notice the rhododendron bush in Deborah's yard.

I bought that for her in celebration of our three-month anniversary. I planted it for her, too. While the bush won't be in bloom, please believe me when I tell you that its flowers are only eclipsed in beauty by Deborah's magnificent emerald green eyes.

7. We will then stand quietly in Deborah's front yard for five min- 8
utes or until Deborah comes out of her house. If any bystander should happen by and ask you what is going on, politely answer, "I'm a fan of doughnuts, and this is the home of the Doughnut Queen."

8. If after five minutes Deborah hasn't come out of her house, I will 9
ring her doorbell. As soon as Deborah opens her door, those people with the "I will never stop lovin' you, Deborah" posters should stoically raise them above their heads. Everybody else will begin singing the Peter Gabriel song "In Your Eyes." Be sure to really sell the tune. No mumbling.

> **WORD POWER**
>
> **stoically**
> not showing any
> emotion

9. My bet is that Deborah will be embarrassed at first. She'll blush 10
and smile and not know what to say. At 6:19 lower the signs and stop singing. It's then when I'll ask her to take me back. However, I'm sure that Deborah, being Deborah, will break my heart yet again. When she does, those holding the "Why do you insist on ruining my life?" post-ers will raise them up. Everyone else will then sing "Love Bites" by Def Leppard. If you want to try to hum the guitar solo part feel free.

10. This will no doubt make Deborah upset, and her ugly side will 11
soon be on display for all to see. Don't be afraid; just stand your ground and continue singing. She'll probably say means things like, "He still owes me $927.00 for back rent," or "He tried to French kiss my sister," but pay her no mind. I'm not even attracted to her sister. Honest.

11. Any better-looking-than-me guy in a sad clown mask that tries 12
to take advantage of the situation by offering to console Deborah will be asked to leave.

12. As Deborah's calling the police, those holding the "Please don't 13
throw out my comic book collection" posters will raise them up. Every-body else will sing "If You're Happy and You Know It Clap Your Hands."

13. At 6:23 p.m. or when we hear the sirens, whichever comes first, 14
we will disperse in an orderly manner. I may stick around for a bit, but don't bother waiting for me; I'll be curled up and crying by the rhodo-dendron bush. I feel it is something I just need to do. So go on. I'll be all right.

Thanks! I look forward to seeing you tomorrow. It'll be great. Things 15
are really starting to look up for me. I can feel it. In the slight chance Deborah is not home when we get to her front yard we will return to Crazy Pizza, get something to eat, and try again later.

Focus on Meaning

1. What does the writer hope to accomplish by organizing this flash mob? What has led to his decision? Is this really a "desperate cry for help" or something else? Explain.

2. Why does the writer set the arrival time at "6:13 p.m. sharp" (paragraph 6)? Why does he ask participants to "notice the rhododendron bush" (7)? That Deborah has an "ugly side" (11)? What do these details reveal about the writer?

3. Based on clues in this essay, why do you think Deborah ended the relationship?

Focus on Strategy and Critical Thinking

1. This essay is written as a set of instructions. Why? How else could it be organized?

2. Why do you think the writer keeps mentioning the physical appearance of the men and women in the group? What does this tell you about him—and, perhaps, about his relationship with Deborah?

3. In his conclusion, the writer says, "Things are really starting to look up for me. I can feel it." Is he right?

Focus on Language and Style

1. Several times in this essay, the writer includes a very short sentence—for example, "Be tough" (6), "No mumbling" (9), and "So go on" (14). What does this stylistic strategy accomplish?

2. Why does Monks use the word *desperate* in his title? Is he being ironic or serious? What other word might more accurately describe this "cry for help"?

Writing Practice

1. Write an essay in which you trace the stages of the writer's relationship with Deborah from first meeting to breakup. Give each stage in the relationship a descriptive title. Include a thesis statement that sums up the lesson the writer learned (or should have learned) from this relationship. (If you like, you can write from Deborah's perspective.)

2. Write a humorous essay that explains how to organize a flash mob for another "desperate cry for help"—for example, demonstrating for a job promotion or a higher grade.

WHAT REALLY KEEPS WOMEN OUT OF TECH

Eileen Pollack

Eileen Pollack is a fiction and essay writer whose books include the short story collection *In the Mouth* (2008), the nonfiction book *Woman Walking Ahead: In Search of Catherine Weldon and Sitting Bull* (2003), and the novel *Breaking and Entering* (2012). Her most recent book, *The*

Only Woman in the Room: Why Science Is Still a Boys' Club (2015), explores the discrepancy between the number of women and men in math- and science-based industries, a subject she also discusses in the following 2015 essay from the *New York Times*. As you read, think about what you know about the roles of men and women in the tech industry and whether or not this article changes your ideas.

Technology companies know they have a gender and diversity problem 1 in their work force, and they are finally taking steps to try to fix it. But where are those new employees going to come from if women and minority students aren't opting to study computer science or engineering?

Figuring out why people who choose not to do something don't in 2 fact do it is like attempting to interview the elves who live inside your refrigerator but come out only when the light is off. People already working for a company might tell you what makes them unhappy. But these complaints won't necessarily pinpoint the factors that keep women and minorities away from studying computer science in the first place.

As a woman who earned a bachelor of science degree in physics 3 in the 1970s but left the field because I felt I didn't belong, I have long been interested, and focus here, on women in science and math. I was fascinated, but not surprised, to learn that many young women today avoid studying computer science because they, too, fear they won't fit in.

For the past six years, Sapna Cheryan, a psychology professor at the 4 University of Washington, has been studying why girls in high school are significantly less likely than boys to sign up for a class in computer science, take the Advanced Placement exam in that subject, or express interest in computer science as a career, and why female college students are four times less likely than men to major in computer science or engineering, even though they test extremely well in math.

Over and over, Dr. Cheryan and her colleagues have found that 5 female students are more interested in enrolling in a computer class if they are shown a classroom (whether virtual or real) decorated not with "Star Wars" posters, science-fiction books, computer parts and tech magazines, but with a more neutral décor—art and nature posters, coffee makers, plants and general-interest magazines.

The researchers also found that cultural stereotypes about com- 6 puter scientists strongly influenced young women's desire to take classes in the field. At a young age, girls already hold stereotypes of computer scientists as socially isolated young men whose genius is the result of genetics rather than hard work. Given that many girls are indoctrinated to believe that they should be feminine and modest about their abilities, as well as brought up to assume that girls are not innately gifted at science or math, it is not surprising that so few can see themselves as successful computer scientists.

In another experiment, Dr. Cheryan and her colleagues arranged for 7 female undergraduates to talk to an actor pretending to be a computer

WORD POWER

indoctrinated taught to accept certain beliefs without questioning

WORD POWER

innately naturally

science major. If the actor wore a T-shirt that said "I CODE THEREFORE I AM" and claimed to enjoy video games, the students expressed less interest in studying computer science than if the actor wore a solid shirt and claimed to enjoy hanging out with friends—even if the T-shirt-clad actor was another woman.

Such superficial stereotypes might seem laughably outdated. And yet, studies show that the public's image of a scientist hasn't changed since the 1950s. And such stereotypes do have a basis in reality. Who could fail to notice that only one of the eight people awarded Nobel Prizes in science or medicine last week was a woman? 8

The percentage of women studying computer science actually has fallen since the 1980s. Dr. Cheryan theorizes that this decline might be partly attributable to the rise of pop-culture portrayals of scientists as white or Asian male geeks in movies and TV shows like *Revenge of the Nerds* and *The Big Bang Theory*. The media's intense focus on start-up culture and male geniuses such as Steve Jobs and Bill Gates might also have inspired more young men than women to enter the field. 9

Men sometimes scoff that if young women let such nebulous factors deter them from careers in physics or computer science, the women are exercising their own free choice, and if girls were tough enough, such exaggerated stereotypes and feelings of discomfort wouldn't discourage them. 10

Yet I wonder how many young men would choose to major in computer science if they suspected they might need to carry out their coding while sitting in a pink cubicle decorated with posters of *Sex and the City*, with copies of *Vogue* and *Cosmo* scattered around the lunchroom. In fact, Dr. Cheryan's research shows that young men tend not to major in English for the same reasons women don't pick computer science: They compare their notions of who they are to their stereotypes of English majors and decide they won't fit in. 11

All this meshes with my own experience. Even though I felt more comfortable wearing a T-shirt and jeans than a skirt and high heels, after four years of studying physics at Yale I felt so much pressure to dress and act like a man that I became extremely uncomfortable about my identity as a woman. I loved teaching myself to program the university's new IBM mainframe. What a miracle it seemed that boxes of punched cardboard cards could produce pages and pages of a printed simulation of a collision between a K meson and a proton. 12

But the summer I worked as a programmer at Oak Ridge National Laboratory in Tennessee, I felt out of place among my mostly male colleagues because I hated drinking beer and didn't like being mocked for reading novels. Not to mention that the men who controlled access to the computer made me listen to a barrage of sexist teasing if I wanted to be given that day's code to run my program. 13

WORD POWER

attributable resulting from a specific cause

WORD POWER

nebulous vague

WORD POWER

meshes matches

Despite my passion for physics, I didn't feel what Dr. Cheryan calls 14
"an ambient sense of belonging" and left science. As this new research
demonstrates, young women today still are avoiding technical disci-
plines because, like me, they are afraid they won't fit in.

WORD POWER

ambient related
to the immediate
surroundings of
something

To make computer science more attractive to women, we might 15
help young women change how they think about themselves and what's
expected of them. But we might also diversify the images of scientists
they see in the media, along with the décor in the classrooms and offices
in which they might want to study or work.

As Dr. Cheryan points out, stereotypes are only partly true, and 16
women who actually take classes in computer science don't hold the
same prejudices as women who get their ideas from pop culture.

This is why Mayor Bill de Blasio's recent announcement that within 17
ten years all of New York City's public schools must offer at least some
training in computer science is so important. All students will have the
opportunity to decide for themselves if they like this work.

At the college level, some fairly simple changes have proved 18
stunningly effective. At Harvey Mudd College, strategies such as creating separate introductory classes for students with no programming
experience and renaming courses ("Introduction to programming in
Java" became "Creative approaches to problem solving in science and
engineering using Python") led to an increase in the percentage of computer science majors who are female, from 10 to 40 percent, in four
years.

Computer scientists and engineers are going to be designing the 19
future that everyone inhabits. We need women and minorities to enjoy
an ambient sense of belonging in those professions if the future they
create is going to be one in which all of us feel at home.

Focus on Meaning

1. According to Pollack, what factors "keep women out of tech"? What
   changes does she propose to improve this situation?

2. According to Pollack's summary of Cheryan's research, "young men
   tend not to major in English for the same reasons women don't pick
   computer science" (paragraph 11). What are those reasons? Does
   your own experience support this claim?

Focus on Strategy and Critical Thinking

1. Where does Pollack include information about her own experiences? Do you find these passages irrelevant or distracting, or do
   you think they help her make her point? Explain.

2. Is Pollack's explanation of the problem—largely based on Cheryan's
   research—convincing? Oversimplified? What other factors might
   explain why so few women enter tech fields?

3. In paragraphs 1 and 2 and in her conclusion, Pollack suggests that minorities face the same challenges as women in tech. Do you think she should delete these references and just focus on women? Change her essay's title? Weave a more thorough discussion of minorities in tech into her essay? Explain.

Focus on Language and Style

1. If you were writing a flyer for an open house for prospective computer-science majors, what adjectives would you include to attract women? Which words would you avoid? Why?

2. In paragraph 2, Pollack explains a concept by comparing it to "the elves who live inside your refrigerator but come out only when the light is off." Is this a useful description? Is it appropriate for this essay?

Writing Practice

1. In paragraph 8, Pollack mentions stereotypical views of scientists. What is your image of a scientist? Write an essay explaining how your experiences shaped this view.

2. What fields do you see as female? Why? What factors keep men from entering these fields in greater numbers? What steps can (or should) be taken to make them more appealing to men?

AN OPEN LETTER TO ALL MY MALE FRIENDS
Estelle Tang

Estelle Tang is a writer and editor whose work has appeared in the *New Yorker*, *Rookie*, the *Hairpin*, and *Jezebel*. She is also a literary scout for children's books. Before moving to the United States, Tang was an editor for Oxford University Press in Australia, where she also received her degree in English literature. In this 2015 essay, which appeared in the *Guardian*, Tang highlights the challenges women confront on a daily basis. As you read, think about the kinds of challenges you or women you know have had to face because of gender.

To all my male friends,   1

I want to tell you about something that happened to me today.   2

I was walking to the gym when a guy on a bike rode past and said,   3
"baby, can I smack that ass?" I am used to this kind of behavior in my
New York City neighborhood, so I usually ignore it. Trust me—if I had
it out with every man who said things like this to me, I'd have a much
shorter, much more annoying day. So I just kept walking. He said it

again, but before I could even decide what to do (or if I should do any-thing) about it, I felt his hand on my butt.

That's right. He rode up to me on his bike so he could touch my   4
arse.[1] Then, again before I could think about doing anything, he rode away.

I was, and am still, so angry. At the time, I felt a bit sad and scared   5
but then quickly grateful that nothing worse happened. Soon after the initial fear subsided, I started thinking about whether I *should* go to the gym at all. Maybe I should stay home and never leave the house again. That would be safer. Silly, no?

Since I moved to New York City from Melbourne,[2] I've been sub-   6
jected to street harassment with a regularity that almost defies belief. To begin with, I chalked it up to the bigger population in the city, and didn't want to make a big deal out of it. I felt—and still feel—extremely grate-ful that I've rarely suffered any worse than catcalling, and it seemed like something I could just deal with and move on.

But eventually, I realized it was happening every day. It's so predict-   7
ably a part of my life now that I cringe in anticipation whenever a man looks at me. I internally genuinely bless every man who turns his face away from me when I walk past. I've tried dressing down and wear-ing no make-up when I leave the house, which hasn't helped. It should go without saying that I don't want to be the one who has to alter my behavior to go unnoticed, and I hate that I even felt like I should try—but results say it's a useless exercise, in any case.

And because of recent awful events, the harassment I receive has   8
seemed like the gentler side of a spectrum that has a much more violent and destructive end. By now, you've heard the news that 22-year-old Elliot Rodger posted a video and wrote a manifesto about his hatred of and planned retribution towards women, before shooting and kill-ing seven people, including himself in California. Within days of this, a man shot at three women after they refused to have sex with him and his friends. This terrifies me. Every time a man whistles me up on the street, murmuring that I'm gorgeous or sexy, I ignore him. And doesn't that mean I'm rejecting him too? Could I be in the same kind of danger one day?

I realize this doesn't have much to do with you. Most of you are   9
back at home in Australia, and you'd have no reason to know what a day in my life is like. But I want you to know. A few months ago, I avoided telling my boyfriend about these incidents, thinking it would sound like contextless boasting: "Look how many men think I'm hot!" But I've started telling him about more and more of these incidents. In fact, I want to start telling him about every single one. Not because I'm delighted to hear about how attractive I am to these men, or because I

WORD POWER

manifesto a public declaration of beliefs

WORD POWER

retribution revenge

---

1. British slang for "butt."
2. A major city in Australia.

want people to feel sorry for me. I just want him—and you—to know. That harassment and violence against women is a very real thing, and that it affects its victims daily.

I don't want you to think that this is something that only happens 10 in America. Sure, it's constant here, but my female friends are catcalled back home in Melbourne, too.

Then there was that time the guy on the train tried to fondle me. 11 I'm not sure I ever told you about that. When I told a group of female friends about this on Facebook (in all caps; I was very angry), I found I wasn't the only person with such experience. One girl I know in London told me that she had had a very similar thing happen to her. While she was jogging, a boy on a bike slapped her on the bum. "I still feel rage and I feel rage for you," she said. Another girl I know, in Poland, had literally also just walked home from the gym and been approached by a drunken man who tried to attack her. He verbally abused her as she walked away. "The saddest part is that I saw it coming," she added. "I had this reflex as soon as he made eye contact with me, steeling myself for the inevitable, calculating what was the worst that could happen, and how to make that not happen."

I was moved, yet also chilled to see an Instagram post in writer 12 Durga Chew-Bose's feed this week that reflected the danger women face in our lives every day: a screenshot of safety check-ins that she and her friends routinely sent each other. When texting each other last thing before bed, these women said not good-bye, or goodnight, but things like "Home! You?" or "Get home safe."

It's understandable how much responsibility we women take upon 13 ourselves in these situations. We want to be able to move around freely, but we don't want to be hurt.

Honestly, I don't want to spend too much time thinking about what 14 happened to me today. But there is another aspect to it. Legally speaking, in Australia this kind of thing is illegal. It's assault, as is force of any kind visited upon an unconsenting person.

Anyway, thanks for listening. I'm winding up now. I know you are not 15 the guys doing this. I'm not trying to make you feel bad for being a man. Believe me, I know there are good and awesome guys out there. But I suppose I wanted to explain a bit about what it's like to be a woman. And while I'm at it, perhaps this goes a little way to explaining why I'm always a killjoy about your rape jokes (sorry, I will never laugh at those). I'm not asking you to become my personal vigilante force, or anything like that, either.

What do I want? I'm not sure. Maybe keep your eye out; read 16 the #yesallwomen hashtag for more examples of what women have to deal with on a daily basis; don't pay attention to the people who said Rodger's wasn't a misogynistic crime; and don't make rape jokes?

I'm not entirely sure. I guess I just wanted you to know. 17

Love, 18

Estelle 19

WORD POWER

misogynistic
expressing a hatred or dislike of women

Focus on Meaning

1. Tang begins her essay by saying she wants to tell her male friends about something that happened to her. What does she hope to achieve by telling them about her experience? Do you think this open letter will have the effect she wants it to have? Why or why not?

2. What is Tang's reaction to the incident she describes in paragraphs 3–5? Do you think she is overreacting? Do you think her reaction should have been stronger? Explain.

3. How has the "street harassment" (6) Tang describes changed her? What steps has she taken to change her own behavior in response to her experiences?

Focus on Strategy and Critical Thinking

1. This essay is written in the form of a letter addressed "To all my male friends." How do you think her male friends would react to her letter? Why?

2. In paragraph 8, Tang discusses a shooting. What connection does she make between this shooting and her own experiences? Is this connection justified? Why or why not?

3. In paragraph 15, Tang tells her male friends, "I know you are not the guys doing this." Should she have given them this reassurance earlier in the essay? If so, where?

Focus on Language and Style

1. Tang's letter is addressed to "all my male friends." What other term could she have used instead of *male friends*? How would this new term change the tone of the essay? How might deleting the word *all* change the tone?

2. Tang signs her letter "Love, Estelle." Is this a good choice? What alternatives does she have?

Writing Practice

1. Write a letter to a group of people you believe do not understand how you feel about an important issue. Support your thesis by discussing incidents from your own experiences

2. Assume that you are one of Tang's male friends. Write an essay in which you answer her letter, demonstrating why you are one of the "good and awesome guys out there" (15).

Appendix A: Strategies for College Success

College can be challenging, exposing you to new experiences and new responsibilities. It can also motivate you to develop new skills and new habits as well as new strategies for becoming a better student and achieving a rewarding work-life balance. The tips on the following pages can help you to meet these goals.

A1 Time-Management Strategies

Learning to manage your time is very important for success in college. Here are some strategies you can adopt to make this process easier.

1. ***Use an organizer.*** New electronic tools are constantly being developed to help you stay organized. For example, Schoolbinder, a free online organizer, can help you manage your time and create a study schedule. If you have trouble blocking out distractions when you are studying, a site like StudyRails can be helpful. For a small monthly fee, this site will help you plan a study schedule and alert you to when it's time to focus on schoolwork. It can also be programmed to block your go-to recreational sites during hours when you should be studying.

    You can use the calendar function on your smartphone to keep track of deadlines and appointments (see the example on page 669). At the beginning of the semester, enter key pieces of information from each course syllabus—for example, the date of every quiz and exam and the due date of every paper. As the semester progresses, continue to add assignments and deadlines. In addition, enter information such as days when a class will be canceled or will meet in the computer lab or in the library, reminders to bring a particular book or piece of equipment to class, and appointments with instructors or other college personnel.

2. ***Use a calendar.*** Buy a large wall calendar, and post it where you will see it every morning—on your desk, on the refrigerator, or wherever you keep your phone, your keys, and your ID. At the beginning of the semester, fill in important dates such as school holidays, work commitments, exam dates, and due dates for papers and projects.

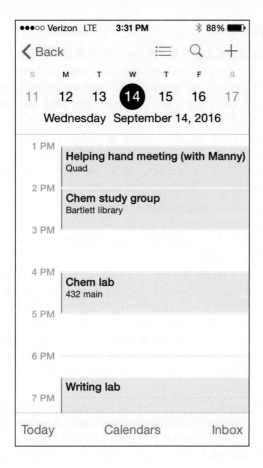

When you return from classes each day, update the calendar with any new information you have entered into your organizer.

3. ***Plan ahead.*** If you think you will need help from a writing center tutor to revise a paper that is due in two weeks, don't wait until day thirteen to make an appointment; all the tutoring slots may be filled by then. To be safe, make an appointment about a week in advance.

4. ***Learn to enjoy downtime.*** When you have a free minute, take time for yourself—and don't feel guilty about it.

A2 Note-Taking Strategies

Learning to take notes in a college class takes practice, but taking good notes is essential for success in college. Here are some basic guidelines that will help you develop and improve your note-taking skills.

During Class

1. ***Come to class.*** If you miss class, you miss notes—so come to class, and come on time. Sit where you can see the board or screen and hear the instructor. Do not feel you have to keep sitting in the same place in each class every day; change your seat until you find a spot that is comfortable for you.

2. ***Develop a system of shorthand to make note taking faster and more efficient.*** You can use texting abbreviations and even symbols in your notes, but remember not to use such abbreviations in your college writing.

3. ***Date your notes.*** Begin each class by writing the date at the top of the page. Instructors frequently identify material that will be on a test by dates. If you do not date your notes, you may not know exactly what to study.

4. ***Know what to write down.*** You cannot possibly write down everything an instructor says. If you try, you will miss a lot of important information. Listen carefully *before* you write, and listen for cues to what is important. For example, sometimes the instructor will tell you that something is important or that a particular piece of information will be on a test. If the instructor emphasizes an idea or underlines it on the board, you should do the same in your notes.

5. ***Include examples.*** Try to include an example for each important concept introduced in class—something that will help you remember what the instructor was talking about. (If you do not have time to include examples as you take notes during class, add them after class when you review your notes.) For instance, if your world history instructor is explaining *nationalism*, you should write down not only a definition but also an example, such as "Germany in 1848."

6. ***If you take notes by hand, write legibly and use helpful signals.*** Use blue or black ink for your note taking, but keep a red or green pen handy to highlight important information, jot down announcements (such as a change in a test date), identify gaps in your notes, or question confusing points. Do not take notes in pencil, which is hard to read and not as permanent as ink.

7. ***Ask questions.*** If you do not hear (or do not understand) something your instructor said, or if you need an example to help you understand something, *ask!* Do not, however, immediately turn to another student for clarification. Instead, wait to see if the instructor explains further or if he or she pauses to ask if anyone has a question. If you are not comfortable asking a question during class, make a note of the question and ask the instructor—or send an email—after class.

After Class

1. *Review your notes.* After every class, try to spend ten or fifteen minutes rereading your notes, filling in gaps and examples while the material is still fresh in your mind. You might also recopy or retype important information from your notes to reinforce what you have learned.

2. *Copy announcements* (such as quiz dates) onto your calendar.

3. *Enter reminders* (for example, a note to schedule a conference before your next paper is due) into your organizer.

4. *Write questions* you want to ask the instructor at the top of the next blank page in your class notebook.

Before the Next Class

1. *Reread your notes.* Leave time just before each class to skim the previous class's notes. This strategy will get you oriented and will remind you of anything that needs clarification or further explanation. (You might want to give each day's notes a title so you can remember the topic of each class. This strategy can help you find information when you study.)

2. *Ask for help.* Call or email a classmate if you need to fill in missing information; if you still need help, see the instructor during his or her office hours, or come to class early to ask your question before class begins.

A3 Homework Strategies

Doing homework is an important part of your education because it gives you a chance to practice your skills and measure your progress. If you are having trouble with the homework, chances are you are having trouble with the course. Ask the instructor or teaching assistant for help *now*; do not wait until the day before the exam. Here are some tips for getting the most out of your homework.

1. *Write down the assignment.* Do not expect to remember your assignment. If you are not exactly sure what you are supposed to do, check with your instructor or with another student.

2. *Do your homework, and do it on time.* Teachers assign homework to reinforce classwork, and they expect homework to be done on a regular basis. It is easy to fall behind in college, and trying to do three—or five—nights' worth of homework in one night is not a good idea.

3. *Be an active reader.* Get into the habit of highlighting and annotating your textbooks and other material as you read. (See Chapter 1 for information on active reading.)

4. *Join study groups.* A study group of three or four students can be a valuable support system for homework as well as for exams. If your schedule permits, regularly review homework assignments or class notes with other students. In addition to learning information, you will learn different strategies for doing assignments.

A4 Taking Exams

Preparation for an exam should begin well before the exam is announced. In a sense, you begin this preparation on the first day of class.

Before the Exam

1. *Attend every class.* Regular attendance in class—where you can listen, ask questions, and take notes—is the best possible preparation for exams. If you do have to miss a class, arrange to copy—and read—another student's notes *before the next class* so you will be able to follow the discussion.

2. *Keep up with the reading.* Read every assignment, and read it before the class in which it will be discussed. If you do not, you may have trouble understanding what is going on in class.

3. *Take careful notes.* Take careful, thorough notes, but be selective. If you can, compare your notes on a regular basis with those of other students in the class; working together, you can fill in gaps or correct errors. Establishing a buddy system will also force you to review your notes regularly instead of just on the night before the exam.

4. *Study on your own.* When an exam is announced, adjust your study schedule—and your priorities—so you have time to review everything. (This is especially important if you have more than one exam in a short period of time.) Over a period of several days, review all your material (class notes, readings, and so on), and then review it again. Make a note of anything you do not understand, and keep track of topics you need to review. Try to predict the most likely questions, and—if you have time—practice answering them.

5. *Study with a group.* If you can, set up a study group. Studying with others can help you better understand the material. However, do not come to group sessions unprepared and expect to get all the information you need from the other students. You must first study on your own.

6. ***Make an appointment with your instructor.*** Make a conference appointment with the course instructor or teaching assistant a few days before the exam. Bring to this meeting any specific questions you have about course content and about the format of the upcoming exam. (Be sure to prepare for the conference by reviewing all your study material in advance.)

7. ***Review the material one last time.*** The night before the exam is not the time to begin your studying; it is the time to review. When you have finished your review, get a good night's sleep.

During the Exam

By the time you walk into the exam room, you will already have done all you could to get ready for the test. Your goal now is to keep the momentum going and not do anything to undermine all your hard work.

WORD POWER
undermine make less effective

FYI

Taking Essay Exams

If an exam question asks you to write an essay, remember that what you are really being asked to do is write a **thesis-and-support essay**. Chapter 13 tells you how to do this.

1. ***Read through the entire exam.*** Be sure you understand how much time you have, how many points each question is worth, and exactly what each question is asking you to do. Many exam questions call for just a short answer—*yes* or *no*, *true* or *false*. Others ask you to fill in a blank with a few words, and still others require you to select the best answer from among several choices. If you are not absolutely certain what kind of answer a particular question calls for, ask the instructor or the proctor *before* you begin to write.

2. ***Budget your time.*** Once you understand how much each section of the exam and each question are worth, plan your time and set your priorities, devoting the most time to the most important questions. If you know you tend to rush through exams, or if you find you often run out of time before you get to the end of a test, you might try checking your progress when about one-third of the allotted time has passed (for a one-hour exam, check after twenty minutes) to make sure you are pacing yourself appropriately.

3. ***Reread each question.*** Carefully reread each question *before* you start to answer it. Underline the **key words**—the words that give specific information about how to approach the question and how to phrase your answer. (These key words are listed in the FYI box on page 674.)

Remember, even if everything you write is correct, your response is not acceptable if you do not answer the question. If a question asks you to *compare* two novels, writing a *summary* of one of them will not be acceptable.

4. ***Brainstorm to help you recall the material.*** If you are writing a paragraph or an essay, look frequently at the question as you brainstorm. Quickly write down all the relevant points you can think of— what the textbook had to say, your instructor's comments, and so on. The more information you can think of now, the more you will have to choose from when you write your answer.

5. ***Write down the main idea.*** Looking closely at the way the question is worded and at your brainstorming notes, write a sentence that states the main idea of your answer. If you are writing a paragraph, this sentence will be your **topic sentence**; if you are writing an essay, it will be your **thesis statement**.

6. ***List your key supporting points.*** You do not want to waste your limited (and valuable) time making a detailed outline, but an informal outline that lists just your key points is worth the little time it takes. An informal outline will help you plan a clear direction for your paragraph or essay.

7. ***Draft your answer.*** You will spend most of your time actually writing the answers to the questions on the exam. Follow your outline, keep track of time, and consult your brainstorming notes when you need to—but stay focused on your writing.

8. ***Reread, revise, and edit.*** When you have finished drafting your answer, reread it carefully to make sure it says everything you want it to say—and that it answers the exam question.

FYI

Key Words

Here are some words that can help you decide how to approach an exam question that calls for a paragraph or an essay.

analyze	give examples	illustrate
argue	identify	recount
compare	identify or explain	summarize
contrast	causes, origins,	support
define	contributing	take a stand
demonstrate	factors	trace
describe	identify or explain	
evaluate	results, effects,	
explain	outcomes	

Appendix B: Strategies for Doing Research

B1 Finding and Evaluating Information

When you do research, you—like most students—probably go straight to the Internet. If you do this, however, you are shortchanging yourself. Your college library gives you access to valuable resources that are available nowhere else. In addition, unlike the material on the Internet, where anything and everything is posted, the material in the library has been screened by librarians (as well as instructors) and, in many cases, conforms to academic standards of reliability. For this reason, you should always begin your research by visiting the library's website.

Finding Information in the Library

Once you connect to the library's website, you should consult the library's **online catalog**—a database of all the library's holdings. Many libraries subscribe to a **discovery service**—an online research tool that allows you to use a single search box to access all of the library's print and electronic holdings—including print books, e-books, full-text journal articles, government documents, streaming video, and DVDs. The result is a Google-like search experience that ranks results by relevancy.

You search the online catalog (or discovery service) just as you would search the Internet: by carrying out a *keyword search* or a *subject search*.

1. You do a **keyword search** the same way you would search using Google—by entering your keywords in a search box to retrieve a list of books, periodicals, and other materials that are relevant to your topic. The more specific your keywords are, the more focused your search will be. Thus, the keywords *Facebook privacy* will yield more specific (and useful) results than the words *social networking* would.

2. You do a **subject search** by entering a subject heading related to your topic. Unlike keywords, subject headings are predetermined and come from a list of subject headings published by the Library of Congress. Many online catalogs provide lists of subject headings you can use. A subject search is best when you want information about a general topic—for example, *rap music*, *discography*, or *Mark Twain*.

675

As you carry out your search, make sure you look at the material in the library's electronic databases (such as InfoTrac and ProQuest). These databases enable you to access articles from newspapers, magazines, and journals that you cannot freely access on the Internet. In addition, database sources usually contain the full text of articles as well as complete bibliographic information, sometimes in the form of a works-cited entry.

If your library subscribes to a discovery service, you can search all the library's electronic databases at once from a search box. If not, you will have to search each database individually. (Most online catalogs list the databases to which your college library subscribes.)

Evaluating Library Sources

Even though the sources in the library are generally more reliable than those on the Internet, they still need to be evaluated. In other words, you have to determine their usefulness and reliability before you use them in your essay.

> **WORD POWER**
>
> **tabloid** a newspaper that emphasizes stories with sensational content

- First, determine the **credibility** (believability) of a source. For example, an article in a respected periodical, such as the *New York Times* or the *Wall Street Journal*, is more credible than one in a tabloid, such as the *National Enquirer* or the *Sun*.
- Next, look at the date of publication to decide if the book or periodical is up-to-date.
- Finally, consider the author. Is he or she an expert in the subject the source explores? Does the author strive for objectivity, or does he or she seem to be advancing a particular point of view?

Your instructor or college librarian can help you select sources that are both appropriate and reliable.

Finding Information on the Internet

The Internet can give you access to a great deal of information that can help you support your ideas and develop your essay. Unlike the resources available in your college library, however, no one is responsible for checking the accuracy of information or the credentials of people who post on the Internet. For this reason, it is your responsibility (and obligation) to determine the trustworthiness of an Internet source and decide whether it is appropriate for your paper.

Once you are online, you need to connect to a **search engine**, which helps you find information by sorting through the millions of documents that are available on the Internet. Among the most popular search engines are Google, Yahoo!, and Bing.

There are two ways to use a search engine to access information.

1. *You can do a keyword search.* All search engines let you do a keyword search. You type a term (or terms) into a box, and the search engine looks for documents that contain the term, listing all the hits that it finds.

2. *You can do a subject search.* Some search engines, such as About .com and Yahoo!, let you do a subject search. First, you choose a broad subject from a list: *Humanities*, *Arts*, *Entertainment*, *Business*, and so on. Each of these general subjects then leads you to more specific subjects, until you eventually get to the subtopic that you want.

Evaluating Internet Sources

You evaluate Internet sources the same way you evaluate library sources. With the Internet, however, you have problems you do not have with the sources in your college library. Because anyone can post information on a website, it can be difficult—if not impossible—to judge the credentials of an author or sometimes even to identify an author. Dates can also be missing, so it may be difficult to tell when information was posted and when it was updated. Finally, it can be challenging to determine whether or not the information on a website is accurate. For example, is the site trying to sell something or to advance a political or social agenda? If it is, it may contain information that is misleading, biased, or incorrect.

You can evaluate websites (and the information posted on them) by asking the following basic questions.

- *Who is the author of the site?* Avoid information written by unnamed authors or by authors with questionable credentials.

- *Who is the sponsoring organization?* Be especially careful of using information from websites that are sponsored by companies trying to sell something or organizations that have a particular agenda.

- *Can you verify information posted on the site?* Make sure that you are able to check the source of the information. For example, you should see if an article on a site includes documentation. Also, cross-check information you find there. Does the same information appear in other sources that are reliable?

- *Does the site contain errors?* In addition to factual errors, look out for mistakes in grammar or spelling. Errors such as these should raise a red flag about the accuracy of the information on the site you are visiting.

- *Do the links on the site work?* Make sure that the links on the site are "live." The presence of "dead" links is a good indication that a site is not being properly maintained.

- *Is the information up-to-date?* Make sure that the site's information is current. Avoid sites that contain information that seems old or outdated. A reliable site will usually include the date information was posted and the date it was revised.

When in doubt, the surest strategy for determining whether a website is reliable is to check with a reference librarian or with your instructor. Unless you can be certain that a site is reliable, do not use it as a source.

FYI

Using Wikipedia as a Source

Most college students regularly consult Wikipedia, the open-source online encyclopedia. The rationale behind Wikipedia is that if a large number of people review information, errors will eventually be discovered and corrected. Because there are no full-time editors, however, Wikipedia articles can (and do) contain inaccurate as well as biased information. In addition, anyone—not just experts—can write and edit entries. Understandably, some instructors distrust—or at least question—the accuracy of Wikipedia entries. Be sure to check the accuracy of the information you find in Wikipedia by comparing it to the information in other sources you are using. (Keep in mind that many instructors do not consider articles from any encyclopedia—print or electronic—acceptable for college research.)

B2 Using Paraphrase, Summary, and Quotation

Once you have gathered your source material, you need to transfer relevant information into computer files or onto index cards. **Taking notes**, however, involves more than simply copying down or cutting and pasting information. As you record information, you should put it into a form that you can use when you write your essay. This strategy allows you to keep track of your source material and eliminates the possibility of accidentally committing plagiarism. For this reason, when you take notes, you should *paraphrase, summarize,* or *quote* the information from your sources.

FYI

Avoiding Plagiarism

When you transfer information from websites into your notes, you may carelessly cut and paste text without recording where the material came from. If you then copy this material into your essay without citing the source, you are committing **plagiarism**—stealing someone else's ideas. Also keep in mind that you must document *all* material that you get from the Internet, just as you document material that you get from print sources. For information on documentation, see B4. For information on plagiarism, see B3.

Paraphrasing

When you **paraphrase**, you use your own words to convey a source's key ideas. You paraphrase when you want to include detailed information from the source but not the author's exact words. Paraphrasing is useful when you want to make a difficult discussion easier to understand while still presenting a comprehensive overview of the original.

Writing a Paraphrase

1. Read the passage until you understand it.
2. Note the main idea of the passage, and list key supporting points.
3. Draft your paraphrase, beginning with the source's main idea and then presenting the source's most important supporting points.
4. When you revise, make sure you have used your own words and phrasing, not the words or sentence structure of the original. Use quotation marks to identify any unique or memorable phrases you have borrowed from the source.
5. Document your source.

Here is a passage from the article "Hot Fakes," by Joanie Cox, followed by a student's paraphrase.

ORIGINAL

Always pay close attention to the stitching. On a Kate Spade bag, the logo is stitched perfectly straight; it's not a sticker. Most designers stitch a simple label to the inside of their purses. On Chanel bags, however, the interior label is usually stamped and tends to match the color of the exterior. Study the material the bag is made from. A real Chanel Ligne Cambon multipocket bag, for example, is constructed from buttery lambskin leather, not vinyl.

PARAPHRASE

It is often possible to tell a fake designer handbag from a genuine one by looking at the details. For example, items such as logos should not be crooked. You should also look for the distinctive features of a particular brand of handbag. Counterfeiters will not take the time to match colors, and they may use vinyl instead of expensive leather (Cox).

Note that this paraphrase does not simply change a word here and there. Instead, the student has taken the time to fully understand the main idea and supporting points of the passage and has restated ideas in her own words.

Summarizing

Unlike a paraphrase, which presents the key points of a source in detail, a **summary** is a general restatement, in your own words, of just the main idea of a passage. For this reason, a summary is always much shorter than the original.

Writing a Summary

1. Read the passage until you understand it.
2. Jot down the main idea of the passage.
3. As you write, make sure you use your own words, not those of your source.
4. When you revise, make sure your summary contains only the ideas of the source.
5. Document your source.

Here is a student's summary of the original passage on the previous page.

SUMMARY

Buyers who want to identify fake handbags should check details such as the way the label is sewn and the material the item is made from (Cox).

Quoting

When you **quote**, you use an author's exact words as they appear in the source, including all punctuation and capitalization. Enclose all words from your source in quotation marks—*followed by appropriate* *documentation.* Because quotations can distract readers, use them only when you think that the author's exact words will add to your discussion.

> **When to Quote**
>
> 1. Quote when the words of a source are so memorable that to put them into your own words would lessen their impact.
> 2. Quote when the words of a source are so precise that a paraphrase or summary would change the meaning of the original.
> 3. Quote when the words of a source add authority to your discussion. The exact words of a recognized expert can help you make your point convincingly.

Here is how a student writer incorporated a quotation from the original passage on page 679 into her notes.

QUOTATION

Someone who wants to buy an authentic designer handbag should look carefully at the material the purse is made from. For example, there is a big difference between vinyl and Chanel's "buttery lambskin leather" (Cox).

Working Sources into Your Writing

To show readers why you are using a source and to help you blend source material smoothly into your essay, introduce paraphrases, summaries, and quotations with **identifying tags** (sometimes called *signal phrases*)—phrases that name the source or its author. You can position an identifying tag at various places in a sentence.

As one celebrity fashion columnist points out, "A real Chanel Ligne Cambon multipocket bag, for example, is constructed from buttery lambskin leather, not vinyl" (Cox).

"A real Chanel Ligne Cambon multipocket bag, for example," says one celebrity fashion columnist, "is constructed from buttery lambskin leather, not vinyl" (Cox).

"A real Chanel Ligne Cambon multipocket bag, for example, is constructed from buttery lambskin leather, not vinyl," observes one celebrity fashion columnist (Cox).

FYI

Identifying Sources

Instead of repeating the word *says*, you can use one of the following words or phrases to identify the source of a quotation, paraphrase, or summary.

admits	concludes	points out
believes	explains	remarks
claims	notes	states
comments	observes	suggests

Synthesizing

When you **synthesize**, you combine ideas from two or more sources with your own ideas. The goal of a synthesis is to use sources to develop your own point about a topic. In a synthesis, then, your own ideas, not those of your sources, should dominate the discussion. In a sense, every time you weave together paraphrase, summary, and quotation to support a point, you are writing a synthesis.

Writing a Synthesis

1. Decide on the point you want to develop.
2. Select at least two or three sources to support your point.
3. Read each source carefully, taking note of how they are alike, how they are different, and how they relate to your point.
4. Begin your synthesis by clearly stating the point you are going to develop.
5. Use specific examples (paraphrases, summaries, and quotations) from your sources to support your point.
6. When you revise, make sure that you have used appropriate transitions to indicate the movement from one source to another. Also be sure that you have clearly identified each source that you discuss.
7. Document all words and ideas that you borrow from your sources.

B3 Using Sources Responsibly

As a rule, you must **document** (give source information for) all words, ideas, or statistics from an outside source. You must also document all visuals—tables, graphs, photographs, and so on—that you do not create yourself. (It is not necessary, however, to document **common knowledge**—factual information widely available in various reference works.)

When you present information from another source as if it is your own (whether you do it intentionally or unintentionally), you commit **plagiarism**—and plagiarism is theft. Although most plagiarism is accidental, the penalties can still be severe. You can avoid plagiarism by understanding what you must document and what you do not have to document.

FYI

What to Document

You should document the following.

- All quotations from a source
- All summaries and paraphrases of source material
- All ideas—opinions, judgments, and insights—of others
- All tables, graphs, charts, and statistics from a source

You do not need to document the following.

- Your own ideas
- Common knowledge
- Familiar quotations

Read the following passage from "The Facts on Fakes!," an article by Adele R. Meyer, and the four rules that follow it. This material will help you understand the most common causes of plagiarism and show you how to avoid it.

ORIGINAL

Is imitation really the sincerest form of flattery? Counterfeiting deceives the consumer and tarnishes the reputation of the genuine manufacturer. Brand value can be destroyed when a trademark is imposed on counterfeit products of inferior quality—hardly a form of flattery! Therefore, prestigious companies who are the targets of counterfeiters have begun to battle an industry that copies and sells their merchandise. They have filed lawsuits and in some cases have employed private investigators across the nation to combat the counterfeit trade. A quick search of the Internet brings up dozens of press releases from newspapers throughout the country, all reporting instances of law enforcement cracking down on sellers of counterfeit goods by confiscating bogus merchandise and imposing fines.

Rule 1: Document Ideas from Your Sources

PLAGIARISM

When counterfeits are sold, the original manufacturer does not take it as a compliment.

Even though the student writer does not quote her source directly, she must identify the article as the source of this material because it expresses the article's ideas, not her own.

CORRECT

When counterfeits are sold, the original manufacturer does not take it as a compliment (Meyer).

Rule 2: Place Borrowed Words in Quotation Marks

PLAGIARISM

It is possible to ruin the worth of a brand by selling counterfeit products of inferior quality—hardly a form of flattery (Meyer).

Although the student writer cites the source, the passage incorrectly uses the source's exact words without quoting them. She must quote the borrowed words.

CORRECT (BORROWED WORDS IN QUOTATION MARKS)

It is possible to ruin the worth of a brand by selling "counterfeit products of inferior quality—hardly a form of flattery" (Meyer).

Rule 3: Use Your Own Phrasing

PLAGIARISM

Is copying a design a compliment? Not at all. The fake design not only tries to fool the buyer but also harms the original company. It can ruin the worth of a brand. Because counterfeits are usually of poor quality, they pay the original no compliment. As a result, companies whose products are often copied have started to fight back. They have sued the counterfeiters and have even used private detectives to identify phony goods. Throughout the United States, police have fined people who sell counterfeits and have seized their products (Meyer).

Even though the student writer acknowledges Meyer as her source, and even though she does not use the source's exact words, her passage closely follows the order, emphasis, sentence structure, and phrasing of the original.

In the following passage, the student writer uses her own wording, quoting one distinctive phrase from the source.

CORRECT

According to "The Facts on Fakes!," it is not a compliment when an original design is copied by a counterfeiter. The poor quality of most fakes is "hardly a form of flattery." The harm to the image of the original manufacturers has caused them to fight back against the counterfeiters, sometimes using their own detectives. As a result, lawsuits and criminal charges have led to fines and confiscated merchandise (Meyer).

Note: The quotation does not require separate documentation because the identifying tag—According to "The Facts on Fakes!"—makes it clear that all the borrowed material in the passage is from the same source.

Rule 4: Distinguish Your Ideas from the Source's Ideas

PLAGIARISM

Counterfeit goods are not harmless. Counterfeiting not only fools the consumer but also destroys confidence in the quality of the real thing. Manufacturers know this and have begun to fight back. A number have begun to sue "and in some cases have employed private investigators across the nation to combat the counterfeit trade" (Meyer).

In this passage, it appears that only the quotation in the last sentence is borrowed from the article by Meyer. In fact, however, the ideas in the second sentence also come from Meyer's article.

In the following passage, the student writer uses an identifying tag to acknowledge the borrowed material in the second sentence.

CORRECT

Counterfeit goods are not harmless. According to the article "The Facts on Fakes!," counterfeiting not only fools the consumer but also destroys confidence in the quality of the real thing. Manufacturers know this and have begun to fight back. A number have begun to sue "and in some cases have employed private investigators across the nation to combat the counterfeit trade" (Meyer).

B4 Documenting Your Sources

When you **document** your sources, you tell readers where you found the information you used in your essay. The Modern Language Association (MLA) recommends the following documentation style for essays that use sources. This format consists of *parenthetical references* in the body of the paper that refer to a *works-cited list* at the end of the paper.

Parenthetical References in the Text

A parenthetical reference should include enough information to lead readers to a specific entry in your works-cited list. A typical parenthetical reference consists of the author's last name and the page number (Brown 2). Notice that there is no comma and no *p* or *p.* before the page number.

Whenever possible, introduce information from a source with a phrase that includes the author's name. (If you do this, include only the page number in parentheses.) Place documentation so that it does not interrupt the flow of your ideas, preferably at the end of a sentence.

As Jonathan Brown observes in "Demand for Fake Designer Goods Is Soaring," as many as 70 percent of buyers of luxury goods are willing to wear designer brands alongside of fakes (2).

Here are some specific guidelines for special situations.

1. WHEN YOU ARE CITING A WORK BY TWO AUTHORS

   Instead of buying nonbranded items of similar quality, many customers are willing to pay extra for the counterfeit designer label (Grossman and Shapiro 79).

2. WHEN YOU ARE CITING A WORK WITHOUT PAGE NUMBERS

   A seller of counterfeited goods in California "now faces 10 years in prison and $20,000 in fines" (Cox).

3. WHEN YOU ARE CITING A WORK WITHOUT A LISTED AUTHOR OR PAGE NUMBERS

More counterfeit goods come from China than from any other country ("Counterfeit Goods").

Note: Material from the Internet frequently lacks some publication information—for example, page or paragraph numbers. For this reason, the parenthetical references that cite it may contain just the author's name (as in example 2) or just a shortened title (as in example 3) if the article appears without an author.

4. WHEN YOU ARE CITING A STATEMENT BY ONE AUTHOR THAT IS QUOTED IN A WORK BY ANOTHER AUTHOR

Speaking of consumers' buying habits, designer Miuccia Prada says, "There is a kind of an obsession with bags" (qtd. in Thomas A23).

FYI

Formatting Quotations

1. **Short quotations**   Quotations of no more than four typed lines are run into the text of your essay. End punctuation comes after the parenthetical reference, which follows the quotation marks.

   According to Dana Thomas, customers often "pick up knockoffs for one-tenth the legitimate bag's retail cost, then pass them off as real" (A23).

2. **Long quotations**   Quotations of more than four lines are set off from the text of your essay. Begin a long quotation on a new line, indented one-half inch from the left-hand margin, and do not enclose it in quotation marks. Do not indent the first line of a single paragraph. If a quoted passage has more than one paragraph, indent the first line of each paragraph (including the first) an extra one-quarter inch. Introduce a long quotation with a complete sentence followed by a colon, and place the parenthetical reference one space *after* the end punctuation.

   The editorial "Terror's Purse Strings" describes a surprise visit to a factory that makes counterfeit purses:

   > On a warm winter afternoon in Guangzhao, I accompanied Chinese police officers on a raid in a decrepit tenement. We found two dozen children, ages 8 to 13, gluing and sewing together fake luxury-brand handbags. The police confiscated everything, arrested the owner and sent the children out. Some punched their timecards, hoping to still get paid. (Thomas A23)

The Works-Cited List

The works-cited list includes all the works you **cite** (refer to) in your essay. The following sample works-cited entries cover the situations you will encounter most often.

Periodicals

JOURNALS

A **journal** is a periodical aimed at readers who know a lot about a particular subject—literature or history, for example.

When citing an article from a journal, include the journal's volume number and issue number, as well as the season and year of publication. Following the date of publication, include page numbers, if there are any. Include the name of the online database (such as Academic Search Premier) if you used one to find the source. For all web sources, add the URL or **DOI** (digital object identifier) for the source.

Article in a Print Journal

> Gioia, Dana. "Robert Frost and the Modern Narrative." *Virginia Quarterly Review,* vol. 89, no. 2, Spring 2013, pp. 185–93.

Article in a Journal Accessed through a Library Database

> Coles, Kimberly Anne. "The Matter of Belief in John Donne's Holy Sonnets." *Renaissance Quarterly,* vol. 68, no. 3, Fall 2015, pp. 899–931. *JSTOR,* doi:10.1086/683855.

MAGAZINES

A **magazine** is a periodical aimed at general readers, rather than people who already know a lot about a subject. Frequently, an article in a magazine is not printed on consecutive pages. For example, it may begin on page 40, skip to page 47, and continue on page 49. If this is the case, your citation should include only the first page, followed by a plus sign.

Article in a Print Magazine

> Poniewozik, James. "Why I Watch Reality TV with My Kids." *Time* 17 June 2013, pp. 54–55.
>
> Isaacs, Matt. "Sheldon Adelson Goes All In." *Mother Jones* March/April 2016, pp. 18+.

Article in a Magazine Accessed through a Library Database

> Sharp, Kathleen. "The Rescue Mission." *Smithsonian,* Nov. 2015, pp. 40–49. *OmniFile Full Text Select,* web.b.ebscohost.com.ezproxy.bpl.org/.

NEWSPAPERS

List page numbers, section numbers, and any special edition information (such as "late ed.") as provided by the source. If the article falls into a special category, such as an editorial, a letter to the editor, or a review, add this label to your entry, after the title.

Article in a Print Newspaper

> Shah, Neil. "More Young Adults Live with Parents." *The Wall Street Journal* 28 Aug. 2013, p. A2.

Article from a Newspaper Accessed through a Library Database

> "The Road toward Peace." *The New York Times*, 15 Feb. 1945, p. 18. Editorial. *ProQuest Historical Newspapers: The New York Times*, search .proquest.com/hnpnewyorktimes.

Books

Books by One Author

List the author with last name first. Italicize the title. Include a shortened form of the publisher's name—for example, *Bedford* for *Bedford/ St. Martin's*. Use the abbreviation *UP* for *University Press*, as in *Princeton UP* and *U of Chicago P*. Include the date of publication.

> Mantel, Hilary. *Bring up the Bodies*. Holt, 2012.

Books by Two or More Authors

For books with more than one author, list second and subsequent authors with first name first, in the order in which they are listed on the book's title page.

> Mooney, Chris, and Sheril Kirshenbaum. *Unscientific America: How Scientific Illiteracy Threatens Our Future*. Basic, 2009.

For books with more than three authors, you may list only the first author, followed by the abbreviation *et al.* ("and others").

> Heti, Sheila, *et al. Women in Clothes*. Blue Rider Press, 2014.

Two or More Books by the Same Author

List two or more books by the same author in alphabetical order according to title. In each entry after the first, use three unspaced hyphens (followed by a period) instead of the author's name.

> Eggers, Dave. *The Circle*. Random, 2013.
> ---. *A Hologram for the King*. McSweeney's, 2012.

Edited Book

Austen, Jane. *Persuasion: An Annotated Edition*. Edited by Robert Morrison. Belknap-Harvard UP, 2011.

Anthology

Adler, Frances P., Debra Busman, and Diana Garcia, editors. *Fire and Ink: An Anthology of Social Action Writing*. U of Arizona P, 2009.

Essay in an Anthology or Chapter of a Book

Weise, Matthew J. "How the Zombie Changed Videogames." *Zombies Are Us: Essays on the Humanity of the Walking Dead*. Edited by Christopher M. Moreman and Cory James Rushton, McFarland, 2011, pp. 151–68.

Internet Sources

Full source information is not always available for Internet sources. When citing Internet sources, include whatever information you can find—ideally, the name of the author (or authors), the title of the article or other document (in quotation marks), the title of the site (italicized), the sponsor or publisher, and the date of publication or last update.

It is necessary to include a web address (URL) when citing an electronic source.

Document within a Website

Enzinna, Wes. "Syria's Unknown Revolution." *Pulitzer Center on Crisis Reporting*, 24 Nov. 2015, pulitzercenter.org/projects/middle-east -syria-enzinna-war-rojava.

Entire Website

Railton, Stephen. *Mark Twain in His Times*. Stephen Railton/U of Virginia Library, 2012, twain.lib.virginia.edu/.

Article in an Online Reference Book or Encyclopedia

Hall, Mark. "Facebook (American Company)." *The Enyclopaedia Britannica*, 2 Jul. 2014, www.britannica.com/topic/Facebook.

Article in an Online Newspaper

Crowell, Maddy. "How Computers Are Getting Better at Detecting Liars." *The Christian Science Monitor*, 12 Dec. 2015, www.csmonitor.com/Science /Science-Notebook/2015/1212/How-computers-are-getting-better-at -detecting-liars.

FYI

Preparing the Works-Cited List

■ Begin the works-cited list on a new page after the last page of your essay.

■ Number the works-cited page as the next page of your essay.

■ Center the heading "Works Cited" one inch from the top of the page; do not italicize the heading or place it in quotation marks.

■ Double-space the list.

■ List entries alphabetically according to the author's last name.

■ Alphabetize unsigned articles according to the first major word of the title.

■ Begin typing each entry at the left-hand margin.

■ Indent second and subsequent lines of each entry one-half inch.

■ Separate major divisions of each entry—author, title, and publication information—by a period and one space.

B5 Model MLA-Style Essay

On the pages that follow is an essay on the topic of counterfeit designer goods. The essay uses MLA documentation style and format and includes a works-cited page.

Compton 1

May Compton

Professor DiSalvo

English 100

29 Apr. 2016

The True Price of Counterfeit Goods

At purse parties in city apartments and suburban homes, customers can buy "designer" handbags at impossibly low prices. On street corners, sidewalk vendors sell name-brand perfumes and sunglasses for much less than their list prices. On the Internet, buyers can buy fine watches for a fraction of the prices charged by manufacturers. Is this too good to be true? Of course it is. All of these "bargains" are knockoffs—counterfeit copies of the real thing. What the people who buy these items do not know (or prefer not to think about) is that the money they are spending supports organized crime—and, sometimes, terrorism. For this reason, people should not buy counterfeit designer merchandise, no matter how tempted they are to do so.

People who buy counterfeit designer merchandise defend their actions by saying that designer products are very expensive. This is certainly true. According to Dana Thomas, the manufacturers of genuine designer merchandise charge ten times more than what it costs to make it (A23). A visitor from Britain, who bought an imitation Gucci purse in New York City for fifty dollars, said, "The real thing is so overpriced. To buy a genuine Gucci purse, I would have to pay over a thousand dollars" (qtd. in "Counterfeit Goods"). Even people who can easily afford to pay the full amount buy fakes. For example, movie stars like Jennifer Lopez openly wear counterfeit goods, and many customers think that if it is all right for celebrities like Lopez to buy fakes, it must also be all right for them, too (Malone). However, as the well-known designer Giorgio Armani points out, counterfeiters create a number of problems for legitimate companies because they use the brand name but do not maintain quality control.

Include your last name and the page number in the upper right-hand corner of every page.

Center your title; do not italicize or underline.

Include your name, instructor's name, course title, and date on first page.

Introduction

Thesis statement

Paragraph combines paraphrase, quotation, and May's own ideas.

Compton 2

What most people choose to ignore is that buying counterfeit items is really stealing the work of the original designer and manufacturer. Between 2002 and 2012, 325 percent more counterfeit goods were seized than in the previous decade (O'Donnell 3b). The FBI estimates that in the United States alone, companies lose about $250 billion as a result of counterfeits (Wallace). In addition, buyers of counterfeit items avoid the state and local sales taxes that legitimate companies pay. Thus, New York City alone loses about a billion dollars every year as a result of the sale of counterfeit merchandise ("Counterfeit Goods"). When this happens, everyone loses. After all, a billion dollars would pay for a lot of police officers and teachers, would fill a lot of potholes, and would pave a lot of streets. Buyers of counterfeit designer goods do not think of themselves as thieves, but that is exactly what they are.

Buyers of counterfeit merchandise also do not realize that the sale of knockoffs is a criminal activity. Most of the profits go to the criminal organization that either makes or imports the counterfeit goods—not to the person who sells the items. In fact, the biggest manufacturer and distributor of counterfeit items is organized crime ("Trafficking"). Michael Kessler, who heads a company that investigates corporate crime, makes this connection clear when he describes the complicated organization that is needed to make counterfeit perfume:

> They need a place that makes bottles, a factory with pumps to fill the bottles, a printer to make the labels, and a box manufacturer to fake the packaging. Then, they need a sophisticated distribution network, as well as all the cash to set everything up. (qtd. in Malone)

Kessler concludes that only an organized crime syndicate—not an individual—has the money to support this illegal activity. For this reason, anyone who buys counterfeits may also be supporting activities such as prostitution, drug distribution, smuggling of illegal immigrants, gang warfare, extortion, and murder (Nellis). In addition, the people who make counterfeits often work in sweatshops where labor and environmental laws are ignored. As Dana Thomas points out, a worker in China who makes counterfeits earns only a fraction of the salary of a worker who makes the real thing (A23).

Paragraph synthesizes May's own ideas with material from three articles.

Long quotation is set off one-half inch from the left-hand margin. No quotation marks are used.

Compton 3

Finally, and perhaps most shocking, is the fact that some of the money earned from the sale of counterfeit designer goods also supports international terrorism. For example, Kim Wallace reports in her *Times Daily* article that during Al-Qaeda training, terrorists are advised to sell fakes to get money for their operations. According to Interpol, an international police organization, the bombing of the World Trade Center in 1993 was paid for in part by the sale of counterfeit T-shirts. Also, evidence suggests that associates of the 2001 World Trade Center terrorists may have been involved with the production of imitation designer goods (Malone). Finally, the 2004 bombing of commuter trains in Madrid was financed in part by the sale of counterfeits. In fact, an intelligence source states, "It would be more shocking if Al-Qaeda *wasn't* involved in counterfeiting. The sums involved are staggering—it would be inconceivable if money were not being raised for their terrorist activities" (qtd. in Malone).

Consumers should realize that when they buy counterfeits, they are actually breaking the law. By doing so, they are making it possible for organized crime syndicates and terrorists to earn money for their illegal activities. Although buyers of counterfeit merchandise justify their actions by saying that the low prices are impossible to resist, they might reconsider if they knew the uses to which their money was going. The truth of the matter is that counterfeit designer products, such as handbags, sunglasses, jewelry, and T-shirts, are luxuries, not necessities. By resisting the temptation to buy knockoffs, consumers could help to eliminate the companies that hurt legitimate manufacturers, exploit workers, and even finance international terrorism.

Paragraph contains May's own ideas as well as a paraphrase and a quotation.

Conclusion contains May's original ideas, so no documentation is necessary.

Compton 4

Works Cited

"Counterfeit Goods Are Linked to Terror Groups." *The International Herald Tribune,* 12 Feb. 2007, www.nytimes.com/2007/02/12/business /worldbusiness/12iht-fake.4569452.html?_r=0.

Malone, Andrew. "Revealed: The True Cost of Buying Cheap Fake Goods." *Daily Mail,* 29 July 2007, www.dailymail.co.uk/news/article-471679/Revealed -The-true-cost-buying-cheap-fakegoods.html.

Nellis, Cynthia. "Faking It: Counterfeit Fashion." *About.com Style,* fashion .about.com/cs/tipsadvice/a/fakingit.htm. Accessed 24 March 2016.

O'Donnell, Jayne. "Counterfeits Are a Growing—and Dangerous—Problem." *USA Today,* 6 June 2012, p. 3b.

Thomas, Dana. "Terror's Purse Strings." *The New York Times,* 30 Aug. 2007, p. A23. Editorial. *Proquest,* search.proquest.com/hnpnewyorktimes.

"Trafficking in Illicit Goods and Counterfeiting." *Interpol,* www.interpol.int /Crime-areas/Trafficking-in-illicit-goods-and-counterfeiting/Trafficking -in-illicit-goods-and-counterfeiting. Accessed 24 March 2016.

Wallace, Kim. "A Counter-Productive Trade." *TimesDaily.com,* 28 July 2007, timesdaily.com/opinion/editorials/counter-productive-trade.

Works-cited list starts a new page.

This Internet source has no listed author, so it is alphabetized in the list by the title.

First lines of entries are set flush left; subsequent lines are indented one-half inch.

Acknowledgments

Index

Note: Page numbers in **bold** type indicate pages on which terms are defined.

PARTS OF SPEECH

Bailey

The English language has eight basic parts of speech: nouns, pronouns, verbs, adjectives, adverbs, prepositions, conjunctions, and interjections.

Nouns   A noun names a person, an animal, a place, an object, or an idea.

Christine brought her dog Bailey to obedience school in Lawndale.
noun   *noun noun*   *noun*   *noun*

Pronouns   A pronoun refers to and takes the place of a noun or another pronoun.

Bailey did very well in her lessons and seemed to enjoy them.
noun   *pronoun noun*   *pronoun*

Verbs   A verb tells what someone or something does, did, or will do.

Sometimes Bailey rolls over, but earlier today she refused.
verb   *verb*

Maybe she will change someday.
verb

Adjectives   An adjective identifies or describes a noun or a pronoun.

This dog is a small Beagle with a brown and white coat and long ears.
adj noun   *adj*   *noun*   *adj*   *adj noun*   *adj noun*

Adverbs   An adverb identifies or describes a verb, an adjective, or another adverb.

Bailey is old now, so she moves very slowly and seldom barks.
verb adverb adverb   *adverb*   *verb*

Prepositions   A preposition is a word—such as *to*, *on*, or *with*—that introduces a noun or pronoun and connects it to other words in a sentence.

Bailey likes sitting quietly in her box at the foot of the stairs.

Conjunctions   A conjunction is a word that connects parts of a sentence.

People say you can't teach an old dog new tricks, but Bailey might be an exception.

Interjections   An interjection is a word—such as *Oh!* or *Hey!*—that is used to express emotion.

Wow! Bailey finally rolled over!

The eight basic parts of speech can be combined to form sentences, which always include at least one subject and one verb. The subject tells who or what is being talked about, and the verb tells what the subject does, did, or will do.

Bailey graduated from obedience school at the head of her class.
s   *v*